Knowledge Networks:
The Social Software Perspective

Miltiadis Lytras
University of Patras, Greece

Robert Tennyson
University of Minnesota, USA

Patricia Ordóñez de Pablos
Universidad de Oviedo, Spain

T0345104

Information Science
REFERENCE

INFORMATION SCIENCE REFERENCE

Hershey · New York

Director of Editorial Content:	Kristin Klinger
Director of Production:	Jennifer Neidig
Managing Editor:	Jamie Snavely
Assistant Managing Editor:	Carole Coulson
Typesetter:	Amanda Appicello
Cover Design:	Lisa Tosheff
Printed at:	Yurchak Printing Inc.

Published in the United States of America by
Information Science Reference (an imprint of IGI Global)
701 E. Chocolate Avenue, Suite 200
Hershey PA 17033
Tel: 717-533-8845
Fax: 717-533-8661
E-mail: cust@igi-global.com
Web site: http://www.igi-global.com

and in the United Kingdom by
Information Science Reference (an imprint of IGI Global)
3 Henrietta Street
Covent Garden
London WC2E 8LU
Tel: 44 20 7240 0856
Fax: 44 20 7379 0609
Web site: http://www.eurospanbookstore.com

Copyright © 2009 by IGI Global. All rights reserved. No part of this publication may be reproduced, stored or distributed in any form or by
any means, electronic or mechanical, including photocopying, without written permission from the publisher.

Product or company names used in this set are for identification purposes only. Inclusion of the names of the products or companies does
not indicate a claim of ownership by IGI Global of the trademark or registered trademark.

Knowledge networks : the social software perspective / Miltiadis Lytras, Robert Tennyson, and Patricia Ordonez de Pablos, editors.

   p. cm.

  Includes bibliographical references and index.

  Summary: "This book concentrates on strategies that exploit emerging technologies for the knowledge effectiveness in social networks"--
Provided by publisher.

  ISBN 978-1-59904-976-2 (hardcover) -- ISBN 978-1-59904-977-9 (ebook)

  1. Knowledge management. 2. Social networks. 3. Organizational learning. I. Lytras, Miltiadis D., 1973- II. Tennyson, Robert D. III.
Pablos, Patricia Ordonez de.

  HD30.2.K63955 2009

  658.4'038--dc22

                          2008024193

British Cataloguing in Publication Data
A Cataloguing in Publication record for this book is available from the British Library.

All work contributed to this book is original material. The views expressed in this book are those of the authors, but not necessarily of the
publisher.

*If a library purchased a print copy of this publication, please go to http://www.igi-global.com/agreement for information on activating
the library's complimentary electronic access to this publication.*

List of Reviewers

Marc Alier
Sciences of Education Institute, UPC, Spain

Bonnie F. Bryson
U.S. Army Engineer Research and Development Center, USA

Yiwei Cao
RWTH Aachen University, Germany

Joseph T. Chao
Bowling Green State University, USA

Mohamed Amine Chatti
RWTH Aachen University, Germany

Angelo Corallo
University of Salento, Lecce - Italy

Mariano Corso
Polytechnic of Milano (Italy)

Virginia L. Dickerson
U.S. Army Engineer Research and Development Center, USA

Gianluca Elia
University of Salento, Lecce - Italy

Pascal Francq
Université Libre de Bruxelles, Belgium

Alexandros Gkikas
Greek Ministry of Education & Religious Affairs, Greece

Seppo J. Hänninen
Helsinki University of Technology, Finland

Stefan Hrastinski
Uppsala University, Sweden

R. Scott Jackson
U.S. Army Engineer Research and Development Center, USA

Matthias Jarke
RWTH Aachen University, Germany

Ilkka Kauranen
Asian Institute of Technology, Thailand

Ralf Klamma
RWTH Aachen University, Germany

Dimitris Konetas
University of Ioannina, Greece

Wendelin Kuepers
Massey University, Auckland, New Zealand

Niki Lambropoulos
London South Bank University, UK

Georgia Lazakidou
University of Piraeus, Greece

Jeanette Lemmergaard
University of Southern Denmark, Denmark

Miltiadis D. Lytras
University of Patras, Greece

Antonella Martini
University of Pisa (Italy)

Patricia Ordóñez de Pablos
University of Oviedo, Spain

Sofia Papadimitriou
*Greek Educational Television, Greek Ministry of
Education & Religious Affairs, Greece*

Kevin R. Parker
Idaho State University, USA

Kathleen Perales
*U.S. Army Engineer Research and Development
Center, USA*

Ourania Petropoulou
University of Piraeus, Greece

Alessandro Piva
Polytechnic of Milano (Italy)

Symeon Retalis
University of Piraeus, Greece

Max Senges
USA

Marc Spaniol
Max Planck Institute for Computer Science, Germany

Pekka Stenholm
George Mason University, USA

Robert Tennyson
University of Minnesota, USA

T. J. Vapola
Helsinki School of Economics, Finland

Marianna Vivitsou
University of Helsinki, Finland

Charalambos Vrasidas
*CARDET-Centre for the Advancement of Research & De-
velopment in Educational Technology LTD, Cyprus*

Table of Contents

Detailed Table of Contents

Chapter I

Gianluca Elia, University of Salento, Lecce – Italy
Angelo Corallo, University of Salento, Lecce – Italy

Many classifications and taxonomies of knowledge management tools highlight mainly specific characteristics and features of a single tool, by ignoring the holistic and systematic dimension of the classification, and the explicit elements of linking with the knowledge management strategy. This chapter aims at proposing a general framework that integrates the technological side of knowledge management with the strategic one. Thus, this framework could represent a powerful instrument to guide knowledge engineers in the implementation phase of a knowledge management system, coherently with strategical choices for knowledge management. Chapter is articulated in two main parts: the first one is focused on reminding some relevant approaches to knowledge management (Hoffmann 2001; Skyrme 2000; Ruggles 1997; Radding 1998; Maier 2002); the second part presents the framework, with a detailed description of its components.

Chapter II

Mohamed Amine Chatti, RWTH Aachen University, Germany
Matthias Jarke, RWTH Aachen University, Germany

Recognizing that knowledge is a key asset for better performance and that knowledge is a human and social activity, building ecologies that foster knowledge networking and community building becomes crucial. Over the past few years, social software has become an important medium to connect people, bridge communities, and leverage collaborative knowledge creation and sharing. In this chapter we explore how social software can support the building and maintaining of knowledge ecologies and discuss the social landscape within different social software mediated communities and networks.

This chapter introduces wikis in the context of social software, focusing on their powerful information sharing and collaboration features. It begins by defining the wiki concept and then discussing the evolution of wikis, explaining how they first emerged and how they have evolved over time. The social software aspect of wikis is then analyzed, examining how wikis can engender collaborative efforts. It investigates ways in which wikis help to develop communities of users, and finally some of the features that enhance the appeal of wikis as social software. The authors hope that by examining a software tool that users may have already encountered, that they will be better able to understand the basic concepts and value of social software. Further, as future trends are discussed, it is hoped that readers will be able to see the value of incorporating social aspects into both existing and as yet undeveloped software applications.

The success of knowledge sharing heavily depends on the capabilities of an information system to reproduce the ongoing discourses within a community. In order to illustrate the artifacts of a discourse as authentic as possible it is not sufficient to store the plain information, but also to reflect the context they have been used in. An ideal representation to do so is non-linear storytelling. The Web 2.0 in its "bi-directional" design therefore is an ideal basis for media centric knowledge sharing. In this article we present a novel solution to this issue by non-linear storytelling in the Virtual Campfire system. Virtual Campfire is a social software that allows a modular composition of web services based on a Lightweight Application Server in community engine called LAS. Hence, Virtual Campfire is capable of fully exploiting the features of the Web 2.0 in a comprehensive community information system covering web-services for geo-spatial content sharing, multimedia tagging and collaborative authoring of hypermedia artifacts.

The Internet is today a widely used platform to exchange information and share knowledge. In this chapter, we propose a prospective study of the use of the Internet as support for e-democracy processes. The history of the Internet shows that social software has always been developed to support knowledge sharing among net surfers. Since participating in political issues implies knowledge sharing, the Internet was rapidly used as a political medium. The concept of e-democracy, i.e. the use of information and communication technologies to allow citizens to participate in the democratic process, is a natural evolution of this situation. Several examples demonstrate that e-democracy can be deployed for local decision purposes. The experiences have also shown several limitations, in particular concerning the on-line tools currently offered. We argue that solutions exist to overcome these limitations and that their integration in social software environments may enhance the concept of e-democracy in order to apply it to more complex decision-taking situations.

This chapter focuses on the Community and Collaboration tools as means of creating business Communities of Practice (CoPs). First, it is provided the state-of-the art of these tools, in terms of diffusion and usage, and then emergent Communities are analysed in terms of targets, goals, models and barriers. The research is based on 16 retrospective case studies that cover more than 50% of the banking sector in Italy by number of employees and which correspond to 33 Communities. The findings provide interesting elements and suggestions to develop a Community in a banking context. The authors aim to develop actionable knowledge to support management in understanding how to manage a business CoP, in order to create value for both the organization and its members.

Knowledge sharing and knowledge transfer have a strong effect on the success of the born-globals. The objective of the present chapter is to create a better understanding of the impacts resulting from knowledge sharing within technology-intensive knowledge networks. The study builds on co-opetitive theory which has its underpinnings in the cooperative game theory. The present study is based on 51 interviews within 31 companies that have business operations in Finland and that have participated in the Fenix technology program financed by the Finnish Funding Agency for Technology and Innovation Tekes. All the companies were small or medium-sized. Because of the small size of the sample, the study is to some extent a multi-case study. The interviewees from companies were technology directors or research and development directors as well as general directors of the companies. According to the results, having discussions with technology partners positively correlated with conducting discussions concerning technology within the companies themselves. This can be an indication that technology companies depend on their partners as regards to technology development. There also was a positive correlation between having discussions with competitors and conducting discussions within the companies themselves. In addition, having discussions with sales partners was positively correlated with having discussions with technology partners and customers. These correlations can be a sign that in technology development sharing information with various stakeholders, including competitors, can create win-win partnerships.

This chapter looks at the concept of sociograms that has great illustrative importance in some circumstances, especially for studying small knowledge networks. It is argued that the sociogram approach might be particularly useful for those who view learning and participation in knowledge networks as an inherently social phenomenon. After giving a basic introduction to the concept of sociograms, examples of different types of sociograms, and their benefits and limitations, are discussed. The chapter also includes an exercise, web resources, further readings, and suggestions for possible paper titles.

Social web asynchronous communication environments provide the space for content creation, idea sharing and knowledge construction within a participatory and collaborative framework that encourages online community establishment and evolution. However, community development is a long-term process and necessitates the adoption of appropriate theoretical principles to support a developmental scheme ensuring the community's exploratory, knowledge-based and reflexively expanding character. This chapter discusses and analyses the techniques and tools used in an online course aiming to enable Greek teachers develop their pedagogical and digital skills in order to keep update, form new relationships and grow professionally. To this end, e-course design was based on formal learning principles underlying the virtual classroom activities during which a collaborative culture was built. Also, the course structure involved informal learning principles, which were integrated into social web activities implemented on weblog and wiki artefacts created and used by participants as individual and collaborative learning tools. Through the analysis of quantitative and qualitative data gathered during the study it became evident that weblogs and wikis contributed to the growth and evolution of Greek educational networked communities and that a new online identity emerged.

Based on a phenomenological understanding of knowing and knowledge in organisation, this chapter aims to contribute to an integral perspective on conceptual and methodological research development. Adopting an advanced phenomenological approach, knowing is argued to be an embodied and emotional process. Furthermore, an integral "pheno-practice" is proposed, allowing a more comprehensive and inclusive approach, analyse, and interpretation for investigating processes of knowing in organisations.

Following a dynamic, processual turn, the concept of an "inter-knowing" is discussed by which knowing is understood as a relational emerging event. By concluding, some implications for theory and research are provided.

Ourania Petropoulou, University of Piraeus, Greece
Georgia Lazakidou, University of Piraeus, Greece
Symeon Retalis, University of Piraeus, Greece
Charalambos Vrasidas, CARDET, Cyprus

There is a growing need for systematic evaluations of computer-supported collaborative learning environments. The present chapter focuses on the evaluation of the learning effectiveness of the interactions that take place in computer-supported problem solving environments. This chapter emphasizes the need for supporting evaluators of such environments with holistic evaluation conceptual frameworks and tools that can facilitate the analysis of data gathered during the evaluation process. We discuss in detail such a holistic framework which has been tested through a primary education case-study.

Jeanette Lemmergaard, University of Southern Denmark, Denmark

This chapter introduces inter-organizational knowledge acquisition and sharing as a means to facilitate benchlearning within the field of human resource management. The chapter presents an interactive web-based portal and demonstrates how valuable knowledge can be released from organizational "silo centers" and be passed around to the benefit of both organizations and academia. In general, human resource departments struggle to demonstrate their validity to the business and their ability to accomplish business objectives. In addition, human resource departments generally lack the ability to speak of their accomplishments in a business language. The presented portal assists human resource professionals in making more efficient and qualitative decisions that are not based on good guesswork or mere instinct, but on facts and knowledge. The portal is novel in its approach of facilitating benchlearning across organizational boundaries and within the soft area of human resource management.

Max Senges, Dachsweg 4a, Germany
Marc Alier, Sciences of Education Institute, UPC, Spain

This chapter discusses the potential of three dimensional virtual worlds as venue for constructivist learning communities. To reach a balanced answer to the question whether virtual worlds are likely to evolve into satisfying educational instruments (1) Authors retrace the historic trajectory of virtual world development and computer based learning, second they describe how (2) learning communities function in general and how virtual worlds in particular can be exploited for collective educational experiences.

With this basis, authors then present (3) a structured analysis of the strenghts, weaknesses, opportunities and threats (SWOT) found to bound the potential of SecondLife for institutionalized learning based on their expertise from working and teaching in virtual worlds. In conclusion authors argue that a critical but optimistic approach towards virtual learning environments (and SecondLife in particular) is adequatee. In their assessment virtual worlds bear great opportunities for educational purposes; however most of today's educational institutions will be challenged to encompass the informal and holistic learning scenario.

    Bonnie F. Bryson, U. S. Army Corps of Engineers, USA
    M. Kathleen Perales, U. S. Army Corps of Engineers, USA
    R. Scott Jackson, U. S. Army Corps of Engineers, USA
    Virginia L. Dickerson, U. S. Army Corps of Engineers, USA

This chapter describes the development of a knowledge management-based website that serves a community of practice within a federal agency, the U.S. Army Corps of Engineers Natural Resources Management Community of Practice. Content development workshops that are conducted as an effective method of creating new content and updating existing content on the website are also described. This successful model may be used by other agencies and organizations to develop and share organizational information in an easily retrievable manner.

    Cynthia T. Small, The MITRE Corporation, USA
    Andrew P. Sage, George Mason University, USA

This paper describes a complex adaptive systems (CAS)-based enterprise knowledge-sharing (KnS) model. The CAS-based enterprise KnS model consists of a CAS-based KnS framework and a multi-agent simulation model. Enterprise knowledge sharing is modeled as the emergent behavior of knowledge workers interacting with the KnS environment and other knowledge workers. The CAS-based enterprise KnS model is developed to aid knowledge management (KM) leadership and other KnS researchers in gaining an enhanced understanding of KnS behavior and its influences. A premise of this research is that a better understanding of KnS influences can result in enhanced decision-making of KnS interventions that can result in improvements in KnS behavior.

    Reinhard Bernsteiner, University for Health Sciences, Medical Informatics and
        Technology, Austria
    Herwig Ostermann, University for Health Sciences, Medical Informatics and
        Technology, Austria
    Roland Staudinger, University for Health Sciences, Medical Informatics and
        Technology, Austria

This article explores how social software tools can offer support for innovative learning methods and instructional design in general, and those related to self-organized learning in an academic context in particular. In the first section, the theoretical basis for the integration of wikis, discussion forums, and Weblogs in the context of learning are discussed. The second part presents the results of an empirical survey conducted by the authors and explores the usage of typical social software tools that support learning from a student's perspective. The article concludes that social software tools have the potential to be a fitting technology in a teaching and learning environment.

An important dimension in education is interaction, that is, the coming together of a number of people to discuss, debate, and deliberate about issues of common concern. In distance education, such social environments are as much present in online learning contexts as they are in face-to-face learning contexts such as tutorials. This chapter expands the notion of teacher-student interaction to focus on integrating human computer interaction in the curriculum. This is done through the use of online discussion forums at Open University Malaysia that help build collaborative online communities using common principles of teaching and learning. Citing a recent case in point, this chapter demonstrates how the Open University Malaysia-Collaborative Online Learning Model for online interaction helped cultivate learner-centric virtual discussions and supported an interactive online community that showcased characteristics of social interdependence and instructional support. This chapter takes a social constructivist view of human computer interaction by proposing an instructional model supported by collaboration, guidance, interdependence, cognitive challenge, knowledge construction, and knowledge extension. The Introduction section of this chapter provides the rationale for human computer interaction and gives an overview of current-day perspectives on the online classroom. This is followed by a trenchant review of recent research on online interaction with a view to outlining the theoretical premise for the use of computers to develop thinking and collaborative or team skills. This section also provides a rationale for the use of online forums and gives a frame of reference for the role of the instructor in this enterprise.

This article adds to the discussion on knowledge management (KM) by focusing on the process of knowledge sharing as a vital part of KM. The article focuses on the relationship between knowledge, learning, communication, and participation in action, and the role of social interaction and technical media in the knowledge sharing process. We develop an initial theoretical framework of knowledge sharing on the basis of a literature study. Drawing on an empirical study of knowledge sharing in a software development company, we discuss what supports and what hinders knowledge sharing in software development. Finally, we use this knowledge to improve the theoretical framework.

Chapter XIX

Ned Kock, Texas A&M International University, USA

Virtual worlds can be defined as technology-created virtual environments that incorporate representations of real world elements such as human beings, landscapes and other objects. Recent years have seen the growing use of virtual worlds such as Second Life and World of Warcraft for entertainment and business purposes, and a rising interest from researchers in the impact that virtual worlds can have on patterns of e-collaboration behavior and collaborative task outcomes. This article looks into whether actual work can be accomplished in virtual worlds, whether virtual worlds can provide the basis for trade (B2C and C2C e-commerce), and whether they can serve as a platform for credible studies of e-collaboration behavior and related outcomes. The conclusion reached is that virtual worlds hold great potential in each of these three areas, even though there are certainly pitfalls ahead.

Chapter XX

Peter H. Jones, Redesign Research, USA

Since Nonaka's (1991) concept of the knowledge creating company, businesses have attempted to organize knowledge as a resource or asset of the firm, with the purpose of creating competitive advantage based on knowledge. Recent surveys and industry trends show that, after a decade of development of knowledge management (KM) as a technology enabler for organizational learning.

Foreword

Social Networks, Social Software and Web 2.0, a phrase coined by O'Reilly Media in 2004, refers to a perceived or proposed second generation of Internet-based services—such as social networking sites, professional communities of practice, wikis, communication tools, and folksonomies—that emphasize the creation of knowledge and intellectual capital, online collaboration and sharing among users. This new emerging era poses critical challenges for the development of Interactive Learning Environment. Let's briefly explore the topics of knowledge management, intellectual capital and technology enhanced learning.

Managing knowledge-based resources is not a new problem and there have been other theories that have tried to tackle it. Intellectual capital is the latest development in this line of research. In particular, the theoretical roots of intellectual capital come from two different streams of research: strategy and measurement. While the first stream studies knowledge management –knowledge creation, acquisition, diffusion, capitalization, conversion, transfer and storage-, the second stream of research focuses on the measuring of intellectual capital. This stream has advanced towards the building of intellectual capital statements and the development of international standards on intellectual capital measuring and reporting.

Knowledge Management is the set of processes that allow using knowledge as a key point to add and generate value. Moreover, it includes not only processes of creation, acquisition and transference of knowledge but also the reflection of that new knowledge in the organization's behaviour. Whilst organizations recognize the importance of creating, managing and transferring knowledge, so far they have been unable to translate this competitive need into organizational strategies. In broad terms, two major types of knowledge management could be identified: operational knowledge management and strategic knowledge management. First, the main concern of operational knowledge management is to connect people to the system being used for the distribution and transfer of knowledge. Second, strategic knowledge management is a process that links organizational knowledge with 1) the design of organizational structures that foster knowledge, 2) business strategy and 3) the development of knowledge workers.

On the other hand, a broad definition of intellectual capital states it is the difference between the company's market value and its book value. Knowledge-based resources that contribute to the sustained competitive advantage of the firm form intellectual capital. However these resources are not registered in the financial accounts. In contrast with tangible resources, the payoff and value of investments in firm's current stock of knowledge (intellectual capital) will not appear in the financial accounting until later on. By all these reasons, knowledge-based resources must now being identified, dissected and analyzed.

Intellectual capital is formed by three components or subconstructs: human capital, structural capital and relational capital. Human capital reflects the set of knowledge, capabilities, skills and experience of the employees of the company. It represents the accumulated value of investments in employee training, competence and future.Structural capital represents organizational knowledge that has moved from individuals or from the relationships between individuals to be embedded in organizational structures, such as organizational routines, policies, culture or procedures. Generally structural capital is divided into technological capital and organizational capital. Technological capital represents industrial and technical knowledge, such as results from R&D and process engineering. Organizational capital includes all aspects that are related with the organization of the company and its decision making process, for example organizational culture, organizational structure design, coordination mechanisms, organizational routines, planning and control systems, among others. Finally relational capital reflects the value of organizational relationships. In general, it has been accepted that these relationships were mainly focused on customers, suppliers, shareholders, and the Administrations, among others, without including the employees, and therefore adopting an external perspective.

Technology enhanced learning is the best term to describe the domain of knowledge society technologies as applied in the learning context: "Learning for anyone, at any time, at any place". With the shift towards the knowledge society, the change of working conditions and the high-speed evolution of information and communication technologies, peoples' knowledge and skills need continuous updating.

Learning, based on collaborative working, creativity, multidisciplinary, adaptiveness, intercultural communication and problem solving, has taken on an important role in everyday life. The learning process is becoming pervasive, both for individuals and organisations, in formal education, in the professional context and as part of leisure activities. Learning should be accessible to every citizen, independent of age, education, social status and tailored to his/her individual needs. To meet these social challenges is a leading issue of research on the use of technology to support learning (e.g. The Technology Enhanced Learning Action within the 7th Framework Program for Research and Technological Development).

In the context of the knowledge society, the focus of research in this area has been set on applications of technologies for user-centered learning, building on the concept of human learning and on sound pedagogical principles, with the key objectives to be:

- To increase the efficiency of learning for individuals, groups
- To facilitate transfer and sharing of knowledge in organisations
- To contribute to a deeper understanding of the learning process by exploring links between human learning, cognition and technologies
- To promote humanistic visions for a better world based on open learning for all

According to the ideas mentioned above, the book *Knowledge Networks: The Social Software Perspective* has three main goals: 1) To promote the state of the art on Social software exploitation for Interactive Learning Environments as a milestone enabled by the evolution of Web 2.0 technologies and approaches; 2) To provide a reference edition for the area with main emphasis to be paid on social network analysis for Learning; and 3) To become a reference edition for people (policy makers, government officers, academics and practitioners) thirsty for knowledge on Social Software for Learning.

The book is formed by 14 chapters which include hot topics such as Collaborative tools for learning groupware as Interactive Learning Environments, Design variables and conditions for knowledge sharing and creation systems, Knowledge Management Strategies at Artifact/ Individual/ Team / Organizational/ Inter-organizational Levels, New forms of interaction in knowledge sharing and creation systems, Blogging and enterprise blogs as a new strategic tool, Collaborative filtering, Analysing social interaction for finding knowledge among Web users, Semantic Desktops, Social Network Analysis to support implicit learning and sharing within educational environments, Learning and Knowledge Communities within higher education, Analysis of Large Online Communities for Building Intellectual Capital, Web Communities of Practice for Sharing, Creating, and Learning, Network Analysis for Building Social

Networks within Learning Communities, Implicit, Formal, and Powerful Semantics in Communities of Practice,Metadata and Annotation Techniques for Automated Support of Collaborative Learning, Folksonomies, tagging and other collaboration-based categorisation systems and Wikis, semantic Wikis and other collaborative knowledge creation systems, among other topics.

Additionally we also include further readings of a complimentary nature to the contents of the rest of our publication. As an added value to our readers, the further readings are to provide additional related data in support of the book's comprehensive concepts, principles and results, as well as studies that build upon the appeal of this publication as a one-stop reference source

Finally, before closing this foreword of the book **Knowledge Networks: The Social Software Perspective**, we would like to invite all our colleagues interested in Application for the Human and The Society, Information Systems &Information Technology, Knowledge Management and E-Learning, Libraries, Digital Culture and Electronic Tourism, E-Business, E-Government and E-Banking, Politics and Policies for the Knowledge Society, Sustainable Development for the Knowledge Society and New Competitive Resources (Culture, Tourism and Services) to pay attention to an important event organised by **OPEN RESEARCH SOCIETY** in 2009: **"The 2nd Athens World Summit on The Knowledge Society"** (Athens, Greece, September 2009). Website: http://www.open-knowledge-society.org/summit. htm Additionally if you are interested in 1st International Conference for the Web Science, please have a look at http://icws2009.org

Miltiadis D. Lytras, Robert Tennyson and Patricia Ordonez de Pablos

Figure 1. Pillars for the 2nd Athens World Summit on the Knowledge Society (Source: Open Research Society)

Chapter I
A Knowledge Strategy Oriented Framework for Classifying Knowledge Management Tools

Gianluca Elia
University of Salento, Lecce – Italy

Angelo Corallo
University of Salento, Lecce – Italy

ABSTRACT

Many classifications and taxonomies of knowledge management tools highlight mainly specific characteristics and features of a single tool, by ignoring the holistic and systematic dimension of the classification, and the explicit elements of linking with the knowledge management strategy. This chapter aims at proposing a general framework that integrates the technological side of knowledge management with the strategic one. Thus, this framework could represent a powerful instrument to guide knowledge engineers in the implementation phase of a knowledge management system, coherently with strategical choices for knowledge management. Chapter is articulated in two main parts: the first one is focused on reminding some relevant approaches to knowledge management (Hoffmann 2001; Skyrme 2000; Ruggles 1997; Radding 1998; Maier 2002); the second part presents the framework, with a detailed description of its components.

Copyright © 2009, IGI Global, distributing in print or electronic forms without written permission of IGI Global is prohibited.

EXISTING APPROACHES FOR KNOWLEDGE MANAGEMENT TOOLS CLASSIFICATION

This brief review starts with the classification proposed by Hoffmann (Heisig et al., 2001), based on the concept that categories of knowledge management tools miss of an explicit reference to the knowledge strategy they enable. These categories are: *search engines / categorization tools / intelligent agents; portals; visualizing tools; skill management; complete knowledge management suites; toolkits for developing individual solutions; learn and teach; virtual teams / collaboration.*

The only one relation with the knowledge strategy is the knowledge management process that each tool enables, chosen among the processes characterizing the knowledge management model of CCKM Fraunhofer Institute of Berlin (Heisig et al., 2001): *knowledge creation, knowledge storing, knowledge delivery, knowledge application.* Table 1 shows this relation:

Another approach is the Skyrme's classification of the *hard* tools for knowledge management, that highlights some categories of technological macro-functionalities, by associating to them some specific strategical impact (Skyrme D. J., 2000). This classification is mainly based on three groups of tools (*Information Resource Management, Knowledge Bases* and *Collaborative Technologies*), and it is not inspired to a pure technological perspective, since the categories are not homogeneous in terms of size and they are not strictly aligned with the market offer and the operative tools known by ICT expert.

Also Ruggles (Ruggles, 1997) proposes a classification characterized by a processes-oriented approach. He distinguishes three principal categories of knowledge management tools:

- *Knowledge Creation* tools, represented by tools that encourage individuals to think beyond their current limits. In particular, this category includes acquisition tools, synthesis tools for integrating different sources

Table 1. Processes-categories mapping (Hoffmann)

KM Process / Tools Categories	Creation	Storing	Delivery	Application
Search Engines / Categorization Tools / Intelligent Agents				X
Portals		X	X	X
Visualizing Tools				X
Skill Management		X	X	
Complete Knowledge Management Suites	X	X	X	X
Toolkit for developing individual solutions	X	X	X	X
Learn and Teach	X			
Virtual teams / Collaboration	X	X	X	

of knowledge to obtain new ideas, creation tools for stimulating users' creativity and encouraging a new thinking style, out of classic and traditional mental schemas.

- *Knowledge Codification* tools, that concern knowledge representation in order to enable and simplify its accessibility and transferring. This category contains knowledge bases and knowledge maps (in order to identify *just-in-time* the necessary knowledge to perform an activity and to represent knowledge flow within the organization), dictionaries and thesauri (to create common language inside the organization), simulators (to understand previous experience and design possible future scenarios).

- *Knowledge delivery* tools, allow going over temporal, geographic, physic and social distance inside the organization, such as virtual spaces, groupware and web-learning systems.

The main limit of these classifications is the excessive emphasis to explicit knowledge, neglecting aspects mainly connect to tacit knowledge, that represents a fundamental component of organizational knowledge. In fact, for example, some informal organization models, such as *community of practices* (Wenger E. C., 1998), are characterized by strong tendency to learning and innovation, often created by exchange of tacit knowledge (Maier R., 2002).

In the classification proposed by Radding (Radding, 1998), the technological infrastructure of knowledge management is slightly correlated with strategic elements. In fact, the categories of this approach are: *Networks, Storage, Capture and Collection, Dissemination, Access, Sharing, Middleware, Information Processing, Information Analysis.* Each category is formed by subcategories, which are organized strongly in a technological perspective and don't give precise information about the strategy they can support (for example, the *Dissemination* category includes

these tools: *e-mail, data warehouse* and *data mart, publishing and subscribe, push, groupware, computer based technology, web*).

The Maier's (Maier, 2002) approach, instead, provides a more clear vision about the direct and indirect bonds between knowledge management technologies and knowledge management strategies. In a general architecture of a knowledge management system, Maier joins the elementary classes of each tool to some knowledge management processes. For example, Maier connects the visualization process with some technological tools as knowledge maps, taxonomies, directory systems and catalogues; another example is the relationship between the discovery process and search agents, push technologies, profiling and filtering tools.

The proposed architectural schema matches the *theory-driven* approach with *market-driven* approach. The former is essentially based on: i) models that describe, in an abstract way, the knowledge types; ii) processes supported potentially by ICT; iii) the organizational levels of these processes (individual, group/community, organization, global scale). The latter is based on specific functionalities offered by a knowledge management system (repository, discovery and mapping, web learning, search engines, portals, community, collaboration and interaction, visualization). Moreover, Maier proposes a first schematic attempt to link technological knowledge management tools and strategical knowledge management approaches, by introducing *integrative* and *interactive* functions of a knowledge management system. The *integrative* functions provide a technology-oriented perspective about knowledge management systems, focusing on explicit knowledge and on search functionalities, access, presentation, acquisition, publication and organization; the *interactive* functions provide a human-oriented perspective, preferring the exchange, sharing and delivery of tacit knowledge through communication, cooperation, interaction and learning functionalities.

3

In the Maier's model, this relationship is not always immediately identifiable and often the architectural design is mixed with technological and functional features of the tool.

THE PROPOSED FRAMEWORK FOR KNOWLEDGE MANAGEMENT TOOLS CLASSIFICATION

The following framework tries to join the technological aspects and the strategical one in a systemic way. This framework is constituted by a functional and technological structure, which represents the *General Facilities* layer, and it is divided into three components:

- *Enabling Infrastructure:* hard infrastructure concerning the aspects of connectivity of the system;

- *People & Task Management Tools:* tools about management and coordination of activities and human resources;
- *Knowledge Map:* tools that guide the users towards processes of knowledge search and recovery.

This *General Facilities* layer includes both typologies of knowledge management tools, which are linked to the two Hansen's approaches (Hansen, 1999) for knowledge management, then discussed by Zack (Zack, 1999):

- *people-to-people tools*, essentially focused on processes concerning tacit knowledge;
- *people-to-document tools:* essentially focused on processes concerning explicit knowledge.

The following figure shows the logic structure of the framework.

Figure 1. Logic structure of the proposed framework

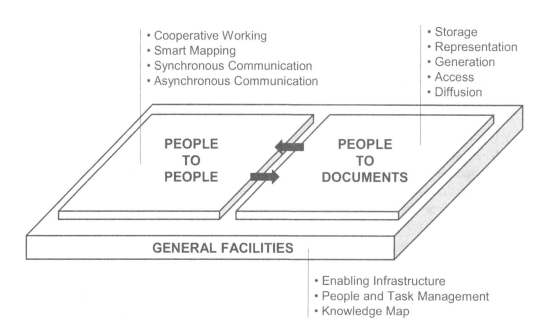

General Facilities level assures the basis functionalities, on which other knowledge management tools linked to strategic approaches are integrated (*people-to-people tools* and *people-to-document tools*).

For each typology of tools, the framework proposes some dimensions and parameters to analyse it. In particular:

- for people-to-people tools, the proposed dimensions are connected to the typologies of communication that are enabled, and to mechanisms that activate the relationships among individuals (*relationship trigger*);
- for people-to-document tools, the proposed dimensions are related to processes and typologies of knowledge resources which are managed by tool (*knowledge resources*).

In the following sections, a detailed description of the three levels of the framework is provided.

General Facilities

The General Facilities of the proposed framework can be described along three main directions:

- *Enabling Infrastructure*: hard infrastructure concerning the connectivity of the system;
- *People & Task Management Tools*: tools for management and coordination of activities and human resources;
- *Knowledge Map*: tools that guide the users towards processes of knowledge search and recovery.

Enabling Infrastructure

The hard infrastructure concerning the connectivity of the system can be represented by its components, that are:

- *Host networks* – networks used to communicate and transfer data generated by heterogeneous systems.
- *Local Area Networks* (LAN) – networks that connect clients and servers of the organization. They constitute the backbone of the network, through which the codified knowledge is transferred and shared into the organization.
- *Wide Area Networks* (WAN) – networks that connect physically different LANs geographical distributed in order to share the access to informative resources or knowledge. WAN carry out a key role to allow access to geographical distributed data sources and knowledge repositories. Usually, the WAN architectures include tools and technologies to guarantee the security of the communication (integrity, confidentiality, authorization, authentication, non repudiation).
- *Intranet* – networks based on TCP/IP protocol and operating on LAN, accessible only by authorized users. In according to the user profile, a *personal knowledge workspace* is automatically and dynamically defined, constituted by reachable services, allowed contents, and authorized relationship.
- *Extranet* – networks constituted by secure integration of a set of Intranets (customers, suppliers, partners). So, extranet becomes a shared space in which organizations interact each other, by sharing information and knowledge. Usually, a firewall guarantees the privacy of communication and the security of all involved Intranets.
- *Internet* – public, global and interactive channel of communication, which promotes the access and sharing of information and explicit knowledge at global level, through its services (WWW, FTP, IRC, newsgroup, telnet, e-mail, etc.).

All the introduced components can be framed and used in a wired or wireless or mixed context, in according to needs and special features of organizational and operational areas.

People & Task Management Tools

Tools for managing and coordinating activities and human resources allow increasing effectiveness and efficiency in the use of knowledge assets in the organization. This category includes tools of *workflow*, *project management* and *competence assessment*.

Workflow tools allow defining the relationships and the interfaces among different process' activities or phases. The identification and definition of the priority among activities and the setting of dynamics of evolution / control and coordination allow systematizing work processes, communication flows and human resources planning. In this way, modelling and activities' parameter set up, together with the analysis of the specifications and mechanisms of activation / execution / control, create a favourable context for defining a strategic and operational framework to enhance knowledge flows, conceived as result of interaction and relationships among people, processes and contents.

Project management tools provide a set of functionalities to support processes management, by ensuring an effective usage of resources, an high level of control for project timing, a careful risk management and a constant quality monitoring.

A more important and strategic aspect, that the traditional project management tools are trying to embed, concerns the management of individual competences. Integration interfaces, more and more rich and complete, allow connecting traditional project management functionalities with monitoring of human resources competences, in order to consider typology and know-how requested for tasks execution as a fundamental driver in the staffing phase of the project team. This integration process points out the aspects of tracking, monitoring and individual competences development for a more careful project planning.

In this way, project planning functionalities include both quantitative aspects (number of available resources, available budget, etc.) and qualitative aspects (kind and level of required competences, acquired experience, etc.). So, apart from traditional functionalities, such as gantt, pert, resources management, notice mechanisms for meeting set up, alert mechanisms, monitoring and costs sheets, calendar, task-list and cash flow reporting, project management tools became integrated more and more with Human Resource Management (HRM) and web-learning tools, in order to provide a better support for competitive knowledge-based enterprise.

Finally, the more and more increasing requirement to concentrate strategic management of the projects in a single professional profile (multi-project manager), generates new requirements (and so new functionalities) that a traditional tool for project management doesn't support, among which:

- budget controlling to optimize cash flows;
- verification of the existence of economy of scale or economy of scope among different projects to optimize the use of the resources and so the profitability of the projects;
- optimization of the available knowledge heritage, through the improvement of existing and available knowledge assets;
- development and improvement of new knowledge and competences, in the perspective of future organizational strategies for value creation.

Competence assessment tools allow monitoring dynamically and real-time the competences level achieved by each member of the organization, extracting useful information through techniques of user tracking applied to carried out activities, used application, produced documents/reports, in order to identify and analyze the knowledge gap and, potentially, propose ad-hoc learning path.

Knowledge Map

Knowledge maps allow representing, in a certain moment, the knowledge heritage existing into the organization, potentially comparable with the knowledge heritage of other competitors. Analysing these maps, it is possible to identify the specific competences of an organization, the competences which require reinforcement or those will disappear in the next future. Apart from the typology and the level of those competences, the knowledge maps allow identifying also the organizational areas they are located in, and the sources (individuals, documents, electronic files, journals, internal and external data repositories).

Another important characteristic of a knowledge map is the possibility to manage intellectual right property of different knowledge sources of the organization, defining the rule and application of the contents, access and distribution policy, update and publication bonds. To this end, Digital Rights Management (DRM) systems allow to manage these features in a complete and advanced way.

So, the knowledge maps allow to monitor dynamically the whole knowledge heritage of an organization, identifying sources, flows, bonds and relationships, in order to optimize the identification and retrieval processes. Moreover, the knowledge maps constitute the basis for recommendation systems, which give a high proactive level to the system, through suggesting services/contents/people organized coherently with user's profile and context.

People-to-People Tools

The knowledge management tools that support people-to-people approach are focused on tacit component of the knowledge. These tools intend to activate interaction and socialization processes among individuals in order to strengthen existing (evident or/and latent) bonds and relations among them. Indeed, these tools aim at creating and strengthening social network through configuration of contexts that enable knowledge sharing and knowledge transfer processes.

The following table lists the two category of knowledge management tools oriented to *people-to-people* approach:

- Category characterized by typology of communication (synchronous or asynchronous);
- Category characterized by mechanisms of activation of the relationships among individuals – relationship trigger (cooperation or expertise search);

Synchronous and Asynchronous Communication Tools

The following figure shows classification matrix of tools related to synchronous and asynchronous communication, completed by the presence or not of a moderator. So, this matrix illustrates four sub-class of tools:

1. *Moderate Synchronous tools*: knowledge management tools that realize instantaneous

Table 2. People-to-people tools

Communication typology	Relationship trigger
Synchronous Communication Tools	Cooperative Working Tools
Asynchronous Communication Tools	Smart Mapping Tools

communications among users that are on line at the same time. The presence of a moderator assures immediate interventions oriented to promote and management the communication, accepting new users or excluding someone from the current session. This sub-class contains virtual classrooms, audio-video conference systems (one-to-one and many-to-one) and chat rooms.

2. *Moderate Asynchronous tools*: knowledge management tools that enable communication among users geographically distributed not only in space (as in the synchronous tools) but also in time. In fact, for these tools, the simultaneous presence of all users is not necessary, since everyone can contribute to discussions and activate communication in a postponed way, both individually and collectively. The presence of the moderator (especially if he is an instructor or tutor) guarantees that all contributions are coherent with the topics of the discussions and they

have been introduced in appropriate and clear way. This subclass includes assessment tools (test, evaluation and verification tools), forums, newsgroups, mailing lists, web training tools supporting web-learning processes.

3. *Non Moderate Synchronous tools:* tools that support unstructured, instantaneous and no moderation communication. Spontaneity and rapidity of the interactions constitute the main strength of these tools. Integrated components to store discussion sessions can increase further the effectiveness of such tools. Typical example of this category are chat, both one-to-one and one-to-many and many-to-many. The integration of these tools with Voice Over IP systems increases the potentiality and effectiveness of the communication, by ensuring multimedia communication channels.

4. *Non Moderate Asynchronous tools:* knowledge management tools with strong func-

Figure 2. Synchronous and asynchronous communication tools

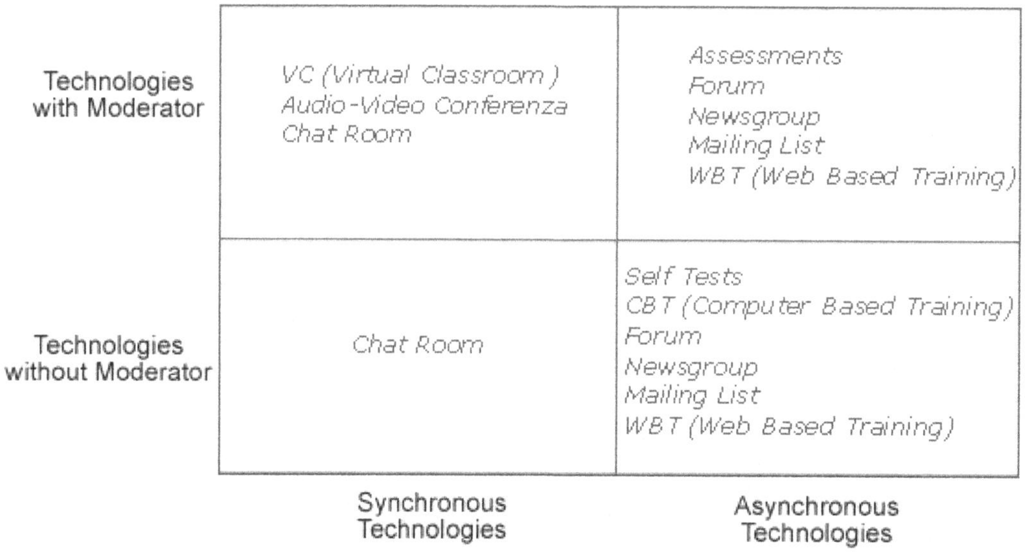

	Synchronous Technologies	Asynchronous Technologies
Technologies with Moderator	VC (Virtual Classroom) Audio-Video Conferenza Chat Room	Assessments Forum Newsgroup Mailing List WBT (Web Based Training)
Technologies without Moderator	Chat Room	Self Tests CBT (Computer Based Training) Forum Newsgroup Mailing List WBT (Web Based Training)

tional characteristics that exalt individual and collective aspects of the interactions. In fact, the absence of a moderator overburdens the individual actions of the user when he uses the tool and accesses to contents. The asynchronous way allows a good level of examination and elaboration, both for contents that are proposed and brought in the discussion, and contents that are accessed by specific tool. This subclass contains self-test tools (for auto-test and auto-evaluation), forums, newsgroups, mailing lists, computer training and web training tools to support individual and collective web-learning processes.

New emerging tools that are obtaining considerable importance in the area of asynchronous communication tools are blogs.

Blogs are virtual environment for communication and interaction in which the personal dimension emerges compared with group dimension. Advanced blogs supply services for user's profiles recommendation, in order to promote the creation of Learning Community and community of knowledge practices.

Cooperative Working Tools

This category includes all tools that enable interdisciplinary groups of individuals, geographically and temporally distributed, to interact each other for carrying out a common activity or joint elaboration of a solution. Examples of these tools are e-meeting systems with audio-video conferences, desktop sharing systems and, in general, application sharing systems, shared tools for activities scheduling (calendars or virtual agendas), forums.

Beyond these systems, there are the traditional systems of document management to manage entire documents life cycle, from their initial creation to their filing. This management consists of structuring of documental workflow according

to the different typologies of documents, in addition to definition of access policies to different work areas (personal and shared). Also, these systems offer a set of tools to support retrieval, manipulation, notice, delivery and documents versioning processes.

Very interesting cooperative working systems are the Group Decision Support Systems (GDSS), which combines communication and processing aspects with decision making processes. After the GDSS have contributed to the removal of communicative limits and obstacles, they propose models and techniques of "collaborative decision making", creating an operative context to support joint and assisted formulation and elaboration of solutions about unstructured and not understandable or defined problems.

Smart Mapping Tools

The category of Smart Mapping Tools includes all tools that support user to accelerate search and retrieval of specific competence profiles to establish a relation with. The quality, effectiveness and efficiency of these tools depend on indexing and classification techniques. To this end, it is possible to distinguish automatic and semi-automatic indexing techniques. Automatic techniques present a low level of "user intrusion". They are based on analysis of user's behaviours with reference to contents and/or documents accessed previously, the typologies of activated communication, users' profile involved in the communication, number and type of documentation shared in that communication, value of proposals suggested in the meeting by participants.

Semi-automatic techniques, instead, require active and explicit (also periodic) intervention and participation by user aimed to update own profile of competences, interests and skills.

Both techniques allow to associate single individual with a set of metadata that contributes to organize and describe the human capital of an organization in a complete way.

Usually, Smart Mapping tools incorporate and improve both semi-automatic indexation techniques and automatic techniques, trying to increase effectiveness of the search processes carried out by users. The result is a more virtuous integration of human capital with knowledge resources (structural capital), in order to maximize the effectiveness of the social dynamics (social capital).

Smart Mapping tools exploit the potentiality of semantic layer of an organization (represented typically by ontologies, thesauri and taxonomies) in order to drive user through an intelligent and problem-driven exploration of the intellectual capital, also utilizing three-dimensional representation of the specific domain (example: yellow-pages).

People-to-Document Tools

Knowledge management tools, that support people-to-document approach, are focused essentially on the explicit knowledge.

These tools aim to strengthen mainly the processes of retrieval, transfer, use and application of the knowledge that is already created, represented and codified in documents, database, manuals, reports, deliverables, software, learning paths. For this purpose, two phases have particular importance:

- to identify 'core' processes to support and feed with such tools;
- to structure, systematize, characterize knowledge resources on which such tools operate.

Concerning the former phase, the proposed framework is based on a process-oriented analysis of some knowledge management approaches (Heisig et al., 2001; Maier, 2002; Tiwana, 2000). This analysis allows identifying the main processes on which it's necessary to focus in order

to transform knowledge in a value creation source.

Concerning the second phase, the framework is based on existing differences (both structural differences and typology / contextual ones) among several types of knowledge resource (Davenport, Prusak, 1998; Maier, 2002; Radding, 1998; ADL, 2001).

In the proposed framework, the process-based dimension is articulated into five levels:

- *Storage*: level of processes directly related to an effective organizing and structuring storage of the knowledge resources into appropriate data structure, which are capable to maintain logic and semantic links among several and heterogeneous resources, in the course of time.
- *Representation*: level of processes oriented to an effective representation of knowledge resources according to the specific user's, in order to maximize the performance of understanding and elaboration processes.
- *Generation*: level of processes focused on knowledge generation, from the acquisition and integration of external knowledge sources (experts, documents, books, journals, patents, database, events and initiatives as conferences, meetings, workshops, projects, benchmarking, best-practices and special interest groups). Knowledge generation processes are based also on internal knowledge sources that feed learning processes and development of new skills, idea and innovative projects. Socialization and externalization processes (Nonaka, 1995) contribute positively to success of generation processes.
- *Access*: level of processes related to access, search and recovery of knowledge assets in an organization. For this purpose, the processes of resources identification are very

important, both at intra-organizational and inter-organizational level.

- *Diffusion*: level of processes focused on distribution of knowledge to involved users, both through push and pull modalities. The knowledge-broker presence, together with personalization techniques - based essentially on user profile - represent two fundamental drivers for success of such processes. Combination and internalization processes (Nonaka, 1995) contribute positively to achieve the objectives of the diffusion processes.

Concerning the knowledge-resource based dimension, it is articulated into four levels:

- *Data*: level dedicated to collection and management of raw data, conceived as objective measures of the properties of an object (for example temperature, price, …), in relation to a specific event.

- *Document*: level dedicated to elaborated, aggregated and contextualized information, in relation to a specific objective, which are represented in the form of text with images, graphics, tables, comments, etc.

- *Multimedia object*: level of objects characterized by contextualized knowledge in the form of text, dynamic images, audio and video sources, interactive graphics, hypertext, dynamic links with other objects.

- *Learning object*: level dedicate to all resources and digital links, that can be used to support learning processes, organized in learning paths with specific objective to achieve and competences to acquire. These learning objects are constituted by

Table 3. People-to-document tools

KR Tipology / Processes	Data	Document	Multimedia Object	Learning Object
Storage	Database, File System	Database, File System	Database, File System	Database, File System
Representation	Data Warehouse, Data Mart	Documental Knowledge Base	Multimedia Knowledge Base (Mediateca)	Multimedia Knowledge Base (Learning Object)
Generation	Data Integration Tools, Data Extraction Tools	Authoring Tools, Validating Tools, Indexing Tools, Workflow Tools	Authoring Tools, Validating Tools, Indexing Tools, Workflow Tools	Authoring Tools, Validating Tools, Indexing Tools, Workflow Tools
Access	Data Processing Tools, Data Analysing Tools	Search & Retrieval Tools, Graphic Map	Search & Retrieval Tools	Virtual Learning Environment, Managed Learning Environment
Diffusion	Help Desk, Query & Reporting Tools, Linkopedia	Publishing Tools	Publishing Tools, Streaming Tools	Virtual Learning Environment, Managed Learning Environment

structured grouping of data, documents and multimedia objects, on which a structural and contextual metadata set is associated, to answer effectively to educational and pedagogical requirements of single learner.

The following figure shows classification of knowledge management tools, according to the above cited description.

A short description of each category of knowledge management tools, is follow presented.

Database, File System

Database and file systems represent main data structure for storing of the knowledge resources (data, documents, multimedia objects and learning objects).

In particular, according to resources typologies, some choices can be more appropriate than the other (for example, object oriented database is used for multimedia resources, relational database is used for banking transaction, or XML-based database for complex search into big and widen documental source). In all case, database becomes at the same time point of arrival of normal routine activities and point of departure for the creation of new multi-dimensional data structures. The database, often, is integrated with external data sources organized on file systems: hybrid structures for storing of different types of knowledge resources are so created.

Data Mart, Data Warehouse

Data Mart and Data Warehouse tools allow to create data structures, that are complex, mission-oriented, integrated, changeable in time, not volatile and that sustain and support activities of analysis and decision making. Data, contained in

Figure 3. OLAP and OLTP systems

CHARACTERISTICS	OLTP	OLAP
• Number of users	Many	Limited
• Typology of users	Operators	Manager
• Typology of operations	Atomic (1 record at a time) (Creating-Updating-Retrieving record)	Aggregated/multidimensional view (Drill down - Drill cross)
• Frequency of data feeding	Real time	Batch
• Access	R/W	R
• Data volatility	High	Low
• Metrics	Throughput	Execution time
• Time reference	Present	Past
• Database dimension	Ferom MB to GB	From GB to TB
• Data structure	Optimized for multi-user accesses	Optimized for analysis
• Focus	Process & Application oriented	Subject & Business oriented (DSS)

a data warehouse, come from heterogeneous and distributed sources and derived from OLTP (On Line Transactional Processing) activities.

Data mart represents a particular "view" on a data warehouse, built to optimize the access of high number of users to context-specific and problem-oriented data and information.

Data mart and data warehouse interact each other both in initial phase, during their creation with top-down and bottom-up approach, and at regime to support OLAP (On Line Analytical Processing) systems in the multi-dimensional analysis on data, by performing:

- 'Slice e Dice' operations (for the visualization of data at various aggregation levels and with different perspectives);
- 'Drill-Down' operations (for data analysis from aggregated and detailed forms);
- 'Rotation' operations (for the reversal of the axis of graphic representation related to data visualization);
- 'Trend Analysis' operations (for the prevision about data performance on temporal base).

The following table reports the main distinctive characteristics of OLAP and OLTP systems.

Knowledge Base (Documental – Multimedia – Learning Object)

Knowledge base allows systematizing the heritage of cognitive resources of an organization in a organic, systemic, logically structured and interconnected way. Knowledge base offers multifaceted semantic views on the same heritage of knowledge resources, which is created by processes of storing data, documents, multimedia objects and learning objects into file system or database. These views are obtained by introducing a semantic layer in the traditional data structure. This layer is constituted by ontologies, taxonomies, thesauri, metadata structures, through which realize real cognitive

maps that provide a flexible, intelligent and user-centric representation of knowledge resources of an organization.

Data Integration and Data Extraction Tools

Data integration and data extraction tools, usually, take part in construction and generation of new data structures from existing sources. An example of tools of this category are ETL (Extract – Transform – Load) softwares that extract raw data stored in the original sources, submit them to cleaning process for the validation and store them in new data structures on which data mining algorithms and OLAP systems operate. EAI (Enterprise Application Integration) tools have particular relevance, since they realize integration of data, applications and entire informative systems, both intra-organizational and inter-organizational level, generating new informative structures, which are fed in a coherent way and aligned with operative processes of the organization.

Authoring, Validating, Indexing and Workflow Tools

Documents, multimedia and learning objects creation tools can be grouped into four main categories:

- *Authoring tools*: software tools for the 'physic' creation of specific knowledge resource. These tools can be very simple, as Office Automation suite (example: Microsoft Word or Microsoft Power Point) for the creation of text document or dynamic presentation, or can be complex, as Adobe Premiere for the realization of a multimedia object, or as IBM Content Producer (or Docent Outliner) for the realization of a web-learning path with assessment. Regardless of specific tool, it is fundamental that authoring tools are user/friendly, have a set of standard templates which can be extended and personalized, have an IDE (Integrated Development Environment), offer the opportunity to recover and reuse contents already developed, generate output which respect the standard, support the collaborative development of the resources, give the opportunity to consult help on line and FAQ (frequently asked question) in a flexible way.

- *Validation tools*: tools for knowledge resources validation, by producer and by third parties. These tools allow also to highlight significant parts of the resources and to associate notes, comments and references for further elaboration.

- *Indexing tools*: tools for the indexing process of knowledge resources that associate a resource to a set of simplex metadata or complex semantic annotations, coherently to the structure of the adopted semantic layer. These tools can be stand-alone or web-based tools, owned by a single company or completely open source, used on internal knowledge base (example: intranet) or on public and shared knowledge base (example: web), automatic or semi-automatic or manual.

- *Workflow tools*: tools that define production process of knowledge resources, in relation to phases to complete, states to plan, version to produce, role to define, action to perform. Also, workflow tools act as coordination tools in the resources generation processes.

Recently, the four categories of resources above cited, constitute the main assets at the base of the architecture of a Content Management System (CMS). In fact, CMS allows organizing all processes of contents management, from the contents creation to publishing and storing, in a web environment, by coordinating the activities of all involved actors in the different phases of the content life cycle.

Particular tools that are acquiring considerable importance relative to CMS tools are wikies.

Wikies are web based tools characterized by distributed processes for the content creation (wiki-pages). The collaborative dimension of wikies characterizes site identity and users/navigators/authors identity.

Usually, wikies are outlined as self-organized environment, in which everyone contributes as authors or readers, respecting an explicitly or implicitly defined behaviour.

Data Processing and Data Analyzing Tools

Data processing and data analyzing tools constitute main point of access to sources of raw data. In fact, these tools allow to launch elaborations on huge amount of data, in order to extract useful information for operative and/or decisional processes. The elaborations are based on techniques of simulation, artificial intelligence, statistics, clustering, pattern recognition, decisional trees and 'what if' scenario analysis.

Search and Retrieval Tools

Search and retrieval tools drive users toward localization of knowledge resources more adapt in relation to the problem to solve and/or to solution to formulate. For this purpose, traditional search (and meta-search) tools based on keywords or statistic algorithms often reveal insufficiencies and innovative approaches based on artificial intelligence and Semantic Web begin to complement the first ones. The tools of this category can use both push technologies (newsletter, mailing list, etc.) and pull technologies (web browsing, search engines, navigators, forums, etc.) and usually they are used to guarantee direct access to documents, multimedia objects and people.

Virtual and Managed Learning Environment (VLE, MLE)

Virtual Learning Environment is a virtual and interactive learning community on the web. The VLE represents the main point of access for delivering learning paths and it proves to be effective in the realization of non-hierarchical learning groups, aimed to share idea, opinions, projects and know-how, remaining active also after the institutional time deadline of training and learning. The VLE seems to be effective in the education, especially if it is in relation with on-line education of first generation (CBT – Computer Based Training), but it still presents some difficulties in the organization of learning contents, in the retrieval and reuse phases depending on educational needs of specific user profile. The production, classification and organization of learning contents represent a strong point of the Managed Learning Environment (MLE).

MLE aims to manage, in an integrate way, a complete system of analysis, competences development and evaluation, learning paths planning and organization, roles and virtual classes description, processes definition and results evaluation. In the MLE, the aspects related to privacy protection and DRM (Digital Rights Management) policies are relevant for the recognition of intellectual properties of available resources and for the allowed operation on these resources. Also, the elements that permit the semantic description of learning contents and its intelligent classification (oriented to application and user profile), are fundamental to maximize effectiveness of learning processes through the use of web learning technological platforms.

Help Desk, Query and Reporting Tools, Linkopedia

Help desk, query and reporting tools, linkopedia are particularly adapt for knowledge dissemination processes. These three typologies of tools allow individuating, organizing and delimitating intervention area, offering right aggregate data to user requirements.

The help desk captures a great quantity of information about products, systems and operative processes. After initial organization, these information are disseminated and distributed in different ways in order to make them rapidly accessible to users (for example customer care operator), by providing so immediate solutions.

Query and reporting tool supports users in the structured questions on the available data sources. The results of these questions are standardized with personalized reports (electronic and paper based) for the different users' categories. For electronic reports, the tools for dynamic visualization of the data are very important, in order to look subset of data on-line, creating report on demand.

The linkopedia allows to organize and structure a set of links to web resources (identified by URL or URI) through the association of descriptive parameters that represent content, purpose and possible use.

Publishing Tools and Streaming Technologies

Publishing tools aim mainly to diffuse and delivery on Intranet, Extranet or Internet documents and multimedia contents (as reviews, elaborations, editorials, comments, seminars, multimedia events and objects in general) about interesting topic for users. Publishing process requires an high level of flexibility, easiness and immediacy, and it has not to require specific and technological competence about web editing. Forms, templates and models guarantee the efficiency in the publishing processes. Feedbacks about the quality of published contents guarantee high levels of effectiveness. Notification services of effective publication of a content increase both effectiveness and efficiency of the tool.

In this context, streaming technologies are particularly effective in order to increase the interest of final user, enhancing the level of understanding and elaboration of the distributed knowledge resources. If on the one hand this aspect is true, on the other hand it is necessary that the final user is appropriately 'equipped' (in term of bandwidth and available multimedia devices) in order to live emotions in the use of streaming of multimedia contents.

REFERENCES

ADL, Ottobre 2001, "SCORM 1.2 – Overview, Content Aggregation Model, Run Time Environment" (http://www.adlnet.org)

Damiani E., Corallo A., Elia G., Ceravolo P.,"Standard per i learning objects: Interoperabilità ed integrazione nella didattica a distanza", Convegno internazionale: "eLearning: una sfida per l'Universita' - Strategie Metodi Prospettive", 11-13 Nov., 2002.

Davenport T. and Prusak L. 'Working Knowledge. How organization manage what they know', (Boston: Harward Business School Press,1998)

Delphi Consulting Group, "Delphi on knowledge management. Research and perspectives on today's knowledge landscape", Boston, MA, USA, 1997"

Fugini M., Maio F., Plebani P., "Sicurezza dei sistemi informatici", Milano, Apogeo, 2001

Hansen M. T., Nohria N., Tierney T., "What's Your Strategy for Managing Knowledge?", Harvard Business Review, March-April 1999.

Heisig P., Mertins K., Vorbeck J., (2001), "Knowledge Management – Best Practices in Europe", Springer

IEEE LTSC, Luglio 2002, "Draft Standard for Learning Object Metadata" (http://ltsc.ieee.org)

Immon W. H., "Building the Data Warehouse", New York, Wiley, 1996.

Kerzner H., "Project Management: A Systems Approach to Planning, Scheduling, and Controlling", Wiley, 2003.

Maier R., 'Knowledge Management Systems, information and communication technologies for Knowledge Management, (Springer-Verlag Heidelberg, 2002).

Nonaka I. and Takeuchi H., 'The Knowledge Creating Company', (New York: Oxford University Press ,1995).

Radding A., (1998), "Knowledge Management – Succeding in the Information based Global Economy", Computer Technology Research Corp.

Ruggles R., "Knowledge Tools: Using Technology to Manage Knowledge Better", 1997.

Saint-Onge H., Wallace D., "Leveraging Communities of Practices for Strategic Advantage", Butterworth Heinemann, 2003.

Schwartz P., Kelly E., Boyer N., "The emerging global knowledge economy", in "The Future of the Global Economy: Towards a Long Boom?", Parigi, OECD, 1999.

Skyrme D. J., "Developing a Knowledge Strategy: From Management to Leadership", in "Knowledge Management Classic and Contemporary Works", Boston, MIT Press, 2000.

Tiwana A. 'The Knowledge Management Tool Kit' (Prentice- Hall Upper Side River , 2000)

Zack M. H., 'Developing a Knowledge Strategy', (California Management Review, Vol. 41, N° 3, Spring 1999)

Wenger E. C., "Communities of Practice", Cambridge University Press, Cambridge, 1998.

Chapter II
Social Software for Bottom–Up Knowledge Networking and Community Building

Mohamed Amine Chatti
RWTH Aachen University, Germany

Matthias Jarke
RWTH Aachen University, Germany

ABSTRACT

Recognizing that knowledge is a key asset for better performance and that knowledge is a human and social activity, building ecologies that foster knowledge networking and community building becomes crucial. Over the past few years, social software has become an important medium to connect people, bridge communities, and leverage collaborative knowledge creation and sharing. In this chapter we explore how social software can support the building and maintaining of knowledge ecologies and discuss the social landscape within different social software mediated communities and networks.

INTRODUCTION

Peter Drucker, among others, argues that in the emerging economy, knowledge is the primary resource for individuals and for the economy overall; land, labour, and capital. He further argues that improving front-line worker productivity is the greatest challenge of the 21st century (Drucker, 1999). Knowledge management has become an important topic for the CSCW community within the last couple of years (Davenport and Prusak 1998). A specific contribution of CSCW to the

Copyright © 2009, IGI Global, distributing in print or electronic forms without written permission of IGI Global is prohibited.

knowledge management field has been to draw attention to the social aspect of knowledge. Within the CSCW community, some important research emphasises the social properties of knowledge and how it is shared among and between communities and networks (Wenger, 1998a; Engeström et al., 1999; Zager, 2002; Nardi et al., 2002; Stahl, 2005). Over the past few years, social software has become a crucial means to connect people not only to digital knowledge repositories but also to other people, in order to share knowledge and create new forms of social networks and communities. In this chapter, we explore how the emerging social software technologies can support collaborative knowledge creation and sharing and discuss the social landscape within different social software mediated communities and networks.

KNOWLEDGE, COMMUNITIES, AND NETWORKS

The Social Aspect of Knowledge

Many researchers have provided different definitions for the term knowledge. Nonaka and Takeuchi (1995) define knowledge as justified true belief. Davenport and Prusak (1998) view knowledge as a fluid mix of framed experience, values, contextual information, and expert insight that provides a framework for evaluating and incorporating new experiences and information. It originates in the minds of knowers. In organizations, it often becomes embedded not only in documents or repositories but also in organizational routines, processes, practices, and norms. Drucker (1989) states that Knowledge is information that changes something or somebody, either by becoming grounds for actions, or by making an individual (or an institution) capable of different or more effective action. Drucker further distinguishes between data, information and knowledge and stresses that information is data endowed with relevance and purpose. Converting data into infor-

mation thus requires knowledge. And knowledge, by definition, is specialized. Naeve (2005) defines knowledge as "efficient fantasies", with a context, a purpose and a target group, with respect to all of which their efficiency should be evaluated. Recently, Siemens (2006) points out that due to the nature of knowledge, it is very difficult to find a common definition and states that knowledge can be described in many ways; an entity and a process, a sequence of continuums: type, level, and application, implicit, explicit, tacit, procedural, declarative, inductive, deductive, qualitative, and quantitative.

Different views of knowledge exist and many researchers have developed classifications of knowledge, most of them in form of opposites (Hildreth and Kimble, 2002). A distinction that is often cited in the literature is made between explicit and tacit knowledge. Explicit knowledge is systematic knowledge that is easily codified in formal language and objective. In contrast, tacit knowledge is not easily codified, difficult to express and subjective. Examples of tacit knowledge are know how, expertise, understandings, experiences and skills resulting from previous activities (Nonaka and Takeuchi, 1995; Nonaka and Konno, 1998). Similarly, Davenport and Prusak (1998) differentiate between structured and less structured knowledge. Seely Brown and Duguid (1998) adopt the terms know what and know how, while Hildreth and Kimble (2002) distinguish between hard and soft knowledge.

Although there is no common definition of the term knowledge, there is a wide agreement that knowledge is social in nature. Many researchers emphasise the social, collective and distributed aspect of knowledge. Polanyi (1967) places a strong emphasis on dialogue and conversation within an open community to leverage tacit knowledge and one of his three main theses is that knowledge is socially constructed. Nonaka and Takeuchi (1995) state that the dynamic model of knowledge creation is anchored to a critical assumption that human knowledge is created and expanded through social interaction between tacit knowledge and explicit knowledge. They further note that this conversion is a social process between individuals and not confined within an individual. Wenger (1998a) points out that knowledge does not exist either in a world of its own or in individual minds but is an aspect of participation in cultural practices. He uses the term participation to describe the social experience of living in the world in terms of membership in social communities and active involvement in social enterprises. Participation in this sense is both personal and social. It is a complex process that combines doing, talking, thinking, feeling, and belonging. It involves our whole person, including our bodies, minds, emotions, and social relations. Wenger stresses that participation is not tantamount to collaboration. It can involve all kinds of relations, conflictual as well as harmonious, intimate as well as political, competitive as well as cooperative. Paavola et al. (2002) propose the metaphor of collective knowledge creation. They discuss three models of innovative knowledge communities; Nonaka and Takeuchi's model of knowledge-creating organization, Engeström's expansive learning model, and Bereiter's theory of knowledge building and point out that all of these models agree that knowledge creation is a fundamentally social process in nature. More recently, Stahl (2005) points out that beliefs become knowledge through social interaction, communication, discussion, clarification and negotiation and that knowledge is a socially mediated product. Siemens (2006) stresses that the challenge today is not what you know but who you know and states that knowledge rests in an individual and resides in the collective. Recognizing that knowledge is a key asset for better performance and that knowledge is a human and social activity, building and maintaining communities and networks that support collaborative knowledge creation and sharing become crucial.

Communities and Networks

Siemens (2006) defines a community as the clustering of similar areas of interest that allows for interaction, sharing, dialoguing, and thinking together. Lave and Wenger (1991) point out that community does not imply necessarily co- presence, a well-defined, identifiable group or socially visible boundaries. It does imply participation in an activity system about which participants share understanding concerning what they are doing and what that means in their lives and for their communities. Quoting Packwood (2004), White (2005) states that a community is present when individual and collective identity begins to be expressed; when we care about who said what, not just the what; when relationship is part of the dynamic and links are no longer the only currency of exchange. The concept of community is very close to the concept of social network. Siemens (2006) defines a network as connections between entities to create an integrated whole. The power of networks rests in their ability to expand, grow, react, and adapt. A network grows in diversity and value through the process of connecting to other nodes or networks. A node in a network can consist of a person, a content resource, or other networks. Nardi et al. (2002) stress that a network is not a collective subject. A network is an important source of labour for the formation of a collective subject. The authors further define a social network as a complex, dynamic system in which, at any given time, various versions of the network exist in different instantiations. Part of the network may be actively embodied through intense communications as a major project is underway. Other parts of the network are instantiated differently, through less intense communications as well as acts of remembering.

Social networks and communities have been viewed from different perspectives and diverse social forms have been introduced in the CSCW literature. These include "communities of practice" (Wenger, 1998a), "knots" (Engeström et al., 1999), "coalitions" (Zager, 2000), and "intensional networks" (Nardi et al., 2002). As a special type of community, Wenger (1998a) introduces the concept of **communities of practice** (CoP). Wenger defines CoP as groups of people who share a concern or a passion for something they do and learn how to do it better as they interact regularly. According to Wenger, a CoP is characterised by: (a) The domain; a CoP has an identity defined by a shared domain of interest. Membership therefore implies a commitment to the domain, and therefore a shared competence that distinguishes members from other people. (b) The community; in pursuing their interest in their domain, members engage in joint activities and discussions, help each other, and share information. They build relationships that enable them to learn from each other. A website in itself is not a community of practice. (c) The practice; members of a community of practice are practitioners. They develop a shared repertoire of resources: experiences, stories, tools, ways of addressing recurring problems, in short a shared practice. This takes time and sustained interaction. To differentiate between CoP and network, Wenger (1998b) states that a CoP is different from a network in the sense that it is about something; it is not just a set of relationships. It has an identity as a community, and thus shapes the identities of its members. A CoP exists because it produces a shared practice as members engage in a collective process of learning.

Within an activity theory framework, Engeström et al. (1999) note that a great deal of work in today's workplace is not taking place in teams with predetermined rules or central authority but in work communities in which combinations of people, tasks and tools are unique, of relatively short duration. The authors introduce the concept of **knotworking** to describe temporal situation-driven combinations of people, tasks, and tools, emerging within or between activity systems. According to the authors, the notion of

knot refers to rapidly pulsating, distributed, and partially improvised orchestration of collaborative performance between otherwise loosely connected actors and organizational units. Knotworking is characterized by a movement of tying, untying, and retying together seemingly separate threads of activity. In knotworking the centre does not hold, meaning that the tying and dissolution of a knot of collaborative work is not reducible to any specific individual or fixed organizational entity as the centre of control or authority . The authors contrast knots to communities of practice, noting the differences between the two in terms of knots' loose connections, short duration of relationships, and lack of shared lore. They also contrast knots to networks, stating that a network is commonly understood as a relatively stable web of links or connections between organizational units, often materially anchored in shared information systems. Knotworking, on the other hand, is a much more elusive and improvised phenomenon.

Zager (2002) explores a collaboration configuration called a **coalition** and notes that coalitions are temporary collaborative groups where shared concerns and interests connect constituent individuals and teams. Constituents are part-time members of the coalition, making the coalition loosely bound. At any moment, the coalition's membership is fluid and diffuse, and communications among constituents may be non-existent, hindering coordination of the coalition. The organization of the coalition is bottom-up, comprising independent participants acting on their own, with little or no reference to the other participants. Nardi et al. (2002) point out that coalitions share many of the characteristics of knots in being temporary, loosely bound, and fluid. The authors further note that while knots and coalitions are similar, it is worth making a distinction between smaller, more discrete knots where certain kind of interactions are possible, and more distributed coalitions. Coalitions differ from knots in that they occur in large distributed organizations where people involved in the knot are in separate parts of the organization and often out of communication with one another.

Nardi et al. (2002) note that the most fundamental unit of analysis for computer supported cooperative work is not at the group level for many tasks and settings, but at the individual level as personal social networks come to be more and more important. The authors develop the concept of **intensional networks** to describe the personal social networks workers draw from and collaborate with to get their work done. The authors further use the term **NetWORK** to refer to the ongoing process of keeping a personal network in good repair. Key netWORK tasks include (1) building a network, i.e. adding new contacts to the network so that there are available resources when it is time to conduct joint work; (2) maintaining the network, where a central task is keeping in touch with extant contacts; (3) activating selected contacts at the time the work is to be done. Nardi et al. compare intensional networks to communities of practice, knots, and coalitions. The authors note that intensional networks differ considerably from communities of practice stating that Intensional networks are personal, more heterogeneous, and more distributed than communities of practices. According to the authors, intensional networks also differ from knots in several ways. First, intensional networks often involve long-term relationships. Second, the joint work may last for long or short periods of time. Third, the knotworking that occurs within established institutions is more structured in terms of the roles it draws upon. In contrast, work that is mediated by intensional networks results in more flexible and less predictable configurations of workers. Fourth, in intensional networks, workers are not thrown together in situation dependent ways or assembled through outside forces. Instead, work activities are accomplished through the deliberate activation of workers' personal networks. Nardi et al. further point out that intensional networks differ from coalitions on the dimension of intentionality. An intensional network is a deliberately

configured and persistent personal network created for joint work, whereas a coalition is highly emergent, fluid, and responsive to state changes in a large system.

SOCIAL SOFTWARE: TECHNOLOGY FOR COMMUNITIES

Web 2.0 and Social Software

Over the past few years, the Web was shifting from being a medium into being a platform that has a social dimension. We are entering a new phase of Web evolution: The read-write Web (also called **Web 2.0**) where everyone can be a consumer as well as a producer of knowledge in new settings that place a significant value on collaboration. Web 2.0 is a new generation of user-centric, open, dynamic Web, with peer production, sharing, collaboration, distributed content and decentralized authority in the foreground. **Harnessing collective intelligence** has become the driving force behind Web 2.0. Jenkins et al. (2006) define collective intelligence as the ability to pool knowledge and compare notes with others towards a common goal. Levy (1999) sees collective intelligence as an important source of power in knowledge communities to confront problems of greater scale and complexity than any single person might be able to handle. He argues that everyone knows something, nobody knows everything, and what any one person knows can be tapped by the group as a whole. Collective intelligence is similar to the concept of the **wisdom of crowds** introduced by James Surowiecki in his book with the same name. Surowiecki (2004) explores the idea that large groups of people are smarter than an elite few, no matter how brilliant. He argues that the many are better at solving problems, fostering innovation, coming to wise decisions, and predicting the future than the few.

Social software, also called **social media**, has emerged as the leading edge of Web 2.0 and has become a crucial medium to connect people not only to digital knowledge repositories but also to other people, in order to share and collaboratively create new forms of dynamic knowledge. Rapidly evolving examples of social software include wikis, blogs, Web feeds, media sharing, social tagging, and pod/vodcasting. Social software is however not restricted to these technologies. Below we provide a brief outline of characteristics of each social software technology.

Recently, wikis have seen a growing mainstream interest. A wiki is a collaborative Web site which can be constantly edited online through the web browser by anyone who cares to contribute. Once created, a wiki can be revised collaboratively, items can be added or deleted easily, and changes can be made quickly, thereby building a shared knowledge repository.

Another form of Web publishing, which has seen an increase in popularity over the past few years, is blogging. Blog creation is rapidly growing. In contradiction to wikis, where anyone can add and edit items, a blog can only be edited by one individual (personal blog) or a small number of persons (group blog or organizational/business blog). A blog is a frequently updated Web site made up of dated entries presented in reverse chronological order, addressed as posts. The posts normally consist of texts, often accompanied by pictures or other media, generally containing links to other blog entries recommended or commented by the author. Each post can be assigned one or multiple tags/keywords as well as a permanent pointer (permalink) through which it can be addressed later. Older posts are moved to a searchable tag-based archive. Additionally, displayed on the sidebar of a blog, there often is available a list of other blogs that the author reads on a regular basis, called blogrolls. Readers can attach comments to a particular blog post. Trackbacks enable to track citations and references to a blog post from other posts in other blogs and automatically link back to these references. New variants of blogs are gaining more popularity each day. Examples include

photoblogs (phlogs) which have photographs as primary content, video blogs (vlogs) which focus on videos and mobile blogs (moblogs) which offer a way for users to post content (e.g. pictures, video and text) from a mobile or portable device directly to their blogs. An enhancement of blogs are Web feeds e.g. RSS and Atom feeds. Web feeds are a new mode of communication that allows e.g. blog-authors to syndicate their posts and gives blog-readers the opportunity to subscribe to selected blogs with topics they are interested in and receive new published content.

Another popular example of social software is media sharing and social tagging. Today, Web users are sharing almost everything: ideas, goals, wish lists, hobbies, files, photos, videos, bookmarks. Additionally they are using tags to organize their own digital collections. Tagging can be defined as user- driven, freeform labelling of content. Users create tags in order to be able to classify, categorize and refind their own digital collections at a later time. Tagging is implemented on the most popular social sites such as on Flickr to organize photos, on YouTube to classify videos, on del.icio.us or Yahoo's My Web to categorize bookmarks, and on 43 things to describe lifetime goals.

Podcasting is also becoming mainstream. The term is a combination of the two words iPod and broadcasting and refers to digital audio files that are recorded by individuals and then made available for subscription and download via Webfeeds. These files can then be accessed on a variety of digital audio devices. A variant of podcasting, called vodcasting (the "vod" stands for "video-on-demand"), works in an almost identical way but offers videos for streaming and download.

Social software offers new opportunities for social closeness and foster changes in the ways how people network and interact with each other. In the next section, we discuss the social landscape within different social software mediated communities.

Social Software Mediated Communities

Social software has been opening new doors for social knowledge networking and dynamic community building. Social software mediated communities are organized from the bottom up. Bottom-up communities are co-constructed and maintained by individual actors. They emerge naturally and are derived from the overlapping of different personal social networks. In contrast, top-down communities are hierarchical social structures under the control mechanisms of outside forces. The social structures evolving around social software are close to Engeström's knots. In fact, social software enables the formation of networks between loosely connected individual actors using distributed tools. These networks have no centre or stable configuration and are characterized by distributed control and coordinated action between individual actors. Furthermore, social software supports the netWORKing perspective in Nardi et al. (2002); that is building and maintaining personal social networks. Social software driven networks are similar to what Nardi et al. describe as intensional networks in that they arise from individual actors that self-organize in flexible and less predictable configurations of actors. The social software networking model is based on personal environments, loosely joined. Rather than belonging to hierarchical and controlled groups, each person has her own personal network. Based on their needs and preferences, different actors come together for a particular task. They work together until the task is achieved and thereby do not have a permanent relationship with a formal organization or institution. Owen et al. (2006) point out that an important benefit from social software is the ability to cross boundaries. People might be able to join communities that they would not otherwise join. They have the opportunity to move beyond their geographic or social community and enter other communities and at the same time others

can move into theirs. Moreover, there is no barrier to be member of communities that contain other ages, cultures and expertise.

Blogs, Web feeds, wikis, podcasts, and social tagging services have developed new means to connect people and link distributed knowledge communities. Blogging began as a personal publishing phenomenon and evolved into a powerful social networking tool. Besides their usage as simple personal publishing tool, blogs can be used as (a) personal knowledge management system to help us capturing, annotating, organizing, reflecting, and exchanging our personal knowledge; (b) distributed knowledge repository that we can use to access and search for appropriate knowledge resources; (c) communication medium that enables us to comment, rate, review, criticize, recommend and discuss a wide range of knowledge assets with peers worldwide; and (d) community forming service to sustain existing social ties and develop new social ties with others sharing similar practices or interests. Moreover, blogging is a good example of a technology that starts with individuals and supports bottom-up dynamic building of personal social networks. Commenting on blog posts makes the interaction between blog-authors and -readers possible and can lead to interesting discussions. New blog-readers can then join the discussion by commenting or writing a post on their own blog with a reference to the blog post that they want to comment on. Trackbacks detect these remote references and enable to establish a distributed discussion across multiple blogs. Web feeds offer a powerful communication medium that enables people to keep track of various blogs and receive notification of up-to-date content. Through comments, citations, trackbacks and Web feeds, a social network from people with similar practices or interests can be created and even enlarged by blogrolls. White (2006) identifies three types of blog based communities: (a) the Single Blog/Blogger Centric Community emerging around a single blogger where readers return to the bloggers' site, comment and get to know not only the blogger, but the community of commentors; (b) the Central Connecting Topic Community that arises between blogs linked by a common passion or topic. What links them is hyperlinks, in the form of blogrolls, links to other blogs within blog posts, tagging, aggregated feeds, trackbacks and comments; and (c) the Boundaried Community where blogs are hosted on a central site or platform. Typically members register and join the community and are offered the chance to create a blog. The communities that emerge from blogging establish their own rules and roles. Citing Cross and Parker (2004), White (2006) points to different roles in blog based communities; i.e. Central Connectors, Unsung Heroes, Bottlenecks, Boundary Spanners and Peripheral People.

Wikis have evolved in recent years to become a simple and lightweight tool for knowledge capturing, asynchronous collaborative content creation, information organization, peer editing, and working on a team project. A wiki is also an important community service that has the potential to build communities coming in from the bottom up. A wiki can connect multiple authors across organizations and institutions. Everyone is able to post, edit, delete, and comment content. Over time, a collaborative social space and a shared knowledge repository will emerge. The most successful model for a wiki is surely the open and freely editable encyclopaedia Wikipedia. Additionally, several wiki-like, more professional services, such as Google Docs, have emerged as collaborative writing tools which let users come and work together on a shared project and rapidly create a new collaborative space. The fact that knowledge created by many is much more likely to be of better value makes wikis a key technology in collective intelligence communities that ensures that the captured knowledge is up-to-date and more accurate.

Media sharing sites, e.g. Flickr, YouTube, del.icio.us, Digg, Slideshare, CiteULike provide innovative collaborative ways of organizing media. These sites have powerful community features.

Users can upload, rate, tag different media, post comments, interact with other members by forming groups, and track their activities by adding contacts. Social tagging is being used by most of the media sharing sites to classify, categorize, and manage media in a collaborative, emergent, and dynamic way. This classification scheme has been referred to as "folksonomy", a combination of "folks" and "taxonomy", which implies a bottom-up approach of organizing content as opposed to a hierarchical and top-down taxonomy. The folksonomy is a good example of the collective intelligence at work. Media sharing, social tagging and folksonomies provide a powerful way to foster bottom-up community building as users share, organize, filter interesting information for each other, browse related topics, discover unexpected resources that otherwise they would never know existing, look for what others have tagged, subscribe to an interesting tag and receive new content labelled with that tag via Web feeds, and find unknown people with similar interests.

SOCIAL SOFTWARE AND SOCIAL NETWORK ANALYSIS

As social software becomes important for building and bridging communities, tools that enable people to manage, analyze, and visualize their social software mediated networks gain popularity. Thereby, different social network analysis methods have been applied. Social network analysis (SNA) is the quantitative study of the relationships between individuals or organizations. Social network analysts represent relationships in graphs where individuals or organizations are portrayed as nodes (also referred to as actors or vertices) and their connections to one another as edges (also referred to as ties or links). By quantifying social structures, social network analysts can determine the most important nodes in the network (Wasserman and Faust, 1994). One of the key characteristics of networks is centrality.

Centrality relates to the structural position of a node within a network and details the prominence of a node and the nature of its relation to the rest of the network. The centrality of a node is influenced by the following factors: (a) degree, which determines the root by identifying the object with the most direct connections to other objects within the network. This finds the object with the most influence over the network, (b) closeness, which determines the root as the object with the lowest number of links to all other objects within the network. This finds the object with the quickest access to the highest number of other objects within the network, and (c) betweenness, which determines the root as the object between the most other linked objects. This measure finds objects that control the information flow of the network (Siemens, 2005).

Our literature survey on the analysis of social software mediated networks has revealed that there is limited empirical work on the analysis of social networks issued through wikis or social tagging. There is however a growing interest in blog social network analysis. Recognizing that blogging is a highly social activity, recent blog research has focused on citations, comments, trackbacks, and blogrolls as indicators of cross-blog conversational activities and has employed social network analysis techniques to detect the linking patterns of blogs, the development of blog based communities, and the popularity of blog-authors. In fact, comments, trackbacks, and blogrolls are a measure of reputation and influence of a blog-author, as an interesting blog post will be frequently commented or cited in other blogs and a popular blog will be often listed in the blogrolls. Blog social network analysis research has adopted different metrics for blog analysis, i.e. the link mass metric, the converstaion mass metric, and the content and conversation mass metric. Different studies have used the link structure of the blogosphere for authority detection and community identification (link mass). For example Marlow (2004) assumes that links to a given blog

are a proxy to the authority of that blog and uses the social network analysis metrics in-degree (links in) and out-degree (links out) to identify authoritative blog authors. Similarly, Adar et al. (2004) propose the use of link structure in blog networks to infer the dynamics of information epidemics in the blogspace and show that the PageRank algorithm identifies authoritative blogs. Kumar et al. (2005) examine the structure of the blogosphere in terms of the bursty nature of linking activity. By comparing two large blog datasets, Shi et al. (2007) demonstrate that samples may differ significantly in their coverage but still show consistency in their aggregate network properties. The authors show that properties such as degree distributions and clustering coefficients depend on the time frame over which the network is aggregated. McGlohon et al. (2007) observe that the usual method of blog ranking is in-links and stress that simply counting the number of in-links does not capture the amount of buzz a particular post or blog creates. The authors argue that the conversation mass metric is a better proxy for measuring influence. This metric captures the mass of the total conversation generated by a blogger, while number of in-links captures only direct responses to the blogger's posts. Similarly, Ali-Hasan and Adamic (2007) notice that most of the blog research to date has only focused on blogrolls and citation links. The authors stress that much of the interesting interaction occurs in comments and point out that reciprocal blogroll links indicate possibly only a mutual awareness, whereas reciprocal comments and citations imply a greater level of interaction. Bulters and de Rijke (2007) point out that traditional methods for community finding focus almost exclusively on topology analysis. The authors present a method for discovering blog communities that incorporates both topology- and content analysis (content and conversation mass). The proposed method builds on three core ingredients: content analysis, co-citation, and reciprocity.

CONCLUSION

In this chapter, we mainly discussed how social software can support the building and maintaining of ecologies that foster knowledge networking and community building. We explored the social structures emerging around social software and found out that social software mediated communities are organized from the bottom up. Finally, we would like to stress two important issues. Firstly, a sole social software technology cannot build a community. Often, relationships start with a social software technology and then extend to other communication media such as email, instant messaging, and face-to-face meetings. Secondly, successful community building and effective knowledge sharing are not primarily dependent on social software technologies. Key prerequisites for knowledge sharing are (a) trust and (b) a participatory culture that allows knowledge to flow and rewards rather than punishes collaboration initiatives. Collaboration has to become the norm and a meaningful part of the performance evaluation of knowledge workers.

REFERENCES

Adar, E., Zhang, L., Adamic, L. A, & Lukose, R. M. (2004). Implicit structure and the dynamics of blogspace. In *Workshop on the Weblogging Ecosystem*, New York, NY, USA, May 2004.

Ali-Hasan, N. F., & Adamic, L. A. (2007). Expressing Social Relationships on the Blog through Links and Comments. *Proceedings of International Conference on Weblogs and Social Media*, Boulder, Colorado, USA, March 26-28, 2007.

Bulters, J., & de Rijke, M. (2007). Discovering Weblog Communities. *Proceedings of International Conference on Weblogs and Social Media*, Boulder, Colorado, USA, March 26- 28, 2007.

Cross, R., & Parker, A. (2004). *The Hidden Power of Social Networks: understanding how work really gets done in organizations*. Harvard Business School Press, Boston.

Davenport, T. H., & Prusak, L. (1998). *Working Knowledge: How Organizations Manage What They Know*. Harvard Business School Press, Boston, MA, USA.

Drucker, P. F. (1989). *The New Realities: In Government and Politics, in Economics and Business, in Society and World View*. Harper & Row, New York.

Drucker, P. F. (1999). *Knowledge Worker Productivity: The Biggest Challenge*. California Management Review, Vol.1 No. 2, pp. 79-94.

Engeström, Y., Engeström, R., & Vähäaho, T. (1999). When the Center Doesn't Hold: The Importance of Knotworking. In: S. Chaiklin, M. Hedegaard, and U. Jensen (editors). *Activity Theory and Social Practice: Cultural-Historical Approaches*. Aarhus, Denmark: Aarhus University Press, 1999.

Hildreth, P.J., & Kimble, C. (2002). The duality of knowledge. *Information Research*, 8(1), paper no. 142.

Jenkins, H. et al. (2006). Confronting the challenges of participatory culture. *MacArthur Foundation*, 2006.

Kumar, R., Novak, J., Raghavan, P., & Tomkins, A. (2005). On the bursty evolution of blogspace. *World Wide Web*, 8 (2):159–178, June 2005.

Levy, P. (1999). *Collective Intelligence: Mankind's Emerging World in Cyberspace*. New York: Perseus.

Marlow, C. (2004). Audience, structure and authority in the weblog community. Paper presented at the *International Communication Association Conference*, May 27-June 1, New Orleans, LA.

Naeve, A. (2005). The Human Semantic Web – Shifting from Knowledge Push to Knowledge Pull. *International Journal of Semantic Web and Information Systems (IJSWIS)*, 1(3), pp. 1-30.

Nardi, B., Whittaker, S., & Schwarz, H. (2002). NetWORKers and their Activity in Intensional Networks. In: *Computer Supported Cooperative Work* 11: 205–242, 2002.

Nonaka, I., & Konno, N. (1998). The concept of "Ba": Building foundation for Knowledge Creation. *California Management Review*, 40(3).

Nonaka, I., & Takeuchi H. (1995). *The Knowledge-Creating Company: How Japanese Companies Create the Dynamics of Innovation*, New York: Oxford University.

Owen, M., Grant L., Sayers S., & Facer K. (2006). Social Software and Learning. *FutureLab*: Bristol, UK.

Paavola, S., Lipponen, L., & Hakkarainen, K. (2002). Epistemological Foundations for CSCL: A Comparison of Three Models of Innovative Knowledge Communities. *Proceedings of the Computer-supported Collaborative Learning 2002 Conference*, Hillsdale, N.J.; Erlbaum (2002), pp. 24-32.

Packwood, N. (2004). Geography of the Blogosphere: Representing the Culture, Ecology and Community of Weblogs. In *Into the blogosphere: Rhetoric, community, and culture of weblogs*, eds. L.J. Gurak, S. Antonijevic, L. Johnson, C. Ratliff, & J. Reyman.

Polanyi, M. (1967). *The Tacit Dimension.* New York, Anchor books (based on the 1962 Terry lectures).

Seely Brown, J., & Duguid, P. (1998). Organizing knowledge. *California Management Review*, 40(3), 90-111.

Shi, X., Tseng, B., & Adamic, L. A. (2007). Looking at the Blogosphere Topology through Different Lenses. *Proceedings of International Conference on Weblogs and Social Media*, Boulder, Colorado, USA, March 26-28, 2007.

Siemens, G. (2005). Connectivism: Learning as Network-Creation. *Elearnspace*. Retrieved May 24, 2007, from http://www.elearnspace.org/Articles/networks.htm

Siemens, G. (2006). *Knowing Knowledge*, Lulu.com, ISBN: 978-1-4303-0230-8.

Stahl, G. (2005). *Group Cognition: Computer Support for Collaborative Knowledge Building*. Cambridge, MA: MIT Press.

Surowiecki, J. (2004). *The wisdom of crowds: Why the many are smarter than the few and how collective wisdom shapes business, economies, societies, and nations* (1st ed.). New York: Doubleday.

Wasserman, S., & Faust, K. (1994). *Social network analysis: Methods and applications*. Cambridge University Press, Cambridge, United Kingdom, 1994.

Wenger, E. (1998a). *Communities of Practice*. Cambridge, Eng.: Cambridge University Press.

Wenger, E. (1998b). Communities of practice. Learning as a Social System. *The Systems Thinker*, 9(5). Community Intelligence Labs.

White, N. (2005). *How Some Folks Have Tried to Describe Community*. Retrieved May 21, 2007, from http://www.fullcirc.com/community/definingcommunity.htm

White, N. (2006). Blogs and Community - launching a new paradigm for online community? *The Knowledge Tree e-Journal of Learning Innovation*. Edition 11, September 2006.

Zager, D., Whittaker, S., & Schwarz, H. (2002). Collaboration as an Activity. In: *Computer Supported Cooperative Work* 11: 181–204, 2002.

Chapter III
Weaving a Knowledge Web with Wikis

Kevin R. Parker
Idaho State University, USA

Joseph T. Chao
Bowling Green State University, USA

ABSTRACT

This chapter introduces wikis in the context of social software, focusing on their powerful information sharing and collaboration features. It begins by defining the wiki concept and then discussing the evolution of wikis, explaining how they first emerged and how they have evolved over time. The social software aspect of wikis is then analyzed, examining how wikis can engender collaborative efforts. It investigates ways in which wikis help to develop communities of users, and finally some of the features that enhance the appeal of wikis as social software. The authors hope that by examining a software tool that users may have already encountered, that they will be better able to understand the basic concepts and value of social software. Further, as future trends are discussed, it is hoped that readers will be able to see the value of incorporating social aspects into both existing and as yet undeveloped software applications.

INSIDE CHAPTER

This chapter explores the wiki, an emerging media concept that allows collaborative content creation on the web. Wikis are a form of social software because they facilitate collaborative work. The objective of this chapter is to explain what a wiki is, how it evolved, and how it can be used in education, government, and business to promote collaborative efforts and knowledge sharing. When a wiki is used for content creation, no longer is a single individual responsible for the

Copyright © 2009, IGI Global, distributing in print or electronic forms without written permission of IGI Global is prohibited.

information provided by a site. For additional readings on wikis the authors recommend a search of Wikipedia, the most successful example of knowledge sharing through wikis. When perusing the history of the incarnation of the wiki concept, readers should bear in mind how the vision of a single individual can lead to new tools that greatly increase productivity.

INTRODUCTION

A wiki is a collaborative and interactive website whose contents can be created and edited using a web browser by anyone granted access. It is one of many software tools that comprise Web 2.0, the emergent generation of web tools and applications (Adie, 2006). Web 2.0 complements, enhances, and adds new collaborative dimensions to social networking. Web 2.0 technologies such as blogs, wikis, podcasts, and RSS feeds are commonly referred to as "social software" because they are characterized by a high degree of connectivity, affording users an opportunity to collaboratively develop web content (Alexander, 2006).

Web 2.0 tools are designed for ease of use and rapidity of deployment, making possible powerful information sharing and straightforward collaboration (Boulos et al., 2006). Further, these tools do not require advanced technical skills to use their features, allowing users to focus on the information exchange and collaborative tasks themselves without first mastering a difficult technological environment (Kirkpatrick, 2006). Such "transparent technologies" (Wheeler, Kelly, & Gale, 2005) allow the user to concentrate more on the task because they can "see through" the technology with which they are interacting.

As shown in Figure 1, the objective of this chapter is to explain the concept of wikis, how wikis evolved, and how wikis work. Once those concepts are understood the social aspects of

Figure 1. Chapter topics

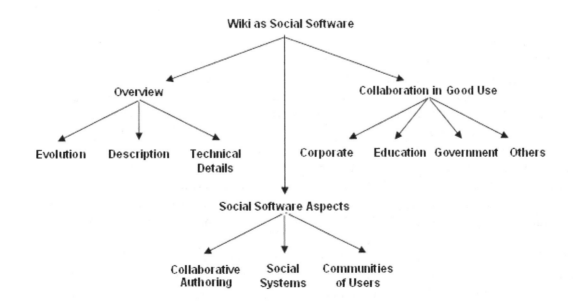

wikis can be explored, including how they can be used for collaborative content creation, how they establish social relationships over a domain of social actions, and how they create communities of users.

BACKGROUND

Evolution of Wikis

The concept of the wiki, or a collection of reader-modifiable web pages, was first envisioned by Howard "Ward" Cunningham. His WikiWikiWeb first became available on the Internet in March, 1995. The WikiWikiWeb was so named because Cunningham thought of his project as a quickly evolving web, or quick web, and remembered encountering a Wiki Wiki bus, Honolulu airport's inter-terminal shuttle bus, on a previous trip to Hawaii. "Wiki wiki" is a Hawaiian phrase meaning quick, and he preferred the sound of wiki wiki web over quick web. The original site's URL abbreviated WikiWikiWeb to wiki, and the short form began to be commonly used. In fact, the word "wiki" is now included in the Oxford English Dictionary and is defined as "A type of web page designed so that its content can be edited by anyone who accesses it, using a simplified markup language."

Wikipedia, the open-access, web-based encyclopedia is, without question, the largest and most widely known wiki project on the web (Lamb, 2004). It is a multilingual, free content encyclopedia project written collaboratively by volunteers, and serves as an excellent illustration of a well-executed wiki. Wikipedia was formally launched in January, 2001. Wikipedia has over six million articles in approximately 250 languages (List of Wikipedias, 2007). Anyone with a web browser can create an article, or edit an article created by someone else. It currently ranks as the ninth most-visited website worldwide (Alexa Traffic Rankings, 2007). The accuracy of encyclopedic entries on scientific topics in Wikipedia is surprisingly good; the number of errors in a typical Wikipedia entry is only slightly higher than a comparable entry in Encyclopaedia Britannica, often considered the gold-standard entry-level reference work. (Wiki's wild world, 2005; Giles, 2005).

Wiki Defined

As noted above, a wiki is a collection of reader-modifiable web pages. Wikis enable users to collaboratively create and edit web content directly, using a web browser. In other words, a wiki is a collaborative web site whose content can be edited by anyone visiting the site, allowing them to easily create and edit web pages collaboratively (Chao, 2007). Wikis can serve as a source of information and knowledge, as well as a tool for collaborative authoring. Wikis allow visitors to engage in dialog and share information among participants in group projects, or to engage in learning with each other by using wikis as a collaborative environment in which to construct their knowledge (Boulos et al., 2006).

As defined in Leuf and Cunningham (2001), the proper term "Wiki" is used to refer to the essential concept rather than to any particular implementation, the latter being called simply a "wiki". From a technical standpoint, the Wiki concept rests on the World Wide Web, and the underlying HTTP protocol defines how the client-server communications occur (Leuf & Cunningham, 2001). At the functional level, Leuf and Cunningham (2001) summarize the essence of Wiki as follows:

- A wiki invites any and all users to edit any page or to create new pages within the wiki site, using only a simple web browser without any additional add-ons.
- Wiki encourages meaningful topic associations between pages by making the creation of page links almost intuitively easy.

- Rather than serving as a carefully crafted site for casual visitors, a wiki seeks to involve the visitor in an ongoing process of creation and collaboration that constantly changes the web site content.

Wiki is essentially a powerful collaboration space that provides a way to organize and cross-link knowledge (Leuf & Cunningham, 2001). Some additional features of wikis include the following:

- Wikis were originally intended for multiple users to create knowledge repositories.
- Wikis are designed for collaborative authoring by everyone and allow the public to edit topics directly.
- Wikis encourage knowledge sharing around topics.
- Wikis typically organize information into topics, which are expected to evolve and often expand into something of a permanent knowledge base.
- Wikis show what information is related and make it easy to browse (Woolf, 2006).
- Wikis are useful when information is intended to be modified and enhanced as part of a collaborative effort (Mader, 2006).

How Wikis Work

Wikis are web based, making navigation intuitive. Locating and utilizing information is quick and easy, because wiki content can be linked and cross-linked. Further, wikis enable users to easily edit or update an existing webpage. As the user browses a topic to which they can make a contribution, they can immediately begin editing the page by clicking the appropriate link and making changes from within their browser. It is easy to create pages and links, and there is no fixed taxonomy of the information since the organization of a wiki is based on user contributions and their collective personality (Howley, 2007).

Wikis have two types of writing modes: document mode and thread mode. Document mode allows users to create collaborative documents, usually written in third person. All users leave their additions to the wiki document unsigned. Multiple authors edit and update the content of the document, and over the passage of time the content becomes a representation of the shared knowledge or beliefs of all contributors. Thread mode permits users to carry out discussions in the wiki environment by posting signed messages to which others respond, and eventually a group of threaded messages evolves (Leuf & Cunningham, 2001).

Because wikis are reader-modifiable web pages, they require certain features. Wiki modifications are easy because the processes of reading and editing are both quite simple. In essence, a wiki is a simplification of the process of creating HTML web pages. Simply clicking an "edit this page" link allows instant revisions (Lamb, 2004). Wikis are editable through a browser, and the editing interface is generally simple and easy to use.

Wikis provide a mechanism to record every change that occurs over time as a document is revised. Each time a person makes changes to a wiki page, that revision of the content becomes the current version, and an older version is stored. Versions of the document can be compared side-by-side, and edits can be "rolled back" if necessary. This means that it is possible to revert a page (if necessary) to any of its previous states.

Further, the administrator of the site has control over access, determining which portions are user-editable. Some wikis restrict editing access, allowing only registered members to edit page content, although anyone may view it. Others allow completely unrestricted access, allowing anyone to both edit and view content (Olson, 2006).

Wiki design is based on eleven principles originally formulated by Cunningham (2007), shown in Table 1 below.

Table 1. Wiki design principles

Principle	Explanation
Open	Should a page be found to be incomplete or poorly organized, any reader can edit it as they see fit.
Incremental	Pages can cite other pages, including pages that have not been written yet.
Organic	The structure and text content of the site are open to editing and evolution.
Mundane	A small number of (irregular) text conventions will provide access to the most useful page markup.
Universal	The mechanisms of editing and organizing are the same as those of writing so that any writer is automatically an editor and organizer.
Overt	The formatted (and printed) output will suggest the input required to reproduce it.
Unified	Page names will be drawn from a flat space so that no additional context is required to interpret them.
Precise	Pages will be titled with sufficient precision to avoid most name clashes, typically by forming noun phrases.
Tolerant	Interpretable (even if undesirable) behavior is preferred to error messages.
Observable	Activity within the site can be watched and reviewed by any other visitor to the site.
Convergent	Duplication can be discouraged or removed by finding and citing similar or related content.

Many wiki systems are adding functionalities such as web-based spreadsheets, calendars, documents, photo galleries, private workspaces, hierarchical organization, WYSIWYG (what you see is what you get) web editing, importing Word or Excel files, and even integration with centralized content management systems (Lamb, 2004). WikiMatrix (2007) provides a tool to compare the features of various popular wiki engines. Wiki selection will be discussed more fully in a later section.

MAIN THRUST OF THE CHAPTER

Social Software Aspect

The concept of social software can be traced to the 1960s, when Licklider and Taylor (1968) noted a need for some way of facilitating communication among the people who can contribute effectively to a solution without bringing them together in one place. Allen (2004) notes that the phrase "social software" seems to have been coined in the early 1990s but didn't come into common usage until 2002 probably due to the "Social Software Summit" in November of that year.

As noted earlier, social software is software that connects users, allowing them to develop content collaboratively (Alexander, 2006). Social software offers powerful information sharing and collaboration features, acting as cognitive reflection and amplification tools, and aiding the construction of meaning through the act of self-design of knowledge databases (Jonassen, Peck, & Wilson, 1999). Social software helps to bring about the original vision of the web as a medium in which anyone can participate (Schaffert, Gruber, & Westenthaler, 2006).

Wikis epitomize the definition of social software because they are characterized by a variety of unique and powerful information sharing and collaboration features (Parker & Chao, 2007). Wikis are expressly designed for collaborative authoring, allowing anyone to edit topics directly and encouraging knowledge sharing around topics.

Globalization

Widespread globalization is forcing businesses to rely increasingly on distributed knowledge and distributed work teams that cannot easily meet face to face (Davies, 2004). This displacement of teams into virtual environments intensifies the importance of knowledge sharing (Tilley & Giordano, 2003). Fortunately, wikis have the ability to disseminate knowledge to various domains that are spread across time, distance, and organizations (Gonzalez-Reinhart, 2005).

Organizational Complexity

Evans (2006) asserts that "the scale and complexity of organizations and supply chains have grown beyond the capabilities of typical command-and-control, top-down hierarchies." Companies are realizing that collaborative technologies like wikis offer new ways to tap the creative energy of the critical important stakeholder groups—customers, suppliers, and employees (Evans, 2006). In addition, wikis can be used to facilitate the connection between the business and technology environments to ensure that opportunities for efficiency and effectiveness are not overlooked (Pawlowski & Robey, 2004; Newman & Robey, 1992; Gonzalez-Reinhart, 2005). As open systems, wikis' reach extends far beyond departmental or organizational limits, allowing for the expression of the interests from virtually any community (Lamb, 2004).

Social System

Wikis enable extremely rich, flexible collaborations that have positive psychological consequences for their participants and powerful competitive ones for their organizations (Evans & Wolf, 2005). Wikis encourage information sharing by letting everybody take equal responsibility for the information published (Brännström & Mårtenson, 2006). Wiki-style collaborative efforts work within communities of users because they establish systems of trust and reputation (Evans, 2006).

Wikis help to establish social relationships over a domain of social actions that stem from the acceptance, objection, or rejection of a contribution (Korfiatis & Naeve, 2005). In this social software approach the aspirations of individuals to belong and contribute in a group atmosphere are technically supported (Boyd, 2003; Gonzalez-Reinhart, 2005). Such voluntary group participation is believed to create social connections that help realize personal goals (Boyd, 2003; Gonzalez-Reinhart, 2005).

Wiki pages mirror physical communities through socialization and the exchange of information, leading to the creation of conversational knowledge (Gonzalez-Reinhart, 2005). The collaborative document editing effort that characterizes wikis relies on the contributions of multiple authors in a concurrent system that combines the contributions of the collective in an effective way (Korfiatis & Naeve, 2005). The system is democratic because everyone has an equal voice; anyone who uses the wiki can contribute content or even make modifications to content contributed by someone else (Korfiatis & Naeve, 2005). This fosters the social ties vital for knowledge sharing (Boyd, 2003; Gonzalez-Reinhart, 2005). Each revision is the result of a community effort that involves a certain amount of social interactions embedded in the content modification used as a mean of expressing them (Korfiatis & Naeve, 2005).

The most interesting feature from a social research point of view is the implicit negotiation process involved in writing and structuring an article. For example, if a user makes a contribution that is not accepted and therefore erased, the user may be able to review the change log to determine how long their contribution persisted and whether one or multiple individuals were responsible for the change. They can resubmit their contribution, either in its original or modified form, and continue the negotiation process. In this submission and assessment process there are interactions that characterize the dynamics of the negotiation process (Korfiatis & Naeve, 2005). This open feature of wikis allows for communication, collaboration, and negotiation to reach a determination of what is collectively considered accurate and pertinent knowledge (Gonzalez-Reinhart, 2005).

Communities of Users

Wikis create a platform for Communities of Practice that facilitates process-spanning exchange of knowledge (Fuchs-Kittowski, Köhler, & Fuhr, 2004). A Community of Practice refers to a group of people who share an interest in a specific area or practice, and who further their knowledge through interacting with each other. Thus, community knowledge is developed within the community itself as community members try to explain their latent knowledge (Campanini, Castagna, & Tazzoli, 2004).

Wikis can be used as a supporting technology for a Community of Practice because they enable users to discuss and provide feedback on concepts, they adapt to situations in which knowledge changes quickly, and they are convenient for those who want to contribute (Campanini, Castagna, & Tazzoli, 2004). Because the success of such communities rises and falls with the participation rate of active users, Hoisl, Aigner, and Miksch,

(2006) study how users can be motivated to participate by means of social rewarding techniques. However, the Community of Practice itself helps users to feel part of a greater project, an important motivational factor that should not be overlooked (Campanini, Castagna, & Tazzoli, 2004).

Communities of Practice can be formed for any area of interest. For example, Farkas (2005) shows how they can be used to engage a community of library patrons. She points out that they can be used to enhance subject guides by adding to the collection of useful resources and removing any dead links that they encounter. Likewise, patrons can participate in annotating the catalog by posting synopses and reviews for books they have read, allowing other patrons to capitalize on their reading experiences to help them make informed reading decisions from the library catalog.

Examples of Collaboration in Good Use

The most recognizable uses of wikis are as reference sites like Wikipedia. However, there is a multitude of other uses for wikis, and some of those have been listed by Wikia, a confederation of wiki communities that create free content with the MediaWiki software (Uses of a wiki, 2007). Their list is shown in Table 2.

The list is very thorough (and it should be, since it is the product of a collaborative effort) but there are still more uses that can be found.

Corporate Use

Corporate use of wikis has often been coincidental – someone in the company learns about or has used a wiki before, and believes that it would be useful in a particular situation. Even so, the popularity of wikis in workplaces has increased exponentially in recent years.

Leuf and Cunningham (2001) presented a number of interesting cases in which wikis are

Table 2. Uses of a wiki

Use	Example(s)
Creating a knowledge base on a specific topic	Creatures, Wikimac
Writing documentation or a FAQ	Category:Documentation
Brainstorming	Scratchpad
Collaborative writing	fiction, comedy, poetry, Storypedia
Learning writing through online collaboration	schools
Product reviews and comparisons	beer, Cafe Review, Facial Cleansing Products, shopping, TechCompare
Creating specifications and architecture documents for software or other projects	Scoop
Creating how-tos	How To
Creating promotional material	Mozilla Community
Developing new languages	Baby Sign Language Dictionary, conlang)
Sharing tips and advice	quit smoking, Answers
Translating documents together	Translation
Coordinate and help fill needs of charities, for donations and services or volunteers	fundraising
Sharing tips with gaming communities	Category:Gaming
Discussion of theories	Abaeté
Publishing	academia, Metodologia Científica
Bringing together a community for activism	activism
Consumption guides	Altereco
Exploring fictional worlds	Alternative History, Conworld
Fan sites or fan clubs	Ashlee Simpson, CamarilaRequiem
Developing patterns or best practices	Best Practices, engineering
Support groups	Cancer Help, Celiac Resources, Quit smoking
Parody	Désencyclopédie, Homestar Runner Wooky
Planning and documenting events, maintaining a calendar of local events, or real-time reports on conferences	events, conferences
Developing software features and other inventions	FeatureGarden, inventions, Software testing and development
A meeting place for language communities	Ladino, Ido Korea, Cantonese, Translation
Political campaigns	VoteRice, Eagle Party
Communication between and within communities	
Creating an easily searchable, linkable, and editable website	
Community news and group announcements	
Information and policies about a project	
Easy refactoring of communication on forums and mailing lists (by turning the thread mode of these discussions into a more useful document mode).	
Meeting agendas and notes for organizations	
Project collaboration	
Enriching existing text documents by editing them collaboratively and adding multimedia	

continued on following page

Table 2. Uses of a wiki (continued)

Use	Example(s)
Solidifying an existing community through collaboration and increased connections	
Supporting a shared community goal	
And even for playing games	games

used in workplaces such as RoleModel Software, Inc., New York Times Digital (NYTD), TakeFive Software (now a Wind River company), and Motorola. In most of the cases, they found wikis useful, powerful and successful. Based on the case studies, Leuf and Cunningham recommend a guideline of Wiki workplace essentials covering the areas of wiki planning, wiki selection, wiki implementation, and day-to-day operations.

Majchrzak, Wagner, and Yates (2006) surveyed over 150 corporations about wiki usage. The most common work activities mentioned were:

- Software development
- E-learning
- Project management
- Posting of general information and knowledge management
- Communities of practice and user groups.
- Ad-hoc collaboration
- Tech support
- Marketing and customer relationship management
- Resource management
- Research and development

Other professional uses found across the Internet include

- Defining and describing procedures, policies, etc.

- Requesting feedback, as used in some seminars for post-presentation comments
- Product planning and development
- Procedure documentation
- Brainstorming marketing ideas
- Coordinating event planning
- Collating attendee availability for a meeting across organisations
- Self-updatable staff directory
- News site for company announcements
- Collaborative journalism
- Writing assistance tools when gathering background data or observer comments

Wikis have been adopted as knowledge creation and management tools as well as for organizational coordination in such widely varied industries as management consulting, retail, manufacturing, and software development (Organizational uses, 2006). Wiki use is increasing in the software development industry. Louridas (2006) suggests that wikis can be used as intranet-based applications for corporate projects, and for software activities such as requirement management, defect tracking, test-case management, and project portal. Wikis have also been used in student software project collaboration with positive feedback (Chao, 2007).

A cursory search of wiki sites reveals that wikis are often used for

- Building a company knowledge base.
- Offering support documentation to product users.
- Managing communication for a project.
- Creating a community news website.
- Providing tech support for developers
- Building data dictionaries for databases
- Developing collaborative documentation (Rapid Document Prototyping)
- Providing a knowledge base for IT stuff
- Sharing various materials (guides, training documents, etc)
- Posting and refining user specs
- Developing collaborative annotation
- Scheduling conferences
- Serving as a simple Content Management System
- Communicating company policy, history, and new ideas
- Providing an interactive user help tool
- Serving as a project notes repository

This is by no means an exhaustive list, but rather a representative list identified by an informal search of wiki sites.

Education

Educational benefits of wikis revolve around the fact that they offer an online space for easy interaction and collaboration. Both teachers and students can easily create web pages using wikis without prior knowledge or skill in web development or programming, eliminating the extra time necessary to develop these skills. A wiki offers the ability to interact with evolving text over time as well, allowing teachers and learners see assignments as they are drafted, rather than commenting only on the final draft. Considering the complications of scheduling after-hours meetings for students, a wiki can also be extremely useful for communication within groups. Further, as more organizations adopt wikis for internal and external collaboration and information dissemi-

nation, interacting with them at the educational level builds important work skills.

With some ingenuity and creativity, the uses of wikis in education are endless. Duffy and Bruns (2006) list several possible educational uses of wikis:

- Students can use a wiki to develop research projects, with the wiki serving as ongoing documentation of their work.
- Students can add summaries of their thoughts from the prescribed readings, building a collaborative annotated bibliography on a wiki.
- A wiki can be used for publishing course resources like syllabi and handouts, and students can edit and comment on these directly for all to see.
- Teachers can use wikis as a knowledge base, enabling them to share reflections and thoughts regarding teaching practices, and allowing for versioning and documentation.
- Wikis can be used to map concepts. They are useful for brainstorming, and editing a given wiki topic can produce a linked network of resources.
- A wiki can be used as a presentation tool in place of conventional software, and students are able to directly comment on and revise the presentation content.
- Wikis are tools for group authoring. Often group members collaborate on a document by emailing to each member of the group a file that each person edits on their computer, and some attempt is then made to coordinate the edits so that everyone's work is equally represented; using a wiki pulls the group members together and enables them to build and edit the document on a single, central wiki page.

Tonkin (2005) identifies four different forms of educational wikis:

1. Single-user wikis allow an individual to collect and edit his or her own thoughts using a web-based environment.
2. Lab book wikis allow students to keep notes online with the added benefit of allowing them to be peer reviewed and changed by fellow students.
3. Collaborative writing wikis can be used by a team for joint writing.
4. Knowledge base wikis provide a knowledge repository for a group.

Finally, Parker and Chao (2007) elaborate on additional educational uses for wikis

*   Supporting writing instruction
*   Project planning and documentation
*   Facilitating online learning groups
*   Semantic wiki to serve as a mathematical resource
*   Icebreaker tool
*   Course textbook writing
*   Student software project collaboration

Lamb (2004) describes various examples of wiki use outside the classroom. Placement centers can use wiki pages to store and organize content for job postings and career development. Wikis can be provided by the university to act as a sounding board so that students can voice opinions about university policies.

Government Uses

Wikis are being used by various governmental bodies as well. Wikis can help government agencies in at least three ways: (1) building a consensus that is crucial for much of the government's work, (2) filling in knowledge gaps to create more complete documents, (3) promoting fairness by representing all sides of an issue (Sternstein, 2005b). For example, the U.S. Chief Information Officers Council posts ongoing revisions to the federal enterprise architecture's data reference model and allows online visitors to read and take part in discussions (Sternstein, 2005a). A U.S. National Aeronautics and Space Administration (NASA) wiki allows users to look at satellite imagery and suggest modifications to the program (Sternstein, 2005a).

Miscellaneous Uses

There are some less easily categorized uses of wikis that are relatively informal. Wikis have been used for such things as

*   Organizing class reunions
*   RSVPing for events
*   Planning weddings
*   Training partners for sporting events
*   Sharing enthusiasms or passions
*   Posting informal classified ads

Again such uses were determined by an unstructured search of current wiki sites.

Industry Examples

Dresdner Kleinwort Wasserstein (DrKW), the international investment banking arm of Dresdner Bank, installed an intranet wiki in 1997 to better link their large number of employees scattered across a broad geographic area. The wiki has since evolved into an enterprise application used primarily for project tracking by frontline employees working with customers, i.e., customer service staff working on customer files (McAfee & Sjoman, 2006).

Ziff Davis Media, one of the largest technology magazine publishers in the United States, uses a wiki for Agile Strategic Planning. They used the tool to plan the development of a new version of their website. The wiki was used to brainstorm ideas for the new site, allowing them to draw upon expertise from social networking, blogging, gaming, and software development, and they estimate that it reduced development time by 25% (Ziff Davis, 2007).

Truong, Herber, Liguori, and Barroso (2005) describe their experiences using a wiki to prepare and upgrade task-based training courses. The wiki served both as a repository for training materials as well as a daily communication vehicle for multiple co-authors working in both Canada and Austria.

Wiki Selection

There are literally hundreds of wikis available on the market, each with various set of features. Determining the best wiki for a particular situation can be a challenge in itself. Ward (2005) offers the following easy steps for selecting a wiki:

1. Determine your subject matter
2. Define your target audience
3. Establish objectives and measurable goals
4. Determine the required feature set and functionality of your wiki
5. Select the most appropriate technology
6. Set up the wiki and arrange hosting
7. Begin writing
8. Invite other contributors

While most of the steps are reasonable, the tasks in steps 4-5 may leave some question marks. A good starting point for wiki novices might be PBWiki or Wetpaint, two popular free hosted wikis for non-technical users. WikiMatrix (2007) offers an excellent tool enabling users with little or no wiki experience to make an informed decision on selecting a wiki. The WikiMatrix Choice Wizard helps in this process by allowing users to select options that narrow down the number of wikis to choose from. If you know the objectives of your application and are armed with certain criteria, the task of selecting the right wiki can be less daunting. For example, wiki security might

be a major concern for business applications, and WYSIWYG editing might be essential for maximizing non-technical user participation. Other major considerations include licensing, page history, page permissions, product maturity, intended audience, usability, system requirements, data storage, development support, programming language, etc.

FUTURE TRENDS

Wiki functionality continues to evolve as more and more useful features such as those discussed in the previous section are offered by individual tools. In addition, the wiki concept itself continues to evolve.

Semantic wiki is a wiki enhanced with technologies developed by the Semantic Web community in order to encode more knowledge than just structured text and hyperlinks (Ontoworld, 2007). Most wikis cannot naturally support structured contents, and this lack of structure can potentially cause information overload and other problems in some Wiki applications. Semantic wiki enhancement allows wiki content to be organized semantically and can make wiki contents easily understood and processed by machines, thus reducing the overhead of wiki management. For example, Klein, Hoecht, and Decker (2005) presented the concept of "Wikitology", which combined a wiki and an ontology for maintaining software engineering knowledge. Decker, Ras, Rech, Klein, and Hoecht (2005) extended the concept by developing a semantic wiki enhanced with an ontology to support self-organized reuse of software engineering knowledge.

As wiki use becomes more widespread and the advantages of wiki technology become better known, wiki features may be incorporated into other applications. Szybalski (2005) predicts that wiki-inspired functionality will likely be incorporated into word processors or blogs, allowing documents to be editable and viewable by a large number of people over the Internet. He goes on to note that these technology enhancements will result in more large knowledge bases like Wikipedia, and "will also affect the way people work on smaller-scale projects, many of which will be less open than today's wikis."

Lamb (2004) points out that "wikis might simply represent the latest advance in online interaction—a cost-effective and readily adopted knowledge management tool." He further notes that collaborative creativity promises to be a key business skill in upcoming years.

CONCLUSION

The use of wikis proliferates and becomes more commonplace as insightful individuals continue to envision innovative uses. This widespread use has led to the concept being considered more mainstream, with wikis becoming accepted as another option in the gamut of productivity software tools available today. The ascent of social software provides new avenues and new opportunities for increased participation and collaboration. The educational, governmental, and business communities stand to benefit from wise use of wikis and the opportunities for collaboration that they offer. New media formats such as wikis and blogs have given rise to virtual communities and are beginning to fill a gaping void in existing practice (Lamb, 2004). As a major component of Web 2.0, the Wiki has continued to live up to its promise of connecting people through interaction and collaboration, empowering users through its openness and flexibility.

REFERENCES

Adie, C. (2006). Report of the information services working group on collaborative tools. Retrieved May 27, 2007 from http://www.is.ed.ac.uk/content/1/c4/10/46/CollaborativeToolsAndWeb2%200.pdf

Alexa Traffic Rankings: Global Top 500 (2007). Retrieved May 27, 2007 from http://www.alexa.com/site/ds/top_sites?ts_mode=global&lang=none

Alexander, B. (2006). Web 2.0: A new wave of innovation for teaching and learning? *Educause Review, 41*(2) (March/April). Retrieved April 19, 2007 from http://www.educause.edu/ir/library/pdf/ERM0621.pdf

Allen, C. (2004) Life with alacrity: Tracing the evolution of social software, http://www.lifewithalacrity.com/2004/10/tracing_the_evo.html

Boulos, M.N.K., Maramba, I., & Wheeler, S. (2006). Wikis, blogs and podcasts: A new generation of web-based tools for virtual collaborative clinical practice and education, *BMC Medical Education, 6*(41). Retrieved April 19, 2007 from http://www.biomedcentral.com/content/pdf/1472-6920-6-41.pdf

Boyd, S. (2003). Are you ready for social software? Retrieved April 19, 2007 from http://internettime.com/blog/archives/000554.html

Brännström, M., & Mårtenson, C. (2006). Enhancing situational awareness by exploiting wiki technology. Proceedings of the Conference on Civil and Military Readiness 2006 (CIMI 2006), Enköping, Sweden, 16-18 May, Paper S3.2. Försvarets Materielverk, Stockholm. http://www.foi.se/infofusion/bilder/CIMI_2006_S3_2.pdf

Campanini, S.E., Castagna, P., Tazzoli, R. (2004). Platypus wiki: A semantic wiki wiki web. Proceedings of Semantic Web Applications and Perspectives (SWAP) - 1st Italian Semantic Web Workshop, 10th December 2004, Ancona, Italy http://semanticweb.deit.univpm.it/swap2004/cameraready/castagna.pdf

Chao, J. (2007). Student project collaboration using Wikis. *Proceedings of the 20th Conference on Software Engineering Education and Training (CSEE&T 2007)*, Dublin, Ireland: July 3-5.

Cunningham, W. (2007). Wiki design principles. Retrieved April 19, 2007 from http://c2.com/cgi/wiki?WikiDesignPrinciples

Davies, J. (2004). Wiki brainstorming and problems with wiki based collaboration. Unpublished Masters Thesis, Department of Computer Science at the University of York, Heslington, York, UK. Retrieved May 27, 2007 from http://www-users.cs.york.ac.uk/~kimble/teaching/students/Jonathan_Davies/wiki_collaboration_and_brainstorming.pdf

Decker B., Ras E., Rech J., Klein B., & Hoecht C. (2005). Self-organized reuse of software engineering knowledge supported by semantic wikis. Proceedings of the Workshop on Semantic Web Enabled Software Engineering (SWESE), at the 4th International Semantic Web Conference (ISWC 2005), November 6-10, 2005, Galway, Ireland.

Duffy, P. & Bruns, A. (2006). The use of blogs, wikis and RSS in education: A conversation of possibilities. Proceedings of the Online Learning and Teaching Conference 2006, Brisbane: September 26. Retrieved April 19, 2007 from https://olt.qut.edu.au/udf/OLT2006/gen/static/papers/Duffy_OLT2006_paper.pdf

Evans, P. (2006). The wiki factor. *BizEd*, January/February, 28-32. Retrieved May 27, 2007 from http://www.aacsb.edu/publications/Archives/JanFeb06/p28-33.pdf

Evans, P. & Wolf, B. (2005). Collaboration rules. *Harvard Business Review*, July-Aug, *83*(7): 96-104. Retrieved April 19, 2007 from http://custom.hbsp.com/b02/en/implicit/viewFileNavBeanImplicit.jhtml?_requestid=34699

Farkas, M. (2005). Using wikis to create online communities. WebJunction. Retrieved May 27, 2007 from http://eprints.rclis.org/archive/00006130/01/wikiarticle_mfarkas.pdf

Fuchs-Kittowski, F., Köhler, A., & Fuhr, D. (2004). Roughing up processes the wiki way – Knowledge communities in the context of work and learning processes. Proceedings of the International Conference on Knowledge Management (I-KNOW '04) Graz, Austria, June 30 - July 2. 484-493. Retrieved May 27, 2007 from http://publica.fraunhofer.de/eprints/N-25285.pdf

Giles, J. (2005). Internet encyclopedias go head to head. Nature, 438(7070), 900-901 (15 Dec 2005). Retrieved May 27, 2007 from http://www.nature.com/news/2005/051212/full/438900a.html

Gonzalez-Reinhart, J. (2005). Wiki and the wiki way: Beyond a knowledge management solution. Information Systems Research Center, Bauer College of Business, University of Houston, 1-22. Retrieved May 27, 2007 from http://www.uhisrc.com/FTB/Wiki/wiki_way_brief%5B1%5D-Jennifer%2005.pdf

Hoisl, B., Aigner, W., & Miksch, S. (2006). Social rewarding in wiki systems – Motivating the community. 2nd Austrian Symposium on Wiki Systems and Applications (Wikiposium 2006), Vienna, Austria November 25. Retrieved May 27, 2007 from http://www.donau-uni.ac.at/imperia/md/content/department/ike/ike_publications/2006/hoisl_2006_wikiposium_social_rewarding.pdf

Howley, D. (2007). What is a wiki? MindTouch White Paper. Retrieved April 19, 2007 from http://www.mindtouch.com/sites/mindtouch.com/themes/mt2/resources/Mindtouch%20What%20Is%20A%20Wiki.pdf

Jonassen, D.H., Peck, K.L., & Wilson, B.G. (1999). *Learning with Technology: A Constructivist Perspective*. Columbus, OH: Prentice Hall.

Kirkpatrick, M. (2006). The flu wiki: A serious application of new web tools. Retrieved May 27, 2007 from http://marshallk.blogspot.com/2005/07/flu-wiki-serious-application-of-new.html

Klein, B., Hoecht, C., & Decker, B. (2005). Beyond capturing and maintaining software engineering knowledge - „Wikitology" as shared semantics. Workshop on Knowledge Engineering and Software Engineering, at Conference of Artificial Intelligence 2005, Koblenz.

Korfiatis, N., & Naeve, A. (2005). Evaluating wiki contributions using social networks: A case study on wikipedia. Proceedings of the First on-Line Conference on Metadata and Semantics Research (MTSR'05). Rinton Press.

Lamb, B. (2004). Wide open spaces: Wikis, ready or not. EDUCAUSE Review, 39(5) (September/October), 36-48. Retrieved May 27, 2007 from http://www.educause.edu/pub/er/erm04/erm0452.asp?bhcp=1

Leuf, B. & Cunningham, W. (2001). The Wiki Way: Quick Collaboration on the Web. Boston, MA: Addison Wesley.

Licklider, J.C.R & Taylor, R.W. (1968). The computer as a communication device, Science and Technology, 76, 21-31.

List of Wikipedias (2007). Retrieved April 19, 2007 from http://meta.wikimedia.org/w/index.php?title=List_of_Wikipedias&oldid=517497

Louridas, P. (2006). Using wikis in software development. IEEE Software, 23(2), 88-91. Retrieved May 27, 2007 from http://ieeexplore.ieee.org/Xplore/login.jsp?url=/iel5/52/33727/01605183.pdf

Mader, S. (2006). Wiki vs. Blog. Retrieved April 19, 2007 from http://www.businessblogwire.com/2006/03/stewart_mader_wiki_vs_blog.html

Majchrzak, A., Wagner, C., & Yates, D. (2006). Corporate wiki users: Results of a Survey, Proceedings of the 2006 international symposium on Wikis (WikiSym'06), August 21–23, Odense, Denmark. 99-104. Retrieved May 27, 2007 from http://www.wikisym.org/ws2006/proceedings/p99.pdf

McAfee, A.P., & Sjoman, A.. (2006). Wikis at Dresdner Kleinwort Wasserstein: (A). Harvard Business School Case 606-074.

Newman, M. & Robey, D. (1992). A social process model of user-analyst relationships. MIS Quarterly (16:2), 249-266.

Olson, G. (2006). New tools for learning. Retrieved April 19, 2007 from http://faculty.eicc.edu/golson/tools.htm

Ontoworld.org (2007). Semantic wiki. Retrieved April 27, 2007 from http://ontoworld.org/wiki/Semantic_wiki

Organizational uses of wiki technology. (2006). Proceedings of Wikimania 2006, Retrieved April 27, 2007 from http://wikimania2006.wikimedia.org/wiki/Proceedings:KL1

Parker, K.R. & Chao, J. (2007). Wiki as a teaching tool. International Journal of Knowledge and Learning Objects, (3), 57-72. Retrieved April 27, 2007 from http://ijklo.org/Volume3/IJK-LOv3p057-072Parker284.pdf

Pawlowski, S.D., & Robey, D. (2004). Bridging user organizations: Knowledge brokering and the work of information technology professionals. MIS Quarterly (28:4), 645-672.

Schaffert, S., Gruber, A. & Westenthaler, R. (2006). A semantic wiki for collaborative knowledge formation. In S. Reich, G. Güntner, T. Pellegrini, A. & Wahler (Eds.): *Semantic Content Engineering*, Austria: Trauner Verlag. Retrieved May 27, 2007 from http://www.salzburgresearch.

at/research/gfx/SemWikiForCollKnowForm_20060120.pdf

Sternstein, A. (2005a). Online collaborative sites open to everyone enable the sharing of ideas. FCW.com. Retrieved May 27, 2007 from http://www.fcw.com/article88467-04-04-05-Print

Sternstein, A. (2005b). Wiki advocate sees government uses. FCW.com. Retrieved May 27, 2007 from http://www.fcw.com/article89069-06-03-05-Web

Szybalski, A. (2005). Why it's not a wiki world (yet). Retrieved April 19, 2007 from http://andy.bigwhitebox.org/papers/wiki_world.pdf

Tilley, P.A., & Giordano, G.A. (2003). Knowledge management strategies and cultural dimensions. Proceedings of the Ninth Americas Conference on Information Systems, 2003, pp. 2618. Retrieved April 19, 2007 from http://aisel.isworld.org/password.asp?Vpath=AMCIS/2003&PDFpath=03HE20.pdf

Tonkin, E. (2005). Making the case for a wiki. Ariadne, Issue 42, January. Retrieved April 19, 2007 from http://www.ariadne.ac.uk/issue42/tonkin/

Truong, Q.S., Herber, N., Liguori, C., & Barroso Jr., H. (2005). Using wikis as a low-cost knowledge sharing tool. Institute of Nuclear Materials Management 46th Annual Meeting in Phoenix, Arizona. Retrieved May 27, 2007 from http://saturn.eton.ca/wiki/index.php/INMM2005/Paper231

Uses of a wiki. (2007). Wikia, Inc. Retrieved May 27, 2007 from http://www.wikia.com/wiki/Uses_of_a_wiki

Wheeler, S., Kelly P., & Gale, K. (2005). The influence of online problem-based learning on teachers' professional practice and identity. ALT-J 2005, 13(2):125-137.

Wiki's wild world (2005). Nature. 438(7070), 890 Retrieved April 15, 2007 from http://www.nature.com/nature/journal/v438/n7070/pdf/438890a.pdf

WikiMatrix - Compare Them All. (2007). Retrieved April 19, 2007 from http://www.wikimatrix.org/

Woolf, B. (2006). Wiki vs. Blog. *IBM developerWorks*. Retrieved April 19, 2007 from http://www-03.ibm.com/developerworks/wikis/display/woolf/Wiki+vs.+Blog

Ziff Davis Media Speeds Projects Cycles, Slashes Group Email. (2007) SocialText Enterprise Wiki. Retrieved May 27, 2007 from http://www.socialtext.com/node/37

APPENDIXES

Internet Session: "Citizendium vs. Wiki"

http://www.citizendium.org/essay.html
http://www.nature.com/news/2005/051212/full/438900a.html

Read the essay and the special report in the links above. Provide an argument supporting Sanger's position, and then take the opposite side and attempt to refute his points. Is there a problem with Wikipedia in its current form?

Case Study

A. Protecting Wiki Content

Because wiki content can be modified by anyone, wiki vandalism is quite common. The most common types of vandalism include the addition of obscenities to pages, page blanking, or the insertion of bad (or good) jokes or other nonsense.

Read the wikipedia page on vandalism (http://en.wikipedia.org/wiki/Wikipedia:Vandalism) and other pertinent pages on the Internet .

Watch the video on vandalism at

http://www.nature.com/news/2005/051212/full/438900a.html

Questions

1. If you are a corporate IT manager, what precautions can you take to limit vandalism and to protect corporate knowledge assets?
2. Wikis are designed for knowledge sharing. From a corporate perspective, what are the advantages and disadvantages of knowledge sharing via a wiki?
3. What features would you add to a wiki to prevent vandalism and to insure that content is accurate and up to date? What features are currently available?

Useful URLs

1. Wiki Papa-Ward Cunningham: http://en.wikipedia.org/wiki/Ward_Cunningham
2. Wiki History: http://c2.com/cgi/wiki?WikiHistory
3. Wiki Innovations: http://c2.com/cgi/wiki?WikiInnovations
4. Social Software: http://www.usemod.com/cgi-bin/mb.pl?SocialSoftware
5. More Social Software: http://james.seng.cc/wiki/wiki.cgi?Social_Software
6. Wiki Matrix: http://www.wikimatrix.org/
7. Wikis in education: http://www.wikiineducation.com

Further Readings

Choate, M.S. (2007). *Professional Wikis.*Hoboken, NJ: Wrox Press.

Huettner, B., Brown, M.K., & James-Tanny, C. (2007). *Managing Virtual Teams: Getting the Most from Wikis, Blogs, and Other Collaborative Tools.* Plano, TX: Wordware Publishing, Inc.

Jonassen, D.H., Peck, K.L., & Wilson, B.G. (1999). *Learning with technology: A constructivist perspective.* Columbus, OH: Prentice Hall.

Klobas, J. (2006). *Wikis: Tools for Information Work and Collaboration.* Oxford, UK: Chandos Publishing.

Leuf, B. & Cunningham, W. (2001). *The Wiki Way: Quick collaboration on the Web.*Boston, MA: Addison Wesley.

Richardson, W. (2006). *Blogs, Wikis, Podcasts, and Other Powerful Web Tools for Classrooms.* Thousand Oaks, CA: Corwin Press.

Tapscott, D. & Williams, A.D. (2006). *Wikinomics: How Mass Collaboration Changes Everything.* New York, NY: Penguin Group.

Chapter IV
Media Centric Knowledge Sharing on the Web 2.0

Marc Spaniol
Max Planck Institute for Computer Science, Germany

Ralf Klamma
RWTH Aachen University, Germany

Yiwei Cao
RWTH Aachen University, Germany

ABSTRACT

The success of knowledge sharing heavily depends on the capabilities of an information system to reproduce the ongoing discourses within a community. In order to illustrate the artifacts of a discourse as authentic as possible it is not sufficient to store the plain information, but also to reflect the context they have been used in. An ideal representation to do so is non-linear storytelling. The Web 2.0 in its "bi-directional" design therefore is an ideal basis for media centric knowledge sharing. In this article we present a novel solution to this issue by non-linear storytelling in the Virtual Campfire system. Virtual Campfire is a social software that allows a modular composition of web services based on a Lightweight Application Server in community engine called LAS. Hence, Virtual Campfire is capable of fully exploiting the features of the Web 2.0 in a comprehensive community information system covering web-services for geo-spatial content sharing, multimedia tagging and collaborative authoring of hypermedia artifacts.

INTRODUCTION

The development of information systems for communities of practice (Lave & Wenger 1991; Nonaka & Takeuchi 1995; Wenger 1998) in different application domains is a challenging issue for several reasons. Principles like legitimate peripheral participation, group knowledge, situated learning,

Copyright © 2009, IGI Global, distributing in print or electronic forms without written permission of IGI Global is prohibited.

informality and co-location have to be taken seriously in the design of the community engine. For that reason, the community engine has to reflect the social learning processes taking place, which differ from community to community. Even more, the information systems need a careful design of the digital media and the related communication/collaboration tools in order to reflect the discursive hypermedia knowledge contained in text, pictures, videos etc. Furthermore, communities are usually not able to express their needs in the very beginning of information system usage. Thus, the communities have to gain experiences "on their own" while applying the technologies in use. In addition, multimedia technologies and the Web 2.0 are rapidly developing, thus creating new requirements on hardware and software. In combination with a trend for multidisciplinary work and research novel approaches for flexible, evolving, adaptable, and interoperable community engines are required. Social software for technology enhanced learning therefore need to reflect the nature of the underlying community processes and their discourses. Consequently, the question is: How to design and orchestrate community information systems in order to fully exploit the features of the Web 2.0?

In order to meet these requirements we have developed in recent years a Lightweight Application Server [LAS] for community information system, which is capable of supporting communities by multimedia services on the basis of the multimedia content description interface MPEG-7. On top of it, Virtual Campfire is a community information system that allows a modular composition of web services for media centric knowledge sharing on the Web 2.0.

In this paper we first introduce a theoretical framework for working and learning in media-supported communities of practice. After that, we introduce concepts of knowledge sharing on the Web 2.0 and explain how these technologies help to create, manage and share knowledge in communities. Then we present Virtual Campfire and its core modules in a scenario of non-linear multimedia storytelling. Here, our social software is applied in a community of professionals for cultural heritage management. The paper closes with a summary and an outlook on further research.

A MEDIA CENTRIC KNOWLEDGE MANAGEMENT THEORY

Snow differentiates between two different trends in collaboration and learning within scientific communities (Snow 1959). First, the 'linear type' of learning that is goal-oriented and transmission-centered. This means, old information in scientific communities is being replaced by new one as soon as this appears. Second, there is a 'non-linear type' of learning. This type is media centric and reflects the nature of the ongoing discourse. It doesn't replace old information but keeps it and might be applied in a different context later on. Here, information is not simply transmitted for learning, but it is presented based on the underlying theory in use. Our collaborative research center on "Media and Cultural Communication" (cf. http://www.fk-427.de) has given us a detailed insight into the importance of proper media support in knowledge sharing. The description and [loose] classification of medial artifacts is probably the most important part of the methodological perception process to make social software work. This means that a continuous perception of activities in communities of practice is necessary for them in order to gain new knowledge. The question therefore is: How to resemble working practices in communities of practice by means of social software?

A media-specific theory developed in the center helped us understand digital media support for discourses in the cultural sciences. It is based on the following three media operations (Jäger & Stanitzek 2002; Fohrmann & Schüttpelz 2004):

- *Transcription* is a media dependent operation to make media collections more readable.
- *Localization* means an operation to transfer global media into local practices. We distinguish between *formalized localization* within information systems [in digital community media] and *practiced localization* [in communities of practice] among humans.
- The term of *[re-] addressing* describes an operation that stabilizes and optimizes the accessibility in global communication.

In the following, we will now synthesize these media specific operations with learning processes of communities of practice. The result is a media centric re-formulation of the previously introduced media operations on knowledge creation and social learning processes adopted from Nonaka and Takeuchi (Nonaka & Takeuchi 1995) and Wenger (Wenger 1998).

Figure 1 brings together both approaches in media centric theory of learning and in communities of practice. It combines the two types of knowledge, tacit and explicit knowledge (Nonaka & Takeuchi 1995; Polanyi 1985), and the process within knowledge creation and learning processes with the media theory developed in our collaborative research center including its media specific operations [*transcription, formalized* as well as *practiced localization,* and *[re-] addressing*]. In the upper section we focus on actions performed by humans. Starting with an individual who has internalized some media-specific knowledge there are two ways to communicate with others. On the one hand, there is an option to present this information to others by human-human interaction in *practiced localization,* which allows the content's socialization within the communities of practice and vice versa which is equivalent to the development of a shared history. On the other

Figure 1. Media centric theory of learning in communities of practice

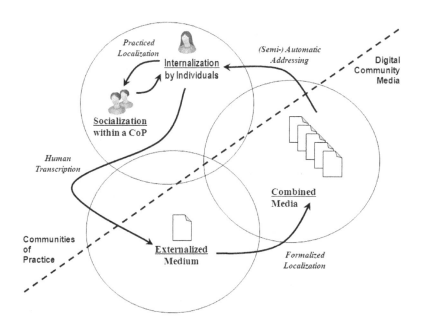

hand, individuals may also perform a *human transcription* of their knowledge by generating new medial artifacts. This operation brings us into the lower section where digital community media are processed. The <u>externalized</u> artifacts of an individual are now further processed by the information system. This is done by *formalized localization* of the medial artifacts. In contrast to its high-level transcription by an individual, here, a technical computer supported recombination of medial artifacts takes place. As a result, the set of medial artifacts from various data types are <u>combined</u> within the information system. The final *[semi-] automatic addressing* closing the circle is the context depending presentation of the medial artifacts or a cross-medial concatenation. From then on, the process might be repeated infinitely oscillating between tacit and explicit knowledge on the epistemological axis and between indi-

viduals and the communities of practice on the ontological axis.

In order to make knowledge sharing a success for any kind of community of practice, independent of size or domain of interest, a generic community engine for social software is needed. That is exactly the point where social software is being applied in order to support the *formalized localization* process. While the previous media centric theory is based on the distinction between tacit or procedural and explicit or declarative knowledge, the importance of storytelling becomes visible after a further distinction between semantic and episodic knowledge (Tulving 1978; Ullman 2004) has been undertaken. In Figure 2 we depict a hierarchy of knowledge types with examples on the individual and community level. While semantic knowledge represents semiotic and conceptual knowledge such as documenta-

Figure 2. Individual and community/organizational levels of knowledge processing [Adapted from (Nonaka & Takeuchi 1995) with refinements on declarative knowledge done by (Ullman 2004)]

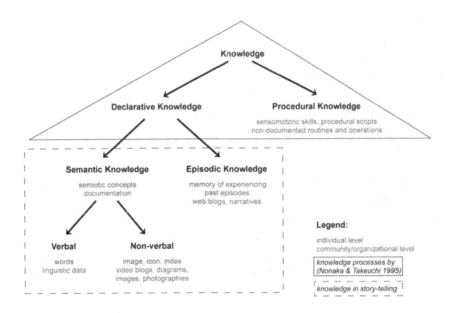

tion in organizational charts, business process definitions and so forth, episodic knowledge is knowledge about experiences such as episodes and narratives, e.g. war stories. This distinction is also being debated. Nevertheless, our claim is that a combination of semantic and episodic knowledge can be used more effectively in organizations. While situational context may be lost by externalizing stories, outreach and impact of stories may be enhanced by this process. Documentation as a means of semantic knowledge can further be classified as verbal [linguistic data] and non-verbal [e.g. visual image, video, and diagram].

The Digital Storytelling Association [DSA] defines storytelling as follows: "Digital Storytelling uses digital media to create media-rich stories to tell, share and to preserve. Digital stories derive their power through weaving images, music, narrative and voice together, thereby giving deep dimension and vivid color to characters, situations, and insights" (DSA 2002). This illustrates that storytelling can be used not only for entertainment, but also for sharing knowledge. It intertwines semantic knowledge, i.e. already reified concepts of communities stored as documents, by linking it with the narrative experiences gained from episodic knowledge (Tulving 1978). Thus, storytelling can be seen as an approach to developing learning histories (Roth & Kleiner 1999) by creating knowledge hyper stories (Royrvik & Bygdas 2002). Consequently, storytelling is an important aspect for knowledge sharing and learning in communities of practice (Wenger 1998). Therefore, telling, sharing and experiencing stories are common ways to knowledge creation in communities of practice.

However, in the Web 2.0 (O'Reilly 2005) the power of storytelling has not been fully explored, yet. Particularly the opportunities of social software in combining contextualized knowledge with multimedia support in stories, is thus far marginally exploited. For that purpose we will introduce the key concepts of the Web 2.0 in the following.

KNOWLEDGE SHARING ON THE WEB 2.0 – THE POWER OF STORIES

While the Internet in general and the especially the web is assumed to be one of the really big media revolutions like the invention of book printing by Gutenberg in the 15th century, the wheel is still spinning. After only roughly 15 years of existence, the now so-called Web 1.0 is replaced by the Web 2.0, a term coined by Tim O'Reilly. Projects like Wikipedia let users become knowledge prosumers [consumer and producer "in parallel"] of wikis, replacing old-fashioned content management systems in organizations. Interoperability between content and services is realized by syndications tools [RSS]. In order to highlight the differences between the "new" and the "old" Web paradigms, we introduce the core Web 2.0 knowledge management presented in O'Reilly's seminal article (O'Reilly 2005). We will not repeat all features of the Web 2.0 here, but put forward the power of stories for knowledge sharing on the Web 2.0.

Participation instead of publishing. "Data are the new Intel Inside" is one of the slogans in the Web 2.0 (O'Reilly 2005), but communities get even more focus than data itself does. From del.icio.us, flickr, youTube, to mercora which are collections for bookmarks, photos, videos and music, the communities can subscribe to or rank the bookmarks' masters, photographers, video makers or DJs. Thus, social networks are built up to get a bundle of information instead of a single piece of information. In the information world, one can get whatever information he wants, when he finds the right community. Social navigation, social recommendation and social filtering techniques are even more important in a multimedia web, while classical information retrieval techniques deliver only limited support. Remix (cf. http://www.manovich.net/IA/index.html) of existing content is a technique which can easily be applied on existing Web 2.0 multimedia repositories like flickr and youTube. In the fact, digital storytelling can only happen within communities of story tellers and the audience. Storytelling as a community activity is based on participation, not necessarily similar to classical storytelling approaches but more to a many-to-many approach.

Syndication instead of stickiness. Lately, Web 2.0 is also featured as a kind of attitude with which people handle the web. More and more web sites support RSS instead of placing a button labeled with "Set this page to your home page". It has become natural and a kind of fashion to integrate third-party web services like google, yahoo and del.icio.us etc. Web services and syndication will be even more important in ubiquitous contexts when learners need support based on their location, their connectivity, their device capabilities and their usage context. Content has to be adapted to the various unreliable or unpredictable contexts of the learners instead of delivering the same content to every learner in every situation. For storytelling this implies more possibilities but also more care about media sets for stories. We already know that the narratives for mobile TV are much shorter than narratives in home TV where story parts e.g. in telenovelas are told in half hour rhythms. But based on adaptation strategies we have to prepare different media sets and even different narratives (Franz & Nischelwitzer 2004) for telling the same story in a different context.

Wikis instead of content management. Control freaks are worrying about the principal openness of the new social software applications like many wikis, but it turned out that participation is increased just by those low barriers. Even if inappropriate content is uploaded or created or existing content is modified or even vandalized, the communities have some self-repair strategies in place which are more flexible than any technological approach to protecting content. When these repair strategies do not work anymore, the community may have a problem by itself and will disappear eventually. This openness ac-

cepts various types of multimedia. It is possible to reuse multimedia, which takes advantage of well-rated community media. Open standards are widely employed but also here simple standards are preferred over complex ones. Storytelling in the Web 2.0 will depend on community strategies to maintain their media. Stories will evolve over time, but even the disruption of stories by other users has to be dealt with by the communities in the Web 2.0.

Folksonomies instead of taxonomies. Web 2.0 often uses tagging technologies to categorize multimedia content. For multimedia content-based retrieval techniques are of limited use, since they only work efficiently enough on a limited amount of materials, and even with large collections, only a limited number of retrieved materials has a high ratio in terms of precision and recall. Tags can inform multimedia retrieval and vice versa. Even if users misuse tagging and create false or misleading tags for multimedia content, content based retrieval techniques can be used to validate retrieval results based on simple keyword search. Multimedia and Web 2.0 technologies have to converge for storytelling on the Web 2.0. We need tagging technologies for retrieving interesting stories but we also need some kinds of emergent semantics for multimedia stories which are based on the content.

Contextualized Storytelling. Digital media allows fast creation, sharing and consumption of interactive content. What makes digital media most suitable for storytelling is the ability to recombine various media types, making stories more effective and interactive. Web-based systems are the ultimate step in the evolution of storytelling by making interactive multimedia contents not only available 24/7, but also allowing community-wide distribution.

As demonstrated in the concepts above, the Web 2.0 allows more and more knowledge to be created, managed and shared by communities themselves. Because Web 2.0 technologies were not intended specifically for digital storytelling, many challenges are raised by the readiness of communities to accept these technologies. However, already on the "classical" Web the power of storytelling was well recognized. There exist a lot of virtual communities like Fray.com (cf. http://fray.com/is/) whose content is solely built of personal stories shared by the community members. Software like MemoryMiner (cf. http://www.memoryminer.com/) is capable of facilitating the authoring of digital stories even for non-experienced computer users. In oral history research web archives like the shoa archive (cf. http://www.shoahproject.org/) or the Densho project (cf. http://www.densho.org/) were created to preserve generational knowledge. In the context of corporate learning storytelling is also known and used (Nonaka & Takeuchi 1995; Davenport & Prusak 1998, Brown & Duguid 2000). A very comprehensive collection of resources is available on the Internet (cf. http://tech-head.com/dstory. htm). For the sake of clarity, we will now introduce and compare existing storytelling and analyze their capabilities for knowledge sharing on the Web 2.0.

Storytelling Environments Reviewed

There are many software tools and models for storytelling available on the Web. However, most of them are commercial products and do not incorporate any Web 2.0 methodologies. Even more, most of them aim at creation of fiction instead of sharing knowledge. Our overview will focus on these systems that are most suitable for sharing semantic and episodic knowledge in communities.

Dramatica is a comprehensive framework suitable to create multimedia stories (Phillips and Huntley 2001). However, it does not allow any kind of non-linearity. In Dramatica a story represents a particular model called the "story mind". It is left to the creativity of the authors to express their episodic knowledge as a linear story so that dedicated aspects of the story are

filled with content. Dramatica is also capable of supporting semantic knowledge. Because of its mostly individual conception, Dramatica does not provide many Web 2.0 features.

Adaptive Digital Storytelling [Adaptive DST] is a computer-based form of narration that tries to integrate basic principles of narratives and dramatic art into interactive digital stories (Franz and Nischelwitzer 2004). Adaptive DST subdivides episodic knowledge into selected- and must-phases, and specifies their interdependencies. Another key concept in Adaptive DST is the option to manipulate the story a-priori. Here, a variation of a story can be generated based on pre-defined tags used to specify the level of information a user wants to obtain. Based on a 4-ary classification scheme users can select from a superficial to a fine-grained story adaptation. Thus, non-linearity is only supported to a certain extent. The existing "core story" might not be changed completely in its outcome, but might be altered depending on the user's interest in the topic. While the concept is applicable to knowledge sharing on scholarly level, in general, it is doubtful that such a labor-intense, and mostly unguided creation process might be applicable in a community, or at a larger scale. Even more, Adaptive DST does not support collaboration features for Web 2.0 technologies.

Storylining Suspense and **Story Engine** are closely related systems for the creation and consumption of non-linear multimedia stories. While Storylining Suspense is an approach to a new authoring method for interactive storytelling (Schneider et al. 2003), Story Engine is used to capture episodic knowledge by narrating interactive non-linear stories [e.g. created by Storylining Suspense] (Braun 2004). The focus in Storylining Suspense is on authoring of non-linear stories based on a set of morphological functions defined by Vladimir Propp (Propp 1958). These functions are mapped within the system based on a scene model thus creating variants of a story based on the underlying model and the user's interaction.

Additionally, there are options to store semantic knowledge about multimedia contents, but it is left open, whether these contents are available only to support the creation process or will be accessible upon consumption as well. Thus, despite their client/server structure, Storylining Suspense and Story Engine are suited only on a limited scale for multi-authoring and, consequently, the Web 2.0.

Hypermedia Novel [Hymn] is a new storytelling approach that extends the classical narration concept of Graphic Novel (Heiden et al. 2001). Hymn is a modular concept that allows the creation and consumption of hypermedia stories. The main concept of Hymn is the so-called narration module which can be accessed by an authoring tool. A narration module captures the episodic knowledge and stands for a scene within a story. These modules may be linked with other narration modules thus defining the story graph. Because of its openness in creating and sharing knowledge Hymn incorporates Web 2.0 methodologies. Despite its clear graph oriented narration structure, Hymn does not seem to apply any theoretical concepts. The "Hymnplayer" is a conventional web-browser using the Java Media Framework. Here, different media might be visualized but there is currently no support to store and retrieve semantic knowledge within media related metadata.

The **Digital Storytelling Cookbook and Travelling Companion** [DSC] is considered to be a handbook for the creation of digital stories based on the "heuristics" gathered in a community of users associated with the center for digital storytelling (Lambert 2003; Center for Digital Storytelling 2005). For that purpose, the DSC breaks down episodic knowledge of digital stories into subcomponents and gives practical advices how to make stories out of user experiences. Besides some practical advices on how to find ideas about stories there are seven theoretical elements specified which should be fulfilled in a good story. However, there are no concepts

described suitable to process media related semantic knowledge. On the technical level, the DSC only gives hints on how to use proprietary software. A common technical platform to create and share stories has not yet been developed. For that reason, DSC can not be considered as Web 2.0 software. In general, the DSC is suitable to support digital storytelling in various areas of application without going into details.

The **Movement Oriented Design** [MOD] paradigm (Sharda 2005) is a new methodology for the creation of linear and non-linear multimedia stories. Its core idea is to bring different theories, models and tools under one roof. Thus, it integrates features from Dramatica (Phillips and Huntley 2005) as well as the Aristotelean Poetic (Aristotels 2000). The result is a novel methodology and formalism in order to create multimedia stories by combining three facets of stories: Motivation [verbal and non-verbal knowledge], Exigency [semantic knowledge] and Structure [episodic knowledge]. Thus, the MOD methodology is a comprehensive framework for the creation of non-linear digital stories. However, a prototypical implementation is missing yet. Consequently, MOD can not be considered as a Web 2.0 implementation.

In the previous subsections we have introduced several implementations and methodologies applied in the area of storytelling. As we have pointed out, current approaches are not suitable to combine Web 2.0 features with a comprehensive methodological concept to process **semantic and episodic knowledge**. Table 1 gives a condensed overview on these approaches by highlighting their key features. For the sake of a comparison among these features, our approach of a Storytelling in Virtual Campfire, which contains the theoretical concepts of MOD [cf. (Spaniol et al. 2006) for details], is included. Thus, Virtual Campfire is a social software that allows a modular composition of web services for media centric knowledge sharing. We will now introduce the core modules in a scenario of non-linear multimedia storytelling applied in a community of professionals for cultural heritage management.

VIRTUAL CAMPFIRE – SOCIAL SOFTWARE APPLIED

Despite the huge number of social software on the web, users face many problems when trying to apply these technologies for more sophisticated means of knowledge sharing than the simple tagging of pictures (e.g. http://flickr.com/) or

exchange of bookmarks (e.g. http://del.icio.us/). However, what is really needed is to orchestrate services like these in an arbitrary manner. Therefore, our approach here is to go one step further by making multimedia contents available to others by interoperable multimedia metadata standards like MPEG-7 (ISO 2003; Kosch 2003). In order to allow community members browsing multimedia artifacts, collections and thus any kind of hypermedia, we use MPEG-7 for the capturing of explicit knowledge. For the purpose of combining interoperability and server side computations,

Table 1. Storytelling environments and methodologies compared

		Dramatica	Adaptive Digital Storytelling	Storylining Suspense & Story Engine	Hypermedia Novel	Digital Storytelling Cookbook and Travelling Companion [DSC]	Movement Oriented Design [MOD]	Storytelling in Virtual Campfire
Story concept		n.a.	Must & should dependencies	Morphological functions	Extended Graphic Novel	Community "heuristics"	Motivation, Exigency and Structure	Motivation, Exigency and Structure
Semantic Knowledge		Verbal & non verbal	Available	Available	n.a.	n.a.	Verbal & non verbal	Verbal & non verbal
Episodic Knowledge		???	Linear	Linear & non-linear	Linear & non-linear	n.a.	Linear & non-linear	Linear & non-linear
Product Type		Commercial	Viewer: Public Editor: Commercial / Proprietary	???	Viewer: Public Editor: ???	Not implemented	Not implemented	Research
Validation		Advices only	n.a.	Automatic consistency checks	n.a.	Not implemented	Not implemented	Automatic validation of MOD compliance
Web 2.0 features	Creation	Individual	Individual	Individual	Community wide	Not implemented	Not implemented	Community wide
	Sharing	n.a.	Proprietary Webserver	Integrated Story Engine	Proprietary Webserver	Not implemented	Not implemented	Affiliated Community Webserver

Adopted from MOD (rotated, spanning Story concept through Episodic Knowledge rows of last column)

Virtual Campfire is based on Lightweight Application Server [LAS] for MPEG-7 Services in community engines. Thus, we will first introduce the basic concepts of LAS before describing the core services applied in Virtual Campfire.

LAS: A Lightweight Application Server for Social Software

LAS is a platform independent Java implementation of a lightweight middleware platform for service oriented architectures [SOA] developed at our chair for the purpose of providing network services which can be shared among various tools supporting the work of communities in practice. The LAS Java API and its concepts are used to build the server's functionality and thus allow arbitrary server extensions by three basic element types: Connectors, components and services. Figure 3 shows a simplified diagram of the LAS architecture and the interrelations between server elements described in the following. A connector realizes the server side for client-server communication using a particular protocol, e.g. HTTP or SOAP. Components encapsulate func-

tionality for common tasks shared by services or other components. Services define the actual functionality that LAS offers to its clients. Public service methods are available to clients through one of the connectors inside a session context. Service methods can be invoked by clients using a connector client for any of the available communication protocols [HTTP/SOAP]. Access to service methods as well as to arbitrary secured objects is controlled on server side by an internal security management that is based on users, groups and roles. Access rights can be defined on different levels of granularity, i.e. per-service, per-service-method or per-method-signature. Therefore, a client simply connects to the LAS using one of the available connector clients and invokes LAS service methods remotely, possibly involving secured objects.

Semantic Zapping Services: Exploration of Multimedia Contents

Semantic Zapping Services in Virtual Campfire tries to bridge the gap between "folksonomy-style" high-level semantic knowledge about multimedia

Figure 3. Simplified LAS architecture

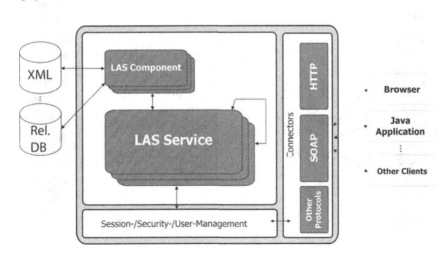

and purely technical low-level content descriptions. These services are intended to support collaboration in communities by the exchange of multimedia contents and their low and high-level semantic descriptions. In order to ensure interoperability among the contents described multimedia metadata standards are being incorporated. In this aspect, the Dublin Core [DC] metadata standard (Dublin Core Metadata Initiative 1999) has been a step forward, as it is an easy to understand and concise method for media annotations. Nevertheless, DC is not suitable for temporal and media specific annotations of multimedia contents. For that reason, we try to overcome these limitations by a combination of the loose classifications in DC with more sophisticated description elements for time based media in MPEG-7. Thus, our Semantic Zapping Services are based on an excerpt of the extensive MPEG-7 multimedia metadata standard. Even more, we provide services for a

semi-automatic conversion from DC to MPEG-7 while an affiliated FTP server is used for an automated up- and download of multimedia artifacts by the community to the common repository. Consequently, the Semantic Zapping Services of Virtual Campfire allow the community members to search and browse for multimedia contents described by MPEG-7.

Collaboration Services: Authoring of Multimedia Contents

Externalization of knowledge in Virtual Campfire is supported by annotating, tagging and sharing multimedia contents within the community. Contrary to a conventional categorization system, multiple concepts are used for one piece of information. Other than Flickr.com [cf. http://flickr.com) all metadata generated in Virtual Campfire is MPEG-7 compliant and generated using MPEG-7

Figure 4. Keyword and semantic tagging of multimedia contents

LAS service methods. For that purpose, Virtual Campfire offers two types of tagging: keyword- and semantic tagging (cf. figure 4). Keyword tagging enables users to assign a set of plain keywords to an image like it can be done in Flickr. From the technical point of view, keyword tagging is covered by the methods of MultimediaContentService. Semantic tagging goes a step further by allowing users to define semantic entities and to assign semantic entity references to an image. These are more expressive than plain keywords, because they carry additional semantics. For example one could not derive from a plaintext keyword "Buddha", that it describes an agent, while for semantic tagging, "Buddha" has been modeled as a semantic entity of type agent. Semantic entities are defined using methods of SemanticBasetypeService. Semantic references are assigned to images using methods of MultimediaContentService.

Similarly, retrieval is based on the multimedia descriptions. For retrieval by plain keyword tags

users can formulate keyword search expressions as propositional logic formulae using keywords as atomic propositions. For example, the keyword search expression "Buddha and Bamiyan and not(Destroyed or Taliban)"would retrieve all images having been assigned the keywords Buddha and Bamiyan, but none of the two keywords Destroyed or Taliban. The above concepts are transferable to the more expressive semantic tagging, which can be easily realized on the basis of the MPEG-7 services.

Storytelling Services: Re-Contextualization of Episodic Knowledge

For re-contextualization of episodic knowledge Virtual Campfire provides dedicated Storytelling Services. In order to help even an "untrained" user in creating useful stories (from a structural point of view), the MOD paradigm is being applied as a

Figure 5. A non-linear story created in Virtual Campfire

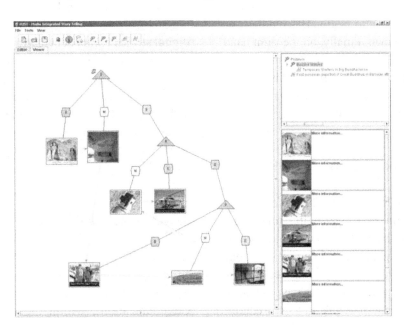

theoretical basis (cf. Section 3). For that purpose two dedicated user interfaces are available for the Storytelling Services: An editor and a player. The editor allows users to create new or edit already existing multimedia stories. The player is used for the consumption of existing multimedia stories. Besides the explicit knowledge contained in the multimedia contents themselves the high-level semantic tags are accessible. These contents can thereafter be temporally arranged as they depend on a certain context they belong to. When creating a story the author can now create paths covering different problematic aspects along the contents. Thus, the problems addressed depend on the path selected and lead consequently to different results in a story. Figure 5 shows the editor consisting of three main elements [from left to right]: Storyboard, plot and semantic annotations. The plot in the middle represents the declarative knowledge captured in a story. It is rendered as a tree hierarchy, which allows the further decomposition into sub-problems. In addition, problems addressed in a multimedia story can be linked to related multimedia contents. The storyboard on the left hand side shows a visualization of episodic knowledge as paths between content elements. In addition, the decomposition of stories according to MOD paradigm into begin (B), middle (M), and end (E) is shown. Finally, on the right hand side, additional semantic annotations can be added to any multimedia element. Thus, users may express verbal-knowledge being associated with non-verbal knowledge.

CONCLUSION AND OUTLOOK

With the further development of the Web 2.0 and social software (in particular) digital storytelling becomes a central knowledge sharing and learning technology again. Especially, in situations where direct interaction is not possible, the new social software application offers the possibility to share multimedia materials in a community-centered style. Like the creation of new knowledge is a discursive and multistage process, the user requirements are rapidly changing and several new features need to be integrated into community information systems. In contrast to existing implementations the methodology and architecture Virtual Campfire is more flexible to assess the community needs over time and to integrate the community members in the development process. Even more, the multimedia services of Virtual Campfire based on MPEG-7 provide interoperability and exchangeability of learning contents. Thus, the usage of LAS simplifies the community support process for the communities of practice drastically and on the same time offering more influence on the development process. However, the direct support of computer scientists and community designers is still needed. In future, graphical editing support for community web sites could leave even more responsibility on the community side.

Another topic of ongoing research is the assessment and analysis of stories. Since the stories are created by communities we need community-centered assessment tools beyond the level of simple rating tools. Our stories are related to a problem-solving space created by a hierarchical presentation of problems. Non-linear digital stories components have to cover at least all sub-problems in the problem space. This can be tested automatically by some algorithmic approach while the emotional movement of learners and their problem-solving skills are much harder to test. This is clearly interdisciplinary research which can be performed in an organizational or psychological framework.

ACKNOWLEDGMENT

This work was supported by German National Science Foundation (DFG) within the collaborative research centers SFB/FK 427 "Media and Cultural Communication", within the research cluster established under the excellence initiative of the German government "Ultra High-Speed Mobile Information and Communication (UMIC)" and by the 6th Framework IST programme of the EC through the Network of Excellence in Professional Learning (PROLEARN) IST-2003-507310. We thank our colleagues Nalin Sharda and Georgios Toubekis for the inspiring discussions. In addition, we thank our students D. Renzel, H. Janßen, M. Pienkos, P. M. Cuong, D. Andrikopoulos and A. Hahne for the implementation of the Virtual Campfire services.

REFERENCES

Andrienko, N. and Andrienko, G. (2005). Exploratory Analysis of Spatial and Temporal Data -- A Systematic Approach. Springer.

Aristoteles (2000). "Poetics" (translated by S. H. Butcher). http://classics.mit.edu/Aristotle/poetics.html, {25.7.2006}.

Braun, N. (2004). "Kontrolliertes Erzählen von Geschichten mit integrierten, Videobasierten Hyperstories". In: R. Keil-Slawik, H. Selke, and G. Szwillus (eds.), Mensch & Computer 2004: Allgegenw¨artige Interaktion, Oldenbourg. pp. 157–167.

Brown, J.S. and Duguid, P. (2000). The Social Life of Information. Harvard Business School Press. Boston, MA.

Center for Digital Storytelling (2005). Homepage, http://www.storycenter.org/index1.html, {25.7.2006}.

Cox, S. and Daisey, P. et al. (eds.) (2005). OpenGIS Geography Markup Language (GML) Encoding Specification. Open Geospatial Consortium, Inc.

Davenport, T. and Prusak, L. (1998). Working Knowledge: How Organizations Manage What they Know, Cambridge, MA, Harvard Business School Press.

Digital Storytelling Organization (DSA). (2002). "Defining Digital Storytelling". http://www.dsaweb.org/01associate/ds.html {25.7.2006}.

Dublin Core Metadata Initiative (1999). "Dublin core metadata element set, version 1.1: Reference description". Technical report, Dublin Core Metadata Initiative. http://dublincore.org/documents/dces/ {25.7.2006}.

Franz, K. and Nischelwitzer, A. (2004). "Adaptive Digital Storytelling: A Concept for Narrative Structures and Digital Storytelling build on Basic Storytelling Principles, Adaptive Story Schemas and Structure Mapping Techniques". In L. Zimmermann (ed.): Multimedia Applications in Education Conference (MApEC) Proceedings. Graz. pp. 28-33.

Fohrmann, J. and Schüttpelz, E. (eds.) (2004). "Die Kommunikation der Medien". Niemeyer, Tübingen (in German).

Gröger, G., Kolbe, T. H. and Czerwinski, A. (eds.) (2006). Candidata OpenGIS CityGML Implementation (City Geography Markup Language). OGC 06-057r1. Open Geospatial Consortium, Inc.

Heiden, W., Frühling, C. and Deuer, H. (2001). "Hypermedia Novel - Hymn. A New Storytelling Paradigm". Proceedings of CAST '01. pp. 345-348.

ISO. (2002). "Information technoloy – Multimedia content description interface – Part 8: Extraction and use of MPEG-7 descriptions". Technical Report ISO/IEC TR 15938-8: 2002(E).

ISO (2003). "Information Technology – Multimedia Content Description Interface – part 5: Multimedia description schemes". Technical Report ISO/IEC TR 15938-5:2003.

Jäger, L. and Stanitzek, G. (eds.) (2002). "Transkribieren - Medien/Lektüre". Wilhelm Fink Verlag, Munich (in German).

Kosch, H. (2003). Distributed Multimedia Database Technologies Supported by MPEG-7 and MPEG-21. Auerbach Publication.

Kraak, M.-J. and Ormeling, F. (2003). Cartography. Pearson Education Limited, England.

Lambert, J. (ed.) (2003). "Digital Storytelling Cookbook and Travelling Companion". Digital Diner Press, 4.0 edition, (Excerpt).

Lave, J. and Wenger E. (1991). Situated Learning: Legimate Peripheral Participation. Cambridge University Press, Cambridge, UK.

Lynch, K. (1960). The Image of the City. The MIT Press.

Martínez, J.M., Gonzández, C., García, C. and de Ramón, J. (2002). "Towards Universal Access to Content using MPEG-7". Multimedia '02. December 1-6, Juan-les-Pins, France.

Nonaka, I. and Takeuchi, H. (1995). "The Knowledge-creating Company". In: Oxford University Press, Oxford.

O'Reilly, T. (2005). "What Is Web 2.0 - Design Patterns and Business Models for the Next Generation of Software". http://www.oreillynet.com/pub/a/oreilly/tim/news/2005/09/30/what-is-web-20.html {3.7.2006}

Phillips, M. A. and Huntley, C. (2001). "Dramatica—A New Theory Of Story". Screenplay Systems Inc., 4th edition, 2.

Polanyi, M (1985). "Implizites Wissen". Suhrkamp, Frankfurt/Main (in German).

Propp, V. (1958). "Morphology of the Folktale". International Journal of American Linguistics, 24(4, Part II).

Roth, G. and Kleiner, A. (1999). "Car Launch: The Human Side of Managing Change". Oxford University Press, New York.

Royrvik, E.A. and Bygdas, A.L. (2002). "Knowledge Hyperstories — The Use of ICT Enhanced Storytelling in Organizations". 3rd European Conference on Organizational Knowledge, Learning and Capabilities. Athens, Greece. http://www.alba.edu.gr/OKLC2002/Proceedings/pdf files/ID260.pdf {2.10.2006}.

Schneider, O., Braun, N. and Habinger G. (2003). "Storylining suspense: An authoring environment for structuring non-linear interactive narratives". In WSCG, http://wscg.zcu.cz/wscg2003/Papers_2003/I53.pdf {25.7.2006}.

Sharda, N. (2005). "Movement Oriented Design: A New Paradigm for Multimedia Design". International Journal of Lateral Computing (IJLC), 1(1):7–14, 2005.

Snow, C. P. (1959). "The Two Cultures". Cambridge University Press, Cambridge.

Spaniol, M., Klama, R., Sharda, N. and Jarke, M. (2006). "Web-Based Learning with Non-Linear Multimedia Stories", 5th International Conference on Web-based Learning (ICWL 2006), July 19-21. Penang, Malaysia.

Tulving, E. (1978). "Episodic and semantic memory". In E. Tulving and W. Donaldson (Eds.), Organization of Memory, New York: Academic Press, pp. 381-403.

Ullman, M. T. (2004). "Contributions of memory circuits to language: the declarative/procedural model". Cognition, 92:231 – 270.

Wenger, E. (1998). "Communities of Practice: Learning, Meaning, and Identity". Cambridge University Press, Cambridge, UK.

Chapter V
E–Democracy:
The Social Software Perspective

Pascal Francq
Université Libre de Bruxelles, Belgium

ABSTRACT

The success of the Internet has launched McLuhan's idea of the global village. Over the years, the Internet has become a real political medium which has inspired the emergence of the concept of e-democracy. Despite some successful applications, many limitations prevent its wide expansion. Some of these limitations can be solved with social software, in particular with the emerging Web2.0 applications. This kind of applications may contribute to a better application of e-democracy processes for local political decisions.

INSIDE CHAPTER

The Internet is today a widely used platform to exchange information and share knowledge. In this chapter, we propose a prospective study of the use of the Internet as support for e-democracy processes. The history of the Internet shows that social software has always been developed to support knowledge sharing among net surfers. Since participating in political issues implies knowledge sharing, the Internet was rapidly used as a political medium. The concept of e-democracy, i.e. the use of information and communication technologies to allow citizens to participate in the democratic process, is a natural evolution of this situation. Several examples demonstrate that e-democracy can be deployed for local decision purposes. The experiences have also shown several limitations, in particular concerning the on-line tools currently offered. We argue that solutions exist to overcome these limitations and that their integration in social software environments may enhance the concept of e-democracy in order to apply it to more complex decision-taking situations.

Copyright © 2009, IGI Global, distributing in print or electronic forms without written permission of IGI Global is prohibited.

INTRODUCTION

With the expansion of available information and the diversity of communication and information technologies, the Internet is a medium support that cannot be ignored. Limited to scientists during its early days, the Internet became a platform for knowledge sharing and collaboration for a variety of domains due to the multitude of social software developed. In particular, the political domain was always present on the Internet and political movements have often used this medium to support their actions. Today, with one billion net surfers around the world, many people claim that the idea of "global village" popularized by Marshall McLuhan in the late 1690s (McLuhan & Fiore, 1967) is a reality. Now that it becomes possible to engage in discussions with everybody around the world across geographical and temporal boundaries, many people believe in the Internet as a virtual place where different cultures may peacefully coexist. From this dream there emerged, in the late 1990s, the concept of **e-democracy**. The main idea is to use the information and communication technologies to make citizens participate more directly in the democratic process. Several examples of the application of this concept for local decision-taking (decisions concerning a part of a city or a town) seem to demonstrate that the idea of e-democracy is no longer utopian. Moreover, with the emergence of the "Web2.0" concept, there is an increased use of social software by net surfers. This chapter proposes a prospective view of the application of social software to support e-democracy processes. In fact, we argue that social software can already be useful in this context. Moreover, we believe that it may be enhanced by integrating existing technologies to overcome certain limitations related to the current tools supporting e-democracy processes. Concretely, the second section proposes a short historical overview to show how the Internet, initially developed to support knowledge networks, was rapidly used as a political medium. The third section presents the concept of e-democracy, some examples and the main limitations of the current applications. The fourth section proposes an overview of how modern social software can be used in the context of e-democracy, and which technologies should be integrated to propose on-line tools enhancing the application of e-democracy processes. Since these evolutions solve some of the e-democracy limitations, the fifth section briefly analyses in which context the concept of e-democracy should be deployed. Finally, the sixth section proposes some conclusions.

FROM KNOWLEDGE NETWORKS TO POLITICAL MEDIA

The history of the Internet studied in section 2.1 shows that new collaboration tools and methodologies were continuously developed to increase knowledge sharing among social networks (scientific ideas, software, electronic resources, ...). Based on these emerging social networks, communities of net surfers have collaborated through the Internet on many different projects (section 2.2). As soon as the Internet allowed net surfers to freely exchange ideas, it was rapidly used to discuss political issues. The result is the evolution of the Internet to a real political medium (section 2.3).

Internet as Knowledge Networks

The Arpanet computer network, the ancestor of today's Internet, was designed to help researchers to collaborate. Tools such as e-mail and newsgroups were developed in the late 1960s to allow researchers to discuss their ideas, present their results and take scientific decisions. Initially limited to the military research area, the access to Arpanet was rapidly extended the whole research community.

In the 1980s, Arpanet became the collaboration platform for many research teams around the world. The result of this evolution was the creation in the late 1980s of the Internet as known today. The main problem with the communication tools existing that time was their asynchronous dimension which strongly limits the interactions between people. With the increased use of the Internet during the 1990s, new synchronized communication applications were developed: instant messaging tools and chat rooms. These tools provided a new level of interactions in the communication process between net surfers. As studied by Rheingold (2000), this technology has permitted the emergence of **virtual communities** of net surfers sharing similar interests. Once communities have emerged, it is possible to make them live through all modern communication supports. With the evolution of communication tools, in particular the net meeting applications, it has become possible to efficiently organize discussions involving participants that are not presented at the same place[1]. Initially developed at the beginning of 1990s as simple diffusion tools for scientific results at CERN, Web sites have become over the years real knowledge dissemination tools. Today, the number of Web sites containing interesting information has exploded making the localization of the relevant information a crucial issue. Since several technologies have increased the interactivity between Web sites and net surfers, the Web can be considered as a social environment and many modern Web sites have become real social software.

The Internet as Collaboration Platform

With the increasing number of net surfers and the availability of synchronous communication tools, the Internet evolves to a collaboration platform. Built upon virtual communities, net surfers have started to collaborate, in particular to build freely available artefacts (software, books, music tunes, ...). Emerging in the early 1980s, the free and open source software movements are the best examples of free collaboration through the Internet. By combining social software with specific collaboration tools, such as source code managing tools, complex software projects[2], comparable in quality and features to well established commercial software, were successfully developed (Raymond, 2001). One surprising aspect of these projects is their ability to manage long-term decisions and to self-organize the work division across a dozen of individual developers. Most of the time, when conflicts appear concerning important decisions in a given project, such as the choice of a project leader, a democratic approach is privileged by the community. This new production process has been successfully applied to other domains than software development. Founded in 2001, Wikipedia[3], the free content encyclopaedia project, is the best known example of the application of the concept of open source to other content than source code. Despite some problems concerning the control of the quality of part of the content[4], everybody agrees that Wikipedia demonstrates that high quality knowledge can be built in a collaborative way. In particular, on-line writers must sometimes reach a comprise as they elaborate articles discussing controversial issues. Since the early 2000s, and the emergence of the "Web2.0" applications[5], a new dimension in on-line collaboration is proposed. In fact, the role of the net surfer has dramatically changed: he or she has been transformed from a "passive consumer of information" to an active organizer of the Internet content. The new paradigm behind this social software is that net surfers should collaborate to manage shared resources (such as bookmarks, contacts, videos, ...) they find relevant. Since current search tools have difficulties treating the amount of available information on the Internet, this approach proposes a sort of "human indexing" of its content and its users.

The Internet as Political Medium

Since it is possible to communicate and collaborate through the Internet, it seems natural that it is a place where political issues may be discussed. A close look at the history of the Internet shows that its use as a political medium is as old as the Internet itself. In fact, as pointed out by Rosenzweig (1998), it is hard to believe that the creators of the Arpanet were unaware of the political context on the late sixties in the USA, in particular the protests against the Vietnam War mobilizing the American universities campuses. Moreover, some authors claim that the success of the Internet can only be understood if we consider that the first net surfers have adopt it as a democratic and interactive communication platform (Hauben & Hauben, 1997). This latest theory finds an echo with an analysis of the content of the messages exchanged in newsgroups carried out in 1998. This study showed that 12% of the total number of messages on Usenet were dedicated to political subjects (Hill & Hughes, 1998). The fact that political issues were discussed in newsgroups is not surprising since it was certainly the first virtual place where any kind of subjects were discussed. But, the amount dedicated to politics reveals of the political awareness of many net surfers at that time and the existence of politically-oriented virtual communities. With the growing popularity of the Web as mass communication and diffusion medium, many "politically-oriented" organizations have understood the potential of the Internet as an internal and external communication tool. Internally, it provides a collaboration platform and is a source of information for members and sympathizers. Externally, the goal is to spread their ideas on the Net and to sensitize net surfers to their points of view. With the multiplication of blogs, it becomes very easy for everybody to publish their political ideas and to create a new genre of journalism (Wall, 2005). Conscious that the Internet is becoming widely used among the

population in some countries, in the late 1990s, different public authorities deployed **e-government** projects, i.e. using information and communication technologies to better communicate with their citizens. Today, in some countries, citizens can use the Internet to access the debates of parliament, to ask for administrative documents or to fill their tax returns. In the e-government approach, the Internet is only used as a communication medium for governments, but there are no real interactions between citizens and public authorities.

E-DEMOCRACY: APPLICATIONS AND LIMITS

If the Internet was used very early to discuss political issues, it took some time before these discussions were transformed into real political actions. The concept of e-democracy emerged from Internet in the late 1990s (section 3.1) and was successfully applied to several situations (section 3.2). But, as analysed in section 3.3, there are actually some important limitations.

Concept of E-Democracy

There exist several definitions in the literature for the concept of e-democracy (sometimes called cyber-democracy). Nevertheless, all authors agree that it is related to the use of information and communication technologies to involve citizens, sometimes called **e-citizens**, in the political decision-making processes. If the idea of using technologies to build a better and more humane society is not new (Wiener, 1965), the actual development of the Internet in our modern societies makes its realization partially possible. Besides the multiple theoretical definitions, it is also possible to define e-democracy as a wide range of actions that should be available for citizens through the Internet: voting for people, participating in online referendums, intervening in public debates, etc. Since we are discussing e-democracy applications rather than the concept itself, we will adopt this approach. In particular, we choose the definition proposed by Vedel (2003) suggesting that the concept of e-democracy includes three levels of interactions between e-citizens and public authorities:

1. Access to information to ensure transparency in political decisions.
2. Build debates and discussion places between citizens in order to coordinate political actions.
3. Participate in public deliberations and decision-making.

Today, the concept of e-democracy is quite successful in Northern countries. Two elements may explain this:

1. Many citizens in these countries are petitioning for a more participative democracy.
2. In the collective conscience of these countries, the Internet is widely accessible for most citizens, even through if the reality is somewhat different.

Some Examples

The Public Electronic Network (PEN), which started in Santa Monica in 1989 (Rogers, Collins-Jarvis & Schmitz, 1994) is often cited as the first example of e-democracy application. By providing a network of terminals, the American city gave the opportunity to its citizens to discuss problems together. One of the results of these discussions was a project to help the homeless people of the city. Since this experience, several other cities or regions have deployed some of the principles of e-democracy (OECD, 2003). Most of these experiences can be categorized into two types of democratic interactions:

1. The creation of Internet portals where citizens can not only consult information (already available with e-government applications), but also interact directly with politicians, for example by sending e-mails or commenting on proposals.
2. The use of electronic consultations to get the opinion of citizens. Nevertheless, in most cases, there is not always an obligation for public authorities to take the results of these consultations into account.

If most of e-democracy applications were organized by public authorities, new situations emerge today where the e-democratic initiatives are directly launched by citizens themselves. The fact that Internet is more and more used to promote e-petitions (electronic petitions) is certainly the visible part of this for most net surfers. Successful uses of e-petitions in the context of local politics were already pointed out (Macintosh, Malina & Farrell, 2002). Moreover, some e-petitions have influenced more global political decisions, such as during the debate on software patents at the level of the European Parliament where it was one of the methods used by the opponents to sensitize the parliamentarians. Despite the criticism concerning the electronic vote[6], several initiatives have been successfully organized. For example, during the primary votes of the Democrats in Arizona in 2002, nearly 50% of the votes were cast using the Internet (Solop, 2002). The important point of such initiatives is that Internet should never be the only way to interact, but one of the possible ways. In fact, since people can participate from "their homes", the Internet may support the participation of people who would not participate without it. Some initiatives were more ambitious and aim to influence global political stakes. During the 2004 US presidential campaign, a Web site allowed net surfers all over the world "to vote" for their candidate[7]. 500.000 net surfers participated in this virtual election with, of course, no influence at all on the final results. But, this can be seen as an interesting experience of e-democracy at a global level.

Main Limitations

Despite some successful e-democracy applications, there are several important limitations that impede a generalized deployment. The main limitation is, of course, the reality of the digital divide. Many people have not (or rarely) access to the Internet. This makes e-democracy, in practice, a preserve for "rich" populations. If this difference is evident between the South and the North (geographical digital divide), among the Northern countries, many people cannot use, at least regularly and correctly, the Internet (social digital divide). Besides, several authors claim that e-democracy will only be available for a small part of the population which can then control the political choices (Barber, 2004). Apart from these problems "outside of the technological sphere", the current examples of e-democracy are always related to very specific issues due to the lack of adequate integrated solutions. Of course, everybody would agree that deploying technologies will never solve all the real problems. Our point is that some of these problems are directly related to the underlying tools. To illustrate this, we propose to study the main limitations associated to the different levels of interactions proposed by Vedel (2003). The first category of interactions is related to the access of the relevant information for citizens. If the e-government initiatives can be seen as a first attempt to offer an access to public information, most of the time, e-government portals are not well structured. The consequence is a difficulty in finding all the relevant information related to a given problem. Moreover, all necessary information to build a real political culture is not available on e-government portals. It is also useful to access studies in universities, documents of political parties, citizens' testimonies, etc. Accessing other

sources of information, such as the Internet, is an important issue. But the Internet is characterized by an increased quantity of available information, and current search solutions, in particular search engines, cannot face this complexity (Fogarty, & Bahls, 2002). Beside this problem of quantity of information, the quality of the proposed information is also problematic, in particular for search engines which are the most popular search tools. Most Internet search engines rank highly the documents which are the most pointed by hyperlinks on the Web (Brin & Page, 1998). Since hyperlinks can be interpreted as human assessments on a given document, i.e. assessments on the ideas defended by a "politically-oriented" document, search engines have a tendency to always propose the documents containing ideas shared by the majority of net surfers. This problem explains the frequent criticism that the Internet acts as support for a certain form of single thought. We believe that the current search methods should be enhanced, in particular to ensure the diversity of the points of view presented to net surfers. The second category of interactions is related to the creation of places where citizens can debate over political issues. As explained earlier, newsgroups and chat rooms are powerful tools for discussions. Participating in on-line discussions can make communities emerged (Rheingold, 2000), in particular net surfers sharing similar ideas and collaborating with a unique political goal. In fact, newsgroups were already successfully used for public on-line consultations (Rosen, 2001). But, the multiple existing communication channels where such communities may exist are a brake for the emergence of large communities of organized citizens, which is the core of the e-democracy concept. Of course, if there is a fixed political reference for a group of people, such as the Web site of a party or any politically-oriented organization, a community exists *de facto*. On the other hand, limiting the communities built around existing entities is somewhat reductive. We believe that networking tools should help people build new communities and that political portals should be used to coordinate political actions around specific subjects. The third category is related to participating in public debates and decision-making. For simple decision-making, such as answer a simple question (yes/no, for/against) or choose a candidate, Internet technologies can be used without any major technical problems. But, for more complex decision-taking, such as drawing up a budget for a town or writing a bill, there is a real lack of well-established on-line tools. We believe that existing methods managing complex decision-taking should be integrated in political portals.

BUILDING AND ORGANIZING POLITICAL NETWORKS

In the previous section, the short overview of the concept of e-democracy has shown the main actual limits of its application and some possible directions for enhancement to solve some of these limitations. These enhancements should support the building and organization of political networks not only to group net surfers sharing the same ideas, but also to provide a discussion environment where people having different points of view on a same topic can hold a debate. Today, there is a need for independent **political portals**. Such portals should be sources for information related to specific political subjects (environment, democratic participation, education, ...). They should reference information coming from e-government applications (since many official political documents are public) but also from alternative sources. They should be build upon content management systems to provide an environment for debates and collaborative writing of documents. We argue that a combination of these political portals with other social software, in particular in the context of the emerging Web2.0 applications, may contribute to solve three major problems:

1. Ensure diversity of points of view.
2. Create political networks.
3. Organize complex decision-taking.

Diversity of Points of View

One of the main stakes behind the concept of e-democracy is to access to information representing different points of view on a given problem. As already explained, the e-government portals currently developed by several countries should help to make official information more accessible. But, it is also necessary for e-citizens to read information coming from other sources and comment this information with other people, which is the role of the political portals. Since they must reference relevant information concerning a particular political subject, they should be combined with applications helping to access to interesting information available on the Internet. Several emerging Web2.0 applications propose some solutions to the access of information by providing a platform for a **social indexing** of the Web. Social bookmarking applications, such as del.icio.us, are well known examples. When net surfers find interesting documents on the Web, they tag them with keywords. It is then possible to find all the documents tagged, thus humanly assessed as relevant, with a given set of keywords. We already know that applying the social bookmarking principle can help net surfers (citizens) to access relevant (political) content. But this principle can also help citizens to have a more open mind. In fact, since political issues are characterized by a diversity of points of view, it is evident that a given document, a law or a study for example, may be interpreted in several ways depending on its readers. This diversity of points of view on a given document will probably correspond to different keywords used to tag this document. So, since net surfers will see all the keywords used by others to tag the same documents, it will be possible for them to have an overview of the different points of view by analysing the different sets of keywords used. Once these documents are tagged, they could be discussed on political portals. Everyone would agree that the major problem concerning Internet is related to the quality of the on-line content. For example, many Web sites around the world diffuse racist ideas. Currently, there is no technology that proposes a real solution to this problem, but several approaches have been proposed to limit its impact. One of them, used by several portals such as Internet marketplaces, is to propose a rating system of users (Chen & Singh, 2001). This system gives the opportunities to users to express a degree of trust to others based on their experiences of the interactions with them (for example buying something from them). This approach could be used in another way in our context: users would rate the people whom they do not trust. The idea of rating the non-trusted people rather than rating the trusted people is to avoid the limitation of the diversity of points of view. In fact, if users rated people by trust, it is probable that they would rate well people sharing the same points of view, and the consequence would be to connect with people that reinforce their opinions rather than open them to diversity. By rating non-trusted people, it will be possible to identify groups of people who are never considered as trusted by most users. This information will be used to filter the information proposed or, at least, to inform net surfers that some political contributions were written by very untrustworthy people and should be taken with caution.

Building Political Networks

The e-democracy concept claims that e-citizens should be able to act on political decisions. It seems therefore evident that they must coordinate their actions. Such a coordination can be built upon "politically-oriented" virtual communities through political portals. If several tools exist to make these communities live (for example

newsgroups) and could be integrated in portals, building these **political networks** remains a challenge. In the previous section, we have explained how social bookmarking applications may be used in the context of e-democracy. Moreover, some researchers have shown that it is possible to cluster the net surfers based on the keywords they used to tag documents (Paolillo, & Penumarthy, 2007). But, as already explained, the tags used represent a certain points of view of the tagged document. There is therefore a risk that doing a clustering on a tag-basis will lead to regroup people sharing the same point of view on a particular topic, which will reduce the access to a diversity of points of view. In fact, we need to build communities of people sharing the same interests on a given topic and not sharing the same points of view on a given topic. The clustering of net surfers into communities must therefore be based on the content of the information. The GALILEI platform is one of the solutions that proposes a solution for this problem (Francq, 2007). This platform implements an approach based on **social browsing**. In this approach, the net surfers define different interests, called profiles, and assess the documents they consider as relevant for their profiles. The system computes descriptions for the different profiles of the net surfers based on the relevance assessments on documents and a content analysis. The profiles are then clustered on the basis of their descriptions: similar profiles are grouped together in order to define a number of communities of interests. If this approach is applied with a corpus of political documents, the communities will group people sharing common interests on different political subjects.

Organize Complex Decision-Making

One of the main ideas behind the concept of e-democracy is to make citizens participate in political decisions-making. In the different examples existing today, this participation is limited to making a "simple choice", such as voting for a candidate. For more complex decision-making, there is a lack of on-line tools. A good example of complex decision-making process is to decide how to organize the allocations of a given budget. To solve this problem it is not only necessary to evaluate the priorities of each citizen, but also several constraints influence the choice such as the total budget available. In fact, within a given budget, a situation may occur where two choices can be financed: either project with priority 1 or projects with priority 2 and 3. Choosing between these two possibilities is not as easy as choosing a unique candidate for an election. Another complex problem is for several people to reach a compromise. The collaborative writing of a local policy is a typical example of this kind of problem. A first approach for dealing with complex decision-making is to gather more information from the participants and to integrate this information in the final decision. The domain of operations research has provided a huge number of methods that help take decisions (Winston, 2003), in particular computer-aided methods for multiple criteria decision-making. But, in the context of e-democracy, these computer-aided decision systems have nevertheless several drawbacks. Since most citizens do not have the competences to understand the methods implemented in these systems, they will probably not correctly understand how their information will be used to take the final decision. This means that these systems can favour the small number of citizens that know which information they have to give to defend their points of view, which is one of the criticisms often made against e-democracy. Moreover, these systems cannot solve every form of complex decision-making, such as agreeing to a comprise. A second approach is to integrate in political portals methods developed to help a group of people dealing in complex decision-making. One of the known method is Delphi (Linstone & Turoff, 1975). This method structures the group communication process of a group of individuals

in order to make them solve a complex problem as a single entity. This method was successfully applied in several contexts, including:

- building a common interpretation of historical events.
- evaluating possible budget allocations.
- delineating the pros and cons associated with potential policy options.

An on-line Web system implementing the Delphi approach was already developed (Kenis, 1995). It organizes the communication between a set of users using an interactive process:

1. Each user gives its opinion to a question asked.
2. A moderator proposes a compromise based on the different answers.
3. The compromise is submitted to every user. They can accept it or reject it (and give their comments).
4. If a given majority does not accept the proposition, the process is reiterated beginning from the second step.

Many problems remain for this type of approach, in particular the role of the moderator of the process, the authentication of the net surfers participating in the debate or the democratic control of the process. But, we believe that integrating such a system can propose a new democratic approach for solving some complex problems.

E-DEMOCRACY: WHICH CONTEXT?

It is difficult to evaluate the status of e-democracy. The paradigms of the global village (McLuhan & Fiore, 1967) and the capacity of computers to help human beings (Wiener, 1965) have created many hopes in the Internet to solve the problem of the confidence crisis of most modern democracies. Since the information and communication technologies have demonstrated their capacities to make people exchange and collaborate, many people believe that the e-democracy concept must be promoted. On the one hand, several different initiatives of this concept have been successfully applied, in particular to local political decisions. Moreover, the previous sections have shown that a combination of specific social software and political portals may solve some of the limitations of the application of e-democracy. On the other hand, many limitations cannot currently be solved. Firstly, technologies cannot best organize all forms of decision-making. Secondly, it is necessary to build new control mechanisms to ensure that the way technologies are used respects the democratic process. But, the main limitation is without doubt the (geographical and social) digital divide. To think that, from now to the middle of the twenty-first century, applications of e-democracy will be widely used seems nowadays utopian. Knowing that the geographical digital divide will not be solved rapidly, it is yet possible to limit locally the social digital divide. Therefore, two main categories of applications of e-democracy will probably be developed in the future:

1. For political local choices related to problems concerning small socially homogeneous communities of citizens, typically the management of a town. If e-citizens have a similar level of access and mastering of the Internet, on-line collaboration tools can increase the commitment of the citizens to final political decisions.
2. For decision-making in organizations where most members have a regular access to the Internet, such as the free and open source community. For nongovernmental organizations, it may also help since most of their decisions centres are located in Northern countries.

We can therefore fear to see in the next decades an asymmetrical deployment of e-democracy applications.

CONCLUSION

The Internet was originally built as a knowledge sharing platform for scientists. Its decentralized schema and the increased facility of content creation and information access have contributed to its use as political medium. The concept of e-democracy was born with the idea of using information and communication technologies to help citizens to interact more directly in political decision-making. In fact, if some examples of e-democracy processes have successively been applied in local areas, despite some utopian attempts, the actual on-line solutions have limitations. Today, some of these limitations can be solved by using and enhancing political portals and social software. Firstly, the emerging Web2.0 applications propose collaboration solutions to manage the information on the Internet. If applied to political content, it may help people to find information on their political interests as well as ensure the diversity of points of view. Moreover, community creation approaches can be used to link people sharing similar political interests. Finally, by integrating on-line methods for complex decision-making on political portals, it is possible to organize on-line collaboration for a group of people in order to take complex decisions. The e-democracy concept has emerged because of the increased use of the Internet. With the digital divide existing today, it is impossible to apply this approach to a wide range of applications. If all democratic constraints must be respected, only specific local or social contexts exist where a real e-democracy process can be applied. Despite the unsolved limitations, this approach proposes a real participative democratic process and should be developed wherever it is possible.

REFERENCES

Barber, B.R. (2004). *Strong Democracy: Participatory Politics for a New Age.* University of California Press.

Brin, S., & Page, L. (1998). The antaomy of a large-scale hypertextual Web search engine. *Computer Networks and ISDN Systems*(33), 107-135.

Chen, M., & Singh, J.P. (2001). *Computing and using reputations for internet ratings.* Tampa, Florida, USA : ACM Press.

OECD (2003). *Promise and Problems of E-democracy: Challenges of Online Citizen Engagement.*

Fogarty, M., & Bahls, C. (2002). Information Overload : Feel the pressure? *The Scientist, 16*(16).

Francq, P. (2007). *The GALILEI Platform: Social Browsing to Build Communities of Interests and Share Relevant Information and Expertise.* In M.D. Lytras & A. Naeve (Editors), *Open source for knowledge and learning management : strategies beyond tools.* Idea Group Publishing (319-342).

Hauben, M., & Hauben, R. (1997). *Netizens: On the History and Impact of Usenet and the Internet.* IEEE Computer Society Press.

Hill, K.A., & Hughes, J.E. (1998). *Cyberpolitics: Citizen Activism in the Age of the Internet.* Rowman & Littlefield Publishers, Inc.

Kenis, D.G.A. (1995). *Improving group decisions: designing and testing techniques for group decision support systems applying Delphi principles.* Universiteit Utrecht.

Linstone, H.A., & Turoff, M. (1975). *The Delphi Method: Techniques and Applications.* Addison-Wesley Pub. Co., Advanced Book Program.

Macintosh, A., Malina, A., & Farrell, S. (2002). Digital Democracy through Electronic Petitioning. *Digital Government. Dordrecht: Kluwer.*

McLuhan, M., & Fiore, Q. (1967). *The Medium is the Massage : An Inventory of Effects* (G. Press, Éd.). Jerome Agel.

Paolillo, J.C., & Penumarthy, S. (2007). The Social Structure of Tagging Internet Video on del. icio. us. *System Sciences, 2007. HICSS 2007. 40th Annual Hawaii International Conference on,* 85-85.

Raymond, E.S. (2001). *The Cathedral and the Bazaar: Musings on Linux and Open Source by an Accidental Revolutionary.* O'Reilly & Associates.

Rheingold, H. (2000). *The Virtual Community.* MIT Press.

Rosen, T. (2001). E-Democracy in Practice: Swedish Experiences of a New Political Tool. *Stockholm, Swedish Association of Local Authorities and Swedish Federation of County Councils and Regions, Department of Democracy and Self-Government.*

Rogers, E.M., Collins-Jarvis, L., & Schmitz, J. (1994). The PEN project in Santa Monica: Interactive communication, equality, and political action. *Journal of the American Society for Information Science, 45*(6), 401-410.

Roy Rosenzweig. (1998). Wizards, Bureaucrats, Warriors, and Hackers: Writing the History of the Internet. *The American Historical Review, 103*(5), 1530-1552.

Solop, F.I. (2002). Digital Democracy Comes of Age: Internet Voting and the 2000 Arizona Democratic Primary Election. *PS: Political Science and Politics, 34*(02), 289-293.

Vedel, T. (2003). L'idée de démocratie électronique: Origines, Visions, Questions. *Le désenchantement démocratique, La Tour d'Aigues: Editions de l'Aube,* 243-266.

Wall, M. (2005). 'Blogs of war': Weblogs as news. *Journalism, 6*(2), 153.

Wiener, N. (1965). *Cybernetics:: Or Control and Communication in the Animal and the Machine.* Mit Pr.

Winston, W.L. (2003). *Operations Research.* Duxbury P.,U.S.

CASE STUDY

BetaVote.com—What if the Whole World could Vote in the U.S. Presidential Election?

During the 2004 US presidential elections, two Americans, Daniel Young and Kevin Frost, claimed that since the decisions of the United States influence the whole world, every citizen in the world should participate to the vote of its president. They have therefore created a Web site where net surfers could choose between John Kerry and George W. Bush. Around 500,000 net surfers participated in this virtual election, and 88% of them chose senator Kerry as US president. Also, although these Internet results did not influence the real results, this initiative can yet be seen as an experience in e-democracy at a global level. Nevertheless, it illustrates the problem of the digital divide. The percentage of voters is relatively low in comparison to the total number of net surfers (evaluated to one billion). Beyond the digital divide, the low number of participants also illustrates the lack of relay for such initiatives on the Internet. Secondly, in the US, the results of the on-line vote (around 70,000 net surfers participated) gave the victory to John Kerry while the real vote gave the victory to George W. Bush. Since some studies have shown that the Americans who voted for John Kerry were mostly "highly educated", the results of the e-democracy approach seem to confirm that using the Internet as a political medium may be the preserve of a given "elite", which is one of the criticisms against

e-democracy. It will be interesting to reiterate this experience during the next US presidential campaign and make comparisons with the one of 2004. In particular, the total number of net surfers participating should be analyzed as well as their geographical distribution.

USEFUL URLS

1. Communauté de communes de Parthenay: A French example of e-democracy portal, http://portail.cc-parthenay.fr/Portail2007
2. Council of Europe Forum for the Future of Democracy, http://www.coe.int/t/e/integrated_projects/democracy/
3. E-Democracy.Org/Minnesota E-Democracy, http://www.e-democracy.org
4. Villes Internet, Villes Internet – agir pour un internet citoyen, http://www.villesinternet.net
5. What if the whole world could vote in the U.S. presidential election?, http://www.betavote.com

FURTHER READINGS

Everard, J. (2001). Virtual states: the Internet and the boundaries of the nation state. Routledge.

Habermas, J. (1991). The Structural Transformation of the Public Sphere: An Inquiry Into a Category of Bourgeois Society. The MIT Press.

Rheingold, H. (2002). Smart Mobs: The Next Social Revolution. Perseus Books Group.

ENDNOTES

[1] The digital divide is, of course, a problem since every participant should have an access to the Internet, a sufficient bandwidth and

the corresponding hardware (microphone, webcam, etc.).

2   Linux, Mozilla, OpenOffice.org, Apache or K Desktop Environment are well known examples of software deployed on millions of computers today.

3   Wikipedia project: http://www.wikipedia. org

4   The main criticism concerning Wikipedia is the difference of quality between the articles. Some of them may be written by a team of experts of the corresponding domain, while others can be written by people without a real expertise. Many net surfers do not verify which authors have written which articles, and suppose that all articles have the same level of quality.

5   Many "Web2.0" applications appear on the Internet such as del.ico.us, LinkedIn, etc.

6   The democratic control of how technologies are deployed in the context of the electronic vote is an important issue. We believe that this is an "organisational" problem, since it is possible to control how the information is gathered and how the software manages this information. In democracies, independent commissions should organize this control and ensure the necessary transparency.

7   Section 8 analyses this case.

Chapter VI
Community and Collaboration Tools to Frame the New Working Environment:
The Banking Industry Case

Mariano Corso
Polytechnic of Milano, Italy

Antonella Martini
University of Pisa, Italy

Alessandro Piva
Polytechnic of Milano, Italy

ABSTRACT

This chapter focuses on the community and collaboration tools as means of creating business communities of practice (CoPs). First, the state-of-the art of these tools is presented with respect to diffusion and usage, and then emergent communities are analysed in terms of targets, goals, models and barriers. The research is based on 16 retrospective case studies that cover more than 50% of the banking sector in Italy by number of employees and refer to 33 communities. The findings provide interesting elements and suggestions to develop a community in a banking context. The authors aim to develop actionable knowledge to support management in understanding how to manage a business CoP, in order to create value for both the organization and its members.

Copyright © 2009, IGI Global, distributing in print or electronic forms without written permission of IGI Global is prohibited.

THE CHALLENGE OF A NEW WORKING ENVIRONMENT

Since KM became a prominent topic in management literature, various perspectives have been developed: ranging from a first, technology-focused view to the taxonomic-based standpoint; from '*knowledge as what is known*' to the later *socio-practical* concept. Each perspective embodies a different role of ICT: which may be a classical information system (IS) which allows users to translate knowledge into information, as well as to extrapolate knowledge from information (technology-focused view), or the need to transfer non-codified knowledge (taxonomic-based standpoint), or a backward role with respect to managerial and organizational levers in the what is known perspective (knowledge lies in the individual mind).

Our perspective on organizational knowledge is socio-practical, and considers knowledge as a common good rather than a mere individual asset (Von Krogh, 2002). Knowledge creation and sharing are interpreted as social processes, in which the most important role is played by individuals and their relationships with others (Senge, 1990; Brown e Duguid, 1998). The creation and transfer of knowledge are considered as social phenomena and an integral part of a community (Brown et al., 1998, Wenger, 1998a). Indeed, individuals choose other individuals with whom to cooperate from beyond their structures and formal ties (i.e. departments, divisions, etc.), so creating informal networks that overlap formal, and top-down designed structures within the organization.

Among the different types of informal networks, Communities of Practice (CoPs) are the most interesting from a knowledge management point of view.

New Needs from Workers

Through communities, individuals find the answers to those needs of sociality, belonging and experience-sharing that organizations find increasingly difficult to satisfy. Moreover, through communities, firms see the possibility of finding new ways to connect people, so overcoming the geographical and organizational bonds of traditional company structures. This is a growing need considering the 'mobile workers phenomenon', which represents an increasingly more important share of the total workforce (Drucker, 2002; Laubacher and Malone, 2003; Corso *et al.*, 2006) and requires different solutions compared to the traditional approaches.

It is clear that these developments have a strong influence on the working environment: on the one hand, the very concept of space changes, while, on the other, there is a different relationship between companies and employees. The latter identify less and less with their companies and are left alone with their needs and professional projects. In many cases, being a mobile worker is an obligation rather than a choice and compared to the traditional figure of the worker involves individual qualities such as independence and spirit. At the same time, the distance workers are more interested in their professional development than in personnel development policies.

For companies, all this means finding new ways to respond to the people's needs (safety and identity, membership and sharing, visibility and status, learning and personal development), re-designing the workspace on the basis of a number of guidelines: process re-configurability and layout independence, predominance of people over ICT tools, and finally, operations, collaboration and access. In other words, processes need to be made re-configurable independently of layout and of an organizational structure that is becoming ever more fluid; the focus needs to be on people and competences with the integration of support tools and not the other way round; the system needs to be brought in line with changing operations, allowing people to work and collaborate, and access information and competences wherever they are and under all conditions.

New Opportunities from ICT

From the technological point of view, a great opportunity is offered by the web as the place in which organizations design and manage communities.

The availability of new ICT-enabled services and particularly of web and mobile communication services makes it possible to overcome geographical (the work-place is everywhere the worker is), time (the worker creates value whenever it is required) and organizational barriers (the concepts of colleague, competitor and supplier have to be rethought and become more worker- and relationship-focused). In addition, the IS evolution in terms of interoperability and integration is speeding up the convergence towards the web application usage, while making the borders of the different IS more and more fuzzy. Intranet, ERP and CRM, which were once distinct ICT application systems, are merging and overlapping, while developing increasingly into communication and collaboration tools. In this sense, collaborative tools are the next generation of knowledge management projects (Andriessen *et al,*. 2002; Wenger and Snyder, 2000).

As a result of this continuous evolution, the emerging IS is not just a sum of its components, but it can be a working 'space' which gives complete support to workers' multidimensional needs. This vision is what we have called *virtual workspace* (Corso *et al.* 2008): a creative and open working space focused on workers, their needs, specific working conditions and interaction with others.

To exploit the potential of the technology, we need to look at people and the 'way' they construct the environment in which they work and interact. Accordingly to this line of research, the role – and the challenge – of ICT is, therefore, to recreate a social reality made up of interpersonal relationships, collaboration and communication flows, and possibly enhance this reality by emphasizing openness and collaboration.

New Challenge for Management

However, the challenge is at the organizational and managerial level: Communities of Practice are emerging as self-organizing entities that management can encourage and support, gaining great advantages, without owning or controlling them totally (Brown and Duguid (1998), Wenger and Snyder (2000), Magnusson and Davidsson (2001), Andriessen et al. (2002)). If Knowledge Management is about "… creating an environment that encourages people to learn and share knowledge by aligning goals, integrating bits and pieces of information within and across organizational boundaries, and producing new knowledge that is usable and useful to the organization" (Corso *et al.* 2004; 2006), Community-based Knowledge Management means *designing the right set of communication tools, incentives, motivation, organizational and managerial mechanisms that, without being intrusive, follow and guide community life and evolution.*

This working environment is the result of technical, organizational and managerial choices with which the company influences people's behavior in all phases of the knowledge lifecycle, including the acquisition, transfer and sharing, capitalization and reuse of knowledge. This environment has to be designed to fit the internal and external context of the organization.

The challenge for management theory is, therefore, clear: to provide empirically grounded and actionable knowledge for companies to design and implement new ICT-enabled (virtual) working environments able to extend the boundaries of their knowledge creation to their mobile workers, customers and suppliers. At the same time, only anecdotal evidence about the good practices is available today. To address those needs in 2003 we set up the Intranet Observatory.

The chapter considers the above issues, and focuses on communities and collaboration (C&C) tools in the Italian banking industry.

In Italy, the banking industry is experiencing an organizational and technological metamorphosis. The evolution from a predominantly hierarchical model to a mainly professional structure with horizontal relations makes the development of C&C tools (such as forum, chat, e-room, mailing list, etc) a strategic area of interest.

RESEARCH CONTEXT AND BACKGROUND

The study presented in this chapter is part of the larger Intranet Bank Observatory initiative which has been analyzing the Intranets of the leading Italian banks since 2004. In 2006, the Observatory examined the Intranets in 50 banks, representing almost 80% of the workforce in the industry. The topics of the investigation were Communities and collaboration tools.

In recent years, the Italian banking system has experienced a rapid evolution in the tools and modes of work. There have been significant investments in technology, not only to increase and develop the range of products and services aimed at customers, but also to improve, simplify and computerize operations for employees.

The banks are moving more and more towards a networked management of core processes with levels of integration within a 'single virtual working environment' that vary in function of the awareness of the strategic role of Intranets and the presence of integrated development plans for the entire bank Information System.

The diffusion of C&C tools on Intranet is a remarkable signal of the Intranet evolutions. Indeed, if on the one hand, the extension of coverage and support of core processes gives Intranets a place alongside other IS, integrating the latter and, in some cases, overcoming many of the traditional limits, their essential nature of pervasive tools oriented to people makes Intranets into ideal tools to support horizontal and vertical relations, facilitating the sharing of knowledge

and collaboration with the network and among the various professional families.

Accompanying operational support with collaboration and communication means Intranets have an important opportunity to acquire a fundamental strategic and organizational role. In this way, they can combine the working and relational spaces, becoming in effect the very layout of the networked organization.

Indeed, the evolution of the banking system is beginning to reveal forces pushing towards single and integrated working environments:

- the need to re-design the organization and its processes in the light of phenomena such as M&A and internationalization;
- the need to develop and manage new skills and geographically dispersed professional families;
- the need to control and improve processes within increasingly complex and geographically dispersed networks of competence.

Given these requirements, the availability of advanced Intranets is a powerful means to re-design banking organizations making them more flexible, dynamic and re-configurable.

C&C tools can be a fundamental communication channel that enables horizontal collaboration, fostering knowledge exchange between different branches of the organisation and the creation of a common business culture. However, to develop and implement a Community and Collaboration strategy in a bank may become very difficult, because of its culture, policies, hierarchy and inertia.

RESEARCH METHODOLOGY

The research is based on case study methodology: 16 cases are reported, which refer to 33 Communities (12 of them are in the start-up phase), as there may be more than one Community in a bank. Given the high level of concentration in this service industry, the 16 case studies cover more than 50% of the employees in the industry in Italy.

Multiple data collection methods, both qualitative and quantitative (Yin, 1984), were use in order to obtain the triangulation of the information acquired.

Data were collected in order to acquire as much information as possible about the bank, the Collaboration tools and the single Communities. In particular, data were gathered from the following sources:

- Documentation about the bank analyzed;
- A questionnaire to the Community manager and to the IT manager;
- Semi-structured interviews with the Community manager and informants in the department in which the Community exists;
- On line analysis of the Collaboration tools and of the activities of members.

The questionnaire used closed questions, but with an open field for comments or more in-depth explanations.

The use of semi-structured interviews gave a good deal of freedom to the interviewer and interviewee, but at the same time assured that all relevant subjects were discussed and all the required information collected. Two different check-lists (one for key informant people and another for community coordinators) were therefore used to define the subjects to cover. However, the order of the questions, the topics to study in depth, the level of detail, and the words to use, etc. were decided by the interviewer during the meeting. A report was written for each case study after the interview.

HOW DIFFUSED AND USED ARE C&C TOOLS?

Community and Collaboration tools have been divided in two different set:

- *Synchronous tools* that allow communication and collaboration in real time and need the simultaneous presence of the participants: e.g. chat, instant messaging, video-conference, presence awareness, virtual Collaboration workplace;
- *Asynchronous tools* that allows participants to communicate with each other even if they are not on line at the same time: e.g. mailing lists, forums, file sharing systems, tools for project management, expert searches, virtual work places, SMS (sent from the intranet), blog, wiki.

The analysis confirms the growing popularity of C&C tools. Only 2 of the 16 banks in the sample declared that they did not currently have C&C tools and have not planned their introduction in the near future.

On the other hand, in most of the banks analyzed, there is already a good presence of asynchronous tools, and future plans envisage strengthening and integrating these with synchronous tools, which are currently less widespread.

Indeed, in comparison to the asynchronous tools, which are very popular and well-accepted, the synchronous applications, e.g. chat and instant messaging, still seem to be met with diffidence and prejudice and therefore require greater organizational maturity. In particular, there is a fear that these tools are inappropriate to working environments, as they could potentially constitute a distraction and lead to a loss of employee productivity.

Even the diffusion of synchronous tools is limited to traditional applications, while more advanced systems such as blogs and wikis are not used, despite their growing international popularity.

The most common tools are, for the main part, directed towards collaborative working (i.e. project management, shared diaries and document management among the asynchronous supports, and videoconferencing for synchronous applications), while forums and mailing lists are the most widespread systems among the tools directed towards community and knowledge management.

Cross-referencing the present and future presence of C&C tools, three different C&C groups emerge (Figure 1):

- "Marginal" or "niche" tools with low level of current and planned presence, such as SMS via the intranet, expert search, chat and virtual work space;
- "Commodity" tools, with a high level of current presence, but no particular planned evolution;
- Emergent tools, growing rapidly, some not so common so far (e.g. instant messaging,

presence awareness), others more widspread (e.g. file sharing systems, project management tools, diary sharing).

Cross-referencing the current presence and the utilization level of C&C tools (Figure 2), it is possible to make some interesting considerations on the effectiveness of these tools in banks:

- Some of the less used tools are also the most widespread ones (forum, mailing list, videoconference). Following introduction (generally on the iniative of the Information Systems department), these systems, previously defined as commodities, are often abandoned or relegated to marginal environments little related to core business;
- Some tools that are less widespread than others have a good utilization level (e.g. asynchronous one-to-one SMS via intranet or synchronous instant messaging). The introduction of these tools can be useful

Figure 1. Current and future presence of C&C tools

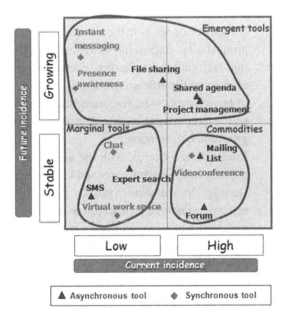

Figure 2. Utilization level of C&C tools

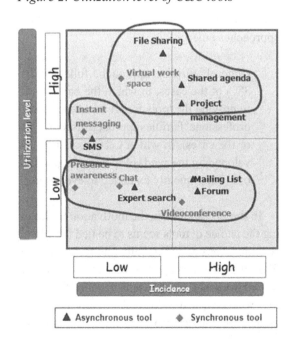

to spread the collaboration culture among employees;

- Tools with acknowledged effectiveness and high utilization levels are those oriented towards supporting collaborative work, such as file sharing systems, virtual work places, diary sharing and project management tools.

THE EMERGING OF COMMUNITIES

The success of C&C tools depends to a large extent on their effective response to the needs of specific target users within the organization. Tools which appear to be not very widespread in the banking sector could in fact be of fundamental importance for a specific group of users.

This means that the analysis must go into greater detail and consider the use of C&C tools by specific targets and, subsequently, identify the emergence of communities.

What are the Targets and Goals for the Communities?

From the analysis, two Community introduction approaches emerged:

- General purpose approach, followed by 38% of the cases, in which the bank tends to provide the tools for all its employees;
- professional families approach (used in 62% of the cases), in which C&C tools are developed for the needs of specific targets and only subsequently extended to everybody.

In the first approach, the motivation underlying the choice of tools seems to be tied mainly to considerations of opportunity and technological feasibility. In many cases, tools such as forums or shared workspaces have been introduced because they were easy to develop and 'already available' on the technological platform employed. In these

cases, there is a risk that the 'organizational' complexity of the systems and the needs in terms of governance and change management will be underestimated, so potentially undermining the success of the initiative and generating prejudices that are difficult to reverse.

In this respect, the case of the forum is particularly significant. Forums are often introduced as an experiment without any management policy, and subsequently 'closed' because they are not used, or not very effective or 'critical' regarding the management of company relations.

In the second approach, on the other hand, the introduction of the system is preceded by a more accurate and conscious needs analysis stage among the individual professional families, resulting in specific combinations of tools and introduction schedules.

Subsequently, the strong 'viral' effect that C&C tools have been seen to possess is exploited: the introduction of a successful community sets off word-of-mouth and imitation mechanisms that bring other professional families to promote the development of new communities.

The major users of these tools or the targets on which the banks have declared an intention to concentrate their investments include (Figure 3):

- branch personnel, with the aim of increasing productivity, improving skills and updating, facilitating the sharing of knowledge, improving the efficiency and effectiveness of branch processes, re-connecting people and overcoming barriers determined by geographic dispersion;
- Information Systems, with the aim of improving company processes and knowledge sharing. Information Systems generally serve as a test-bed for these new technologies, which in some cases manage to spread if they find organizational encouragement from line management;
- General and regional head office managers, where the main need is for interaction

Figure 3. Main targets of C&C tools

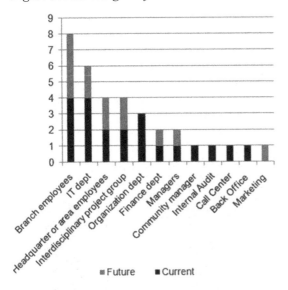

between experts with the aim of sharing and developing knowledge, and improving and innovating processes;

• Inter-functional project groups that often involve staff from head office, marketing, sales and customer service that seek to increase the productivity of resources and improve processes and the level of co-ordination;

• The Organization function, with the aims of improving processes and sharing knowledge.

There are some further, less widespread but especially interesting tests, e.g. Internal Audit to support experts in mobility activities, Call Center to resolve practical problems in real time, and community administrators for the exchange of best practice.

The most frequent aims related to the introduction of Community and Collaboration tools in banks are: to improve effectiveness or efficiency, share knowledge, define or consolidate a shared corporate culture and identity (in particular after reorganization or merger/acquisition operations), and improve planning and process control abilities.

The marketing, sales, and customer service and support functions are the most involved, while the use of C&C in senior management and operations functions is less common.

If we analyze in detail the different target groups, some common characteristics emerge. The groups are almost always geographically dispersed, but show high levels of interaction, characteristics which constitute the ideal terrain for the creation of communities. The introduction of C&C tools makes it possible to overcome communication barriers between people who need to collaborate and exchange data.

What are the Models for the Communities?

To analyze the nature of communities, we looked in depth at the aims and objectives in terms of two fundamental aspects:

• **the time scale:** short-term objectives directed to problem-solving or long-term questions linked to the creation of skills or process innovation;

• **focus:** specific roles/tasks of individuals or, in a wider sense, that involve entire processes.

Given these two aspects, four different types of community have been identified (Figure 4):

• reciprocal help (short-term objective tied to the task). Within a specific professional, the individuals look for the help of colleagues to resolve similar daily work problems;

• individual learning (long-term objective tied to professional development); individuals interact by exchanging knowledge to improve their own training and professional preparation in the long-term;

• process support (short and medium-term objectives) involving individuals working on the same process who interact with the

Figure 4. Community models

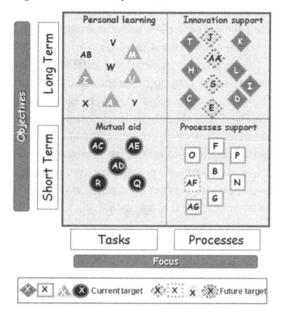

Figure 5. Community present and future

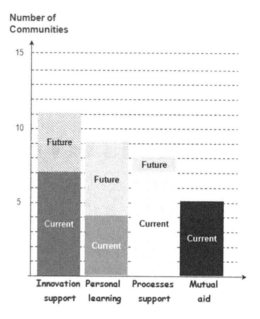

aim of improving overall performance in the short-term;

- innovation support (long-term objective) which seeks to develop a company's knowledge and capacity to innovate and attracts individuals with key competences,

The analysis of the 33 communities revealed a clear predominance of long-term objectives linked to individual learning (9 cases) and innovation (11 cases).

This prevalence of long-term objectives appears to be more the result of a low perception of the 'practical' benefits of the communities (regarding the processes supported), together with a significant presence of staff from the training and human resources departments in their set up and development (regarding support of job tasks), than of a strategic view of the role of communities.

The four types of community do not particularly differ in terms of the C&C tools used, indicating, in many cases, the lack of a strategic definition and of careful analysis of the needs of the targets prior to introduction. Those communi-

ties with short-term, problem-solving objectives would probably present more synchronous tools, while in those with long-term objectives, asynchronous systems, which can manage the entire knowledge cycle, would be more common.

Sponsorship, Commitment and Barriers

In addition to the target, other key variables in an effective introduction of community and collaboration tools are the sponsorship of top management, and the presence of supervisory roles in the development and management.

Cross-referencing these variables, three models emerged (Figure 6; some Communities are still in a design phase):

1. introduction not organizationally mature, with low top management sponsorship and no definition of any roles;
2. growing communities with high sponsorship, but roles so far not defined;
3. introduction organizationally mature, with

Figure 6. Sponsorship and community management roles

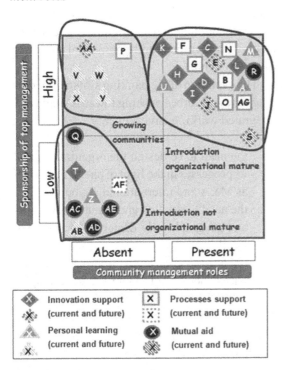

mitment. These are the two key variables for the introduction phase from a change management point of view: working on these two aspects can help to solve many of the barriers cited above.

Cross-referencing these two dimensions and mapping the Communities analyzed, it is possible to define three main groups (Figure 7):

- Start-up initiatives with a good commitment from the organization that have to involve members;
- Initiatives with limited organizational commitment but with a good level of participation; in these cases, it becomes essential to obtain support from top management by illustrating the benefits generated by the Community for the organization;
- strategic initiatives with high commitment and members' involvement; in the banking industry, this is the largest cluster.

roles defined and a high level of commitment from top management.

Type 3 model is the most diffused in banking and there seems to be a good awareness of the potential benefits of these tools among top management.

There are many barriers or "alibi" to the development and the diffusion of C&C tools. Some frequently cited examples are: limited knowledge about these tools (5 cases); lack of understanding of potential benefits (4 cases); knowledge dispersion (3 cases) and user resistance (2 cases). Other barriers are related to the difficulties in quantifying benefits in relation to costs (usually well defined), limited experience in using these kinds of tools, a predilection for personal relations (not mediated by tools).

Those barriers can be divided into two main classes: barriers related to members' involvement and barriers related to lack of organizational com-

Figure 7. Organizational commitment and members' involvement

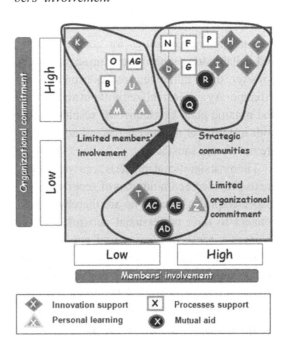

The research highlights that when Community management roles are defined and animation and promotion plans are implemented, i.e. when a governance strategy is defined, members' commitment grows. In particular, it is possible to notice a direct relation between the systematic definition of governance and the utilization level of Community and Collaboration tools.

FINAL REMARKS: DEVELOPING COMMUNITIES IN THE BANKING INDUSTRY

The challenge emerging from the research seems to be that of creating integrated workspaces where people can find what they need to work, to know, to inform themselves and to integrate. Although the realization of this objective still appears to be some way off, there are already many signs confirming a convincing trend in this direction: one indication is the implementation on Intranets of Community and Collaboration tools. Following an incremental path that often starts with the introduction of simple, asynchronous tools and then moves to increasingly sophisticated, synchronous means of collaboration, banks incorporate ever greater opportunities for communication and collaboration within their Intranets. Often, however, these initiatives are experimental and extemporary and are realized without a conscious and organic plan. Consequently, results to date both in terms of use and perceived advantages are not always satisfactory.

The most significant impact is seen where tools are used to create communities of geographically dispersed professionals who are thereby able to connect to their professional network and rediscover a sense of identity and opportunities for exchanges and relations that staff turnover and geographic distance often negate. From an organizational point of view, the development of community environments for specific professional groups is a growing trend of particular interest.

A further step towards an integrated work and relation space will be taken when the banks undertake genuine and in-depth integration of the collaboration and communiction environments with operations and commercial processes (web-counters).

The evolution of the banking system is beginning to reveal forces pushing towards single and integrated working environments:

- the need to re-design the organization and its processes in the light of phenomena such as M&A and internationalization;
- the need to develop and manage new skills and geographically dispersed professional families;
- the need to control and improve processes within increasingly complex and geographically dispersed networks of competence.

Given these requirements, the availability of advanced Intranets is a powerful means to re-design banking organizations making them more flexible, dynamic and re-configurable.

However, a considerable increase in awareness among those who govern the Intranets is necessary. Intranet systems must not be viewed with the eyes of people who design 'desktops, drawers and blinkers'. We have to look beyond the 'narrow space of the screen' and provide new environments for relations and opportunities in which people are free to move, find stimuli and possibilities for growth, develop professionally and build networks of contacts. In this way, Intranets will become the virtual workspace, through which companies will be able to stimulate and direct among staff effective attitudes to innovation, collaboration and sharing.

This research provides interesting elements and suggestions to develop Communities in the banking sector:

- in the strategic concept definition, it emerges that it is convenient to focus attention on geographically dispersed targets with a stable belonging level, a good level of interaction between members and an heterogeneous level of experience;

- in governance definition, there is a clear correlation between the systematic nature of the governance and the level of use and, consequently, of the benefit achievable. In the day-by-day operations, animation and promotion levers are fundamental in obtaining a high level of member involvement;
- with regards design, implementation and launch, some good practices seem to release asynchronous tools first and then subsequently enrich the system with synchronous facilities;

Finally, it is interesting to note that these tools have a strong "viral power". The successful introduction of a Community triggers imitation mechanisms that lead to the creation of new Communities, so fostering a Collaboration and knowledge sharing culture in the organization.

The research reported in this chapter is a first step in designing a roadmap to help management to create, develop and run a Community is presented.

REFERENCES

Andriessen, E., Soekijad, M., & Keasberry, H.J. (2002). *Support for knowledge sharing in communities*. Delft University Press.

Brown, J.S., Collins, A., & Duguid, S. (1998). Situated cognition and the culture of learning. *Educational Researcher, 1*, 32-42.

Brown, J.S., & Duguid, P. (1998). Organizing Knowledge. *California Management Review. 40*(3), 90–111.

Corso, M., Giacobbe, A., & Martini, A. (2008). Community and collaboration tools in the Ital-

ian banking industry. *International Journal of E-Banking, 1*(1), 60-72.

Corso, M., Giacobbe, A., & Martini, A. (2008). Rethinking Knowledge Management: the Role of ICT and the Rise of the Virtual Workspace. *International Journal of Learning and Intellectual Capital. 5*(4)

Corso, M., Giacobbe, A., Martini, A., & Pellegrini, L. (2006). What Knowledge Management for Mobile Workers?. *Knowledge and Process Management Journal, Special Issue on Continuous Innovation and Knowledge Management. 13*(3), 206-217.

Corso, M., Martini, A., Paolucci, E., & Pellegrini, L. (2004). Knowledge Management Systems in Continuous Product Innovation. in Leondes, CT (Ed.), *Intelligent knowledge-based systems. Business and Technology in the New Millennium. Volume 1 Knowledge-Based Systems*, Chapter 2. Kluwer Academic Press, pp. 36-66.

Drucker, P.F. (2002). *Management Challenges for the 21st Century*. New York: Harper Business.

Magnusson, M., & Davidsson, N. (2001). Creating and managing communities of knowing. *International Conference on Entrepreneurship and Learning*, 21-24 June 2001, Naples, Italy.

Laubacher, R., & Malone, T.W. (2003). Retreat of the firm and the rise of guilds: the employment relationship in an age of virtual business. In *Inventing the Organization of the 21st Century*, Malone T.W., Laubacher R. and Scott-Morton M.S. (eds). Boston: MIT Press.

Senge, P.M. (1990). The Leader's New Work: Building learning organizations. *Sloan Management Review*. Fall, 7-23.

Von Krogh, G. (2002). The communal resource and information systems. *Journal of Strategic Information Systems*. 11, 85-107.

Wenger, E. (1998), *Communities of practice. Learning, Meaning and Identity.* Cambridge: Cambridge University Press.

Wenger, E.C., & Snyder, W.M. (2000). Communities of practice: The organizational frontier. *Harvard Business Review. 1*, 39–145.

Chapter VII
Who Talks with Whom:
Impact of Knowledge Sharing in the Value Network of Born Globals

Seppo J. Hänninen
Helsinki University of Technology, Finland

Pekka Stenholm
George Mason University, USA

T. J. Vapola
Helsinki School of Economics, Finland

Ilkka Kauranen
Asian Institute of Technology, Thailand

ABSTRACT

Knowledge sharing has a strong effect on the success of the born globals. The objective of the chapter is to create a better understanding of the impact of knowledge sharing in the value network of born globals. The study builds on co-opetitive theory, which has its underpinnings in the cooperative game theory. The present study is based on 51 interviews within 31 companies that have participated in a technology program financed by an agency funding technology and innovation development. All the companies were small or medium-sized. In the study, correlations between having discussions with various stakeholders are analyzed. The tentative empirical results are in line with the essential nature of co-opetitive relationships in which various actors engage in knowledge sharing regardless of whether they are competing or not.

Copyright © 2009, IGI Global, distributing in print or electronic forms without written permission of IGI Global is prohibited.

INSIDE THE CHAPTER

Knowledge sharing has a strong effect on the success of the born globals. The objective of the chapter is to create a better understanding of the impact of knowledge sharing in the value network of born globals. The study builds on co-opetitive theory, which has its underpinnings in the cooperative game theory.

The present study is based on 51 interviews within 31 companies that have business operations in Finland and that have participated in the Fenix technology program financed by the Finnish Funding Agency for Technology and Innovation TEKES. All the companies were small or medium-sized. Because of the small size of the sample, the study is to some extent a multi-case study. The interviewees from companies were technology directors or research and development directors as well as general directors of the companies.

According to the results, having discussions with sales partners positively correlated with having discussions with technology partners and with customers, This and other results give support to the proposition that competitors' opinions on consumer trends may proactively change the technological preferences, which are recommended for customers. In parallel, the results give confirmative evidence that technological perspectives are not shared with competitors as widely as ideas on consumer trends.

There were two additional interesting results as regards to the objective of creating a better understanding of the impact of knowledge sharing in the value network of born globals. Having discussions within the companies themselves positively correlated with having discussions with competitors and having discussions with technology partners. These results may be a sign that there do exist co-opetitive relationships in the value networks of born globals in which knowledge sharing with various stakeholders, including competitors, can create win-win partnerships. These tentative empirical results are in line with the essential nature of co-opetitive relationships in which various actors engage in knowledge sharing regardless of whether they are competing or not.

INTRODUCTION

The present chapter focuses on knowledge sharing in technology-intensive value networks of born global high-technology companies. Knowledge sharing and knowledge transfer have an effect on the success of the born globals (Levy, Loebbecke and Powell, 2003). In any value network, knowledge sharing with the partners is typical (Dyer and Nobeoka, 2000). However, it is very difficult to say which companies or other actors are not partners of a company. Competitors typically cooperate to standardize technologies but compete in other functions of the same business. For example, the GSM mobile technology standardization alliance consisted of such companies as Nokia, Siemens and Ericsson. These companies were fierce competitors in the GSM business as soon as the common GSM standard was approved.

Knowledge has two very different components: tacit knowledge and explicit knowledge. Tacit knowledge means such knowledge as skills, capabilities and feelings. Tacit knowledge is difficult to communicate and share. Explicit knowledge means measurable knowledge such as numeric data. (Nonaka and Takeuchi, 1995) The knowledge sharing literature defines knowledge sharing as an internal feature of a company (Adenfelt and Lagerström, 2006; Hansen, 1999; Makela, Kalla, and Piekkari, 2007). An important and common reason for limited knowledge sharing is that there is lack of trust among network partners (Abrams et al, 2003; Li, 2005; Ariño, Torre, and

Ring, 2001). Knowledge transfer is a term the meaning of which is similar to the meaning of the term knowledge sharing. However, knowledge transfer has a wider meaning, which includes, in addition, for example the transfer of patents (Agrawal and Henderson, 2002).

There are two theoretical perspectives in this present chapter. On the one hand, the theoretical perspective concerning the interaction between firms that has both cooperative and competitive behavioral elements is based upon the co-opetitive theory (Brandenburger and Nalebuff, 1996). On the other hand, the theoretical perspective describing knowledge sharing is based on the resource-based view by Wernerfeld (1984) and Barney (1986) and on the knowledge-based view by Kogut and Zander (1992), Grant (1996) and Spender (1996). These views suggest that the competitive advantage of a company is based on knowledge the company manages. A central process concerning knowledge is information absorbing. Cohen and Levinthal (1990) have found that it is easier for companies to absorb information if they already are familiar with related information. This means that previous knowledge is needed in order to absorb more.

Knowledge sharing can be measured, for example, by the number of patents utilized together by two or more companies (Agrawal and Henderson, 2002). In the present chapter, the measure of knowledge sharing is the importance that companies assign to the discussions that they have had with their value network partners.

Knowledge sharing has a strong effect on the success of the born globals. The objective of the chapter is to create a better understanding of the impact of knowledge sharing in the value network of born globals. An empirical sample is collected from Finnish companies, which have taken part in partly government supported technology programs. The study makes a contribution both on new theory development and on empirical verification of the theories.

THEORY ON CO-OPETITION

Extant literature tends to view cross-functional relationships as primarily cooperative or competitive in nature, but not both. In contrast, this present chapter focuses on the simultaneous occurrence of cooperation and competition in strategic interactions between firms. The co-operative game theory's free-form interaction between players corresponds well with active search for value creation and appropriation opportunities (Brandenburger and Stuart, 1996, 6 – 7), which appears to provide a fruitful baseline for an analysis of the impact of knowledge sharing interactions between partners.

Co-opetitive theory has its underpinnings in the cooperative game theory (Brandenburger and Nalebuff, 1996). Co-opetition refers to simultaneously cooperative and competitive behavior of firms (Tsai, 2002), when firms are also considered as utility maximizers (Hartwig, 1998). There are multiple sources that can be credited for coining the term: Sam Albert of IBM (DeMarzo, 2003) and Ray Noorda of Novell (Williams, 2004). It is clear, however, that Brandenburger and Nalebuff (1996) brought the term to a wide attention. They gave a spin to this economic theory unknown to most managers, and it has been named to be the latest big idea in management thinking (Dearlove, 2004). Zineldin (2004) argues that the co-opetitive partnerships provide a more effective response to changed environmental threats and opportunities of today's marketplace than traditional forms of interaction.

According to Brandenburger and Nalebuff (1996), a co-opetitive game consists of five strategic levers: players, added-value of each player, rules of the game, tactics used by each player in the game, and the scope of the game. These levers operate within the value network. The value network provides an interesting tool for analyzing the strategies applied by the players when embedded in the external network.

Value network is an important addition to Porter's (1985, 5) five forces model analyzing industry dynamics, because it redirects strategic thinking from a specific focus on competitors to the broader economic environment (Hartwig, 1998). A value networks illustrates the relationships between a focal firm and other players, which can play multiple roles: customers and suppliers, competitors and complementors, depending on the particular circumstances (Brandenburger and Nalebuff, 1996). The primary advancement is the realization of the role the complementors can play in the value creation (Armstrong, 1997). Further, a value network also reveals that symmetrical roles are played by customers and suppliers, as well as by competitors and complementors (Katz, 1996).

While the term co-opetition (Armstrong, 1997) originally was above all aimed helping practitioners, it has also spurred an interest to apply the theory to academic context as well. A number of researchers have used the co-opetitive theory in their studies of strategic interaction between different players. Among others, it has been used in analyzing government-university-industry research and development (R&D) partnerships (Carayannis and Alexander, 1999), the effectiveness of coordination mechanisms on knowledge sharing in intra-organizational networks (Tsai, 2002), the interaction of local firms in tourist destinations (von Friedrichs Grangsjo, 2003), relationships in the grocery industry (Kotzab and Teller, 2003), knowledge sharing between small and medium sized enterprises (SMEs) (Levy et al., 2003), interactions between European biotechnology firms (Quintana-Carcias and Benavieds-Velasco, 2004), the exploration of the smart card industry (M'Chirgui, 2005), the contingency of small and medium sized enterprise (SME) network structures and the environment in the publishing industry (Lin and Zhang, 2005), relationships between geographically dispersed sub-units of globally coordinated multinational corporations (MNC) (Luo, 2005), and the innovation constel-

lations in telecommunications industry (Vapola and Seppälä, 2006).

APPLYING THE THEORY OF CO-OPETION TO KNOWLEDGE SHARING IN VALUE NETWORKS

Drawing on a social network perspective of organizational coordination, this present chapter investigates the effectiveness of coordination mechanisms on knowledge sharing in value networks that consist of both collaborative and competitive ties between different organizations. Luo (2005) suggests that the performance impact of applying the co-opetitive strategy is mediated by an underlying market learning mechanism. Increasing cooperation is taking place in the form of heightened interdependence in resource sharing or knowledge sharing, value-chain rationalization, and common function integration (ibid). Cooperation is done in pursuit of synergistically collective gains. At the same time, there is competition for resources, support, position, and market expansion (ibid).

Internal knowledge sharing within a multi-unit organization requires a formal hierarchical structure and informal lateral relations as coordination mechanisms. Using sociometric techniques, it has been analyzed how a formal hierarchical structure and informal lateral relations influence knowledge sharing and how inter-unit competition moderates such coordination mechanisms and knowledge sharing in large, multi-unit companies. Results show that a formal hierarchical structure, in the form of centralization, has a significant negative effect on knowledge sharing. Furthermore, the results show that informal lateral relations, in the form of social interaction, have a significant positive effect on knowledge sharing among units that compete with each other for market share, but not among units that compete with each other for internal resources. (Tsai, 2002)

Although presently documented only as a firm-level phenomenon involving sharing of proprietary technical knowledge, informal knowledge sharing seems relevant to and may currently exist in many other types of situations. Indeed, informal knowledge sharing may be applicable to any situation in which individuals or organizations are involved in such competition where possession of proprietary knowledge represents a form of competitive advantage. (von Hippel, 1987).

Von Hippel's (1988) collaboration strategy considers the issue of working together with the key lead users to be able to understand better the actual technological change needs in an early phase and thus gain technological leadership in the development of corresponding products. In high tech industries, the world moves so rapidly that using lead users for testing novel products is essential for accurate market need forecasting (Vapola, 2000). When applied to born global value network context, it is expected that firms will have discussions concerning technology with their sales partners in order to gain insights on the future technological possibilities (Vapola et al., 2008). Furthermore, it is expected that in order to gain competitive advantage from the knowledge gained from sales partners, a firm will need to understand and potentially influence its upstream and downstream partners on the new technological opportunity (Hänninen, 2007; Hänninen and Kauranen, 2007). To do this, firms are expected to collect information from technology partners and from customers to form their view for successful future technologies. Hence, it is expected that there is a positive correlation between having discussions with sales partners, on the one hand, and having discussions with technology partners and customers, on the other hand. Hence, the following hypothesis is put forward:

Hypothesis 1: There is a positive correlation between having discussions with sales partners, on the one hand, and having discussions with technology partners and customers, on the other hand.

Von Hippel (1987) also showed that people at rival organizations, when they are in contact, share their knowledge. They mainly do this for personal motives. When an executive thinks sharing certain knowledge can be valuable for him or her, now or in the future, knowledge will be shared. In parallel, the executive receiving information from an executive in a competing firm may seek the applications of such knowledge that can increase the competitive advantage of the firm of the receiving executive. For example, if discussions concerning consumer trends are shared between competing firms, the receiving firm probably seeks use that knowledge to improve its position in the customer interface. Typically, the competitors' opinions on consumer trends can proactively change the technological preferences, which are recommended for customers of each one of the competing firms. This can be done in the form of having discussions concerning technology with customers, aiming to influence the technological choices of these customers. The behavior is in line with von Hippel's (1988) original work, which indeed suggests locking in key customers to the supplier's technological solution. Hence, the following hypothesis is put forward:

Hypothesis 2: There is a positive relationship between having discussions with competitors, on the one hand, and having discussions with customers, on the other hand.

RESEARCH METHOD

The present study is based on 51 interviews within 31 companies that have business operations in Finland and that have participated in the Fenix technology program financed by the Finnish Funding Agency for Technology and Innovation TEKES.

The majority of the companies have a home base in Finland. In five cases, their headquarters were elsewhere and the company located in Finland was a foreign subsidiary. All the companies were small or medium-sized. Because of the small size of the sample, the study is to some extent a multi-case study.

The interviewed companies were chosen with the help of the Internet site of the Fenix technology program and thus, the sample was not random. The companies were chosen to represent different types of technology-intensive businesses, typical examples being computer game software, mobile telecommunication software, and open-source software.

The interviewees from companies were technology directors or research and development directors as well as general directors of the companies. The interviews were structured with an interview scheme and involved probing issues further depending on the situation of each firm. The interviews took place in 2005. The hypotheses presented were tested by confirmatory factor analysis using the AMOS 7.0 statistical software package.

RESULTS

Despite the small sample size (n=51), the statistical model was deemed to be good enough for the analyses. Bollen's (Bollen, 1989) incremental fit index (IFI) value .899 was very good. The comparative fit index (CFI) value .960 as well as Tucker-Lewis index (TLI) value .889 means that the model is good. The root mean square error of approximation (RMSEA) value .062 indicates moderate model fit. The probability of getting as large a discrepancy as occurred with the present sample p value .148 ($\chi^2 (22) = 28.89$) is good even though the sample was small.

The results of the statistical analyses are as follows. In the present results section, β is used to

symbolize standardized parameters and r is used to symbolize model correlations. As hypothesized in hypothesis 1, there was an indicative positive correlation between having discussions with sales partners and having discussions with technology partners (r=.39, p=.061) and with customers (r=.44, p=.063).

In a closer analyses of the various discussions that the companies had had, the relative importance of discussions concerning technology and discussions concerning customer trends was analyzed. In discussions with sales partners, discussions concerning customer trends (β=.97, p<.05) were more important than discussions concerning technology (β=.77, p<.05). In discussions with technology partners, discussions concerning technology (β=.94, p<.05) were more important than discussions concerning customer trends (β=.65, p<.05). In discussions with customers, discussions concerning technology (β=.85, p<.05) were more important than discussions concerning customer trends (β=.72, p<.05).

Concerning hypothesis 2, the results show a different outcome than anticipated. There was practically no correlation between having discussions with competitors and having discussions with customers. As stated above, in discussions with customers, discussions concerning technology were more important than discussions concerning customer trends. In stead, in discussions with competitors, discussions concerning customer trends (β=.96, p<.05) were more important than discussions concerning technology (β=.75, p<.05).

The results revealed also other correlations, in addition to the hypothesized relationships. The strongest observed correlation was a strong positive correlation (r=.64, p<.01) between having discussions with technology partners and having discussion within the companies themselves. There also was an indicative positive correlation between having discussions with competitors and having discussion within the company itself (r=.35, p=.090). As regards to the closer analyses of the discussions, in discussions within the companies themselves, there were no meaningful differences between the relative importance of discussions concerning technology (β=.82, p<.05) and the importance of discussions concerning customer trends (β=.80, p<.05).

CONCLUSION

Having discussions with sales partners had an indicative positive correlation with having discussions with technology partners and with customers, as hypothesized in the hypothesis 1. Closer analyses showed that customer trends were more important than technology in the discussions with sales partners and in the discussions with competitors. On the contrary, technology was – not surprisingly – more important than customer trends in discussions with technology partners, and – surprisingly – also in discussions with customers. These results give support to the proposition that competitors' opinions on consumer trends may proactively change the technological preferences, which are recommended for customers. In parallel, the results give confirmative evidence that technological perspectives are not shared with competitors as widely as ideas on consumer trends.

There was practically no correlation between having discussions with competitors and having discussion customers. Therefore, hypothesis 2 did not get empirical support.

There were two additional interesting results as regards to the objective of creating a better understanding of the impact of knowledge sharing in the value network of born globals. Having discussions within the companies themselves positively correlated with having discussions with competitors and having discussions with technology partners. These results may be a sign that there do exist co-opetitive relationships in the value networks of born globals in which

knowledge sharing with various stakeholders, including competitors, can create win-win partnerships. These tentative empirical results are in line with the essential nature of co-opetitive relationships in which various actors engage in knowledge sharing regardless of whether they are competing or not.

MANAGERIAL IMPLICATIONS

The results of the present chapter have important managerial implications. Managers of the born global high technology companies should not refrain from knowledge sharing with competitors but try to build co-opetitive win-win type relationships. For example, sharing knowledge of consumer trends can benefit both parties by increasing the fit of their technologies to the customers' future needs.

ACKNOWLEDGMENT

The statistical analysis contribution of Ilkka Mellin to this book chapter is very warmly acknowledged. The financial support of the Jenny and Antti Wihuri Foundation and the Finnish Cultural Foundation is acknowledged.

REFERENCES

Abrams, L. C., Cross, R., Lesser, E. and Levin, D.Z. (2003). Nurturing interpersonal trust in knowledge-sharing networks, *Academy of Management Executive*, 17(4), 64-77.

Adenfelt, M. and Lagerström, K. (2006). Knowledge development and sharing in multinational corporations: the case of a centre of excellence and a transnational team, *International Business Review*, 15(4), 381-400.

Agrawal, A. and Henderson, R. (2002). Putting patents in context: exploring knowledge transfer from MIT, *Management Science*, 48(1), 44-60.

Ariño, A., Torre, J.D.L. and Ring, P.S. (2001). Relational quality: managing trust in corporate alliances, *California Management Review,* 44(1), 109–31.

Armstrong, S.J. (1997). Co-opetition, *Journal of Marketing*, 61(2), 92-95.

Barney, J.B. (1986). Strategic factor markets: expectations, luck, and business strategy, *Management Science*, 32, 1231-1241.

Bollen, K.A. (1989). A new incremental fit index for general structural equation models, *Sociological Methods and Research*, 17, 313-316.

Brandenburger, A.M. and Nalebuff, B.J. (1996). *Co-opetition*, New York, New York, USA: Currency-Doubleday.

Brandenburger, A.M. and Stuart, H.W. (1996). Value-based business strategy, *Journal of Economics & Management Strategy*, 5(1), 5-24.

Carayannis, E.G. and Alexander, J. (1999). Winning by co-opeting in strategic government-university-industry R&D partnerships: the power of complex, dynamic knowledge networks, *Journal of Technology Transfer*, 24(2-3), p. 197.

Cohen, W. M. and Levinthal, D. A. (1990). Absorptive capacity: a new perspective on learning and innovation, *Administrative Science Quarterly*, 35(1), 128-152.

Dearlove, D. (2004). Origins and blasphemies, *Business Strategy Review*, 15(2), 2-4.

DeMarzo, R.C. (2003). Today's top channel execs set corporate strategy - the chief channel officer is on par with the CFO or CIO in many companies, *VARbusiness*, Mar 3, 2003, 10.

Dyer, J.H. and Nobeoka, K. (2000). Creating and managing a high-performance knowledge-sharing network: the Toyota case, *Strategic Management Journal*, 21(3), 345-367.

Friedrichs Grangsjo, von, Y. (2003). Destination networking: co-opetition in peripheral surroundings, *International Journal of Physical Distribution & Logistics Management,* 33(5), 427-449.

Grant, R.M. (1996). Toward a knowledge-based theory of the firm, *Strategic Management Journal*, 17(1), 109-122.

Hansen, M.T. (1999). The search-transfer problem: The role of weak ties in sharing knowledge across organization subunits, *Administrative Science Quarterly*, 44(1), 82-111.

Hartwig, R.J. (1998). Cooperation and competition: a comparative review, *The Journal of Business and Economic Studies,* 4(2), 71-76.

Hänninen, S. (2007). The 'perfect technology syndrome': sources, consequences, and solutions, *International Journal of Technology Management*, 39(1-2), 20-32.

Hänninen, S. and Kauranen, I. (2007). Product innovation as micro-strategy, *International Journal of Innovation and Learning*, 4(4), 425-443.

Katz, Jeffrey P. (1996). Co-opetition, *The Academy of Management Executive*, 10(4), 118-119.

Kogut, B. and Zander, U. (1992). Knowledge of the firm, combinative capabilities, and the replication of technology, *Organization Science*, 3(3), 383-397.

Kotzab, H. and Teller, C. (2003). Value-adding partnerships and co-opetition models in the grocery industry, *International Journal of Physical Distribution & Logistics Management,* 33(3), 268-282.

Levy, M., Loebbecke, C. and Powell, P. (2003). SMEs, co-opetition and knowledge sharing: the role of information systems, *European Journal of Information Systems*, 12(1), 3-18.

Li, L. (2005). The effects of trust and shared vision on inward knowledge transfer in subsidiaries' intra- and inter-organizational relationships, *International Business Review*, 14(1), 77-95.

Lin, C.Y. and Zhang Z. (2005). Changing structures of SME networks: lessons from the publishing industry in Taiwan, *Long Range Planning*, 38(2), 145-162.

Luo, Y. (2005). Toward coopetition within a multinational enterprise: a perspective from foreign subsidiaries, *Journal of World Business*, 40(1), 71-90.

Makela, K., Kalla, H.K. and Piekkari, R. (2007). Interpersonal similarity as a driver of knowledge sharing within multinational corporations, *International Business Review*, 16(1), 1-22.

M'Chirgui, Z. (2005). The economics of the smart card industry: towards Coopetitive Strategies, *Economics of Innovation & New Technology*, 14(6), 455-477.

Nonaka, I. and Takeuchi, H. (1995). *The knowledge-creating company: how Japanese companies create the dynamics of innovation*, New York, New York, USA: Oxford University Press.

Porter, M. (1985). *Competitive advantage: creating and sustaining superior performance,* New York, New York, USA: The Free Press.

Quintana-Carcias, C. and Benavieds-Velasco, C.A (2004). Cooperation, competition, and innovative capability: a panel data of European dedicated biotechnology firms, *Technovation*, 24(12), p. 927.

Spender, J.C. (1996). Making the knowledge basis of a dynamic theory of the firm, *Strategic Management Journal*, 17(1), 45-62.

Tsai, W. (2002). Social structure of "coopetition" within a multiunit organization: coordination, competition, and intraorganizational knowledge sharing, *Organization Science*, 13(2), 179-190.

Von Hippel, E. (1987). Co-operation between rivals: informal know-how trading, *Research Policy,* **16**, 291–302.

Von Hippel, E. (1988). The source of innovation, New York, New York, USA: Oxford University Press.

Vapola, T.J. (2000). *Technological leadership and competitive strategy: A case of shaping the future,* M.Sc. Thesis, Helsinki, Finland: Helsinki School of Economics.

Vapola, T.J. and Seppälä, T.T. (2006). The performance impact of membership in a global alliance: evidence on the revenue growth rate of mobile operators, Benito G. & Greve, H.R. (eds), *Progress in International Business Research*, London, United Kingdom: MacMillan.

Vapola, T.J., Tossavainen, P. and Gabrielsson, M. (2008). The battleship strategy: the complementing role of born globals in MNC's new opportunity creation, *Journal of International Entrepreneurship,* 6(1), 1–21.

Wernerfelt, B. (1984). A resource-based View of the Firm, *Strategic Management Journal*, 5(2), 171-180.

Williams, S. (2004). The brave new world of coopetition, *CircuiTree*, 17(11), 40-41.

Zander, U. and Kogut, B. (1995). Knowledge and the speed of the transfer and imitation of organizational capabilities: an empirical test, *Organization Science*, 6(1), 76-92.

Zineldin, M. (2004). Total relationship and logistics management, *International Journal of Physical Distribution & Logistics Management*, 34(3-4), 286-301.

Chapter VIII
Illustrating Knowledge Networks as Sociograms

Stefan Hrastinski
Uppsala University, Sweden

ABSTRACT

This chapter looks at the concept of sociograms that has great illustrative importance in some circumstances, especially for studying small knowledge networks. It is argued that the sociogram approach might be particularly useful for those who view learning and participation in knowledge networks as an inherently social phenomenon. Then, the sociogram approach is described and benefits and limitations of different approaches are discussed. The chapter also includes an exercise, web resources, further readings, and suggestions for possible paper titles.

INTRODUCTION

In the 1930s, Jacob Moreno (1934) founded sociometry, later defined as "the measurement of interpersonal relations in small groups" (Wasserman & Faust, 1994, p. 11). It is a precursor to social network analysis, which has been developed ever since and now provides a set of techniques for understanding patterns of relations between and among people, groups and organizations (Garton, Haythornthwaite & Wellman, 1999). Social network data is initially organized in *sociomatrices*. For example, such a matrix might include data

on who communicate with whom. Sociomatrices might then be used for quantitative analysis or drawing *sociograms* or *graphs*. Sociograms have been of great illustrative importance ever since the 1930s (Moreno, 1934). In this chapter, the concept of sociograms is discussed. It is argued that sociograms have great illustrative importance in some circumstances.

In the next section, different perspectives on learning in knowledge networks are discussed. It is argued that the sociogram approach might be particularly useful for those who view learning and participation in knowledge networks as

Copyright © 2009, IGI Global, distributing in print or electronic forms without written permission of IGI Global is prohibited.

an inherently social phenomenon. In the third section, a basic introduction to the concept of sociograms is presented. Then, different examples of sociograms, and their benefits and limitations are discussed.

FROM OBJECTIVIST TO SOCIAL PERSPECTIVES ON KNOWLEDGE NETWORKS

There are many different perspectives on learning, and the perspective of learning that the managers and members of a knowledge network subscribe to will both explicitly and implicitly influence participation and learning in the knowledge network. In this section, a brief review, which describes how the emphasis has shifted from objectivist perspectives on learning towards more social perspectives on learning, is presented.

Learning has traditionally been based on *objectivist* theories on learning. The objectivist tradition assumes that knowledge is an object that can be absorbed (Duffy & Jonassen, 1992). This assumption originates from the psychological school of behaviourism. The key theory of behaviourism was that of stimuli and response, where stimuli, and combinations of stimuli, were argued to determine reactions (Watson, 1925/1997). The aim was "to be able to reproduce [a] reaction at another time (and possibly in other individuals as well)" by determining "what the situation is that causes this particular reaction" (ibid, p. 20). When applying ideas originating from the objectivist tradition, the goal of the participants of a knowledge network becomes to transfer "knowledge objects" (Duffy & Jonassen, 1992; Leidner & Jarvenpaa, 1995). Prior experiences and human interpretation is not of interest since it is seen as leading to partial and biased understandings (Duffy & Jonassen, 1992). Technology is used to transmit knowledge with limited possibilities for conversations among members of the knowledge network (Edelson, Pea & Gomez, 1996).

In the beginning of the 1990s, *constructivist* theories on learning gained popularity. The argument of constructivism is that there is no correct "meaning" of the world that we are striving to understand. Instead, it is argued that there are many ways to structure the world, and there are many meanings or perspectives for any event or concept (Duffy & Jonassen, 1992). Individually oriented constructivist models assume that the main objective when managing knowledge networks should be to support the members in gaining experiences rather than aiming to transfer "knowledge objects" between the members of the knowledge network (Säljö, 2000). Thus, constructivist theories have moved away from the knowledge transmission model towards an active learner model. However, like objectivism, constructivism has "commonly focused on the learner as an individual, learning in isolation from other learners" (Edelson et al., 1996, p. 151).

Social theories on learning (e.g., Wenger, 1998; Vygotsky, 1978) have gained renewed interest since the beginning of the 1990s (Heeren, 1996) and emphasize that learning is dialogue, both internal and by social negotiation (Jonassen & Land, 2000). Rather than being solely based on experience with the physical world, the construction of knowledge and understanding is seen as a fundamentally social activity (Littleton & Häkkinen, 1999, p. 24). There exists different perspectives but the most common ones share a focus on participation as a condition for learning (Jaldemark, Lindberg & Olofsson, 2006).

The basic premises and implications of the three theoretical perspectives on learning that have been discussed are summarized in Table 1. Jonassen and Land (2000) argue that never before have so many learning theories shared so many assumptions and common foundations. Nowadays, most researchers agree upon that knowledge not only exists in individual minds but also "in the discourse among individuals, the social relationships that bind them, the physical artefacts that they use and produce, and the theories, models

Table 1. Summary of the three perspectives on learning (adapted from Leidner & Jarvenpaa, 1995)

Theoretical perspective	Basic premise	Implication for managing knowledge networks
Objectivist	Learning occurs by absorbing objective knowledge.	The manager(s) of a knowledge network should transfer knowledge to its members.
Constructivist	Learning occurs by constructing knowledge individually.	The manager(s) of a knowledge network should support rather than direct its members.
Social	Learning occurs by participating in the social world.	The manager(s) of a knowledge network should encourage communication among its members.

and methods they use to produce them" (Jonassen & Land, 2000, p. vi).

Each of the three theoretical perspectives on learning inspires different people to a different extent. In the next section, the social network approach of sociograms is discussed. This approach is especially useful for studying participation and learning in knowledge networks from a social perspective.

ILLUSTRATING KNOWLEDGE NETWORKS AS SOCIOGRAMS

Sociograms have been of great illustrative importance ever since the 1930s (Moreno, 1934). In social network analysis, *relations* describe particular types of resource exchange between *actors*. A *social network* is defined as "a finite set or sets of actors and the relation or relations defined on them" (Wasserman & Faust, 1994, p. 20). The resources exchanged among pairs of actors can be of many types, including tangibles such as goods, services, or money, or intangibles such as information, social support, or influence (Haythornthwaite, 1996, p. 323). As illustrated in Figure 1, there are four levels of measurement in relational data.

In a sociogram, each *node* represents a member of the network and lines show which others each node is tied to. For example, some participants of a knowledge network may give more information to peers or it may be experienced as they do. Differences in reporting of relationships are often found in situations where an actor is a prominent figure of a network (Haythornthwaite, 1996).

Ties may be directed and then arrows, instead of just lines, are used. Assigning a numeric value to each arrow can denote the strength of the ties, for example, the frequency of communication. An alternative approach is to use thinner (weak ties) and thicker (strong ties) lines (Hrastinski, 2006a, 2006b). Standard works on social network analysis (Scott, 1991; Wasserman & Faust, 1994) suggest that a number is assigned to each line to denote strength. However, as discussed in the next section, this can make a sociogram difficult to interpret.

In Figure 2, an example of a fictive sociogram is presented. Let us say that the sociogram illustrates perceived information exchanges in an online knowledge network, which communicate in a discussion board, during a week. It seems

Figure 1. Levels of measurement in relational data (Scott, 1991, p. 48)

		Directionality	
		Undirected	Directed
	Binary	1	3
Numeration			
	Valued	2	4

like the most prominent member of the knowledge network is B, who gives information to and receives information from A and D, and gives information to E. Node C and E seem to mostly receive information, rather than contributing with information to the others.

EXAMPLES OF SOCIOGRAMS

Social or knowledge network data is commonly organized in sociomatrices. Such matrices can then be transformed to sociograms. In this section, it will be drawn on Daugherty and Turner (2003) who analysed sociomatrices to assess group dynamics in a web-based course. Benefits and limitations of the sociogram approach will be

Figure 2. A binary and directed sociogram

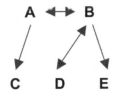

distinguished, by converting one of their sociomatrices to sociograms of different types.

Daugherty and Turner argued that sociometry is a useful approach for assessing group dynamics. This claim was based on a study of a web-based college graduate course on educational research. Ten of the eleven enrolled students responded to a "sociometric survey" of 13 questions. For example, the first question was: Who from the class would you like to be around in college course settings? Students were asked to limit their choices to 1-2 classmates per question.

Drawing on the results, a sociomatrix that reflects the number of nominations students reported and received by person was created (see Table 2). By analysing the table, Daugherty and Turner drew several conclusions: "First, the recipients of numerous choices from others and who, therefore, held positions of popularity were identified. [The table] showed that the most frequently chosen students (D and K) each received almost three nominations per respondent with mean choice selections of 2.89 and 2.8, respectively. ... It was also evident ... that class members infrequently chose 2 students. These 2 students (A and E) received, on average, less than one nomination per respondent, .78 and .67, respectively. ... [The table] also showed chains of interconnectedness between students. Pairs or individuals that nominated each other frequently were clearly evident. Seven dyads (A/F, A/J, C/E, C/I, D/H, D/I, F/G) were shown in which each selected the other a minimum of three times." (p. 269).

It is clear that Daugherty and Turner could draw conclusions, which might be essential in understanding group dynamics. Notably, many of the conclusions were proposed after studying the means of nominations. In Figure 3-5, sociograms have been created, by using the software Ucinet 6 (Borgatti, Everett & Freeman, 2002), to graphically illustrate the sociometric data collected by Daugherty and Turner. In the figures, arrows, instead of just lines, were used to illustrate the direction of perceived exchanges. This may be important since differences in reporting of relationships are often found in situations where some actors are prominent figures of a network (Haythornthwaite, 1996).

Example 1: Directed Values Sociogram

In Figure 3, a directed valued sociogram is presented (type 4). Note that student K was excluded because he or she did not answer the questionnaire. This type of sociogram seems primarily to be useful for analyzing small knowledge networks. However, the sociogram illustrates that every member of the knowledge network interact with other members of the network. D and H reciprocally selected each other many times. H selected E six times, while E never selected H. These findings can be derived from Table 2 but it can be assumed that different people would prefer to study the matrix of Table 2 while others would prefer the sociogram of Figure 3.

Example 2: Directed Binary Sociogram

In Figure 4, a directed binary sociogram is presented (type 3). The sociogram illustrates strong ties by only displaying the arrows with a value of 3 or higher. This makes the sociogram easier to interpret, but a weakness of this approach is that more detailed information is lost. As identified by Daugherty and Turner, the sociogram tells us that seven pairs of actors (A/F, A/J, C/E, C/I, D/H, D/I, F/G) reciprocally selected the other a

Table 2. Nominations received by respondent (Daugherty & Turner, 2003, p. 268)

Recipient	A	B	C	D	E	F	G	H	I	J	Mean	SD
A		1	0	0	0	3	0	0	0	3	0.78	1.3
B	1		0	0	0	6	1	2	2	1	1.44	1.88
C	0	0		0	4	0	0	0	6	0	1.11	2.26
D	1	1	6		3	0	4	5	3	3	2.89	2.47
E	0	0	3	1		0	0	0	2	0	6.7	1.12
F	3	2	0	0	0		3	1	0	0	1	1.32
G	1	0	0	2	0	4		0	0	2	1	1.41
H	1	1	2	7	6	0	2		1	0	2.22	2.54
I	0	4	3	3	6	0	0	1		0	1.89	2.2
J	5	9	0	0	0	3	0	0	0		1.89	3.22
K	5	4	0	4	0	3	8	0	0	4	2.8	2.74

minimum of three times. The sociograms also illustrates that all members of the knowledge network maintained at least one relation with a class member. Thus, among other things, it can be learnt that the problem of *isolates* was not apparent in the network.

Example 3: Directed Sociogram with Varying Line Widths

The sociogram of Figure 3 gives more detail by denoting each arrow with a numeric value, while the sociogram of Figure 4 is easier to interpret but gives less detail. Figure 5 presents a compromise between these two approaches. The strength of the ties, measured as frequency of communication, is denoted by thin (weak ties) and thick (strong

ties) lines. As mentioned earlier, this has not been the most common approach. The sociogram was created using Ucinet 6 (Borgatti et al., 2002), the software can represent tie strength as line width rather than by numeric values.

CONCLUSION

In this chapter, it has been argued that the sociogram approach might be particularly useful for those who view learning and participation in knowledge networks as an inherently social phenomenon. After giving a basic introduction to the concept of sociograms, three examples of different types of sociograms were put forward. This chapter has showed that essential questions

Figure 3. A directed valued sociogram

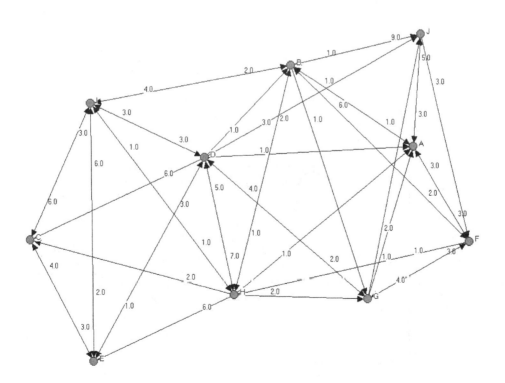

Figure 4. A directed binary sociogram

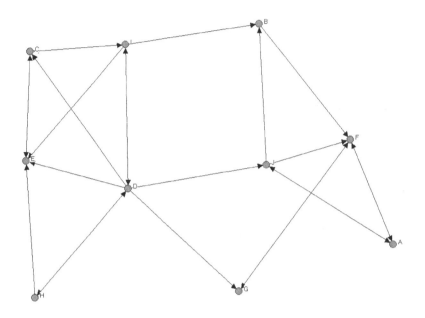

Figure 5. A directed sociogram, which illustrates strong and weak ties

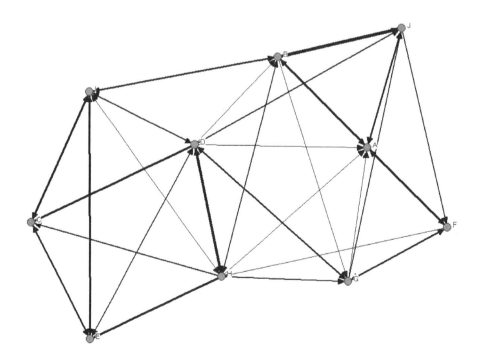

to ask when studying knowledge networks are: Can sociograms be used to aid in illustrating and understanding the knowledge network under investigation? Which type(s) of sociograms can aid in understanding the knowledge network under investigation?

INTERNET SESSION: "SOCIAL NETWORKS OF AN ONLINE COMMUNITY"

Choose an online community, which is a typical example of a knowledge network. For example, Microsoft's forums include many knowledge networks: http://forums.microsoft.com/msdn/.

Interaction

Create three sociograms (see Example 1-3) that illustrate the exchanges among the members of the knowledge network. If the community is large, illustrate a subset of the network by creating an ego-centered network, which illustrates all exchanges from and to one or a few actors. Which were the benefits and limitations of each type of sociogram you chose to create?

Useful URLs

1. Analytic Technologies: Software for analyzing social networks and creating sociograms, http://www.analytictech.com/
2. Netlab: scholarly network studying computer networks, communication networks, and social networks, http://www.chass.utoronto.ca/~wellman/netlab/
3. International network for social network analysis, http://www.insna.org/

Further Readings

Scott, J. (1991). *Social network analysis: A handbook.* Newbury Park, CA: Sage Publications.

Wasserman, S., & Faust, K. (1994). *Social network analysis: Methods and applications.* Cambridge: Cambridge University Press.

Garton, L., Haythornthwaite, C., & Wellman, B. (1999). Studying on-line social networks. In S. Jones (Ed.), *Doing Internet research: Critical issues and methods for examining the net* (pp. 77-105). Thousand Oaks: Sage Publications.

Haythornthwaite, C. (1996). Social network analysis: An approach and set of techniques for the study of information exchange. *Library and Information Science Research, 18*(4), 323-342.

REFERENCES

Borgatti, S. P., Everett, M. G., & Freeman, L. C. (2002). *Ucinet 6 for Windows: Software for social network analysis.* Harvard: Analytic Technologies.

Daugherty, M., & Turner, J. (2003). Sociometry: An approach for assessing group dynamics in web-based courses. *Interactive Learning Environments, 11*(3), 263-275.

Duffy, T. M., & Jonassen, D. H. (1992). Constructivism: New implications for instructional technology. In T. M. Duffy & D. H. Jonassen (Eds.), *Constructivism and the technology of instruction: A conversation.* New Jersey: Lawrence Erlbaum.

Edelson, D. C., Pea, R. D., & Gomez, L. (1996). Constructivism in the collaboratory. In B. G. Wilson (Ed.), *Constructivist learning environments: Case studies in instructional design* (pp. 151-164). Englewood Cliffs, New Jersey: Educational Technology Publications.

Garton, L., Haythornthwaite, C., & Wellman, B. (1999). Studying on-line social networks. In S. Jones (Ed.), *Doing Internet research: Critical issues and methods for examining the net* (pp. 77-105). Thousand Oaks: Sage Publications.

Haythornthwaite, C. (1996). Social network analysis: An approach and set of techniques for the study of information exchange. *Library and Information Science Research, 18*(4), 323-342.

Heeren, E. (1996). *Technology support for collaborative distance learning.* Doctoral thesis, University of Twente, Twente.

Hrastinski, S. (2006a). Introducing an informal synchronous medium in a distance learning course: How is participation affected? *Internet and Higher Education, 9*(2), 117-131.

Hrastinski, S. (2006b). The relationship between adopting a synchronous medium and participation in online group work: An explorative study. *Interactive Learning Environments, 14*(2), 137-152.

Jaldemark, J., Lindberg, J. O., & Olofsson, A. D. (2006). Sharing the distance or a distance shared: Social and individual aspects of participation in ICT-supported distance-based teacher education. In M. Chaib & A. K. Svensson (Eds.), *ICT in teacher education: Challenging prospects* (pp. 142-160). Jönköping: Jönköping University Press.

Jonassen, D. H., & Land, S. M. (2000). Preface. In D. H. Jonassen & S. M. Land (Eds.), *Theoretical foundations of learning environments* (pp. iii-ix). New Jersey: Lawrence Erlbaum.

Leidner, D. E., & Jarvenpaa, S. L. (1995). The use of information technology to enhance management school education: A theoretical view. *MIS Quarterly, 19*(3), 265-291.

Littleton, K., & Häkkinen, P. (1999). Learning together: Understanding the processes of computer-based collaborative learning. In P. Dillenbourg (Ed.), *Collaborative learning: Cognitive and computational approaches* (pp. 20-30). Oxford: Elsevier Science Ltd.

Moreno, J. L. (1934). *Who shall survive? A new approach to the problems of human interrelations.* Washington, DC: Nervous and Mental Disease Publishing Company.

Säljö, R. (2000). *Lärande i praktiken: Ett sociokulturellt perspektiv (Learning in practice: A sociocultural perspective.* Stockholm: Prisma.

Wasserman, S., & Faust, K. (1994). *Social network analysis: Methods and applications.* Cambridge: Cambridge University Press.

Watson, J. B. (1925/1997). *Behaviorism.* New Jersey: Transaction Publishers.

Wenger, E. (1998). *Communities of practice: Learning, meaning, and identity.* Cambridge: Cambridge University Press.

Vygotsky, L. S. (1978). *Mind in society: The development of higher psychological processes.* Cambridge, Massachusetts: Harvard University Press.

Chapter IX
Web 2.0 Collaborative Learning Tool Dynamics

Marianna Vivitsou
University of Helsinki, Finland

Niki Lambropoulos
London South Bank University, UK

Sofia Papadimitriou
Greek Educational Television, Greek Ministry of Education & Religious Affairs, Greece

Alexandros Gkikas
Greek Ministry of Education & Religious Affairs, Greece

Dimitris Konetas
University of Ioannina, Greece

ABSTRACT

Social web asynchronous communication environments provide the space for content creation, idea sharing and knowledge construction within a participatory and collaborative framework that encourages online community establishment and evolution. However, community development is a long-term process and necessitates the adoption of appropriate theoretical principles to support a developmental scheme ensuring the community's exploratory, knowledge-based and reflexively expanding character. This chapter discusses and analyses the techniques and tools used in an online course aiming to enable Greek teachers develop their pedagogical and digital skills in order to keep update, form new relationships and grow professionally. To this end, e-course design was based on formal learning principles underlying the virtual classroom activities during which a collaborative culture was built. Also, the course structure involved informal learning principles, which were integrated into social web activities

Copyright © 2009, IGI Global, distributing in print or electronic forms without written permission of IGI Global is prohibited.

implemented on weblog and wiki artefacts created and used by participants as individual and collaborative learning tools. Through the analysis of quantitative and qualitative data gathered during the study it became evident that weblogs and wikis contributed to the growth and evolution of Greek educational networked communities and that a new online identity emerged.

INTRODUCTION

The term Web 2.0 has generated debate and actually the need for its very existence has been questioned by representatives in the fields of computer science and sociology and by non-experts as well. Nevertheless, the appeal of Web 2.0 technologies and applications worldwide is an undeniable fact. Indeed, relevant entries in search engines come with lists of millions of: weblogs; an increasing number of targeted wikispaces; awards for user-friendly, knowledge-based environments; diverse content finding its way to the e-audience through different types of media; networked communities of users sharing common interests, knowledge and experiences.

Web 2.0 is a signpost indicating a new state of mind of using information as in Web 1.0 but this development is not confined to a change in terminology. It has affected the way we connect to other people; the way we interact, we acquire information; the way we think and the way we learn. At the end of the day, it seems that the essence of the challenge lies in the principles underlying the educational change that follow the World Wide Web impact. Apparently, the Web 2.0 effect has a multidisciplinary nature, as the exploitation of second generation WWW services challenges existing theories and methods applied in pedagogy-related domains, such as human-computer interaction and knowledge management. Yet, as Baudrilliard (2002) puts it,

we are obliged to change, but changing is something other than becoming, they are different things. We are in a "changing" time, where it is the moral law of all individuals, but changing is not becoming. Baudrilliard, 2002 (online interview)

Attempting to interpret Baudrilliard's words in educational terms, we should admit that in order to avoid the reproduction of traditional frameworks in the field, and thus fail to '*become*', we need to reconsider the parameters upon which online education is structured. These relate to the qualities that Web 2.0 technologies bring forward and involve: knowledge distribution, networking /interconnectedness and ability for information access, collaboration, content creation, reshaping and redistribution.

Through the lines of this chapter we aim to present the rationale and implementation of the 'Project Method' online course aiming to encourage active learning and participation, reflective thinking and collaboration within the framework of the online learning community of Greek teachers that was developed during the course. At the other end of the continuum, values and attitudes incarnate through actions and symbolic representations mediated by different types of artefact acting as media for meaning construction and communication. Therefore, to achieve our overall pedagogical goals, we included a variety of synchronous and asynchronous tools in the curriculum; however, for the purposes of this chapter the focus will be cast upon the use of Web 2.0 environments, namely weblogs and wikis, and their dual role in the online learning process, as products and as media.

PARTICIPATORY LEARNING IN ONLINE TEACHER EDUCATION

The Educational Social Network

The connective network technologies of Web 2.0 have provided space for social engagement and significantly increased the mass of users who appreciate the joys of *sharing content, communicating* or *accessing information.* Along with activating user participation, these technologies lower the threshold for collective action and enable cooperative peer-to-peer production – of knowledge, of tools, of power. Yet, sociologists and critics (e.g. Coleman, 2008; Scholz et al., 2008) of the social web[1] point out the danger of decay if the context of interaction is the production of commodities to be consumed. Instead, the challenge for the social web is to foster platforms which would engage users in not being productive just simply to produce, but to be productive in the sense that Fromm (2003) defines the term– where one uses one's capacities in order to better oneself through interaction. Social web is based on an unstable social contract (Bauwens, 2005), which brings forward the necessity for users to be aware that content creation is an exploratory and reflective process. A deeper insight of participation and knowledge of underlying policies encourages this type of awareness and urges the users to express their true powers, not simply reproduce consumer products in a mechanical way. As Coleman (2008: para. 12) argues, referring to social justice activists, they "*... have no choice but to turn to these technologies that do facilitate interactions and collaborations. But they* [technologies] *also must be built, disseminated, and hosted by the very people who would most benefit from the tools. Otherwise, they* [users] *risk losing control over design features and as a result become vulnerable to security and privacy breaches.*"

Extending the above observations and assertions onto the educational field, we cannot avoid considering the fact that it is educators that can play the mediating role between participation systems and the society, i.e. existing and potential users, by introducing their learners into the principles that characterize active, reflective and informed engagement. This is feasible by blending media education with classroom practices aiming to activate cognitive, aesthetic, emotional and moral mechanisms (Potter, 2005). At the same time in-service teachers need to keep informed of developments in both the pedagogical and technological fields in order to be able to adapt their teaching to the expectations of the digital generation. Therefore, educational institutions need to incorporate into their curricula principles that promote the development of skills that are necessary for constant change management within a context that favours continuous, active learning. However, research findings (Guskey, 2002) clearly show the limitations of conventional training and reinforce the view that online education can offer an alternative path. The incorporation of Web 2.0 technologies into teacher education course design can serve this perspective, as they encourage the development of knowledge networks.

Based on a non-static concept of knowledge, that of a 'flowing utility' in networks, Downes (2007) claims that learners learn through connections. In this sense, networks are compared to ecosystems and as such, unlike groups, are characterised by diversity, autonomy, openness and interaction. As Siemens (2004) puts it, learning does not only take place internally but can also '*reside outside of ourselves (within an organization or a database), is focused on connecting specialized information sets, and the connections that enable us to learn more are more important than our current state of knowing*'. Educational networks (Lieberman, 2000) are organized around the interests and needs of their participants, building agendas sensitive to their individual and collective development as educators. The quality of fluidity that characterizes networks allows them to change quickly and invent new structures and activities that are responsive to their members.

Networked Educational Communities: A New Identity

The age of high modernity, sociologists (e.g. Giddens, 1991; Wittel, 2001) point out, is characterised by the collapse of community and the onset of individualization. 'Individualization' presumes a removal from historically prescribed social forms and commitments, a loss of traditional security with respect to rituals, guiding norms and practical knowledge (Beck, 1999). Although freeing, this new situation requires that individuals must actively construct social bonds. On the other hand, the internet provides the platform for a complex set of relationships to emerge, as well as opportunities for exploration and flexibility (Huffaker, 2004). In other words, the evolving Web 2.0 infrastructure and architecture and its emerging participation systems have facilitated the rise of a new type of social engagement, the 'virtual community'. The term was introduced by Rheingold (1993) to describe the situation where individuals with a common interest meet online in order to exchange opinions, to collaborate, to learn. When users who share a common passion (i.e. for their profession) and a common jargon, and communicate on a regular basis in order to construct knowledge and devise new professional practices online, they constitute a Community of Practice (CoP) (Lave et al., 1991). The results of research conducted on a virtual, university-based learning CoP (Allan et al., 2006) provided insights into the long term impact of the community on individual careers and also the impact of the community on performance in the workplace. Although the very concept of a virtual community has been challenged (Wittel, 2001), the researchers identified the importance of the VLC in providing a comfort zone from which members could innovate and take risks. Participation in the community enabled some members to transform their professional identities and career trajectories, while some members embraced the opportunity to develop and enhance their careers in an evolutionary manner. Based upon the results of this study, we argue that the significance of this new reality does not solely lie in the VLC members' transformation of professional identities but, most importantly, in the emergence of an altogether new identity: the networked community identity.

In an online community individuals view this scheme as something external to them and are willing to transform themselves for the sake of the community, thus associating sociality with the qualities of a process to be engaged in for its own sake, i.e. as an intrinsic good. This type of virtual CoP is a self-regulatory and self-organized entity, in the sense that very often communities supersede the aspirations of their creators and do something novel (Scholz et al., **2008**), thus rendering themselves independent entities. This principle reflects the Aristotelian idea that we are only fully human when we are engaging in the governance of our community. Contrary to the potential generated for a citizen in the physical world, nowadays users simultaneously engage in numerous online communities with widely varying forms of governance. So instead of conforming with or arguing against one type of regime, a community participant builds up new community networks while at the same time navigates the advantages, disadvantages, and rules of appropriate action from community to community. In addition, participants bring their experiences and expectations with them from community to community.

This multiple-identity and community mobility ultimately creates a participant- citizen who is much more sensitive to the joys and challenges of an actively engaged life through a growing political awareness and social engagement. Yet, the new media field contains subjects with a diversity of educational and geographical backgrounds. People are 'lifted out' of their contexts and reinserted in largely disembedded social relations, which they must at the same time continually construct (Wittel, 2001). Therefore, the challenge for Web 2.0 users is actually to become social web active and productive participants, thus constructing a new identity, both individual and collective. To do so, users also need to redefine their virtual self insomuch as the internal (i.e. in terms of interpersonal characteristics, such as self-definition) as well as the external experience (i.e. in terms of communal manifestations, such as social roles, relationships with others or shared values, Calvert, 2002; Erikson, 1993; Freud, 1989) is concerned. Consequently, for the development of participatory networked educational communities, teachers also need to create proximity and a common history or narrative of the collective while at the same time constructing an online personal biography, a persistent and coherent, though flexible, self-identity (in a sense that follows Giddens' (1991: 244) definition of the term: '*the self as reflexively understood by the individual in terms of his or her biography*'). In this interplay of the individual and the collective both elements (identities) are in a process of ongoing transformation.

In the case of Greek teachers-participants in the PM e-course, the emergent identity presents multiple characteristics and is defined in terms of the digital tools exploited, the interaction generated, the artefacts (both symbolic and objects) created and the participants' own evaluative comments generated at the initial and post-course phases. The emergence of this new identity has been encouraged in a social online environment through the application of collaborative techniques and is: active, interactive, reflective, analytic, synthetic, productive and multi-dimensional.

Collaboration in Networked Educational Communities

Using the iceberg metaphor, we consider it essential to note at this point that the multiple net-

worked identities emerged through a process of increased interactive participation following the introduction of Web 2.0 tools into the e-course curriculum. This strategy aimed to encourage participants to familiarise with popular social web platforms that facilitate collaboration and networking so that e-learners can form connections, construct new social bonds and develop individual and collective identities. Seemingly, collaboration is a fundamental issue for the entire operation and constitutes the connecting tissue among the members of the community; yet its definitions present variations with regard to the time parameter that frames the occurrence of collaborative episodes.

Koschmann (1996) defines collaborative learning (CL) as the practices of meaning making in the context of joint activity, and the ways in which these practices are mediated through designed artefacts. Roschelle & Teasley (1995: 70) define collaboration as "...*a coordinated, synchronous activity that is the result of a continued attempt to construct and maintain a shared conception of a problem*". However, Dillenbourg (1999) challenges the notion of synchronicity and argues that the four criteria that characterise a collaborative setting are: situation, interactions, processes and effects. Along with a more complex, procedural view of collaboration, Dillenbourg (1999) relates CL to joint problem solving and defines this type of learning as the outcome of problem solving activities. In this chapter we focus upon collaboration as an asynchronous activity, which, therefore, heavily depends upon volition, i.e. participants' willingness to share thoughts and ideas with colleagues towards the common, though not in real time, attempt for the solution of problems (e.g. the creation of e-environments, the preparation and presentation of assignments etc). To this end, we aimed for maximization of engagement by blending pedagogical and technological issues in the course content and anticipated that cognitive mechanisms would be sequenced by the activation of emotional, aesthetic and moral domains, thus fulfilling the whole-person involvement approach of the strategic planning of the e-course.

The principles of social constructivism also defined the theoretical background of the PM online course. These consider learning as the internal process of constructing and restructuring mental schemata within a social context. The vygotskian view (Vygotsky, 1978) of knowledge mediated by meaningful artefacts, both physical (i.e., tools) and symbolic (e.g. linguistic) was also considered. Therefore, in order to achieve the pedagogical goals of the course, we set up a virtual classroom on the Moodle learning management system aiming to encourage knowledge building (Scardamalia et al., 1991) through input data retrieval and processing. Moreover, this environment aimed to provide a 'dialogic space' (Dillenbourg et al., 1996) so that participants' cognitive mechanisms would activate through interaction allowing for the exploitation of higher order thinking skills (e.g. negotiation, argumentation etc). Nevertheless, although discussion forums allowed for reflexivity and the emergence of constructive dialogue, we judged it was critical to extend participants' activities into the social web platforms for the establishment of a collaborative culture, which, notably, is lacking from real educational settings. Indeed, the social web resembles real-life society bearing its own risks and opportunities for sociality, new relationships and knowledge construction. The difference lies in the fact that, being a relatively new medium and, therefore, still highly unstructured, the social web needs to develop upon ideals that promote active, participatory, multi-dimensional practices that safeguard the democratisation of the medium.

Concluding, we claim that a collaborative culture underlies the philosophy of the social web which is founded upon the social activist movement and the ideal of active citizenship. By adopting and indulging in collaboration-based techniques and tools, users can gain a dynamic

learning experience and manage the transformation of their life-perspective (Mezirow, 2003) through the challenge of pre-established ideas and beliefs leading to an improved awareness of reality and acting as a springboard for individual and collective initiative. Therefore, it can be said that building a collaborative culture is synonymous to constructing an environment that favours active engagement, skills development and contextualized learning, and promotes critical thinking and co-creativity. In short, this process unlocks the potential of evolution of the initial community into a more independent scheme, i.e. an open, transformative network of collaboration and learning.

The following section aims to present the Web 2.0 tools that contributed to the transition phase of the Greek teachers' online community. Yet, due to the ephemeral nature that characterises tools, it should be borne in mind during reading this chapter that the dynamics generated during the course should actually be attributed to underlying principles and the overall context, not the specific web platforms per se that actually played a mediating role.

Weblogs and Wikis as Social Collaborative Learning Tools

The potential of Web 2.0 software for creative knowledge construction was a basic criterion for selection, as, being dynamic social websites, weblogs and wikis allow for personalisation and user-generated content. Additionally, being artefacts whose shaping depends upon the creators' decisions or the consensus among the members of a team of authors, these types of software encourage reflexivity, interaction and the development of individual and collective online identities. More particularly:

- A weblog (or blog) is a website where entries are made in journal style and displayed in reverse chronological order. An important characteristic of many blogs is the ability for readers to leave comments in an interactive format. Researchers in the field of online social networking (or blogosphere - http://en.wikipedia.org/wiki/Blogo-sphere) coincide in the view of weblogs as knowledge-based environments: Efimova (2004) claims that a blog is the place where the individual, the community and people's ideas blend and considers it ideal for knowledge management; Sessums (2006) recommends weblogs for data collection, communication and collaboration; Warlick (2005) concludes that a blog is a more effective collaborative tool than a discussion forum; Mortensen και Walker (2002) add the quality of a research tool, while the research conducted by neuroscientists Eide and Eide (2005) underpins the positive results the use of weblogs can have in the development of critical and analytical thinking. Considering all the above features we add that, due to the personality-centred quality of blogs, blogging can contribute to the generation of a principally individual identity of the owner, which can be:

○ Active (keeping a blog on a regular basis is itself an on-going activity)

○ Interactive (e.g. through exchanging ideas using comments, interconnecting using blogroll)

○ Analytic, synthetic, productive (posting ideas, news etc presupposes the activation of the thinking process and the use of perceptive and productive skills)

○ Reflective (e.g. through the consideration of comments and/or the reconsideration of post content)

○ Multidimensional (i.e. through the analysis, presentation etc of a variety of thematic areas, the development of digital skills etc)

• Although personality plays a central role in weblogs (Efimova 2005), the wiki is the environment where the social element prevails for the sake of collaboration and collective knowledge construction. Wikis are beginning to be used in many innovative ways across a broad range of subject areas while they provide unique collaborative opportunities for education. Several factors have been identified in the successful implementation of educational wikis. Wikis allow each contributor to both author and edit collaboratively. Combining freely accessible information, rapid feedback, simplified HTML, and access by multiple editors, wikis are being rapidly adopted as an innovative way of constructing knowledge. However, the characteristic that has most strikingly set wikis apart from other web-based forums and discussions is that of multiple contributors. Unlike a blog, for example, which has one main identifiable author, a wiki web page may be authored and edited by a number of people. Not only may an individual contributor edit their own work, but also the work of others. User-friendliness and ease of interaction make a wiki a dynamically effective tool for collaborative writing as the software provides the means to monitor the process of editing and revising and at the same time allows for an on action evolution of the collective identity. In this asynchronous collaborative mode, the individual blends with the communal while their interplay, as an ongoing process of meaning negotiation and decision making, contributes to the emergence of new identity qualities online.

Apparently, both Web 2.0 software provide the space for the generation of discourse, in the sense of language-in-use that exploits linguistic and non-linguistic (e.g. images, video etc) elements (Gee, 1999) for meaning construction and communication. Therefore, in addition to the expressive means used by e-learners to convey meaning, the genres of text and types of weblogs and wikis of the e-course will be examined through the lines of this chapter. Moreover, a quantitative analysis of data gathered through questionnaires given to participants at the initial and post-course stages in correlation with a qualitative analysis of collaborative episodes traced in the learner-generated environments will also aim to explore the following areas:

- The themes that interest and motivate Greek teachers
- The role of weblogs and wikis in community development
- The interactive relation between online collaborative work, self-expression and cognitive development through artefact creation and content editing
- The degree to which weblogs encourage the collaborative process
- The way(s) in which the use of the wiki software contributes to the collaborative process

E-COURSE BACKGROUND: CONTEXT, OVERALL GOALS AND TOOLS

This section presents the background of the Project Method e-course to indicate the evolutionary process of the Greek teachers' online community. Apparently, this is a learning community and bears the characteristics of a CoP, as defined by Lave and Wenger (1991). Yet, as the results of the study show, the evolution of a CoP into multiple networked communities is a long-term process based upon sustained action, interaction and reflexivity and built on multi-disciplinary approaches.

The 'Project Method' (PM) online course was implemented on the e-learning platform (http://e-learning.sch.gr) of the Greek Schools Network (GSN) (www.sch.gr), the national intranet that interconnects and offers a variety of pedagogically informed telematic services to Greek state school teachers in primary and secondary education. One of the Network's overall goals is to promote online teacher education by providing the necessary platform and the opportunity to researchers and educators specialising in the use of ICTs to implement experimental online courses addressing the needs of its teachers-members. For e-learning purposes, the GSN operates the Moodle learning management system (www.moodle.org).

The emergence of the second cycle of the PM e-course sequenced the series of lessons during the first cycle (PM1), and was based upon realisations resulting from our own participatory observation:

- the limitations of conventional in-service teacher education when pressure urged upon teachers to extend their knowledge and develop existing skills in order to introduce project-based learning into their classroom practice. The pressure came in the form of curricular requirements aiming towards a more learner-centred educational paradigm and following the Reform that was institutionalised in 2003 (Law 303 & 304 /13-03-2003). Other contributing factors were:
- increased participation in PM1 as compared with the overall rate of participation in the e-courses offered by the GSN;
- the conclusions drawn at the post-implementation phase of the course (Vivitsou et al., 2008) concerning the integration of educational technology into pedagogical models as well as of informal elements into the online learning process;

Table 1. The Project method e-course 1 & 2: Differences

PM 1	PM 2
Data-driven	Content-driven
Discussion forum, chatroom, virtual classroom, e-mail	PM1 + Blog, wiki, videoconferencing
Asynchronous and synchronous interaction individually and/or in groups, mainly tutor driven	Networking
Product – oriented	Process - oriented
Formal e-learning principles	Formal and informal principles as well

- the rising popularity of social networking technologies and the impact of their integration into educational curricula.

As shown in Table 1 below, the main differences in the planning of the two cycles of the e-course were:

In the second phase, our ultimate pedagogical goal was to enable teachers-participants to extend and transfer their skills and competencies from the password-protected Moodle environment to that of online social networking and, thus, establish a framework for continuous, collaborative, participatory online learning. In this way, we also aimed for the empowerment of the e-learners and the transformation of the Greek teachers' online community into community 2.0. This type of community has a coherent and persistent collective identity, being the sum of distributed online presence of its members, and expands into flexible networks depending upon participants' needs, interests and priorities.

THE GREEK EDUCATIONAL ONLINE COMMUNITY: A CASE STUDY

The Context

The second cycle of the 'Project Method' e-course (PM2) lasted 4 consecutive weeks (from February to March 2007), each of which corresponded to a pre-determined thematic unit. The core structure of the syllabus evolved around the creation and use of personal weblogs for publication and sharing of experiences, ideas and thoughts and reflection upon them, as well as interlinking among e-course participants; collaborative content creation, editing, revision and publication on thematically-oriented wikis; presentation and evaluation of the process and the outcomes of the learning experience during pre-scheduled video-conferencing sessions. The framework was based on the stages for project design and implementation proposed by Frey (1987) and formed the plateau to accommodate the creation of artefacts on the one hand, and meaning construction and negotiation on the other. Therefore, for active participation encouragement, it was left to course participants to decide upon the design (aesthetic domain) and content (cognitive, emotional, moral domain) of the Web 2.0 environments, tailoring them to own needs and interests. During the course 39 personal weblogs, 4 multi-authored and 5 personal wikis were created by participants.

Methodology

The aim of this study is to explore the degree to which weblogs and wikis contributed to and promoted collaborative online learning. Also it seeks to explore whether these digital artefacts, the creation and development of which constituted a course requirement, played a role in the teachers' online community evolution. For the analysis both quantitative and qualitative approaches were used. The data were retrieved from different sources: the questionnaires administered to participants at the initial and post-course phases; participants' log-ins in the GSN environment; their contributions to the virtual classroom during the weblog and wiki module and the participants' social web artefacts.

Participants' Profile

Demographic Data

PM2 had 128 participants in all: 121 registered e-learners and 7 e-tutors. Out of the total number of questionnaires administered during the initial and final stages of the course, 47 were returned via e-mail (36,7%). Of the total number of respondents (47), 35 were male (74%) and 12 female (26%). One e-learner was between 20-30 years of age (2%), 15 were between 30-40 years old (32%), and 31 between 40-65 years old (66%). 4 participants responded that they had 1-5 years of service (9%) in state education, 9 participants 6-10 years (19%), 22 participants 11-20 years

(46%) και 12 participants had more than 20 years of service (26%).

Previous E-Learning Experience

The participants' overall experience of using computers ranged between 6-20 years (74%) while internet access, which was estimated to one to two connections per day (54%), showed a 6% increase during the e-course. The majority of e-participants (78%) had no previous experience in using learning management systems (LMS), such as Moodle@GSN, and lacked training (70%) in LMSs. Nevertheless, 74% of the total number of respondents estimates that the integration of such environments into e-learning courses is of high priority. Generally, the Greek teachers had a positive stance towards the introduction of Information and Communication Technologies into traditional classroom practices, even though half of the respondents (50%) had no previous experience in e-learning and 43% of them had never worked in a similar collaborative mode before.

Techniques and Activities

The pedagogical methods and techniques led to activities that took place both within the virtual classroom and beyond closed walls and included:

- Newsletters (aiming to set up activities and keep e-learners informed of the e-course progress; sent via e-mail)
- Resources (learning input uploaded in the virtual classroom)
- Asynchronous and synchronous discussions (use of Moodle discussion forums and chats for input processing)
- Personal messages (input processing / Moodle environment)
- Social web tasks

- ○ Thematic unit 1 (creation of personal blogs, division into teams according to participants' interests)
- ○ Thematic unit 2 (group work using wikis)

Virtual Classroom Activities Resources

The content of resources (25 in total: 14 for weblogs and 11 for wikis) uploaded in the virtual classroom can be categorized as follows:

- Articles discussing the use of the tools and their pedagogical value
- Hyperlinks leading to websites with tips and information about the creation and improvement of blogs and wikis
- Hyperlinks to model blogs and wikis

As the e-course logs indicate, the material attracted the participants' interest (there were 134, 316 and 822 hits in the weblog resources and 135, 208 and 210 in the wiki resources). The material was highly valued by the participants as far as coverage and usability is concerned (36 estimated that coverage was very high, 9 average and 2 low) (43 estimated that usability was very high, 2 average and 2 low).

Asynchronous Discussions

The discussions created in the virtual classroom forums can be analysed on the basis of two categories: general (e.g. news, problems-solutions etc) and focused on the course thematic units (modules). More particularly, the analysis of the focused discussions revealed:

Weblog Forum

Two discussions were created and 64 topics were developed in this forum concerning the presentation of personal weblogs, difficulties encountered during creation and suggested solutions. The first discussion with the overall title 'Weblogs in education' had 61 topics with 173 replies (1-17 replies to each topic), while 47 of them were initiated by the e-learners (31 topics by unique participants). The second discussion evolved around technological issues (e.g. the HTML code) and had 3 topics (1-2 replies to each), which were initiated by the e-tutors. The first message was sent by the e-tutor AG on 26-02-07, and the last one by the e-learner NV on 01-04-07, while, notably, the thematic unit on blogs was concluded on 8-03-07.

Asynchronous interaction was mainly of a tutor-learner type, while one of the topics introduced by the former had replies by 5 unique e-learners. Additionally, 5 topics initiated by the latter received responses by more than one e-learners. The content of the interaction was mainly related to the integration of the tool into the teaching syllabus, overall pedagogical goals and specific teaching aims. Moreover, skepticism was expressed as to the effective exploitation of the tool and the blending of face-to-face and online learning, while there were suggestions for implementation (e.g. the use of weblogs as a tool promoting communication and collaboration among students from schools in different / distant geographical locations). Finally, questions were posed concerning the use of the software (e.g. text editing, hyperlink entries, file uploads etc).

Participants' contributions to both discussions were generally well-structured and frequently well-elaborated and, therefore, they achieved to communicate meaningful messages through argumentation (see Hybrid Synergy episodes). On the e-tutors' part the discourse produced was supportive and encouraging, which facilitated a teaching presence (Garrison et al., 2001) aiming rather to establish a sense of reliability and coherence than to actually offer solutions. E-tutors' replies aimed to facilitate understanding and problem solving and to establish a realistic social atmosphere in the virtual environment, while frequently sustained the intended meaning conveyed through written

Figure 1. 'Weblogs in education' forum: Comprehensive view

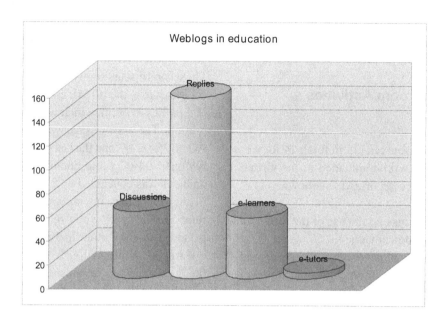

Figure 2. Technical issues blog forum: Comprehensive view

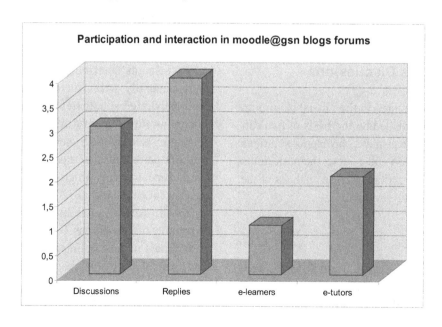

text by the use of emoticons. Respectively, the e-learners posed questions, made references to background personal experience and to how they dealt with problems and suggested solutions, thus working towards the fulfilment of learning objectives and knowledge gap elimination.

The diagrams (figure 1 & 2) below aim to present a comprehensive view of participation and interaction created in the weblog forums.

As the ratio of e-learners' participation increases (fig. 1), it is evident that Greek teachers chose to focus on general and issues that had a pedagogical value to them, in their effort to construct the new mental schema of building and using a weblog. However, we believe that this fact could not be considered as indicative of a tendency to neglect the more technical issues; rather we view it as a tendency to organize learning in a way that would encourage the generation of ideas and the emergence of concepts qualifying

the e-learners' educational identity in the online community. Compared with PM1 (Vivitsou et al., 2008), increased participation and interaction in the PM2 forums also shows that the collaborative culture in the community is reinforced. This observation is sustained when considering the rate of e-learner participation in synchronous communication (chats), which boosted on 1 March 2007, i.e. during a period that the weblog module was still in progress (fig. 3).

Wiki Forum

Eight wiki-related discussions were created in the virtual classroom. Three of them were accommodated in the 'General issues' forum, had 19 topics and 45 replies. In the wiki forum there were 5 discussions with 13 topics and 26 replies. As the following diagram (fig. 4) shows, the participants' showed a greater interest in practi-

Figure 3. Participation in chats

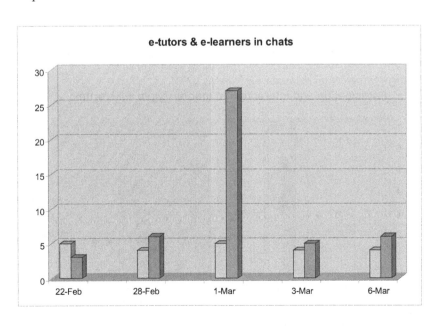

Figure 4. Wiki-related forums: e-tutors' and e-learners' participation

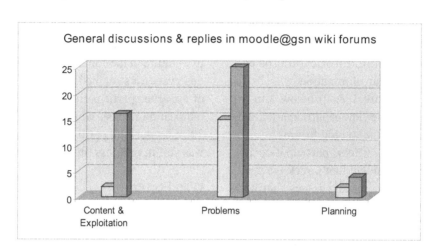

cal problem solving, which is attributed to the complexity of managing the software per se, as compared with the weblog.

This observation is confirmed through the data in figure 5, which also indicates that the overall e-learner active participation through messages in the wiki module is lower when considering the number of replies posted in the weblog-related forums.

Figure 5. Wiki-related forums: overall view

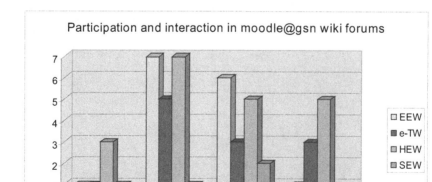

Besides software complexity, another possible reason justifying the activity in the wiki module can be the complexity of the writing process and the difficulties individuals face in producing coherent and well-organized written speech. Compared with the spontaneity and 'casualty' that frequently characterize the discourse developed in blogs, content intended to be uploaded in a wiki needs to be carefully planned prior to the editing process that follows publication.

Social Web Activities

In the Greek Educational Blogosphere

The weblogs (39) of the e-course were hosted on several free platforms (e.g. blogger.com, pblogs and wordpress.com) and their presentation involved different templates, layouts and formatting, depending on the owners' preferences (see two examples of screenshots below). Image files were uploaded for aesthetic purposes and for the reinforcement of the owner's intended message. Links to suggested websites were added in the sidebar and e-learners were interconnected using the blogroll. During the course these 39 weblogs were visited by participants and received positive and encouraging comments.

As figure 6 shows, learning about weblogs activated the interest of teachers specializing in different domains, which underpinned the multidisciplinary nature of the blogging task. Most digital artifacts were created by primary school teachers (9) and computer science teachers serving in secondary education (8).

Moreover, an overview of posts reveals that teachers have a tendency to focus on a variety of thematic areas, such as topics of personal interest (22), school projects (6), pedagogy (15), theology (2), the environment (1) and geographical locations (3). The texts posted mainly had an informative character. Two of the blogs were used by the owners for blended learning purposes, involving actively their 1st Grade Junior High school students to support classroom teaching.

Wikifying Learning

Through the content of weblogs emerged four focal areas indicating the e-learners' special interests. Based on this observation we created 4 thematic wikis, while 5 teachers decided to set

Screenshot 1. Biology for everyone

Screenshot 2. Life-long learning

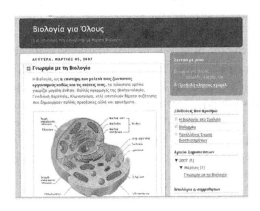

Figure 6. Blogs per educational specializing domain

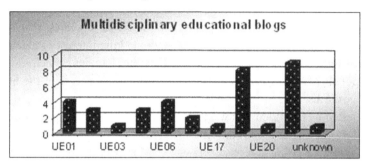

up personal wikis in order to experiment on the environment. During the course the 'E-twinning' wiki had 95 views and 64 content edits by 12 unique logged in users of whom 9 were registered and 1 administrator. The 'Health Education' wiki had 174 views and 62 content edits by 6 unique authors (4 registered) and 1 administrator. The group wiki discussing special learning needs had 60 views and 14 content edits by 3 unique authors (1 administrator and 2 non-registered users). The fourth group wiki discussed environmental issues and had 176 views and 119 content edits by 14 unique authors and 1 administrator. These social wiki data highlight participants' access and contributions until module conclusion, are in accordance with the data retrieved from the module-related discussion forums and confirm the participants' interest in the chosen topics.

There are 1,320 total pages in the database of the 'environmental' wiki, which exhibited the highest activity. This includes "talk" pages, pages about the focal topic, minimal "stub" pages, redirects, and others that cannot be assessed as content pages. Excluding those, there are 8 legitimate content pages. Today there have been a total of 7,478 page views, and 316 page edits since the wiki was setup in February 2006. That comes to 0.24 average edits per page, and 23.66 views per edit. Moreover, there are 34 registered users of whom 2 (or 5.88%) are administrators.

Therefore, despite the conclusion of the related thematic unit and the e-course, the wiki remains an environment open for update, editing and meaning construction as well as an information resource space.

Content Analysis: Asynchronous Interaction and Collaboration

Weblog Forum Episode

For the qualitative analysis we used Hybrid Synergy (Lambropoulos et al., 2008) to analyse an episode from the weblog forum. Hybrid Synergy works on the argumentation stages of information, social cues and emotions, ideas exploration, evaluation and assessment, and overviews.

This Hybrid Synergy episode investigates the issues needed by a new user when setting up a blog. Following the suggestions in the course, CC had to reason against the very purposes of having the blog as well as the targeted audience. His co-participants encouraged and helped him with suggestions building on each other. They also provided evaluation in order to direct and encourage him for his decisions. As there were 5 episodes in the blog section with a total of 61 threads and 3,541 words, this episode is an example of the Hybrid Synergy methodology.

Table 2. Hybrid Synergy Episode I

Hybrid Synergy	Analysis
Information	Participant CC continued the issues about creating a blog from the chat discussion. He presented the reasons why he chose: • the specific host: the environment is in Greek • the blog as a tool as such: being able to write in Greek • the target: share ideas • specific title: be honest with the target • time of use: time of computers and Web 2.0, ergonomics and upgrading • ways of use: simple and experimental to start with
Social cues and emotions	• Dear CC… • Good luck! • Waiting for your news! • Time to return the favour and help you… • It will be great if you do it this way!
Ideas exploration	Based on CC's thoughts on the time of use, participant MV suggested starting with these specific issues. For example, describing and defining the concepts and suggesting examples to students. In this way, he will create a flow of thoughts that could lead to his answers without getting frustrated (justification). Participant JC suggested that instead of 'learning by doing' to try 'teaching from knowing it'. This means to attract students who actually work on the subject in the Secondary school and let them to teach it to the younger students using the blog (justification). JC continued by justifying the previous suggestion. She said that the students actually like doing this but we never let them (justification). She actually provided the way; i.e. by providing students with the main guidelines. Participant MV built on JC and suggested to CC that he should change the settings in the blog in order to allow the students to work this way.
Evaluation and assessment	• Excellent, CC! • Very good, CC! • Bravo! • Very good idea, JC, well done! • 2 comments already! Imagine having more resources! • Very good, CC!
Overviews	Participant NL agreed with all previous suggestions.

Social Web Wiki Episode

According to the diagrams (fig. 7 &8) below, the 4 e-learners with the highest number of wiki uploads during the course extended their activity to the community portal of the environment, thus producing a social collaborative learning episode.

As in the blog forum episode, the wiki community portal episode is based on the Hybrid Synergy model working upon common areas (i.e. social cues and emotions, evaluation and assessment, and overviews). This model also covers areas that reveal the propositional content of entries (information) expressing intended collaboration sustain (ideas exploration) and indicating the

Figure 7. Most active e-learners in the 'Environmental' wiki

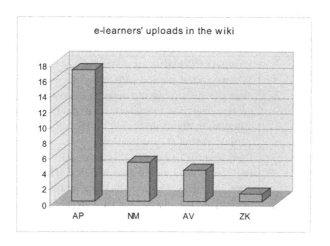

Figure 8. 'Environmental' wiki community portal: E-learners' contributions

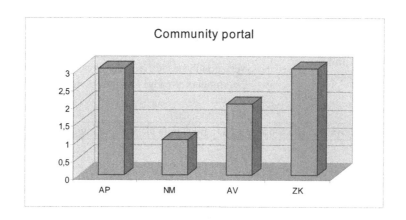

Table 3. Hybrid Synergy Episode II

Hybrid Synergy	Analysis
Information	Participant AP states the purpose of the wiki environment (communication, idea exchange, joint problem solving, socializing) AV informs his colleagues about a new upload and addresses a direct invitation for comments on his article; also he expresses his intention for further exploration of the issue (the ozone hole). ZK expresses her intention to expand networking capabilities through the introduction of a new tool; invites for ideas for conferencing meetings
Social cues and emotions	• Hello wiki co-e-learners!!! • Good morning, my name is ... • Good luck!!! • But I don't manage ...! Could someone help? • Did you like it (the upload)? • If not, please edit.
Ideas exploration	ZK gives the background and sets a problem (internal link entries). AP provides solutions and alternatives (e.g. using the 'help' hyperlink). ZK builds upon AP's suggestions and confirms digital skills development (text and image file uploads, link entries etc); also she checks her understanding of the wiki module task to be completed. AP sets a problem (page entries) NM offers an idea and elaborates by illustrating the meaning through details (internal hyperlink entries etc). AP elaborates on his idea of the wiki software and uses a metaphor to illustrate his intended meaning: the wiki is like 'syrtaki' dance; it starts slowly and gradually you get surprised by the crazy tune!!!
Evaluation and assessment	• Congratulations! • Wonderful article and very interesting links!!! • Congratulations on your initiative to set up this space for wiki members' communication facilitation!!! • So simply!
Overviews	All participants agreed on the quality of the work produced (encouragement, agreement, consensus)

participants' disposition as well as their (explicitly stated or implied) aim to work out joint solutions and to construct social bonds through a multiple networking experience.

Contrary to the blog episode, in which participant CC was the central figure as the discussion developed on the basis of his argumentation, the community portal contributions unveil multiple interaction foci: participant AP establishes a collaborative culture and explores the wiki software management, ZK introduces ideas for networking tools exploitation, and AV and NM invite their colleagues to evaluate and edit their entries, thus disclosing the emergent sense of trust among the members of the group.

Questionnaires

The questionnaires were sent to e-course participants via e-mail at the initial and the post-course phase and included closed and open items. As figure 9 shows, according to the analysis of closed items, teachers value positively the usability of the digital tool and the perspective of integrating its use in the teaching syllabus.

Similarly, teachers view positively the educational use of wiki as a tool enhancing collaboration towards the production of written speech while a high percentage of them (79%) assert that they frequently used the tool, as shown in figures 10 and 11 respectively.

Obviously, Greek teachers through the questionnaire responses acknowledge the perspective of pedagogical integration of the tool; yet, the fact that 15 of them (32%) make no explicit contributions in the open item area related to suggestions for implementation is indicative of a sense of embarrassment against this issue (fig. 11). In addition, the lack of effective descriptions or illustrations of terms, such as cross-curricular learning, project-based learning etc, referring to complex concepts, sustains this sense. This observation is in accordance with the analysis of overall participation data in the wiki module and also indicates that the applicability of tools in teaching and learning settings correlates with the degree of familiarization with the software and the development of cognitive and digital skills. The more skillful the user becomes with social web environments management, the more think-

Figure 9. Participants' responses in questionnaires (blog)

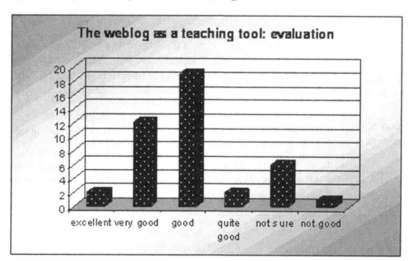

Figure 10. Participants' responses in questionnaires (wiki)

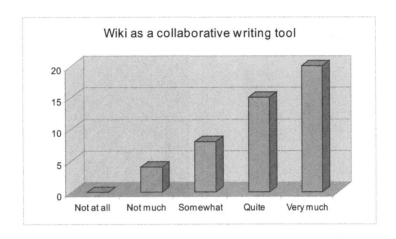

Figure 11. Participants' responses in questionnaires (wiki, frequency of use)

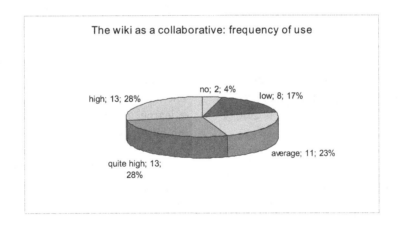

ing domains are activated (cognitive, aesthetic, emotional, value).

Overall, the analysis of responses to open questionnaire items concerning suggestions as to the exploitation of the tools in the educational field indicates that teachers mainly focused on four areas:

• Awareness (suggestions were made as to the need for institutionalized training on the use of the tools for blended learning purposes organized by the Ministry of education, teachers' unions etc; manual and newsletter development for teachers and students)

Figure 12. Participants' responses in questionnaires (wiki, future trends)

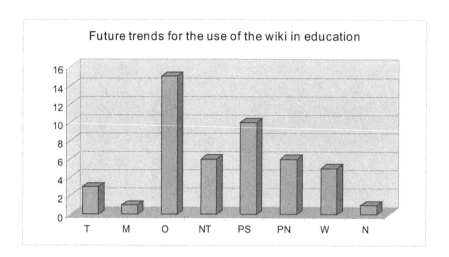

- Pedagogical integration and use (ideas were offered as to the use of the tools in project-based learning aiming to provide space for communication and collaboration among students)
- Safe navigation (worries were expressed and suggestions were offered concerning the development of a security policy against offensive and inappropriate content)
- Software development (e.g. suggestions were offered for new themes development, file upload, multimedia embedment)

DISCUSSION

From an educational perspective, research findings not only bear implications for online course design but also indicate the dynamics of blogs and wikis as social web environments and the potential of their pedagogical use. Qualities, such as multidisciplinarity, that characterise the

social web and reinforce user governance over the medium, accord with educational principles. The multidisciplinary character of participants' (e-learner and e-tutor) group composition did not inhibit the learning process; on the contrary, it encouraged interaction in virtual classroom and social web activities while the exchange of knowledge deriving from diverse areas of expertise enriched the intellectual capital produced within the community.

Moreover, data analysis gathered from the study clearly shows that the Greek teachers involved in the Project Method e-course evaluate highly Web 2.0 tools and favour their integration into school curricula to supplement conventional classroom practices; and into networked educational settings in order to keep informed, to share, to communicate. Certainly, there are still numerous parameters that need to be investigated, such as the role of personality and learning style in the selection and effective use of online learning technologies. In this way, we will be able to draw conclusions as to the degree to which 'change' and 'becoming' have been attained. To this end, it is essential that we experiment, gain new experience, evaluate, and test new hypotheses on a systematic basis, if we aim for educational frameworks founded on a value system that promotes reflective participation and active citizenship. Therefore, future research orientation might include areas such as:

- the use of weblogs and wikis as learning tools in blended situations and in groups of learners with specific interests,
- the development of multi-authored blogs for collaborative learning purposes,
- the integration of multimedia into Web 2.0 environments and their role in learning and a
- longitudinal study where the practice of e-learners can be measured and researched across timeframes beyond a single semester.

The analysis of data also offers insight to online community evolution into a self-regulatory, self-organised entity, able to transform and expand depending on the members' priorities, interests and needs. The Community of Interest that formed during the first phase of the e-course transformed into a Community of Practice in the second phase, as new teaching practises emerged and stronger social bonds were constructed. The community was built on an equalitarian model reflecting the democratic ideals of open, non-hierarchical participation, relying on the members' volition, knowledge repertoire and skilfulness as well as the strong wish to explore new, virtual worlds, thus transferring the dialogue from face-to-face interaction to the social web and vice versa. This new type of sociality was first launched in the Moodle environment and was subsequently injected into the social web through blogs and wikis. Blending formal (virtual classroom activities) and informal (social web activities) elements

in the course facilitated the evolutionary process. In it, e-tutors acted as mediators between the two types of learning using academic and empirical knowledge, a role normally assumed by online community moderators. The dynamic development of the e-tutors' group, which is built upon the same principle of participation, sharing, expertise and initiative, followed the transformation of the larger community and the transition into innovative networked schemes in the social web.

The core educational online community generated multiple networked schemes of online communication, collaboration and knowledge building. During the period following course conclusion and until the time of writing this chapter, participants have enhanced their web presence by setting up new blogs with increased interaction, have made new connections and have become involved in projects (e.g. training in ICTs) giving them the opportunity to create new agendas for professional development. These networks constitute evolutionary stages and sustain the viability of the educational community being based on its member's initiative and action. This whole operation brought innovations in the overall Greek educational context, such as the announcement of a contest for students-bloggers in primary and secondary education (http://www.kseblogare.gr/) and generated the expressed need for training in using Web 2.0 tools. Also the decision of the Greek educational authorities to institutionalise the use of weblogs through the setting up of a blogging platform in the Greek Schools Network portal (http://blogs.sch.gr/) manifests the interplay between the real and the virtual and indicates a bottom-up innovation opening up new perspectives for Greek teachers. Today there are 168 blogs (http://blogs.sch.gr/allblogs/) in this growing community, the policy of which allows students to participate and create their own blogs.

As it became evident through the study, this dominance of blogs over wikis is a phenomenon that can be attributed to factors such as software complexity. Yet, we believe that the power of blogs can be also justified through the consideration of another factor: building and maintaining a blog gives the opportunity to users to create their own narrative and build own biographies, thus constructing a self-identity, an online one. Through this process active users gradually create a distributed, multiple and coherent presence (Turkle, 1995). By becoming skilful active social web participants, users build networked communities, thus constructing the narrative of the collective. Collective identities, although highly diversified (Castells, 1997), are essential for social transformation when existing structure can no longer satisfy people's needs.

CONCLUSION

The rise of the social web has taken place during an era that requires the redefinition of self-identity. At the same time the virtual world provides a complex set of relationships, opportunities for exploration and a context where a new identity emerges through the blending of distributed presence online. Despite limitations arising from the need for a representative sample, which affects the generalisation of conclusions, the study of the Greek teachers' learning community provides evidence that Greek teachers, having established a coherent, interactive and reflective web presence, are in the process of building networked communities. These virtual schemes encapsulate their members' experiences and generate new practices, ideas and values. Through this process the online self-identity acquires new qualities and becomes more concrete while a collective identity becomes apparent.

This study is actually a first attempt to interpret the mechanisms that led to the evolution of the core Greek educational community of learning and collaboration; yet, it provides initial evidence of the fact that the social web ideal depends on three major factors: the individual, the collective and the medium. From an educational perpective,

a pedagogical scenario for the establishment of a collaborative learning community should involve:

- an awareness of social software and tools developments
- an awareness of and sensitisation to participants' needs and expectations,
- a holistic approach towards learning as a process within a social context and
- an integrative approach to life as a reflective, social and political act.

Being the change process of constructing a sense of identity (Wiszniewski et al., 2002) and the context aiming for the promotion of democratic participation and active citizenship, education can play a significant role in the process of approaching the ideal within dynamic networked communities aiming to serve this goal.

REFERENCES

Allan, B., Lewis, D., (2006). Virtual learning communities as a vehicle for workforce development: A case study. *Journal of Workplace Learning, 1356-5626, Vol. 18 (6) pp 367-383.*

Baudrillard, J. (2002). Between Difference and Singularity: An open discussion with Jean Baudrillard. Available: http://www.egs.edu/faculty/baudrillard/baudrillard-between-difference-and-singularity-2002.html. Retrieved: 02-10-07.

Bauwens, M. (2005) Peer to Peer and Human Evolution. Available online: http://integralvisioning.org/article.php?story=p2ptheory1. Retrieved: 6-04-08

Beck, U. (1999). *Individualization.* London: Sage.

Calvert, S. L. (2002). Identity Construction on the Internet. In S. L. Calvert, A. B. Jordan & R.

R. Cocking (Eds.), Children in the Digital Age: Influences of Electronic Media on Development (pp. 57 - 70). Wesport, Connecticut: Praeger.

Castells, M. (1997). *The Power of Identity.* Oxford: Blackwell.

Coleman, G. (2008). Toward a positive critique of the social web. Available online: http://www.re-public.gr/en/?p=288. Retrieved: 6-04-08.

Dillenbourg, P., Baker, M., Blaye, A. & O'Malley, C. (1996). The evolution of research on collaborative learning. In E. Spada & P. Reiman (Eds) *Learning in Humans and Machine: Towards an interdisciplinary learning science.* (pp. 189-211). Oxford: Elsevier.

Dillenbourg, P. (1999). What do you mean by collaborative learning?. In P. Dillenbourg (Ed) *Collaborative-learning: Cognitive and Computational Approaches.* (pp.1-19). Oxford: Elsevier.

Downes, S. (2007). E-Learning 2.0 in Development. Brandon Hall Conference, San Jose, September 25, 2007. Available: http://www.downes.ca/. Retrieved: 02-10-07.

Efimova, L. (2004). Discovering the iceberg of knowledge work: a weblog case. Proceedings of Fifth European Conference on Organizational Knowledge, Learning and Capabilities (OKLC04), Innsbruck, 2-3 April 2004.

Efimova, L. and S. Hendrick (2005). In Search for a virtual settlement: An exploration of weblog community boundaries. Communities and Technologies 05. Available: https://doc.telin.nl /dscgi/ds.py/Get/File-46041. Retrieved: 07-09-07.

Eide F., and Eide B. (2005). Brain of the Blogger. Available: . Retrieved: 03-09-07.

Erikson, E. H. (1993). Childhood and Society. New York: W.W. Norton & Company.

Freud, S. (1989). Civilization and Its Discontents. New York: W.W. Norton & Company.

Frey, K. (1987). *The project method.* Thessaloniki: Kyriakidis (in Greek).

Fromm, E. (2003). Man for Himself, an Inquiry into the Psychology of Ethics. Routledge

Garrison, D. R., Anderson, T., & Archer, W. (2001). Critical thinking, cognitive presence, and computer conferencing in distance education. *American Journal of Distance Education 15*(1), 7-23.

Gee, J. P. (1999). *An introduction to discourse analysis: theory and method.* London: Routledge

Giddens, A. (1991). Modernity and Self-identity: Self and Society in the Late Modern Age. Cambridge, UK: Polity Press

Guskey, T. R. (2002). Does It Make a Difference? Evaluating Professional Development. Educational Leadership, 59(6), 45-51.

Huffaker, D. (2004). Gender similarities and differences in online identity and language use among teenage bloggers. Unpublished MA Thesis. Available online:

Koschmann, T. (1996). Paradigm shifts and instructional technology: An introduction, In T. Koschmann (Ed.), CSCL: Theory and practice of an emerging paradigm, 1-23, Mahwah, NJ: Lawrence Erlbaum Associates.

Lambropoulos, N., Kampylis, P., Papadimitriou, S., Vivitsou M., Gkikas, A. Minaoglou, N. & Konetas, D. (2008). Hybrid Synergy for Virtual Knowledge Working. In Salmons, J. & Wilson L. (Eds) (2008), Handbook of Research on Electronic Collaboration and Organizational Synergy, Hershey, PA, USA: IGI Global Publications.

Lieberman, A. (2000). Networks as learning communities: Shaping the future of teacher development. *Journal of Teacher Education, Vol. 51, No. 3, May/June 2000, 221-227.* American Association of Colleges for Teacher Education

Mezirow, J. (2003). Transformative Learning as Discourse. *Journal of ransformative Education, Vol.1, No 1, Jan. 2003, 58-63.* London: Sage publications.

Philip, D. (2007). The Knowledge Building paradigm: A model of learning for Net Generation students. *Innovate* 3 (5). Available: http://www.innovateonline.info /index.php?view=article&id=368. Retrieved: 06-07-07.

Potter, J. W. (2005). Media Literacy. Sage Publications: London.

Rheingold, H. (1993). *The Virtual Community.* Reading: Addison-Wesley.

Roschelle, J. & Teasley S.D. (1995). The construction of shared knowledge in collaborative problem solving. In C.E. O'Malley (Ed), *Computer-Supported Collaborative Learning.* (pp. 69-197). Berlin: Springer-Verlag.

Scardamalia, M., & Bereiter, C. (1991). Higher levels of agency in knowledge building: A challenge for the design of new knowledge media. *Journal of the Learning Sciences, 1,* 37-68.

Sessums, C. (2006). Weblogging and teacher learning: getting the most out of the online social networks. Available: http://eduspaces.net/csessums/weblog/134953.html. Retrieved: 31-08-07.

Siemens, G. (2004). Connectivism: A Learning Theory for the Digital Age. Available: http://www.elearnspace.org/Articles/connectivism.htm (updated: 05-04-2005). Retrieved: 02-10-07.

Scholz, T. & Hartzog, P. (2008). Toward a critique of the social web. Online interview available: http://www.re-public.gr/en/?p=201. Retrieved: 6-04-08.

Turkle, S. (1995). *Life on the Screen: Identity in the Age of the Internet.* New York: Simon and Schuster.

Vivitsou, M., Lambropoulos, N., Konetas, D., Paraskevas, M., Grigoropoulos, E. (2008). The Project

Method e-course: the use of tools towards the evolution of the Greek teachers' online community. *Int. J. Cont. Engineering Education and Lifelong Learning,* Inderscience Enterprises Ltd.

Vygotsky, L. (1978). *Mind in society.* Cambridge, MA: Harvard University Press.

Warlick, D. (2005). Four reasons why the blogsphere might make a better professional collaborative environment than discussion forums. Available: http://davidwarlick.com/2cents/2005/08/15/four-reasons-why-the-blogsphere-might-make-a-better-professional-collaborative-environment-than-discussion-forums/. Retrieved: 31-08-07.

Wegerif, R. (2006). A Dialogic Understanding of the Relationship between CSCL and Teaching Thinking Skills. Computer Supported Learning, Springer Science and Business Media, Inc.

Wiszniewski, D., & Coyne, R. (2002). Mask and Identity: The Hermeneutics of Self-Construction in the Information Age. In K. Ann Renninger & Wesley Shumar (Ed.) Building Virtual Communities (pp. 191-214). New York, New York: Cambridge Press.

Wittel, A. (2001). Toward a Network Sociality. *Theory, Culture & Society, Vol. 18(6): 51–76.* London: SAGE

ENDNOTE

[1] The Social Web refers to two related concepts: a description of web 2.0 technologies that are focused on social interaction and a proposal for a future network similar to the World Wide Web (http://en.wikipedia.org/wiki/Social_Web#The_Social_Web_as_a_future_network)

Chapter X
Knowing in Organizations:
Pheno–Practical Perspectives

Wendelin Kupers
Massey University, New Zealand

ABSTRACT

Based on a phenomenological understanding of knowing and knowledge in organisation, this chapter aims to contribute to an integral perspective on conceptual and methodological research development. Adopting an advanced phenomenological approach, knowing is argued to be an embodied and emotional process. Furthermore, an integral "pheno-practice" is proposed, allowing a more comprehensive and inclusive approach, analyse, and interpretation for investigating processes of knowing in organisations. Following a dynamic, processual turn, the concept of an "inter-knowing" is discussed by which knowing is understood as a relational emerging event. By concluding, some implications for theory and research are provided.

INTRODUCTION

The contemporary debates concerning knowledge in organisations represent a heterogeneous discourse involving many different perspectives. The 'nature' of knowledge, the degree to which knowledge is separable from or related to practice, where knowledge resides, and the status and relation of explicit and implicit knowledge are investigated and interpreted in diverse ways. Basically knowledge is a necessary constituent for business activities, added-value and organisational competitiveness. Consequently, it has become operationalised in a plethora of so called "Knowledge Management" concepts and strategies with corresponding application in the business practice. This has led to various agreements or disagreements and critiques among researchers concerning the ontological, epistemological, and political dimensions involved (e.g. Choo, 1998; Easterby-Smith & Lyles, 2003; Styhre, 2003). Such debates have stimulated an on-going search

Copyright © 2009, IGI Global, distributing in print or electronic forms without written permission of IGI Global is prohibited.

for criteria for evaluating approaches, frameworks and methodologies with regard to various knowledge management issues (e.g. Assudani, 2005; Metaxiotis, et al., 2005) and balanced reviews (e.g. Despres & Chauvel, 2000).

However, much of the current literature about the knowledge-based economy and knowledge-management has been predicated upon reductionistic assumptions about the nature of knowledge. Reductionistically, organisational knowledge is conceptualised either as a codified and transferable asset, that is as an "object"; or as generated by an autonomous subject or inter-subjective interactions. Following either "objective" or "(inter-)subjective" orientations, different types of knowledge have been identified and examined "taxonomically" (Tsoukas, 1996, 13). What prevails in conventional discourses are various classifying distinctions and dichotomies of dualistic thinking about knowledge (e.g. Grant, 1996; Nonaka & Takeuchi, 1995, Teece, 1998). With this, knowledge are understood either as resource or as process, as "objective" or "subjective", as implicit or explicit, as internal or external, immanent or transcendent etc. Furthermore, with cognitive bias, bodily and emotional dimensions of knowing are misinterpreted or seen merely as pragmatic functions to get more effective means for generating, sharing, and managing knowledge in organizations.

Both underlying paradigms - the empiristic-objective tradition of "realism" and the rationalistic-subjective discourse of "idealism" and representationalism (Aadne, et al., 1996) - are eminently limited and problematic in their one-sidedness (Merleau-Ponty, 1962, 28). A great many of current approaches to knowledge management hold to these paradigmatic underpinnings and are primarily rational in orientation, thus neglecting or underestimating bodily and emotional aspects. What is needed instead a more inclusive and processual understanding of knowing and knowledge and integration of embodied and emotional dimensions. The challenge will be to consider

the experiential constituencies of the knowing process and to see where and how the objectifying codification and entitative approaches reduce these constituencies to some simplistic "subject-object" constructs. For developing a more integral approach and practice of knowledge management and research about the underlying dynamics, we need to shift from the prevailing modes of thinking. Accordingly, the aim of the following is to contribute to a conceptual and methodological research development of knowing and knowledge in organisations.

Specifically, this chapter tries to show in particular how advanced phenomenology (Merleau-Ponty, 1962, 1995) helps to reach a deeper understanding of organisational knowledge, by rearticulating an account of the lived body and emotions in relation to knowing. Based on a phenomenology of embodied and emotional knowing, a corresponding integral "pheno-practice" will be presented. Integral pheno-practice offers a conceptual framework and methodological map for generating a more comprehensive analysis and interpretation of knowing in organisations. Following a processual turn, perspectives on what will be called "inter-knowing" will be outlined. Finally, some implications and research perspectives will be discussed.

PHENOMENOLOGY OF THE KNOWING BODY AND EMBODIED "KNOWLEDGE"

In general, phenomenology represents a philosophical discipline that has been has been central to the tradition of continental European thinking throughout the 20th century and still provides a relevant contemporary purview (e.g. Hammond et al. 1995; Küpers 2008; Macann 1993). Literally, "phenomenology" is the study of "phenomena": that is, the appearances of things as they appear in human experience. Thus, it concerns ways how humans experience phenomena and meanings involved. The very term "phenomeno-logy" itself, is derived from the two Greek words "phainom-enon" (an "appearance") and "logos" ("reason" or word", hence a "reasoned inquiry"). Accordingly, phenomenology is a reasoned inquiry; a method of scientific philosophy in general, which tries to discover the essences of appearances, that is, to anything of which human beings can become conscious. Classical phenomenology - as initiated by Edmund Husserl (1859 – 1938) approaches phenomena by studying conscious experience from the "subjective" or "first person point of view" along with relevant conditions and horizons of experience within the unified field of a person's consciousness and existence. The inspiration of phenomenology has undergone significant development and change through the work of different successors. Various criticisms have been raised concerning the limitations of classical phenomenology, including the retained implicit Cartesianism, transcendental idealism, essentialism, monism and solipsism (Küpers 2008). Advanced (post-Husserlian) phenomenology attempts to overcome many of these limitations. For example, one important further development is represented by Alfred Schütz's (1899-1959) "mundaned" social phenomenology of acting respectively a phenomenology of the social world (Schütz 1972).

Phenomenology has been used as a new way of viewing organizational research and as a qualitative research approach that seeks to make explicit the implicit structure and meaning of human experience and meaning in organizational life-worlds (Sanders, 1982). "Applied phenomenology" has been related to different other issues of organizations (Harmon, 1990)[a], by which members within organizations are understood as active, intentional, and social. Accordingly it has been used in studies on qualitative research in organizational behavior (e.g. Burgoyne and Hodgson, 1983), and research on organizational culture (e.g. Allaire and Firsirotu, 1984) as well as organizational development (White, 1990).

From a phenomenological perspective, organisations are life-worlds, in which also processes of organising and knowing take place through experiential processes. Phenomenologically, the main intention is to go back to "knowing it-self", to the present, living act of knowing as embedded practice and process. To return to things themselves and to their life-worldly situatedness is to turn to that world, which precedes knowledge, of which knowledge always speaks, and in relation to which every scientific schematization is an abstract and derivative sign-language, "as is geography in relation to the countryside in which we have learnt beforehand what a forest, a prairie, or a river is" (Merleau-Ponty, 1962, ix). Returning to such life-worldly knowing is to relate to a meaningful world, in which an embodied knower meets and co-creates with her lived-in experience the like-wise embodied known. Thus, phenomenologically all knowledge is always embodied and mediated by the living process of knowing.

EMBODIED KNOWING: ADVANCED PHENOMENOLOGY OF MERLEAU-PONTY

The advanced phenomenology of Merleau-Ponty (1962, 1995) offers an important interpretative approach for assessing the interlacing role of bodily, perceptual and expressive dimensions involved in knowing. According to this phenomenologist we are first and foremost embodied beings. We are both a part of the world and coextensive with it, constituting but also constituted (Merleau-Ponty 1962, 453). We find the life-world meaningful primarily with respect to the ways in which we act within it, and which acts upon us as engaged and perceiving "body-subjects" (Crossley, 1996, 101). This kind of acting and enactment implies that we can never know about things or encounters independent of our lived experiences as "bodily-interwined" beings. With this orientation "embodiment" does not simply mean "physical manifestation." Rather, it means that the knower is being "grounded" in everyday, mundane experience and integrally connected to herself and her environment in an ongoing sensual inter-relation.

The knowing subject of the organising processes is situated in his or her environment in a tactile, visual, olfactory or auditory way through their embodied selves. Whatever s/he thinks, feels or does, s/he are exposed to a synchronised field of inter-related senses (Merleau-Ponty, 1962, 207). S/he lives in the midst of a world of touch, sight, smell, and sound. It is through the body that members the organisational processes directly reach their perceived and handled "objects" and relations at work. Moreover they "know" while being situated pre-reflectively and spontaneously in accordance with their bodies and within their embodiment. For this reason, the embodied experience and knowing practices are built upon an original, ambiguous "ground" or genuine horizon on which the knower perceives and "body-forths" his or her possibilities into the world, in which s/he is enmeshed. These primordial constituents of the lived world are not (only) "objective" properties, but situated modes of "being-in-the-world". Consequently, these situations are as much part of the "subject" as they are of the "world". Moreover, both the "subject-side" and the "object-side" are inextricably linked to each other through an embodied pre-reflexive, yet active communion with the world.

From an advanced phenomenological perspective, not only is knowing embodied, but being embodied is always already a way of knowing and acting through "lived situations". Within this situatedness, the "living body" mediates between "internal" and "external" or "subjective" and "objective" as well "individual" and "collective" experiences and meanings of knowing. This body-mediated knowing coordinates the relations between individual behaviour, social relations and 'artefacts, and 'institutions', including language and communication as expressive media (Merleau-Ponty, 1962, 197). Thus, it is the vivid body and the embodiment which "knows" and understands experientially. Knowing, then, is seen as a "function" and emergent process of a "bodily subject" and embodied situatedness. It is an embodied life-world, in which knower and knowing are actively involved and passively taking part. Therefore, neither "subjective", "inter-subjective" nor "objective" dimensions can be isolated from the dynamics of intermediated, embodied knowing. This view of knowing as an encroachment and infringement between knower and known directs individual perception and actions as well as inter-subjective knowing and "objective knowledge" in a fluid, integrative fashion. Thus the corporeally constituted status of perceiving knowers, with their embodied "pre-interpretation" and situated embedment, provides a profound ontological and epistemological as well methodological base for approaching and interpreting knowing also in organisations.

However, the body and embodiment have been marginalised as medium of organisational practice and theory (Hassard, et al., 2000; Casey, 2000). Facing the prevailing separation of body and consciousness (Dale & Burrell, 2000; Dale, 2001) and considering the "absent presence" of the body (Leder, 1990; Shilling, 1993) in social and organisational theory, there is a need for a "re-membering" between body, embodiment and organisations. Only this re-joining allows re-integrating lived, embodied experiences and processes of knowing. Following the embodied turn in social and organisational science (Hassard, et al., 2000, 12), advanced phenomenology offers possibilities for developing such an understanding of a (re-)embodied organisation (Styhre, 2004) and corresponding embodied knowing as a specific practice.

EMBODIED INTENTION AND RESPONSIVENESS WITHIN KNOWING AS PRACTICE

In order to approach processes of knowing, they can be understood as embodied intention and responsiveness. All organizing processes involve encounters between bodies that are oriented, from or towards a specific point of seeing feeling, hearing or touching and acting. With an intentional and responsive orientation of the bodily organs and consciousness, the agent within the sphere of knowing does not feel primarily only "I think", but also "I relate to" or "I do" (Macmurray, 1957, 84). In other words, the atmosphere within knowing is situated is not only what people "think about" it, but primarily what they "live through" with their "operative intentionality" (Merleau-Ponty, 1962, xviii) and within a "responsive order" (Gendlin, 1997). This implies that the "I can" (or cannot) - and "I feel" (or don't feel) - precedes and conditions the possibility of the "I know" (Merleau-Ponty, 1962, 137). With this understanding of embodied-based knowing, there is a close link between what is intended and what is actually given, between intention, and the knowing situation and corresponding responses.

As a living body, the "knower" not only intends, but also responds to meaningful questions, problems or claims posed to him through embodied conditions and situational contexts. Therefore, studying processes of knowing in organizations requires capturing a sense of "phenomenological presence" and considering life-worldly practices, both as source and "outcome" of human knowing. As we have seen knowing arises from direct and engaged participation in the embodied act of organising. Accordingly, phenomenology is an appropriate "praxis philosophy", in that it makes theory of action and engagement primary, preceding and grounding all theory of knowing and "knowledge". This understanding of practise

("praxis") corresponds to the 'practice turn' in contemporary theory (Schatzki, et al., 2001), and practice-based theorizing on knowing-in-organising (Blackler, 1995; Gherardi, 2000). Practice-oriented approaches to knowing, organizing, knowing, learning, action and practice are all mutually constitutive processes (Gherardi, 2001; Nicolini, et al., 2003). They are all part of the micro dynamics of a "knowledge-in-use". As an on-going "individual" and "social" accomplishment and dynamic process, knowing is not a static embedded capability or stable disposition of actors, but constituted and reconstituted in the dynamics of everyday practice, hence a "knowing-in-practice" or "knowing-as-doing" (Orlikowski, 2002, 252, 271). As capacity to act, knowing is the ability of actors to 'intervene' or to "let go" in a flow of action, respectively to change the course of events in situated contexts. These again consist of embodied, historical, social, and cultural "con-+-Texts" (Küpers, 2008), in which knowing manifests in a variety of forms, and by use of different media. Practices of knowing are circumscribed as a bricolage of material, mental, social and cultural resources (Gherardi, 2001). Therefore, the meaning of everyday practices of knowing is related to local ways of knowing. Thus, we do not experience our practice as "knowledge"; rather we realise our practice as experience, and "experience is knowing" (Levinas, 1969, 62). 'Meanings of knowing' and a 'knowing of meanings' are both "found in" the world and co-created by embodied "subjects" and their active dealings with themselves, other "subjects" and "objects'". In an embodied state of being, the material and the ideational, the active and the passive are intimately linked. Therefore knowing as practice cannot be conflated into merely isolated "object" or "subject"-bound paradigm, for "there is no meaning which is not embodied, nor any matter that is not meaningful" (Crossley, 1994, 14). Not only does the "knowing body" provide an access to the world; but "knowledge" and processes of knowing inhere also in the "things" themselves and within concrete lived action (Schön 1983, 49). Therefore, any "knowledge base" of an organisation does not only include "bodies of knowledge", but also "knowing" and "knowledgeable bodies"; not only enacted "knowledge" but also "knowledge" that is already action, not only situated and contextual knowledge, but also knowledge that inheres in situations and relations. The following table summarizes in an 'ideal-typical' contrasting way, conventional and phenomenological view on knowledge and knowing:

The phenomenological approach has gained popularity particularly in clinical practice and among nurse researchers, investigating empirical,

personal, and socio-political nursing knowledge development and utilization of that knowledge in practice (van der Zalm & Bergum 2000). Furthermore, Orr's ethnographic study (1996) showed the enacted practices and embodied knowledge by repair technicians in their every-day dealings by using stories (non canonical knowledge) and not the manual (the canonical knowledge). Narratives provide sense-making devices and foster knowledge transfer: knowledge is created day-by-day through problem solving and maintained through the circulation of success stories which contributes to building the technician's identity as a competent worker. Using a phenomenological approach Patriotta (2003a,b) explored empirically narrative-based processes of sense-making and

Table 1. Conventional and phenomenological views on knowledge and knowing

	Conventional focus on decontextualised knowledge	**Phenomenological focus on embodied knowing**
Framing of Research / Status of knowledge	Knowledge as asset is disembodied	Knowing as process is always already embodied
	Dichotomizing objective or (inter-)subjective knowledge; duality of interior and exterior, knower and known	Post-dichotomous encroachment and infringement of knowing *between* subject and object, inside and outside, knower and known.
Status of body and embodiment	Privileging of the disembodied intellect leads to an epistemological preoccupation with a particular form of knowledge where the body only figures as a necessary yet cumbersome intermediary.	Living body and embodiment are both constitutive and inter-mediating media and "subject" of knowing and "knowledge"
Basic Orientation	Instrumental and objective orientation, following logic of efficiency and control	Embodied intention and responsiveness within life-world as source and "outcome" of knowing
Relation to praxis	Separation between knowledge and praxis as each having distinct identity	Inter-Relation between knowing & acting; praxis of "knowledge-in-use" & "knowing-as-doing" in situated practice
	"Bodies of knowledge" opposite of the world	"Knowing" and "knowledgeable bodies" being-in-the-world

organisational knowledge in the making that is creation, utilization, and institutionalization within the 'life world' of organizations (Küpers 2006). Pentland (1992) has empirically shown how knowledge and action cannot be separated in service operations. His study of software support hot lines showed also that situations are the most appropriate level for and "moves" as unit of analysis. Actually, the situation provides the point of contact between the individual and the organisation (Pentland 1992: 529). Adopting a phenomenological perspective also Dall'Alba and Barnacle (2005), have empirically explored the notion of embodied knowing as it relates to higher education programs and, more specifically, the ways in which information and communication technologies are used in these programs. Also Friesen (2002) provides an account of how presence and embodiment can be experienced in an online course in a way that brings to the fore some opportunities and limits of the human-technology relation in question.

PHENOMENOLOGY OF E-MOTIONAL KNOWING

The outlined embodied orientation needs further also to "re-turn" to fundamental questions concerning the emotion-related quality of knowing, to the felt practices and relationships of the knower that is to emotional knowing. Phenomenologically, feelings, emotions and moods are basic structures and processes of human existence in general and organising and knowing in particular. Emotions and an emotional atmosphere permeate almost all ways of self-knowledge and social transactions within organisations. Being a vital part of organisational life, emotions inform, shape and reflect the life-world of organizations (Fineman, 2000, 2003). As emotions are an immutable part of everyday life they also influence the process of knowing and ways of developing and dealing it. Hence, the way members of organisations can

or do feel angry, guilty, envious, or satisfied, proud etc. co-determines the quality of knowing processes in organisational settings. Moreover, as an essential dimension of organisational culture (van Maanen & Kunda, 1989), emotions do not just have an impact on "knowledge", but co-constitute the knowing process itself.

"Emotion" – like the body – has been a neglected topic in the organizational behaviour literature (Muchinsky, 2000) as well as in studies of organisation (Fineman, 2003; Küpers & Weibler 2005) and knowledge management (Spender, 2003). In organisational research on and practice emotions have been consistently marginalized, devalued as illegitimate or inappropriate to organisational life, while a dis-embedded and/or disembodied rationality is privileged (Putnam & Mumby, 1993, 39). Specifically, emotions have been and are still seen as disturbing and interfering factors (Oatley & Johnson-Laird, 1987, 30) or as a barrier to rational and effective organisation and management (Ashforth & Humphrey, 1995). Seen as incalculable and irrational as well as unruly, undesirable culprits, emotion are eliminated, contained or controlled and managed in the workplace. This is done in order to reduce unpredictability, and ensure rationality and order incompatible with modern economic reasoning, which is separating the (masculine) "rational" and the (female)"emotional" as incompatible and binary opposites (Parkin, 1993).

Despite the increased theoretical and empirical attention given to emotion in various disciplines, much disagreement remains on precisely how emotion should be defined. Emotion is a dynamic and multi-dimensional event that eludes mainstream scientific treatment (Kleinginna & Kleinginna, 1981).

Phenomenologically, one central attribute of emotions is that they are directed toward or engaged with the world and include self and others in a "moving" way. The very term 'emotion' is derived from the Latin, "e-movere", "e-motum"; that is "to move out." This kinaesthetic understanding already refers to the fact that to experience an emotion is to realize or to 'enact' an intentional and responsive world relation. Emerging as 'potential movement' implies a particular bodily, relational and transformational orientation to the world and to others. Thus, emotions can be considered as dynamical dispositions for and realisation of intentions, expressions and actions, rather than only some inner state of being or set of beliefs about the world.

In terms of a phenomenology related to body-based "e-motions" (Mazis, 1993), "feeling" presupposes an embodied, tactile sensitivity. Accordingly, "feeling" refers to a "felt sense" which is encompasses bodily sensation and intention. Emotionality then refers to the ways sensations-feelings emotions are integrated in lived experience (Denzin, 1984, 113-120). Contrary to naturalistic or essentialist views, emotions are irreducible to their physiological and/or psychological components. Furthermore, emotions are always situated in historical and social contexts (Stein & Trabasso, 1992). However, they are realised not only as a mere "cultural constructions" (Gergen, 1994, 221), but are always an embodied and expressive, hence living communicative process (Merleau-Ponty, 1962). Another important function of emotion is that it involves evaluations. As a kind of value judgment, emotions attached significance to external phenomena and, in so doing, affect such things as goals and our intended goals and the prioritisation. This implies that emotions are ways of seeing patterns of salience among objects of attention, lines of inquiry, and inferential approaches (de Sousa, 1987). They assist in finding, creating and employing appropriate strategies (Solomon, 1980). For example Perrone and Vickers (2004) have shown in a larger phenomenological study that employees use feelings as a strategic tools of defence against a vindictive, aggressive and hostile work place as a protective response. As a kind of "embodied cognition" emotions reduce the number of alternatives that need to be considered by sifting out options that are irrelevant.

By this kind of appraisal they are increasing the accuracy and efficiency of deliberative processes and thereby have particular importance in the context of knowing within organisations.

EMOTION AND KNOWING IN ORGANISATIONS

As many knowledge management approaches take a mental and representationalistic perspective and emotional dimensions and the interplay between emotional and rational processes are often undervalued. It seems that for a long time there has existed a "autism of knowledge management" (Lambe, 2002) in relation to the "uncomfortable knowledge" of emotional dimensions of knowing. Such a situation recognises neither the actual working environment as an experiential life-world nor the emotion-based knowing process itself. Moreover, the lack of integrating emotions may also be responsible for sub-optimal knowledge (management) processes and performances.

However, as "presentational" acts, emotions influence the way that members of organizations perceive, develop, interpret, control, evaluate and resist their organisational actions (Waldron, 1994), and, hence, they also shape the process of knowing and knowledge. Thus emotions co-constitute, energise and organise co-ordinated states, and focus the energies of an organization and its members. Correspondingly, emotion "intermediate" important opportunities for creating, developing, sharing and evaluating knowing and knowledge. Not only do knowledge deficiencies produce emotional responses as they 'arrest' rational decision making (Spender, 2003). Emotions contribute crucially for defining ends and priorities while generating and using knowledge as well as influencing information-processing mechanisms (Öhmann 1992).

Similar as for the process of learning (Vince 2001, 2002) emotions exert specific influences and effects on the knowing and practices of "knowledge management". These influences can be helpful or harmful, depending on the kind of emotions and the respective context involved. Following Scherer and Tran (2001, 385) the next table groups various emotions into five major classes, which all have both positive and negative effects on knowing of individuals, groups and the entire organisations:

A blend of theses various classes of emotion, particularly with regard to the positive effects, is what fosters optimal knowing processes, depending on the situation in which an organization itself and its members find themselves, e.g. the role of emotions or emotional capabilities and performances in knowledge-intensive work groups (Reus, 2004) or the on a broader level the quality of an emotional climate (Tran, 1998). Both embodied and emotional knowing are emerging out of processual nexus that require to be approached by an integral "pheno-practice" of knowing, outlined in the following.

INTEGRAL "PHENO-PRACTICE" OF KNOWING

As we have seen, understanding and enacting knowing in organisations demands a comprehensive, practice-oriented approach that is suited to investigating the complex, inter-related processes involved. What is required is a more pluralist epistemology (Spender, 1998) that takes an integral perspective on knowing. In moving towards this, the following presents an integral "pheno-practice" of embodied and emotional knowing. This "pheno-practice" is understood as a special employment and application of (advanced) phenomenology (Küpers, 2008). Like classical phenomenology, pheno-practice is basically driven by the intention to clarify and understand what is at issue; that is, what appears as phenomena, here of knowing. In the present case, what appears as phenomena with regard to the complex inter-relating process of knowing and its various

Table 2. Effects of emotions on knowing (Scherer & Tran, 2001, 385, modified)

• **Approach emotion** (interest, hope, joyful anticipation); Effects: foster exploration and development of knowledge, provide motivational underpinning for sustained goal-directed activity of e.g. knowledge acquisition and generation
• **Achievement emotions** (relief, satisfaction, contentment, joy, pride, elation); Effects: positively reinforce knowing processes, and sharing of knowledge, responses to positive chance outcome may imply over-attribution of personal merit and encourage stagnation;
• **Deterrence emotion** (anxiety, fear, distress, pessimism); Effects: serve as warning of imminent danger or negative consequences based on generalizations from past experiences; may prevent further development, block exploration, and generally inhibit knowing and learning processes;
• **Withdrawal emotions** (sadness, resignation, shame, guilt); Effects: serve to facilitate restoration of forces and internal adaptation after an uncontrollable loss or the discovery of a major personal shortcoming requiring dissimulation, repair, or both in oneself; may deprive organism of energy and drive it to vigorous pursuit of learning or acting on knowledge,
• **Antagonistic emotions** (irritation, anger, hate, aggressiveness); Effects: Serve to forcefully overcome obstacle to goal achievement and assert individual or organizational interest and status in relation to knowledge, may lead to self-assertion becoming aim in itself and conflict hampering or permanently damaging normal relations and interactions, e.g. knowledge sharing.

meanings. In this sense, pheno-practice strives for making accessible, describable, interpretable and practical the implicit and explicit settings and meanings of knowing for individuals, groups and organisations. Integral pheno-practice represents a specific research orientation and methodology, understood as a practice of researchers, striving to portray phenomena of knowing from various different perspectives. Furthermore, pheno-practice focuses on offering critical and practical perspectives for creative and transformative processes of situated knowing in organisations. Thereby, it strives to bridge the gap between theory and practice by providing a conceptual and practice-oriented approach to the complexities involved in knowing in a more integral way. For being "integral" the concept of pheno-practice considers various conceptual orientations towards realities of knowing and knowledge. The term *"integral"* here refers to the "completeness" of a comprehensive and inclusive approach, in which the constituent "parts" and "wholes" of and within knowing in organisation are not fragmented or reduced to each other. Thus briefly stated, integral means a bringing together and strategically linking of seemingly divergent facets, perspectives, concepts, and practices in the attempt to create a realistic, workable, fluid, and dynamic understanding and practice. Specifically, it accommodates equally the subjective, inter-subjective and objective dimensions of knowing as a holonic event. Holons are integrative 'entities' or processes which are both wholes and parts of bigger wholes at the same time (Koestler, 1967). As emerging events holons evolve to complex orders of whole/partness by virtue of specific dynamic "patterns" that they exhibit. Furthermore, the holon construct is based on the distinctions between the higher (transcendence) and the lower (immanence), and between the dynamics of agency (preservation) and of communion (adaptation) (Wilber, 1999; Edwards, 2005). Holonically, knowing comprises processes and structures which are simultane-

ously autonomous and dependent, characterized by differentiation (generation of variety) and integration (generation of coherence). A holonic understanding of knowing utilises different lenses including interior and exterior dimensions as well as the individual and collective perspectives of embodied and emotional knowing. Holons can be used to represent inner levels of knowing and external, behavioural aspects of "knowledge" of individuals as well their collective dimensions within an organizational culture and system. Because it includes many different conceptual lenses, a holonic modelling can be used to accommodate and assess the scope and adequacy of approaches towards knowing and "knowledge". Holons are in a sense, a conceptual maps or tools for holding various understandings in juxtaposed relationship. Moreover, holonically different dimensions and levels of knowing can be brought together in an integral probable scheme (Wilber, 1999, 2000).

For example an integral pheno-practice considers simultaneously the inner, tacit knowing of the individual knower and his enacted "knowledge", the roles and actions as well as the collective orientations of a community of knowers or "knowledge-"culture and the corresponding structures and functions of the material infrastructure. Thus, an integral conceptualisation provides a framework into which disparate contents and approaches of knowledge can be placed and integrated (Goodall et al. 2004).

Following an inclusive orientation various facets and areas are all considered cohesively including interconnected processes between them within an "Integral Cycle" in organisations (Edwards, 2005; Cacioppe & Edwards, 2005). Thus, seen from an integral pheno-practical and holonic perspective different dimensions of knowing are not only complementarily, but co-create each other and are unfolding together.

With such orientation an integral approach helps to critical analyse the ways in which knowing and „knowledges" are related and exercised within organisational settings. For instance, an integral investigation will include not only the empirical observations of individuals' behavioural enactments but also their subjective experiences, meanings and projections of individuals as they perform the relational acts of managing, facilitating, co-ordinating. An integral approach also allows investigating the ordering and normalising disciplinary techniques and processes of knowing used at the collective level. This may include controlling norms or group resistance within organisational culture or governing functional and structural aspects within organisational system. Investigating critically the interrelation of different levels and spheres, an integral approach can reveal how knowledge and knowing plays a fundamental role in rendering aspects of existence thinkable, calculable, desirable and amenable to intervention, that is, manageable. Additionally, using an integral inquiry of this type can diagnose various problems, pathologies and conflicts with regard to knowledge generation, distribution and/or evaluation as well as provide ways for dealing with them. One of the advantages of a pheno-practical approach is that with its focus on embodied and emotional dimensions of knowing it enables to consider these often neglected dimensions and its impact systematically.

Furthermore, an integral pheno-practical modelling of knowing considers also systematically, a series of different *developmental lines* of knowing subjects and "knowledge" practices. These developmental lines concern complex developments, like - among others - spatio-temporal, object-relations, cognitive, emotional, learning, interpersonal, behavioural developments and ethical lines. As shown before conventional approaches of knowledge management and also those of organisational learning follow mostly cognitive lines. This explains the prevailing difficulties to integrate embodied tacit and implicit knowing and emotional dimensions as constitutive for knowing and learning (Küpers, 2005, 2006).

By applying varied perspectives, pheno-practical researchers are better equipped to shed light on tensions that come along with knowledge practices by, for example, exposing conflicting demands and disparities as complementary, and by demonstrating that apparently opposing interests are actually interwoven. Thus pheno-practice provides a clearer, more comprehensive picture of occasions of knowing in organisations and a base for a processual turn towards a relational understanding of "inter-knowing".

PROCESSUAL TURN TOWARDS INTER-RELATIONAL KNOWING: THE IN-BETWEEN OF KNOWING

A processual orientation of knowing links up advanced phenomenology and the outlined action- and practise-oriented understanding of embodied and emotional knowing with a radical relational orientation. Such a relational approach sees knowing as an emerging event, that is, as a dispersed and "inherently indeterminate" process which is continually reconfiguring itself (Tsoukas, 1996, 13, 22; Cook & Brown, 1999). Through this relationality it becomes possible to transcend both a possessive subjectivism and an obsessive objectivism. Knowledge is not then reductively seen as an identifiable entity sui generis based on the individual, respectively intersubjective or made objectively measurable. With a relational intelligibility in place we can shift our attention from what is "contained" within individuals, communities or an "organisational knowledge base" to what transpires between people and their "artefacts-in-use". With this orientation, knowing becomes factually based on embodied and emotional relational processes that are jointly or "dialogically" structured and responsive activities (Shotter, 1993; Stacey, 2001). Thus, knowing refers to an ongoing event of relating and responding. As such it develops out of a complex set of inter-actions and "inter-passion" or inter-relations between "subjects" and "objects". It is through these inter-relations that feelings, cognitions and meanings, communities as well as structures and functions of knowledge are continually created, re-created, questioned and re-negotiated. All of these components are processed as a relational chiasmic and reversible nexus (Merleau-Ponty 1968, 130).

Ultimately, this "space in-between" (Bradbury & Lichtenstein, 2000), is the birth-place of knowing, of individual and collective identity and social relationships. Here also is the source for creativity, innovation and added value in organisations. Therefore, the inclusion of embodied and emotional knowing as relational event provides renewed possibilities for developing deeper, richer more textured experiences and understandings of how the "knower" and the "known" are enfleshed with each others. In this processual space or intermediating realm of the in-between, all parties involved in the knowing process meet in an on-going relational activity. By recognising the primacy of relational processes, these become media, in which knowing is continuously created and changed in the course of being practised. Thus, any knowing and knowledge always depends on a set of relationships to other knowing and knowledges´ in continuous and dynamic (ex-)changes and transformation.

Understanding organisations and knowledge-related phenomena as dynamic constellations of relationships allows us to see that knowing processes are not substantively fixed, but rather are a shifting cluster of variable elements throughout a decentred, configured mesh. This mesh of knowing is distributed and moving in dynamic sets of relations within influential historical, embodied and emotional, social and structural dimensions. Therefore, knowledge, knowing, the knower, and the known interrelate and co-create each other within an "inter-world" of integral and processual "inter-knowing".

IMPLICATIONS AND PERSPECTIVES: CONCLUSION

The previous text has tried to show the significance of a phenomenological and "pheno-practical" approach of knowing in organisations. Such an approach represents an integrative response to the shortcomings of traditional concepts and discourses of "knowledge" and knowledge-management. Following the phenomenological "re-turn" to "knowing it-self", the embodied, emotional and practice-oriented dimensions of knowing have been discussed with the aim to open up the possibility for an integral "pheno-practice" and processual understanding of *"inter-knowing"*. In describing the complexities and nuances of a more inclusive comprehension of organisational knowledge, this chapter has certainly generated more openings than closings. Nevertheless it is hoped, to have made evident that knowing is not only realised through experiential processes, but that embodied and emotional experiences are always a kind of knowing and that such processes are already enacting a specific practice itself. The outlined integral model of pheno-practice and the processual understanding of "inter-knowing" have attempted to not only reconceive the experiential "base" of knowing, but also open up new ways of analysing and interpreting how knowing takes place and co-evolves.

A pheno-practical integral approach to knowing has tremendous practical, as well as theoretical and methodological implications. First, it opens up the possibility for generating *practical actions*. As individual, social and organizational knowing and knowledge are being processed in changing inter-related practices, it is necessarily provisional and thus there cannot be a given, stable or manageable "knowledgeability", i.e. fixed entity of "knowledge". Therefore embodied and emotional knowing cannot be simply organised, managed or controlled. Instead of being designed directly; it can only be designed for, that is, facilitated or, encouraged. For this to occur antecedent conditions need to be considered, which are likely to support a context where embodied and emotional knowing can be applied and flourish. The challenge will be to create circumstances and support relationships that generate practices of integrative knowing. In other words, what is required are all those shaping possibilities, for developing or upgrading more fulfilling embodied and emotional experiences and relationships of knowing in every-day life-work. These implications refer to targeted facilitations, creating supportive conditions and processes for each of the outlined "pheno-practical" spheres of knowing on a situation-specific basis.

These applications may include specific tasks, policies and actions of integral informed measurements, creating and endowing lived knowing processes. For supporting the development and sharing of knowing processes and knowledge, the inner individual knowing sphere can be enhanced for example by training in self-observation, reflective practices of self-management; or the outer individual knowing sphere by development of competencies via coaching, trainings and forms of experiential learning (Boud & Miller 1997) and practices of emotion management (Erickson, 1997). Examples for developing the inner collective knowing sphere refer to the cultivating of communal knowing relations e.g. via team-development (Druskat and Pescosolido, 2002; Edmondson, 1999) and supporting communities of (knowing) practice. The outer collective knowing sphere may be improved e.g. by restructuring, organisational arrangements like formal structures, functioning workflow and knowledge-supportive technologies and emotional designs (Norman 2004).

Importantly, all possible interventions in the four fields of application require an adjustment and coordination according to the embodied knowers' and organisation's particular settings to achieve a sustainable leveraging of potentials and capabilities. One practical benefit of pheno-practice lies in opening up an innovative understanding of inter-related and responsive practices (Küpers 2007) of enacted knowing informing and adapting in the course of pragmatic actions. Practically, the integral framework helps designing the roll-out of knowledge management initiatives so that they consider individuals and collectives particularities in their different but interrelated ways. This orientation also allows diagnosing reasons for failures of interventions and possible solutions to problems directly related to real knowledge management issues and objectives, supporting more effective planning and implementation (Goodall et al. 2004).

With regard to *theoretical and methodological implications* and future research, the proposed phenomenological approach and pheno-practical, integral and processual framework provides a "bedrock" for more rigorous theory building and theory testing. In terms of methodology, advanced phenomenology offers an alternative approach for understanding the intricate nature of the processes and patterns of knowing in organisations.

Phenomenology can bring the researcher in closer touch with "real-word" of knowing processes, while recognising the heterogeneous dimensions involved. As reminders of the lifeworld's multifaceted wholeness phenomenology and an integral pheno-practice of knowing serve as helpful antidotes to partial views and reductionist methods.

As a way of doing phenomenology (Spiegelberg, 1975), pheno-practice refers to a specific research methodology striving to portray phenomena from the personal, inter-subjective and contextual perspectives of those who experience them. Thus, in addition to phenomenology-oriented first-person perspectives (Giorgi 1997), it would be therefore be conscquent to extend research towards second- and third- persons (singular and plural forms) for understanding the complex dimensions of relationality and of knowing in organizations. For example a second-person approach would including all those interpersonal and team -based experiences of knowledge and knowing can be approached via group-feedback assessments. The third-person world of objective methods focuses on the empirical, behavioural and outcomes-based methods of quantitative analysis. Here the emphasis is on the behavioural investigation of enacted knowledge through such means as psychometrics, situational analysis and detailed observation. Third-person methods can be used for investigating influencing conditions and factors of knowledge and knowing related to both action-related cultural and systemic spheres by generating quantitative data with rigor. Thus an integral methodology and corresponding research designs recognize the validity of behavioural and functionalist analyses and quantitative investigations.

Methodologically, an empirical tested integral approach can contribute not only to re-examine the implications of variations in qualitative techniques (Kvale 1983; Küpers, 2008), but complementing rigorous empirical methods for generating and quantitative, and multiple triangulations (Jick, 1979), including longitudinal studies und multiple case studies (Yin 1994).

In terms of contents, for a further application and development of the integral model it would be challenging to link different dimensions of the integral pheno-practice of knowing with those of learning (Küpers 2004, 2006). For example, it would be interesting to see how specific dimensions of knowing and learning inter-relate reversibly to each other. Embodied and emotional knowing are intimately linked with the concepts of implicit and tacit knowing (Polanyi, 1966, 1969)[b], implicit and transformative learning (Berry 1997; Reber 1993; Gunnlaugson 2005), and narratives (Küpers, 2005). Exploring the connections between these fields may prove to be a very important avenue for further research. Moreover, research work needs to be undertaken on how the outlined concepts might be used investigating change interventions or self-organising processes

for developing an integrally informed knowing-oriented and learning organisation.

With regard to future research on conditions, developments and effects of an embodied and emotional knowing, it would be worthwhile to analyse how these processes are regulated, ordered and sustained. For example, investigating the influence of power and socio-political tensions could provide new insights into how interconnections emerge between inner knowing and external "knowledge" and learning on both individual and collective levels.

Basically, it is hoped that the phenomenological and integral pheno-practical frame-work and research agenda, as proposed here, may provide possibilities to re-assess, re-think and further investigate the deeper relevance of embodied and emotional processes of knowing and acting in life-worlds of organisations. It can be assumed that taking into account the various inter-relational dimensions will attain a more comprehensive and creative understanding of the constitution and development of knowing in organisations. Thus, the integral phenomenological and phenopractical approach presented here can be used to illustrate, interpret, and re-conceive the experiential and interrelated "base" of knowing processes in organisations. By including conventional orientations within a more comprehensive integral pheno-practice, researching the lived experience of (inter-)knowing is a challenging endeavour. However, further applied research on pheno-practice will be worthwhile undertaking, as it contributes to feasible and sustainable practices and ways of thinking, imagining and "living" knowing in organisations and through this to future social realities.

REFERENCES

Aadne, J.H., von Krogh, G., & Roos, J. (1996). `Representationism, The Traditional Approach to Cooperative Strategies`. In von Krogh, G. & Roos,

J. (Eds.). *Managing Knowledge: Perspectives on Cooperation and Competition*, pp. 9-31; London: Sage Publications.

Acker, J. (1990). Hierarchies, Jobs, `Bodies: A Theory of Gendered Organizations', in *Gender and Society*, 4(2) 139-158.

Allaire, Y. & Firsirotu M.E. (1984). Theories of Organizational Culture, *Organization Studies*, 193-226.

Ashforth, B.E. & Humphrey, R.H. (1995) Emotion in the workplace. A reappraisal'. *Human Relations*, 48. Jg. (1995) 2, S. 97–125.

Assudani, R.H. (2005). Catching the chameleon: understanding the elusive term "knowledge". *Journal of Knowledge Management, 9*(2), 31-44.

Berry, D. C. (ed.) (1997). *How Implicit is Implicit Learning?* Oxford; Oxford University Press.

Blackler, F. (1995). Knowledge, Knowledge Work and Organizations: An Overview and Interpretation. *Organization Science, 16*(6), 1021-46.

Boud, D. and Miller, N. (Eds.) (1997). *Working with Experience: animating learning*, Routledge, London.

Bradbury, H., & Lichtenstein, B.M.B. (2000). Relationality in organizational research: Exploring The Space Between. *Organization Science, 11,* 551-564.

Burgoyne, J. G. & Hodgson, V. E. (1983). Natural learning and managerial action: A phenomenological study in the field setting, *Journal of Management Studies,* 20 (3): 387-399.

Cacioppe, R., & Edwards, M. (2005). Adjusting blurred visions: a typology of integral approaches to organizations. *Journal of Organizational Change Management, 18*(3), 230-246.

Casey, C. (2000). Sensing the Body: Revitalizing a Dissociative Discourse, in Hassard, J., Holliday,

R., & Wilmott, H. (2000). *Body and Organisation,* (pp. 52-70). London: Sage.

Choo, C.W. (1998). *The Knowing Organization.* New York: Oxford University Press.

Cook, S.D., & Brown, J.S. (1999). Bridging epistemologies: The generative dance between organizational knowledge and organizational knowing. *Organization Science, 10,* 381-400.

Crossley, N. (1994). *The Politics of Subjectivity: Between Foucault and Merleau-Ponty.* Aldershot, England: Brookfield USA, Avebury Series in Philosophy.

Crossley, N. (1996). *Intersubjectivity: The Fabric of Social Becoming.* London: Sage.

Dale, K. (2001). *Anatomising Embodiment and Organisation Theory.* Basingstoke: Palgrave.

Dale, K., & Burrell, G. (2000). What shape are we in? Organization theory and the organized body, in J. Hassard, R. Holliday, & H. Willmott (Eds.), (2000). *Body and organization,* (pp. 15-30). London: Sage.

Dall'Alba, G. & Barnacle, R. (2005). Embodied knowing in online environments. *Educational Philosophy. and Theory*, 37(5), 719–744.

de Sousa, R. (1987). *The Rationality of Emotions.* Cambridge, MA: MIT Press.

Denzin, N.K. (1984). *On understanding emotion.* San Francisco, CA: Jossey-Bass.

Despres, C., & Chauvel, D. (2000). *Knowledge Horizons. The Present and the Promise of Knowledge Management.* New York: Butterworth-Heinemann.

Druskat, V. U. and Pescosolido, A. T. (2002). The content of effective teamwork mental models in self-managing teams: Ownership, learning, and heedful interrelating, *Human Relations*, Vol 55, pp. 283-314

Easterby-Smith, M., & Lyles, M.A, (Eds.), (2003). *The Blackwell Handbook of Organizational Learning and Knowledge Management*. Malden, MA; Oxford: Blackwell Publishing.

Edmondson, A. C. (1999). Psychological safety and learning behavior in work teams, *Administrative Science Quarterly*, Vol 4 No 2, pp. 350-383

Edwards, M.G. (2005). The integral holon: A holonomic approach to organisational change and transformation. *Journal of Organizational Change Management, 18*(3), 269-288.

Erickson, R. J. (1997). Putting emotions to work, in Erickson, R. J. and Cuthbertson-Johnson, B. (Eds.), *Social Perspectives on Emotion*, JAI Press, Greenwich, CT, pp. 3-18.

Fineman, S. (2000). *Emotion in organizations*. London: Sage.

Fineman, S. (2003). *Understanding emotion at work*. London: Sage.

Friesen, N. (2002). Is There a Body in this Class? in: M. van Manen (ed.), Writing in the Dark: Phenomenological studies in interpretive inquiry, Ontario: Althouse Press.

Gergen, K.J. (1994). *Realities and Relationships. Soundings in Social Construction*. Cambridge: Harvard University Press.

Gherardi S. (2001). From organizational learning to practice-based knowing. *Human Relations, 54*(1), 131-139.

Gherardi, S. (2000). Practice-based Theorizing on Learning and Knowing in Organizations. *Organization, 7*(2), 211-223.

Gill, J.H. (2000). *The Tacit Mode*. Albany: State University of New York Press.

Giorgi, A. (1997), The theory, practice, and evaluation of the phenomenological method as a qualitative research procedure. *Journal of Phenomenological Psychology*, 28(2), 235-260.

Goodall, A. Taylor, R. & Pollack, S. (2004). Towards Integral Culture Change Initiative to support Knowledge Management In: Truch, E. (ed) (2004) *Leveraging Corporate Knowledge*, (pp. 158-177) Aldershot, Gower.

Grant, R.M. (1996). Toward a Knowledge-Based Theory of the Firm. *Strategic Management Journal, 17,* 109-122.

Gunnlaugson, O. (2005), Toward Integrally Informed Theories of Transformative Learning, Journal of Transformative Education, Vol. 3, No. 4, 331-353 (2005).

Hammond, M. Howarth, J. & Kent, R. (1995). *Understanding Phenomenology,* Oxford: Blackwell.

Harmon, M. M (1990). Applied phenomenology and organization. *Public Administration Quarterly,* 14 (1): 10-17.

Hassard, J., Holliday, R., & Wilmott, H. (2000). *Body and Organisation*. London: Sage.

Hosking, D.M., Dachler, H.P., & Gergen, K.J. (1995). *Management and Organization. Relational Alternatives to Individualism*. Averbury: Aldershot.

Jick, T. D. (1979), Mixing Qualitative and Quantitative Methods: Triangulation in Action," *Administrative Science Quarterly*, 24,4 (1979),602-611

Kleinginna, P.R., & Kleinginna, A.M. (1981). A categorized list of emotion definitions, with suggestions for a consensual definition. *Motivation and Emotion, 5*(4), 345-379.

Koestler A. (1967). *The Ghost in the Machine*. London: Hutchinson.

Küpers, W. & Weibler, J. (2005). *Emotion in Organisationen*. Stuttgart: Kohlhammer

Küpers, W. (2004). Learning Organization and Leadership, in Burns, J.M., Goethals, R.R., &

Sorenson, G.J. (2004). *Encyclopaedia of Leadership,* (pp. 881-886). Thousand Oaks: Sage.

Küpers, W. (2005). Phenomenology and Pheno-Practice of Embodied Implicit and Narrative Knowing. *Journal of Knowledge Management, 9*(6), 113-133.

Küpers, W. (2006). "Integrales Lernen in und von Organisationen" ("Integral Learning in and of Organisations"), In: *Integral Review*, 2, pp. 43-77.

Küpers, W. (2008). Phenomenology and Integral Pheno-Practice of responsive Organizations and Management. In: Barry, D., & Hansen, H. (Eds.), (2008). *New Approaches to Management and Organization.* London: Sage (forthcoming).

Küpers, W. (2007), *"Inter-Practice-Perspectives on an Integral "Pheno-Practice" in Responsive Organisations",* paper presented at stream "Practice, Practicing and Practising" at EURAM Conference, Paris, 05. 2007.

Kvale, S. (1983). The qualitative research interview: A phenomenological and a hermeneutical mode of understanding. *Journal of Phenomenological Psychology, 14* (2), 171-196.

Lambe, P. (2002). *Autism of knowledge management.* see: www.straitsknowledge.com.

Lanzara, G. F. & Patriotta, G. (2001). Technology and the courtroom: An inquiry into knowledge making in organizations, *Journal of Management Studies*, 38(7): 943-971.

Leder, D. (1990). *The absent body.* Chicago: University of Chicago Press.

Levinas, E. (1969). *Totality and Infinity: An Essay on Exteriority. Translated by Alphonso Lingis.* Pittsburgh: Duquesne University Press.

Macann, C. (1993). *Four Phenomenological Philosophers: Husserl, Heidegger, Sartre, Merleau-Ponty*, New York: Routledge

Macmurray, J. (1957). *The Self as Agent.* London: Faber.

Mazis, G.A. (1993). *Emotion and Embodiment: Fragile Ontology.* New York: Lang.

Merleau-Ponty, M. (1962). *Phenomenology of Perception.* London: Routledge.

Merleau-Ponty, M. (1995). *The Visible and the Invisible.* Evanston: Northwestern University Press.

Metaxiotis, K., Ergazakis, K., & Psarras, J. (2005). Exploring the world of knowledge management: agreements and disagreements in the academic/practitioner community. *Journal of Knowledge Management, 9*(2), 6-18.

Muchinsky, P.M. (2000). Emotions in the workplace: The neglect of organizational behaviour. *Journal of Organizational Behavior, 21,* 801-805.

Nicolini, D., Gherardi, S., & Yanow, D., (Eds.), (2003). *Knowing in Organizations: A Practice-Based Approach.* Armonk: Sharpe.

Nonaka, I., & Takeuchi, H. (1995). *The Knowledge-creating Company.* New York: Oxford University Press.

Norman, D. (2004). *Emotional Design:* New York: Basic-Books.

Oatley, K., & Johnson-Laird, P.N. (1987). Towards a cognitive theory of emotions. *Cognition and Emotion, 1,* 29-50.

Öhman, A. (1992). Fear and anxiety as emotional phenomena: clinical, phenomenological, evolutionary perspectives, and information-processing mechanisms, in: Lewis, M./Haviland, J. M. (Eds.): *Handbook of the Emotions*, New York, S. 511-536.

Orlikowski, W.J. (2002). Knowing in practice: Enacting a collective capability in distributed organizing. *Organization Science, 13,* 249-273.

Orr, J. E., (1996). *Talking about machines: An ethnography of a modern job*, Ithaca and London: Cornell University Press.

Parkin, W. (1993). The public and the private: Gender, sexuality and emotion, in Fineman, S. (Eds.). *Emotion in organizations,* (pp. 167-189). London: Sage.

Patriotta, G. (2003a), *Organization knowledge in the making: How firms create, use, and institutionalise knowledge*, Oxford & New York: Oxford University Press.

Patriotta, G. (2003a). *Organization knowledge in the making: How firms create, use, and institutionalise knowledge*, Oxford & New York: Oxford University Press.

Patriotta, G. (2003b), Sensemaking on the shop floor: Narratives of Knowledge in organizations, *Journal of Management Studies*, 40(2): 349-375.

Patriotta, G. (2003b). Sense-making on the shop floor: Narratives of Knowledge in organizations, *Journal of Management Studies*, 40(2): 349-375.

Pentland, B. T. (1992). 'Organizing moves in software support hot lines'. *Administrative Science Quarterly*, 37, 4, 527–48.

Perrone, J. and Vickers, M. H. (2004). Emotions as Strategic Game in a Hostile Workplace: An Exemplar Case, *Employee Responsibilities and Rights Journal* Volume 16, Number 3 / September 2004 167-178Polanyi, M. (1966). *The Tacit Dimension.* London: Routledge.

Polanyi, M. (1969). *Knowing and Being.* Chicago: The University of Chicago Press.

Polanyi M., & Prosch H. (1975). *Meaning.* Chicago: Univ. of Chicago Press.

Putnam, L.L., & Mumby, D.K. (1993). Organisations, emotions and the myth of rationality, in Fineman, S. (Eds.). *Emotion in Organisations,* (pp. 36-57). London: Sage.

Reber, A.S. (1993). *Implicit learning and tacit knowledge.* Oxford University Press.

Reus, T.H. (2004). Rhyme and Reason: Emotional Capability and the Performance of Knowledge-Intensive Work Groups. *Human Performance,* 17(2), 245-266.

Sanders, P. (1982). Phenomenology; A New Way of Viewing Organizational Research', *Academy of Management Review,* 7 (3): 353-360.

Schatzki, T.R., Knorr-Cetina, K., & von Savigny, E. (Eds.), (2001). *The Practice Turn in Contemporary Theory.* London: Routledge.

Scherer, U., & Tran, V. (2001). Effects of emotions on the process of organizational learning, in Dierkes, M., Antal, A.B., Child, J., & Nonaka, I. (Hrsg.): *Handbook of organizational learning and knowledge,* (pp. 369-394). Oxford: OUP.

Schipper, F. (1999) 'Phenomenology and the Reflective Practitioner'. *Management Learning,* 30 (4): 473-485.

Schön, D. A. (1983). *The Reflective Practitioner,* Basic Books.

Schütz, A. (1972). *The Phenomenology of the Social World*, New York. Humanities Press.

Shilling, C. (1993). *The Body and Social Theory.* London: Sage.

Shotter, J. (1993). *Cultural Politics of Everyday Life: Social Contructionism, Rhetoric, and Knowing of the Third Kind.* Toronto: Open University Press.

Solomon, R.C. (1980). Emotions and choice, in Rorty, A. (Eds.). *Explaining emotions, Berkeley,* (pp. 251-281). University of California Press.

Spender, J.-C. (1998), Pluralist Epistemology and the Knowledge-Based Theory of the Firm, *Organization*, Vol. 5, No. 2, pp. 233-256.

Spender; J.C. (2003). Exploring uncertainty and emotion in the knowledge-based theory of the firm. *Information Technology and People Volume, 16,* 266-288.

Spiegelberg, H. (1975). *Doing phenomenology.* The Hague/Netherlands: Martinus Nijhoff.

Stacey, R. (2001). *Complex Responsive Processes in Organizations: Learning and Knowledge Creation.* London: Routledge.

Stein, N.L., & Trabasso, T. (1992). The organization of emotional experience: Creating links among emotion, thinking and intentional action. In N. Stein, & K. Oatley (Eds.). *Cognition and Emotion (special issue), 6,* 225-244.

Styhre, A. (2003). *Understanding Knowledge Management: Critical and Postmodern Perspectives.* Copenhagen: Copenhagen Business School Press.

Styhre, A. (2004). Rethinking Knowledge: A Bergsonian Critique of the Notion of Tacit Knowledge. *British Journal of Management, 15*(2), 177-188.

Teece, D.J. (1998). Capturing value from knowledge assets: The new economy, markets for know-how, and intangible assets. *California Management Review, 40,* 55-79.

Tran, V. (1998). The role of the emotional climate in learning organizations. *The Learning Organization, 5*(2) 99-103.

Tsoukas, H. (1996). The firm as a distributed knowledge system: a constructionist approach. *Strategic Management Journal, 17,* 11-25.

van der Zalm, J. & Bergum, V. (2000). Hermeneutic-phenomenology: providing living knowledge for nursing practice Journal of Advanced Nursing 31 (1), 211–218.

van Maanen, J., & Kunda, G. (1989). Real Feelings: Emotional expression and organizational culture. *Research in Organizational Behavior, 11,* 43-103.

Vince, R. (2001). Power and Emotion in Organizational Learning. *Human Relations, 54*(10), 1325-1351.

Vince, R. (2002). The Impact of Emotion on Organizational Learning, in: *Human Resource Development International,* 5. Jg. (2002): 1:73–85

Waldron, V. (1994). One more, with Feeling: Reconsidering the Role of Emotion in Work, in Deetz, S. A. (Eds.). *Communication Yearbook, 17,* (pp. 388-416). Thousands Oaks: Sage.

White, J. D. (1990). Phenomenology and Organizational development, *Administrative Science Quaterly,* Spring.

Wilber, K. (1999). *Collected Works of Ken Wilber: Volumes 1-4.* Boston: Shambhala.

Wilber, K. (2000). *Collected Works of Ken Wilber: Volumes 5-8.* Boston: Shambhala.

Yin, R.K. (1994). *Case study research: Design and methods* (2nd ed.). Thousand Oaks, California: Sage Publications.

ENDNOTES

[a]   By "applied phenomenology," Harmon means the activity of ferreting out practical lessons from what is best characterized loosely as a phenomenological attitude. This phenomenological attitude suggests an understanding of organizing as process of sense-giving and -making about what people have been doing, what they might want to do in the future, including (but not limited to) how they might want to do it (Harmon, 1990, 11). Accordingly, there is a similarity between the phenomenological meanings of the practical activity of organizing and

theorizing. "Theorizing becomes an act of organizing, first, when it is a cooperative activity shared in by several or even all of the actors in an organizational setting and, second, when its purpose is to reveal hidden or novel possibilities for acting cooperatively. Organizing is cooperative theorizing and vice versa. The practical implications of the phenomenological attitude for organizing, then, are deductible from the criterion of good - which is to say, practical - theorizing" (Harmon, 1990, 11). By viewing organizing as logically and ontological prior in organization, Harmon discourages researchers from mistakenly regarding organizations as "things" or reified "entities". In addition to a preference of verbs over nouns, applied phenomenology, according to Harmon, also sensitises for a preference for action over behaviour, as well as for a preference of consensual organizing and for active listening.

[b] Polanyi (1966, 1969, 147) has already emphasised the role of the body in our contact to the world and throughout the act of knowing in particular (Gill, 2000, 44-50) as the necessary somatic equipment referring to "the trained delicacy of eye, ear, and touch" (Polanyi & Prosch, 1975:31). As Polanyi stated, "the way the body participates in the act of perception can be generalized further to include the bodily roots of all knowledge and thought. (…) Parts of our body serve as tools for observing objects outside and for manipulating them" (Polanyi, 1969, 147). However, the status of Polanyi's body as a masculine, rational-instrumental ideal, as standardised body of 'man the knower' who is disengaged, emotionally under-control, lacking desire, isolated in its own performance and disassociated from itself (Acker, 1990) need to be investigated critically. This includes other a-rational forms of knowing, e.g. carnal, affective, erotic, intuitive, and spiritual and situated power relations in the micro-morphological flows of perception, desire, and action, conducting the structure and dispositions for the knowledge in organisations.

Chapter XI
Evaluating the Learning Effectiveness of Collaborative Problem Solving in Computer–Mediated Settings

Ourania Petropoulou
University of Piraeus, Greece

Georgia Lazakidou
University of Piraeus, Greece

Symeon Retalis
University of Piraeus, Greece

Charalambos Vrasidas
CARDET, Cyprus

ABSTRACT

There is a growing need for systematic evaluations of computer-supported collaborative learning environments. The present chapter focuses on the evaluation of the learning effectiveness of the interactions that take place in computer-supported problem solving environments. This chapter emphasizes the need for supporting evaluators of such environments with holistic evaluation conceptual frameworks and tools that can facilitate the analysis of data gathered during the evaluation process. We discuss in detail such a holistic framework which has been tested through a primary education case-study.

Copyright © 2009, IGI Global, distributing in print or electronic forms without written permission of IGI Global is prohibited.

INTRODUCTION

Collaborative problem solving is used widely in all grades of education (Stanic and Kilpatrick, 2003; Jonassen et al., 2003; Schoenfeld, 2006). Tutors try new practices to develop their students' problem solving skills through collaboration. A number of powerful Computer Supported Collaborative Learning (CSCL) tools (either synchronous or asynchronous) have already been developed and used to foster learner's skills. They help the development of networked learning communities whose members communicate and interact to build a shared understanding of a domain (Schwartz, 1995). In a networked community problem solving, learners and tutors, share knowledge, experiences and resources for finding the most appropriate problem solving techniques as well as the solution to a given problem.

People promoting computer supported collaborative problem solving environments generally target the acquisition of higher-order thinking skills, problem solving abilities, epistemic fluency and the collaborative improvement of knowledge within a field of practice (Oliver and Herrington, 2003, p.115; Goodyear, 2002, pp.58-63). Evaluation of the learning effectiveness of such environments is not an easy task. This is why very few systematic and complete evaluation studies in authentic educational environments have been reported in the literature (Wallace, 2003). Evaluation is a systematic process which tries to give insight in how the interactions within networked learning communities affect learning (TELL, 2005). There is a need for defining a framework and accompanied methods and tools which can help evaluators collect, analyze and interpret data about the interactions within networked learning communities. The scope of this paper is to present a holistic conceptual framework for evaluating interactions within networked community problem solving which has been tested and validated in primary education.

The rest of this paper is organized as follows. In the next section we make a brief overview of the theoretical foundations for the added value of community problem solving while we refer to school projects using collaborative problem solving. Then we continue with a short overview of current approaches in the evaluation (methods and tools) of interactions within networked community problem solving, summarizing the strengths and weaknesses of each one. We then propose a conceptual framework for holistic analysis of interaction during a networked collaborative problem solving activity. We present a concrete case study illustrating how this framework been applied in primary schools. Finally, we draw some conclusions and outline future lines of research in the area of evaluation of interactions within networked community problem solving.

EXPLOITATION AND THEORETICAL ISSUES OF PROBLEM SOLVING LEARNING COMMUNITIES

Collaborative problem solving has been variably exploited in schools from the first grades and in all disciplines. A great number of projects have been funded in order to explore collaborative problem solving as it is considered as a special style of teaching and learning (Johnston et al., 2000). The first and most cited project is the *Jasper Project*: an anchored instruction of mathematical problem solving that was developed by the Cognition and Technology Group at Vanderbilt (CTGV, 1997). According to this project solvers explore and model a problem space involving mathematical problems for extended periods of time and from a diversity of perspectives; the problem spaces offer opportunities for cooperative learning and discussion in small groups, as well as for individual and whole-class problem solving. Another well-known project that was developed by the University of Pittsburgh (1998) is the *Belvedere* approach (http://lilt.ics.hawaii.edu/belvedere/index.html). According to this project solvers working in groups conduct a scientific inquiry and find answers to various challenging problems such as finding out the cause of a strange disease, solving a problem for evolutionary theory in the Galapagos Islands, etc. Another example of using collaborative problem solving is in teaching of algorithms in Secondary Education (Voyiatzaki et al., 2004). In this study fifteen-year old solvers used the Synergo tool (http://hci.ece.upatras.gr/synergo/synergo.php) to represent flowcharts for collaborative exploitation and building of algorithms. These are some of the examples of exploiting collaborative problem solving into school settings for educational purposes.

In a community problem solving, it is essential to reach that all learners (members of this community) have an adequate level of mutual understanding of the problem space in order that they reach a common goal (Dillenbourg, 1999; Baker et al., 1999; Veerman, 2000). According to Dillenbourg and Traum (1999), mutual understanding can occur at the linguistic level as well as at the cognitive level. This is inspired by the socio-cultural work of Vygotsky (1962, 1978).

Related to the Soviet socio-cultural psychology is the Activity Theory (AT) according to which strong emphasis is given to collective activities and mediated artifacts. Activity can be considered as a process subdivided into separate interconnected elements or actions. Through the performance of different actions, a learner achieves the conscious goal. These actions could be characterized either as external behavioral or internal mental ones. External behavioral actions include different motions and transform material or tangible objects, whereas mental actions analogously transform images, concepts, or propositions, and nonverbal signs within the mind. Thus the action can be motor or cognitive in nature (Bedny et al., 2001). The main focus of any activity is in the production of an outcome (object), physical or mental.

Using tools (e.g. computer supported collaborative learning tools) the learner tries to accomplish the learning goals. Engeström (1999) considers joint-collaborative activity or practice as the unit of analysis. He is interested in the processes of social transformation and includes the structure of the social world in his analysis whilst taking into account the confliction nature of social practice. It is not only the learner, but the whole community, that is modified through mediated activity (Cole and Engeström, 1993). The differentiation between AT and socio-cultural approach is found in that cultural and historical evolution does not stop at an individual level but encompasses entities like the community, its rules and the division of labor that make the community organized and functioning (Cole, 1996). Consequently, learner's activity can be described as an interdependent system of several components namely: subjects, tools, rules, community and division of labour (Engeström, 1987). Respectively, in a problem solving activity emphasis is given to the activity of learners, thus permitting the analysis of the activity of at various levels of abstraction (Avouris et al., 2004b).

EVALUATION FRAMEWORKS IN PROBLEM SOLVING LEARNING COMMUNITIES

The evaluation of effectiveness of a community problem solving is strongly related to the theoretical framework that supports it (Rummel & Spada, 2005). Evaluation frameworks are not recipes but guides that help evaluators and evaluation stakeholders perform their tasks in a systematic way (Patton, 2002). They can offer guidance about the appropriate steps to follow during the evaluation process, and provide directions for the way of collecting, analysing and documenting the findings based on the requirements of the various stakeholders (Alkin, 1997).

One such a framework –which is inspired by the socio-cultural theory- is the Distance Environment for GRoup ExperiencEs (DEGREE). This is mainly used for conversation-based evaluation. According to the DEGREE (Barros & Verdejo, 2000), peer computer mediated interaction analysis is affected by the quality of the dialogues among learners and tutors. The Kaleidoscope project Interaction Analysis is a European project in which European researchers work together on the purpose of providing methodological and theoretical foundations for interaction analysis supporting learning activity participants and providing developers with means to support participants in a metacognitive level, exploiting new and existing techniques (http://www.noe-kaleidoscope.org/pub/network/communities/jeirp) In this project (Soller et al, 2005) it is attempted to define a set of cognitive and social indicators as a means of convergence all those various approaches of interaction analysis within a computer supported collaborative learning environment.

Another interesting framework is the On-line Community Framework (OCF) which attempts to face the complexity of communicative processes not only from users' but also from designer's perspective in order to conclude if an on-line community is successful. According to the OCF approach (De Souza, & Preece, 2004) semiotic engineering advances the clarification of dependencies among the communication, sociability and usability through a heuristic evaluation of all these. This approach is mainly directed to the technology designers of a CSCL system. It tries to draw their attention to particular interrelated dimensions of online learning communities which affect the quality of the learning process.

Inspired by the AT the object-oriented Collaboration Analysis Framework (OCAF) has been proposed. OCAF studies the activity of each learner who produces objects during a problem solving process (e.g. creates a new node to a concept map, modifies the name of an existing relation in a concept map, etc.). Objects and actions over them become the centre of attention and are studied as entities that carry their own history and are "acted upon" their owners (Avouris et al., 2002, 2003). This approach produces a view of the process, according to which the solution is made of structural components that are "owned" by actors/agents who have contributed in various degrees to their development.

Of course the aforementioned frameworks are not the only ones that can be found in the literature. The reader is advised to study the TELL project (2005) for finding more about the evaluation frameworks and interaction analysis methods in CSCL. It is acknowledged that there is a gap between what we can easily capture and evaluate (technical-computational indicators) and what it is important for learning and pedagogical management (indicators with a psychological or pedagogical meaning) of collaborative activities (Jermann, 2004). This is why the research problem of evaluation frameworks in community problem solving is still unsolved. The following sections deal with a new proposal for such framework which has been tested and validated in primary educational settings.

A PROPOSED CONCEPTUAL FRAMEWORK FOR INTERACTION ANALYSIS IN COMMUNITY PROBLEM SOLVING

The motivation behind the proposal for yet another conceptual framework for interactions analysis in community problem solving is the well known need of a tutor with basic computing skills for simple and useful evaluation "tools". This framework will enable her to perform an in depth analysis and interpretation of various data from the interactions occurred in such communities. The proposed framework suggests that

Figure 1. The proposed conceptual framework consisted of three main axes

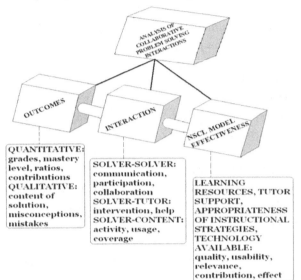

interaction analysis should be conducted along three axes: a) the outcomes of the collaborative problem-solving process, b) the interactive individual and collaborative problem-solving activities and c) the effectiveness of the pedagogical model which has been followed for building and running the problem solving community. Figure 1 illustrates the fundamental axes of our proposed conceptual framework. The proposed framework tries to analyse the interaction holistically, thus covering the three types of interaction defined by Moore (1989): learner-content interaction, instructor-learner interaction, and learner-learner interaction. It also tries to give a holistic view of the learning outcomes and learners' perception of the pedagogical model based on which interaction occurred.

Axes of the Proposed Conceptual Framework

The outcomes of the problem solving process in a CSCL environment refer to the deliverables of individual or group action (e.g. learners' assignments, solutions to given problems, etc.). Both qualitative (i.e. time needed for solving a problem) and quantitative aspects (e.g. type of misconceptions and/or mistakes, etc.) of the problem-solving outcomes should be accounted for.

The quantitative analysis of the problem-solving outcomes could include:

• Grades of problem solver's ongoing and final learning products (such as final reports, tests, exercises, quizzes etc.)

- Group's overall performance in specific task (e.g. group's average score)
- Mastery level of each concept/skill/method/competency (e.g. individual scores that prove the knowledge growth (novice, advanced, expert), individual versus overall score (mean of success/failure)
- Number of steps performed in a multi-step problem (e.g. number of correct, wrong, or incomplete steps)
- Problem Solver's most significant contributions to the task (e.g. first draft of a deliverable, creating of elements in a solution path, all expressed in numbers, or percentages etc.)
- Ratio of correct to incorrect steps per session in correlation with problem difficulty

The qualitative analysis of the problem-solving outcomes could include:

- Quality of the content of problem solver's proposed final solution (such as single/alternative solution presented). Quality indicators might be the solution as such, the clarity of presentation of the solution, the justifications for the proposed solutions, and so on.
- List of most frequent diagnosed mistakes and misconceptions

The second axis refers to the specification of the effects of particular categories of interactions within a collaborative problem solving learning community. These interactions can be classified as (Solver-Solver), Solver-Tutor (S-T) and Solver-Content (S-C) ONES. All three types of interaction play a key role in a community problem solving (Harry et al., 1993). So they need to be captured and analyzed accordingly. Specifically, in terms of **Solver-Solver Interactions (S-S)** we propose the evaluation of the descriptives of participation behavior, which means measuring:

- the total number of actions (e.g. by counting mouse clicks, contributions, etc.)
- the total number of messages that the solvers exchanged each other (per week/per day)
- the total Number of notes (per week/per day)
- the time frequency and sequence of individual and group actions
- the solver's behavior/actions in comparison with that of other solvers-members of the problem solving learning community
- the direction of messages (active/passive participation)

Moreover, we propose the evaluation of the Level of Communication Behavior, which means measuring:

- the direction of the information flow (different kind of communication among the participants)
- the total number of follow-up postings
- the total number of thread initiations

We also propose the evaluation of the type and the quality of Collaboration by measuring:

- the number and the nature of contributions to the task (per solver)
- the content of solver' contributions in terms of :
  ○ Division of labor among participants
  ○ Role playing (equal contribution/leading role within a group, number of social nets)
  ○ Mutual engagement of participants in a coordinated effort to solve a problem
  ○ Development of trust, social cohesiveness, sense of belonging
  ○ Ratio of social activities to overall activities

○ Number of relationships established among a group of solvers
○ Members' motivational and emotional support to their peers
○ Number of solver's help requests

Concerning the **Solver-Tutor Interactions** (S-T) the following issues should be measured:

Intervention

- Time and Reason of tutor's intervention (Netiquette, provision of feedback, instructions, opinions, summary of solvers' comments, discourse facilitation, encouragement, acknowledgement or reinforcement of a solver's contribution, diagnosis of misconceptions)
- Type of intervention (actions, messages etc.) during an on-line activity
- Recipient(s) of tutor's intervention
- Tutor's participation patterns
- Total number of notes posted (per week/per day)

Help Services

- Timely help
- Relevance of help to the solver's needs
- Conception of tutor help by solvers
- Application of tutor help by solvers

The **Solver-Content Interactions (S-C)** are mainly illustrated by the solver's navigational behavior and include:

Total Usage & Activity Times

- Amount of time a solver spends within the network (per session)
- Number of sessions
- History of past usage

Activity Types

- Average time interval spent on each activity
- Activity types distributions
- History of past activity patterns

Course Coverage

- Percentage of available material read
- Percentage of available exercises tackled
- History of past percentages

Problem-Solving Content Usage

- Amount of time spent per concept/skill/method/competency
- Number of problem-solving activities per concept/skill/method/competency
- The sequential problem-solving paths per session (theory, example, exercise etc.)
- History of past problem-solving contents
- Solvers' preferences over concept/skill/method/competency
  ○ List of accesses (and potentially) read course material
  ○ List of most frequently looked-up terms
  ○ Solver classification
  ○ History of past solver classification

The third axis of our proposed framework refers to the **effectiveness of the applied pedagogical model** for building and running/maintaining the collaborative problem solving learning community. The applied model is considered to be influenced by a number of variables (Innes, 2007; Retalis et al., 2005; Avouris et al., 2003; Johnston et al., 2000). The effectiveness of the applied pedagogical model is tightly coupled with the quality of problem-solving resources, tutor support, and appropriateness of instructional strategies according to problem-solvers and technology available. The evaluation of the applied pedagogical model should include the measurement of the:

- Relevance of the NSCL model to the solvers' body
- Effect of the NSCL model to solvers' learning styles with respect to educational settings, problem-solving strategies, assessment methods, etc.
- Contribution of the problem-solving resources to the acquisition of knowledge and skills with respect to their problem-solving objectives
- Effect of the NSCL model to the acquisition of knowledge and skills
- Quality of the problem-solving resources
- Quality of the instructional support services provided by the human agents in respect to the solver's acquisition of knowledge and skills
- Usability of the technological systems used

Evaluation Methods and Tools

Interaction analysis has been the centre of current research and several tools have been developed to support it. The recent trend is to perform inter-action analysis using mixed method approaches (Martinez et al., 2003). Thus, the proposed conceptual framework accords with this trend and suggest the use of various analysis methods and tools in a consistent way. More analytically, every method and every tool is coupled with the indicators of the proposed framework as illustrated below:

- Social Network Analysis (SNA): SNA is a method that seeks to identify and describe patterns of relationships between participants, to analyze and represent the structure of these patterns by tracing the flow of infor-

mation (De Laat et al., 2005). This method is based on studying the developed relations among peers or groups, and the investigation of solvers' social roles. Moreover, through SNA results may be represented graphically with the aid of sociograms in which nodes represent solvers and linking lines represent their relations.

- Observation: This method refers to the systematic observation of learning processes in specific problem-solving environments aiming at recording peer interactions, their behaviors while communicating with each other, the direction of their communication patterns and how these factors influence their task performance.
- Log Files Analysis (LFA): LFA is a method which allows the restoration and analysis of solvers' navigation paths in an on-line environment. The results are represented through a variety of indicators such as participation, number of visits per solver/group/activity/day etc. Our framework is supported by a specified analytic tool which is called CosyLMSAnalytics (Retalis, et al., 2006). This tool has been tested for analyzing learners' behavior in Moodle LMS. More specifically, it can:
  - Produce usage statistics such as count of visits, average time interval spent on an activity, and offer them in various formats such as cross tabs and charts.
  - Provide more detailed information regarding discussion forum statistics.
  - Exploit solvers' sequential patterns by drawing the exact paths being followed by each solver individually or in groups.
  - Show deviations of individual solvers from the typical series of activities performed by their group.
  - Perform Path Analysis with the cre-

ation of more complex queries that reveal interesting correlations and association rules among solvers' problem-solving paths.

- Collaborative Analysis Tool (ColAT): ColAT is a tool, which is tightly coupled with Synergo CSCL tool that permits the analysis of data of multiple types (e.g. chat messages, drawing objects created, changed or deleted) which can be interrelated. The analysis process involves interpretation and annotation of the collected data (Avouris et al., 2004a).

- Usage of Pre-Post Questionnaires: According to this technique solvers answer open/closed questions before and after the problem-solving process and their answers work as data resources for their tutor/evaluator. Then a tutor by comparing them can reach useful conclusions about the efficacy of the instructional choices made with respect to the attained problem-solving goals. Questionnaires extract specific information related to: problem-solving outcomes, problem-solving activities, quality of collaboration, and solvers' satisfaction in correlation with their needs or expectations.

- Think Aloud Protocol (TAP): TAP is a method which is widely used when a researcher needs to elicit the inner thoughts or cognitive processes that illuminate what's going on in a solver's head during the performance of a task (Erickson, & Simon, 1980). There are two approaches in the TAP technique: the concurrent approach and the retrospective approach. The first approach concerns the verbalization of one's thoughts while engaging in an activity. The second approach concerns the explanation of one's thoughts and reasoning after doing whatever they are doing. But, both approaches provide the researcher with the sole opportunity for conclusions about participants' cognitive

model while they collect comparative data about their strategies before and after their engagement in problem-solving tasks.

A CASE-STUDY FOR VALIDATING THE PROPOSED FRAMEWORK

In order to investigate the applicability and validity of the aforementioned conceptual framework of interactions analysis we applied it in a recent study in primary education. According to the pedagogical model of this study a solver should develop his/her problem-solving skills through a multi-step method:

- observation of an exemplary problem solving model created by the teacher,
- collaboration in a group of 4 students to solve a similar problem,
- collaboration in a group of 2 students to further practice the model of problem solving and
- semi-guidance to advance the adoption of exemplary model of problem solving.

All activities were designed to take place via the synchronous collaborative learning tool Synergo (Avouris et al, 2002; 2003). Synergo allows the collaborative problem solving activity through its shared space and chat tool. During all problem-solving steps solvers had access to related learning resources (e.g. explanations of the given problem, solutions of similar problems, calculators, etc.), meaningfully organized and integrated into the Moodle Learning Management System (http://www.moodle.org). The following table (table 2) illustrates how the problem-solving tools had been exploited in the study.

Participants and Duration: The case-study took place during the course subject of Mathematics. 24 learners (15 girls and 9 boys) of the fourth grade of a primary school in a Greek rural region

Table 1. The problem-solving tools and resources which solvers accessed while exploiting the multi-step method

PROBLEM-SOLVING STEPS	PROBLEM-SOLVING TOOLS	PROBLEM-SOLVING RESOURCES
OBSERVATION	Synergo LMS Moodle	The exemplary model of problem solving Support Educational Material
COLLABORATION IN 4	Synergo LMS Moodle	Shared Space for 4 Chat Support Educational Material
COLLABORATION IN 2	Synergo LMS Moodle	Shared Space for 2 Chat Support Educational Material
SEMI-STRUCTURED GUIDANCE	Synergo LMS Moodle	Guided Solution Support Educational Material
SELF-REGULATION	Synergo LMS Moodle	Space for Individual Solution Support Educational Material

participated to this study. The tutor had adequate basic computer skills. She had great interest in teaching using collaborative problem-solving techniques. Solvers and tutor had not previous experience in using the Synergo or the Moodle system. Thus they attended a two-hour session on how to use them before the beginning of the collaborative learning process. The study lasted for 10 collaborative problem solving learning sessions of 45 minutes during the period of April the 10th till June, the 10th, 2006.

Data Analysis and Findings: In order to examine the effectiveness of the collaborative problem solving learning activities, we applied the proposed framework. For the purposes of tracking the problem solvers' learning progress

we used a pre and a post test of four mathematical problems in order to derive the problem solvers' problem solving capacity. Also, we used five tests during the study which were graded by the tutor. To conclude if the results of 5 different grades per problem solver were statistically significant we used Analysis of Variance (ANOVA). Post hoc analyses were used to discover the differences among the sessions. Through all these tests we concluded the problem solvers' ongoing and final problem-solving outcomes. Moreover, we could derive the mean of success of class from every problem solver's progress. The means from the pre and the post tests were compared. It was noticed a statistically significant (the confidence interval of the difference varied from -3.5 to -1.3) increase

Figure 2. The improvement in solvers' performance over ten sessions

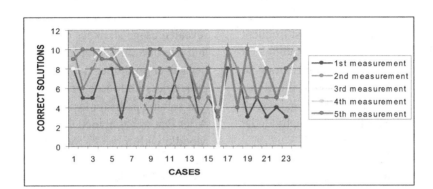

of 2.4 degrees. These degrees expressed as a percentage define the recorded gain from the study that is .024. The following figure (fig.2) illustrates problem solvers' progress during our study.

The repeated measures ANOVA confirmed that solvers' performance improved over the ten sessions, $F(4,104)=5,65$, $p<.01$. Post hoc analyses indicated significant differences between the first and third, fourth and fifth measurement of sessions

$(p=.005, p=.003, p=.004$ respectively). This allows us to make conclusions about the relationship between the time measurement and the problem solvers' performance. Namely, problem solvers' performance was generally being increased over time despite the gradual increase of difficulty of problems. This finding confirms the findings of pre and post test comparison.

Then, we collected all participants' contribu-

Figure 3. The total number of wrong and right steps during individual problem-solving

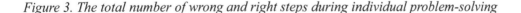

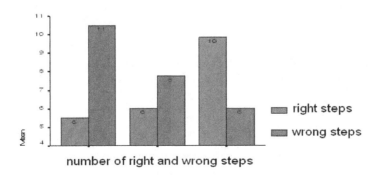

tions to the completion of tasks and we used ColAT to get quantitative results about the number of steps completed for each task. Being able to "re-play" one session we could evaluate the most frequent presented mistakes and misunderstandings as well as every problem solver's contribution to the task. The following figure (fig.3) illustrates the number of problem solvers' right and wrong steps while solving a problem individually in the first and last day of case-study.

Having analyzed the various outcomes of the collaborative problem solving learning process, we proceeded in evaluating the grid of interactions, using two main tools: the ColAT and the CosyLMSAnalytics. Specifically, the study of solver-to-solver interaction through the ColAT revealed the total number of messages exchanged, number of actions, nature of actions (such as emotional, motivational, cognitive, metacognitive etc. support), role playing, sequence of roles, help seeking attempts, and ratio of social activities to overall activities (as shown in fig.4).

The study of Solver-to-Tutor interaction through ColAT revealed the number of teacher's messages exchanged between the teacher and her problem solvers, the time, reasons and acceptance of her interventions as well as the most frequent

recipient of teacher's intervention. Finally, the data collection and analysis through CosyLMSAnalytics for evaluation of Solver-to-Content interaction revealed usage statistics (such as count of visits and average time interval spent on an activity per solver/group per day/week), problem solver preferences and most frequent sequential problem-solving paths for every session and activity. After that we combined the analyzed log files of Moodle with those of Synergo to conclude the usefulness of every single problem-solving resource in Moodle. The following snapshot (fig.5) of CosyLMSAnalytics tool presents the discrete solvers' preference for problem-solving resources. Problem-solving resources (especially the representation resources) were mostly preferred as a first and second problem-solving path. CosyLM-SAnalytics tool helps us easily and quickly see which resources had been accessed by learners at which stage of their problem solving task. At the specific experiment, we observed that some resources had not been used much, so we regard them as "useless" for this pedagogical model.

Social Network Analysis (SNA) method was finally used to perform the evolution of solvers' coherence while collaborating in the group of four. For the SNA we used the UCINET- a social

Figure 4. A comparative table of overall activities during an educational scenario

#	Group name	Whole duration	Number of sessions	Number of all events	Partners
1	Amathima	00:54:36	1	341	kafetzis
2	Bsynergasia4	02:52:26	4	206	kafetzis, gata, alexi 1, e.x.e., xat...
3	Cetairikh_synergasia1	01:04:39	3	131	kafetzis, zigene, alexi 1, xatzi, pa...
4	Detairikh_synergasia2	01:52:19	3	157	zigene, alexi 1, papad
5	Eodhgies	01:46:48	3	150	kafetzis, kantzoyra
6	Obhmata	00:19:28	1	168	kafetzis
7	problem1	00:01:51	1	37	kafetzis

The whole duration of all sessions is 08:52:07
The total number of sessions is 16
The average duration of all sessions of a group is 01:16:01
The average number of sessions is 2.3
The average duration of a session is 00:33:15

Figure 5. A snapshot of CosyLMSAnalytics tool for solvers' problem-solving paths

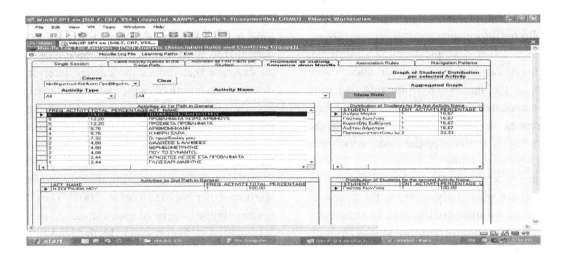

Figure 6a. Sociogram representing the social coherence of groups while collaborating in four during the first day of study

Figure 6b. Sociogram representing the social coherence of groups while collaborating in four during the last day of study

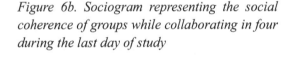

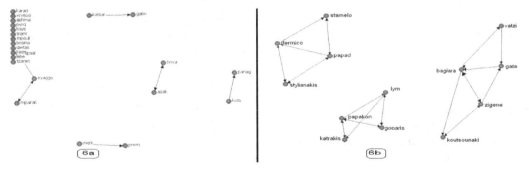

network analysis tool. The figure below represents the first and the last day of the study. The referred names are only passwords and have no relation with their real names or surnames.

As it is derived from the diagrams above all problem solvers were finally participated in problem solving process despite their initial reluctance and passive acceptance of the problem solving process. Their relationship – as members of the same group – was much closer over time attempting to exceed the collaboration rules and propose new steps in solving a problem.

To evaluate the effectiveness of the pedagogical model we used a questionnaire which was given to the tutor and solvers before and after the study. We collected information about their expectations, judgments on various topics (such as helpfulness, usefulness, easiness, etc.), opinion about every aspect of the model (environments, learning tasks and content of the problems, etc.) and their preferences. In general, both the tutor and the solvers highly appreciated the model which was found very stimulating.

The application of the proposed framework in the above pilot study supports the necessity of adopting a framework like this. In a computer supported collaborative problem-solving environment there are numerous variables that should be taken into account, analyzed and evaluated in order to achieve an in-depth understanding of the problem-solving process and draw related conclusions. On the other hand the application of the framework requires appropriate and integrated technological support if one attempts to analyze interactions in CSCL problem solving settings.

CONCLUSION

This chapter studied the community problem-solving by evaluating the interactions which occur among the problem solvers and tutors. It is evident that holistic evaluation frameworks and accompanied methods and tools are needed which can allow tutors and evaluators collect, analyze and interpret vast amount of data in an effective way. This is consistent with Tennyson and Schott's (1997) proposal for future tutor's involvement in the process of formative evaluation. In this chapter we proposed a framework that aims to facilitate the evaluator's work by equipping him with an easy-to-apply tools and techniques for in-depth analysis of occurred interactions. Our framework has been successfully applied in a pilot study in primary education: It helped the tutor reach conclusions about the learning effectiveness of

a pedagogical model which is based on building collaborative community problem-solving. However, it was time consuming since various tools had been utilized. Luckily the tools do not demand too much technical know how. One such an example that proves the current interest in developing related tools is the Integrated Participation Evaluation Tool (iPET) that is a Web-based application combining social network analysis and visualization to enable distance learning instructors and students to improve their participation in online discourse and so improve their overall learning experience (Saltz et al., 2007). The iPET system may be integrated with web-conferencing systems and its features includes the definition of participation rules, the view of community and participant activity, and the provision of automated participation reports to each individual. One more tool is the Discussion Interaction Analysis System (DIAS) which has been developed to offer extended interaction analysis support, by providing a wide range of indicators (individual, group and general –totally 52 indicators) jointly used in various learning situations, to all discussion forae users (individual students, groups, teachers or even researchers), appropriate for their various roles in different learning activities (Bratitsis and Dimitrakopoulou, 2005). All indicators are displayed in graphical and text format. All these efforts emerge the need for an integrated environment for interaction analysis of CSCL settings.

REFERENCES

Alkin, M. (1997). Stakeholder Concepts in Program Evaluation. In Evaluation for Educational Productivity, edited by A.Reynolds & H.Walberg. Greenwich, CT: JAI.

Avouris, N., Komis, V., Margaritis, M., Fiotakis, G.(2004a). An environment for studying collaborative learning activities, Journal of International Forum of Educational Technology & Society, 7(2), 34-41.

Avouris N., Komis V., Fiotakis G., Dimitracopoulou A., Margaritis M. (2004b). Method and tools for analysis of collaborative problem-solving activities. Proceedings of ATIT2004, First International Workshop on Activity Theory Based Practical Methods for IT Design , Denmark, September 2004, 5-16.

Avouris N.M., Dimitracopoulou A., Komis V., (2003). On analysis of collaborative problem solving: An object-oriented approach, Computers in Human Behavior, 19(2), 147-167.

Avouris N.M., Dimitracopoulou A., Komis V., Fidas C., (2002). OCAF: An object-oriented model of analysis of collaborative problem solving, G. Stahl (ed), Proceedings CSCL 2002, pp.92-101, Colorado, January 2002, Erlbaum Assoc. Hillsdale, NJ, 2002.

Baker M., Hansen, T., Joiner, R., & Traum, D. (1999). The role of grounding in collaborative learning tasks. In P.Dillenbourg (Ed.): Collaborative learning: Cognitive and computational approaches. UK: Elsevier Science/Pergamon.

Barros, M., Verjedo, M., (2000). Analysing learner interaction processes in order to improve collaboration. The DEGREE approach. International Journal of Artificial Intelligence in Education, 11, 221-241.

Bedny, G., Karwowski, W., & Bedny, M. (2001). The principle of unity of cognition and behavior: Implications of activity theory for the study of human work. International Journal of Cognitive Ergonomics, 5(4), 401-420.

Bratitsis, T., & Dimitrakopoulou, A. (2005). Data recording and usage interaction analysis in asynchronous discussions: The DIAS system. Proceedings of the 12th International Conference on Artificial Intelligence in Education AIED, Workshop "Usage Analysis in Learning Systems", Amsterdam, The Netherlands (2005).

Cognition and Technology Group at Vanderbilt (1997). The Jasper Project. Lessons in curriculum, instruction, assessment, and professional development. Mahwah, NJ: Erlbaum.

Cole M. (1996). Cultural psychology: a once and future discipline. Cambridge, Mass.: Belknap Press of Harvard University Press.

Cole M., & Engeström, Y. (1993). A cultural-historical approach to distributed cognition. In Learning, working and imagining: twelve studies in activity theory. Helsinky: Orienta-Konsultit Oy.

De Laat, M., Lally, V, Lipponen, L. and Simons, P.R.J. (2005). Patterns of interaction in a networked learning community: Squaring the circle. Manuscript submitted for publication (Submitted) http://eprints.soton.ac.uk/17267/.

De Souza, C., S., Preece, J. (2004). A framework for analyzing and understanding online communities. Interacting with Computers. The Interdisciplinary Journal of Human-Computer Interaction, downloadable at http://www.ifsm. umbc.edu/~preece/Papers/Framework_de-souza_preece2003.pdf. Paper retrieved on May 30th, 2007.

Dillenbourg, P. (1999). Collaborative Learning: Cognitive and Computational Approaches. Elsevier Science, Oxford.

Dillenbourg, P., & Traum, D. (1999). Does a shared screen make a shared solution? Paper presented at the Computer Supported Collaborative Learning Conference (CSCL'99), December 1999.

Engeström, Y. (1999). Innovative Learning in Work Teams: Analysing cycles of knowledge creation in Practice. In Y. Engeström, R. Miettinen, & R.L. Punamaki (Eds.): Perspectives on Activity Theory, Cambridge University Press.

Engeström, Y. (1987). Learning by expanding: An activity theoretical approach to developmental research. Helsinki: Orienta-Konsultit Oy.

Ericsson, K. A. & Simon, H. A. (1980). Verbal reports as data. Psychological Review, 87, 215-251.

Goodyear, P. (2002). Psychological foundations for networked learning. In C. Steeples & C. Jones (Eds.): Networked learning: Perspectives and issues. London, Springer-Verlag.

Harry, Keith, John Magnus, Keegan, Desmond. (1993). Distance Education: New Perspectives. Rutledge in London and New York.

Innes, R.B. (2007). Dialogic communication in collaborative problem solving groups. International Journal of the Scholarship of Teaching and Learning, 1(1), 1-19.

Jermann, P., (2004). Computer support for interaction regulation in collaborative problem solving, Phd Thesis, Switzerland.

Johnston, C.G., James, R.H., Lye, J.N., & McDonald, I.M. (2000). An evaluation of collaborative problem solving for learning economics. Journal of Economic Education, Winter 2000, 13-29.

Jonassen, D.H., Howland, J., Moore, J., & Marra, M. (2003). Learning to solve problems with technology: A Constructivist Approach. (2nd Ed.), NJ: Merill Prentice Hall.

Martínez, A., Dimitriadis, Y., & De La Fuente, P. (2003). Contributions to analysis of interactions for formative evaluation in CSCL. In Llamas, M., Fernandez, M.J., & Anido, L.E. (Eds.): Computers and education. Towards of lifelong learning society, The Netherlands: Kluwer Academic, 227-238.

Moore, M. G. (1989). Three types of interaction. The American Journal of Distance Education, 3(2), 1-6.

Oliver, R., & Herrington, J. (2003). Exploring technology-mediated learning from a pedagogical perspective. Interactive Learning Environments, 11(2), 111-126.

Patton, M. Q. (2002). Qualitative Research & Evaluation Methods. (3rd Ed)Sage Publications.

Retalis, S., Papasalouros, A., Psaromiligkos, Y., Siscos, S., & Kargidis, T., (2006). Towards Networked Learning Analytics – A concept and a tool, Proceedings of the 5th International Conference on Networked Learning 2006, Lancaster UK.

Retalis S., Psaromiligkos, Y., & Siassiakos K. (2005). The 'why', 'what', 'when' and 'how' of a summative evaluation method about the learning effectiveness of web-based learning systems. THEMES in Education, Universiy of Ioannina. Athens: Ellinika Grammata 6(2), 207-222.

Rummel, N., & Spada, H. (2005). Learning to Collaborate: An Instructional Approach to Promoting Collaborative Problem Solving in Computer-Mediated Settings. Journal of the Learning Sciences, 14(2), 201-241.

Saltz, J.S., Hiltz, S.R., Turoff, M., & Passerini, K. (2007). Increasing participation in distance learning courses. IEEE Internet Computing, 11(3), 36-44.

Schoenfeld, A.H. (2006). Mathematics teaching and learning. In P.A. Alexander & P.H. Winne (Eds.), Handbook of Educational Psychology (2nd Ed.). Mahwah, NJ: Lawrence Erlbaum Associates, 479-495.

Schwartz, D.L. (1995). The emergence of abstract dyad representations in dyad problem solving. The Journal of the Learning Sciences, 4(3), 321-354.

Soller, A., Martinez, A., Jermann, P., & Muehlenbrock, M., (2005). From mirroring to guiding: a review of state of the art technology for supporting collaborative learning. International Journal on Artificial Intelligence in Education. 15(4), 261-290.

Stanic, G.M.A., & Kilpatrick, J. (2003). A history of school mathematics. Reston, VA: National Council of Teachers of Mathematics, Vols.1–2.

TELL Project. (2005). Introducing a Framework for the Evaluation of Network Supported Collaborative Learning, WP1 Deliverable, Project number: EAC/61/03/GR009 eLearning Initiative, EU: European Commission Downloadable at: http://cosy.ted.unipi.gr/tell/media/WP1_deliverable.pdf

Tennyson, R.D., & Schott, F. (1997). Instructional design theory, research, and models. In R.D.Tennyson, F.Schott, N.M.Seel, & S.Dijkstra (Eds.), Instructional design: International perspective. Mahwah, NJ: Lawrence Erlbaum Associates, Inc, 1-18.

Veerman, A.L. (2000). Computer-supported collaborative learning through argumentation. Enschede: Print Partners Ipskamp. Downloadable at: http://eduweb.fss.uu.nl/arja/

Voyiatzaki E., Christakoudis Ch., Margaritis M., Avouris N. (2004). Teaching algorithms using a collaborative computer environment. Proceedings 4th ETPE Conf., Athens, vol B, pp. 641-647, October 2004 (in GREEK).

Vygotsky, L.S. (1962). Thought and language. Cambridge, MA: MIT Press. (Original work published in 1934).

Vygotsky, L.S. (1978). Mind in Society: The development of higher psychological processes. Cambridge, MA: Harvard University Press.

Wallace, R. (2003). Online learning in higher education: a review of research on interactions among teachers and students. Education, Communication & Information, 3(2), 241-280.

Chapter XII
Acquiring and Sharing Knowledge Through Inter–Organizational Benchlearning

Jeanette Lemmergaard
University of Southern Denmark, Denmark

ABSTRACT

This chapter introduces inter-organizational knowledge acquisition and sharing as a means to facilitate benchlearning within the field of human resource management. The chapter presents an interactive web-based portal and demonstrates how valuable knowledge can be released from organizational "silo centers" and be passed around to the benefit of both organizations and academia. In general, human resource departments struggle to demonstrate their validity to the business and their ability to accomplish business objectives. In addition, human resource departments generally lack the ability to speak of their accomplishments in a business language. The presented portal assists human resource professionals in making more efficient and qualitative decisions that are not based on good guesswork or mere instinct, but on facts and knowledge. The portal is novel in its approach of facilitating benchlearning across organizational boundaries and within the soft area of human resource management.

INTRODUCTION

In order to stay innovative and be competitive under rapid environmental changes, it is essential for organizations to continually develop strategic and organizational flexibility (Sampler, 1997). Thus, critical knowledge acquisition is crucial for organizations' continual development and sustainability. However, knowledge acquisition is essentially related to human action since

Copyright © 2009, IGI Global, distributing in print or electronic forms without written permission of IGI Global is prohibited.

knowledge is created by individuals (Nonaka & Takeuchi, 1995). Yet, organizations can establish a context that supports creation and enlargement of knowledge (Nonaka & Takeuchi, 1995), for example through the use of an information system. The value of such information system, however, can be even greater when applied to a collaborative setting, especially when such setting involves a combination of both professionals and academics.

This chapter suggests that software designed to collect, store, manage, deliver, present, and manipulate data can increase knowledge acquisition and sharing and thus facilitate the process of learning even across organizational boundaries. Academic researchers have increasingly focused on the notion that innovations are often found in the space between organizations (e.g., von Hippel, 1998; Powell et al., 1996). Mostly this research, however, does not address the ways in which information systems can support the joint acquisition of knowledge.

This chapter presents a technological platform (i.e., share2know) that facilitates inter-organizational knowledge acquisition and knowledge sharing within the field of human resource management. Hereby, this chapter answers a request in this specific field, as little theory has dealt with knowledge acquisition and knowledge sharing within human resource management. As Ulrich et al. (1989) argues, progress within the field is little supported by empirical evidence. Furthermore, trends are pushing towards justifying the expenditures and the mere existence of human resource departments leading human resource professionals to become preoccupied with enhancing their knowledge on how to increase their efficiency and visibility within the organizations.

The platform presented is designed as a web-based bench-learning tool (Karlöf et al., 2001). Through inter-organizational knowledge acquisition and sharing, the portal provides organizations with easier access to human resource knowledge, quicker responses to problems, and increased learning curves. The tool facilitates that valuable knowledge is released from organizational "silo centers" and passed around not only to members of the community of human resource professionals (i.e., inter-organizational), but also around intra-organizational members (e.g., CEOs and directors of finance). Equally important, the portal facilitates knowledge acquisition to academia. Through the portal, academic researchers can retrieve data for scientific usage that makes the researchers end-users of the portal as well. In this way, the portal provides both inter-organizational and intra-organizational knowledge acquisition. Moreover, the portal facilitates knowledge generated on the basis of a longitudinal theoretically and empirically driven reflection from academic researchers. It is especially the close collaboration with academia and the fact that the information system is based on scientifically based knowledge combined with practical experience that is rather unique.

BETTER AT KNOWING WHAT IS KNOWN

Knowledge provides a substantial input to all business activities whether it is production, sales, logistics, or human resource management. The ability to acquire and share the specific knowledge that provides competitive advantages is a key factor in gaining success. However, knowledge acquisition and sharing is not simply a question of distributing informative reports and sharing 'best practices' (Marshall et. al, 1997). The general view is that knowledge acquisition is closely related to experiences for example in the form of organizational learning (e.g., Fiol & Lyles, 1985; Huber, 1991), and as such knowledge acquisition is closely related to internalization. However, the ability to exploit external knowledge sources is a critical component related to organizations' innovative capabilities since a broader knowledge base is preferred when the aim is to increase flexibility and adaptability to environmental changes (Bierly & Chakrabarti, 1996). Not only is external knowledge required to keep abreast of for example cutting-edge technologies (Bierly & Chakrabarti, 1996), external knowledge is also critical to the innovation process as most innovations come from borrowing rather than from inventing (Cohen & Levinthal, 1990).

Within the field of economic research, knowledge sharing has been a major topic over the last thirty years. Theoretically, the importance of sharing is well established. An organizational knowledge base is critical to innovative thinking and to keep up with industry trends. Organizational knowledge largely depends on external sources and is essential to economic growth (Griliches, 1992). At the organizational level, the theory of knowledge sharing mainly deals with attracting knowledge generated by various external resources (e.g., competitors, universities, and governmental research organizations). Theory mostly deals with innovation of technological design and desires within various industries (e.g., Monjon & Waelbroeck, 2003; Desrochers, 2001; Baise & Stahl, 1999). Further, knowledge sharing has mainly been addressed within a certain industry and not across industry boarders. Finally, studies have explored the impact of progression and innovation on strategic interaction among organizations and on endogenous growth (Aghion & Howitt, 1997). For example, research on the sources of innovation supports the observation that imitation is an important means of technological diffusion and change (Cohen & Levinthal, 1990).

Many organizations have valuable knowledge hidden in financial systems, databases on customers, and in production systems. However, only if this knowledge is used and combined across different knowledge sources, it is possible to learn, innovate, and develop. The purpose of knowledge acquisition and sharing is, therefore, to improve accessibility. By exploiting the existing knowledge and creating new knowledge, future activities are likely to be performed faster, more efficiently, and probably more predictably. Mediated through technology the full potential of an organization's existing system-base knowledge can be used and shared. Knowledge sharing – as is the case with human resource management – is recognizable by the argument of better usage of existing resources.

FROM HEART TO HEAD MANAGEMENT

Management involves planning, budgeting, implementing, tracking, and measuring. However, knowledge management goes far beyond the storage and manipulation of data. Knowledge management requires a commitment to create new task-related knowledge, disseminate it throughout the organization, and embody it in products, services, and systems (Nonaka & Takeuchi, 1995). Organizations are used to dealing with for example technical efficiency, productive efficiency, and allocative efficiency. For example, managerial accounting practice has a strong tradition of budgeting based on historical projecting of facts and rational expectations for the future. The marketing department uses the same combination of measures and good guesswork about the future when making decisions.

Within the human resource management department, however, the same tradition for measuring is not common. The human resource department used to be the feel-good department that is oddly disconnected from the rest of the organization (Tracey & Nathan, 2002). Recently, human resource professionals, however, have experienced changes in their need to demonstrate the added value of the human resource department to the organization, and if the human resource department is not a profit centre, then it should at least be able to justify return on investment. Despite a general agreement that adequate management of the human resources is essential for survival in an increasingly competitive and global market, and that increasingly more information is stored in electronic formats, turning this information into valuable knowledge is rarely happening. Demonstrating statistically significant relationships between measures of human resource practices and organizational performance has become a dominant issue within the field of human resource management, but what is easy to measure is more often measured than what is right to measure (Ulrich & Brockbank, 2005).

Generally, too few measures are being made within the field of human resource management, and decisions are most often made on the background of traditions, existing procedures, by mere chance, or instinct. The argument is that it is much easier as a sales manager to report that a new order has been accepted that will raise this years profit with a certain percentage than it is for the human resource professionals to demonstrate the value of an increase in employee satisfaction. This challenge is further intensified due to the fact that the individual human resource departments each have their own unique way of measuring. Hereby, comparisons across organizations are impossible to perform. Nevertheless, only through measurement can the human resource activities be tangible and get a businesslike character. The human resource department must demonstrate its validity to the business, its ability to accomplish business objectives, and its ability to speak of accomplishments in business language (Phillips, 1996). If human resource departments are not adding value to organizational performance, they may be viewed merely as cost departments with the risk of being minimized or outsourced (Andersen et al., 2006).

From the literature, it is clear that there are many different methods for measuring and valuating the human resources. Statistical and financial evaluations of the human resource contributions are best suited to evaluating particular human resource practices or programs. However, the absence of a widely accepted measure of "progres-

sive" or "high performance" human resource management practices makes it difficult to compare findings across studies and across organizations (Andersen et al., 2006). However, one method to evaluate a human resource management system is to use benchmarks. Benchmarking is a systematic process of measuring an organization's products, services, and practices against recognized excellent organizations. Benchmarking gathers the tacit knowledge that explicit knowledge often misses through a process of identifying, learning, and adapting outstanding practices and processes from excellent organizations. Hereby, benchmarking helps create and initiate the need for change as it identifies what an organization needs to do to improve its performance relative to the human resource strategy of excellent organizations (Phillips, 1996).

BENCHLEARNING AS OPPOSED TO BENCHMARKING

In the management literature, benchmarking is often associated with Xerox's learning experiences about their Japanese competitor Canon (Karlöf et al., 2001). In the late 1970s, Xerox realized that Canon was selling comparable products for less than the productions price of Xerox. In order to get back into the game, Xerox compared its operations to those of Canon. Xerox simply bought some of Canon's products and put them on a bench with the purpose of taking them to pieces. In this way, Xerox acquired knowledge about the design and construction of Canon's products. Xerox learned that Canon used clips instead of screws that were both cheaper and faster to insert. Xerox also learned that Canon used identical parts for different models that gave larger batch sizes and reduced the need for storage. Moreover, Xerox even realized that Canon's products had a higher quality than their own products. This knowledge inspired Xerox to improve their production methods, and brought Xerox back into business.

Today, the concept of benchmarking is synonymous with successful performance, and many organizations use benchmarking to measure and compare business processes and practices. The self-analysis inherent in the benchmarking process encourages the identification of more efficient ways of operating, and monitoring other organizations often leads to more efficient alternatives to the current practices. However, one of the main criticisms of benchmarking is the implicit assumption of 'best practice' being generalizable and not organization specific (Meyer & Rowan, 1977; Becker & Gerhart, 1996). In a benchmarking perspective, organizational policies and practices are adopted based on a few legitimate organizations that serve as models for others to imitate. However, many practices, that are typically not included in 'best practice,' may be a source of new 'best practices' and the potential for new competitive advantages. Consequently, critics of benchmarking argue that exactly the inclusion of practices from outside the mainstream sets of 'best practices' might provide an opportunity to complement and extend prior 'best practice' (Rodwell et al., 2000).

The critics of benchmarking indirectly argue for the concept of benchlearning. Benchlearning builds on the pedagogic of benchmarking and team learning. Similar to benchmarking, it aims at improving business performance and concurrently creates a system for continuous learning and improvement (Karlöf et al., 2001). However, benchlearning is not imitation, but a method of finding inspiration for continuous learning and change. If benchmarking can be characterized as a boost to efficiency with learning as a rare and limited by-product, then benchlearning can be characterized as learning with efficiency as an important ingredient (Karlöf et al., 2001). The portal, presented in this chapter, builds on the concept of benchlearning, although it also builds on the assumption that there is no single 'best practice', as all organizations are different in some way either in missions, cultures, environments,

or in technologies. However, despite differences, organizations can learn from each other, and in a knowledge-management framework, this relates to knowledge acquisition and sharing.

HUMAN RESOURCE MANAGEMENT BENCHLEARNING

Progress within the field of human resource management is little supported by empirical evidence (Ulrich et al., 1989) and theory dealing with knowledge acquisition and sharing in the field of human resource management is rare. But trends have slightly occurred towards justifying expenditures and existence of the human resource department. Consequently, human resource professionals have become preoccupied with enhancing their knowledge on how to increase efficiency of the human resource departments (Pfeffer, 1997; Ulrich, 1997). Just as benchlearning of manufacturing, distribution, and marketing practices help organizations improve, human resource benchlearning can boost value adding for a number of reasons.

First, benchlearning enables a company to calibrate how it is delivering its human resource practices. Learning from the successes and mistakes of other organizations might increase the business economic value. Through knowledge acquisition and sharing across organizational boarders, organizations can learn by imitating and borrowing from competitors (March & Simon, 1958). Through exchange and adjustment of understandings and actions between human resource professionals from different organizations, the community as such will be better equipped to deal with mismatches. Measuring, valuation, and benchlearning are likely to direct actions and initiatives towards better human resource management practices. The process will enhance organizational learning (i.e., benchlearning), and subsequently lead to higher performance.

Second, benchlearning helps set priorities and track performance. Measures should obviously not be performed for their own sake, but need to be supported by the management of an organization. Hereby, measures can be the key to most quality-improving initiatives. Measures will increase the knowledge of an organization, but it is the actual activities that create value. The process that follows introducing measurement includes setting, pursing, and reaching goals. Setting goals leads to focus and continuity, pursuing goals leads to feedback and learning, and subsequently, reaching goals lead to the feeling of success.

Too often, measuring is a matter of trouble-shooting, and hereby the value of measuring success is lost. By only focusing on errors, measuring can easily become a pillory. Measures on successful activities, however, generate focus that can further lead to alertness and interest. This can be compared to the top athlete who sets a goal and reaches that goal only to set a new and higher goal. For the athlete it is both the path towards the goal and the goal itself that comprise the satisfaction. A measurable goal gives focus and direction, and it generates the possibility of experiencing success. Accepted goals are needed to change behavior, and changed behavior and attitude can be accomplished by imitating others. Unelected imitation in the traditional benchmarking way, however, is not preferred. Human resource professionals should aim at imitation in the benchlearning tradition, as benchlearning is more a method of finding inspiration for continuous learning and change. In other words, action counts more than plans and concepts.

Third, benchlearning enhances professional development and cultivates credibility. Human resource professionals generally remark on the difficulty they have in gaining respect at the top-management level. Rather than being involved in the planning phases, human resource professionals are often consulted after major decisions have been made. Not until later in the change

processes are the human resource professionals asked to contribute to the implementation process. This frustration of not being involved sooner in the planning process is partly due to lack of insights in and visibility of the human resource value proposition. Part of the reason why human resource professionals are often not part of the top-management team is that only few organizations have implemented elaborate systems to track human resource management goals and measures.

A WEB-BASED LEARNING PORTAL

The motivation for engaging in the interactive web-based portal presented here (i.e., share2know, see www.share2know.dk) is knowledge acquisition, sharing, and coordination primarily concerning human resource management practices and processes. The platform enables knowledge management, by assisting in a systematic and objective analysis of human resource practices. The portal bridges organizational silos and enhances inter-organizational interaction in what could be compared to a virtual community. The portal facilitates both measurement and valuation leading to learning and inter-organizational knowledge sharing. The community brings together members from different and sometimes competing organizations that have not previously collaborated or shared knowledge. The community consists of three collaborators; the organization, other organizations, and academia. The basic idea of the platform is that organizational conditions that promote fundamental contributions to the practice of human resource management need to be identified, as does the role of the human resources in relation to strategic planning. The platform facilitates mutual knowledge acquisition, structures spontaneity, and brings together what may be fragmented practice into a coherent whole. It serves as a mechanism that allows the community to think outside the box and combine linear and random insights on human resource management routines and practices.

The knowledge-sharing portal gives the community the possibility of critically acquiring and handling knowledge within the field of human resource management in a systematic and coordinated form, designed in accordance with the specific needs of the individual organization. This provides the human resource department with a number of possibilities for concentrating on and applying to value creation in line with the overall business strategy that is essential for continual development and sustainability of organizations. More specifically, organizational data stored on the web-portal provides human resource professionals with extensive quantitative data and information on integrated consistent bundles of human resource practices that should help the human resource professionals to handle the human resource challenges. In this way, the portal is a decision-support system that can be used for defining and discussing problems and solutions, building a shared understanding of a situation, discussing shifting priorities and external pressure, interpreting ambiguous signals, and socializing the community members.

The portal provides the human resource professionals with one joint tool that through measures can help describe and make visible the value that the human resources generate for the organization. At the same time, the tool can improve and develop the human resource initiatives and hereby in the longer term, the tool can improve and develop the organization in general. The greatest benefit of the portal, however, is its application to the more sophisticated human resource management activities (e.g., personnel planning, recruitment and selection, and staff development) in relation to the overall business strategy. The portal supports gathering and systematizing the knowledge that for a large part is already intuitively known. What makes the difference are the systematization and the argumentation that the portal provides.

Of course, the actual human resource activities are most important. The portal only functions as a supporting tool.

NOT AN AUTOPILOT

The portal is not an autopilot that solves all human resource related activities. On the contrary, the performed measures are important as background knowledge that needs to be followed by a dialog about which activities and combination of activities to be carried out. Through the knowledge acquired and generated via the portal it is possible to measure substitution effects and hereby give qualified arguments on cause-effect relationships that are very often non-existent within the field of human resource management. More specifically, the portal highlights which human resource practices that are interchangeable, to what degree they are interrelated, and whether some activities eventually are getting in each other's way.

Among human resources professionals, there is a general disagreement regarding whether or not it is at all possible to measure human resource activities and processes. For some organizations, it is natural to measure, for others it will require a cultural change to conduct clear, concise, measurable measures – and to follow up on these. Often feelings and beliefs are brought into the game when discussing measures with human resource professionals and employees for that matter. Measurements are provoking hesitations often linked to doubts as to whether a result-oriented culture is desired, whether measures are twisting the truth, or whether measurement gives such a strong focus on what is measurable, that creativity, flexibility, and learning will decrease. Above all, measurement often appears to be too controlling.

However, it is an old cliché within management, that if something cannot be measured, it cannot be managed. This cliché is both false and inconsequent. It is false in the sense that an organization always has leadership over for example employees, moral, and strategy, which essentially cannot be measured. It is inconsequent in the way that everybody and everything within business – including employees, moral, strategy, and so on – in some way are included in the accounts (Andriessen, 2004). It is generally agreed that measurement evaluations are complicated to perform. Nevertheless, no matter how difficult it is to measure human resources, it is the measures that make the effect of activities visible. The human resource departments must demonstrate their contribution and value added to the organization and provide useful knowledge that clearly indicates the outcomes of the human resource strategy in a meaningful manner comparable with those of other departments (e.g., department of accounting and department of marketing).

The portal encompasses a broad range of capabilities needed to logically capture, organize, share, and use knowledge elements in order to recognize problems and suggest possible solutions. The portal collects knowledge practices ranging from human resource planning, recruitment and selection to human resource development and reward management. However, when focus is put on specific goals, there is a risk of non-measured activities being less prioritized, and subsequently the quality in general is falling. This has led organizations to the apparent belief that the more things they measure, the more they will get done. This, however, is not the case. A few measures that are directed at critical process outcomes are better than a plethora of measures that only serve to produce a lack of focus, confusion about what is important, and what is not important (Ahmed et al., 2002). In addition, it is necessary to realize who is using the measurements and for what purpose. It is very important that ownership is created for the measures. Therefore, measures and criteria for success need to be decided on before imitating the process in order to make the evaluation relevant, useful, and reliable. Finally, it is important to notice that goals might be reached without the plans of action being carried into ef-

fect, and sometimes plans of action are carried into effect without the goals being reached.

PARTICIPATION AND TRUST

One of the benefits of the portal is that it enables inter-organizational collaboration without the costs (i.e., significant investment in establishment, formalized agreements and contracts, and legal requirements) of supporting specific partnership arrangements. For a portal to be able to evolve, participation through contributions from its members is necessary. Consequently, users must provide an input of knowledge in order to get access to the output side of the portal.

By answering an online survey, organizations report knowledge to the web portal. Subsequently, organizations can download standard reports or self-designed reports relating their own human resource activities and performance to data from other organizations. The self-designed reports enable the user to restructure the knowledge structures within the knowledge base. Both the standard and the self-designed reports are intended to be used as aiding tools in the benchlearning process, rather than serving as some specific piece of cutting-edge knowledge. Keeping in mind that human resource professionals in spite of interest and enthusiasm are always looking for quick, efficient, and timesaving answers, the portal is built on a rather simple technical system for the user. This way the user does not consider the portal as time consuming when figuring out how the system works. Top-ten standard reports are available for the quick-user, whereas the advanced user has the possibility of downloading extended versions or even constructing his or her own reports based on the input.

For the community to evolve, the portal also needs 'participation' from the outside. Therefore, the portal has gateways through which knowledge from non-members can pass. It is when external or new knowledge is brought into the community that tension is created between the accepted and institutionalized community knowledge. This tension is a prerequisite for learning and progressive evolvement (Wenger, 1999). Researchers, who add new theoretical human resource knowledge to the portal, create tension. The organization data stored on the web portal provides researchers with extensive quantitative material for scientific use resulting in the researchers being end-users as well. In this way, the explicit and tacit knowledge and expertise on how human resource is applied in reality provided by the human resource professionals is combined with theoretical developments, and hereby knowledge from two worlds (i.e., theory and practice) is continuously combined.

NO ROOM FOR FREE RIDERS

A limiting factor, however, is competitive logic that can prevent organizations from committed participation in the knowledge-sharing community. Inter-organizational knowledge-sharing requires a great deal of trust. Trust provides the foundation for a successful implementation and operation of a community. Although trust is the key coordinating mechanism in the community form, experiences from existing communities show that many communities fail to meet the requirements upon which trust is established. In the research literature, there appears to be general consensus on the importance of trust. However, there seems to be an equally widespread disagreement on an appropriate definition of the concept. Trust is a complex, multifaceted phenomenon. Definitions of trust have become "a confusing potpourri of definitions applied to a host of units and levels of analysis" (Shapiro, 1987).

From an IT systems view, trust is often linked to reputation where a user builds reputation and hence a basis for trust. In using reputation as part of the basis of trust, there is the question of what reputation should be based on, particularly when participants do not have detailed knowledge of each other. In e-commerce systems, for example, reputation is linked to ratings generated as feedback to transaction-type financial interactions. However, in the knowledge-sharing community presented here the specific knowledge sharing goals are not linked to financial transactions. The quality of knowledge sharing related to improving politics, processes, and strategies depends on the quality, reliability, and level of detail of knowledge provided.

From social sciences research, three types of trust are generally identified when dealing with generation of trust among unfamiliar actors. First, interpersonal trust (e.g., Deutsch & Krauss, 1962; Wichman, 1970; Pruitt & Kimmel, 1976; Good, 1988) that is to be found at the personal level and is both an agent- and context specific concept. Trust is a function of relatively rational decision-making processes, rather than personality characteristics. Trusting behavior appears when the long-term interests of the participants are stressed initially, where only small initial rewards are at stake, where there is no potential for threat, and there is great potential for successful communication. This form of trust is common to many business relationships and is important to the goals of strategic alliances based on collaborative sharing of strategy amongst peers for shared competitive advantage against external rivals.

Second, system trust (e.g., Zucker, 1986; Shapiro, 1987) is based on the perceived property or reliance on a system or institution within which trust exists. The belief that proper impersonal structures are in place (e.g. safeguards as regulations, guarantees, or contracts) generates system trust. System trust also refers to the belief that proper structures of one's own role and that of others in the situation have been defined. This is particularly relevant in the presented portal where a community facilitator needs to be a trusted third party who stores and enforces community roles and policies. Members of the community need to trust the facilitator to act for the benefit of the community.

Third and finally, dispositional trust describes the general attitude of the person seeking trustworthiness towards trust. This is also called basic trust and is independent of any other party or context. This trust is built on two basic assumptions. The first assumption is that others are generally trustworthy people. The second assumption is that irrespective of whether people are good or not, one will obtain better outcomes by trusting them as individuals develop their propensities to trust and predilections affect their thoughts and actions (e.g., Hardin, 1993; Rotter, 1980).

Participants of the community do usually not participate in all activities and functionalities of the portal from day one. They are anticipated to follow a path, where they begin by using the portal only for self-referral. Once accustomed to the functionalities of this area, participants are expected to move on to inter-organizational referrals. A reputation system is linked to ratings that reflect how well a member participates in and contributes to the community. The portal is oriented towards a phase/stage build-up of participation and commitment in the community adding a time dimension to the building of trust. This is contrary to trust seen from a theoretical perspective, as trust has usually been studied as a static rather than a dynamic variable.

IT TAKES MORE THAN A COMPUTER

At a more general level, Martinsons (1997) addresses the difficulties of computerizing human resource management due to its perceived softness that makes it difficult to quantify. In addition, uncertainty as to whom the information should be reported and lack of interest in this area by senior management are important barriers to be overcome. Other barriers to the valuation of human resources are lack of time and resources to pursue the area, lack of understanding of the areas, and lack of understanding by others in the organization. Often organizations are complaining that they do not have the time needed for capturing and organizing their knowledge, but time as such is not the problem. The problem is that it is complicated to measure. Under a constant time pressure, it is difficult to prioritize the time, and short-time goals are often selected at the expense of more long-term goals. It is important that time-outs are built into the everyday routines, for example through implementation of knowledge-management technologies as the portal presented here. It takes time to create the preliminary statement of measurement, but what is gained from sharing knowledge and applying knowledge later in the process makes it all worth.

Besides the organizational obstacles, also a number of difficulties regarding the system as such might cause significant barriers. First, lack of reliable and valid measures that are not overly complex and difficult might be a barrier. Second, lack of widely accepted measures and models, concerns as to quantifying people, and lack of expertise by the human resource department in relation to valuation of human resource is important. However, what are most important are factors of credibility and user-friendliness. The mentioned barriers are of key interest especially in the context of human resource management, as human resource professionals in general are not yet comfortable with measuring and valuating how their own departments contribute to the organization. Whereas operational aspects (i.e., outputs, faster processes, etc.) are measured, human resource professionals find the intangible aspects (i.e., employee motivation, competency gaps, hiring effectiveness, etc.) excessively complex and, therefore, difficult to measure. Compounding the problem, organizations find it difficult to establish (and maintain) the complete frameworks that create common measurement criteria across the organization.

CONCLUSION

Human resource professionals are to an increasing degree required to justify, in a systematic way, the cost of their activities, and they are looking to human resource performance indicators to express the added value of their activities to the success of the organization. Knowledge sharing generates learning that facilitates input into strategic planning, access to professional networks and formation of human resource standards, preparing the knowledge sharing, and constructing a circulation system. However, often knowledge-management systems are too general and thereby irrelevant. Information might not confer a competitive advantage and the knowledge-sharer might, therefore, not wish to share knowledge. The presented portal answers a call for a human resource system that is designed to overcome these problems. What moreover makes the presented portal unique is that it is developed in close collaboration among human resource professionals and academics.

This chapter investigates how an inter-organizational human resource knowledge-management system, in contrast to an intra-organizational system, may assists organizations in evaluating their human resource practices. In general, the system encompasses the broad range of capabilities needed to logically capture, organize, share, and use knowledge elements in order to recognize problems and suggest possible solutions. It is pointed out that in order to gain from knowledge sharing and obtain organizational learning, the system should contain both measurement and valuation.

The importance of benchlearning in contrast to traditional benchmarking is emphasized. Implicit in the distinction between benchlearning and benchmarking is the belief that obsession of simply creating databases does not cause knowledge management. The success criterion for an inter-organizational IT benchlearning system is not only related to inter-organizational knowledge creation and sharing, but also to the suggestion of

how such a tool can assist professionals in more efficient and qualitative decision-making.

The presented portal is novel in its approach of facilitating benchlearning across industry boundaries and within a soft area (i.e., human resource management). The argument against measuring intangible assets such as human resource practices is that the processes are too complex to be put into tangible goals, actions, and measures. However, the chapter questions this argument by presenting a portal that supports organizations in bringing new perspectives into the human resource area based on inter-organizational knowledge sharing.

REFERENCES

Aghion, P. & Howitt, P. (1997). A Schumpeterian Perspective on Growth and Competition. In D. M. Kreps & K. F. Wallis (Eds.), *Advances in Economics and Econometrics: Theory and Applications, Vol. 2* (pp. 279-317). New York, NY: Cambridge University Press.

Ahmed, P. K, Kok, L.K, & Loh, A.Y.E (2002). *Learning Through Knowledge Management.* Oxford: Butterworth-Heinemann.

Andersen, T., B. Eriksen, J. Lemmergaard, & L. Povlsen (2006). The Many Faces of Fit – An application to strategic human resource management, Chapter 5 (pp. 85-101). In Burton et al., 2006, *Organization Design. The Evolving State-of-the-Art.* LLC, USA: Springer Science+Business Media.

Andriessen, D. (2004). IC Valuation and Measurement: Classifying the State of the Art. *Journal of Intellectual Capital*, 5(2), 230-242.

Baise, M. & Stahl, H. (1999). Public Research and Industrial Innovations in Germany. *Research Policy*, 28, 397-422.

Becker, B. & Gerhart, B. (1996). The Impact of Human Resource Management on Organizational

Performance: Progress and prospects. *Academy of Management Journal*, 39(4), 779-801.

Bierly, P. & Chakrabarti, A. (1996). Generic Knowledge Strategies in the US Pharmaceutical Industry. *Strategic Management Journal*, 17(1), 123-135.

Cohen, W.M. & Levinthal, D.A. (1990). Absorptive Capacity: A New Perspective on Learning and Innovation. *Administrative Science Quarterly*, 35(1), 128-152.

Desrochers, P. (2001). Local Diversity, Human Creativy, and technological Innovation. *Growth and Change*, 32, 369-394.

Deutsch, M., Krauss, R.M. (1962). Studies of Interpersonal Bargaining. *Journal of Conflict Resolution*, 6, 52-76

Fiol, C.M. & Lyles, M.A. (1985). Organizational Learning. *Academy of Management Review*, 10(4), 803-813.

Good, D. (1988). Individuals, Interpersonal Relations, and Trust. In Gambetta, D. (Ed.): *Trust: Making and Breaking Cooperative Relations* (pp. 31-48). Basil Blackwell: New York.

Griliches, Z. (1992). The Search for R&D Spillovers. *Scandinavian Journal of Economics*, 94(Supplement), 29-47.

Hardin, R. (1993). The Street-Level Epistemology of Trust. *Politics and Society*, 21, 505–529.

Huber, G.P. (1991). Organizational Learning: The Contributing Processes and a Review of the Literature. *Organization Science*, 2, 88-117.

Karlöf, B., Lundgren, K., & Froment, M. E. (2001). *Benchlearning – forbilleder som løftestang for udvikling* København: Børsens Forlag A/S.

March, J. G. & Simon, H. A. (1958). *Organizations*. New York: John Wiley & Sons.

Marshall, C., Prusak, L., & Shpilberg, D. (1997). Financial Risk and the Need for Superior Knowledge Management. In Prusak, L., *Knowledge in Organizations* (pp. 227-251). USA: Butterworth-Heinemann.

Martinsons, M. G. (1997). Human Resource Management Applications of Knowledge-based Systems. *International Journal of Information Management*, 17(1), 35-53.

Meyer, J. W. & Rowan, B. (1977). Institutionalized Organizations: Formal Structure of Organizations as Myth and Ceremony. *American Journal of Sociology*, 83(2), 340-363.

Monjon, S. & Waelbroech, P. (2003). Assesing Spillovers from Universities to Firms: Evidence from French Firm-Level Data. *International Journal of Industrial Organizations*, 21, 1255-1270.

Nonaka, I. & Takeuchi, H. (1995). *The Knowledge-Creating Company – How Japanese Companies Create the Dynamics of Innovation*. Oxford, UK: Oxford University Press.

Pfeffer, J. (1997). Pitfalls on the Road to Measurement: The Dangerous Liaison of Human Resources With the Ideas of Accounting and Finance. *Human Resource Management*, 36(3), 357-365.

Phillips, J. (1996). *Accountability in Human Resource Management*. Houston: Gulf Publishing.

Powell, W. W., Koput, K. W., and Smith-Doerr, L. (1996). Interorganizational Collaboration and the Locus of innovation: Networks of Learning in Biotechnology. *Administrative Science Quarterly* (41), 116-145

Pruitt, D.G., Kimmel, M.J. (1976). Twenty Years of Experimental Gaming: Critique, Synthesis and Suggestion for the Future. *Annual Review of Psychology*, 28, 363–392.

Rodwell, J.J., Lam, J. & Fastenau, M. (2000). Benchmarking HRM and the Benchmarking of Benchmarking. Best Practices from outside the Square in the Australian Finance Industry. *Employee Relations*, 22(4), 356-374.

Rotter, J.B. (1980). Interpersonal Trust, Trustworthiness, and Gullibility. *American Psychologist*, 35, 1–7.

Sampler, J. L. (1997). Information Specificity and Environmental Scanning: An Economic Perspective. *MIS Quarterly*, 21(1), 25-53.

Shapiro, S. P. (1987). The Social Control of Impersonal Trust. *American Journal of Sociology*, 93(3), 623–658.

Tracey, B.J. and Nathan, A.E. (2002). The Strategic and Operational Roles of Human Resources: An emerging model. *Cornell Hotel and Restaurant Administration Quarterly*, 43(4), 17-26.

Ulrich, D. (1997). *Human ressource Champions - The next agenda for adding value and delivering results*. London: Harvard Business School Press.

Ulrich, D. & Brockbank, W. (2005). *HR The Value Proposition*. United States of America: Harvard Business School Press.

Ulrich, D., Brockbank, W., & Yeung, A. (1989). Beyond Belief: A Benchmark for Human Resources. *Human Resource Management*, 28(3), 311-335.

von Hippel, E. (1998). Economics of Product Development by Users: The impact of "sticky" local information. *Management Science*, 44, 629-644.

Wenger, E. (1999). *Communities of practice: learning, meaning and identity*. Cambridge: Cambridge University Press.

Wichman, H. (1970). Effects of Isolation and Communication on Cooperation in a Two Person Game. *Journal of Personality and Social Psychology*, 16, 114–120.

Zucker, L.G. (1986). Production of Trust: Institutional Sources of Economic Structure, 1846-1920. In: B.M. Staw, and L.L. Cunnings (Eds.), *Research in Organizational Behaviour* (pp. 53-111). JAI Press: Greenwich, CT *8*, 53-111.

Chapter XIII
Virtual Worlds as Environment for Learning Communities

Max Senges
Dachsweg 4a, Germany

Marc Alier
Sciences of Education Institute, UPC, Spain

ABSTRACT

This chapter discusses the potential of three dimensional virtual worlds as venue for constructivist learning communities. To reach a balanced answer to the question whether virtual worlds are likely to evolve into satisfying eductional instruments (1) we retrace the historic trajectory of virtual world development and computer based learning, second we describe how (2) learning communities function in general and how virtual worlds in particular can be exploited for collective educational experiences. With this basis, we then present (3) a structured analysis of the strenghts, weaknesses, opportunities and threats (SWOT) found to bound the potential of SecondLife for institutionalized learning based on our expertise from working and teaching in virtual worlds. In conclusion we argue that a critical but optimistic approach towards virtual learning environments (and SecondLife in particular) is adequat. In our assessment virtual worlds bear great opportunities for educational purposes, however most of today's educational institutions will be challenged to encompass the informal and holistic learning scenario.

INTRODUCTION

As it is the intention of this chapter to delve on the constructivist knowledge networking paradigm, the authors believe that it is more appropriate to develop an optimistic scenario while aware of this biased perception than restraining the description and analysis to what is feasible today.

In his paper on the future of education Lombardo argues for educational approaches that allow

Copyright © 2009, IGI Global, distributing in print or electronic forms without written permission of IGI Global is prohibited.

for a more holistic understanding of knowledge (as in wisdom): "Where in the past emphasis was on memorization, drill, and mechanical learning, education today should facilitate the development of interpretative skills and deep understanding" (Lombardo, 2007). Far from being a reality in 2007, virtual worlds are assessed to be suitable complements to presential education and apprenticeship training because the are "facilitating collaborations, community and experiential learning" (Dickey 2005).

ICT IN EDUCATION: FROM TECHNOLOGY TO COMMUNITY

Over the years, the use of ICT in education has shifted its focus from a perspective that attempted to use software and hardware as means of knowledge transmission (the Computer Based Training or Computer Based Learning approach), to a perspective where ICT is deployed to provide an improved environment for creative knowledge construction (Computer Enhanced Learning). Todays e-learing paradigm no longer regards the web as only a pipe to deliver content, but also as a meeting point, a place to 'be' with others, where all sort of communities are conjugated (as communities of practice, or communities of interest). In the radical constructivist approach promoted, all experiences serve as basis for reality construction and thus all places are learning environments. It depends on the environments architect to create the atmosphere for discourse and inquiry and to provide the tools to empower the constituents to effectively communicate, take decisions, and own their creations.

JUST A GAME

3D games have been around at least since Wolfeinstein 3D (1986) precursor of the famous

Doom. But, despite the technical evolutions, first person "shoot em up" games have almost exclusively captured the attention of young male gamers. Learning communities are not about 3D and rendering quality.

After the boom of PAC-MAN and Space Invaders (which rendered Japan in a sudden shortage of coins) it is hard to find games that captured such a wide social spectrum of players. We need to look for games like "SimCity" or "The Sims", specially to capture female audiences. These games are more about "what can I create with this game?" than "what is the experience that this game will deliver?" The latter seems to be more what young males are interested in.

SimCity and The Sims are about creating things. They came in a time when thousands of newbie computer users needed to learn how to interact with technology to access information and build knowledge objects. Constructivism reminds us how creating is a good way of learning.

The online gaming, brings the next big hit in gaming comes with the MMORPG where the social elements comes into the equation. While shoot em up players use the network to kill each other in online 3D environments, the players of MMORPG such as Everquest, WoW, Guild Wars, Hellgate London, and others.

The communities transcend the virtual space of the 3DVE when the members meet in conventions, form *guilds*[1] or *clans*[2], and start to collaborate, trade (even with real money[3]) and interact in the "real world".

The current generation of videogames has established genres that use narrative, competitive strategies and game structures built around community-based interaction. In this environment, not few players have *made good friends*[4] or [5] with people they got to know inside the game.

"We are on the cusp of a new generation where parents telling their children about the circumstances of how they met will not revolve around

college parties[...]. Instead, they will tell their children how they met each other, battling gnolls in subterranean caverns or slaying the undead in forgotten crypts while pretending to be warriors or clerics" (Yee 2007)

Many players consider their online friends *comparable or even better*[6] than their real life friends. Though it may seem strange that such a strong relationship can develop in an environment where everyone is pretending to be someone else, it is exactly that social setting what facilitates relationships.

CYBERSPACE EVOLVING

Obviously the formation of online communities is not a local phenomena of the gaming world. So far the online communities have been gathering in the various formats of cyberspace (Gibson 1984): first in networks like *Compuserve* or the home breed network of BBS's[7] in the 80's and 90's, then later the WorldWideWeb enabled more sophisticated and graphically appealing environments like forums, chats, IRC, and lately even more collaborative tools like wikis invented by Ward Cunnigham, in 1996, or identity centric personal media like blogs. These most recent additions, dubbed by Tim Oreilly with the term Web 2.0, emphasized the social aspect to the web. However, while there has been an vibrant development of media presence, 'Being' on a website always involves the imagination of Becoming textual, but over the last years also three dimensional places emerged in Cyberspace; places not un-alike Stephenson's Metaverse (Stephenson 1992) where immersive ICT environments build a distorted version of the "real world".

The "Metaverse", is a concept conceived by Neal Stephenson and described in his book "Snow Crash" a visionary cyberpunk book published 1992 when the World Wide Web was just created

and the Internet was available to limited government and educational establishments. Stephenson describes a virtual world called the Metaverse which people log into from their computers or roaming devices using sophisticated interfaces to experience it. In the Metaverse, each one's self is represented by an *avatar* or autoimage. In the Hindu philosophy the Sanskrit word avatar, refers to the bodily manifestation (or incarnation) of a divine being (deva). The world of computing takes this antique metaphor to explain the digital entity that allows a human being to "exist" in a virtual world.

In Stephenson's Metaverse main place is the Street, the central road which loops around the "equator" of the Metaverse. The Street is lined with buildings and bright neon signs, there are side roads off the Street and people (builders) with planning permission can create virtual homes and offices, but also everything from night clubs to shops and residential buildings. Anyone who "is someone" has an address in the Metaverse.

Stephenson foresees in his novel the future value of the "place" in the virtual environments. Today we are familiar with the cybersquatter phenomena and legal battles for a domain name. A virtual real estate market appears naturally in all representations of cyberspace, which seems to mimic the universe we call reality.

In 2003 Linden Labs started to create Second Life, a virtual world that mimics Stephenson's Metaverse to a surprising detail - taking todays technology available to the users into consideration. Second Life rapidly developed into the most widely known of the Virtual Worlds. Especially during the years 2006 and 2007 Second Life has experienced an exponential growth in registered users and a not so pronounced, but always ascending, curve in active members [8].

Since the foundation of Second Life educational institutions, companies, and all kinds of organizations have developed increasing interest in learning about the potential of Second Life to

Figure 1. Vishnu with his 10 avatars (incarnations): Fish, Tortoise, Boar, Man-Lion, Dwarf, Rama with the Ax, King Rama, Krishna, Buddha, and Kalkin. Painting from Jaipur, India, 19th century; in the Victoria and Albert Museum, London. (Source http://en.wikipedia.org/wiki/Image:Avatars.jpg image without copyrigth because it has expired)

Figure 2. The number of hours spent by users in Second Life grows steadily (Based of information available in SecondLife.com)

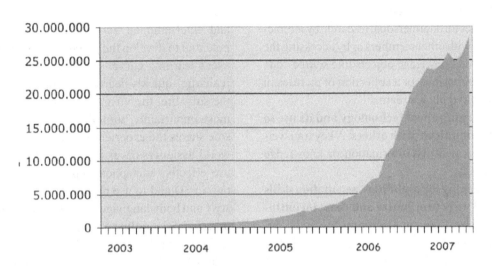

promote their mission and many have setup a presence. There's the feeling in the air that after the Web 2.0 and the spreading of the internet to the mobile devices, the next big step will be the virtual worlds.

LEARNING IN VIRTUAL WORLDS

Online Learning Communities

Communities built in social software environments (in all their different configurations and levels of integration) are proving to be an outstanding catalyst for the development of knowledge and information artifacts such as software

(e.g. moodle), encyclopedias (e.g. wikipedia) or special interests such as a way to find gold in almost depleted mines (Tapscott & Williams, 2006). Members participate in communities relevant to the pursuit of their own interests (Poe, 2006) but also in pursuit of a common goal such as building an online free encyclopedia. Hence knowledge related communities become also learning communities.

All the mentioned social environments have one element in common: The collective ownership of the knowledge generated within the community. Licenses such as GPL or the Creative Commons are providing a comprehensive way of granting both universal access to the knowledge generated as well as "moral" rights to the author.

Learning communities evolving around exclusive or blended ICT interaction provide learning opportunities in more than one level

- **Learning specific knowledge related to the community objectives.** This learning comes through personal research, by interaction with other members or by accessing the shared knowledge objects like source code in a repository or a collection of pictures in a shared photostream.
- **Learning about technology and its use to communicate with others**. A key transversal skill in the information or knowledge society.
- **Learning social abilities, negotiation skills and ways to organize and react to contingencies.** Communities are made of individuals and organizations, each one with their own focus an purpose, thus governance of the communities and the relationship with other communities and organizations is always a challenge to handle. The survival of the community as such or as one entity depends on how good the community is able to deal with it.
- **Learning to be part of the community, as the comunity builds its own culture of shareing knowledge.** The tech-geeks have been depicted as strange guys always surrounded by computers and technology and apart from social interaction. It is ironical that this collective, the tech-geeks, is the one that has pioneered the new ways of creating social communities in an urban society that is loosing its sense of community our ancestors had in the villages.

Thus *online communities* become automatically *learning communities,* even if the purpose of the community is not learning as such. In addition to that, most online communities leave a digital trace of their experience and give away the knowledge objects they create (Linux, Wikipedia, Moodle, etc.)

3D virtual environments (3DVE) seem to bee among the candidates to become the next scenario where social networks will thrive and develop themselves. Evolved in the context of gaming and entertainment 3D environments have the potential to develop the practices to optimize the user's learning curve. The user, almost without realizing, quickly learns how to interact with the software, the virtual environment and, and most importantly, the other users, with whom s/he shares the experience of the 3DVE. Virtual world designers haver learned over the years to use effective metaphors representing information in 3D and to use more channels (i.e. avatar style and body language) of communication than traditional flat online environments. That's why specialists in Business Intelligence are looking at the control panels used in Massive Multiplayer Online Role Playing Games (MMORPG), such as Blizzard's Word of Warcraft (WoW)[9].

Communities in Virtual Worlds

MMORPG's are a terrific framework to create communities and social bounds among the players. And this happens between online gamers who do know that they are in a gaming scenario (even though they take the game very seriously). But what happens when we stop calling it a game and we call it our Second Life? Then we are building a virtual world and what happens there is as serious as we want it to be.

The reason of existence for virtual worlds such as Second Life is to breed online communities that inevitably become communities of practice and thus learning communities (Alier, 2007). They are open to the mainstream public unlike MMORPG that are focussed on fans of some kind of fantasy or science fiction story. (While WoW is the MMORPG for JRR Tolkien like fantasy fans, StarWars, Startrek or "The Matrix" have their own MMORPG's.)

A key difference between virtual worlds (VW) and MMORPGsis that in VWs there are no pre-created storylines nor a defined ways of how the residents should carry out a task, or have fun. A WoW player is supposed to gain experience, goods, and skills for his/her character (who's detached from the player), to do so he/she must complete quests, e.g. kill dragons and other kinds of beasts. In a VW this is different, the resident has his/her self projected on the VW (the avatar) and the VW is there for him to do what s/he wants. The residents need to figure out what to do there.

In VWs like Second Life the residents are the creators of what's around them. Like we saw in the Sims, the resident's can build their house (if they buy land to build it, of course) and can design, create and use virtual objects like furniture, a boat, or clothing. In SL the residents are owners of the information objects they create inside (houses, avatar designs, clothes, cars, rayguns, action movies, pictures, etc.) and they are free to sell them (in Linden Dollars the currency of SL, with an exchange rate in real money), give them away or share them under licenses such as Creative Commons. So the VW, in this case, is created and shaped by its residents.

Opportunities for Learning Enhancement in Virtual Worlds

Communities and communities of practice are bred mostly spontaneously in VW. But how can these communities be turned into true learning communities ? The following list compiled by Driscol[10] identifies several sensibilities that can help to enhance learning in VW's.

- The Sense of Self. In short, you are your avatar when in a VW, and your emotional attachment to that avatar will surprise you!
- The Death of Distance. Avatars can teleport through cyberspace from one place to another "at the speed of light". Like using

a StarTrek transporter. So in VW there is space but no distances.

- Environment created by the learners: SL's landscape is constructed by residents themselves. Other VW such as ProtoSphere (link) comes with pre-built classrooms, lecture halls, and meeting spaces, which can be useful as starting point but over time does not deliver enough potential for interaction, VW residents want to shape the environment they live in.
- Social interaction. Virtual worlds foster the social interaction between users. When avatars spend time together they have (virtual) presence, sense of space, and capacity interact, while they co-create things and, or engage in social activities.
- The Pervasiveness of Practice. Second Life it's not only a virtual social world, but it is a world that particularly fosters a culture of collaborative learning. "Sandboxes abound where slightly more experienced Second Lifers share what they know with others. In every corner you see chat interactions that start with the wonderful learning question 'How do I...?'" (is this a quote?) In VW all the cultural attributes of peer-to-peer creation and learning are present just like in the traditional web, but they are so in a way that is more natural for us as human beings: a 3D environment.

Neither web based nor mobile learning replaced other forms of learning. Instead of asking "How do I build a virtual classroom?" we might ask, "What can this technology do that will enhance the learner's experience that my current learning technology portfolio cannot?" (Driscol[11])

In the following we consider the case of a teacher who wants to extend the classroom space with a VW. What kind of activities can be designed to improve the learning experience. The "Cool Cat teacher" (Davis, 2007) explains in her blog what opportunities we have in VW to improve our portfolio of learning practices:[12]

- **You can go places that cannot be visited today.** What if the students could go to ancient Rome and what if we could go there as well? If experience is the greatest teacher, what if we could give our students a SAFE way to experience such things! Think of the potential!

  You can overcome stereotypes Fashion, physical appearance and public exhibition of one's family power of acquisition create strong social differences between children at school. The creation of an avatar can allow students to escape the stereotypes of their daily lives .**Authentic Assessment / Project Based Learning Possibilities.** What if students had to research and create a village as it did in the time of Shakespeare. Even further, what if a whole school district or schools around the world created this. How much would they learn?

- **Role Playing.** Students can role play and become what we want to teach. Court cases (like the one shown above), decision making, character development, plot, metaphors, and so many things can be taught in such an environment.

- **Potential for group synergies (collaboration among teachers)** Teachers of different places (schools, towns even countries) can put their classes to work together for common projects. This has been a common educational practice that started with the exchange of mail (the one that requires paper and to actually send atoms, not only bits) among students; the Internet with email, chat, forums and wikis gave new ways to collaborate and provided a more synchronous experience. Virtual worlds offer an environment for this collaboration to take place.

- **Scenario Simulation.**

- **Digital Storytelling.** Machinima is the act of making real movies in virtual worlds. Your students can role play, you can film and share it and critique it. The possibilities are unlimited!There are accounts of psychologisits who use SL to treat autism, and agrophonbia, as well as to simulate schizophrenia[13].

The possibilities for innovative learning scenarios are virtually unlimited, but potential is only realized in case it is nurtured and surrounded by a supporting environment.

A Meeting Point Between Two E-Learning Paradigms

But let us step back a moment and consider how ICT's have been used for learning: **content driven vision**. Hypertext, multimedia and 3D simulation contents are considered as the channel to use to deliver knowledge to the students. The Virtual Campus is the framework where the contents are delivered to the student, and the teacher assumes the role of a tutor, just monitoring and grading the students progress. The content is, like software, also a valuable resource expensive to produce and something to protect as intellectual property or to be shared as Open Learning Objects.

This notion of working with illustrative content or simulations is hardly a new phenomenon of cyberspace. As Herbert Simone already acknolwedged in the 1960's, "simulation, as tequnichnique for achieving understanding and predicting the behavior of systems, predates of course the digital computer. The model basin and the wind tunnel are valued means for studying the behavior of large systems by modeling them in the small, and it is quite certain that Ohm's law was suggested to its discoverer by its analogy with simple hydraulic phenomena" (Simone, 1996,)

A social constructionist vision. Where communities of practice as conceptualized by Wenger[14] are gathering around a shared interest and continuously provide learning experiences to each other. The fundamental constituents of this vision are according to Martin Dougiamas[15]:

- All of us are potential teachers as well as learners - in a true collaborative environment we are both.
- We learn particularly well from the act of creating or expressing something for others to see.
- We learn a lot by just observing the activity of our peers.
- By understanding the contexts of others, we can teach in a more transformational way (constructivism)
- A learning environment needs to be flexible and adaptable, so that it can quickly respond to the needs of the participants within it.

Virtual worlds can be applied in both paradigms since Virtual Worlds are designed to experience digital contents like no other framework ever and as a "place" to interact with others.

Reality and Virtuality are Being Mashed

In a project with the aim to identify and describe future forces that affecting education, the Knowledgeworks Foundation and the Institute for the Future write: "Life and learning become serious games. As the barriers between physical and digital spaces come down, people will move seamlessly between digital game spaces and urban neighborhoods. The intermingling of world building (alternate reality) games and real-life interactions in physical–digital space will create a culture of layered realities, where strategies from the worlds of gaming and simulation will increasingly be employed in non-game situations. For learning, this means that the cooperative, critical-thinking, and problem-solving practices encouraged in digital games make serious games a key form of pedagogy[16]." Today the serious

gaming momvement is gaining acceptions in the educational community and never had any problems developing traction with the learners. Recently we see whole conferences dedicated to social change through digital games are being held[17].

So what are the 'new' properties of virtual 3D environments like SecondLife?

As repeatedly alluded to the fundamental conditions of being in a virtual world are different from two dimensional online spaces. The consultancy Gartner has published[18] five laws meant to facilitate good practice and understanding in virtual worlds:

- The first law is that **"virtual worlds are not games"**. In virtual worlds there is no global artificial narrative and purpose or quest to be pursued by the users.
- The second law deals with the fact that **"every avatar is a real person"**. At least for now there is only real people maneurving avatars in virtual worlds. This might change with the advances and application of computational intelligence, but in 2007 it is a matter of politeness and social competence to interact with the fellow participants.
- The third law enters into normative propositions to construct a rich and rewarding experience:: **"Be relevant and add value"**. This assertion paraphrases the heart of all social software environments. They only function when many participants add value by contributing relevant information or activities.
- The forth law raise an important point which is all to often neglected because of the optimistic, sometimes euphoric attitudes of entreprencurial creators: **"contain the downside"**. It is a matter of media literacy that people are aware of the 'negative' possibilities in virtual worlds. Company branding material such as T-shirts might be burned or worn by people engaging in

ethically questionable activities and young learners might be poking into the extensive redlight district. There are endless possibilities for what can be considered bad behavior within a given usage scenario, but it helpful to remember the analogy put forward by Jimmy Wales (2006): When thinking about designing a social software the old software architecture paradigm applied in the context of e.g. developing a banking software "seal all potential chances for exploitation" is not valid anymore. Rather he proposes to see the architecture of a social software like the design for a restaurant. Just because knifes are weapons and can potentially be used to attack other customers nobody designs a restaurant with blunt knifes or individual security cells. Instead social software needs flexible to tackle issues when they arise and to give the participants the tools to self-manage the community.

- Last but not least the fifth law highlights a point that is made throughout this chapter also: the development and experience of virtual worlds is at its beginning or as the Gartner experts put it, "**it is a long haul**". There will be major changes in the technical and social design of the métier.

Two obvious innovative characteristics have to do with SL's integration in the real world: The first aspect that is assessed to have a significant impact on the expectations and motivation of the participants of the virtual world is that **in Second Life there is a real money economy** with all the associated components like a property, a market, and means of production. In Second Life economics have been an innate part since very early in its existence and while many users come to Second Life to be part of an innovative community project, the majority of the users either come for entertainment or attracted by the Sirenes singing about becoming rich in what is marketed as the next virtual goldrush.

The second aspect is that it is an environment that is integrated with the rest of the media-sphere (i.e. websites, email, online video and audio). Especially the popular platform Second Life intended from the beginning to facilitate integration websites and email as well as with so called web 2.0 applications by including possibilities to record video as a standard client feature and having in-world messages delivered to users email accounts. Due to the (relative) openness of the programming environment third parties are also able to add functionalities such as streaming video and audio into and from the virtual world.

In this line Second Life made Open Source its client in 2007 and currently is moving to the Mono platform (Open Source runtime environment for Microsoft's .Net). This opens possibilities for versatile developments and integrations of third party systems, but it still keeps closed the server part closing the door for many more interesting possibilities, specially for integration with educational institutions who might want to have control over his virtual land.

In our opinion: Second Life should open the server side software and allow other companies to provide service in their virtual world, just like the World Wide Web, if they don't other Virtual World platforms will do it and might win "the game" and become "the" virtual world platform.

What is really changing the character of the environment is that it is setup to be build by its users. Creation is a key entertainment factor, and the commitment and relation of the builders as community of learners paramount. So in short, virtual worlds are a combination allowing for learning through role-play, simulation and, and what is really new, "real virtuality". Real virtuality in this case means that the learning experience happens in a virtual classroom that is, because of the three dimensions of VLs much more like a real room than any 2D web based virtual classroom can ever be. Hence it is the challenge for online education to construct a similarly rich experience as in presential educational settings, while at the same time exploiting the specifically positive conditions of digital environments. Compared to traditional two-dimensional web environments (which had limitations on navigation) virtual worlds provide a more versatile and at the same time seamless experience which makes them more natural and hence immersive and engaging to be in.

SECOND LIFE FOR LEARNING: A SWOT ANALYSIS

Naturally what educational institutions did first was 'replicate' their real world understanding and transpose their campus into a virtual copy. Some SL properties change the experience from a 2D web-video cast - such as that you see the other participants with their avatars. But that is not the

Table 1. SWOT analysis for learning in Second Life

Strengths	Weaknesses

1. authentic learning
2. social learning
3. Intrinsic motivated learning
4. Reflective learning
5. Educational purposes for which virtual worlds are well suited:
   1. all artistic performances can stage fantastic works without static, material costs, space limitations
   2. Project management, negotiation, dealing with ambiguity, entrepreneurship
   3. Media literacy & critical thinking
   4. Simulations
   5. all kinds of practice training for which role-play can be used (ethics, examinations, acting)
   6. three dimensional perception and imagination
	1. Relevance & Correctness
	2. Emerging Technology
	3. Weak meshability (technology integration)
	4. High demands on the client
	5. No pedagogy is established
	6. Educational purposes for which virtual worlds are not well suited:
	   1. transmission of a targeted learning experience
	   2. following linear presentations (frontal teaching)

Opportunities	**Threats**
1. to allow learners to experiment with and 'feel' other identities (e.g. culture, gender, race, etc.) 2. to allow learners to experiment with and act out roles (e.g. entrepreneur, researcher, architect) 3. higher engagement 4. Reduce social boundaries 5. Increase Idea production 6. cosmopolitan learning environments 7. Integrate disadvantaged learners 8. Business as motivation	1. Accuracy 2. Complexity 3. Non-standard Technology 4. Business model 5. Need for fundamental change (Eg. Examination methods)

interesting aspect of this learning environment.

A virtual campus does not need to share many visual and spatial aspects with its brick and mortar doppelgraenger. Instead the challenge is to use the special strengths and develop the opportunities of SL for learning. But one has to be cautious, there are weaknesses and traps as well. Therefore in the following we list considerations regarding potential benefits as well as the risks and benefits for educational institution's engagement in SecondLife. An overview of the assessed education scenario in SecondLife is illustrated in Table 1. It is important to point out that the strengths of virtual worlds are developed in a hypothetical way elaborating on the potential rather than today's possibilities. When developing the weaknessess, the arguments are meant to mitigate the risks rather than painting a worst case scenario.

Strengths

1. **Authentic learning** - SL is an open learning environment meaning that learning can happen in 'real' scenarios rather then in a closed up e-learning platform or a classroom. Mason and Moutahir (2006) assess that SL is a good setting for learning projects which "provide a "hand-on" opportunity for students to address real-world problems in a multidisciplinary, collaborative environment. This has been shown to increase student engagement and provide intrinsic motivation for authentic, relevant learning. (Bradford, 2005)"
2. **Social learning** – virtual worlds are suitable for collaborative activities because you actually experience the other in the same spot – rather than a mere 'presence'-indicator, there is movement, gestures etc.
3. **Intrinsic motivated learning** - Because of the complexity of the environment virtual worlds are more suitable for self-motivated learning projects which are supported by self-developed learning strategies

4. **Reflective learning** - Because of the 'detachment' of the virtual experience of oneself, reflective or critical thinking is likely to be triggered. Critical thinking has been described as "the art of thinking about your thinking while you are thinking in order to make your thinking better" (Paul, Binker, Adamson, & Martin, 1989).
5. **Educational purposes for which virtual worlds are explicitly well suited:**
   - All artistic performances can stage fantastic works without static, material costs, space limitations
   - Project management, negotiation, dealing with ambiguity, entrepreneurship
   - C. Media literacy & critical thinking
   - Simulations - Learning content is experienced rather than looked at. For example Doherty et al (2006) found that "scale models that are difficult to represent in a book or on a flat computer screen become easy to build and interesting to explore in Second Life".
   - All kinds of practice training for which role-play can be used (ethics, examinations, acting)
   - F Three dimensional perception and imagination

Weaknesses

1. **Relevance & Correctness** - Because learning environments are not controlled learners are potentially exposed to a wide array of unnecessary or even 'false' information.
2. **Technology is not ready for prime time** (e.g. chat instead of voice)
3. **Technology is still not well integrated with other media.** The client is quite big and even though (1) links to locations as well as (2) in-world recordings can be made,

overall integration is still low. SLoodle[19] is the first initiative that intends to setup one integrated solution.

4. **There are high technical demands and proprietory software needed on the client computer** (which are met by approximately one quarter of western PC users in 2008). The choosing of DirectX as 3D acceleration platform closes the door with the OpenGL market preeminent on the Apple computers and Linux based desktops.

5. **No didactic methodologies are established** - learning depends inmensly on the skill and methodology deployed and for virtual worlds there is simply not enough experience for tested methodologies to be available. Educators are experimenting and pioneering their pedagogy on a trial and error basis. This situation is probable to continue for the next years as the new pedagogy has to be developed, tested and verified before it can become dominant. However given the rapid technological development and hence the rapid development of features and conditions of virtual worlds, it is more likely that teaching and learning will maintain an entrepreneurial activity, with the state-of the art always prone to be overthrowing by the next improved opportunity.

6. **Educational purposes for which virtual worlds are not well suited:**Transmission of a targeted learning experience (as in book or video). Virtual worlds need to be interactively explored hence pure theory and memorization tasks are more difficult to design (except if they can and are visualized and made interactive adequately, as is the case for language learning).

   • Following all kinds of linear presentations and frontal teaching methods. Because of the plentifull communication channels and the potential to "go and do" it seems not prudent to have the learner be passive and simply follow the activities and speech of someone.

   • Clark Aldrichs[20] gives ten reasons explaining why virtual worlds are not yet ready to deliver their potential for real skillz simulation. Most of them have to do with missing hardware and especially interface and experience controllers. Among the features he demands are support for After Action Reviews (AARs), heads up displays (HUD) to support specific learning goals, as opposed to navigation, or dynamic AI Characters.

Opportunities

1. **To allow learners to experiment with and 'feel' other identities** (e.g. culture, gender, race, etc.). This role playing is particularly useful for all social skills such as needed in all service providing professions. Given that the role asumed is not the least influenced by age, race or any other physical or communication feature the learner has role playing can be used in a much more effective setting then most real life experiences.

2. **To allow learners to experiment with and act out roles** (e.g. entrepreneur, researcher, architect (explore choice and consequence Jenkins (2006))). Virtual worlds have an enormous potential to empower the users to start any kind of project within the environment. Everything from a lemonade stand to an architecture agency can be planned and setup at virtually no cost.

   • Higher engagement - to create learning environments that are fun to be in (and are adequate for digital natives). Virtual worlds are true multi-media combining action, images, sounds, and words Gee (2006) and as these elements are situated in one setting, the learners experience how the concepts work in context

- Reduce social boundaries amongst learners because of in-world equality. As alured to already, in virtual worlds the physical features and communication habits as well as disorders are completely leveled and distinction based on appearance is be impossile. This is a clear opportunity to create multi-cultural learning experiences and foster cosmopolitan learning.
- Increase Idea production and imagination through the expanded possibilities of virtual worlds
- to allow a richer experience for learners with disabilities (or otherwise constrained e.g. isolation)
- The fact that SL allows for real money business activities is likely to cause some students to be more motivated to engage in learning.
  - building an intergenerational knowledge corpus
  - holografic camera

Threats

- Accuracy - Learners might make an experience that makes them embrace a false believe. E.g. SL is most definitely not the right place to learn about sexuality.
- Complexity - Learners and professors might loose their time as initial 'orientation' might be quite complex (depending on previous experience)
- Non–standardized programming language and object descriptions - SL might very well not turn out to lead the way into a standardized 3D web infrastructure. In this case some aspects learned in SL might be worthless. Generally there is no need to bet on SL; most of the learning can also be setup on similar platforms such as croquet,

or Active Worlds. An informal comparison has been conducted here

- Business-model - The SL business model may cause some students to focus more on creating "business skills" rather than "learning skills". Setting in which students exploit education time for business development where it is not adequate can be imagined.
- Need for fundamental change - Traditional examination and subsequently certification methods are not easily transferred into virtual worlds. This poses a challenge for educational institutions to amend their examination scheme. Some insights might be gained by looking at examination methods in artistic disciplines.

VIRTUAL WORLDS IN THE EDUCATIONAL KNOWLEDGE ECOSYSTEM

After reflecting about the various opportunities and threats regarding virtual worlds and learning, we lastly situate education in virtual worlds within the wider learning experience created by the internet. Figure 3. illustrates how virtual worlds and the activities within them are surrounded by "traditional" collaborative learning tools such as wikis, blogs and fora. On the bottom of the model we have the learning commmunity giving input from their existing experience about whatever the target learning subject is. During the virtual world expirience they learners activities are recorded and they report about them. Sometimes in a conversation with community members who are not part of the virtual excursion team. Afterwards the experience in the virtual world is codified and thereby made more tangable and transferable to the wider community of learners. Just like this chapter is the report of two educators experimenting and erflecting about their teaching and learning ventures in SecondLife.

Figure 3. Virtual worlds within online education ecosystem

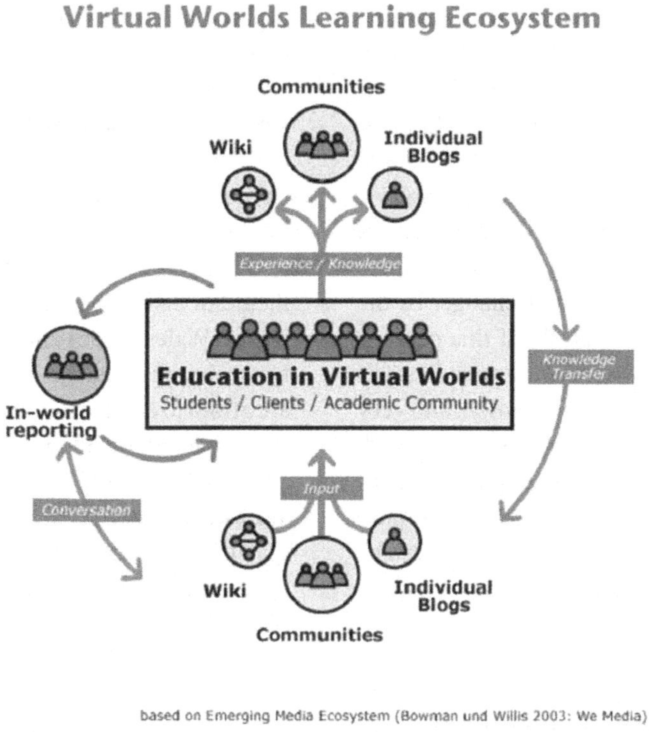

CONCLUSION

In conclusion we acknowledge the potential of virtual worlds as holistic learning environments. We share Diehl's (2007) evaluation that 3DVE encompas many challenges and opportunities, but many traditional fundamental educational practices and especially formal education following traditional standards in evaluation will need to be amended and revised in order to exploit the grand potential for learning in the metaverse.

So what needs to happen to make the most out of virtual worlds for learning? Yochai Benkel, the author of the seminal work on co-production in the network society "The Wealth of Networks" poses the right forward looking questions in his text "Common Wisdom: Peer Production of Educational Materials": "The questions around the long-term importance of this medium from the perspective of production can be divided into two. First, there is the question of the extent to which the platform or engine will be developed in an open, collaborative way. The second is whether, if this precondition is fulfilled, there is reason to think that richly-rendered learning objects and educational experience contexts will in fact be developed for this platform." (Benkler, 2005)

Education has long been acknowledged as one of the key sectors for the application of new innovations, especially ICT based innovations. However the visions and expectation of the observers have seldom been realized or at least not been realized to the degree and within the timeframe specified. Radical optimist the eminent scientist, entrepreneur, and futurologist Ray Kurzweil has envisioned the future of education as follows: "Because of current bandwidth limitations and the lack of effective three-dimensional displays, the virtual environment provided today through routine Web access does not yet fully compete with 'being there', but that will change. In the early part of the second decade of this century visual-auditory virtual-reality environments will be full immersion, very high resolution, and very convincing. Most colleges will follow MIT's lead, and students will increasingly attend classes virtually. Virtual environments will provide high-quality virtual laboratories where experiments can be conducted in chemistry, nuclear physics, or any other scientific field. Students will be able to interact with a virtual Thomas Jefferson or Thomas Edison, or even to become a virtual Thomas Jefferson. Classes will be available for all grade levels in many languages. The devises needed to enter these high-quality, high-resolution virtual classrooms will be ubiquitous and affordable even in third world countries. Students at any age, from toddlers to adults, will be able to access the best education in the world at any time and from any place" (Kurzweil, R., 2005, The singularity is near, p. 337). As stated, this radial position has to seen with skepticism as most of these kind of visions turn out wrong. For example the very Thomas Edison mentioned in the above quote proclaimed in 1913: "Books will soon be obsolete in schools ... It is possible to teach every branch of human knowledge with the motion picture. Our school system will be compeletly changed in the next ten years" (as cited by Reiser, 2001). Traditional media and practices have enormous advantages when it comes to usability and the possibility of inter-generational understanding of the practices.

However we do have a positive answer to Benkler's questions. Our positive outlook towards virtual worlds as learning environments is based on the observation that there is a vibrant and inspired community collaborating on and as we have argued thereby learning in virtual worlds. It is these community members who are developing virtual worlds to be social learning environments and who will be able to inspire and integrate novices.

Wikipedia founder Jimmy Wales brings the theme in a simple equation: "community needs trust" (Wales, 2006) and many of today's executives want the positive effects of community but are afraid to create open systems with open social rules that can be adopted to new circumstances and amended based on experience. According to Wales communities are 'responsible' when you give them the responsibility to decide for themselves and the tools to make decisions collectively (ibid.). From the development of virtual worlds so far it does not seem that the traditional brick & mortar reservations towards community rule are being transposed into this new environment.

Hence we endorse Bates (forthcoming) that in this "volatile context, it is critical that educational organizations have processes in place that encourage dynamic change, innovative uses of technology, and monitoring and evaluation of what works and what does not."

REFERENCES

Alier, M. (2006) "A Social Constructionist Approach to Learning Communities:Moodle" in "Open Source for Knowledge and Learning Management: Strategies Beyond Tools" Militadis D. Lytras, Ambjörn Naeve (Eds). Idea Group INC.

Bates, T. (Forthcoming) Understanding Web 2.0 and its implications for e-learning; in *Web 2.0-Based E-Learning: Applying Social Informatics for Tertiary Teaching*, Lee, M. & McLoughlin, C. (Eds); IGI Global

Benkler, Y. (2005) Common Wisdom: Peer Production of Educational Materials, retrieved on 19. Feb. 2008 from http://www.benkler.org/Common_Wisdom.pdf

Davis, V.A. (2007) "The frontier of education: Web 3D" The Coolcat teacher blog. Online http://coolcatteacher.blogspot.com/2007/03/frontier-of-education-web-3d.html Accesed 13 March 2007

Dickey, M. D. (2005). "Three-dimensional virtual worlds and distance learning: two case studies of Active Worlds as a medium for distance education." British Journal of Educational Technology 36(3): 439-451.

Diehl, W. (2007) The new social networking technologies: educators get a Second Life; in The Twelfth Cambridge Conference on Open and Distance Learning, www2.open.ac.uk/r06/conference/CambridgeConferencePapers2.pdf

Doherty, P., Rothfarb, R., Barker, D. (2006) Building an Interactive Science Museum in Second Life http://www.simteach.com/SLCC06/slcc2006-proceedings.doc

Gibson, W. (1984). Neuromancer. New York: Ace Books.

Kahn, J. (2007) Wayne Gretzky-Style 'Field Sense' May Be Teachable, Wired Magazine, 15.06 http://www.wired.com/science/discoveries/magazine/15-06/ff_mindgames

Lombardo, T. (2007). The Pursuit of Wisdom and the Future of Education [Electronic Version]. Retrieved 28.May.2007 from http://www.mcli.dist.maricopa.edu/dd/wisdom05/pursuit_of_wisdom.pdf.

Marshal Poe. "The Hive". The Altantic Monthly. Magazine September 2006. Online:http://www.theatlantic.com/doc/200609/wikipedia Accessed Setembre 2007

Mason, H., Moutahir, M. (2006) Multidisciplinary Experiential Education in Second Life: A Global Approach http://www.simteach.com/SLCC06/slcc2006-proceedings.doc

Paul, Binker, Adamson, & Martin. (1989). Critical thinking on the web: Definitions [Electronic Version]. Retrieved 29.May.2007 from http://www.austhink.org/critical/pages/definitions.html.

Simon, H. A. (1996). Sciences of the artificial (3rd edition): MIT.

Stephenson ,N. (1992) Snowcrash. New York: Spectra.

Tapscott, D., Williams, A. D. (2006). "Wikinomics: How Mass Collaboration Changes Everything" Portfolio Hardcover.

Wales, J. (2006). Wikipedia, wikia and free culture [Electronic Version]. University of Bergen. Retrieved 29.05.06 from http://academicfeeds.friwebteknologi.org/index.php?id=25

Yee, N. (2007) The Daedalus Project: Psychology of MMOTPGG's. Online http://www.nickyee.com/daedalus/ Accessed 12 March 2008

ENDNOTES

1   In Guild Wars.
2   In the World of Warcraft: WoW
3   The Chinese Farming phenomena consists in the huge number of chinese players that spend lots of hours in the VW to gather virtual resources (gold, items, etc) and sell it through online auction sites like ebay.com.
4   http://www.nickyee.com/daedalus/archives/000523.php
5   http://www.nickyee.com/daedalus/archives/000512.php

6   http://www.nickyee.com/daedalus/archives/000523.php

7   In 1978 Ward Christensen created the software called BBS:Bulletin Board Systems, that allowed a computer to share information and files through the analog telephone line.

8   In Feb 2008 there are 12 milion SL registered users 1 million has been connected during the last month, and 50.000 where logged in when we checked it. http://secondlife.com/whatis/economy_stats.php

9   According to Joi Ito interviewed in Mobuzz-TV on august 2007. http://dailybuzz.mobuzz.tv/shows/the_joi_of_warcraft_1

10   http://informl.com/2007/05/08/another-life-unexpurgated/

11   http://internettime.pbwiki.com/Immersive%20Environments

12   http://coolcatteacher.blogspot.com/2007/03/frontier-of-education-web-3d.html

13   http://ialja.blogspot.com/2007/03/thinking-about-3d-web-or-is-it-web-30.html

14   http://www.ewenger.com/theory/

15   Creator of the Moodle LMS. http://Moodle.org

16   http://www.kwfdn.org/map/map/12/Serious-Games.aspx

17   http://www.gamesforchange.org/

18   http://www.gartner.com/it/page.jsp?id=503861

19   www.sloodle.org/

20   http://clarkaldrich.blogspot.com/2007/05/top-ten-missing-features-of-second-life.html

Chapter XIV
Corps of Engineers Natural Resources Management (NRM) Gateway:
Communities "in" Practice

Bonnie F. Bryson
U. S. Army Corps of Engineers, USA

M. Kathleen Perales
U. S. Army Corps of Engineers, USA

R. Scott Jackson
U. S. Army Corps of Engineers, USA

Virginia L. Dickerson
U. S. Army Corps of Engineers, USA

ABSTRACT

This chapter describes the development of a knowledge management based website that serves a community of practice within a federal agency, the U.S. Army Corps of Engineers Natural Resources Management Community of Practice. Content development workshops that are conducted as an effective method of creating new content and updating existing content on the website are also described. This successful model may be used by other agencies and organizations to develop and share organizational information in an easily retrievable manner.

Copyright © 2009, IGI Global, distributing in print or electronic forms without written permission of IGI Global is prohibited.

INTRODUCTION

This chapter describes the development and maintenance of content in a knowledge management-based website to support a public sector organization's community of practice (CoP). The Natural Resources Management (NRM) Gateway is a website where the NRM CoP integrates its people, policies, programs and practices. The NRM CoP is part of the U.S. Army Corps of Engineers (USACE or Corps), America's largest federal provider of water-based recreation, spanning 42 states and over 450 lakes and river systems (USACE, 2006b). Organizationally, the NRM CoP is a part of a larger Corps Operations and Regulatory CoP. The NRM CoP's diverse responsibilities are described in the following mission statement:

The Army Corps of Engineers is the steward of the lands and waters at Corps water resources projects. Its Natural Resources Management Mission is to manage and conserve those natural resources, consistent with ecosystem management principles, while providing quality public outdoor recreation experiences to serve the needs of present and future generations.

In all aspects of natural and cultural resources management, the Corps promotes awareness of environmental values and adheres to sound environmental stewardship, protection, compliance and restoration practices.

The Corps manages for long-term public access to, and use of, the natural resources in cooperation with other Federal, State, and local agencies as well as the private sector.

The Corps integrates the management of diverse natural resource components such as fish, wildlife, forests, wetlands, grasslands, soil, air, and water with the provision of public recreation opportunities. The Corps conserves natural resources and provides public recreation opportunities that contribute to the quality of American life." *(USACE, 1996, p. 2-1).*

The NRM CoP has three distinct business areas of expertise and responsibility, although many staff members manage some or all of the three within their assigned geographic region: Recreation, Environmental Stewardship, and Environmental Compliance. Each of these business areas traditionally had their own organizational stovepipes for providing information to staff in the 400+ field offices across the nation. Partnerships represent a fourth area of expertise and responsibility that are incorporated within each of the previously listed business areas. The NRM Gateway blurs the lines and provides information to managers regardless of the business area or organizational structure, and emphasizes partnerships within the business lines.

The NRM Gateway website initiative primarily targets the NRM CoP staff, comprised of over 3,000 Resource and Operation Managers, Rangers, Environmental Compliance, Environmental Stewardship (Foresters, Fisheries Biologists, etc.) Specialists, Contract, and Administration staff (USACE, 2006c). The initial design of the NRM Gateway was to provide "information the way managers manage." Besides the NRM CoP, the Gateway serves citizens through visitor pages that describe recreation opportunities at Corps lakes.

The NRM Gateway objectives (USACE, 2005) are to:

- Serve the needs of the NRM CoP, while integrating it into the larger scheme of the recreation and travel industry, environmental stewardship and environmental compliance arenas and the larger agency CoP (see Figure 1);
- Preserve institutional knowledge;
- Develop practical and agency-approved webpages that provide useful and easily retrievable corporate information for the NRM CoP and enhanced citizen access to information about Corps public use facilities;

Figure 1. Community circles instead of stovepipes

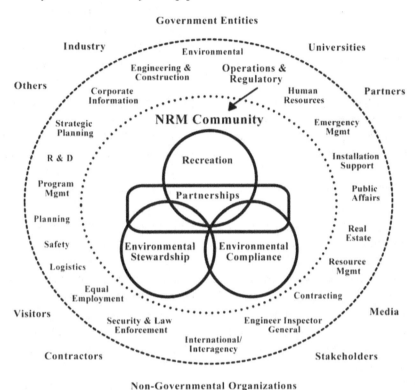

- Integrate policies, standards, program histories, best management practices and lessons learned to support organizational learning;
- Incorporate new technology such as Webcasting and collaborative software to enhance CoP communication; and
- Incorporate budgeting tools to support NRM initiatives.

One of the NRM Gateway operating principles is having many content providers (Content Subject Matter Experts [SMEs]) responsible for small units of knowledge within an area of interest and expertise, in order to maintain manageable components. Workshops are conducted periodically to facilitate building of additional content by the SMEs as well as reviewing and refreshing information that has been posted for any significant period of time.

Moving from communication within the traditional organizational stovepipes to the NRM Gateway's knowledge management-based website in support of a functioning CoP represented a significant shift in this organization's corporate culture. The NRM Gateway, launched in April 2001, was on the leading edge of this shift considering that "USACE 2012" reorganization that promoted use of CoP as part of an agency-wide reorganization was not published until two years later (USACE, 2003). The Corps regulation "The Community of Practice (CoP) in the U.S. Army Corps of Engineers (USACE)" was not officially issued until nearly five years later (USACE, 2006a). The process of building the NRM Gateway and the workshop approach used for content development are described in this chapter. This successful model may be used by other agencies and organizations to develop and share organizational information in an easily retrievable fashion.

BACKGROUND

Background for this chapter is provided by a brief literature review discussing issues relevant to the fields of Knowledge Management, Communities of Practice, and Change Management.

Knowledge Management

Knowledge management (KM) in organizations has received considerable attention in the 1990s and into the first decade of the 2000s. KM attempts to capture the immense volume of knowledge that an organization may posses and convert it so that it can be retrieved and used by everyone within (and sometimes outside) the enterprise. Wiig's (1997) "working definition" of KM is "(1) [t]o make the enterprise act as intelligently as possible to secure its viability and overall success and (2) [t]o otherwise realize the best value of its knowledge assets" (p. 1). Wiig further identifies three areas in which KM helps build organizational superiority: "operational excellence, product leadership, and customer intimacy" (p. 14). Drew (1999) identifies "the key components of successful [KM as] strategy, culture, technology, organization and people (p. 132), and encourages the integration of KM with the company's strategic goals.

Dieng, et al (1999) discusses the importance of KM in retaining "corporate memory." An organization's corporate memory is comprised of "technical memory" (workers' collective skills and abilities), "organizational memory" (including historical progression of the organization's development) and "project memories" (lessons learned). Dieng, et al further distinguish between "internal memory" possessed within an organization and "external memory" that encompasses valuable resources outside the organization (p. 570). "Stakeholder-centered design" is another approach that considers users needs in KM efforts (p. 572). "Knowledge-based corporate memory" discusses building corporate memory that the user retrieves and places "in context" rather than grabbing an "expert system...automatic solution" (p. 578).

Weeks (2004) presents a case study of KM in a large organization with global operations. As part of this organization's KM efforts, new positions known as "*knowledge brokers*" (p. 16) were created. Knowledge brokers channelled knowledge from informal settings to a formal KM process. The persons filling these positions could be at any level of the organization, but the desirable qualifications included "someone with at least five to six years of experience...enthusiasm for the job and respect within the firm. Ideally... a motivator for other members of the team..." (p. 17). Weeks discussed avoidance of the "tragedy of the commons" (p. 23) in which a KM system is owned by everyone but where no one is responsible for contributing to or maintaining the system. Weeks recommended that KM efforts be added to the organization's recognition and performance evaluation systems. Weeks' study identified that a major KM challenge for modern organizations "is to apply knowledge in such a way that context and wider strategic meaning are not lost during transfer throughout the firm and beyond the firm's boundaries" (p. 23).

Soo et al (2002) state that "...all too rarely is...data sifted into the sort of knowledge that can inform business decisions and create positive results" (p. 130), and assert that "formal databases must be treated as strategic tools rather than mere storage facilities" (p138). Soo et al also recommend that the valuable information from "informal networking" within the organization should be provided structure so that it can be retrievable by others (p. 140).

Communities of Practice

Closely associated with KM are CoPs. Snyder and Briggs (2003) define a CoP as "a particular type of network that features peer-to-peer collaborative activities to build member skills as well as organizational and societal capabilities" (p. 5). At the heart of a CoP is the important concept that participation is voluntary. Snyder describes three elements of CoP, (1) domain, which is the core business of what the CoP does and related problematic issues, (2) community, which in the federal government arena necessitates collaboration with a variety of agencies, partners, and stakeholders, and (3) practice, which includes "both methodologies and skills" (p. 9). A variety of CoP tools discussed include teleconferences, various meeting types, email capabilities, and websites that make knowledge available for internal audiences as well as external audiences to include the public.

Wenger, McDermott, and Snyder (2002) describe the stages of CoP development with the following descriptive titles, "potential," "coalescing," "maturing," stewardship," and "transformation" (p. 69). In the transformation phase, events such as significant organizational changes or loss of CoP "energy" can require regression to an earlier development stage or even the death of the CoP (p. 109).

The Corps issued a regulation in 2006 that established policy for CoP in that agency. It describes CoP as follows:

Community of Practice (CoP)--is a group of people who regularly interact to collectively learn, solve problems, build skills and competencies, and develop best practices around a shared concern, goal, mission, set of problems, or work practice. CoPs cut across formal organizational structures and increase individual and organizational agility and responsiveness by enabling faster learning, problem solving, and competence building; great-

er reach to expertise across the force; and quicker development and diffusion of best practices. CoP structures range from informal to formal and may also be referred to as structured professional forums, knowledge networks, or collaborative environments (USACE, 2006a, p. 2)

Bryson conducted a 1999 career development study of the NRM workforce now known as the NRM CoP (Bryson, 1999). This study, conducted two years before the NRM Gateway was launched, revealed that the average age of NRM employees was 42.8 years with an overwhelming majority of the workforce in the baby boomer cohort. Since many of the older members are eligible to retire at age 55, a looming significant loss of expertise was signalled by 33-percent of the 1999 workforce who were already eligible or would reach retirement eligibility by 2009. Many comments received in the qualitative portion of the study indicated that individuals felt their training opportunities were limited due to lack of funds for travel to attend sessions as well as training tuition costs. One particular comment in the qualitative section noted that "...those of us older employees feel a great deal of pressure to make changes that our education and experience has [sic] not prepared us for...Evidently the Corps does not value experience nearly as much as their newly perceived skills that they feel we must have in the new age of computers..." (p. 143). This study provided evidence of a workforce that could benefit from KM and CoP principles to preserve and share institutional knowledge and enhance accessible training opportunities.

Change Management

Change management literature provides valuable insights into successful accomplishment of a cultural shift such as the introduction of KM and CoP principles to an agency like the Corps. In his classic 1995 change management article,

Kotter noted that having observed over 100 organizations in a ten-year span try to change for the better, "the most general lesson to be learned from the most successful cases" is that change requires a lengthy progression through a sequence of stages (Kotter, 1995, p. 2). Kotter identified the following "Eight Steps to Transforming Your Organization" (p. 3):

- "Establishing a Sense of Urgency"
- "Forming a Powerful Guiding Coalition"
- "Creating a Vision"
- "Communicating the Vision"
- "Empowering Others to Act on the Vision"
- "Planning for and Creating Short-Term Wins"
- "Consolidating Improvements and Producing Still More Change"
- "Institutionalizing New Approaches"

In terms of the final stage, Kotter notes that an important factor is ensuring that "the next generation of top management really does personify the new approach" (p. 8). Kotter expanded these concepts in his 1996 book *Leading Change* (Kotter,1996).

Sirkin, Keenan and Jackson (2005) noted that "...contrary to popular perception, our studies show that a long project that is reviewed frequently is more likely to succeed than a short project that isn't reviewed frequently. Thus, the time between reviews is more critical for success than a project's life span" (p. 2). These authors also assert that formal upper level management review of set milestones that impact the success of the project should be done with the development team.

In his 2002 book *The Tipping Point*, Gladwell asserts that "ideas and products and messages and behaviours spread just like viruses do" (p. 7), and extends this concept to "the introduction of any new technology" (Gladwell, 2002, p. 12). Gladwell describes "the Tipping Point" as "the

moment of critical mass, the threshold, the boiling point" (p.12) when a change takes hold in a broad manner. Gladwell credits three special types of people who are crucial to such "epidemics." "In a social epidemic, Mavens are data banks. They provide the message. Connectors are social glue: they spread it. But there is also a select group of people – Salesmen--with the skills to persuade us when we are unconvinced of what we are hearing, and they are as critical to the tipping of word-of-mouth epidemics as the other two groups" (p. 70). This author further asserts that these types of persons are the change agents on whom efforts should be focused when interested in starting such an "epidemic" (p. 246).

THE NRM GATEWAY WEBSITE

The Impetus for an NRM Gateway

In the late 1990s, several recurrent issues and frustrations regarding communication and knowledge gaps surfaced in conversations with NRM community members at all levels of the organization. These issues took on new life when a Recreation Leadership Advisory Team (RLAT) was created in 1999. The RLAT membership represented all levels of the NRM organization and functioned as an ad hoc board of directors for Headquarters (HQ) staff on recreation business area issues. This group legitimized for Headquarters what was previously only anecdotal expressions of dissatisfaction with the status quo on items to include:

- Multiple channels of information abounded, especially with the advent of email and a proliferation of independent-issue websites, but individual staff members were responsible for acting on all of it.
- The lower echelon of staff to include Rangers, administrative and maintenance staff

complained about inconsistently receiving HQ memorandums and other communications about policy matters.

- The lower echelon of staff further complained that their voice could not be heard through the filters of management that their communication attempts are required to flow through for procedural reasons.

- Grave concerns about the amount of institutional knowledge leaving the agency included how difficult this was to overcome at the lake level due to overall staff reductions.

- Staff members spent an inordinate amount of time searching for policy documents, and even when they were able to locate a document, they were still uncertain whether they had the most recent version.

- A significant duplication of effort in the independent development of local websites and public information documents was wasting staff time and giving the public inconsistent information about recreation opportunities at Corps lakes.

The problems described above resulted from technological, demographic, and procedural causes:

- Multiple channels of internal information included email, independent websites developed by various internal teams, and increasingly sporadic hard-copy communications.

- Top-down communications that once circulated throughout any given office in hard-copy format became increasingly available only by email sent to distribution lists that represented members in the upper levels of the organizational hierarchy. Lower echelon staff members only received a copy of the communication if someone in that chain chose to forward it to them.

- Paper files became increasingly incomplete as information sources for policy issues with the evolution to electronic communication. Documents were inconsistently printed and filed for general reference within an office, often staying within an individual's email archives, so that they were not accessible by others.

- The demographic realities of an aging baby-boomer staff legitimized concerns about the amount of institutional knowledge leaving the agency. Additionally, in a 14-year period beginning in 1985, there was a 36-percent decline in the number of Corps NRM positions nationwide. A series of reorganizations left some offices staffed only one person deep and others struggling to keep up with new automation and infrastructure changes.

- The stovepipe organizational structure and local traditions generally required that a lake-level staff member's comments or questions about a national policy issue go through a manager, that manager's manager, district, and then division staff and if deemed worthy by those layers of management, the resulting interpretation of the original communication would reach Headquarters. There were, however, several existing oversight committees for individual programs that were more accessible.

- Meanwhile, the Corps' USACE 2012 initiative mandated an agency-wide reorganization and use of CoP. The *USACE 2012 – Aligning USACE for Success in the 21st Century* report (2003) stated that "CoP will facilitate the maintenance and advancement of our technical expertise and will play a prominent role in moving towards the Corps objective organization" (p. 27).

In response to organizational realities, the RLAT became the proponent for development of an NRM Gateway website as a solution to the changing environment. It was envisioned as a means to improve communications within the NRM community, to enhance communication between the NRM community and the general public, and as an important tool to preserve institutional knowledge in a retrievable manner. It also supported the five key functions of Communities of Practice identified in USACE 2012: a) policy and doctrine storage, b) a capable workforce, c) national and international relations, d) organizational communication, and e) a learning organization (USACE, 2003).

There was some initial organizational resistance to the NRM Gateway concept. Headquarters NRM staff feared it would turn out to be an expensive technological "system" that could not be effectively used or kept up to date. They also expressed concerns about incorrect materials being posted, local managers acting on policy that was appropriate for some regions of the country but not others, and the fear that draft policy would be accessed before it was ready for distribution. Division and district staff and some lake level managers feared loss of control of information and policy that they traditionally filtered for their staff. However, there was clear field level support and significant RLAT support among the members who represented division and district level offices. The initial organizational concerns were addressed, and the NRM Gateway initiative progressed as described in the following section.

The NRM Gateway as a Solution

The NRM Gateway was conceived as a solution to the communication problems and knowledge gaps being experienced by the NRM CoP. Developing and implementing this tool was an exercise in change management and contributed to a functional CoP. The initial development and evolution of the NRM Gateway is outlined below within the framework of the "Eight Steps to Transforming Your Organization" (p. 3.) that were described in Kotter (1995).

1. "Establishing a Sense of Urgency"
   • "Examining market and competitive realities"
   The NRM community issues previously detailed, as well as Bryson's 1999 study of the workforce, describe an organization with a pending mass exodus of institutional knowledge, declining staff resources, and an organization that was increasingly frustrated and overwhelmed by communication issues and knowledge gaps. The RLAT that became the proponent for the NRM Gateway initiative thoroughly understood the culture and on-the-ground realities of this CoP at every level of the organization.
   • "Identifying and discussing crises, potential crises, or major opportunities"
   The RLAT discussed the current state of the NRM organization in detail at their initial meetings in 1999. They identified the loss of institutional knowledge due to pending retirements and communication issues as looming crises for the organization. The NRM Gateway was conceived as a tool for organizational learning and enhanced communication that could help avert crisis in these areas. The USACE 2012 initiative that promoted CoP became a timely opportunity to gain Headquarters level support for the NRM Gateway initiative.
2. "Forming a Powerful Guiding Coalition"
   • "Assembling a group with enough power to lead the change effort"
   The RLAT had legitimacy as an advisory group when they recommended development of the NRM Gateway. Next a Working Group to steer NRM

Gateway development was formed with some RLAT members, other key NRM CoP members, the NRM Gateway Project Leader, Technical Coordinator and Web Developer, and eventually the individuals selected to be Technical Coordinators for the information related to the business areas of Recreation, Environmental Stewardship, Environmental Compliance and Partnerships. The Working Group tapped another powerful group of NRM CoP members to develop the initial content for the website: the chairs of several existing Recreation business area standing committees and teams. These chairs became the first SMEs for the Gateway, the equivalent of Weeks' "knowledge brokers." Collectively these groups of people had connections throughout the organization, and had individuals who demonstrated characteristics of Gladwell's "salesmen," "connectors," and "mavens" who could not only spread the word but "infect" others with the understanding of value and power of the NRM Gateway (2002, p. 88).

- "Encouraging the group to work together as a team"

The RLAT and the Working Group were already established as teams by virtue of their charters. The way that SMEs were brought together as a team proved to be one of the most successful elements of the NRM Gateway development. Rather than ask these persons to independently develop content and deliver it for posting, workshops were held. SMEs from various locations across the country were brought together for a week and they all were briefed on the purpose of the session and the importance of the NRM Gateway initiative. The initial SME group developed and achieved consensus on the look and feel that a typical NRM Gateway page of technical information would display. In subsequent workshops, SMEs would first be led through an exercise to ensure buy-in on the typical page format developed at the first workshop and to adjust the format, if necessary, to accommodate everyone's information. SMEs then would develop their pages of content and the Web Developer would immediately post it on a test area so it could be viewed by the group. Each SME would then present their page to the workshop participants and revisions would be made based on the group's feedback. The SMEs left the workshops with their individual technical expertise captured on webpages and ready for Headquarters review prior to going live on the web. The workshops were a team experience that made them part of the overall NRM Gateway effort.

3. "Creating a Vision"
   - "Creating a vision to help direct the change effort"

   The RLAT developed an initial concept in 1999. The Working Group first met in the summer of 2000 to develop the vision for this effort. During the summer of 2000, the Recreation Technical Coordinator was designated and given a short-term assignment to devote full time to further conceptual development as well as negotiating the administrative requirements to get the site going. A white paper fully outlining the vision was developed to educate Headquarters staff and serve as a platform from which to launch initial development.

The following operating principles were developed as part of the vision for the NRM Gateway:

○   Share knowledge in a manner and method promoting knowledge management;

○   Continually develop and sustain competency in the NRM CoP;

○   Apply the process described in *Leading Change* (Kotter, 1996) by empowering the organization to deliver the information that is shared—allow the field to contribute and have a sense of agility in the day-to-day operation of the public resource;

○   Organize materials around peer review standards and provide the field with skill sets beyond those of our Agency by modeling the NRM Gateway framework around the National Recreation and Park Association (NRPA) Agency Accreditation Model and the Army's Fort Excellence website;

○   Maintain manageable components by having many content providers responsible for small units of knowledge within an area of interest and expertise; and

○   Coordinate with other organizations and initiatives to eliminate duplication of efforts.

•   "Developing strategies for achieving that vision"

"Phased development/deployment" and "small manageable components" were guiding rules to bring the vision to reality. Rather than having only a few technical experts, many SMEs were to deliver and maintain manageable amounts of content. The vision was to develop and launch content for the CoP business areas one at a time. One of the early decisions was to begin development with the Recreation business area since numerous standing committee chairs could serve as SMEs and deliver content fairly quickly. Workshops were initiated as a means of content development and delivery. The initial workshop was conducted in February 2001 for SMEs of topic areas identified as high priority for development and posting on the website, e.g., content to which lake-level CoP members were in dire need of ready access. The website featuring the Recreation program information was officially launched in April 2001. The NRM Gateway incorporated the Environmental Compliance business area launched in 2003, the Corps Lakes Visitor Pages were launched to the public in 2004, and the Environmental Stewardship business area made an initial launch in 2005. At the completion of each stage of Gateway development, presentations were made to the RLAT to verify that the product delivered met expectations, a frequent milestone review similar to that recommended by Sirkin, Keenan & Jackson (2005).

4.   "Communicating the Vision"

•   "Using every vehicle possible to communicate the new vision and strategies"

The vision for the NRM Gateway and the strategies for its development were communicated through various methods, ranging from those as formal as official Headquarters memorandums and fact sheets to as informal as word of mouth by CoP members. The official launch of the website in conjunction with the CoP's biennial national conference received wide publicity. Presentations were made at division and district manager and ranger conferences for internal audiences and at professional conferences for wider audiences. The Project Leader and Technical Coordinator had NRM Gateway information on the back of their business cards, and SMEs began including hyperlinks to their technical areas in the signature blocks of their outgoing emails.

- "Teaching new behaviors by the example of the guiding coalition" RLAT members have helped educate the CoP members under their jurisdiction and have not only strongly encouraged NRM Gateway use, but have facilitated their employees' participation as SMEs, etc. SMEs as well as division and district level staff began giving the following initial response to any policy question that could be answered independently by viewing posted materials: "Have you checked the NRM Gateway?" SMEs shared their success stories of how much time they were saving in answering routine questions in this way with division and district staff members, who began using a similar technique to ensure that the NRM Gateway became the first option to answer a question, learn more about a program or issue, and orient new employees.

One of the more unique educational activities by members of the guid-

ing coalition was initiated by senior division and district level managers. An NRM Gateway "Treasure Hunt" was set up for their respective staffs in which a series of special icons were embedded in various NRM Gateway website pages. Their staffs were then encouraged to explore the website to familiarize themselves with its institutional knowledge, and cash from the managers' own pockets rewarded whoever first found and reported the locations of all the icons.

5. "Empowering Others to Act on the Vision"

- "Getting rid of obstacles to change" The NRM Gateway immediately removed one obstacle to upward communication at the time of its 2001 launch by demonstrating a method by which field personnel could directly comment on draft policy instead of having their comments filtered by layers of management. The Corps was developing new recreation facility standards, and the draft standards manual was ready for review and posted for comment at the time of the NRM Gateway launch. The posting included an electronic format for submitting comments through the website directly to the team that drafted the standards. The standards team then considered and responded to all those field level comments and revised the draft document accordingly prior to posting a final draft that underwent the traditional division, district, field level review and approval process. Subsequent draft policy documents have used this process, which allows direct field comments to be considered in national policy development.

• "Changing systems or structures that seriously undermine the vision"

One threat to the NRM Gateway from the start was concern over consequences of posting of inaccurate information or information that could be misused by the field or public, and security risks. A quality control plan was developed and implemented that minimizes these risks. Disclaimers on Good Enough to Share, Lessons Learned and Frequently Asked Questions pages minimize risk of local policies being interpreted as national policies. A disclaimer on the Related Sites pages prevents the appearance of endorsement of private sector businesses and services. Rigorous attention by the web developer to timely antiviral software updates and following server security protocols minimize the risks of disruption of Gateway availability due to hacking/ viruses, etc.

A rigorous review protocol for content further minimizes these risks (also see Figure 2):

○ All content is reviewed by a Corps editor prior to posting.

○ Headquarters proponents review and approve substantial content postings for consistency with policy prior to authorizing posting.

○ Technical Coordinators review new pages and substantial content postings within their area of expertise prior to forwarding to Headquarters proponents. They also coordinate the formal periodic reviews of their component's pages with Content SMEs and the Web Developer.

○ SMEs periodically review their pages for accuracy and removal/ archival actions on outdated materials

○ An NRM Gateway Field Review Group (FRG) consisting of Division and District Office, as well as project level reviewers periodically accesses and reviews the website and provides specific comments on site functionality and accessibility.

○ Users can comment directly to the SME for individual pages or to the Web Developer using email links provided at the bottom of each page.

○ Routine corrections suggested by the FRG or users are corrected immediately, and other items such as major format change suggestions are referred to the Working Group for consideration.

○ The Web Developer routinely runs software that detects broken links.

○ External audiences such as university students and professors are invited to review and comment.

○ Visitor pages are reviewed for accuracy by local representatives of each lake/lock.

○ Draft policy is located behind firewalls for the internal audience until the final version is approved for public release.

• "Encouraging risk taking and non-traditional ideas, activities, and actions"

The NRM Gateway has opened up several ways that CoP members can

Figure 2. NRM Gateway Website Technical Area Development Process

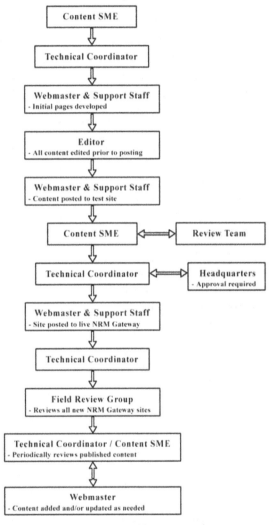

share and learn about local activities and initiatives across the country, including those that are considered nontraditional. Good Enough to Share pages collect and distribute success stories and Lessons Learned pages collect and distribute history on things tried that did not turn out so well. As Soo et al (2002) recommend, structure was provided to informal network-ing to enhance the usefulness of the knowledge being shared. What was once a small informal email group that asked questions and shared information was incorporated into the NRM Gateway as the Ranger Network where all such questions and answers are captured and distributed to the entire CoP for consideration and additional contributions are encouraged.

6. "Planning for and Creating Short-Term Wins"
   - "Planning for visible performance improvements"
     The NRM Gateway vision from the start was for phased development and deployment that would be visible and demonstrate immediate performance improvements due to enhanced communication and organizational learning opportunities.
   - "Creating those improvements"
     The implementation of the phased development and deployment of the NRM Gateway and use of workshops to develop content created a series of highly visible short-term wins. In less than three years the NRM Gateway reached the "tipping point," e.g. it was the widely accepted way in which communication flowed throughout the CoP and where institutional knowledge was located for retrieval.
   - "Recognizing and rewarding employees involved in the improvements"
     Methods of recognition and rewards for proponents and contributors to the NRM Gateway initiative ranged from certificates of appreciation, to ribbons that were worn at national conferences that identified team members. The two managers who initiated the NRM Gateway Treasure Hunts received national recognition in front of their peers at the 2003 national conference. Many individual contributors consider the recognition they get from having their ideas posted on the website as reward in itself.

7. "Consolidating Improvements and Producing Still More Change"
   - "Using increased credibility to change systems, structures, and policies that don't fit the vision"

One method to increase credibility for the NRM Gateway is to conduct studies of its effectiveness and usage. Russi (2005) conducted a study of the use of and perception of the NRM Gateway's value by NRM employees. An external study by Propst, et al (2006) looked at use of the NRM Gateway by non-Corps audiences and recommended modifications to accommodate those users.

   - "Hiring, promoting, and developing employees who can implement the vision"
     The NRM Gateway team consisting of the Project Leader, Web Developer, and Technical Coordinator has remained intact since the inception of the project and has demonstrated a successful mix of technical competence and marketing skills. Additional Technical Coordinators with the expertise and skills to oversee the content development and maintenance of the main business areas are the other critical appointments. There is a continuous recruitment of SMEs to develop new content and fill behind those who retire or otherwise leave an SME position.
   - "Reinvigorating the process with new projects, themes, and change agents"
     The NRM Gateway has had a succession of new projects that reinvigorate the process. The phased development and deployment has contributed to this. Other examples of things that invigorated the CoP were the launch of an NRM SmartBook that connects anyone to program points of contact and SMEs, the launch of the Ranger Network, and e- cards on the Visitor pages.

8. "Institutionalizing New Approaches"
   - "Articulating the connections between the new behaviors and corporate success"
     A variety of presentations to internal and external audiences have marketed and articulated the corporate success of the NRM Gateway. Only two years after launch, the USACE 2012 final report (2003) cited the NRM Gateway as "active in promoting CoP initiatives" (p. 27). The NRM Gateway and its team members have also been recognized with several awards that recognize the corporate success, including a 2006 American Recreation Coalition Beacon Award, a 2002 Corps award for Outstanding Achievement in Technology Transfer, and a 2001 William Penn Mott Award from the National Society of Park Resources.
   - "Developing the means to ensure leadership development and succession"
     A Project Management Plan documents the overall NRM Gateway initiative and the content development workshops establish and institutionalize the process for further development of the project and the leadership of the initiative (USACE, 2005). More importantly, the NRM Gateway is now a part of the CoP culture at all levels of the organization and has strong support at the Headquarters (funding) level. The NRM CoP now has its third leader since the NRM Gateway was initiated. The first NRM Chief who initially resisted the idea in 2000, was a fan by the time he retired in 2002. He was succeeded by one of his senior staff members, who having been in on the NRM Gateway from its inception, utilized and promoted it during his tenure. When he retired in 2006, the person who eventually filled that position – someone who had never worked for the Corps -- says that she used the NRM Gateway to investigate the organization and decide if she wanted the job. This new NRM Chief came on board as a user of the NRM Gateway and fully recognized and utilized its value and power from her first days on the job, actualizing Kotter's prescription for success of making sure that "the next generation of top management really does personify the new approach" (1995, p. 8).

FUTURE TRENDS

As the NRM Gateway matures and develops, the focus moves toward resolving issues noted by Soo et al that "…all too rarely is…data sifted into the sort of knowledge that can inform business decisions and create positive results" (p. 130). Status reports for each of the NRM CoP business lines are being developed that extract information from numerous independent databases that will allow managers to benchmark and evaluate their programs in a strategic way that will enhance performance. The status reports are being developed with a balanced scorecard approach as described by Kaplan & Norton (2001).

The status reports are part of a natural progression that started with a data visualization component of the Visitor Pages, which for the first time allowed those making data input to consistently and easily see data imported from other databases and make corrections. The status reports also bring a wealth of information formerly available only to those well-versed in the individual data systems to any employee with the click of a mouse, which should overcome some technological challenges cited by some older employees who are relatively new to computer usage.

The NRM Gateway model has been extended to the entire Operations CoP and the various Sub-CoPs therein. This model is actually moving up the organizational chain to extend its KM resources to higher levels of the organization.

CONCLUSION

The NRM Gateway is a valuable resource that uses KM principles to serve a CoP and was implemented using solid change management approaches. The NRM Gateway is by no means a static tool, evidenced by content contributions that have seen it grow from an overall file size of 648 MB in 2002 to 7.5 GB in 2007. The site is also heavily utilized, with 101 million hits recorded from April 2001 to July 2008, marking a steady increase in usage from a 2001 level of just over a half-million to a 2007 annual total of 40 million. The NRM Gateway story offers a model that other organizations may consider to capture, manage, and publish information to a variety of stakeholders in an easily retrievable fashion.

REFERENCES

Bryson, B.F. (1999). A study of individual reactions to career plateaus in the natural resources management branch of the Operations Division of the U.S. Army Corps of Engineers. *UMI Dissertation Services.*

Dieng, R., Corby, O., Giboin, A., Ribiere, M. (1999). Methods and tools for corporate knowledge management. *Int. J. Human-Computer Studies,* 51 (567-598).

Drew. S. (1999). Building knowledge management into strategy: Making sense of a new perspective, *Long Range Planning,* 32(1), 130-136).

Gladwell, M., (2002). *The Tipping Point.* Boston: Back Bay Books.

Kaplan, R.S. & Norton D.P. (2001). *The strategy-focused organization: How balanced scorecard companies thrive in the new business environment.* Boston: Harvard Business School Press.

Kotter, J. P. (1995). Leading change: Why transformation efforts fail. *Harvard Business Review,* 73(March/April), 59–67.

Kotter, J.P. (1996). *Leading change.* Boston: Harvard Business School Press.

Propst, D.B., Sales, K., Iyer, V., Perales, M.K., Bryson, B.F. (2006). Extending the Army Corps of Engineers Natural Resource Management Gateway to non-Corps of Engineers audiences: results and recommendations. (In publication).

Russi, J. (2005). *An evaluation of the use and perceived value of the Natural Resource Management Gateway.* Unpublished master's thesis, University of California at Sacramento, Sacramento, CA.

Sirkin, H.L., Keenan, P., and Jackson, A. (2005) The hard side of change management. *Harvard Business Review,* (October): 108-118.

Snyder, W.M. & Briggs, X.S. (2003). Communities of Practice: a new tool for government managers. http://www.businessofgovernment.org/pdfs/Snyder_report.pdf (accessed May 3, 2007)

Soo, C., Devinney, T., Midgley, D., and Deering, A. (2002). Knowledge management: Philosophy, processes, and pitfalls. *California Management Review,* 44(4), 129-150.

U.S. Army Corps of Engineers. (1996). *Project operations – Recreation operations and maintenance policies,* Engineer Regulation 1130-2-550, Washington, DC.

U.S. Army Corps of Engineers (2003). USACE 2012 final report. http://www.hq.usace.army.mil/stakeholders/Final.htm (accessed May 3, 2007)

U.S. Army Corps of Engineers. (2005). Project Management Plan Natural Resources Management (NRM) Gateway Website Initiative. *http://corpslakes.usace.army.mil/employees/gateway/pdfs/05pmp-gateway.pdf* (accessed May 1, 2006).

U.S. Army Corps of Engineers. (2006a). *The Community of Practice (CoP) in the U.S. Army Corps of Engineers (USACE)*, Engineer Regulation 25-1-8, Washington, DC.

U.S. Army Corps of Engineers. (2006b). Natural Resources Management System (NRMS) historical data. Natural Resources Management Gateway, Mike Owen, Subject Matter Expert, CESWF-OD-R. *http://CorpsLakes.usace.army.mil/employees/nrms/nrms.html* (accessed July 10, 2006).

U.S. Army Corps of Engineers. (2006c). Operations and Maintenance Business Information Link (OMBIL) historical data. Natural Resources Management Gateway, Mike Owen, Subject Matter Expert, CESWF-OD-R. *http://corpslakes.usace.army.mil/employees/ombil-rec/ombil.html* (accessed May 6, 2006).

Weeks, M. (2004). Knowledge management in the wild. *Business Horizons*, 47(6), 15-24.

Wenger, E., McDermott, R. A., and Snyder, W. (2002). *Cultivating communities of practice: a guide to managing knowledge.* Boston, Mass: Harvard Business School Press.

Wiig, K.M. (1997). Knowledge management: Where did it come from and where will it go? *Expert Systems with Applications,* 13(1), 1-14.

USEFUL URLS

NRM Gateway. http://corpslakes.usace.army.mil/

Corps Lakes Gateway: Visitor Pages. http://www.CorpsLakes.us

NRM Gateway Initiative. http://corpslakes.usace.army.mil/employees/gateway/gateway.html

NRM Gateway Initiative: Content Development Workshops http://corpslakes.usace.army.mil/employees/gateway/workshop.html

Recreation Budget Simulations: RECreation Budget Estimation SysTem (Rec-BEST). http://corpslakes.usace.army.mil/employees/recbest/recbest.html

Recreation Facility Standards. http://corpslakes.usace.army.mil/employees/facilities/standards.html

Interpretive Services: Tool Box for Interpretive Program Exchange. http://corpslakes.usace.army.mil/employees/interpretive/tools.html

Recreation Network: Questions and Answers. http://corpslakes.usace.army.mil/nrmnetwork/qna.cfm

Economic Impact Analysis. http://corpslakes.usace.army.mil/employees/economic/economic.html

Good Enough to Share. http://corpslakes.usace.army.mil/employees/gets-main.cfm

Career Advancement. http://corpslakes.usace.army.mil/employees/career/career.html

Human Resources. http://operations.usace.army.mil/humanres.cfm?CoP=Ops

Value to the Nation: Recreation. http://www.vtn.iwr.usace.army.mil/recreation/

Federal Enterprise Architecture: E-Gov. http://www.whitehouse.gov/omb/egov/a-1-fea.html

Government Made Easy: USA.Gov. http://www.USA.gov

FURTHER READINGS

Gammelgaard, J. (2007). Why not use incentives to encourage knowledge sharing? Journal of Knowledge Management Practice, 8(1). http://www.tlainc.com/articl127.htm

Alrawi, K. (2007). Knowledge management and the organization's perception: a review. *Journal of Knowledge Management Practice*, 8(1). http://www.tlainc.com/articl131.htm

US Government Services Administration, Intergovernmental Communities. (http://www.gsa.gov/collaborate)

COLAB: An Open Collaborative Work Environment Wiki. http://colab.cim3.net/cgi-bin/wiki.pl?WikiHomePage

Knowledge Management Working Group Wiki. http://colab.cim3.net/cgi-bin/wiki.pl?KnowledgeManagementWorkingGroup

Semantic Interoperability Community of Practice Wiki. http://colab.cim3.net/cgi-bin/wiki.pl?SICoP

Chapter XV
A Complex Adaptive Systems–Based Enterprise Knowledge Sharing Model

Cynthia T. Small
The MITRE Corporation, USA

Andrew P. Sage
George Mason University, USA

ABSTRACT

This paper describes a complex adaptive systems (CAS)-based enterprise knowledge-sharing (KnS) model. The CAS-based enterprise KnS model consists of a CAS-based KnS framework and a multi-agent simulation model. Enterprise knowledge sharing is modeled as the emergent behavior of knowledge workers interacting with the KnS environment and other knowledge workers. The CAS-based enterprise KnS model is developed to aid knowledge management (KM) leadership and other KnS researchers in gaining an enhanced understanding of KnS behavior and its influences. A premise of this research is that a better understanding of KnS influences can result in enhanced decision-making of KnS interventions that can result in improvements in KnS behavior.

CAS-BASED MODELING OF ENTERPRISE KNOWLEDGE SHARING

The enterprise KnS model developed here models enterprise knowledge sharing from a complex adaptive systems perspective. Hypothetical concepts that are fundamental to the development of this CAS-based model and to this research include:

1. Knowledge sharing is a human behavior performed by knowledge workers;

Copyright © 2009, IGI Global, distributing in print or electronic forms without written permission of IGI Global is prohibited.

2. Knowledge workers are diverse and hetero-geneous;
3. Knowledge workers may choose to share knowledge; and
4. The KnS decision is influenced by other knowledge workers and the KnS environment.

Enterprise knowledge sharing is the result of the decisions made by knowledge workers, individually and as members of teams, regarding knowledge sharing. As depicted in *Figure 1*, there are two major decisions (rectangles) that a knowledge worker makes: "Share Knowledge?" and "Type of Knowledge to Share?" This research models the KnS decisions as being influenced by the attributes of the individual knowledge worker, the KnS behavior of other knowledge workers, and the state of the KnS environment. Previous KnS studies and research identify factors that influence KnS behavior. However, few address the heterogeneity of knowledge workers and how the attributes of the individual knowledge worker, and knowledge worker teams, impact KnS behavior. The emergent enterprise KnS behavior, noted by the diamond shape in *Figure 1*, is the result of the interactions of the knowledge worker with the KnS environment and other knowledge workers. Relevant aspects of enterprise KnS behavior and the associated KnS influences are discussed in the sections that follow.

Enterprise KnS behavior takes on many forms. It can be a conversation around a water fountain, e-mail sent to a co-worker or a group forum, a presentation to a small group, an enterprise "best-practice" forum, or documents published to a corporate repository. Murray (2003) categorizes KnS activities into technology-assisted communication (videoconferencing, databanks/intranet, e-mail, and teleconferencing), meetings (face-to-face interaction, seminars and conferences, social events, and retreats), and training and development (mentoring, instructional lectures, video tapes, and simulation games). This research combines

the two types of knowledge (tacit and explicit) and the ontological dimension (individual, group, and organization) of knowledge creation presented by Nonaka and Takeuchi (1995) to derive the types of KnS behavior for the model. The KnS behaviors investigated and incorporated in the enterprise KnS model are as follows:

1. **Individual tacit:** This behavior includes sharing tacit knowledge with an individual or individuals, such as face-to-face interactions in informal or formal meetings.
2. **Individual explicit:** This behavior includes sharing explicit knowledge with an individual or individuals, such as through sending e-mail or hard copy material to select individual(s).
3. **Group tacit:** This behavior includes sharing tacit knowledge with a group, such as face-to-face interactions with a community of interest, community of practice (CoP), or organizational unit.
4. **Group explicit:** This behavior includes sharing explicit knowledge with a group, such as posting or contributing to a community of interest, CoP, or organizational unit repository, Web site, or mailing list server.
5. **Enterprise tacit:** This behavior includes sharing tacit knowledge in an enterprise-wide forum, such as presenting at a technical exchange meeting or other forum that is open to the entire enterprise.
6. **Enterprise explicit:** This behavior includes sharing explicit knowledge in a manner that makes it available to anyone in the enterprise, such as publishing in a corporate-wide repository or enterprise-wide intranet.

While we investigate KnS behavior as being comprised of six different types, both tacit and explicit knowledge are often shared in a given situation. For example, in an enterprise KnS forum, tacit knowledge, such as unrehearsed oral presentations and responses to questions, and explicit knowledge, such as hard copy presenta-tions, are generally both shared.

We investigate three major KnS influences on the associated sharing of knowledge:

1. The enterprise KnS environment,
2. KnS behavior of other knowledge workers, and
3. Attributes of the knowledge workers.

The KnS literature, such as reviewed in Small and Sage (2006), identifies many factors that influence KnS behavior. A discussion of each of the major influences is provided in the sections that follow.

The enterprise KnS environment is closely aligned to the Japanese concept of "ba" which translates into English as "place." Nonaka and Konno (1998) adapted this Japanese concept for their knowledge creation theory. "Ba," as

described by Nonaka and Konno (1998), is the shared space for emerging relationships that can be physical, virtual, mental, or any combination of these. It is the place where knowledge is created, shared, and exploited. The "ba" is comprised of the knowledge resources and the people who own and create the knowledge. The KnS environment or "ba" is comprised of many factors that influence KnS behavior. There are at least six important influence factors in the KnS environment modeled and investigated here. A brief description of each of these factors is appropriate here:

1. **KnS technology:** KnS technologies are those technologies that allow knowledge workers to share tacit or explicit knowledge. Technologies and tools reported (APQC, 2000) as critical to knowledge sharing at best practice firms included: e-mail, intranets, document sharing systems, collaboration

Figure 1. Enterprise KnS influence diagram

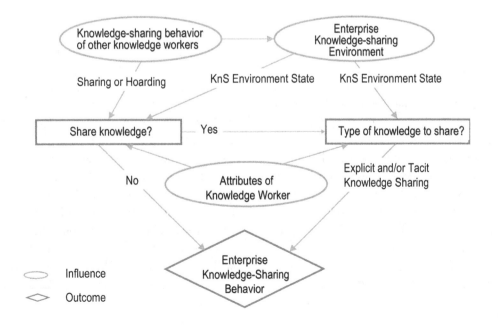

tools, and video conferences. Chu (2003) included e-mail, Internet, intranet, databases, and teleconferences in his listing of these. With the advent of Web 2.0, wikis, blogs, and social networking applications are being used to enable enterprise knowledge sharing (APQC, 2008)

2. **Leadership:** Leaders and managers in an organization impact KnS behavior by directing behavior, rewarding or recognizing behavior, and by setting KnS behavior examples. Many studies indicate that organizations with appropriate KnS leadership behavior have more instances of appropriate KnS behavior than others.

3. **KnS culture:** Culture is an organization's values, norms, and unwritten rules. Most existing KM models and KnS investigations include culture as a critical enabler or influence on KnS behavior. Additionally, cultural issues are regularly cited as one of the concerns held by those implementing KM initiatives.

4. **Human networks:** This factor includes processes, technology, and resources that help to connect knowledge workers or support knowledge networks. Support for human networks, which includes informal and formal forums, is widely practiced among best practice organizations. They are often referred to as communities of practice or community of interests. Organizations can enable these networks with knowledge stewards, online collaboration tools, and tools to facilitate easy publishing.

5. **Rewards and recognition:** This factor includes the approaches organizations use to encourage or reinforce the discipline of knowledge sharing. Approaches include rewards, recognition, alignment with performance assessment and promotion, and conducting visible KnS events. When establishing rewards, organizations must

consider the generic type of behavior they are trying to stimulate. Many organizations have instituted reward and award programs for knowledge sharing and/or have integrated incentives for knowledge sharing with performance appraisals and promotions.

6. **Alignment with strategy:** This refers to the alignment of knowledge sharing with business strategy. Best practice organizations do not share knowledge for the sake of knowledge. Rather, knowledge sharing is deemed critical to achieving business goals and is linked to the business strategy (APQC, 1999). The alignment of knowledge sharing to business strategy can be either explicit or implicit. When organizations have explicit alignment, language regarding knowledge sharing can be found in documents such as strategic business plans, vision or mission statements, or performance measures. Organizations with implicit alignment are evidenced by knowledge sharing embedded in business practices. Fifty percent of the best-practice firms that participated in the APQC benchmarking study (APQC, 1999) on knowledge sharing were explicitly aligned, while the other half were implicitly aligned. Findings of two APQC benchmarking studies found that organizations where knowledge workers understood how knowledge sharing supported the business strategy had stronger KnS behavior.

The behavior of other knowledge workers within an organization affects the KnS decisions of a specific knowledge worker in many ways. Ford (2003) describes sharing knowledge as a risky behavior because the individual does not know how the shared knowledge will be used by the party who obtains it. Trust in, and some knowledge of, what the recipient of the shared knowledge will do with the shared knowledge are critical to knowledge sharing. From an enterprise perspective, knowledge workers must trust the organization not to cast them aside after the knowledge is harvested. From a peer interrelationship perspective, a knowledge worker must trust that the knowledge recipient will make ethical use of the shared knowledge (Bukowitz & Williams, 1999). If a knowledge worker shares and the knowledge recipient misuses the shared knowledge, from the perspectives of the intended purposes for sharing, then the knowledge worker may be reluctant to share knowledge in the future.

The KnS influence of individual knowledge workers attributes is very important because knowledge sharing is a human behavior in which the knowledge worker chooses to share. The decision to share is influenced by interactions. Leonard and Straus (1997), for example, assert that individuals have preferred habits of thought that influence how they make decisions and interact with others. Knowledge workers have many diverse attributes, some of which are fixed and others of which are variable. Some of the individual attributes or human factors identified in the KM and KnS literature include employees' means, ability, and motivation (Ives et al., 2000); job characteristics including workload and content (Chu, 2002); feelings of being valued and commitment to the project (Ipe, 2003); and conditions of respect, justice perception, and relationships with superiors (Liao et al., 2004).

Here, we model enterprise knowledge sharing as emergent behavior that is the result of decisions made by knowledge workers. The decisions, "Share Knowledge?" and "Type of Knowledge to Share?" depicted in *Figure 1* are based on dynamic interactions and are influenced by factors in the KnS environment, KnS behaviors of other knowledge workers, and the individual attributes and perspectives of the knowledge worker. The CAS-based enterprise KnS model integrates the knowledge worker, KnS decisions, and the KnS influences into a CAS-based framework, which consists of two major components:

1. CAS-based enterprise KnS framework
2. Enterprise KnS simulation model (e-KnS-MOD).

A detailed discussion of each of the components is provided in the sections that follow.

CAS-BASED KNS FRAMEWORK

The CAS-based KnS framework is the most critical element of our CAS-based KnS model and distinguishes it from other KM models, such as those described in Small and Sage (2006). The CAS-based KnS framework describes enterprise knowledge sharing from a complex adaptive systems perspective. The properties of a CAS, as described by Holland (1995), are aggregation, diversity, internal models, and non-linearity. Axelrod and Cohen (1999) identify variation, interaction, and selection as the hallmark of complex adaptive systems. Other important concepts of complex adaptive systems include the agent, strategy, population, type, and artifacts. For simplicity, the following constructs of a complex adaptive system have been addressed at the highest level of the enterprise KnS framework: agent, agent attributes, interactions, artifacts, and rules.

The CAS-based KnS framework, illustrated in *Figure 2*, is comprised of the following elements: knowledge worker(s); KnS environment (comprised of KnS influences/enablers and barriers); KnS behaviors; KnS rules; and attributes of the knowledge worker. The KnS behavior results from the interactions of the knowledge workers with each other and the KnS environment. The decision to share is influenced by individual attributes, KnS behavior of other knowledge workers, and the KnS environment. A mapping of the KnS influence diagram in *Figure 1* to the CAS concepts used in the CAS-based framework of *Figure 2* is as follows:

Figure 2. Major elements of the CAS-based KnS framework

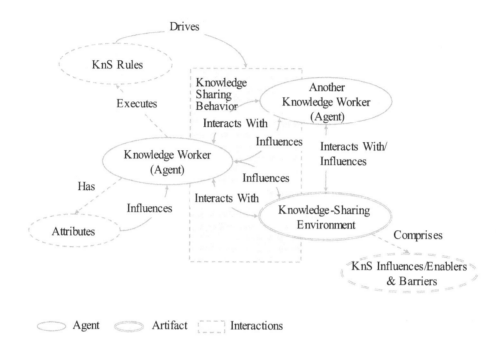

Figure 3. Investigated attributes of knowledge worker

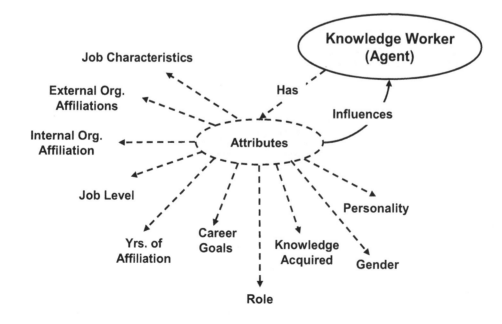

- **KnS Influence Diagram Elements**
  - Knowledge workers
  - KnS Environment
  - KnS Decisions
  - Enterprise knowledge sharing
  - Knowledge worker attributes
- **CAS-Based KnS Framework Elements**
  - KnS Agents
  - KnS Environment (artifacts)
  - KnS Rules
  - KnS Behaviors (interactions)
  - KnS Agent attributes

The knowledge worker is the KnS agent within the CAS-based model. Critical to this concept is the diversity and heterogeneity of this KnS agent. The knowledge worker within an enterprise is diverse in many ways: personality, gender, role, and job level. *Figure 3* associates this segment of the KnS framework with the attributes of the knowledge worker. The KnS decisions (execution of rules) of a KnS agent depend on the agent's attributes and are influenced by the agents' interactions with other knowledge workers and the KnS environment.

The attributes of the knowledge worker investigated here include: personality, gender, level of knowledge acquired, years of affiliation, role, career goals, job level, internal organizational affiliation, external organizational affiliation, and job characteristics. These attributes are described as follows:

1. **Personality:** Such as introvert, extrovert, or a combination.
2. **Gender:** Male or female.
3. **Level of knowledge acquired:** The level of knowledge acquired over time (related to competency) by the knowledge worker.
4. **Years of affiliation:** The number of years a knowledge worker has been affiliated with the enterprise (i.e., number of years at the company).

5. **Role:** The role (s) the knowledge worker has within the enterprise, organization, or project. Examples include manager, technical leader, or technical contributor.
6. **Career goals:** The job or career-related goals possessed by the knowledge worker. Goals investigated as part of this research include: career growth (promotion), knowledge growth opportunities, satisfying customers, satisfying management, recognition, and reward.
7. **Job level:** The job level that is assigned by the company to a given knowledge worker, ranging from entry/junior level people to executive management.
8. **Internal organizational affiliation:** An enterprise usually consists of many organizations. This is the internal organization to which the knowledge worker is assigned.
9. **External organizational affiliations:** The number of external professional organizations with which the knowledge worker is affiliated.
10. **Job characteristics:** This includes number of tasks supported, workload, pace, and content of work.

KnS rules drive the decisions the knowledge worker makes. A knowledge worker has two fundamental KnS decisions: "Share Knowledge?" and "Type of Knowledge to Share?" The KnS rules are the same for all KnS agents. They are parameterized based on the attributes of the agents, behavior or other knowledge workers, and the state of the KnS environment.

An enterprise KnS environment consists of many factors that influence or enable KnS behavior. A KnS artifact is an entity in the enterprise (not a person) with which the knowledge worker interacts that either influences or enables their KnS behavior. An enterprise has many KnS artifacts, including information technology, performance and reward systems, knowledge repositories, and

Figure 4. KnS influences/enablers investigated

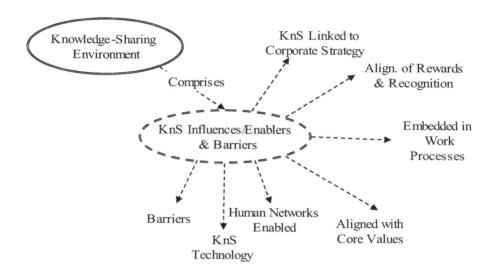

information help desk. The KnS influences or enablers examined here and illustrated in *Figure 4* include: KnS linked to corporate strategy, alignment of rewards and recognition, KnS embedded with work processes, KnS aligned with core values, enabling of human networks, and KnS technology (availability and ease of use). The artifacts that exist in an environment can have different enabling characteristics. A five-state characterization instrument was developed to characterize the KnS environment.

A knowledge worker (KW) gains or acquires knowledge by interacting with the environment and other knowledge workers. Knowledge sharing results in and from a KW interacting with another KW and/or with the KnS environment. Enterprise knowledge sharing is the result of knowledge workers interacting with other knowledge workers and the enterprise KnS environment. Included in the CAS-based framework are the following

KnS behaviors: individual tacit, group tacit, enterprise tacit, individual explicit, group explicit, and enterprise explicit.

MULTI-AGENT ENTERPRISE KNS SIMULATION MODEL (E-KNSMOD)

The Enterprise KnS Model (e-KnSMOD) simulates enterprise knowledge sharing as the emergent behavior of knowledge workers, represented as agents, interacting with the KnS environment and other knowledge workers. The design of the e-KnSMOD is based on the CAS-based KnS framework described here. All of the constructs of the framework (KnS agent, agent attributes, KnS behavior, KnS environment, and rules) are implemented in the simulation model. For simplicity, the simulation model implements a subset of the attributes (level of knowledge, role, career goals, job level, and internal organizational affiliation) of the knowledge worker included in the CAS-based framework. The purpose of the model is to examine the effects of the KnS enterprise environment and behavior of other knowledge workers on the KnS behavior of a heterogeneous population of knowledge workers. Epstein and Axtell (1996) refer to agent-based models of social processes as artificial societies. The design and implementation of this model leverages the agent-based computer modeling of the artificial society known as The Sugarscape Model (Epstein & Axtell, 1996) and the Sugarscape source code developed by Nelson and Minar (1997) using Swarm (Minar et al., 1996; Johnson & Lancaster, 2000; Swarm Development Group, 2004).

The e-KnSMOD model simulates a population of knowledge workers that work in an artificial enterprise. As with Sugarscape (Epstein & Axtell,

1996), the e-KnSMOD leverages the research results that have been obtained using cellular automata (CA) for agent-based modeling. KnS agents represent the knowledge workers, and the CA represents the artificial enterprise, KnS-scape. The KnS agents interact with each other and their environment as they move around the enterprise gaining valuable knowledge (a goal of many knowledge workers). Agents acquire knowledge by engaging in a knowledge creation opportunity or by receiving knowledge shared by other knowledge workers. In order to satisfy their goals, they must continue to generate new knowledge. As conceptually depicted in *Figure 5*, the e-KnSMOD consists of three major elements:

1. KnS agents ("knowledge workers")
2. The artificial enterprise or KnS-scape
3. Interactions (driven by rules).

Figure 5. Major elements of the e-KnSMOD

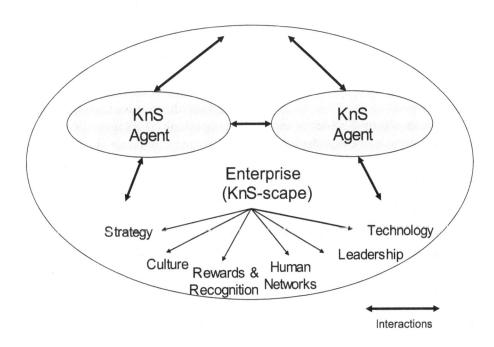

Each of these elements, as implemented in the e-KnSMOD, is described in the following subsections.

KnS Agent

A KnS agent represents a knowledge worker in the artificial enterprise. The KnS agents are heterogeneous. This implementation of e-KnSMOD models the following subset of attributes included in the CAS-based KnS framework: level of knowledge acquired, role, job level, and organization affiliation. Each KnS Agent is characterized by a set of fixed and variable states that vary among the agents. The fixed states include:

1. Level of knowledge acquired (competency)
2. Job level (vision is based on job level) in organization (e.g., Jr. Analyst, Sr. Analyst, Principal, Director)
3. Role in organization (manager, non-manager)
4. Organizational affiliation.

Each agent has the following variable states:

- New knowledge gained
- Location on the KnS-scape
- KnS indicator (indicates if the agent shared in the previous run cycle).

The KnS agent comes to the KnS-scape with a specified competency. Upon entry, the agent is assigned a vision and organizational affiliation. The job level is then based on vision. The KnS agent moves (changes location) around the enterprise in order to participate in knowledge-creation opportunities that allow the KnS agents to gain knowledge. The agent's vision restricts what knowledge creation events the agent can see. The agent decides to share or hoard the knowledge gained. If the agent decides to share, it can participate in one or more KnS behaviors:

individual tacit, individual explicit, group tacit, group explicit, enterprise tacit, and enterprise explicit. The shared knowledge indicator is set when the agent shares knowledge.

KnS-scape: The Artificial "Ba"

The KnS-scape, which represents the "Ba," is represented by a two-dimensional (50 x 50) coordinate grid. The grid is built using the Swarm tool set. The grid has multiple views. Each point (x, y) on the grid has a knowledge-creation opportunity, an organization identifier, and a KnS environment state. The information needed by the model to create these views is read from data files, which can be specified at run time. A KnS agent is randomly placed on the KnS-scape. The organizational unit associated with the agent's initial location on the KnS-scape determines an agent's organizational affiliation. When a KnS agent engages in a knowledge-creation opportunity, it acquires the knowledge associated with the opportunity. An organization view of the KnS-scape would indicate that there are four different organizations within the enterprise. The KnS agents are colored by the organizational affiliation of their initial location on the KnS-scape.

Knowledge-Creation Opportunity

Each location on the KnS-scape, represented by an (x, y) coordinate, has a knowledge-creation event or opportunity. KnS agents interacting with their environment and with other KnS agents create knowledge. One of the ways a KnS agent interacts with the environment is by moving to a location and then acquiring the knowledge associated with a knowledge-creation event. When an agent acquires the knowledge at a given location, the knowledge is depleted (value = 0) until another knowledge creation event occurs. The value of the knowledge creation event is increased on each cycle of the simulation until the maximum value for that location is achieved. The amount of increase on each cycle is controlled by the "alpha" parameter, described later.

KnS Environment State

Each location on the KnS-scape has a KnS environment state. The states are as follows:

1. **Barrier:** KnS environment has a negative impact on KnS behavior.
2. **Neutral:** KnS environment has no or minimum impact on KnS behavior.
3. **Enabled:** KnS environment enables KnS behavior.
4. **Encouraged:** KnS environment encourages KnS behavior.
5. **Aligned:** KnS environment positively influences KnS behavior.

KnS Organization View

Each location on the KnS-scape, represented by an (x, y) coordinate, has an organizational identifier. When an agent enters the KnS-scape, it is given the organizational identifier of the location where it is placed. The organizational identifier is used in group KnS behaviors.

Interactions: Acquiring and Sharing Knowledge

The KnS agent interacts with the KnS-scape and with other KnS agents. As previously described, each KnS agent comes to the KnS-scape with a vision that allows it to see knowledge-creation opportunities. During each simulation cycle, an agent looks out over the KnS-scape and determines the location of the best knowledge-creation opportunity. It then moves there and acquires the knowledge. If the KnS agent acquires enough knowledge to share, the KnS agent then chooses to share or not to share. The KnS agent can participate in six types of KnS behaviors: individual tacit, individual explicit, group tacit, group

explicit, enterprise tacit and enterprise explicit. The impact of each of these KnS interactions is briefly described as follows:

1. Tacit individual: Results in the "current knowledge" attribute of the recipient KnS agent being increased. The physical vicinity of KnS agents restricts this interaction.
2. Tacit group: Results in the "knowledge acquired" attribute of the recipient KnS agents being increased. The "current knowledge" attribute restricts this interaction.
3. Tacit enterprise: Results in the "current knowledge" attribute of all KnS agents being increased. The "organizational affiliation" attribute restricts this interaction.
4. Explicit individual: Results in the "current knowledge" attribute of the recipient KnS agent being increased.
5. Explicit group: Results in an increase of knowledge in the organizational or group repository.
6. Explicit enterprise: Results in an increase of knowledge in the enterprise repository.

The most important aspect of "ba" is interaction. Important to this research is that knowledge is created by the individual knowledge worker as a result of interactions with other knowledge workers and with the environment.

Rules for the KnS-Scape

Eptein and Axtell (1996) describe three types of rules: agent-environment rule, environment-environment rule, and agent-agent rule. There are three types of similar rules in the KnS-scape model:

1. Agent movement rule;
2. Generation of new knowledge creation events rule;
3. KnS rule.

A brief description of each rule is provided here:

- **Agent movement rule:** The KnS agent uses the movement rule to move around the KnS-scape. The movement rule processes local information about the KnS-scape and returns rank ordering of the state according to some criteria. The rules and functions used by the agents are the same for all agents. The values of the parameters change based on the attributes of the agent and the state of the environment. A summary of the movement rule is as follows:
    1. Look out as far as vision (an agent attribute) permits and identify the unoccupied site(s) that best satisfies the knowledge acquisition goal.
    2. If goals can be satisfied by multiple sites, select the closest site.
    3. Move to the site.
    4. Collect the knowledge associated with the knowledge-creation opportunity of the new position.
- **Generation of New Knowledge Creation Events:** A knowledge creation event has a knowledge value. After the knowledge is collected from the site on the KnS-scape, the value goes to zero (it no longer exists). The frequency of new events is driven by the "alpha" parameter. At the end of each cycle, each location on the KnS-scape is incremented by the "alpha" value until it reaches its maximum value.
- **KnS Rule:** After an agent completes the move to the new location and acquires the knowledge there, the KnS rule is executed. The decision to share and the type of knowledge to share is dependent on the KnS behavior of other agents, the KnS environment state, and the "level of knowledge acquired" attribute.
- **E-KnSMOD—Simulation of Enterprise Knowledge Sharing:** Enterprise knowledge

sharing is simulated by the e-KnSMOD. Enterprise knowledge sharing is measured by the number of KnS agents participating in one of the six KnS behaviors, the percent of KnS agents that share, the frequency that KnS agents share, and the number of items deposited into the group or enterprise repositories.

Initializing the e-KnSMOD environment properly is important here. E-KnSMOD, built using the Swarm tool set, has two basic components: the Observer Swarm, and the Model Swarm. Swarms are objects that implement memory allocation and event scheduling. Upon execution of the e-KnSMOD, two probes and a program control panel are displayed. The observer (ObserverSwarm) and model (ModelSwarm) probes consist of default parameters that are modifiable by the user. After the parameters for the Observer Swarm and Model Swarm are processed, the e-KnSMOD environment is established by creating the Observer and Model objects and building the Scheduler. The Observer objects consist of the windows used to display the KnS-scape and KnS agents and other graphs specified by the user. The Model objects consist of the KnS-scape and the KnS agents. These steps are described next:

1. **Creation of the KnS-scape:** The KnS-scape, a 50 x 50 lattice, represents the KnS enterprise environment. Each location (x,y) on the KnS-scape has a knowledge creation opportunity, an organization identifier, and a KnS environment state. The KnS_event, organization, and KnS_environment datafiles (specified in the ModelSwarm probe) are used to build the characteristics of each (x,y) location, respectively. The knowledge creation events, which have a value of 1 through 5, are observable by the user of the KnS model from the KnS-scape window. The value of a knowledge creation (KC) event is distinguishable by color as repre-

sented in the KnS-scape window illustrated in *Figure 6*.

2. **Creation of the KnS Agents:** After the KnS-scape is created, the KnS agents are created and randomly placed on the KnS-scape. The "KnSnumAgents" parameter is used to determine how many KnS agents are created. The model creates a heterogeneous population of KnS agents. Some of the attributes are randomly generated, and others are based on where the agent is placed on the KnS-scape. The agents organizational affiliation is determined by the organization associated with the (x, y) coordinate at which the agent is placed. The initial value of current knowledge is based on the vision, which is randomly generated.

3. **Creation of the Scheduler:** The Observer Swarm and the Model Swarm create a schedule for activities to be performed during each cycle of the model. The Model Swarm schedules the actions to be performed by the KnS agents and the actions to be performed on the KnS-scape. The actions include:

1. KnS Agent: Move and acquire knowledge.
2. KnS Agent: Execute KnS behavior rule.
3. KnS-scape: Update KnS-scape (Knowledge Creation Event View).
4. KnS Repositories: Update group and enterprise repositories.
5. Display: Update KnS-scape display window.
6. Display: Update knowledge distribution graph.
7. Display: Update KnS attributes over time.
8. Summary File: Update KnS summary (metrics) file.

4. **Model Output:** The e-KnSMOD has three primary output windows that are updated after each cycle. The windows include: KnS Agent Attributes Over Time, Agent Knowledge Distribution, and the KnS-scape. Additionally, the model maintains a KnS summary data file that captures the KnS metrics of the KnS agents. This data file is

Figure 6. Knowledge creation (KC) events on the KnS-scape

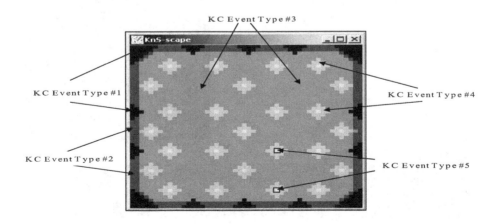

used for additional data analysis outside the e-KnSMOD environment. The following KnS metrics are captured by the model: the number of KnS agents that shared, the number of agents that shared by organization, the average amount of knowledge acquired, the number of items contributed to a group repository, and the number of items contributed to an enterprise repository.

The e-KnSMOD is designed to allow the user to explore possible improvements in enterprise knowledge sharing by observing the impact of KnS influences. The influences identified in the enterprise sharing influence diagram, shown in

Figure 1, are: KnS environment, KnS behavior of other knowledge workers, and attributes of the knowledge workers. *Figure 7* shows the results of a 10-cycle run using the default "alpha" value (alpha = 1), which causes a depleted KC event to increase one unit per cycle until it reaches its maximum capacity. Examination of the KnS Agent Attributes Over Time window shows that an average number of KnS agents sharing during each cycle is approximately 50, with a steady increase of knowledge acquired. By changing the "alpha" parameter to zero (0), for example, the user can examine what the impact of the KC event not reoccurring has on KnS behavior. Here, the results of a 10-cycle run show that the number of

Figure 7. Example run – recurring rate for KC events = 1

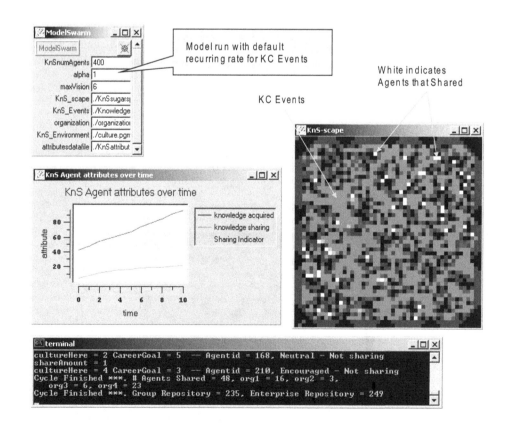

KnS agents sharing began to drop until no sharing occurred. The resulting KnS-scape window shows that there are no KC events.

Sensitivity analysis may be performed on e-KnSMOD by executing the model of several varying conditions in order to determine if small changes to the parameters resulted in unexpected results. Analysis may be performed on the parameters that are used in either the KnS rule or the environment rules. A summary of the findings are:

1. **Number of agents:** the model was tested with the number of agents ranging from 100 to 500 with varying conditions. In most cases, the percent of agents sharing increases slightly ($<1.5\%$) as one increases the number of agents in increments of 50. The number of agents was more sensitive in the range of 100-300 than in the range of 200-500.

2. **Behavior influence:** the model was tested by setting this parameter to 0 and 1. In all the tests conducted the percent of agents sharing decreased in the range of 1.7 to 4.0 percent when the parameter was changed from 0 to 1.

3. **Max vision:** The maximum vision was tested with the values 7, 14 and 28. In most cases, as the vision increased (7 to 14 to 28) the resulting knowledge sharing increased ~ 1 %. However, the percent was higher when the knowledge creation events with high value (part of the KnS_scape) were further apart.

4. **KnS_scape:**– the percent of agents sharing is impacted most by this parameter. The KnS agents acquire knowledge from the KnS_scape and if the agent does not have knowledge, it does not share.

5. **KnS_environment:** the percent of agents sharing is impacted greatly by this parameter. A difference of one state (i.e., barrier to neutral or neutral to enable) can change

the percent of agent sharing from 5 % to 14 %.

Much more detailed discussions of the construction of this simulation model are presented in Small (2006).

As described in this article, the e-KnSMOD, is a simple multi-agent simulation based on simple environment and KnS rules. The environment is represented by three 2-dimentional (50 by 50) lattices: one for the knowledge creation events, one for the organization affiliation, and one for the state of the KnS environment. Many complex relationships among the KWs and the KnS environment are not included in the implementation of e-KnSMOD. The objective of the model is not to predict enterprise KnS behavior, but to be used with the other CAS-based tools to enhance the understanding of enterprise knowledge sharing.

One major use of this KnS model is to improve enterprise knowledge sharing. The CAS-based enterprise KnS model can assist enterprise KM leadership, managers, practitioners, and others involved in KM implementation to characterize the current KnS environment, identify influences of KnS behavior, and better understand the impact of KnS interventions. This model can be applied to enterprises that are about to embark on KnS initiatives, as well as those that have a rich KnS portfolio.

The CAS-based characterization instruments allow a practitioner to characterize enterprise KnS from the perspective of the KW and from that of KM Leadership. Both instruments characterize the frequency of KnS behaviors, the extent of influence of KnS influences and barriers, and the state of the KnS environment. The data gathered using these instruments provide the information needed to characterize and model an enterprise from a CAS perspective.

The KW Profiling Questionnaire is a critical element here. The purpose of the KW Profiling Questionnaire is to determine, from an individual knowledge worker perspective, the answers to four questions:

1. What are your attributes?
2. What is your KnS behavior?
3. What influences your KnS behavior?
4. What is the state of the KnS environment?

The answers to these questions allow a KM practitioner to investigate the extent of KnS influences on the heterogeneous knowledge worker populations. Addressing the attributes of the knowledge worker is a critical aspect of this CAS-based methodology.

The focus of the KM Leadership Characterization Questionnaire is to determine, from the perspective of KM leadership and implementers, the answers to the following four questions:

- Part I: What is the understanding of the KM Leadership Team regarding the KnS needs (mission perspective) and KnS behavior within the organization?
- Part II: What are the KnS influences and the extent of the influences within your enterprise?
- Part III: What is the state of the KnS enablers/influences within your enterprise?
- Part IV: What is the KnS Strategy for Improvement?

Part I and Part IV of the KM leadership characterization instrument relates to the KnS improvement strategy. Part I addresses the importance of KnS to support mission needs, and whether KnS is occurring at the right level (individual, group, enterprise) and frequency. Part IV addresses the KnS strategy, which includes areas of improve-

Figure 8. KM leadership characterization and the CAS-based KnS framework

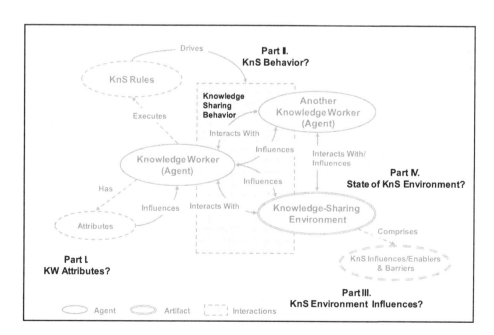

ment and the priority for achievement. The relationships of these questions to the CAS-based KnS framework are depicted in *Figure 8*.

The CAS-based KnS improvement methodology can be used by either an enterprise about to embark on KnS improvement activities for the first time (Initial Stage) or an enterprise that has a KnS strategy and robust KnS portfolio (Learning Stage). The tools described here can be used to identify and prioritize KnS improvement courses of action. The CAS-based methodology consists of five primary steps:

1. Step 1: Determine KnS Needs in Context of Mission Effectiveness. During this step, the KM practitioner determines the importance of KnS to the organization and assesses whether KnS is occurring at the appropriate frequency to support mission needs. Part I of the KM Leadership Characterization Questionnaire is used to gather this information.

2. Step 2: Characterize Current State of KnS. During this step, the KW profiling instrument is used to characterize KnS in the organization from a CAS perspective. The frequency of KnS behavior, KnS influences, and the state of the KnS environment are characterized from the individual knowledge worker perspective.

3. Step 3: Establish KnS Target State. During this step, Part III of the KM Leadership Characterization Questionnaire is used to capture the target state of the KnS environment, identify factors in the KnS environment that need improvement, and to establish priority of their implementation.

4. Step 4: Perform CAS-based Analysis. During this step, population analysis is performed based on KW attributes of interest to the organization. A gap analysis is performed on areas targeted for improvement against the extent of influence of the KnS factors identified by the KWs.

5. Step 5: Develop KnS Improvement Strategy. During this step, the results of the CAS-based analysis are used to develop or align the KnS strategy. The current state of the KnS environment (KW perspective), the target state of KnS environment (KM leadership), and the extent of KnS influence (KW perspective) are used to identify areas of improvement and their priority. The CAS-based simulation model can be used to model the planned improvements to gain insight into the possible impacts on KnS behavior.

The steps of the CAS-based KnS methodology should be integrated into the organizational improvement framework. We describe the CAS-based KnS improvement methodology in the context of the IDEAL[SM] (SEI, 1996) model, an improvement process originally designed for software process improvement. The IDEAL[SM] model consists of five phases:

1. Initiating: This phase lays the groundwork for a successful KnS improvement effort. It includes setting the context and sponsorship, and establishing the improvement infrastructure (organizations). Step 1 is conducted during this phase.

2. Diagnosing: Assessing the current state of KnS in the enterprise and determining where the organization is relative to the target state. Step 2, 3, and 4 are conducted during this phase.

3. Establishing: Developing strategies and plans for achieving the KnS target state. Step 5 is conducted during this phase.

4. Acting: Executing the plan to improve KnS.

5. Learning: Learning from the KnS experience and feedback from mission stakeholders, KM leadership, and knowledge workers.

Figure 9. CAS-based methodology: An IDEAL^{SM} perspective

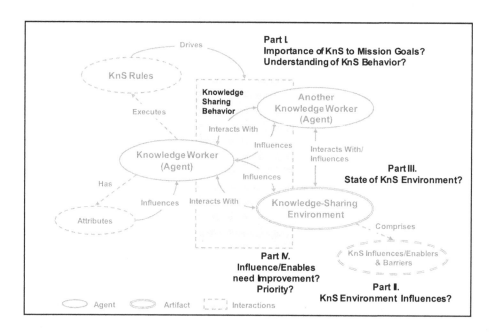

As shown in *Figure 9*, Step 1 occurs during the Initiating phase. Step 2, 3, and 4 occur during the Diagnosing phase, and Step 5 concurs during the Establishing phase.

SUMMARY

A CAS-based enterprise KnS model is described in this article. The model was evaluated for validity and effectiveness in two case studies. The premise of our research was that modeling enterprise knowledge sharing from a complex adaptive systems (CAS) perspective can provide KM leadership and practitioners with an enhanced understanding of KnS behavior within their organization. This research found that the CAS-based enterprise KnS model and methodol-

ogy provides KM leadership with an enhanced understanding of KnS behavior and the KnS influences. In the two case studies conducted in operational environments, members of the KM leadership teams indicated that they had gained a better understanding because of the CAS-based modeling approach. Enhanced understanding of the following was indicated: KnS behavior in their organization; KnS influences in their organization; and the extent of the KnS influences within their organization. KM leadership also indicated that because of the CAS-based modeling, they would either change the target KnS state of the KnS environment or the priority for achieving that state.

The CAS-based enterprise KnS model developed as part of this research was found to be valid. The CAS-based enterprise KnS model was exercised in two case studies. The results of the case studies (Small, 2006) provided support for the validity of the assumptions on which the CAS-based enterprise KnS model was developed. The claims associated with the validity of the CAS-based enterprise KnS model are as follows:

1. Claim 1 (C1): The KnS behavior of other KWs is a significant influence on KnS behavior.
2. Claim 2 (C2): The KnS environment factors are a significant influence on KnS behavior.
3. Claim 3 (C3): The attributes of the KW are related to the frequency of KnS behavior (how often a KW engages in a KnS behavior).
4. Claim 4 (C4): Enterprise KnS behavior can be characterized using a multi-agent CAS model, with a few basic rules that drive agent behavior.

REFERENCES

American Productivity & Quality Center (APQC). (1999). *Creating a knowledge-sharing culture.* Consortium Benchmarking Study -- Best-Practice Report.

American Productivity & Quality Center (APQC). (2000). *Successfully implementing knowledge management.* Consortium Benchmarking Study -- Final Report, 2000.

Anderson, P. (1999). Complexity theory and organization science. *Organization Science, 10*(3), 216-232.

Axelrod, R. (1997). *The complexity of cooperation: Agent-based models of competition and collaboration.* New Jersey: Princeton University Press.

Axelrod, R., & Cohen, M. (1999). *Harnessing complexity: Organizational implications of a scientific frontier.* New York: The Free Press.

Bukowitz, W., & Williams, R. (1999). *The knowledge management fieldbook.* London: Financial Times Prentice Hall.

Epstein, M., & Axtell, R. (1996). *Growing artificial societies: Social science from the bottom up.* Washington D.C.: The Brookings Institution.

Ford, D. (2003). Trust and knowledge management: The seeds of success. In *Handbook on Knowledge Management 1: Knowledge Matters* (pp. 553-575). Heidelberg: Springer-Verlag.

HBSP. (1998). *Harvard Business review on knowledge management.* Cambridge, MA: Harvard Business School Press.

Holland, J. (1995). *Hidden order: How adaptation builds complexity.* MA: Perseus Books Reading.

Holsapple, C.W. (Ed.). (2003). *Handbook on knowledge management 1: Knowledge matters.* Heidelberg: Springer-Verlag.

Holsapple, C.W. (Ed). (2003). *Handbook on knowledge management 2: Knowledge directions.* Heidelberg: Springer-Verlag.

Ipe, M. (2003). *The praxis of knowledge sharing in organizations: A case study.* Doctoral dissertation. University Microfilms.

Ives, W., Torrey, B., & Gordon, C. (2000). Knowledge sharing is human behavior. In *Knowledge management: Classic and contemporary works* (pp. 99-129).

Johnson, P., & Lancaster, A. (2000). *Swarm users guide.* Swarm Development Group.

Leonard, D., & Straus, S. (1998). Putting your company's whole brain to work. In *Harvard*

Business Review on Knowledge Management (pp. 109-136). Boston: Harvard Business School Press.

Liao, S., Chang, J., Shih-chieh, C., & Chia-mei, K. (2004). Employee relationship and knowledge sharing: A case study of a Taiwanese finance and securities firm. *Knowledge Management Research & Practice, 2,* 24-34.

Minar, N., Burkhar, R., Langton C., & Askemnazi, M. (1996). *The Swarm Simulation System: A toolkit for building multi-agent simulations.* Retrieved from http://alumni.media.mit.edu/~nelson/research/ swarm/.

Murray, S. (2003). *A quantitative examination to determine if knowledge sharing activities, given the appropriate richness lead to knowledge transfer, and if implementation factors influence the use of these knowledge sharing activities.* Doctoral dissertation. University Microfilms.

Nonaka, I., & Konno, N. (1998). The concept of Ba: Building a foundation for knowledge creation. *California Management Review (Special Issue on Knowledge and the Firm), 40*(3), 40-54.

Nonaka, I., & Takeuchi, H. (1995). *The knowledge-creating company: How Japanese companies create the dynamics of innovation.* New York: Oxford University Press.

O'Dell, C. (2008). *Web 2.0 and knowledge management.* American Productivity & Quality Center (APQC). Retrieved from http://www.apqc.org.

Small, C. (2006). *An enterprise knowledge-sharing model: A complex adaptive systems perspective on improvement in knowledge sharing.* Doctoral dissertation, George Mason University. University Microfilms.

Small, C., & Sage, A. (2006). Knowledge management and knowledge sharing: A review. *Information, Knowledge, and Systems Management, 5*(3), 153-169.

Software Engineering Institute (SEI). (1996). *IDEAL^{SM}: A user's guide for software process improvement* (Handbook CMU/SEI-96-HB-001). Pittsburgh, PA: Software Engineering Institute, Carnegie Mellon University.

Swarm Development Group. (2004). *Chris Langton, Glen Ropella.* Retrieved from http://wiki.swarm.org/.

This work was previously published in the International Journal of Information Technologies and Systems Approach, edited by M. Mora and D. Paradice, Volume 1, Issue 2, pp. 38-56, copyright 2008 by IGI Publishing, formerly known as Idea Group Publishing (an imprint of IGI Global).

Chapter XVI
Facilitating E-Learning with Social Software:
Attitudes and Usage from the Student's Point of View

Reinhard Bernsteiner
University for Health Sciences, Medical Informatics and Technology, Austria

Herwig Ostermann
University for Health Sciences, Medical Informatics and Technology, Austria

Roland Staudinger
University for Health Sciences, Medical Informatics and Technology, Austria

ABSTRACT

This article explores how social software tools can offer support for innovative learning methods and instructional design in general, and those related to self-organized learning in an academic context in particular. In the first section, the theoretical basis for the integration of wikis, discussion forums, and Weblogs in the context of learning are discussed. The second part presents the results of an empirical survey conducted by the authors and explores the usage of typical social software tools that support learning from a student's perspective. The article concludes that social software tools have the potential to be a fitting technology in a teaching and learning environment.

INTRODUCTION

One major task of higher education is to train students for the requirements of their future work by applying and adapting their knowledge to specific workplace-related requirements and settings. Due to the ongoing pressure on enterprises to cut

Copyright © 2009, IGI Global, distributing in print or electronic forms without written permission of IGI Global is prohibited.

costs, the periods of vocational adjustment in a company will become shorter and shorter.

On the one hand, the rising pressure of innovation and fast-paced development in the economy results in increased demand for continuous employee training. On the other, growing global competition forces enterprises to use available resources very economically so that employee training is considered to be necessary and desired even though it is conducted under considerable time and cost pressure (Köllinger, 2002).

According to these goals, the settings of the education must be changed adequately: "While most of higher education still ascribes to traditional models of instruction and learning, the workplace is characterized by rapid changes and emergent demands that require individuals to learn and adapt in situ and on the job without the guidance of educational authorities" (Sharma & Fiedler, 2004, p. 543).

In the field of higher education, it has become an important goal to develop "digital literacy" and educate learners as competent users and participants in a knowledge-based society (Kerres, 2007), but it can be assumed that there is a new generation of students, the "digital natives," who are accustomed to digital and Internet technology (Prensky, 2001a, 2001b).

Oblinger and Oblinger (2005) characterize next-generation students (called "n-gen," for Net generation) as digitally literate, highly Internet savvy, connected via networked media, used to immediate responses, preferring experiential learning, highly social, preferring to work in teams, craving interactivity in image-rich environments, and having a preference for structure rather than ambiguity.

According to a study conducted by Lenhart and Madden (2005), half of all teens in the USA may be considered "content creators" by using applications that provide easy-to-use templates to create personal Web spaces.

Classical face-to-face learning is seen as rigid and synchronous, and it promotes one-way (teacher-to-student) communication. Thus, it is not surprising that more and more students are opting for Web-based education as a more flexible and asynchronous mode (Aggarwal & Legon, 2006).

The higher education system should provide answers to this new generation of students who enter the system with different backgrounds and skills. They are highly influenced by social networking experiences and are able to create and publish on the Internet (Resnick, 2002).

Educators and teachers therefore have to consider the implications of these developments for the future design of their courses and lectures.

In 2002, a new term, "social software," entered the stage to refer to a new generation of Internet applications. One focus of this new generation is the collaboration of people in sharing information in new ways such as through social networking sites, wikis, communication tools, and folksonomies (Richter & Koch, 2007).

Wikis, Weblogs, and discussion forums will play a central role in the new context, so the areas of application and possibilities will enlarge enormously. It can be assumed that this will also have considerable influence on learning and the usage of these instruments as learning tools.

This article presents the results of an empirical survey in order to highlight the benefits of the above-mentioned Web-based social software tools from the student's point of view; 268 first-semester students, all in the first term of their studies at Austrian universities from different study programs, took part in this survey. The students were asked to use one or more of these tools as a learning tool. Participation in this survey was voluntary.

The presentation of the results of this survey is divided into three parts: first, the use of the tools by the students (before they started their studies); second, the experiences the students had made with the tools during the study; and third, the potential future usage.

The article concludes with a discussion of the results of this survey in contrast with other empirical studies already published. Also, the limitations of this survey and ideas for further research are pointed out.

THEORETICAL FRAMEWORK

This part refers to the necessary theoretical background required for the following empirical study, especially the areas of social software and learning.

Social Software

The term *social software* emerged and came into use in 2002 and is generally attributed to Clay Shirky (2003). Shirky, a writer and teacher on the social implications of Internet technology, defines social software simply as "software that supports group interaction."

Another definition of social software can be found in Coates (2005), who refers to social software as "software that supports, extends, or derives added value from human social behaviour."

Users are no longer mere readers, audiences, or consumers. They have the ability to become active producers of content. Users can act in user and producer positions and they can rapidly change the position.

Nowadays the term *social software* is closely related to "Web 2.0." The term *Web 2.0* was introduced by Tim O'Reilly (2005), who suggested the following definition:

Web 2.0 is the network as platform, spanning all connected devices; Web 2.0 applications are those that make the most of the intrinsic advantages of that platform: delivering software as a continually updated service that gets better the more people use it, consuming and remixing data from multiple sources, including individual users, while providing their own data and services in a form that allows remixing by others, creating network effects through an "architecture of participation," and going beyond the page metaphor of Web 1.0 to deliver rich user experiences.

Web 2.0 technologies such as blogs, wikis, podcasts, and RSS feeds or discussion forums have been dubbed social software because they are perceived as being especially connected and allow users to develop Web content collaboratively and publicly (Alexander, 2006).

Until now, the Internet (Web 1.0) has one big disadvantage: It is easy to get information in it, but it is quite complicated and inconvenient to act as an author and take part in the development of content. Web 2.0 should enable all Internet users to actively take part in the further development of the Internet. Everyone should be able to contribute easily. The focus of Web 2.0 is on the behaviour of the user. It should empower people to communicate, collaborate, contribute, and participate.

This growing phenomenon is very interesting and ought to be examined carefully in order to understand how the Web is evolving and how this continuously regenerative cycle of performance and technological innovation empowers "learning by sharing" (Thijssen & Vernooij, 2002).

Based on the key principle of the architecture of participation, social software can be seen as part of Web 2.0. Wikis, Weblogs, and discussion forums are tools that are seen as social software applications and were selected for further research and the empirical study presented below.

Related Empirical Research

Institutions in the field of higher education have made efforts to introduce various IT-supported learning tools in the daily routine of students and lecturers (Aggarwal & Legon, 2006; Dooley & Wickersham, 2007; Duffy & Bruns, 2006; Evans & Sadler-Smith, 2006; McGill, Nicol, Littlejohn, Grierson, Juster, & Ion, 2005).

Published results of the usage of Weblogs in the Prolearn project (http://www.prolearn-project.

org) have shown that a large majority of respondents considers personalization and adaptation of the learning environment as important and crucial factors. Learning should be individualized to become more effective and efficient. Personalization is a key element of the learning process, and specific problems need specific solutions as students differ greatly in their backgrounds and capabilities.

Learning materials are typically too general in order to cover a very wide range of purposes and personal learning needs. Compared to classical learning, personalization can be the most important added value that e-learning can offer. With it, education can be optimised and adjusted to various working conditions and needs because students have different goals, interests, motivation levels, learning skills, and endurance (Klamma et. al., 2006).

Chao (2007) explored the potential uses of wikis in the field of software engineering (38 participants), especially for software project team collaboration and communication. Overall, 25 students agreed and 1 student disagreed (2 were neutral) that the wiki is a good tool for project collaboration. Concerning the applications of wikis, more than 23 students found that a wiki is a good tool for maintaining a group diary, managing user stories (project requirements), and project tracking and reporting. While a majority of students found that a wiki is a good tool for updating a project plan, managing acceptance tests, tracking defects, and developing user documents, there were also a significant number of students who disagreed.

First results using wikis for collaborative writing (about 40 participants) also reported similar results. In this study, students used wikis to write articles partly together with the lecturer.

After early problems with using the software and writing contributions in the wiki, students were able to write articles by themselves or in teams. The motivation among students was on different levels, so the lecturer had to increase it during lessons. Other students, however, were highly motivated and were creating the content and adding them to the wikis (Bendel, 2007).

Constructivism and Learning: Presentation of the Learning Model

A constructivist point of view focuses on the learning process by looking at the construction of knowledge by an individual. As a consequence, there is a recommendation to align learning environments, especially in the academic context, and associated complex learning objectives with constructivist learning principles (Du & Wagner, 2005; Jonassen, Mayes, & McAleese, 1993; Tangney, FitzGibbon, Savage, Mehan, & Holmes, 2001). Learning is not seen as the transmission of content and knowledge to a passive learner. Constructivism views learning as an active and constructive process that is based on the current understanding of the learner. Learning is embedded in a social context and a certain situation (Schulmeister, 2005).

The constructivist approach shifts learning from instruction and design centered to learner-centered learning and teaching. The role of the educator changes from directing the learner toward supporting and coaching the learner.

Baumgartner (2004) has suggested three different prototypical modes of learning and teaching. These three different modes of learning and teaching can be neutral or specific so they can be applied across all subject domains. Therefore, each teaching model can be used to teach, for example, sociology subjects as well as to teach technical sciences. Learning can be portrayed as an iterative process that can subsequently be subdivided into different phases, which are summarized in Figure 1.

In particular, these three different prototypical modes for learning encompass the following.

Figure 1. Prototypical modes of learning and teaching (Baumgartner, 2004)

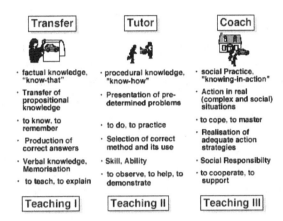

Learning and Teaching I: Transferring Knowledge

At the starting point, the learner needs to be provided with abstract knowledge to lay the theoretical foundations and to understand relevant signposts, road markings, and orientation points. This kind of factual knowledge is static and has little value by itself in real and complex situations. It merely serves as a shortcut to prevent pitfalls and to help to organize the student's learning experiences.

The knowledge of the student is based on knowledge possessed by the teacher. Students have to learn what teachers ask them to learn. The teacher has the responsibility to make the knowledge transfer as easy as possible.

Learning and Teaching II: Acquiring, Compiling, and Gathering Knowledge

In this section of the individual learning career, the student actually applies the abstract knowledge and gathers his or her own experiences. In order to limit the action and reflection possibilities, the learner interacts within a somewhat restricted, artificial environment, which is reduced in complexity and easy to control by the teacher. To provide feedback, the learning environment is designed to include relevant devices where students can deposit their interim products and teachers can inspect them.

The emphasis in this model lies on the learning process of the student. Teachers try to help the students overcome wrong assumptions and wrong learning attitudes, and assist in the reflection process of the subject domain.

Learning and Teaching III: Developing, Inventing, and onstructing Knowledge

Teacher and learner work together to master problems. This model includes problem generation and/or invention. The environment is constructed in such a way that it represents, at least in certain aspects, reality or reality in a constrained form.

This model includes two-way communication on equal terms, using either linguistic representations or other adequate kinds of language.

Teaching III has strong links to constructivism. From a constructivist point of view, learning is considered as an active process in which people construct their knowledge by relating it to their previous experiences in complex and real situations in life. In their practical lives, people are confronted with unique, unpredictable situations whose inherent problems are not readily observable (Baumgartner, 2004).

Students should be enabled to invent new things, and produce or generate new knowledge. Consequently, learning and teaching at universities in most cases can be assigned to the requirements presented in Learning and Teaching II and III. In order to achieve this goal, a special learning environment must be provided.

Consequences for IT-Supported Learning and Teaching

Computer software can be used for all three models, ranging from programmed instruction (Learning/Teaching I) to problem-solving software (Learning/Teaching II), to complex simulations and/or so-called micro worlds (Learning/Teaching III). It is said that the inherent nature of the Internet brings the real world into the classrooms, and with its hyperlink structure it clearly advocates the model of Teaching III (Baumgartner, 2004).

The use of the Internet, especially through its social software, gains importance because it can contribute to exceed the limits of classical teaching models. By adapting learning and teaching models to the new technical possibilities, the roles of learner and teacher are becoming more indistinct because the learner can take a central part in the design and arrangement of the learning process (Kerres, 2006).

Systems that support learners with respect to the Learning Model III are called personal learning environments (PLEs). PLEs are mostly Web-based applications and are based on learning management systems (LMSs; Seufert, 2007).

PLEs are personal and open learning environments, and they are suitable for cross-linking content and people. Learners can use PLEs to manage individual learning progress. They are ideally available for lifelong learning and are supported by the following processes.

- setting up individual learning goals
- planning and controlling one's own learning concerning the content as well as the learning process
- combining formal and informal learning activities
- communicating with peers during the learning process
- establishing social networks or communities of practice
- using Web-based services, for example, syndication
- verifying the learning process with respect to the learning goals

Unlike an LMS, which is usually related to one special institution or to one special course, a PLE is focused on the individual learner. A PLE should combine a broad mixture of different resources and subsystems in a "personally-managed space" (Attwell, 2006).

In the previous decade, learning management systems were developed that moved toward enterprise-level applications, "but the wealth of new, user-friendly, tools in the Web 2.0 environment suggests that the all-in-one monolithic e-learning systems may be entering a phase of obsolescence by the ongoing development of the web" (Craig, 2007).

Social software applications have the potential to cope with these requirements (Brahm, 2007).

DESCRIPTION AND CLASSIFICATION OF SOCIAL SOFTWARE TOOLS

In the following section, three social software tools—Weblogs, discussion forums, and wikis—are described in more detail and the tools are compared. Students were able to select these tools during the empirical study.

Weblog

A Weblog, a compound of *Web* and *logbook*, usually just called "blog," is a Web site that contains new articles or contributions in a primarily chronological order, listing the latest entry on top.

Primarily, a Weblog is a discussion-oriented instrument especially emphasizing two functions: RSS feeds and trackback. RSS feeds, also called RSS files, can be read and processed for further use by other programs. The most common programs are RSS readers or RSS aggregators that check RSS-enabled Web sites on behalf of the user to read or display any updated contribution that can be found. The user can subscribe to several RSS feeds. Thus, the information of different Web sites can be retrieved and combined. Preferably, news or other Weblogs are subscribed to.

Trackback is a service function that notifies the author of an entry in a Weblog if a reference to this contribution has been made in another Weblog. By this mechanism, a blogger (person who writes contributions in a Weblog) is immediately informed of any reactions to his or her contribution on other Weblogs (Hammond, Hannay, & Lund, 2004).

Forum

A discussion forum or Web forum is a service function providing discussion possibilities on the Internet. Usually, Web forums are designed for the discussion of special topics. The forum is furthermore subdivided into subforums or subtopics. Contributions to the discussion can be made and other people may read and/or respond to them. Several contributions to a single topic are called a thread.

The application areas of the two instruments, Weblogs and forums, are quite similar. The most essential differences between Weblogs and discussion forums can be described as follows:

- A forum is usually located on one platform while many bloggers develop their own, individual environments. They connect their Weblogs via RSS feeds and trackback functions.
- Through the integration of RSS files and trackback functions, a discussion process can be initiated and continued, crossing the boundaries of the bloggers' own Weblogs without authors having to observe other Weblogs.
- Weblogs tend to be more people centered whereas forums are more topic focused. Through the use of Weblogs, learner-specific learning environments can be constructed without interfering with the learning environments of others (Baumgartner, 2004).

Wiki

A WikiWikiWeb, shortly called wiki, is a hypertext system for storing and processing information. Every single site of this collection of linked Web pages can be viewed through a Web browser. Furthermore, every site can also be edited by any person. The separation between authors and readers who write their own text, and change and delete it is obsolete as also third parties can carry out these functions (Augar, Raitman, & Zhou, 2004).

Learning Activities Supported by Social Software

The integration of different social software tools offers support in the following learning activities:

- Learning from different perspectives: The integration supports the exchange of ideas as well as finding like-minded people. Furthermore, social software tools simplify the process of establishing connections between people of the same or similar interests. Simultaneously, its open and expandable philosophy supports going beyond the thinking in groups (of a common interest) by supporting diversity and bringing together different perspectives and backgrounds (Efimova & Fiedler, 2004; Schulmeister, 2004).

- Synergies of self-organized and joint learning: Social Software tools provide a personal learning area for their authors. However, this does not force a general learning flow or learning style. Learners are not alone and can profit from the feedback of a community in order to examine and enhance the development of their own ideas (Böttger & Röll, 2004; Efimova & Fiedler, 2004; Fiedler, 2004).

- Digital apprenticeship: Through reading other wikis, forums, or Weblogs regularly, beginners are enabled to learn from experts. At the same time, they can actively participate in discussions beyond geographic or thematic borders (Efimova & Fiedler, 2004; Fiedler, 2004).

- Support for the development of the ability to learn (learning to learn): Through the publication of one's own thoughts and reflections, content is made available for assessment as well as for further development, thereby improving self-observation and self-reflection

skills. The knowledge change of the learner will be improved (Baumgartner, 2005).

- Support for reflexive writing: The simple but efficient and rather robust encoding standard usually used in social software allows for the explicit modeling of content flows, feedback loops, and monitoring procedures of various kinds, thus supporting an ongoing reiterative process of explication and reflection (Fiedler, 2004).

Integration of Social Software Tools and the Learning and Teaching Modes

Baumgartner (2004) has integrated different types of content management systems in relation to the most suitable learning and teaching mode. He clearly states that the boundaries are overlapping and that every tool, in one way or another, could be used for every teaching model. Figure 2 presents the integration of the social software tools and the learning and teaching modes.

Weblogs and forums can be defined as discussion-oriented tools because the discourse and exchange of ideas related to a certain topic is the preeminent aim. Weblogs offer the possibility to support all three phases of the learning process. However, the main focus can be assigned to Modes II and III.

Based on the multitude of interaction possibilities, wikis can be attached to Teaching III (Baumgartner, 2004). Additional functions were added to Weblog tools that go beyond the scope of the central use of Weblogs; for example, longer articles can also be stored. Through the creation of directories, a structured collection of links can be implemented.

Through the additional linking of Weblogs, wikis, and forums, there is the possibility to develop a personal knowledge collection (Kantel, 2003).

Figure 2. Prototypical modes and social software tool

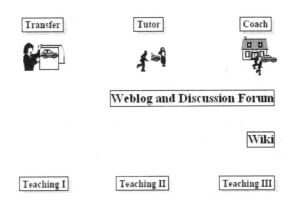

EMPIRICAL SURVEY

The purpose of this survey was to determine if the integration of Web-based social software tools (wikis, discussion forums, and Weblogs) are suitable to foster learning from the student's point of view.

Aim of the Survey and Methodology

Scrutinizing the possibilities and constraints of social software tools (wikis, discussion forums, and Weblogs) as personal learning environments, students at Austrian universities were asked to use one or more of the offered tools for their research, homework, and documentation purposes. In most cases, the collaboration of students was required to perform the assigned tasks.

The students were asked to use the tools for one course only during the winter term of 2006. Furthermore, there was no obligation for the students to use a tool at all; they were just encouraged to do so. Students were also offered the possibility

to use two or three tools; the selection was up to the students.

The courses were organized as blended-learning courses so they included on-campus lessons and off-campus work in which the students could work face-to-face or using the social software tools.

More than 90% of the students attending the courses took part in this survey. In order to give the participants an impression of the functionality and usage of the tools, short presentations of the tools were made by an instructor before the students made their choice.

At the end of the testing phase—after 4 weeks of using the tools—selected students reported their experiences with the tools used. Students who had decided not to use the tools in the first place got an impression about the usage, advantages, and disadvantages of the tools from their fellow students. Following these short presentations, a questionnaire was completed that provided the basic findings for further inspection and research.

A total of 268 first-semester students of different Austrian universities in five selected courses took part in this survey. The majority of the participants were between 18 and 20 years old. The portion of female students was about 17%.

According to a survey conducted by Seybert (2007) concerning gender differences in computer and Internet usage by young people (aged between 16 and 24), there is no gap between men and women in Austria. The proportion of women and men (in the relevant age class) that use a computer (almost) once a day is 72% the same. A study by Otto, Kutscher, Klein, and Iske (2005) indicates that there is a positive correlation between a formal educational background and the usage of the Internet in Germany: "Beside socio-cultural resources like family background, peer structures and social support in general, the formal educational background turns out to be the main factor for explaining differences in internet usage" (p. 219). As a consequence, for the analysis of the results of this survey, no distinction between male and female students was made.

Table 1 presents the distribution of the participants concerning the degree programs the students are attending.

For the further analysis of the results, no distinction according to degree programs will be made.

The questionnaire asked each participant questions about her or his subjective impression of the

Table 1. Distribution of students regarding degree program

	Distribution
Management & Law	17%
Management & IT	31%
Management & Industrial Engineering	22%
Mechanical Engineering, Electronics	30%

application of the tools. It included 5-point Likert scales for rating constructs such as eligibility, perceived quality, or enjoyment.

The study was conducted to find answers about the:

- usage of social software before the study started,
- selection of the offered tools,
- perceived quality of the contributions and the support for learning,
- applicability of the instruments to support communication and community building,
- correlation of the usage for private and educational purposes of the tools,
- fun factor in using the instruments, and
- potential future usage.

The results of the study are presented in three parts:

- Part 1: Analysis of the usage of wikis, discussion forums, and Weblogs of the students before the study was started
- Part 2: Experiences made with the tools during the study
- Part 3: Potential future usage of the tools

Part 1: Tool Selection and Prestudy Usage

Due to the fact that the students could select the tools on their own, the Table 2 shows the results of this selection process.

According to Table 2, the combination of wikis and discussion forums is the most selected combination of tools (42.9%), followed by wikis only (23.1%) and discussion forums only (22.4%). In the end, only five students (1.9%) did not take part in the study; they did not select a tool, although they first had the intention to do so. Only one student used Weblogs only. Generally, Weblogs were not used very intensively by the participants.

Table 2. Tools selected by the students

	Percent	Number
Only one tool selected		
Wikis only	23.1%	62
Discussion forums only	22.4%	60
Weblogs only	0.4%	1
More than one tool selected		
Wikis and discussion forums	42.9%	115
Wikis and Weblogs	1.9%	5
Discussion forums and Weblogs	0.7%	2
Wikis, discussion forums, and Weblogs	6.7%	18
No tool selected		
No tool selected	1.9%	5

Table 3 shows the usage of the tools by the participants before they took part in the study. It indicates that wikis (76%) and discussion forums (78%) are currently the most widely used tools. Weblogs are only used by 11% of the asked students.

The results clearly show that the Weblog hype had not yet reached the surveyed students. Due to the fact that only about 11% of the students are currently using Weblogs, the results for this instrument are not published for the first part of the analysis. When it comes to the potential future usage of the instruments, Weblogs are taken into consideration again.

The following section presents the results for statements used in analyzing the usage in more detail.

Tables 4 and 5 present the current usage of the tools for private and educational purposes. First, the statement "I often use wikis or forums for private purposes" was presented.

Table 3. Students already using the tools

	Wiki	Forum	Weblog
Yes	76%	78%	11%
No	24%	22%	89%

Table 4. Usage for private purposes

	Wiki	Forum
I totally agree	33%	33%
I generally agree	35%	29%
Neither...nor (neutral)	9%	9%
I slightly disagree	16%	17%
I disagree	8%	12%

Table 5. Usage for educational purposes

	Wiki	Forum
I totally agree	57%	22%
I generally agree	33%	29%
Neither...nor (neutral)	3%	12%
I slightly disagree	8%	24%
I disagree	1%	12%

Table 5 presents the results for the statement "I often use wikis or forums for educational purposes."

A huge majority (90%) stated that they use wikis for educational purposes and about two thirds (68%) used wikis for private purposes. Wikis are therefore more intensively used for educational purposes than for private purposes, whereas the usage of forums is exactly the opposite: They are more used for private purposes than for education.

The responses of the students concerning these statements were that wikis are foremost considered as a source of serious information, whereas forums are ideal for getting hints or clues to problems because of their privacy. Questions about computer problems, computer games, leisure activities, and so forth were mentioned. A repetition of this image can be identified when the disagreement with the statement is analyzed; 29% of the students do not or rarely use forums for private purposes compared to 36% for education.

Part 2: Experiences Made During the Study

This section presents the results of the study concerning experiences with the usage of the tools during the study.

Quality and Support for Learning

The following refers to statements concerning the quality of the contributions of wikis and discussion forums and their support for learning.

The results of the statement "The quality of contributions in wikis or forums is in general good" are presented in Table 6. The contributions of wikis are evaluated to be much better than those of forums.

The surveyed pupils had the opportunity to give reasons for their assessment concerning the quality of contributions via additional qualitative feedback. The following summarizes the addressed reasons.

One reason for the excelling grade for the quality of wikis is the "Wikipedian community." The term *wiki* is often seen as a synonym for the free online encyclopedia Wikipedia (http://www.wikipedia.org). Wikipedia is widely used for a great variety of tasks, including research on all topics needed for educational and private purposes.

In contrast to the good evaluation of the contributions of wikis, the open architecture of wikis was also mentioned. In most cases, this open architecture allows everyone to edit entries, which results in the uncertainty of whether the knowledge presented is correct or not. The quality of contributions in discussion forums was rated rather mediocre. Forums are primarily used for technical problems, especially computer-related problems; to get in contact with experts on certain topics, and to get information on online games.

The next statement, "The usage of wikis or forums leads to misunderstandings and confusion," is about the clarity of the contributions.

Only a minority think that the contributions are not clear and may lead to misunderstandings. In this case, wikis are also rated better than forums.

The next statements addressed the support of these instruments for learning. Table 8 summarizes the results for the statement "When reading

Table 6. Perceived quality of contribution

	Wiki	Forum
I totally agree	38%	10%
I generally agree	52%	31%
Neither...nor (neutral)	10%	41%
I slightly disagree	2%	15%
I disagree	0%	4%

Table 8. Reading contributions helps to acquire contents

	Wiki	Forum
I totally agree	23%	8%
I generally agree	36%	21%
Neither...nor (neutral)	32%	31%
I slightly disagree	5%	25%
I disagree	3%	15%

Table 7. Clarity of contributions

	Wiki	Forum
I totally agree	2%	4%
I generally agree	6%	18%
Neither...nor (neutral)	29%	37%
I slightly disagree	34%	27%
I disagree	29%	14%

Table 9. Writing contributions helps to acquire contents

	Wiki	Forum
I totally agree	8%	7%
I generally agree	13%	19%
Neither...nor (neutral)	45%	34%
I slightly disagree	14%	22%
I disagree	19%	17%

contributions in wikis or forums, it is easier for me to acquire the learning contents."

More than half of the students express that reading contributions in wikis is helpful for learning, whereas only about 8% think that it is not helpful. Compared to forums, wikis were again much better evaluated, especially considering the big difference from the negative evaluations of forums.

Table 9 presents the learning support achieved by writing contributions. ("When writing contributions in wikis or forums, it is easier for me to acquire the learning contents.")

A different picture emerges in the statistics when comparing the evaluation of how writing

an article or post supports the learning process. Here, forums take the lead when it comes to positive assessment. In both cases, there was a large number stating that writing is neither positive nor negative. The majority of the students read rather than wrote, while more students wrote in forums than in wikis.

Applicability for Communication and Community Building

The statement was formulated as follows: "Wikis or forums are appropriate to support communication."

Table 10. Applicability for communication

	Wiki	Fo-rum
I totally agree	9%	39%
I generally agree	33%	37%
Neither...nor (neutral)	29%	17%
I slightly disagree	15%	4%
I disagree	15%	3%

Table 11. Support for community building

	Wiki	Forum
I totally agree	10%	28%
I generally agree	25%	32%
Neither...nor (neutral)	39%	23%
I slightly disagree	15%	11%
I disagree	10%	6%

The results clearly demonstrate that discussion forums are made for communication whereas wikis are rather seen as a kind of reference book or encyclopedia, as already mentioned above.

The results of the next statement, "Wikis or forums support the setup of communities," can be seen in Table 11.

Opinions about the applicability of wikis to establish a community is split. About 35% say that wikis are supportive of building a community compared to 25% who said that wikis do not support community building. The support of forums to build a community is rated much better: 50% indicated that forums are well suited to build a community.

These results were to be expected because they confirm the nature of the instruments.

Fun Factor in Using the Instruments

In surveying whether students gain pleasure ("I enjoy using wikis or forums"), wikis again came out on top.

A majority enjoy using wikis (62%) and forums (56%). Considering the percentage of students who said that there is no ("I disagree") or little ("I slightly disagree") fun when using these instruments, wikis (6%) are much better rated than forums (18%).

Part 3: Potential Future Usage of the Tools

The third section of the empirical study deals with the potential usage by students who had not used the instruments before the study. Students gained knowledge and experiences by using the tools during the study by themselves or on the basis of the reported experiences made by their fellow students.

The first statement, "I will use wikis, forums, or Weblogs for educational purposes in the future," yielded the results in Table 13.

According to this study, wikis will have a bright future and will be used often for educational purposes, whereas forums will be used less often. About 54% of the surveyed students had the intention of using wikis more or less often in the future. About 16% did not think that they will use wikis often in the future and 30% are not yet sure if they will use this instrument.

The results for forums and Weblogs indicate no clear trend, but forums were rated slightly higher than Weblogs; 39% of the students stated that they can imagine using forums in the future for their education compared to 36% for Weblogs. At the other end of the scale, 45% did not have the intention to use forums (40% for Weblogs).

Table 12. Fun Factor in using the instruments

	Wiki	**Forum**
I totally agree	26%	19%
I generally agree	36%	37%
Neither...nor (neutral)	31%	26%
I slightly disagree	5%	14%
I disagree	1%	4%

Table 13. Future usage in educational context (current nonusers)

	Wikis	**Forums**	**Weblogs**
I totally agree	18%	16%	13%
I generally agree	36%	23%	23%
Neither...nor (neutral)	30%	16%	24%
I slightly disagree	9%	12%	13%
I disagree	7%	33%	27%

Table 14. Future usage in private context (current nonusers)

	Wikis	**Forums**	**Weblogs**
I totally agree	11%	14%	9%
I generally agree	36%	23%	22%
Neither...nor (neutral)	30%	25%	24%
I slightly disagree	14%	7%	16%
I disagree	9%	32%	28%

The statement "I will use wikis, forums, or Weblogs for private purposes in the future" leads to similar results.

From this point of view, wikis are again the leading instrument, followed by forums and then Weblogs.

It must be said that the responses to this set of statements represented feelings, attitudes, and opinions about instruments that had not yet been used by the asked participants. The purpose of posing these statements was to gain insight into the mind-set in regard to these instruments.

DISCUSSION

The results clearly show that wikis are currently the most often used instrument and furthermore have the greatest potential as a tool for learning and knowledge management in the field of learning; these findings are in line with other empirical studies (Bendel, 2007; Chao, 2007).

Other studies (McGill et al., 2005; Nicol & MacLeod, 2004) report that a shared workspace helps to support collaborative learning; the possibility of being able to access and contribute to the development of resources at any time and from any location was especially appreciated by the students.

The survey at hand made a distinction between reading and writing contributions to wikis and discussion forums. The results show that 59% of students said reading contributions in wikis is helpful for learning (stating "I totally agree" and "I generally agree") while only 21% stated that writing in wikis is helpful for learning. Reading contributions in forums helped 29% of the participants, whereas writing in forums was helpful to 26%. This survey supports the general statement that a shared workspace that supports a constructivist and learner-centered approach is helpful for learning.

The pedagogical value in the context of learning is described in several publications (Babcock,

2007; Hurst, 2005). Weblogs can foster the establishment of a learning and teaching environment in which students and teachers experience a greater degree of equality and engagement. Du and Wagner (2007) published results of a study of an information systems undergraduate course (31 participants). This study indicated that the performance of students' Weblogs was a significant predictor for learning outcomes, while traditional coursework was not. Moreover, individuals' cognitive construction efforts to build their own mental models and social construction efforts to further enrich and expand knowledge resources appeared to be two key aspects of constructivist learning with Weblogs. According to this study, there is a potential benefit of using Weblogs as a knowledge construction tool and a social learning medium.

According to the survey at hand, Weblogs are not yet widely used, and their potential seems to be limited. It can be assumed that these limited prospects will change when the penetration of Weblogs into the daily routine of the students increase—for private as well as for educational purposes.

To avoid possible pitfalls about the application of these instruments in the context of learning, some social and psychological issues must be taken into consideration (Kreijns, Kirschner, & Jochems, 2003). Social interaction is essential for members of a team to get to know each other, commit to social relationships, develop trust, and develop a sense of belonging in developing a learning community. The size and the composition of the learning communities seem to be important factors in how interaction and communication within the learning community will take place (Dooley & Wickersham, 2007). There are also many unresolved issues, like the provision of the technology and the services, intellectual property rights and digital rights management, the security of data, access restrictions to the content, and information ethics (Attwell, 2006; McGill et al., 2005; Sharma & Maleyeff, 2003).

CONCLUSION

The aim of this contribution was to investigate the experiences of students using social software tools in the context of learning. Wikis, Weblogs, and discussion forums are typical social software tools and were used for this survey.

The results clearly show that wikis and discussion forums can support learning and collaboration. The usage of Weblogs in this study was limited and hence no statements about their applicability can be made. In order to assure a successful implementation of these tools, social and psychological issues must be taken into consideration as well.

The results of this study are the basis for the introduction of social software into education to help students set up individual learning environments. These learning environments should support lifelong learning.

There are likely to be other unplanned consequences of the intensive use of the Internet in general and social software especially. Further research is needed to explore possible problems and solutions.

The results of the empirical survey indicate that a long-term study in combination with the further development of social software tools may be promising.

REFERENCES

Aggarwal, A. K., & Legon, R. (2006). Web-based education diffusion. *International Journal of Web-Based Learning and Teaching Technologies, 1*(1), 49-72.

Alexander, B. (2006). Web 2.0: A new wave of innovation for teaching and learning? *Educause Review, 41*(2), 32-44.

Attwell, G. (2006). *Personal learning environment*. Retrieved May 17, 2007, from http://www.

knownet.com/writing/weblogs/Graham_Attwell/
entries/6521819364

Augar, N., Raitman, R., & Zhou, W. (2004, December 5-8). Teaching and learning online with wikis. In R. Atkinson, C. McBeath, D. Jonas-Dwyer, & R. Phillips (Eds.), *Beyond the Comfort Zone*: *Proceedings of the 21ˢᵗ ASCILITE Conference*, Perth, Western Australia. Retrieved May 17, 2007, from http://www.ascilite.org.au/conferences/perth04/procs/contents.html

Babcock, M. (2007). Learning logs in introductory literature courses. *Teaching in Higher Education, 12*(4), 513-523.

Baumgartner, P. (2004). The Zen art of teaching. *Communication and Interactions in eEducation.* Retrieved May 17, 2007, from http://bt-mac2.fernuni-hagen.de/peter/gems/zenartofteaching.pdf

Baumgartner, P. (2005). Eine neue lernkultur entwickeln: Komptenzbasierte ausbildung mit blogs und e-portfolios. In V. Hornung-Prähauser (Ed.), *ePortfolio Forum Austria: Proceedings of the ePortfolio Austria 2005*, Salzburg, Austria (pp. 33-38).

Baumgartner, P., Häfele, H., & Maier-Häfele, K. (2004). *Content management systeme in e-education: Auswahl, potenziale und einsatzmöglichkeiten.* Innsbruck, Austria: Studienverlag.

Bendel, O. (2006). Wikipedia als methode und gegenstand der lehre. In K. Hildebrand (Ed.), *HMD: Praxis der wirtschaftsinformatik: Vol. 252. Social software* (pp. 82-88). Heidelberg, Germany: dpunkt-Verlag.

Böttger, M., & Röll, M. (2004, December 15-17). Weblog publishing as support for exploratory learning on the World Wide Web. In P. Isaias, K. Demetrios, & G. Sampson (Eds.), *Cognition and Exploratory Learning in Digital Age (CELDA 2004): Proceedings of the IADIS International Conference*, Lisbon, Portugal. IADIS Press.

Brahm, T. (2007). Social software und personal broadcasting: Stand der forschung. In S. Seufert & D. Euler (Eds.), *Ne(x)t generation learning: Wikis, blogs, mediacasts & Co. Social software und personal broadcasting auf der spur* (pp. 20-38). SCIL Arbeitsbericht.

Chao, J. (2007). Student project collaboration using wikis. In *Proceedings of the 20ᵗʰ Conference on Software Engineering Education & Training* (pp. 255-261). Washington, DC.

Coates, T. (2005). *An addendum to a definition of social software.* Retrieved March 4, 2007, from http://www.plasticbag.org/archives/2005/01/an_addendum_to_a_definition_of_social_software

Craig, E. (2007). Changing paradigms: Managed learning environments and Web 2.0. *Campus-Wide Information Systems, 24*(3), 152-161.

Dooley, K. E., & Wickersham, L. E. (2007). Distraction, domination and disconnection in whole-class online discussions. *Quarterly Review of Distance Education, 8*(1), 1-8.

Du, H. S., & Wagner, C. (2005). Learning with Weblogs: An empirical investigation. In *Proceedings of the 38ᵗʰ Annual Hawaii International Conference on System Sciences (HICSS'05): Track 1* (p. 7b). Washington, DC: IEEE Computer Society.

Du, H. S., & Wagner, C. (2007). Learning with Weblogs: Enhancing cognitive and social knowledge construction. *IEEE Transactions on Professional Communication, 50*(1), 1-16.

Duffy, P. D., & Bruns, A. (2006). The use of blogs, wikis and RSS in education: A conversation of possibilities. In *Proceedings of the Online Learning and Teaching Conference 2006*, Brisbane, Australia (pp. 31-38).

Efimova, L., & Fiedler, S. (2004, March 24-26). Learning webs: Learning in Weblog networks. In P. Kommers, P. Isaias, & M. B. Nunes (Eds.),

Web based communities: Proceedings of the IADIS International Conference 2004, Lisbon, Portugal (pp. 490-494). IADIS Press. Retrieved May 17, 2007, from https://doc.telin.nl/dscgi/ds.py/Get/File-35344

Evans, C., & Sadler-Smith, E. (2006). Learning styles in education and training: Problems, politicisation and potential. *Education + Training, 48*(2/3), 77-83.

Fiedler, S. (2004). Personal Webpublishing as a reflective conversational tool for self-organized learning. In T. Burg (Ed.), *BlogTalks* (pp. 190-216). Retrieved May 7, 2007, from http://seblogging.cognitivearchitects.com/stories/storyReader$963

Hammond, T., Hannay, T., & Lund, B. (2004, December). The role of RSS in science publishing: Syndication and annotation on the Web. *D-Lib Magazine*. Retrieved April 20, 2007, from http://www.dlib.org/dlib/december04/hammond/12hammond.html

Hurst, B. (2005). My journey with learning logs. *Journal of Adolescent & Adult Literacy, 49*(1), 42-46.

Jonassen, D. H., Mayes, T., & McAleese, R. (1993, May 14-18). A manifesto for a constructivist approach to uses of technology in higher education. In T. M. Duffy, J. Lowyck, D. H. Jonassen, & T. Welsh (Eds.), *Xpert.press: Vol. 105. Designing Environments for Constructive Learning: Proceedings of the NATO Advanced Research Workshop on the Design of Constructivist Learning Environments Implications for Instructional Design and the Use of Technology*, Leuven, Belgium (pp. 231-247). Berlin, Germany: Springer.

Kantel, J. (2003). *Vom Weblog lernen: Community, peer-to-peer und eigenständigkeit als ein modell für zukünftige wissenssammlungen*. Retrieved March 12, 2007, from http://static.userland.com/sh4/gems/schockwellenreiter/blogtalktext.pdf

Kerres, M. (2006). Web 2.0 and its implications to e-learning. In T. Hug, M. Lindner, & P. A. Bruck (Eds.), *Micromedia & E-Learning 2.0: Gaining the Big Picture: Proceedings of Micro-learning Conference 2006*, Innsbruck, Austria. University Press.

Kerres, M. (2007). Microlearning as a challenge for instructional design. In T. Hug & M. Lindner (Eds.), *Didactics of microlearning*. Münster, Germany: Waxmann. Retrieved March 10, 2007, from http://mediendidaktik.uni-duisburg-essen.de/files/Microlearning-kerres.pdf

Klamma, R., et al. (2006). Social software for professional learning: Examples and research. In B. Kinshuk, R. Koper, P. Kommers, P. Kirschner, D. Sampson, & W. Didderen (Eds.), *Advanced Learning Technologies: ICALT 2006*, Los Alamitos, CA (pp. 912-917). IEEE Computer Society.

Köllinger, P. (2002). *Report e-learning in deutschen unternehmen: Fallstudien, konzepte, implementierung* (1. Aufl.). Düsseldorf, Germany: Symposion.

Kreijns, K., Kirschner, P., & Jochems, W. (2003). Identifying the pitfalls for social interaction in computer-supported collaborative learning environments: A review of the research. *Computers in Human Behaviour, 19*, 335-353.

Kutscher, N., Klein, A., & Iske, S. (2005). Differences in Internet usage: Social inequality and informal education. *Social Work & Society, 3*, 215-233.

Lenhart, A., & Madden, M. (2005). Teen content creators and consumers. In *Pew Internet Project Data Memo*. Retrieved June 21, 2007, from http://www.pewinternet.org/pdfs/PIP_Teens_Content_Creation.pdf

Lewinson, J. (2005). Asynchronous discussion forums in the changing landscape of the online learning environment. *Campus-Wide Information Systems, 22*(3), 162-167.

McGill, L., Nicol, D., Littlejohn, A., Grierson, H., Juster, N., & Ion, W. J. (2005). Creating an information-rich learning environment to enhance design student learning: Challenges and approaches. *British Journal of Educational Technology, 36*(4), 629-642.

Nicol, D. J., & MacLeod, I. A. (2005). Using a shared workspace and wireless laptops to improve collaborative project learning in an engineering design class. *44*(4), 459-475.

Oblinger, D., & Oblinger, J. (2005). Is it age or IT: First steps towards understanding the Net generation. In D. Oblinger & J. Oblinger (Eds.), *Educating the Net generation*. Educause. Retrieved June 12, 2007, from http://www.educause. edu/educatingthenetgen/

O'Reilly, T. (2005). *Web 2.0: Compact definition?* Retrieved May 17, 2007, from http://radar.oreilly. com/archives/2005/10/web_20_compact_defini- tion.html

Otto, H.-U., Kutscher, N., Klein, A., & Iske, S. (2005). *Social inequality in the virtual space: How do young people use the Internet? Results from empirical research about online use differences and acquiring patterns of young people.* Retrieved January 16, 2008, from http://www.kib-bielefeld. de/externelinks2005/Social_Inequality%20KIB. pdf

Prensky, M. (2001a). *Digital natives, digital im- migrants: Part 1.* Retrieved April 13, 2007, from http://www.marcprensky.com/writing/Prensky -Digital Natives, Digital Immigrants-Part1.pdf

Prensky, M. (2001b). *Digital natives, digital im- migrants: Part 2.* Retrieved April 13, 2007, from http://www.marcprensky.com/writing/Prensky -Digital Natives, Digital Immigrants-Part2.pdf

Resnick, M. (2002). Rethinking learning in the digital age. In G. S. Kirkman, P. K. Cornelius, J. D. Sachs, & K. Schwab (Eds.), *Global information technology report 2001-2002: Readiness for the networked world* (pp. 32-37). New York: Oxford University Press.

Richter, A., & Koch, M. (2007). *Social software: Status quo und zukunft* (Tech. Rep. No. 2007- 01). Fakultät für Informatik, Universität der Bundeswehr München. Retrieved June 1, 2007, from http://www.unibw.de/wow5_3/forschung/ social_software/

Schulmeister, R. (2004). Diversität von stud- ierenden und die konsequenzen für elearning. In D. Carstensen & B. Barrios (Eds.), *Kommen die digitalen medien in die jahre? Medien in der wissenschaft* (Vol. 29, p. 133-144). Münster, Germany: Waxmann.

Schulmeister, R. (2005). *Lernplattformen für das virtuelle lernen: Evaluation und didaktik* (2. Aufl.). München, Germany: Oldenbourg.

Seufert, S. (2007). Ne(x)t generation learning: Was gibt es neues über das lernen? In S. Seufert & D. Euler (Eds.), *Ne(x)t generation learning: Wikis, blogs, mediacasts & Co. Social software und personal broadcasting auf der spur* (pp. 2- 19). SCIL Arbeitsbericht.

Seybert, H. (2007). *Gender differences in the use of computers and the Internet.* Retrieved Janu- ary 15, 2008, from http://epp.eurostat.ec.europa. eu/portal/page?_pageid=1073,46587259&_ dad=portal&_schema=PORTAL&p_product_ code=KS-SF-07-119

Sharma, P., & Fiedler, S. (2004, June 30-July 2). Introducing technologies and practices for supporting self-organized learning in a hybrid environment. In K. Tochterman & H. Maurer (Eds.), *Proceedings of I-Know '04*, Graz, Austria (pp. 543-550).

Sharma, P., & Maleyeff, J. (2003). Internet edu- cation: Potential problems and solutions. *17*(1), 19-25.

Shirky, C. (2003). *Social software and the politics of groups.* Retrieved May 3, 2007, from http://shirky.com/writings/group_politics.html

Tangney, B., FitzGibbon, A., Savage, T., Mehan, S., & Holmes, B. (2001). Communal constructivism: Students constructing learning for as well as with others. In C. Crawford, D. A. Willis, R. Carlsen, I. Gibson, K. McFerrin, J. Price, & R. Weber (Eds.), *Proceedings of Society for Information Technology and Teacher Education International Conference 2001* (pp. 3114-3119). Norfolk, VA: AACE.

Thijssen, T., & Vernooij, F. (2002). Breaking the boundaries between academic degrees and lifelong learning. In T. A. Johannessen (Ed.), *Educational innovation in economics and business: Vol. 6. Teaching today: The knowledge of tomorrow* (pp. 137-156). Dordrecht, The Netherlands: Kluwer Academic.

This work was previously published in the International Journal of Web-Based Learning and Teaching Technologies, edited by L. Esnault, Volume 3, Issue 3, pp. 16-33, copyright 2008 by IGI Publishing, formerly known as Idea Group Publishing (an imprint of IGI Global).

Chapter XVII
Enlivening the
Promise of Education:
Building Collaborative
Learning Communities
Through Online Discussion

Kuldip Kaur
Open University Malaysia, Malaysia

ABSTRACT

An important dimension in education is interaction, that is, the coming together of a number of people to discuss, debate, and deliberate about issues of common concern. In distance education, such social environments are as much present in online learning contexts as they are in face-to-face learning contexts such as tutorials. This chapter expands the notion of teacher-student interaction to focus on integrating human computer interaction in the curriculum. This is done through the use of online discussion forums at Open University Malaysia that help build collaborative online communities using common principles of teaching and learning. Citing a recent case in point, this chapter demonstrates how the Open University Malaysia-Collaborative Online Learning Model for online interaction helped cultivate learner-centric virtual discussions and supported an interactive online community that showcased characteristics of social interdependence and instructional support. This chapter takes a social constructivist view of human computer interaction by proposing an instructional model supported by collaboration, guidance, interdependence, cognitive challenge, knowledge construction, and knowledge extension. The Introduction section of this chapter provides the rationale for human computer interaction and gives an overview of current-day perspectives on the online classroom. This is followed by a trenchant review of recent research on online interaction with a view to outlining the theoretical premise for the use of computers to develop thinking and collaborative or team skills. This section also provides a rationale for the use of online forums and gives a frame of reference for the role of the instructor in this enterprise.

Copyright © 2007, Idea Group Inc., distributing in print or electronic forms without written permission of IGI is prohibited.

In the next section of this chapter, the Open University Malaysia-collaborative online learning model is described, with details on The Learning Context as well as Group Learning Outcomes, which may be seen as inherent parts of the model. Under the sub-section Knowledge Construction, the chapter carries a qualitative analysis of online interaction for one Open University Malaysia course using a comprehensive list of indigenous categories and sub-categories as well as examples of interactions that match each sub-category. The chapter ends with a Summary, a statement of Acknowledgement, a list of References, and an Appendix. The appendix contains the Task that was used for the course for which online interaction in this chapter was analyzed.

INTRODUCTION

In ancient Roman cities, a forum was an assembly place for judicial activity and public business. Such assembly often took place in a public square or marketplace. This is where orations were delivered, and public meetings and open discussions were held by various people. Similarly, in ancient Greece, a place of congregation—like a marketplace—was known as the agora. Such movements in history have given rise to the human need for discussion, debate and deliberation for the explication of ideas and facts before one can promote or dissuade an idea or event.

As extensions of the forum and the agora, today's online forums and online discussion groups have given rise to various discourse communities (Jonassen, 2002), collaborative learning groups (Dillenbourg and Schneider, 1995) and learning networks (Harasim, Hiltz, Teles, & Turoff, 1995). In these virtual classrooms (Hiltz, 1995), tutors, learners and experts come together to discuss content-related topics, debate on issues of common interest, share resources and deliberate on best solutions to various issues or problems. Such developments in educational practice have had an enormous impact on the way we teach, and on the way we interact with our students. We now view the online or virtual classroom as an extension of the traditional face-to-face classroom, and conversations begun in the latter are continued in the former, and so on. The role of the tutor or teacher has been redefined to include online facilitation, support frameworks and dialogue

(Collison, Elbaum, Haavind & Tinker, 2000). In tandem to this, the learner is expected to play a constructive role in the knowledge s/he builds and in the online learning process s/he is engaged in (Jonassen, Peck & Wilson, 1999). In sum, the historical premise for discussion, debate and deliberation for the explication of ideas and facts remains significant in the classrooms of today.

The brief discussion above demonstrates the way the online classroom has become a significant part of educational practice today, and how human computer interaction has transformed current conceptions of the role of the teacher and the learner. In order to provide a framework for understanding these developments, the next section of this chapter presents a review of research on online interaction and outlines recent developments in the theory of online pedagogy.

(Note: In this chapter the term tutor also refers to a teacher, instructor or facilitator.)

ONLINE INTERACTION

Recent research on constructive pedagogy has drawn attention to the use of online networks to improve thinking and to develop team skills. The thrust of the work in this area comes from the social constructivist view of learning (Bruner, 1986; Shaw, 1994), where learning is perceived as a "personal, reflective and transformative process" leading to the co-construction of knowledge through collaboration, inquiry, invention and knowledge-building activities (Sandholtz, Ringstaff & Dwyer, 1997: 12-13).

One application of this perspective is the use of computers to develop thinking learners (Jonassen, 2002). Referring to selected applications as mindtools, Jonassen encourages learning with computers so that the whole enterprise of learning "becomes greater than the potential of the learner and the computer alone" (Jonassen, 2002 p. 4). Another perspective is forwarded by Anderson's (2004) theory of e-learning which espouses Bransford, Brown, and Cocking's (1999) four credentials of effective learning environments: learner-centredness, knowledge-centredness, assessment-centredness and community centredness. These perspectives recognize the power of collaboration, which is a critical component of interactive online learning.

The work of socio-psychologists who have researched constructive pedagogy (Bruner, 1986) and peer-led instructional support (Keefer, Zeitz, & Resnick, (2000) has shown that collaboration is a powerful learning tool. Research indicates that collaborative activity such as online peer tutoring and team projects increases the knowledge learned and the satisfaction derived from the process (Clark, 2000). Collaborative tasks in online forums are also effective learning tools as they involve discussion and debate, processes which are crucial to understanding the many elements that influence a situation (Laurillard, 1993) Other studies have shown that online collaboration strategies increase students' communicative ability (Andres, 2002), their self-efficacy and academic performance (Sandholtz, Ringstaff & Dwyer, 1997) as well as their motivation to work (Turoff, 1999). Online forums also facilitate discussion, which is significant to learning as it paves the way for the use of domain-specific language and allows learners to generate their own explanations of what is understood or learnt (McKendree, 2002).

Although the use of online forums for discussion and team skills is a relatively recent phe-

nomenon, it has become a part of many teaching and learning programmes in post-secondary education (Spatariu, Hartley & Bendixen, 2004). Many educationists (Collison, Elbaum, Haavind & Tinker, 2000; Kearsley, 2000; Liao, 1996) have extolled the value of online forums in the teaching-learning process because they facilitate transparent discussion, offer direct accessibility to learning resources or materials and utilize learner-centric instructional values. To understand the widespread use of online forums in delivering the promise of education, one must recognise their enormous potential as drivers of learning and as channels of meaningful communication.

To begin, online forums provide the space for individual contribution toward a topic of discussion in a way that traditional classrooms do not. Tutors or facilitators use online facilities to provide fodder for discussion, and learners access these forums as an anytime-anywhere learning facility (Twigg, 2001). Learners can also access the forum as many times as they wish and independently contribute to the discussion. Tutors can examine each and every learner's contributions and provide feedback to groups or to individuals depending on the nature of the task. Learner-led discussions in online forums give learners the latitude to say what they think (and what they mean) without feeling the pressure of adult presence (Johnson, Aragon, Najmuddin & Palma-Rivas, 2000). The teacher as a custodian of correctness or truth (Balester, Halasek & Peterson, 1992) phenomenon diminishes as learners exchange information in learner-led online forums. More importantly, one person's online contributions are accessible to all participants in the learning event, in a way that individual written products in an exercise book are not.

This, above all, is the most liberating influence of the forum: the ability to communicate in an unrestricted time and space, under less restrictive conditions, and to deliver one's thoughts to one or many as a matter of choice. For tutors, this offers an opportunity to exercise group activity and interaction in a way that they can help realise the learning potential of each participating member of the classroom.

Despite the learner-directed nature of online interaction, it is important to realize that the role of the tutor is not attenuated as more and more computer-mediated instruction is used in a learning programme. Tutors play a very active role in designing tasks that are appropriate for collaborative and constructive activity and in participating in online discussion by moderating, modeling, questioning and providing learning support. This active role played by the facilitator, as it were, is summed up by Anderson (2004:271) when he describes what an online teacher has to do: design and organise the learning experience; devise and implement activities to encourage discourse between and among students, between the teacher and the student, and between individual students and groups of students and content resources; add subject matter expertise through a variety of forms of direct instruction; and fulfill a critical credentialing role that involves the assessment and certification of student learning. Thus, while online forums have changed the landscape of teaching and learning in terms of space and process, especially in higher education, it is also significant that the role of participating individuals has been redefined to include meaningful interaction and knowledge construction.

The review of literature above sheds light on the social constructivist view of learning and the theory of e-learning with specific reference to human computer interaction. Of significance is the influence of socio-cognitive processes such as collaboration, discussion and learner-centredness, all of which may be imbibed through carefully selected online tasks and tutor-facilitated online activity. The next section of this chapter presents details of a model for collaborative online learning which was implemented at Open University Malaysia. The implementation of this model helped to realise the ideals of social constructivism and helped build an interactive online learning community using online discussion and collaboration.

A MODEL FOR COLLABORATIVE ONLINE LEARNING

The theoretical premise for a constructivists' view on teaching and learning served as an impetus for the design of a model for online discussion at Open University Malaysia (OUM). This model, which is referred to as the OUM Collaborative Online Learning (COL) Model (Kuldip & Zoraini 2004), was developed to enrich the learning experience of Open University Malaysia's distance learners. Further, it was envisaged that computer-mediated communication would be the most effective way of providing instructional support for distance learners.

In the following sub-sections of this chapter, three aspects of the Open University Malaysia-collaborative online learning model are presented. These are: The Learning Context, which provides a description of how collaborative online learning was implemented; group learning outcomes, which outlines the learning design and the instructional outcomes of one course; and Knowledge Construction, which provides examples of online discussion utilizing principles of collaborative online learning pedagogy.

We begin with The Learning Context, a subsection that describes the learning environment at Open University Malaysia, and provides details of the five components which serve as interactive dimensions of the model itself.

The Learning Context

Learners at Open University Malaysia are required to participate in online activity as part of the total learning solution for a programme of study. For each course they are registered in, learners attend ten hours of face-to-face tutorials, engage in autonomous learning activity using a printed module and participate in online discussions. The online discussion forum is housed within Open University Malaysia's learning management system known as myLMS, which also serves as a repository for teaching-learning resources or sample tests and as a communication channel for all administrative matters. Throughout the year, Open University Malaysia tutors from various learning centres are trained in the finer points of online collaboration and online tutoring. Training of learners incorporates guidelines on the use of the forum to communicate with peers and tutors about academic matters, collaborative strategies, as well as access to online learning resources and notices on administrative matters.

Under the collaborative online learning model, online discussions may be led by a tutor or a learner, but the focus is on an assignment which carries 25% of the marks for the final grade. The assigned task is expected to be completed in six to eight weeks, and often requires extensive reading, deliberation, as well as some amount of research and application. Students are assigned to tutorial groups led by a tutor, and the same group functions as a virtual class in myLMS. Asynchronous discussions on the task begin at the beginning of each semester and learners access myLMS from their home, workplace or an Open University Malaysia learning centre. Either the tutor or a learner may begin a threaded discussion, but both parties are expected to play and active role in the online discussion forum. Using the assignment as a point of departure, tutors and learners focus on explication and inquiry leading to deliberation on best solutions, possible outcomes and findings of individual research. In this way, collaborative online learning helps to build an interactive online learning community aimed at providing instructional support to distance learners.

The fulcrum of the collaborative online learning model is collaboration, which may be defined as a communal process encouraging learners and tutors to work together as part of a larger system rather than as individuals (Kuldip & Zoraini,

2004). This interactive and recursive process draws on characteristics of four other components of the model, namely the task, instructional or learning support, discussion and knowledge construction. The following description of the five components of the collaborative online learning model illustrates its role in shaping the learning experience at Open University Malaysia.

1. **Online collaboration:** Learners and tutors using myLMS to work together toward common goals, which in this case is to co-construct understanding of the requirements of a task, deliberating on ways to perform the task, sharing findings based on task performance and evaluating outcomes of a task;

2. **The task:** An assignment such as a problem, a case study, a debate or a project, designed for learners to apply course content in a real-world situation, or to engage in critical examination of theory and findings of past research;

3. **Learning support:** Provision of online instructional support for the task from the tutor and subject matter expert, and encouraging participation from all learners and guidance on the use of online/printed learning resources;

4. **Discussion:** Active tutor and learner participation through asynchronous threaded discussions, a way for peers to help each other, and for the tutor to facilitate the collective solving of problems or work related to the assigned task; and

5. **Knowledge construction:** The intended outcome of a task which is characteristically (a) something the learner is unable to do independently and (b) represents new knowledge or new learning.

The above components are viewed as interactive dimensions in the Open University Malaysia collaborative online teaching and learning process. Thus a discussion group in Open University Malaysia's myLMS functions as a virtual classroom (Hiltz, 1995) where collaborative activity among tutors, learners and experts is encouraged, as well as deemed necessary. Using guidelines provided by Collison, Elbaum, Haavind & Tinker, (2000), collaborative online learning is designed for tutors to play a significant role in the facilitation of learner deliberations, provision of instructional support frameworks and modeling ways to engage in meaningful communication. In turn, the learner plays a direct role in the construction of knowledge and in gaining new learning experiences (Jonassen, Peck, & Wilson, 1999).

The sub-section above has described in detail the instructional environment that is part and parcel of the Open University Malaysia learning experience. It has also outlined the salient aspects of the implementation of the Open University Malaysia-Collaborative Online Learning Model. In the next sub-section, group learning outcomes for one course for which the model was implemented are described. Of particular importance are the four categories and 16 sub-categories of online interaction that were derived through a qualitative analysis of the data from the discussion forum, myLMS.

Group Learning Outcomes

After an initial round of pilot testing and evaluation (Kuldip & Zoraini, 2004), the collaborative online learning model was implemented for two teaching English as a second language (TESL) courses for in-service teacher trainees at the Open University Malaysia in the year 2005. This chapter uses data from one of the two courses, Introduction to Novels and Short Stories, which was conducted over a 15 week semester. There were 462 students registered in the course in multiple teaching sites. Each of the 21 student groups were led by a tutor and instruction was based on a prescribed module. Five tutorial sessions, totaling ten hours of face-to-face interaction, and self-regulated study were required for the course. In addition to the interaction during face-to-face tutorials, online discussions—another course requirement—related to the contents of the module and a take-home assignment contributed to the bulk of discussion that was held on the contents of the course. The assignment (Appendix A) required students to read and write reviews of texts assigned in the course and to hand in a bound portfolio based on their reading and reviews.

Table 1. Analysis of selected group contributions in myLMS

Contributions	Number and Percentage of Contributions by Tutorial Group			
Total number of contributions analyzed: 288 (100%)	Group 1 total: 85 (29.5%)	Group 2 total: 82 (28.5%)	Group 3 total: 70 (24.3%)	Group 4 total: 51 (17.7%)
Number of tutor contributions analyzed: 117 (41%)	By tutor 1 30 (10.4%)	By tutor 2 37 (12.9%)	By tutor 3 26 (9%)	By tutor 4 24 (8.3%)
Number of student contributions analyzed: 171 (59%)	By 25 group 1 students 55 (19.1%)	By 16 group 2 students 45 (15.6%)	By 15 group 3 students 44 (15.3%)	By 10 group 4 students 27 (9.4%)

Table 2. Categories and sub-categories of online interaction

Category I: GUIDANCE	
Sub-categories	Description
i. Guidance on how to begin an assignment ii. Guidance on how to ask questions	Tutors work with learners to *show how* something is done
iii. Guidance on use of reference materials	Tutors help learners use printed and **online** resources
iv. Guidance on concepts related to course content	Tutors provide support through questions, leads, and simplification of difficult subject matter
v. Guidance on instructions by focusing learner attention	Tutors direct learners' attention to a particular point/topic or area of **discussion**

Category II: INTERDEPENDENCE	
Sub-categories	Description
vi. Peer coaching	Learners collectively answer questions, solve problems, or discuss solutions with assistance from the tutor
vii. Peer tutoring	Learners help each other by answering questions and providing direction without the assistance of a tutor
viii. Sharing	Learners share ideas and a variety of learning materials by telling each other what they know
ix. Utilizing learner expertise	Learners recognize and use each other as a knowledge source
x. Vicarious learning	Learners learn by reading, watching, or 'lurking' without directly contributing to a **discussion**

Category III: CHALLENGE	
Sub-categories	Description
xi. Designing tasks that require multiple skills	Tutors design tasks based on a broad idea of learning outcomes
xii. Pushing the boundaries	Tutors encourage learners to go beyond what they have done or what they think is sufficient for the task
xiii. Inspiriting learner ability	Tutors think of ways to inspirit learners' attempts at performing a task when the task proves too difficult
xiv. Redirecting to encourage greater autonomy	Tutors redirect learner attention to other resources in order to encourage autonomous learning

Table 2. Categories and sub-categories of online interaction (continued)

Category IV: EXTENSION	
Sub-categories	Description
xv. Recasting content learned in course	Learners recast, rephrase, or reformulate recently acquired content Learners seek feedback on content and ideas presented in their own words
xvi. Application of concepts learned in course	Learners use meta-cognitive strategies to analyze and apply theoretical views learned in course Learners view concepts from the social perspective or they relate real life experiences to course content

Figure 1. Interaction within the collaborative online learning model

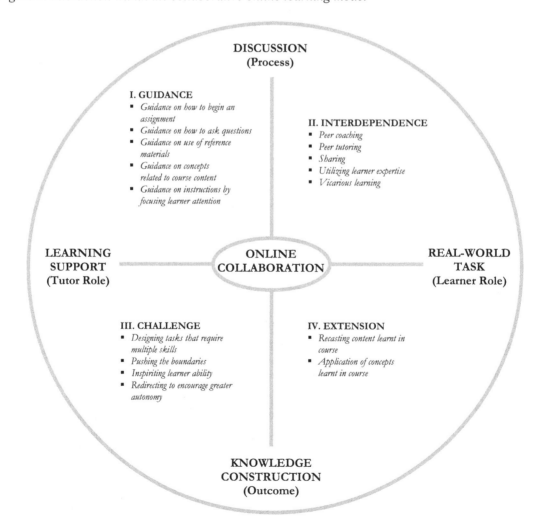

Although threaded discussions in myLMS were held by all 21 groups, this paper utilises data drawn from by the four most active groups. In addition, only contributions related to the assignment part of the course are used in the analysis. Thus, 4 tutors' (19 % of all tutors) and (their) 66 learners' (14 % of all students) contributions in the online forum related to the assignment were analysed. As shown in Table 1, a total of 288 contributions were analysed, of which 117 were from the 4 tutors while 171 were from the 66 students. The tutor-student ratio of contributions was 1:1.46; the average number of postings per tutor was 29.3 while the average number of postings per student was 2.9.

The 288 contributions from the four groups were analysed qualitatively to examine the nature of discussion during collaborative online learning. It was found that discussion threads could be classified under four categories of interaction: guidance, interdependence, challenge and extension. These four data-driven categories are not mutually exclusive, i.e., a single thread may present evidence for one or more categories of interaction. The analysis also revealed that the four main categories could be further divided into 16 subcategories as learners and tutors engaged in a lively discussion on the assignment. The description of categories and subcategories that emerged from the data is presented in Table 2.

The four categories and 16 subcategories categories are linked to all five components of the collaborative online learning model in terms of the specific thinking and learning processes that are brought to bear upon the discussion (Figure 1). In terms of collaboration, guidance was provided by both tutors and learners, and learners were interdependent in terms of their need for input on content, procedure and application of theory. Additionally, the assigned task appeared to have posed a challenge to learners, and learner activity provided evidence of skills extension. In terms of the four quadroons of the collaborative online learning model in Figure 1, guidance and chal-

lenge may be viewed in terms of an active tutor role while interdependence and extension may be viewed as an active learner role.

To summarise, the sub-section above has given the labels and operational definitions of the various categories and sub-categories of online interaction that are directly related to the Open University Malaysia-collaborative online learning model. These categories were derived from the analysis of online discussion during one course at Open University Malaysia. In the following sub-section, Knowledge Construction, vignettes taken from myLMS demonstrate the power of tutors' and learners' discussions in constructing meaning through co-construction and social interdependence.

Knowledge Construction

In order to demonstrate the viability of online interaction in creating a meaningful learning environment for distance learners, this sub-section is focused on discussion during the course Introduction to Novels and Short Stories. In the following pages, the analysis of online interaction is organised by category, vis. guidance, interdependence, challenge and extension (Table 1). Each category is then further explicated using descriptions and vignettes that fall under each sub-category. A 'cue' refers to the comment or contribution that triggers a threaded discussion, while cuer refers to the person who has triggered the thread. Unless otherwise indicated, all cues cited below were provided by learners.

(Note: The names of all contributors have been changed to protect their identity. Excerpts have not been edited for grammatical accuracy and italics in the data are the chapter author's.)

I. Guidance

The collaborative online learning-based interaction showed that tutors play an active role in the discussion by providing instructional support or guidance to learners. This means that they show how a task can be done, help identify and glean information from printed and online resources, use questions and leads to direct understanding, simplify difficult subject matter, and model ways for learners to work together. In many classrooms or other educational contexts, this role of the teacher is oft-times not evident; teachers may get lost in a myriad of paperwork and evaluation-based activity, forgetting that they ought to play a role in showing how to do something—e.g., how to do a sum, write a paragraph or draw a diagram.

Below is a description of the tutors' role in providing guidance is illustrated with examples related to each of the five subcategories of guidance provided to include: how to begin an assignment, how ask questions, the use of reference materials, concepts related to course content, instructions by focusing learner attention.

i. Guidance on how to begin an assignment. In the following vignette, Aris seeks guidance on how she should begin the assignment on the novel The Pearl by John Steinbeck. Her tutor, John, tells her to begin by answering the given questions in sequence, and gives her pointers on what she should not include in her paper.

Cue 1.
Dear Sir, How do we begin the assignment? Should I start a little bit about the review of the Pearl or we just start by answering task 1. That is by just listing down the title, author...? Aris

Response from tutor.
Aris, just start by answering the questions in sequence. The second and third questions form the introduction to your who assignment. You are not required to write things not related to the assignment questions. Rgds., John

Feedback.
Dear Sir, Thank U for shedding some light to me. Aris

ii. Guidance on how to ask questions. In contrast to Aris, another student called Ravin asks a question that is rather vague (Cue 2). As shown in the extract below, the tutor responds by requesting for more specific information. This is an important move to encourage learners to learn how to communicate effectively, and to make students aware of the need to define a problem that they want resolved. Further, as Open University Malaysia assignments may be lengthy or contain several parts, online tutoring is effective if learners are more focused and concise when they raise questions.

Cue 2.
Dear Sir, Please explain about our assignment. Thank you.

Response from tutor.
Dear Ravin, Thank you for your attempt but you can't ask general questions like this. What or which part of the assignment don't you understand? Be specific please so that I can be of help to you. John

iii. Guidance on use of reference materials. In the example below, the tutor, Tuan Hj. Idris, provides a reference and dictionary-based explanation for terminology used in the course. The tutor goes a step further by drawing attention to how the student can deduce the meaning of a concept. Initiatives such as these often benefit more than one student at a time, and have the effect of modeling study skills or information retrieval skills.

Cue 3.
Tuan Hj Idris. What is meant by using stylistic approach in teaching literature in the classroom?

Response from tutor.
Pari, My previous answer was a little hasty. Sorry.

Martin Grey's A Dictionary of Literary Terms, explain the term under style. Style = the characteristic manner in which a writer expresses himself... may be a combination of many different factors... describe by analysis of syntax, tone, imagery, point of view and linguistic features. As such we can always deduce that SA is like DA also Neo-RA i.e., looking at a literary work through the use of words.
Is that OK? Bye.

iv. Guidance on concepts related to course content. In response to questions posed by one student (Cue 4 & 5), a tutor explains concepts that are related to the course. Often such explanations are given when a concept is complex, or if it is new or difficult. If the term is found and well explained in the printed module, or if it is available in an online source, tutors may direct a learner to that specific source.

Cue 4.
Dear Sir, Please explain what the term 'generic conventions' is? Thank you.

Response from tutor.
Hi Nadine, Sorry for the late reply. Well, generic means the class origin - i.e belonging to a class and conventions means the basic characteristics. Therefore generic conventions would be the basic features of a certain type of writing or style or language used etc. For example what are the generic conventions of Shakespearean sonnet. So

here you have to talk about the sonnet and what are the special conventions of the sonnets written by Shakespeare. Boleh faham kan? John.

Cue 5.
Dear Sir, What does the term 'contemporaneous appeal' mean when explaining short stories? Thank you.

Response from tutor.
Hi Nadine, Contemporaneous appeal refers to the current or present day readers/critics' appeal. As opposed to traditional or orthodox preferences. Rgds, John.

v. Guidance on instructions by focusing learner attention. Very often, students ask questions about a task because they have problems interpreting directions or instructions for the task. In the example below, the tutor focuses Salmah's attention on the language used in the directions for the task so that she better understands what she is required to do.

Cue 6.
For question no. 8, do I have to write an analysis of 3 reviews/ essays altogether OR do I have to write it separately thank you

Response from tutor.
Dear Salmah, The question specifically stated, Write a 300 word analysis on THESE reviews... so obviously you have to write on them as one. OK? Bye.

II. Interdependence

The analysis of the threaded discussions also showed that learners work interdependently on the task at hand. They do this by collectively solving problems, discussing solutions, sharing learning materials, answering questions and providing direction as well as by recognising and using each other as a knowledge source. In the case of this course, Introduction to Novels and Short Stories, learners appeared to have had difficulty with the critical review of assigned texts and in accessing material from the internet. Here is how learners demonstrated interdependence during their discussions.

vi. Peer coaching. In the following example, Cue 7 is a call for help on writing a critical review. The tutor responds by referring to an announcement he has posted. However, the students go further to take on the role of a coach or guide by making suggestions, as well as seeking and providing clarification on the task. In the threaded discussion below, four students (including the cuer) are involved in one such coaching event.

Cue 7.
Hai everybody!
I'm having problem to write my critical review of The Pearl. Does anyone has any tips on how to write a good critical review? TQ

Response from tutor.
Chong, Last night I posted an announcement concerning this kind of problem. Refer to the announcement, visit the web and then...? OK? Bye.

Response from peer 1 to cuer.
Saudari Chong, Voice your opinions at the end of every paragraph (6 paragraphs- 6 chapters)!
Suggestions:
Chapter 1- author constructs Kino as an eg. with concerns typical of persons of all social circles, couple symbolic of the Mexican-Indian community
Chapter 2- canoe as provider of income, describe to audience whether in reality will a diver find a big pearl coincidentally

Chapter 3-tempt the readers whether they want to be rich and famous, just like striking a gold mine in real life!
Chapter 4 -6: Request responses from readers by asking realistic Qs!

Response from peer 2 to peer 1.
I thought critical review is writing about the background of the author and the books he had produced. Someone please correct me if I'm wrong.

Response from peer 3 to peer 2.
Lai Fong, a critical review is to write the main events of a text. the ups and downs of life the main character faces. we may include the moral value behind the story; whether the book is worth reading or not; the background info. of the author can be included. hope it helps. all the best. Kim Wee

vii. Peer tutoring. In some instances, the tutor does not get involved in the discussion and learners assume the role of tutor. The analysis of the data showed that peer tutoring is evident in collaborative online learning as a number of learners' views are colligated to refine understanding of a concept. However, it must be noted that peer tutoring does not always cover the full range of questions posed by a cuer as learners focus on what they know and on issues where they have some experience. In the following vignette, Chew, (cuer) gets a satisfactory response to only one of the two questions that he poses. The first question raised by Chew is addressed by a peer (peer 2) but this does not provide a solution to Chew's problem.

Cue 8.
Dear Tn. Haji Idris, 1. Q7 is a headache It requires us to find 3 book reviews on the selected text. I have searched the net but in vain. Must the book reviews be written by well-known critics or just anybody? 2. For our assignment, are we suppose

to present the portfolio in an essay form or in point form according to the steps given as below? Eg. Title of book: The Pearl, Author: John Steinbeck, Year of Publication. 2. Plot Summary: The Pearl is a story......

Response from peer 1.
Answers Question 2: I think we can write both ways.

Response from peer 2.
Addresses Question 2 but does not give a satisfactory answer:
Saudari Chong,
Book reviews concern with research done on the book regarding the plot of the novel like what the researchers think and voice their opinions! Different researchers from different universities explain the contexts from various views!
Haji Idris, pls correct me if I m wrong!

Response from cuer.
Thanks Selvam and Tek Boon. I still cannot find the book reviews.

viii. Sharing. In some instances, two or more learners facing the same problem with the task share their problem in the online forum. This is when multiple level communication and collaboration was evident showing a strong sense of group interdependence. As shown in the threaded discussion below, learners (Cuers 9 & 10) share information on how or where the cuers could get the information they need. For example, cuers trigger a discussion and other classmates exchange information on the topic, aiming to provide as much assistance as possible. Like tutors who use phrases such as have you tried..., learners help the cuers by giving directions e.g. with statements like Try typing in different keywords... However, it must be noted that as in this case, sharing

does not always help every learner access the information needed, even though the discussion on this topic spanned four days.

Cue 9.
11 Oct 2004 02:52:36 AM
Dear Sir and friends,
I"m doing the assignment on short story, "The Pencil". I've tried looking for the book reviews as required but it seems that I"m not successful yet. Can someone help please?

Cue 10.
12 Oct 2004 10:01:33 PM
Hello Sir,
I'm doing the "The necklace" for my assignment but I'm facing problem searching for the reviews. Please give some tips on how to get the reviews. I 've tried using goggles and yahoo.
Eng L.P.

Response from cuer 10 to cuer 9.
12 Oct 2004 10:04:04 PM
Dear Philo, It seems that both of us are in the same boat as I can't find any reviews for the short story I'm doing. Hopefully, both of us will be able to find the reviews soon.

Response from tutor to cuer 9.
14 Oct 2004 03:13:00 PM
Hi there,
Have you tried another search engine, maybe Google? Type different keywords too - eg, Book review + The Pencil, etc. Give it a try.

Response from tutor to cuer 10.
14 Oct 2004 03:15:14 PM
Hi Lai Peng,
Have you tried the search engine recommended by Janice during T3? Try typing in different keywords - Book review of The Pencil, or the author's name, or Book review +Malaysian literature in English, etc.

Response from peer 1 to cuer 10.
15 Oct 2004 05:44:29 AM
Eng,
Just type 'Book Review: The Necklace'. I'm sure you'll see reviews there.

Response from peer 2 to peer 1.
15 Oct 2004 06:07:03 PM
For my case, I've typed book review: The secret life of Walter Mitty". The feedback is very disappointing. I just manage to access a few reviews on that particular story.

The three postings below (Cues 11-13) illustrate how learners shared resources among their peers and with their tutor—purely as a matter of personal initiative.

Cue 11.
Hi tutor and course-mates, I managed to get hold of the texts; Welcome and Return to Malaya. I don't mind making copies for all those interested but I have no idea how many copies to make. Enlighten me please. BTW I am still waiting for Hemmingway's text.

Response from tutor.
Hi Lily! You bring wonderful news. Hurray for you! Kindly make one set for me. I'll pay you later, thank you very much

Cue 12.
Dear all, I found this interesting story on this website: do read and let's enjoy the stories. http://reading.englishclub.com/short-stories.htm

Cue 13.
Dear sir,
http://incontinet.com/two_drugs_fail.htm
The above website is one the sites that offers critical review. What do you think of it. Is it ok enough for our assignment. TQ.

ix. Utilising learner expertise. An important dimension of learner involvement in a discussion is the recognition of the learner as a knowing, able and knowledgeable individual who is capable of providing informed responses to a peer's questions. In the following exchange, the tutor raises this point by validating the ideas that have been put forward by two classmates and by acknowledging that their explanations were indeed 'good.' Learner involvement of this nature is necessary for learners to get feedback on the input they provide and to motivate them to take part in more discussions of this nature.

Cue 14.
Hello Mr Anthony and course-mates,
I'm quite confused and blurry on writing critical review of the text. Could anyone of you please elaborate more on the requirements of the question (3). What is the specific guideline/s needed to answer this question.
Thanks for your worth reply.

Response from peer 1.
Hello, Just to share what I understand about it. It is your respond toward the story. You can also tell what is it that you like in the story, the moral values and setting. You can also tell the part of the story that attract you the most and give reasons.

Response from peer 2
Can I add in some viewpoints here. You can also touch on why you like/dislike the characters in the story. Apart from that, you can also briefly elucidate on the author's writing whether his/her writing of the particular book awesome, breathtaking or even overwhelm. List out the interesting part/s you like most or may bring hatred to you.

Response from tutor.
Hi Marisa, Philomena & Jonathan have given a good explanation about this. Have their expla-

nation helped you a little? It's giving your own personal response to the text and not writing a summary of the story.

x.   Vicarious learning. Learning in many contexts can occur when learners are not involved in the exchange, or are not providing input on a topic of discussion. This is something that may be present but is often not obvious in a traditional classroom. The threaded discussion below is an example of vicarious learning is evident as two class-mates – Bob and Vimala – have benefited from a response from Mahera. As another facet of peer interdependence in myLMS, these learners learn from each other and express their satisfaction about the sharing of individual expertise.

Cue 15.
Hi there tutor and course-mates, I've chosen a short story "The secret life of Walter Mitty" for my assignment. Is it okay if I write these points for my blurb of the story. a. It portrays the stupidity and mild- mannered of a husband by the name of Walter Mitty who merely dares to show his valiant only in his fantasy world. Read more to attain joyfulness and suspense of the story. b. The story is full of humorous and fantasy. c. The story is very entertaining and catchy. Readers are motivated and seemingly enjoy their reading entirely. [Bob]

Response from Peer 1.
Hello dear Bob, First of all, I would like to elucidate on blurbs which means a praising word/s to foster a novel or short story. Therefore, the word stupidity is not really recommended for writing blurb. Anyway, I do agree with your third viewpoint about the blurbs of the story. Nice of you selecting a Walter Mitty secret life for your assignment. Hope to meet your requirements. [Mahera]

Response from peer 2 to peer 1.
Hello Mahera, I was not sure on how to write the blurb a moment ago. At least your comment for Bob had given me some ideas. Thanks. [Vimala]

Response from cuer to peer 2.
Me too Vimala. Now, I've a picture on how to write the blurbs of the story. Hopefully our tutor will go along my path. [Bob]

III. Challenge

At the Open University Malaysia, tutors are encouraged to design goals that challenge learners so that new knowledge is constructed, and learning is extended beyond current ability. The assignment for the course Introduction to Novels and Short Stories appeared to have been a challenging one as evidence by learners' deliberations on the many things that they were required to do for the submission of the portfolio. The subcategories below demonstrate the many areas in which learners were challenged, and how tutors helped by scaffolding the many demands of the task.

xi. Designing tasks that require multiple skills. In the following example, the tutor draws attention to the many skills that will be required to perform the assignment to satisfaction. The posting (Cue 16) was forwarded at the beginning of the semester, and appears to serve as an advance organizer for the tutorial group. It appears too that the tutor is making learners aware of the many cognitive skills that learners will have to exercise in undertaking the task.

Cue 16 from tutor.
After doing an internet search on a keyword form the selected text, choose 2 items about the keyword which you think are useful. Explain why it would be useful to the reader if he/she knows this information when reading the text or how it

would help the reader understand the text better. For instance during T3, Nyet Fah gave us an example. She liked the word 'pearl' in The Pearl. So she did an internet search and came up with many things related to the word pearl. But she decided to choose only 2 items, that is, how pearls are formed and how people dive for pearls. Now ask yourself, if you were reading The Pearl, how would information on these 2 items help you understand the text better? You would be able to imagine the difficulty Kino goes through every time he dives into the sea to look for pearls. You would also know how he holds his breath, how he cuts the pearl from its shell, how long a diver can hold his breath, etc. Does this help you a little?

xii.   Pushing the boundaries. Apart from assigning tasks that challenge learners, tutors also encouraged learners to work harder on their assignment. In the following example, Cuer 15 is told that he has done a good job with part of the task, but he has to do more. It must be noted that the tutor scaffolds the sub-tasks with the use of questions, which will indeed guide Nicholas in the presentation of the paper for the assignment.

Response from tutor to Cuer 15.
Dear Robert, These are nice blurbs you have written. But you can further improve on them. Be more specific. (b) It is humorous and full of fantasy. So what? Why should people read the story? (c) What is catcy? Do you mean catchy? How can readers be motivated and enjoy the reading? This is not clear. Try and improve them, Bob.

xiii.   Inspiriting learner ability. For difficult tasks, learners sometimes need a great deal of encouragement and direction. In the example below, Rahim has a problem with part of his assignment and asks for help. His tutor responds by providing a set of guidelines Rahim can follow, and use to

structure his answer. More importantly, the tutor uses a series of questions to inspirit Rahim's efforts by outlining the kind of information the examiner would like to see in the answer. Notably, Rahim also gets a response from his classmate something he gratefully acknowledges.

Cue 17.
Dear sir & fellow course-mate, Could explain a little bit more on question No.3 & 6. I'm still blurry about these two questions. TQ

Response from tutor.
Dear Rahim, Hi there. May I know what text you have chosen? Q3 requires you to write a critical review about the text which you have read. Writing a review is not writing a report about the story you have read. Notice the word 'critical' here. You should mention things like - what did you like/ dislike in the story? Do you think the story managed to convey its values/ message clearly to the reader? Which character did you like/ dislike? Were the characters effective in the story? What were the strengths/ weaknesses of the story? etc. Q4 requires you to write three 'blurbs' of the story which you have read. (to help promote, encourage other people to read the story) Please refer to the module/ dictionary for the meaning of the word 'blurb'. We have discussed this before. Hope this has helped you a little.

Response from peer 1.
Hi Rahim, Critical review is about in simplest form what you have read, you try to summarise it according to your understanding (the context should be directly from the book) You suppose to sum up according to your own words. Just as Mr. Wong wrote, what you like/or dislike. The 200-250 will inspire you to write a well-compacted review (of course reading and understanding the book helps a lot, no short cut) After your critical review, you need to analyse which caption that

fascinates you and see whether that caption were in the form of authorial or neo-rhetorical criticism and elaborate further. From, Sophia

Response from cuer.
Thanks for the replies. It helps a lot. TQ, again.

xiv. Redirecting to encourage greater autonomy. In the online forum, it was found that several postings were either repetitions or not very well thought out. Generally, questions in these postings had already been dealt with on another occasion by the same tutor. Thus, tutors sometimes redirected learners to sources where they could find the information, or to an earlier response by the tutor or student. This appeared to be a way to challenge learners to seek answers on their own, or to use more self-reliant measures in seeking answers to their questions, as demonstrated in the following examples.

Cue 18.
Dear Mr. Roshan. can you please explain what are the elements that i should put in this critical review? besides the author do i have to write about all the literary devices such as the theme, setting and mood of the text?

Response from tutor.
You may criticise on the use of literary devices, you may see some critical reviews on http://www.pinkmonkey.com/booknotes/ba4rrons/peqrl5.asp Regards, Roshan

Cue 19.
Sir, Can you please explain in detail how to to the assignment in our next tutorial? TQ

Response from tutor.
Got some techniques on writing a review from the forum. You may want to read them. It comes as an attachment. [Attachment]

Response from cuer.
Dear Sir, Thank you for the notes given on writing a review I am sure it will help me and others to write our assignment very well. Thank you Sir. That's all for now .Good bye.

Cue 20.
Sir, Can you please explain what is authorial criticism and neo-rhetorical criticism? Dear Sir,

Response from tutor.
Please refer to Janita's and Gerry's question on this forum Regards, Roshan

IV. Extension

An important—albeit highly desirable—outcome of active learning is the extension of learners' skills or current thinking-learning ability. The analysis of the data showed that learners own attempts at extending their knowledge led to various ways of using course content. In this category, extension, the learner is in focus again as s/he works actively toward the recognition that s/he has to show his understanding of course content. The following examples illustrate learners' efforts at extending their cognitive reach through recasts and application, and their tutors' requests for extension of learner effort.

xv. Recasting content learnt in course. As learners came across new ideas, concepts and issues in their reading, they engaged in sense-making by way of rewording or restating what they read in their own words. Often these recasts, as it were, were accompanied by requests for feedback on their understanding of course content. In the following vignettes, Cuers 21 and 22 recast ideas to show what they have understood from their reading, and request for feedback from the tutor.

Cue 21.

Hi friends and tutor, Generally, the process of literary reading involves: a. pre-reading, b. while-reading, c. post-reading. Based on the process above, I would like to emphasize on pre-reading stage which involves identifying assumptions, interest and pre-conceptions. For this reason, I've chosen a questioning method activity that a teacher can carry out for literary learning.

Response from peer 1.

Jo, I agree with you about the process of literary reading. I also have the same idea like you. Me too state the pre-reading, while-reading and the post-reading as the process of reading literary text. Are we two right?

Response from tutor.

Hi Jo, Your answers are acceptable, but elaborate more in your paper. Be more descriptive. OK?

Cue 22.

Dear tutor and course-mates, A review of a novel is also a response since it normally includes an evaluation of the work. It requires analytic skill but it is not identical with an analysis. Some retelling of the plot is necessary, however, the review is primarily concerned with describing, analysing, and evaluating. Do you agree?

xvi. Application of concepts learnt in course. Another subcategory of extension is the application of theoretical concepts or approaches to what learners are reading or to matters related to their life. In the first case cited below, Putri seeks guidance on understanding the discursive approach to analysis literary discourse (Cue 23). Putri gets a response from the tutor, but another student, Rajesh, is unable to apply the discursive approach to the text he is reading, i.e. The Pearl by John Steinbeck. Rajesh's request on the same topic (Cue 24) is responded to by a peer, Yeo, who is from another OUM

learning centre altogether. Finally Putri (and hopefully Rajesh too) is able to apply the discursive approach to The Pearl.

Cue 23.
01 Oct 2004 06:04:38 PM
Dear Tuan Haji Idris, according to question 5, we are suppose to give a brief definition of both criticisms. But it's not easy to understand about the discursive approach. Can you please explain it? [Putri]

Response from tutor to cuer 23.
01 Oct 2004 08:14:10 PM
Assalamualaikum Putri, Page 34 of the module, try to say something about discursive approach [da],but does not really make you understand it. Well I don't blame you. When you talk about da, you are actually looking at analysis of discourse in literature i.e. you want to see how sense, meaning, idea, fact, truth is built by language, produced by institutions, discipline—science, history etc. Every discourse is situated in an ideology/context; such as political, gender, class etc. When you talk about literary discourse, remember about imagination/ imaginative, rhetorical. Historical discourse has to be based on fact/factual. I hope this is easier to understand. Good luck. Wassalam.

Response from cuer 23 to tutor.
01 Oct 2004 08:31:04 PM
Thank you very much Tuan Hj. Idris, At least I have an idea what the da is.

Cue 24.
01 Oct 2004 09:04:33 PM
Dear Tuan Haji Idris, Can you give an example on how to view "The Pearl" according to discursive analyses. I think this examples will make me understand and apply the method [Rajesh]

Response from peer 1 to cuer 24.
04 Oct 2004 12:47:51 AM
Rajesh, Yeo again fr Seberang Jaya Centre! Dis-

cursive approach is classified under Neo-Rhetorical Approach according to the module which the second app. The first app. is the study of genres which consists of Poetry, Drama, Short stories & Novels as we have learned during Jan. semester (Intro. to Literature). For the module, it seems to me that discursive app. is regarding the possibility of the readers' perception. Thought & action that depends on the minds' structure of a certain meaningful field. It reflects as sense as opposed to incoherent nonsense of the literary texts!

Response from cuer 23 to peer 1 and to cuer 18. 04 Oct 2004 05:38:22 PM
Or can I say it in a simple way, discursive approach is the beauty of the language used in order to convey the message. For example, when the writer wrote 'Kino awakened in the dark night' -the first line of the first page tells you something sad or a tragic scene may happen through out the story as he was awaken in the dark -forwarding. While the last line in the last page mentioned 'And the music of the pearl drifted to a whisper and disappeared' is actually telling us the power of the pearl of the desire towards the pearl is no longer in Kino as it was thrown back to the sea. The author conveys message through his creativity in playing with words and gives deep meaning to the reader. Am I right Tuan Hj Idris? [Putri]

Application of course content was also seen in relevance to matters beyond the classroom. In the following excerpts, we see how two students see the relevance of ideas picked up in the course in terms of personal experience (Cue 25) and in terms of metaphor (Cue 26) related to a short story with a Kelantanese setting (in the north-eastern part of West Malaysia).

Cue 25.
Dear Sir, as I discussed with you earlier I pick up the theme (no 10) caste in my assignment. As i go on doing, it is becoming a very sensitive matter to talk about. What you think? Can I continue with
the same theme? I have almost towards the end of the product.

Response from tutor.
You don't have to worry. When we are discussing caste, we are looking at an academic point of view. Go ahead with the assignment. Regards

Cue 26.
Dear Sir, Here's what I understand of the title of the story of "Pak De Samad's Cinema". The word 'cinema' tells me of many things such as his life and struggles, entertainment, fantasy or maybe a place. Am I right? Thank you.

Response from tutor.
Wow! That's the way to go. You have the basic idea. Expand on that idea in your exam ok. John

The above sub-section on tutor-learner discussion has shown the many ways in which learners have benefited from participation in the online discussion forum. True to the historical premise of the forum, students in thus course (that was the focus of the analysis) engaged in a process that involved inquiry, debate and collaborative activity for the purpose of learning from their tutors and peers. The vignettes also demonstrate the authenticity with which the players approached the task, as well as the integrity that accompanies tutor feedback and peer-led interaction during online interaction. Below, the summary section presents an overview of the chapter, and links the aims of the chapter to the implementation of the model and related outcomes.

SUMMARY

This chapter is centred on the role of online discussion forums in creating meaningful learning experiences for learners in distance learning programmes. The use of a collaborative learning model that helped create an interactive online learning community at Open University Malaysia has been discussed. Within this model, task-directed collaborative activity provided authentic learning experiences and helped learners achieve specified learning outcomes. The chapter also presents exemplars of threaded discussions related to four categories: while guidance and challenge show how tutors play an active role in collaborative online learning, interdependence and extension demonstrate how learners play and active role in task-directed collaborative activity.

The Open University Malaysia-collaborative online learning model is premised upon the understanding that knowledge construction is a result of learners employing many skills simultaneously to carry out authentic, complex and less-structured tasks in culturally relevant learning environments. Thus, learners' skills are developed as they think of ways to resolve issues, define and solve problems, focus on ways to present newly acquired knowledge and actively strive to complete tasks and to achieve learning goals. As an instrument for learning, the discussion on the implementation of the Open University Malaysia-collaborative online learning model has shown how interactive online communities are instrumental in enlivening the promise of education in distance education programmes.

ACKNOWLEDGMENTS

The author thanks colleagues at Open University Malaysia for their help with the implementation of the collaborative learning model at the Open University Malaysia, especially Zoraini Wati Abas, for initial discussions on the collaborative online learning model, and David Lim Chong Lim for writing the task that was used in the course Introduction to Novels and Short Stories.

REFERENCES

Anderson, T. (2004). Teaching in an Online Learning Context. In T. Anderson & F. Elloumi (Eds.), *Theory and practice in online learning* (pp. 271-296). Athabasca: Athabasca University.

Andres, Y. M. (2002). Art of Collaboration: Awesome Tools and Proven Strategies. *Journal of Computer-Mediated Communication, 8*(1), Retrieved January 2005, from http://clp.cqu.edu.au/online_articles.htm

Balester, V., Halasek, K. & Peterson, N. (1992). Sharing authority: Collaborative teaching in a computer-based writing course. *Computers and Composition, 9*(1), 25-40.

Bransford, J., Brown, A., & Cocking, R. (1999). *How people learn: Brain, mind experience and school.* Retrieved April 2005, from http://www.nap.edu/html/howpeople1

Bruner, J. (1986). *Actual minds, possible worlds.* Cambridge: Harvard University Press.

Clark, J. (2000). Collaboration Tools in Online Learning Environments. *ALN Magazine, 4*(2). Retrieved August 2005, from http://www.sloan-c.org/publications/magazine/v4n1/index.asp

Collison, G., Elbaum, B., Haavind, S. & Tinker, R. (2000). *Facilitating Online Learning: Effective Strategies for Moderators.* Madison, WI: Atwood Publishing.

Dillenbourg, P., & Schneider, D. (1995, March 7-10). Collaborative learning and the internet. Paper presented at the *International Conference on Computer Assisted Instruction (ICCAI'95)*. National Chiao Tung University, Hsinchu, Taiwan. Retrieved January 2005, from http://tecfa.unige.ch/tecfa/ research/CMC/colla/iccai95_1.html

Harasim, L., Hiltz, S., Teles, L. & Turoff, M. (1995). *Learning networks: A field guide to teaching and learning online.* Cambridge: MIT Press.

Hiltz, S. (1995, March 7-10). Teaching in a virtual classroom. Paper presented at the *International Conference on Computer Assisted Instruction (ICCAI'95).* National Chiao Tung University, Hsinchu, Taiwan.

Johnson, S., Aragon, S., Najmuddin Shaik, Palma-Rivas, N. (2000). Comparative analysis of learner satisfaction and learning outcomes in online and face-to-face learning environments. *Journal of Interactive Learning, 11*(1), 29-49.

Jonassen, D. (2002). *Computers as mindtools for schools.* Upper Saddle River, NJ: Merrill.

Jonassen, D., Peck, K., & Wilson, B. (1999). *Learning with technology: A constructivist perspective.* Upper Saddle River, NJ: Prentice Hall.

Kearsley, G. (2000). *Online education: Learning and teaching in cyberspace.* Belmont, CA: Wadsworth.

Keefer, M., Zeitz, C., & Resnick, L. (2000). Judging the quality of peer-led student dialogues. *Cognition and Instruction, 18*(1), 53-81.

Kuldip Kaur & Zoraini Wati Abas (2004). Implementation of a collaborative online learning project at Open University Malaysia. *2004 Southeast Asia Association for Institutional Research (SEAAIR) Conference* (pp. 453-462). Wenzhou, China: SEAAIR.

Laurillard, D. (1993). *Rethinking university teaching: A framework for the effective use of educational technology.* London: Routledge.

McKendree, J. (2002). The Role of Discussion in Learning. Poster Presentation at *AMEE 2002*, 29 Aug-1 Sep, Lisbon, Portugal.

Sandholtz, J., Rngstaff, C., Dwyer, D. (1997) *Teaching with technology.* NY: Teachers College Press.

Spatariu, A., Hartley, K. & Bendixen, L. D. (2004). Defining and measuring quality in on-line discussion. *Journal of Interactive Online Learning, 2*(4). Retrieved January 2005, from http://www.ncolr.org/jiol/issues/PDF/2.4.2.pdf

Shaw, A. (1994). Neighborhood Networking and Community Building. In S. Cisler (Ed.), *Ties that bind: Building community networks.* Cuppertino, CA: Apple Computer.

Liao, T. T. (Ed.). (1996). *Advanced educational technology: Research issues and future technologies.* Berlin: Springer-Verlag.

Turoff, M. (1999). An end to student segregation: No more separation between distance learning and regular courses. *Telelearning 99 Symposium*, Montreal, Canada. Retrieved January 2005, from http://eies.njit.edu/~turoff/Papers/canadapres/segregation.htm

Twigg, C. (2001). Innovations in online learning: Moving beyond no significant difference. *The Pew Symposia in Learning and Technology 2001.* Retrieved January 2005, from http://www.center.rpi.edu/PewSym/mono4.html

APPENDIX A: THE TASK

This assignment aims to evaluate your grasp of the discussion in Unit 1 of the HBET4303 module and to facilitate hands-on experiential learning. To answer this question satisfactorily, you will need to (a) conduct library and/or internet-based research; (b) participate in online discussion to share resources and clarify ideas; and (c) apply the theories you have learned in Unit 1 on a literary text of your choice.

The specific aim of this assignment is to evaluate your understanding of the authorial and neo-rhetorical means by which a literary text is given coherence, that is, how we produce meaning from or weave it into a text. Online discussions based on steps (1) to (12) below are important to create an understanding of this task, as well as the process involved in putting together your portfolio.

Bear in mind that unacknowledged use of quotes or extracts constitutes plagiarism, the penalty of which will be severe.

To prepare a bound portfolio for submission to your tutor, follow these steps:

1. Pick a literary text of your choice. List down the title, author, and year of publication. Choose a text discussed in your module or one that is used in the school where you teach. The text you select will form the basis of your research.
2. Write a plot summary of the text you have selected. Your summary should be between 50-60 words.
3. Write a 200-250 word critical review of the text as though you would submit it to a newspaper for publication. Don't just summarise the story in this section. Tell your readers something about the author and the place of the text in the author's oeuvre. Share with your readers your view on why it is worth reading (or not). Highlight standout moments in the text (if they exist in your opinion).
4. Produce three blurbs from your review to be used to promote (not disparage!) the text. Remember that while a blurb always says something positive, the full-text from which it is extracted need not be thoroughly so.
5. Write a brief definition of authorial criticism and neo-rhetorical criticism.
6. Reread your review of the selected text in (2) and analyse whether you have written an authorial and/or neo-rhetorical criticism. Substantiate your answer with appropriate quotes from your review. Your analysis should be between 150-200 words.
7. Conduct a library and/or internet search to find three book reviews (of reasonable length) and/or critical essays on the selected text. Marks will be given on the appropriateness of your choice, i.e. the reviews/essays should be scholarly and varied in response. Photocopy or print them out and compile them in your portfolio.
8. Study the three reviews/essays you have selected and photocopied or printed out. Write a 300-word analysis of these reviews/essays, in the same way that you analysed your own review in (2) above. Remember to think in terms of authorial and neo-rhetorical criticisms.
9. Decide on one keyword which, in your opinion, captures an important thematic aspect of your selected text. Examples: pearl, Mexico, imam, Malaya, colonialism, cross-cultural relationship, gedeber, modernism, love, evil, old age, Japanese occupation.
10. With that one selected keyword in mind, conduct a library and/or internet search for articles, essays, book chapters, and the like which not only revolve around the keyword you have selected but which also probes, unpack and shed light on it. From the mountains of material you are likely to find from various disciplines including history, sociology, psychology, philosophy, anthropology,

cultural studies, and politics, select two items which best illuminate the fictional world of your selected text. Photocopy and/or print them out and append them to your portfolio.

11. Write a 400-word essay on the ways in which the two items in (9) are useful in adding depth to your appreciation of the literary text you selected in (1).

12. Provide a systematic bibliography of all works cited in your portfolio. Refer to guides like Joseph Gibaldi's *MLA Handbook for Writers of Research Paper* (6th edition) (New York: MLA, 2003) or *The Chicago Manual of Style* (15th edition) (Chicago: The University of Chicago Press, 2003).

This work was previously published in Enhancing Learning Through Human Computer Interaction, edited by E. McKay, pp. 132-153, copyright 2007 by Information Science Reference, formerly known as Idea Group Reference (an imprint of IGI Global).

Chapter XVIII
Towards an Integrated Model of Knowledge Sharing in Software Development:
Insights from a Case Study

Karlheinz Kautz
Copenhagen Business School, Denmark

ABSTRACT

This article adds to the discussion on knowledge management (KM) by focusing on the process of knowledge sharing as a vital part of KM. The article focuses on the relationship between knowledge, learning, communication, and participation in action, and the role of social interaction and technical media in the knowledge sharing process. We develop an initial theoretical framework of knowledge sharing on the basis of a literature study. Drawing on an empirical study of knowledge sharing in a software development company, we discuss what supports and what hinders knowledge sharing in software development. Finally, we use this knowledge to improve the theoretical framework.

INTRODUCTION

The KM literature is extensive, but the discussion on how to manage knowledge in organisations is far from over, and new proposals as well as lessons learned are continually being suggested. However, the published literature, especially in the information systems field, is largely grounded in

a view that considers knowledge as an objective commodity which can be collected, represented symbolically and processed like information (Dahlbom & Mathiassen, 1993; Tsoukas, 1998). The literature consequently shows a certain preoccupation with information technology (IT) and technical solutions while it reflects a limited view of individual and organisational knowledge-

Copyright © 2009, IGI Global, distributing in print or electronic forms without written permission of IGI Global is prohibited.

related processes (Swan, Scarbrough, & Preston, 1999). The practice of KM is frequently reduced to the implementation of new IT-based systems, and important organisational aspects, in particular human and social issues, are overlooked. There are, however, exceptions in the literature which reviews KM success and critical success factors (Jennex & Olfman, 2005, 2006). Like Kautz and Thaysen (2001), those who emphasise the important but not privileged role of IT provide a balanced discussion of technical issues related to KM.

This article takes this debate into account and is based on a broader perspective of knowledge and KM. Our focus is on understanding especially the process of knowledge sharing as a vital part of KM and on the relationship between knowledge, communication, and participation in action through either social interaction or technical media in the knowledge sharing process.

By studying the knowledge sharing process in a Danish software development company, we provide an insight into how developers draw from organisational memory (Walsh & Ungson, 1991) to share knowledge in a learning context. We discuss the use of social interaction and technical media in the communication process and provide conclusions on how different forms of knowledge are shared through the two types of media.

Our focus is primarily on the role of people in the knowledge sharing process, but we also include empirical findings on how people use technology to share knowledge.

The article is structured as follows. The next section introduces the concepts of knowledge, learning and communication which inform our understanding of knowledge sharing. The third section presents our research approach and setting. Our empirical findings are described in the fourth section and discussed in the fifth section. Finally in the sixth section, we present our conclusions and the challenges for future research.

THEORETICAL BACKGROUND

We begin by exploring the concepts on which we build our initial theoretical understanding in order to present how we utilise them in this study. Knowledge sharing is a bilateral process in which knowledge is exchanged between individuals and groups (Comas & Sieber, 2001). Knowledge is the outcome of a complex process, a part of which is the gathering and processing of information. This has been described by Kolb (1984) and others as a learning process. Learning is significant for the attainment of knowledge, and thus also for the sharing of knowledge. Information is communicated among people with the aid of a shared language, body language, and actions (Fiske, 1990; Nielsen, 1994) and participation in action and practice builds the foundation for learning (Wenger, 1998). This happens through social interaction and in some cases with the aid of technical media (Thompson & Walsham, 2001). Communication and participation in action are thus also significant for the sharing of knowledge. In the following we revisit the concepts of knowledge, learning communication, and participation in action and their relationship and importance for knowledge sharing in more detail.

Knowledge

Many definitions of knowledge have been presented in the literature. Although they differ in scope and orientation, they seem to agree upon the fact that knowledge is a complex multifaceted concept which can be understood from different perspectives (Cook & Brown, 1999; Kautz & Thaysen, 2001). From a hermeneutic perspective, knowledge is not a commodity which can be collected under controlled conditions and bought or sold on a market (Dahlbom & Mathiassen, 1993). On the contrary, it is subjective enlightenment, a personal property which is grounded in human cognition of things and relations in the world (Nielsen, 1994) and it affords actions (Cook & Brown, 1999).

Nonaka (1994) and Nonaka and Takeuchi (1995) build their model of the dynamics of knowledge creation with its conversion processes socialisation, externalisation, internalisation, and combination, which is a prerequisite for knowledge sharing according to Polanyi (1966), in particular under his concept of tacit knowledge. However, the commonly used sharp distinction between explicit knowledge which can be captured and codified into manuals, procedures, and rules and is easy to disseminate, and tacit knowledge, which cannot be easily articulated and thus only exists in people's hands and minds, and manifests itself through their action, has not been made by Polanyi (Stenmark, 2000). As Stenmark argues, Polanyi (1966) sees explicit and tacit knowledge as intrinsically interrelated and mutually consti-tuted, and views tacit knowledge as the backdrop against which all understanding is distinguished. All knowledge thus has a tacit dimension, and tacit knowledge is the cultural, emotional, and cognitive background of which humans are only marginally aware. This is supported by Tsoukas (1996), who argues that explicit and tacit knowl-edge are inseparably linked, and that they cannot be treated as two separate types of knowledge.

Against this background, the mechanical conversion model as a background for knowledge creation and sharing appears to be an inadequate description of the underlying processes. We follow Cook and Brown (1999), who apply the concepts of explicit and tacit knowledge in the form origi-nally intended by Polyani (1966). Acknowledging the codifiable nature of explicit knowledge which can be transmitted through formal, systematic language, and tacit knowledge, which is rooted in action and difficult to formalise and communicate, they do not promote one distinct kind of knowledge as an ideal for knowledge. Instead they emphasise

the importance and necessity of different forms of knowledge. They distinguish between explicit and tacit knowledge, but also between individual and group knowledge, thereby creating four ba-sic knowledge forms: (1) explicit individual, (2) explicit group, (3) tacit individual, and (4) tacit group knowledge. They see these four forms as distinct forms of knowledge all with equal stand-ing. All four forms are relevant to describe and understand knowledge and knowledge sharing in organisations. In addition to the four knowledge forms, Cook and Brown introduce the concept of knowing, which is the part of an action or practice which deals with the way knowledge is used in in-teraction with the social and physical world. Shar-ing their broader perspective on knowledge, our theoretical framework includes three dimensions of knowledge based on Cook and Brown's (1999) work: explicit/tacit knowledge, individual/group knowledge and knowledge/knowing.

We thus understand explicit knowledge as knowledge which is codifiable and can be ex-pressed directly through language. This means that explicit knowledge is structured and ordered such that it can be described and discussed through speech, scripts, drawings, and other signs and symbols. Tacit knowledge is knowledge which cannot directly be codified, but which can (only) be expressed indirectly through language and action. Tacit knowledge is a "feel" or sense for something or "to be able to do something without being able to explain why" (Brown & Gray, 1995, p. 78). Tacit knowledge is not hidden or inacces-sible—tacit knowledge simply cannot be codified or expressed directly.

Individual knowledge is knowledge held by an individual that is applied in the individual's ac-tions, while group knowledge is knowledge held by a group and applied in the group's actions. Group knowledge is created through the cooperation of the group's members and is part of the group's practice (Brown & Gray, 1995). Group knowledge includes knowledge about how the group works, its social rules, the group's memory about earlier actions, and knowledge about the group's tasks. Not necessarily all members of the group possess the whole group's knowledge; it is the group as a whole that possesses the group's knowledge, and it is the group as a whole that applies this knowledge (Cook & Brown, 1999).

Each of the four types of knowledge presented by Cook and Brown (1999) is associated with a set of knowledge forms (see Figure 1). Explicit individual knowledge is expressed in concepts, rules, equations, and interrelations. This is, for example, knowledge in the form of concepts about the design of a product or a specific procedure to follow. Tacit individual knowledge can be expressed in a person's skills in applying tools or routines for the performance of a particular task (Comas & Sieber, 2001). Explicit group knowledge consists of shared stories about previous successes or failures and of metaphors used for establishing a common understanding of a problem or a task. And finally, tacit group knowledge is related to organisational culture in the form of genres which guide the thoughts and actions of organisational members.

The four types of knowledge can be seen as constituting organisational memory in different forms. According to Walsh and Ungson (1991), organisational memory is both an individual and organisational level construct. Although the definition of organisational memory is far from uniform, it is generally agreed upon that organisational memory consists of mental and structural artefacts which have a consequential affect on performance (Walsh & Ungson, 1991). In its most basic sense, organisational memory refers to stored information from an organisation's history which can be brought to bear on present decisions.

We have knowledge to carry out an action, but at the same time we can have knowledge independently of whether we carry out the action or not. Knowledge is something we possess irrespective of action. Thus knowledge is a tool which can be used in action, but which in itself is not action. The four forms of knowledge created by the dimensions of explicit—tacit and individual—group

Figure 1. Types of knowledge related to knowing based on Cook & Brown (1999)

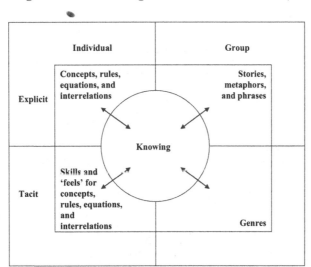

are thus not sufficient to describe the knowledge which is expressed through practice (Cook & Brown, 1999).

Every time someone carries out an action, a combination of many different types of knowledge is used. Each type of knowledge contributes to the action in a way in which the other types cannot. The part of the action which focuses on the application and combination of explicit and tacit knowledge in interaction with the social and physical world is referred to as "knowing" by Cook and Brown (1999). As they put it, "Knowing is to interact with and honour the world using knowledge as a tool" (p. 389). Knowing has a focus on how we use our knowledge in practice. Knowing is not something we have, but something we do, and therefore a part of the actual action.

Figure 1 shows the different forms of knowledge related to the process of knowing.

Having argued for a three-dimensional understanding of knowledge, we now focus on the concept of learning and how this contributes to our understanding of the knowledge sharing process.

Learning: Knowing as a Learning Process

Learning is the process in which we acquire knowledge based on the communication of information and the participation in action. The learning process is thus an antecedent of having knowledge and is important for the sharing of knowledge.

Kolb (1984) has developed a theory of learning according to which learning is based on experience, and takes place through learning cycles. The learning process is a cognitive process in which individuals process new information or actions on the background of existing information or actions. In this process—depicted in Figure 2—information called abstract conceptualisation is obtained though speech and script, or indirectly through action and practice, when it is called concrete experience; thereafter information is processed actively through active experimenting or reflectively through reflection and/or observation. This means that abstract concepts and concrete experience are tested actively in practice or are

Figure 2. Kolb's (1984) learning cycle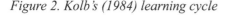

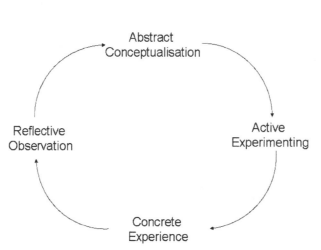

reflected upon. The result of this process is new knowledge.

This learning theory can be related to Cook and Brown's (1999) understanding of knowledge and knowing (Comas & Sieber, 2001). A mutual interplay exists between knowledge and knowing: knowing means that we use our knowledge in new ways, or that we make use of our knowledge in new ways through practice, and thus discover new interrelations or gain a new understanding of our knowledge. Kolb's (1984) learning cycle, which is based on experiential learning, complements Cook and Brown's comprehension of knowing, as it can explain those aspects of knowing which deal with the creation of new knowledge. Comas and Sieber postulate that the four different stages of the learning process indirectly reflect the presence of different states of knowing, and argue that moving through the cycle contributes to what Cook and Brown have called productive inquiry.

There is, however, a difference between the four types of knowledge and how they relate to learning. The learning process depends on the types of knowledge involved, but also on different ways of learning (Nielsen & Kvale, 1999). This is a part of our theoretical framework and it will be discussed next.

The concept of scholastic learning describes the (part of) learning which takes place through verbal and textual instruction detached from practice (Nielsen & Kvale, 1999). This comprises the communication of information which represents explicit knowledge, and as such, concepts, rules, equations, and interrelations are acquired through scholastic learning. This involves learning through concrete institutionalised education, for example, through courses, seminars, or literature studies, but also through verbal and textual instruction among colleagues at the workplace.

Learning of tacit knowledge occurs through active participation in practice as well as general learning in day-to-day life. Wenger (1998) presents a social theory of learning in which participation in practice forms the basis for learning. When

people work closely together, share a practice, a vocabulary to talk about the practice, and an understanding about the practice, tacit knowledge in the form of skills, proficiency, routines, and shared genres is more easily shared (Wenger, 1998; Wenger & Snyder, 2000). Practice learning takes place in communities of practice which are particular areas of activity or bodies of knowledge which a community has organised itself around. It is a joint enterprise inasmuch as it is understood and continually renegotiated by its members who are linked to each other through their involvement in common activities (Wenger, 1998).

Over time, a community of practice builds up an agreed set of communal resources, a shared repertoire which consists of tangible as well as intangible aspects such as procedures, politics, rituals, and values (Wenger, 1998; Wenger, McDermott, & Snyder, 2002).

While scholastic learning is primarily about receiving, processing, and "absorbing" information, practice learning is primarily a question of becoming part of a community (Brown & Gray, 1995).

Individual learning can occur through scholastic as well as practice learning, and it is an individual's learning of explicit and tacit knowledge. Individual learning denotes the acquisition of knowledge which an individual (him/herself) uses in and for his or her actions. An example is knowledge in the form of concepts about the design of a product, or skills in the application of tools or routines for the performance of particular tasks (Comas & Sieber, 2001).

Group learning is learning of tacit and explicit knowledge on a group level. Group learning can also occur through scholastic as well as practice learning. Through group learning, the group acquires knowledge which it uses for its actions. This comprises knowledge in the form of rules for how a task is to be solved, shared stories about successes and failures, routines for how the group distributes tasks, and genres for particular meetings and documents.

Communities of practice (Lave & Wenger, 1991; Wenger 1998) are a prominent example of group learning, being groups of individuals who work together over a period of time. The individuals in these groups may carry out the same job or cooperate on a shared assignment, but they do not have to be a formal or identifiable group (Brown & Gray, 1995). Individuals in communities of practice are bound together through a shared practice and understanding of this practice, and they develop shared knowledge about the practice (Brown & Gray, 1995).

Communication and Active Participation in Action: Knowledge Sharing Through Social Interaction or Technical Media

Knowledge sharing is a process in which knowledge is exchanged between individuals and groups (Comas & Sieber, 2001). The access to and exchange of information is necessary for the acquisition of knowledge (Kautz & Thaysen, 2001), and communication is therefore important for the sharing of knowledge.

We take as a starting point Fiske (1990), who argues that communication can basically be understood as the exchange of information. Fiske relies on Lasswell's (Severin & Tankard, 1997)—Who (says) What (to) Whom (in) What Channel (with) What Effect—and Shannon and Weaver's (1949) rather general and simplistic models of communication, but emphasises that the communication process takes place with the aid of a shared oral and written language, body language, or action. In this model a sender or communicator chooses, combines, and presents data in such a way that it represents the information which he or she wants to communicate. A receiver recognises and takes information in by interpreting the transmitted data on the background of existing knowledge, other information, context, culture, and the rules and pragmatics of the language.

Communication can take place as a dialogue, meaning that the roles of sender and receiver change continuously during the communication, or as a monologue, in which case the roles of the sender and the receiver are fixed throughout the communication session. The roles of sender and receiver of information in the communication process can be held by individuals and by formal or informal groups. Formal groups are groups which are linked to business processes or organisational units and which have been defined by an organisation's management (Brown & Gray, 1995). Informal groups are groups which are connected with informal business processes or built by people who congregate outside or across the formal organisational units.

The differences between how individuals or groups exchange knowledge have an impact upon how and which information can be communicated. Information can not only be found in speech, but is also expressed through body language and action. An individual can obtain information which is embedded in actions and body language by participating in someone else's work. This means that information has different formats, is more or less structured, and is stored in different ways, which all have an influence on how information can be communicated.

Knowledge sharing takes place through inter-subjective and/or technology-facilitated communication (Thompson & Walsham, 2001). Inter-subjective communication takes the form of social interaction, while technology-facilitated communication comes about through technical media. There is a difference between which type of information can be most suitably exchanged and provided through social interaction and technical media (Thompson & Walsham, 2001).

Social interaction as the exchange of information face-to-face between people comprises, for example, formal or informal meetings, verbal presentations, and teaching sessions. In social interaction, information is communicated through speech, body language, or actions; hence, social interaction enables the exchange of information linked to both explicit and tacit knowledge (Nielsen & Kvale, 1999). Explicit knowledge can be codified, and it can thus be expressed verbally (or textually) in a shared language. Tacit knowledge cannot be codified and it can therefore not be expressed verbally or textually; body language and actions are thus important for the learning of tacit knowledge (Nielsen & Kvale, 1999). This indicates that social interaction is suitable for the communication of complex, less structured, and nonformalised information because it provides different possibilities for communicating a message. This happens through the application of a combination of a shared language and speech, body language, and actions which can supplement each other. Social interaction in itself cannot store information, and thus the storing of the exchanged information through social interaction is dependant on the individuals' or the group's capability to "store" across time and place.

Technical media are technologies, especially information and communication technologies, which support the exchange of information in the whole or in parts of the communication process. These can, for example, be telephones, databases, electronic documents, or e-mails. Technologies can "transport" communicated information between the involved parties and simultaneously support the storage of data (Thompson & Walsham, 2001). Technology thereby provides the possibility of making information available across time and space. Technology can also contribute to changes in the format or structure of information in the form of categorisation of documents, composition of document indices, or conversion of analogue sound to a data file. This improves the communication in relation to a situation where technology is not applied.

Technical media are suitable for the communication of codified information (Thompson & Walsham, 2001) as most technical media are based on verbal and textual communication. Some

technologies, such as video, can also reproduce information expressed through body language and action. Technical media are suitable for well structured, well defined, and formalised information such as technical specifications or measurement results. Technical media primarily support the communication of information related to explicit knowledge, and they can only indirectly, and to a limited extent, support communication of information related to tacit knowledge (Thompson & Walsham, 2001). Different strategies are used to access that information depending on the type of knowledge and the background of those who use the medium (Smolik, Kremer, & Kolbe, 2005).

An Initial Theoretical Model for Knowledge Sharing

In summary, in this section we have presented our understanding of knowledge, learning, communication, and participation in action as constituting knowledge sharing via different types of media. In Figure 3 we have integrated these concepts as a step towards a unified model of knowledge sharing.

In the model, learning occurs through scholastic or practice learning, and the learning process is the process which determines how individuals and groups acquire different types of knowledge through the communication of information and participation in practice. The model thus shows how knowledge, organisational memory, and learning are related, and how they influence each other as prerequisites for knowledge sharing. We will use the framework to analyse the relationship between ways of learning and types of knowledge as prerequisites for knowledge sharing in our case organisation, and take it up again later and discuss it in relation to our findings, which resulted in a refinement of the theoretical framework.

We use this model to discuss our empirical findings. In the next section we present the research approach and setting of our empirical study of knowledge sharing in software development as

Figure 3. An integrated model of knowledge, learning, communication and participation in action

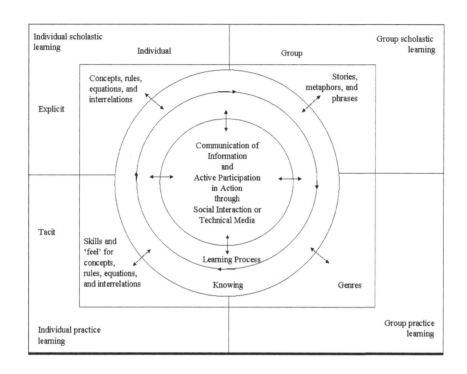

a prelude to the presentation of the findings in the *KNOWLEDGE SHARING IN THE CASE ORGANISATION* section.

RESEARCH APPROACH AND SETTING

The ontological and epistemological assumptions of our work are informed by the interpretive paradigm. The objective of our research was to study and understand the organisational members' knowledge sharing processes within their work and organisational context. In line with Andersen (1999), we chose a case study approach in order to study the process of knowledge sharing in its organisational context. To ensure the validity of our work we largely followed Klein and Myers's (1999) seven principles for interpretive field

research and Eisenhardt's (1989) seven steps for case study research.

Given the resources available to our study, we concentrated on a single case study of knowledge sharing in a large Danish IT company. This approach might be criticised for only generating a local empirical theory which might not be generalisable, but as argued by Hughes and Jones (2003), it contributes to the existing body of knowledge by providing a detailed account of empirical findings. By limiting the study to a single organisation, we were able to examine the case in more detail to understand more thoroughly the interrelationships of separate data, which was our research objective.

The research setting was a Danish subsidiary of a global provider of telecommunication systems. At the time of the study (in 2002), the Danish subsidiary was 23 years old and it had been acquired by the American parent company 6 years earlier. The company's customers are fixed network, mobile network and cable operators who reside in more than 80 countries.

The Danish subsidiary concentrates on the development of new products. The company's products consist of hardware and embedded software which provide the product functionality and management software to access, calibrate, and monitor the products' functions. This is mirrored in the organisation of the company's research and development (R&D) department, which consists of three divisions (access, calibration, and monitoring) which perform the detailed specification and actual development tasks. In addition, the company has a product management department; a product planning and specification department; and a finance department. The company has 420 employees of whom 180 are directly involved in product development.

In agreement with company management and also because of resource restrictions, we agreed to focus our investigation of the knowledge sharing process on one organisational unit—the division of embedded software. The embedded software division consists of some administrative staff, a manager, three project leaders, two team leaders, and 27 staff members. With its position between different departments and divisions, embedded software appeared to be most appropriate and representative for our purpose in light of the resources available for the investigation.

The company was interested in participating in our research study due to increased competition in the market, they had decided to focus on employees' knowledge, learning, and communication both within and across the organisational units with the aim of increasing productivity and quality in the product development process.

The product development process is organised in programmes consisting of projects. The company has about three large and 5-10 minor programmes running at any one time, consisting of

multiple projects of varying length from 6 months to 2 years. The projects are typically carried out in and by the different divisions. The company's development process can be characterised as product-oriented, sequential, and document focused. The process consists of an analysis and design phase, a development phase, a test phase, and a product installation and introduction phase.

A planning team consisting of experienced employees from different departments is responsible for the overall definition of a programme. A so-called core group of project leaders and technical experts performs a feasibility study and produces product and document reviews at the end of each development phase. Finally, a core team which consists of the project leaders of the different divisions in R&D is responsible for conducting and completing the actual projects and products. The development work is performed by the individual divisions and their developers and is coordinated by the project leaders in and across the three divisions and beyond.

The developers in the division were our primary unit of investigation. Within the category individuals and groups within the division under investigation, we differentiated between developers in the division, developers who worked on the same tasks, developers who shared a two-staff office, project groups, subproject groups, informal groups, and experience (exchange) groups. Individuals and groups related to other units were roughly distinguished into individuals in other divisions and departments affiliated with the same project or product, other departments and divisions in the Danish subsidiary, or individuals and groups in other countries.

We collected data through 13 semi-structured interviews with eight developers, our primary group of interest, and one project leader in the unit under investigation. We also interviewed four employees from other divisions and departments. We also performed one group interview with management personnel and two one-workday-long observations where we followed a member of management and a developer. Finally, we have included secondary material in the form of the different kinds of documents used in the organisation.

All interviews were taped, and a summary listing relevant issues from each interview was written. During and after the interviews we produced rich pictures inspired by the Soft Systems Methodology (Checkland & Scholes, 1990) to depict our understanding of the situation with regard to knowledge sharing in the organisation. These rich pictures constructed the basis for the data analysis and were so useful that we only had to return to the tape recording for further consultation in one case.

To analyse the data we used a combination of common sense interpretation, inspired by the Soft Systems Methodology, and theoretical interpretation which related the data to our theoretical framework (Andersen, 1999). For all interviews and observations we identified and coded sensible units of expressions. These statements were then linked to one or more categories which we deduced from our theoretical framework, and by comparing all statements within each category and across categories, a number of recurring subjects emerged, and over 100 issues critical for knowledge sharing in the case organisation were identified. The three main categories, which will also be used in the subsequent in-depth description, were (1) knowledge sharing through social interaction, (2) knowledge sharing through technical media, and (3) (the) different kinds of knowledge (which are) shared.

This allowed for an in-depth understanding and discussion of knowledge sharing in the case organisation, revealing what kind of interaction and which media provide possibilities for sharing different kinds of knowledge. It also revealed what impact the identified issues had on the sharing of knowledge, and it ultimately led to a refinement of our theoretical framework.

KNOWLEDGE SHARING IN THE CASE ORGANISATION

We explore the case study to identify how the software developers draw upon organisational memory to share knowledge. As part of our research question, we investigate how knowledge sharing in software development unfolds in social interaction and via technical media. Our findings provide some interesting insights on these matters and present a more detailed account of the kinds of knowledge which are shared. Another interesting finding concerns how and when the developers rely on formal or informal contacts in the knowledge sharing process. Finally, the findings show a difference in the unfolding of the knowledge sharing process according to individual or group action.

When we refer to knowledge sharing as unfolding through social interaction, we relate to the subjects' knowledge sharing through formal interaction in formal meetings, informal interaction in informal meetings; seminars and courses; presentations; exchange of experience groups; personal networks; and in the offices shared by two or more people.

When we refer to knowledge sharing as unfolding through technical media, we cover the subjects' knowledge sharing by the use of the organisation's document handling system (DHS), the file server, the error reporting system, the version control system, the project management system, e-mail, electronic discussion groups, Internet, intranet, video, whiteboards, paper documents, and literature.

When we refer to kinds of knowledge, we cover the subjects' shared knowledge of technical specifications (particularly requirement specifications and design documents); general project information and technical standards; information about who knows what about previous projects or old products; and information about technical problems and improvement of products.

We then provide a more detailed analysis of how knowledge sharing unfolded between individuals and in and between groups, and what kinds of knowledge are shared. We identify critical issues related to each of the categories and provide some suggestions regarding how some of these issues can be solved. As limitations of space preclude a full description of our analysis, we have chosen two subjects from each of the categories to illustrate our findings.

Knowledge Sharing through Social Interaction: Formal Meetings and Personal Networks

Social interaction in the case study took place through formal meetings and personal networks which are now discussed.

Formal Meetings

The members of the case study organisation participate in various formal meetings dealing with the communication of the status of projects and problems through verbal and textual communication. These formal meetings provide the opportunity for the acquisition of explicit individual and group knowledge. Explicit individual knowledge is shared in the form of coordination, communication of status, and discussions of tasks. Explicit group knowledge is shared in the form of (communication of) management attitudes and opinions; definition of rules; and (communication of) stories about good and bad projects. The formal meetings are also used as "pathfinders" to those developers who hold individual knowledge about, for example, concepts and rules, or who have specific skills. In this way the formal meetings provide the individuals with the possibility of obtaining knowledge about where they can obtain further knowledge. Active participation in formal meetings also provides the opportunity for acquisition of knowledge about the genres which are

related to formal meetings and the acquisition of individual skills about how meetings are run.

The following issues were identified in relation to the formal meetings:

- **The information communicated through project meetings is arbitrary.** This shows that the developers are not sure that the information they need, or which would be helpful to them, is communicated through meetings. It contributes to the project meetings having less value for the developers, and it indicates that the developers are not sure about the genres which are related to formal meetings, or that they lack skills to utilise formal meetings. The study does not provide any evidence that the developers are trained to use formal meetings. The developers therefore communicate to a higher degree through informal meetings which are "held" as the need for particular information arises, or through personal networks. Information about the same subject is thus communicated through many different forms of social interaction and through different technical media. This in itself does not have to be a problem as a certain amount of redundancy increases the chance that everyone will receive the desired or necessary information, but it is problematic when it confuses the developers.

- **There are no project meetings between divisions, and coordination across divisions rarely happens in formal meetings.** These issues indicate that communication between the divisions is generally poor, and that it is limited to taking place through the project leaders' personal networks. This reinforces the organisational divide between the developers in the different divisions and creates a barrier which does not support communication or insights into other developers' work. The communication and the exchange, which happen across the departments and is necessary for the developers, instead comes about through personal networks or written information. The communication between divisions is much more difficult than within a division because one has to be much more precise, as the developers cannot assume that the receiver of their information has the same background knowledge.

Personal Networks

Personal networks are personal relationships between the developers. These are used to communicate information and to instruct each other. Communication of information through personal networks is verbal and textual and provides the opportunity for scholastic learning of explicit knowledge. This is true for both individual and explicit group knowledge because personal networks are directed towards communication of concrete problems, discussions of different possibilities for solutions, and informal education of the individual developer. This knowledge takes the form of concepts and rules related to projects, products, and other technical matters which the developers need for the performance of their work. Good and bad experiences are communicated for this purpose, and phrases are used which are defined by the groups in the organisation. This happens, for example, through informal meetings, which are the links for, and which make the networks visible. The developers communicate information through informal meetings, and at the same time they can identify other developers' personal networks and thereby build and extend their own personal networks.

The developers become actively involved and participate in each others' practice through personal networks, and in so doing they have the opportunity to acquire the genres which are related to personal networks. In addition, the networks give the developers the opportunity to acquire

skills in how personal networks can be used, and skills related to the topics which are communicated. This happens, for example, through the two-staff offices, which facilitate the developers' participation in the same practice. It is common practice in the company that an experienced developer shares an office with a less experienced developer to help him or her to achieve skills and learn genres. This includes helping the less experienced ones by pointing them in the right direction when it comes to searching for information. This occurs in communication about how things work, and where what information can be found, as well as in the form of stories and rules related to work in the divisions.

The following issues were identified in relation to personal networks:

- **The poorer the formal meetings and the technical specifications, the more the developers use their personal networks.** This shows that personal networks are pivotal for communication in the division because many other forms of social interaction and technical media are not adequate and detailed enough for the developers to communicate all the desired or necessary information.

- **The developers gain a "feel" through the personal network for what is important and whom they should go to in order to prioritise resources and tasks.** These issues show the importance of the personal networks; they bind other forms of social interaction and technical media together, and they satisfy the need for communication which is not covered through other social interactions and technical media.

- **Developers depend on personal networks, which are strongest within the division, but more experienced developers have networks which span divisions.** This issue shows that the developers are dependant on their personal networks to be able to perform the work for which they need information from previous projects. This dependency on the personal networks and on the most experienced developers can be problematic when the developers, who have comprehensive knowledge of previous projects and old products, leave the organisation and take their knowledge with them.

- **Personal networks save time**. This shows that personal networks are faster to use than searching in documents. The developers can find what they are looking for faster through their personal networks than through other forms of social interaction or technical media.

- **A good personal network takes time to build.** These issues show that personal networks are created through the developers' daily work, and that a good network takes many years to build up. This is because the developers work on the same projects and with the same colleagues over a long period of time. This contributes to those developers who have broad and comprehensive networks having a lot of information at their disposal, while others with lesser networks have less information. This indicates that not all developers have comprehensive personal networks, which results in less communication of information and less opportunity for the acquisition of new knowledge for these developers.

Some Conclusions on Knowledge Sharing through Social Interaction

The analysis of the examples of social interaction shows that social interaction through verbal and textual communication provides the possibility for scholastic learning of explicit knowledge. Beyond this, the active participation in action in the form of social interaction provides the opportunity to acquire those genres which are related to social interaction and the acquisition of the individual skills for how social interaction can be applied, and the skills related to the topics and themes which are communicated. The investigation shows that the individuals and groups in the investigated division communicate through social interaction, and social interaction thus provides the opportunity to share knowledge in the division.

This finding is interesting, as the analysis also shows that social interaction is not facilitated in a structured way, and that formal forms of social interaction in general are not prioritised. This creates problems, as the developers are uncertain about which information is communicated through which type of social interaction, and the findings show that this results in a high degree of arbitrariness with respect to which information is communicated through which form of social interaction, for example, in courses, presentations, experience groups, or personal networks.

Knowledge Sharing Through Technical Media: The Document Handling System and the File Server

In our case study company, documents used to share knowledge are stored on two kinds of technical media: the DHS and the file server.

The Document Handling System

The DHS provides the opportunity for textual communication. By far the largest part of all technical specifications, analysis documents, and project-related documents is stored in the DHS. This comprises feature plans, functional and object models, and iteration plans, but also how-to documents, technical standards, and presentations. The documents are used by the individual developers in their work as they describe what and how something should be or has been done. The documents are also directed towards groups as they provide the framework and the scope for the groups' collective work. The verbal and textual communication through the DHS offers the opportunity for individuals and groups to acquire explicit knowledge.

Active participation in the form of interaction with and use of the DHS provides the possibility for the developers to gain skills in use of the system to acquire the genres related to it. This comprises which documents are stored in the system, how the documents are structured and categorised, how search functions are applied, and how keywords and indices are linked to documents.

- **Not all documents are stored in the DHS, and as a consequence not all necessary documents are accessible to all developers.** This issue is related to the fact that the DHS is regarded as being for documents which are directly related to projects or the product development process. Other documents which do not comprise formal or project-defining information, such as descriptions of "private" ideas for solutions, experience or general descriptions of problems, are often stored on other media, among others the file server. Only what the individual developer thinks has to be version-controlled is stored in the DHS. The developers have to search for information in many places and to supplement information from the DHS with information from, for example, the file server or their personal networks. This indicates that developers need to have a good overview of the information and have to make an extra effort to gather the quantity and the quality of information they need for their work.

- **The DHS is slow and hard to use, the search functions are poor, and distribution lists are not used to the necessary degree; it is difficult to find the right documents; there is a lack of abbreviations and designations, and the information structure in**

the system is strictly hierarchical. These issues indicate that the actual functionality and the information structure in the DHS hinder the developers' use of the DHS and the communication of information. This limits the developers' chances of sighting all documents and finding all relevant information for a particular task. The strict information structure does not mirror the individuals' and the groups' problem-oriented way of working. Communication of information in the DHS is based on the partition between projects and divisions instead of being based on the structure of the working processes, problems, and solutions.

- **Not all departments are equally engaged in using the system.** This issue reinforces and even increases the problems related to the developers' limited possibilities of accessing all documents and finding all relevant information for a particular task. Although the DHS is the official place for storing and distributing documents, some departments use other technical media, for example databases for technical specifications.

- **Many developers use the system only to the extent to which it has an impact on their communication with other divisions, or when demanded as part of the formal work process.** This indicates that some divisions provide their documents to developers in other divisions only to a very limited extent, and that the division only has an insight into other divisions' documents to a limited extent. The lack of insight into each others' work makes the communication of information across divisions difficult and hinders the sharing and exploitation of explicit knowledge. In the case where the use of the DHS is bypassed to the advantage of other technical media, this also has an influence on the acquisition of tacit knowledge related to the use of the DHS, especially the individual skills related to using the DHS for the storage of technical specifications. This is also true of the acquisition of genres related to the DHS. Information about genres is communicated though the documents in the DHS. When the same information is communicated through different forms of social interaction and technical media, meaning that different genres are used for the same themes, this can lead to a situation where the same information gains different meanings.

The File Server

The file server is primarily used for informal documents such as technical notes, proposals for technical designs, intermediate and temporary versions of documents, standards, product descriptions, third party documents, and so forth, which are not directly or ultimately related to the projects or the product development process. Apart from these documents the file server also contains binary files in the form of programs and video recordings. This shows that the file server is used for textual and verbal—in the form of video recordings—communication, which provides the opportunity for acquisition of explicit knowledge related to the information that is stored on the server. Interaction with and use of the file server provides the opportunity for the developers to acquire skills in the use of the file server and genres related to it. These are implicitly determined by the developers and deal, for example, with which documents and files are to be stored on the server; how they are and should be structured; and which search functions can and should be applied.

The following issues were identified in relation to the file server:

- **The file server is used to store files which should be stored in the DHS.** This problem

is related to the fact that the DHS is regarded as being for documents which are directly linked to the projects or to the product development process. Nevertheless, some older documents have not been transferred to the DHS and are stored on the server. This includes, for example, own ideas and experiences; technical notes; proposals for technical designs; designs; intermediate and temporary versions of documents; standards; product descriptions; third party documents; and so forth, which are not directly or ultimately related to the projects or the product under development. This indicates that information which relates to the same subject is stored and communicated through different technical media: for example, own experience and proposals for technical designs are stored on the file server, while technical specifications related to the same product are stored in and communicated through the DHS. This results in a situation where the developers have to gather information from different places, depending on whether the information is categorised as formal or informal, or whether the information relates to newer or older products. This means that the developers must have a good overview of the information and extra time to gather the necessary quantity and quality of information. As information has an impact on the learning process and ultimately the acquisition of knowledge, the use of the file server hinders the sharing of explicit knowledge, as it functions as a ragbag and as it provides the opportunity to store information in places other than the DHS.

- **The developers' and the divisions' use of the file server is very different.** Some developers never use it; others use it often or store and find much useful information there. The divisions also structure files differently on the server, and this is an obstacle to the sharing of knowledge. The different use of the file server makes the communication of information through this technical medium look arbitrary and dependant on individuals. The different use of the file server holds the risk that the developers do not communicate the same information, and thus that the information accessible to the other developers becomes different. There is a risk that those developers who do not use or do not have knowledge of the information on the file server do not acquire knowledge of the same concepts or stories. This then decreases their later capabilities to act. The developers' different uses of the file server lead to differences in the extent to which the developers acquire skills related to the file server and knowledge of the file server as a genre. This includes skills related to the use of the file server to store and work with technical standards or the handling of video recordings or other binary files on the server. It also includes the genres related to the file server, for example the form in which information in a technical standard is communicated through the medium.

- **It is difficult to find information on the file server; the developers have to know where the information is stored to find it.** The problem with access to information on the file server is emphasised by this issue. This is due to the fact that the file server has limited search functions which only cover searching based on file names, and that the directory structures and naming are very "anarchistic." This means that the developers have to have considerable knowledge of the file server and its contents to be able to search for information there. Information about the file server is communicated through personal networks, but the personal networks take a long time to build up and

seldom cross division boundaries. It is thus difficult for new employees and developers in other divisions to find relevant information on the server.

Some Conclusions on Knowledge Sharing Through Technical Media

All these issues deal with access to information. As information is the basis of the developers' acquisition of knowledge, access to and gathering of information are necessary for the acquisition and sharing of knowledge. The analysis shows that the issues identified in relation to the developers' use of technical media to communicate have a negative influence on the sharing of knowledge between individuals and groups in the company division which was investigated.

Sharing Different Kinds of Knowledge: Technical Specifications and Information about "Who Knows What"

Finally, we shift focus from communication of information and participation in action through social interaction or technical media and emphasise what kinds of knowledge are actually shared, and we concentrate here on technical specifications and on information about "who knows what."

Technical Specifications

Technical specifications comprise feature plans; device transport and management specifications; overview and detailed function and object specifications; and hardware specifications. They are the basis for the acquisition of explicit knowledge, and the developers actually use specific technical specifications for product development. The technical specifications are directed towards the individual developer's work and at the same time define the rules and phrases for the collective, joint, and shared development work. They thereby form the basis for the sharing of explicit knowledge between individuals as well as groups.

The developers, who have been in the division for a long time, can understand and use technical specifications better than others. This indicates that through their daily work, the developers acquire skills and genres in utilising technical specifications. Active participation in action provides the opportunity for the acquisition of tacit knowledge. This means that the developers' use of technical specifications contributes to their skills in utilising technical specifications. Their skills related to the topics that the technical specifications deal w i t h , a n d provide possibilites to the acquisition of genres that are related to technical specifications.

However, not all developers understand the documents equally well. When they do not understand the documents they contact the developers who originally produced the documents and ask them what they were trying to describe and express. This shows that the developers need certain skills and knowledge of the applied genres to be able to use the information which is provided in the technical specification.

The following issues were identified in relation to the use of technical specifications:

- **The developers find it difficult to gain an overview of what has been agreed on, and which of the changes in the specifications have been carried out; changes are sometimes carried out before they are agreed upon and approved; not all changes are documented and reviewed.** These problems show that communication about changes or updates to specifications and documentation is sometimes difficult or defective. Acquisition of knowledge is based on the information which the receiver obtains. Access to and exchange of information is thus necessary for the acquisition of knowledge. The developers' different and nonupdated

information basis therefore has an impact on the explicit knowledge they acquire, and ultimately on their possibilities of action.

- **The change management tool is not used to receive information on updated technical specifications; the document handling system is sometimes bypassed and e-mail is used instead.** These issues show that the communication of these documents and information on updated technical specifications takes place through many "routes" and different technical media. This indicates that the developers are not secure in and certain about the genres which are connected to these technical media, for example, the specifications are communicated through the DHS, but updates to these documents are communicated through the error reporting system, while both types of information should be communicated through the DHS.

- **Sometimes feature plans are not finished when a project starts, which results in guessing and rough estimates; there is no possibility of tracing all features through the whole product development process including the final test of the product.** These issues indicate that the quality of the information which the developers use in their work is insufficient. As noted earlier, access to and exchange of information is necessary for the acquisition of knowledge, and when information is not available, acquisition of knowledge is impeded or hindered.

- **The hardware specifications are difficult for the developers in the division to understand.** The hardware division uses different standards and a different version of the control system; hardware specifications are formulated in a 'slangy' way and are not written in pedagogical form; the schedule seldom leaves the developers an opportunity to dig deeply into the hardware specifications.

These issues also indicate that insufficient information, and information which is difficult to understand, as well as lack of time, hinder the sharing of explicit knowledge and the developers' possibilities of action.

Information on "Who Knows What"

Information on "who knows what" includes information about which employees and colleagues have which skills, and knowledge about projects, products, and technologies. As this information is directed towards the individual developer's seeking of information and simultaneously defines rules for who the developer should turn to, this information is the basis for explicit individual and group knowledge.

Active participation in action provides the possibility of acquisition of tacit knowledge. This means that the developers' utilisation of personalised knowledge contributes to the skills in utilising these skills and in skills to actually find the colleagues in question, and to the acquisition of the genres which are related to the skills and to these people. The study shows that the developers use a lot of time finding out who knows what, and that they do not always succeed. The developers find that knowledge about who knows what comes with time, when they become familiar with other developers.

The following issues were identified in relation to knowledge about "who knows what":

- **Many developers lack insight into who has what information and skills; the developers often only know the skills of those they work or have worked with in projects.** These issues show that many developers have limited knowledge of their associates. However, for development of the technical skills it is important to know whom to ask in the organisation, while formal education is less important. The lack of knowledge of colleagues can thus have a

negative impact on the access to and communication of information, and ultimately on knowledge sharing, as the developers do not have an overview of what information can be found where, and this is even more problematic given that it is most important to know who to ask as part of the development of the skills which the developers require to perform their tasks.

- **The project leaders know who has knowledge; the division's "catalogue of competences" has become too voluminous to be updated; it is difficult to find information about who works in which project.** These issues show that the project leaders are prominent as those who know who has what knowledge. The overview over who has what information and which skills, and therefore the access to other people's information and capabilities, depends on a relatively small number of people. The division's catalogue of expertise is no longer updated, and therefore is of very limited help in this respect. The developers instead use their personal networks to obtain this information. The difficulties in localising information and skills of other developers are reinforced through the fact that the developers have difficulty finding overviews of who works in which project.

- **The developers do not know what other developers and colleagues need to know.** At the same time as they do not find desired or necessary information, the developers do not know what others need to know. This hinders the distribution of information to developers who might benefit from it.

Some Conclusions on Sharing of Different Kinds of Knowledge

In summary, the analysis of technical specifications and information about "who knows what" as exemplars of different kinds of knowledge shows that the identified issues can be detrimental to the sharing of knowledge in the case organisation, as this knowledge is difficult to find, and in part also hard to understand. The developers instead use their personal networks to acquire the knowledge they need. However, as personal networks take time to build, this solution works best for those employees who have been with the company for long time.

DISCUSSION

The study has shown that the integrated model can explain the relationship between the communication of information, participation in action, the learning process, and knowing the different types of knowledge. It thus presents an appropriate basis for a detailed understanding of knowledge sharing. The empirical data provide examples of how different forms of knowledge are shared in social interaction and by using different media.

Our study shows that when there are problems with the communication of information such as missing information, poor access to information, or poor quality of information, this determines the extent to which explicit knowledge can be acquired. Similarly, if active participation and learning in practice are hampered or function poorly, this determines the extent to which tacit knowledge can be acquired.

Our work is based on the assumption that a number of different dimensions and perspectives have to be taken into account in order to create a comprehensive understanding of the knowledge sharing process.

Other authors such as Cook and Brown (1999); Comas and Sieber (2001); Kolb (1984); and Nielsen and Kvale (1999) only deal with the relationship between two dimensions such as communication of information and knowledge, or knowledge and learning, or they consider and describe the dimensions as different perspectives on knowledge

sharing. We take all these different dimensions and perspectives into account.

Cook and Brown (1999) identify types of knowledge and knowing which can exist in an organisation and the relationship between them. They consider knowing primarily as productive inquiry. They do neither relate them to the concept of learning or to the importance of communication of information. Comas and Sieber (2001) discuss managing knowing by describing the relationship between experiential learning and knowing. They argue that managing knowing can be described as an experiential process, and they thus emphasis knowing primarily as a learning process. They do not, however, draw on the importance of what precedes this process, namely communication of information, and the actual situation in which learning takes place. Kolb's (1984) learning cycle also concentrates primarily on the learning process with a focus on individual learning which ignores the group dimension of learning and knowledge. Kolb also emphasises how information is gathered and processed in the learning process, but does not deal with what happens before in the form of communication of information. He thus ignores the problems which can arise when obtaining information.

Nielsen and Kvale (1999) identify scholastic learning and practice learning as well as the explicit knowledge and tacit knowledge to which these ways of learning contribute, but they do not clearly deal with the individual and group dimensions of knowledge and learning. We take all these issues into account.

Finally, our understanding of communication is distinct from the original models (Fiske, 1990) by being explicitly directed towards our focus on knowledge and learning processes, and by viewing communication not as a technical, decontextualised process, but as a social process which takes place in a context. We thus emphasise the concepts of social interaction and technical media instead of the technical term *channel,* and we do not use the terms *sender* and *receiver,* but stress the concepts *individual* and *group* in relation to communication.

In summary, our theoretical framework thus contributes to research within the field of knowledge sharing by integrating different areas related to knowledge sharing.

The theoretical framework does however not clearly show how communication in the form of verbal and textual communication and active participation in practice contribute to the acquisition of knowledge through scholastic and practice learning. Kolb's (1984) learning cycle can contribute to many types of knowledge. His learning cycle and the different types of knowledge focus on the individual's learning and the related cognitive process which, Kolb argues, can be dominated by a particular way of learning and type of knowledge. How far multiple learning cycles can take place simultaneously in the same situation is not evident from Kolb's theory. Comas and Sieber (2001) describe the relationship between experience or experiential learning and knowing, but they do not take a position on either, whether or if so, how many learning cycles take place at one time. Cook and Brown (1999), however, argue with respect to the relationship between tacit and explicit knowledge that these are separate types of knowledge, but that one is or can be used as support to acquire the other. We now provide examples from our study and discuss how different types of knowledge contribute to the acquisition of other types of knowledge, how this can be conceptualised as multiple learning cycles, and the consequences this has for our framework.

The Relationship Between Individual and Group Knowledge

A number of developers in our study explained that they discussed technical problems and solutions with other developers using, for example, personal networks and experience groups. We found that the developers had a shared repertoire of phrases for particular types of technical specifications. This indicates that the developers' individual explicit knowledge about, for example, how technological solutions are specified contributes to the group's use of phrases concerning technical specifications, and thus to explicit group knowledge, about specific types of technical specifications.

We also found that the developers primarily store formal documents, that is, documents which are a defined part of the development process or which are somehow related to projects and products, in the DHS. These documents are placed in a strict hierarchical structure which is ordered according to departments, products, and/or projects. This indicates that the developers' skills—tacit individual knowledge of skills and "feel" for which documents should be stored in the DHS, and where—contributes to the genre, tacit group knowledge with respect to which documents are communicated through the system and how they are communicated.

The study also showed that new developers are trained in use of the system through courses and apprenticeship learning. This indicates that the genre tacit group knowledge related to the DHS contributes to the development of the individual developer's skills in relation to the use of these genres. Figure 4 depicts these relationships.

Figure 4. The relationship between individual and group knowledge

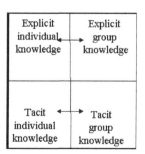

Explicit individual knowledge	Explicit group knowledge
Tacit individual knowledge	Tacit group knowledge

The Relationship Between Explicit and Tacit Knowledge

The relationship between explicit and tacit knowledge is depicted in Figure 5. A number of the developers said that on the basis of books, presentations, and courses they use their understanding of concepts and interrelations to experiment in practice and thereby acquire new skills. This indicates that the individual developers apply explicit knowledge in practice—practice learning which contributes to the acquisition of tacit knowledge in the form of skills. The study also shows that developers who are experts in a particular field tell other developers about how a specific task should be carried out. This can happen through presentations, experience groups, and personal networks, thereby giving other developers the opportunity to gain explicit knowledge about the action related to solving the task in question. This indicates that the developers reflect upon their tacit knowledge and explicate related actions and activities, which they communicate to other developers through scholastic learning.

The study also shows that the project management system which was previously used to plan projects is now only used for general project planning and time registration. According to

Figure 5. The relationship between explicit and tacit knowledge

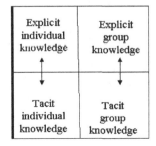

the respondents it ought to be possible to extract estimates for new projects directly from the system, but because the projects are dissimilar, these estimates are hard to use. We also found that some developers had ceased to register time in the system. This indicates that stories—explicit group knowledge—about the deficiencies of the project management system make the developers interpret the information which is communicated through the system in an unfavourable way. They have thus developed a concept of the system which has become tacit group knowledge. The study also shows that the developers reflect over their use of the document handling system as a form of communication in the company which only functions poorly. This contributes to stories among the developers about how their work is made cumbersome by the system, and that necessary documents are hard to find. This shows that the groups reflect on their tacit knowledge and explicate actions related to this knowledge which contribute to the acquisition of stories and phrases in the groups related to the use of genres.

The Relationships between Tacit Individual and Explicit Group Knowledge and Explicit Individual and Tacit Group Knowledge

The relationships between tacit individual and explicit group knowledge and explicit individual and tacit group knowledge are depicted in Figure 6.

We observed how one developer, through use of his skills, developed a browser tool which other developers found useful. It became part of the development toolbox and contributed to the stories and phrases which the members of this group of developers told about useful tools. This shows that developers, through their skills and thus their individual tacit knowledge and its explication in related actions, contribute to the group's stories and phrases, and thus their explicit group knowledge.

Figure 6. The relationships between tacit individual and explicit group knowledge and explicit individual and tacit group knowledge

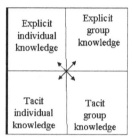

The study also provided examples of how success stories about how to solve a specific task were sometimes transformed into how-to documents, for example how to program in C, which other developers could use to acquire new skills. This indicates that a group's stories enter into individual practice learning which contributes to the development of the individual group member's skills, in this case C programming.

Our findings show that the developers' understanding of the importance of standards for the development work makes them perceive what is communicated as a standard as being specifically important. This indicates that concepts or rules related to the use of a particular form of communication contribute to the development of genres. The study also shows that when developers observe others communicating, they gain knowledge about how, for example, one conducts a presentation or a formal meeting. This indicates that the developer's acquaintance and application of genres contributes to the developers' individual understandings of the concepts, rules, and interrelations which are related to genres.

Knowing as Multiple Learning Cycles

We have shown above how different types of knowledge contribute to the learning of different types of knowledge by drawing from our case study to show how the developers have knowledge which they apply to acquire new knowledge. Figure 7 summarises the relationship between the different types of knowledge and indicates a cyclic connection between them.

The various and different learning situations can also be understood as multiple cycles which can take place simultaneously—in other words, the developers constantly use knowledge to learn in order to create new knowledge. How this relates to the different types of knowledge is shown in Figure 8.

According to Cook and Brown (1999), learning is a process in which an individual or a group processes new information on the basis of existing knowledge which can then be used as a basis for action. The result of the learning process is new knowledge. Following Kolb's (1984) understanding of the learning process and the relationship between different ways of learning and different types of knowledge as expressed in our initial

Figure 7. The relationships between different types of knowledge

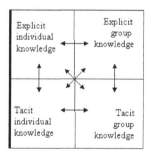

Figure 8. The relationships of different types of knowledge as multiple learning cycles

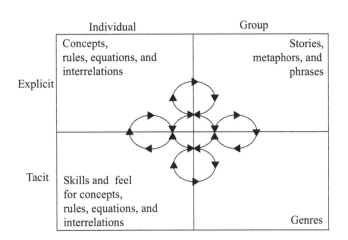

theoretical framework, and relating and comparing these to the relationship of different types of knowledge illustrated as multiple learning cycles and summarised in the preceding paragraph, the following becomes evident:

Tacit knowledge is acquired through practice learning, but when, for example, the developers explain how a task is solved, they reflect upon tacit knowledge. The situation where a developer explains to other developers what he or she has done is scholastic learning. It is not the tacit knowledge itself which becomes explicit through scholastic learning, but the developers acquire new explicit knowledge. This is not the same as being able to solve a particular task. If other developers want to achieve the same tacit knowledge, this can only happen through practice, that is, they themselves must apply the explicit knowledge in practice and participate actively in carrying out the task.

Explicit knowledge can contribute to the acquisition of tacit knowledge through application in practice and through participation in practice learning. At the same time, tacit knowledge contributes to the acquisition of explicit

knowledge through reflection and participation in scholastic learning. Tacit knowledge and explicit knowledge thus supplement each other through reflection and application in practice (see Figure 9). This can be understood as a detailed description of knowing as a learning process. Taking scholastic learning as a starting point, explicit knowledge will always precede an eventual acquisition of tacit knowledge. Taking practice learning as a starting point, tacit knowledge will always precede an eventual acquisition of explicit knowledge. It is a question of whether one starts with scholastic or with practice learning.

The Consolidated Model

The overall relationship between participation in action, communication, learning, and knowledge as the starting point for our theoretical framework was illustrated in Figure 3. On the basis of the study, we have brought together and integrated the theoretical framework's models for knowledge, learning, communication and participation in

303

Figure 9. Learning of explicit and tacit knowledge through scholastic and practice learning

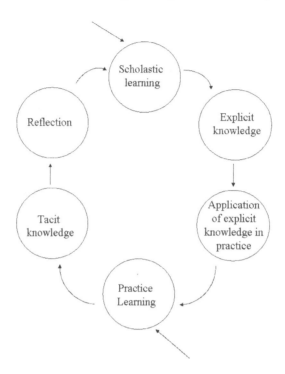

Figure 9. The consolidated model

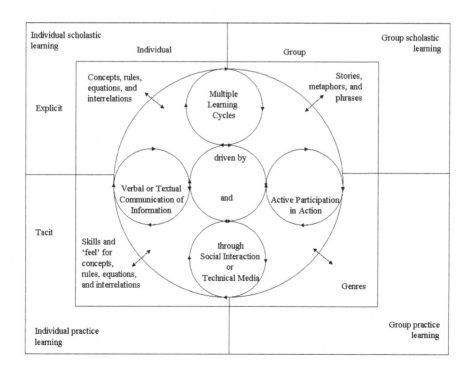

action, and amended them with the evidence for multiple learning cycles explained previously. As a result, the theoretical framework and the study's outcome can be presented in a model of sharing knowledge, where communication consists of verbal and textual communication and active participation in action. Learning comprises learning through scholastic learning, practice learning and multiple learning cycles, and knowledge consists of explicit and tacit individual and explicit and tacit group knowledge.

The model for the sharing of knowledge shows that verbal and textual communication of information through social interaction and/or technical media contribute to individual and group scholastic learning, which thereby contribute to explicit individual and group knowledge. The model also shows that participation in action through social interaction and/or technical media contributes to individual and group practice learning, which thereby contribute to tacit individual and group knowledge. The model for the sharing of knowledge shows in addition how multiple learning cycles and knowing contribute to the acquisition of knowledge.

CONCLUSION AND FUTURE RESEARCH

In the research presented here, we have applied Cook and Brown's (1999) multiple forms of knowledge to an empirical example in software development, emphasising how these forms of knowledge are shared in communication via social interaction or different types of technical media.

Our work resulted in a model of knowledge sharing which can be used to understand and ultimately improve knowledge sharing in practice. Although some concrete advice for improving knowledge sharing could be derived from our analysis, the theoretical framework and our study do not describe how the results of the analysis and

identified areas for improvements can be transformed into concrete organisational or technical improvements, or which strategies organisations should use to improve the sharing of knowledge. Furthermore, we do not include concrete guidelines for the design of information technology and technical media.

Problems related to the technical media lead to limited access to and quality of information. The developers in the case organisation thus use or supplement them with social interaction or other technical media which enable them to gain access to the information or actions which are a prerequisite for their learning processes, and the acquisition of knowledge which is necessary for them to carry out their tasks. How an optimal balance between social interaction and technical media might look has to be decided from case to case, and is again not part of our framework, but it could be constructed with the aid of Hansen, Nohria, and Tierney's (1999) work on codification and personalisation strategies. In this context it is necessary for future research to investigate the relationship between the different types of knowledge in more detail in order to clarify how this relationship can be used to improve the sharing of knowledge.

Finally, the study shows that personal networks play a specific role in the sharing of knowledge, as they link other forms of communication together and compensate for the information which is not communicated through these other forms of communication. The framework does not explain all phenomena related to personal networks with regard to knowledge sharing, and future research based on the framework should thus aim to extend the framework in this respect.

ACKNOWLEDGMENT

With acknowledgments to Dorte Boejstrup and Mads E. Bock, who worked as research assistants on this project during their master's theses.

REFERENCES

Andersen, I. (1999). *The apparent reality—On knowledge production in the social sciences* (3rd ed.) [in Danish]. Copenhagen, Denmark: Samfundslitteratur.

Brown, J. S., & Gray, E. S. (1995). *The people are the company.* Retrieved January 11, 2005, from http://www.fastcompany.com/magazine/01/people.html

Checkland, P., & Scholes, J. (1990). *Soft systems methodology in action.* Toronto, Canada: John Wiley and Sons.

Comas, J., & Sieber, S. (2001). Connecting knowledge management and experiential learning to gain new insights and research perspectives. In *Proceeding of the ECIS 2001,* Bled, Slowenia.

Cook, S. D. N., & Brown, J. S. (1999). Bridging epistemologies: The generative dance between organisational knowledge and organisational knowing. *Organisational Science, 4,* 381-400.

Dahlbom, B., & Mathiassen, L. (1993). *Computers in context—The philosophy and practice of systems design.* Cambridge, UK: Blackwell.

Eisenhardt, K. M. (1989). Building theories from case study research. *Academy of Management Review, 14*(4), 532-550.

Fiske, J. (1990). *Introduction to communication studies* (2nd ed.). London: Routledge.

Hansen, M. T., Nohria, N., & Tierney, T. (1999). What is your strategy for managing knowledge? *Harvard Business Review, 77*(2), 106-116.

Hughes, J., & Jones, S. (2003). Reflections on the use of grounded theory in interpretive information systems research. In *Proceedings of the ECIS 2003 Conference,* Naples, Italy.

Jennex, M. E., & Olfman, L. A. (2005). Assessing knowledge management success. *International Journal of Knowledge Management, 1*(2), 33-49.

Jennex, M. E., & Olfman, L. A. (2006). A Model of knowledge management success. *International Journal of Knowledge Management, 2*(3), 51-68.

Kautz, K., & Thaysen, K. (2001). Knowledge, learning and IT Support in a small software company. *Journal of Knowledge Management, 5*(4), 349-357.

Klein, H., & Myers, M. (1999). A set of principles for conducting and evaluating interpretive field studies in information systems. *MIS Quarterly, 23*(1), 67-93.

Kolb, D. A. (1984). *Experiential learning—Experience as source of learning and development.* New Jersey: Prentice Hall.

Lave, J., & Wenger, E. (1991). *Situated learning: Legitimate peripheral participation.* Cambridge, UK: Cambridge University Press.

Nielsen, J. (1994). Ways to Knowledge [in Danish]. In M. Brorup, L. Hauge, & U.L. Thomsen (Eds.). *Pieces of psychology* (pp. 65-86). Copenhagen, Denmark: Gyldendah.

Nielsen, K., & Kvale, S. (1999). Master-apprenticeship learning: Learning as social practice [in Danish]. Copenhagen, Denmark: Hans Reitzel.

Nonaka, I. (1994). A dynamic theory of organisational knowledge creation. *Organisation Science, 5*(1), 14-37.

Nonaka, I., & Takeuchi, H. (1995). *The knowledge-creating company.* Oxford, UK: Oxford University Press.

Polanyi, M. (1966). *The tacit dimension.* London: Routledge.

Severin, W., & Tankard, J. (1997). *Communication theories* (4th ed.). New York: Longman.

Shannon, C., & Weaver, W. (1949). *The mathematical theory of communication.* Urbana: University of Illinois Press.

Smolnik, S., Kremer, S., & Kolbe, L. (2005). Continum of context explication: Knowledge discovery through process-oriented portals. *International Journal of Knowledge Management, 1*(1), 27-46.

Stenmark, D. (2000). Leveraging tacit organisational knowledge. *Journal of Management Information Systems, 17*(3), 9-24.

Swan, J., Scarbrough, H., & Preston, J. (1999). Knowledge management—The next fad to forget people. In *Proceedings of the ECIS 1999,* Copenhagen, Denmark.

Thompson, M., & Walsham, G. (2001). Learning to value the Bardi tradition: Culture, communication, and organisational knowledge. In *Proceeding of the ECIS 2001,* Bled, Slowenia.

Tsoukas, H. (1996). The firm as a distributed knowledge system: A constructionist approach [Winter special issue]. *Strategic Management Journal, 7,* 11-25.

Tsoukas, H. (1998). The word and the world: A critique of representationalism in management research. *International Journal of Public Administration, 21*(5), 781-817.

Walsh, J. P., & Ungson, G. R. (1991). Organisational memory. *Academy of Management Review, 16,* 57-91.

Wenger, E. (1998). *Communities of practice: Learning, meaning, and identity.* Cambridge, UK: Cambridge University Press.

Wenger, E. C., McDermott, R., & Snyder, W. M. (2002). *Communities of practice—A guide to managing knowledge.* Boston: Harvard Business School.

Wenger, E. C., & Snyder, W. M. (2000). Communities of practice: The organisational frontier. *Harvard Business Review, 78,* 139-145.

This work was previously published in the International Journal of Knowledge Management, edited by M. Jennex, Volume 3, Issue 2, pp. 91-117, copyright 2007 by IGI Publishing, formerly known as Idea Group Publishing (an imprint of IGI Global).

Chapter XIX
E–Collaboration and E–Commerce in Virtual Worlds:
The Potential of Second Life and World of Warcraft

Ned Kock
Texas A&M International University, USA

ABSTRACT

Virtual worlds can be defined as technology-created virtual environments that incorporate representations of real world elements such as human beings, landscapes and other objects. Recent years have seen the growing use of virtual worlds such as Second Life and World of Warcraft for entertainment and business purposes, and a rising interest from researchers in the impact that virtual worlds can have on patterns of e-collaboration behavior and collaborative task outcomes. This article looks into whether actual work can be accomplished in virtual worlds, whether virtual worlds can provide the basis for trade (B2C and C2C e-commerce), and whether they can serve as a platform for credible studies of e-collaboration behavior and related outcomes. The conclusion reached is that virtual worlds hold great potential in each of these three areas, even though there are certainly pitfalls ahead.

INTRODUCTION

Virtual worlds can be defined as environments created by technology that incorporate virtual representations of various elements found in the real world. Among those elements are virtual human beings with whom one can interact, virtual physi-cal environments that include land and oceans, and virtual objects like chairs and tables. Recent years have seen a growing use of virtual worlds for entertainment and business purposes, and a corresponding growing interest from researchers in the impact of virtual worlds on e-collaboration behavior and outcomes (Kock, 2008).

Copyright © 2009, IGI Global, distributing in print or electronic forms without written permission of IGI Global is prohibited.

Some virtual worlds, like Second Life, attempt to replicate elements of the real world with practical applications in mind. Others, like World of Warcraft, are designed with the goal of making people forget about the real world and get immersed in multiplayer games. Users of virtual worlds, sometimes referred to as players or characters, appear to each other as avatars, which are virtual world representations of individuals. Most, but not all, of the avatars have either human or humanoid form; for example, a wolf that walks upright and has hands with opposable thumbs.

The emergence and growing use of virtual worlds begs some interesting questions. Can actual work be accomplished in virtual worlds? Can they provide the basis for trade? Can they serve as a platform for the study of human behavior? This article tries to answer these questions. User interface problems are discussed through a retrospective look at the emergence of online learning courseware several years ago and the discussion of analogies between that and the more recent emergence of virtual worlds. Human evolutionary arguments are put forth for the qualification of the potential of virtual worlds to support modern trade. A discussion of pros and cons to conducting behavioral research in virtual worlds is also presented.

VIRTUAL WORLDS

Virtual reality technologies and artificial worlds created by such technologies may seem now radically new and cutting-edge to many e-collaboration technology users. Yet, Morton Heilig developed an immersive virtual reality technology in the 1950s called Sensorama (see Figure 1), one of the earliest examples of this type of technology. Among other unexpected features for its time, Sensorama simulated odors.

Also, several virtual environments have been conceptualized, designed and used since the 1960s and 1970s for a variety of purposes, notably for

online learning. Those early virtual environments were definitely low-tech when compared with more modern ones, and even modern ones present a great degree of variability in terms of their technology, sophistication and features offered. Strictly speaking, the courseware suites that emerged in the 1990s to support online learning are, in fact, virtual environments, but fall short of the features that characterize virtual worlds.

Virtual worlds are defined here as virtual environments that incorporate most of the elements of the real world, even if those elements are presented in a stylized and somewhat unrealistic manner. Thus, a virtual world would have a terrain, animated things, gravity, and would impose some laws of physics. For example, users could be allowed to fly in the virtual world without the constraints of gravity; but they could also walk, which requires gravity. Two objects would not be allowed to occupy the same physical space at the same time, which is a common requirement for virtual interaction. And so on.

Many virtual worlds exist that can be used through the Internet, each offering different forms

Figure 1. Sensorama virtual reality system

of interaction. The underlying technologies are still evolving. Therefore, it is difficult to place virtual worlds into clearly defined categories, and most classifications likely would not be useful for a long time. Still, there seem to be some clear differences between virtual worlds that attempt to replicate elements of the real world to enable concrete applications, and those that are designed with the goal of making people forget about the real world. The former seem to be designed with more practical purposes in mind, such as to facilitate commercial transactions, while the latter are designed to serve as multiplayer computer gaming platforms.

Second Life, developed by Linden Research (also known as Linden Lab), is a good example of a virtual world that attempts to replicate elements of the real world with practical applications in mind. World of Warcraft, developed by Blizzard Entertainment (a division of Vivendi Games), is a good example of virtual world designed with the goal of making people forget about the real world and become immersed in multiplayer games.

The type of virtual world that is exemplified by Second Life usually contains more human-made elements found in the real world, such as chairs, rooms, buildings, and parks (see Figure 2). Arguably, this type of virtual world is less of a departure from the real world than the type of virtual world represented by World of Warcraft. Also, the elements in the Second Life type of virtual world seem to be easier to reproduce without advanced graphics, which may be one of the reasons why this type of virtual world contains less stunning graphics than the virtual worlds of the World of Warcraft type. Another reason may be simply that video game users expect stunning graphics because they are associated with perceived video game quality. Users in Second Life type virtual worlds appear to each other as avatars, which are virtual world representations of individuals, and most of the avatars have human form. Since users choose the appearance of their avatars, most of the avatars have physical characteristics that many people would consider attractive.

The type of virtual world that is exemplified by World of Warcraft normally contains fewer human-made elements found in the real world, and a great deal more natural elements such as forests, canyons, rivers, mountains, and waterfalls (see Figure 3). The graphics used are generally of higher quality than in the Second Life type of virtual world, and often evoke fantastic and/or

Figure 2. Park scene from Second Life

Figure 3. Dark forest scene from World of Warcraft

mystic themes. Players interact with each other and with artificial intelligence characters, such as monsters, which they often have to fight for the good of a community in the virtual world or simply to remain alive in the virtual world.

Other examples of virtual worlds that could be loosely placed in the same category as Second Life are Active Worlds, There, and ViOS. Other virtual worlds that could be loosely placed in the same category of World of Warcraft are Ever-Quest, Guild Wars, and Ultima Online. Still other virtual worlds that do not fit either category, but lean more toward the World of Warcraft type, are Entropia Universe, Red Light Center (modeled after Amsterdam's Red Light District), and The Sims Online.

USER INTERFACE PROBLEMS

The virtual worlds' theme received quite a lot of attention in the 2007 installment of the International Conference on Information Systems held in December, 2007, in Montreal, Canada. This is the most prestigious conference in the discipline of information systems, which is primarily concerned with the impact of technology on individuals, groups, and organizations. Two panels in that conference focused on the discussion of technological aspects and user perceptions of Second Life and World of Warcraft, as well as one or two lesser known multi-user virtual reality environments.

There was a significant contrast between the perceptions of technology designers and users about virtual worlds. Technology designers, including representatives from IBM and Linden Lab, were quite enthusiastic and positive in their discussions of the technologies that enabled the existence of the virtual worlds. That enthusiasm about technological aspects is arguably well founded since virtual worlds are indeed major technological achievements.

The views from users were quite different, especially when presented by information systems researchers who had conducted apparently disinterested analyses of samples of user perceptions. A constant complaint heard from new users of Second Life is that the interface is rudimentary and the graphics are worse than those found in World of Warcraft and other video games. Users of World of Warcraft, which is much more video game-like than Second Life, also tended to display stronger signs of addiction to their virtual life experiences. Nevertheless, Second Life seems to have many more registered users than World of Warcraft, and concerns about user addiction exist in Second Life as well. Perhaps Second Life has more users because use of World of Warcraft requires purchase of the computer game, while individual use of Second Life is generally free.

It seems from the discussions at the 2007 International Conference on Information Systems that users were much less enthusiastic about the virtual worlds than the technology designers, and that the majority of users had serious problems with the user interfaces. Possibly, the users would have preferred a 1950s Sensorama-like interface updated with today's technology, but it is doubtful that they would be willing to pay what that type of technology would cost now. Other consistent complaints were related to the CPU-intensive nature of the computer programs and the time delays associated with multiple users accessing the systems at the same time over the Internet. Those problems arguably make virtual worlds much less realistic than their designers intended them to be.

Judging from these initial views of Second Life, World of Warcraft and other virtual worlds, it appears that there is a great deal of room for progress in the design of the interfaces. It is likely that a great deal of that progress will happen in the context of video game design, and then be transferred to virtual world technologies that are not inspired in video games. As the huge success of the Nintendo Wii has taught us, one possible direction for progress is improvement in interactivity support through interface devices whose use are more natural than mice and keyboards. The Wii's remote wireless controller, for example, is a handheld pointing device that detects three-dimensional motion and translates that into game actions.

CAN ACTUAL WORK BE ACCOMPLISHED IN VIRTUAL WORLDS?

Several organizations have set up shop in Second Life, and even allow users to buy products and services there using Linden Dollars, the local currency used by Second Life users that is exchangeable by US Dollars. In fact, the designers of Second Life seem to have had support for e-collaboration and e-commerce in the back of their minds when they developed the initial set of features and rules that regulate user interaction. As one can imagine, not everything is possible in Second Life. For example, there are some limits to the size and appearance of avatars, even though users are given many choices. Also, characters in Second Life cannot give themselves just any type of superpowers, even though they can do some supernatural things like flying. All of this begs the question as to whether actual work, which would also include commerce-related work, can be accomplished in virtual worlds like Second Life.

Gary Anthes wrote a very interesting article for Computerworld, an information technology industry magazine, on his experiences in Second Life (Anthes, 2007). What makes the article unique and particularly useful for the discussion presented here is that it is written from the perspective of someone who was looking at the potential of Second Life to serve as an actual e-collaboration and e-business tool. That is, the article looked into whether actual work and commerce could in fact be accomplished in Second Life, and the possible implications for real organizations.

The main conclusion that one can infer from that article is that Second Life is still far from reaching the point at which it will serve as an effective e-collaboration tool for organizations, if it ever reaches that point. Several problems are raised, some of which are related to the design of the virtual environment and many to the way in which organizations use the environment. For example, new users have some obstacles that they need to overcome in order to experience the full interactivity features of Second Life.

Newbies are required to start out doing four simple exercises in a place called Orientation Island. Well three were simple and one was impossible. (Anthes, 2007, p. 31)

After new users overcome the initial obstacles faced at the orientation stage, if they go through the full orientation stage at all (they can skip the full orientation), there are other difficulties related to the use of certain interaction features. As anybody who has participated in Web-based text chat rooms can attest, new users often have a hard time sending their comments to the right people. Often comments are sent to the whole group when they are intended to only one individual or two. The same problem occurs in Second Life.

Many in the audience [of a presentation] apparently didn't realize that the [Second Life] text-chat function allows a user to chat with just one person or with everybody at once. As a result, there were frequent interruptions ... as well as all kinds of random comments. (Anthes, 2007, p. 32)

Additionally, organizations have apparently made mistakes in the establishment of their virtual presence in Second Life, some of which are very basic mistakes. For example, Second Life allows users to jump out of it and into plain Web sites, as long as hyperlinks are properly inserted into it. After all, Second Life runs on an operating system window that can be minimized while its user shifts his or her attention to programs running on other windows or does other things. This is a feature that can be used by companies to turn

an interesting experience in Second Life into a business transaction enabled by a plain e-commerce Web site whose hyperlink is strategically inserted in Second Life. However, that is not always done properly.

I walked into a huge, round auditorium called IBM Theatre I. The seats were all empty, and the stage was bare save for a big whiteboard with some semi-interesting techno-items written on it, each followed by an ordinary Web address. Problem was, the addresses were grayed out, and when I clicked on them, nothing happened. (Anthes, 2007, p. 34)

There are many gems in Anthes' article, which is a relatively long one for an industry magazine. The article also contains inserted in it a rebuttal by Ian Lamont, who agrees with the problems yet is much more enthusiastic about Second Life's future potential. Toward the end of the article, Anthes makes a suggestion that goes to the heart of the problems that many users likely experience in their interactions with companies with a Second Life presence. Following that suggestion could potentially go a long way toward improving their customers' experience.

Each major company location in SL should be staffed by a real person, at least during business hours. (Anthes, 2007, p. 37)

What about World of Warcraft and related virtual worlds? Since they were designed as computer games their potential in their original form to support e-collaboration and e-commerce is much more limited, with some exceptions such as brand development and other selected marketing applications. Nevertheless, a recent event in World of Warcraft points at its potential as a simulation environment that could have real world benefits. The event was the accidental spread of a virtual plague, called the Corrupted Blood plague, which very closely resembled a real world epidemic.

313

Characters affected by the virtual disease, which was contagious, had their abilities impaired in a way that mimicked what would happen if they contracted a disease in the real world. After Blizzard Entertainment contained the disease and confined it to a specific virtual region, researchers started looking at the potential of World of Warcraft for the study of human behavior in response to epidemics. The interest comes in part from recent real world epidemics, such as the severe acute respiratory syndrome (SARS) outbreak in 2002 and 2003, and the apparent lack of preparedness by governments and other organizations in dealing with those epidemics (Ho & Su, 2004).

The prominent emergence of virtual worlds such as Second Life and their rapidly growing user base does not necessarily imply that they have an immediately practical e-collaboration appeal. For a virtual world to have a practical e-collaboration appeal, meaning that actual work can be done in the virtual world, the benefits of e-collaborating through the virtual world must outweigh the costs. Possible benefits are time and dollar savings due to the reduced need for physical transportation to meeting sites. Possible costs are reduced communication fluency and increased communication ambiguity due to cumbersome interfaces and interaction delays.

Past experience tells us that if a virtual community of users is created around a technology and grows beyond a critical mass, then practical e-collaboration applications will follow. One example is the Internet and e-mail, which were initially difficult to use and had little business appeal. Their use is now ubiquitous in business. Any virtual world that attracts a large number of users on a global scale will eventually have a business impact, even if for no other reason than its marketing appeal. This will, in turn, lead to technological improvements that will eventually make e-collaboration through virtual worlds attractive as the benefits of e-collaboration outweigh the costs.

THE FUTURE OF VIRTUAL TRADE: B2C OR C2C?

One of the interesting characteristics of virtual worlds is that they enable interaction between individuals who may be physically far apart from one another (e.g., individuals located in different countries) in a common virtual environment. Those individuals interact as if they were in the same place at the same time, which is sometimes referred to as real-time interaction. Whenever individuals can freely interact in this fashion, one can reasonably expect something to happen. That something is not necessarily falling in love or getting into conflict, although those things may happen as well. That something is a human universal called trade.

A propensity to engage in trade is a human universal in the sense that it is observed in human groups in a wide variety of cultural and physical contexts. In fact, some anthropologists believe that trade is a key element of all human cultures. This means that trade is observed even among non-urban human groups that can individually produce all that they need for their survival. There are many examples of non-urban groups that specialize in the production of items that are consumed by other groups, and that are exchanged by other items produced by the other groups. (The technical term used to refer to this type of exchange is *bartering*, This term is used to indicate any form of trade where money is not used). In non-urban cultures, the reason for this phenomenon seems to be alliance formation rather than the utilitarian need for the items that are traded (the Ricardian model of trade), which in turn reduces the chances of violent conflict among the trading groups (see, e.g., Chagnon, 1977).

In our evolutionary past, this would have increased the reproductive success of the individuals of the groups that engaged in trade compared to groups that did not engage in trade. Violent conflict among any two groups could lead to multiple deaths in both groups. Any environmental element that creates a differential impact on reproductive success also creates the opportunity for genes coding for a related trait to evolve. The trait in this case would be a trading instinct, or a propensity, to engage in trade. The idea here is that all human beings may share genes that induce them to engage in trade. This would explain why, for example, often people buy things that they do not need. Meg Whitman, the long term senior management leader of eBay, has said that trade is in the human DNA. She might not have meant it in the way just discussed here, but that statement is certainly consistent with the notion that trade may well be an evolved mechanism that increased the reproductive fitness of those human ancestors who possessed it.

Trade in virtual worlds is essentially a more sophisticated version of e-commerce, which can be roughly categorized into two main types: business-to-consumer (B2C) and consumer-to-consumer (C2C). There is a growing trend for both B2C and C2C trade to take place on the Web, and many companies have emerged and done quite well in terms of revenues and profits by providing the infrastructure on which e-commerce can take place. Good examples are Amazon, Craigslist, and eBay.

Virtual worlds have the potential to be the new infrastructure providers for B2C and, particularly, C2C. Virtual worlds are likely to be particularly effective at promoting C2C trade because they are exceptionally effective at putting individuals who are geographically dispersed into virtual contact with each other. That, in turn, has the potential to support the growth of virtual worlds, by bringing in users interested in trade who would not otherwise join them, in a closed feedback loop process. Processes that benefit from self-reinforcing feedback loops often experience exponential growth. In this respect, Second Life and similar virtual worlds are perhaps better positioned than their World of Warcraft type counterparts, since the former have apparently been designed to support

virtual trade and work involving geographically dispersed individuals.

One of the reasons why virtual worlds may be particularly appealing as enablers of trade is that they offer a more natural environment than existing Web sites for C2C trade, which is a mode of e-commerce that has been experiencing significant growth recently. If human beings possess a trading instinct, as discussed earlier, then the genes that evolved to code for that instinct did so in what is referred to by evolutionary psychologists as the environment of our evolutionary adaptation (Barkow, et al., 1992; Buss, 1999). In that environment our ancestors interacted face-to-face, since there was no e-mail, instant messaging, or videoconferencing in the Pleistocene or before that. Therefore, one could reasonably expect that the trading instinct will operate more effectively in a face-to-face-like environment today. Second Life provides a more face-to-face-like environment for interaction than Amazon, Craigslist or eBay. Of course, those companies can set up shop in Second Life and get ready for the opportunity that will face them as the self-reinforcing feedback loop process gets started. If the line of reasoning presented here is correct, that would be a wise line of action.

Another interesting conclusion that one can infer from the discussion presented here is that trade growth in virtual worlds is likely to be moderated by human intervention in the form of virtual sales representatives. As pointed out in Gary Anthes' article discussed earlier, it may be quite frustrating for a potential buyer to visit a company-sponsored area in Second Life and not find a sales representative avatar there to help the potential buyer.

The reason is probably analogous to the reason why people generally dislike emoticons when they are used in e-mails to express emotions. In the same way that emoticons are a poor approximation of facial expressions, often perceived as idiotic and/or mocking little faces, a company branch in Second Life without helpful sales representatives is a poor approximation of a real company branch.

Our species evolved a very complex web of facial muscles, probably more complex than that of any other species (Bates & Cleese, 2001; McNeill, 1998). Nearly all of the evidence available suggests that the complex web of muscles has been evolved almost exclusively for communication through facial expressions in various situations. Given this, poor approximations of faces (e.g., emoticons) are likely to be particularly frustrating because of the significant amount of information given off by, and likely sought from, real faces. If the hypothesis that our species also evolved a trading instinct is correct, then one would expect trade in virtual worlds to depend not only on the existence of an environment that is similar to the real world, but on human interactions that are also similar to those found in the real world where our human ancestors lived. In that ancient world one would not exchange spears for bananas by following instructions on a cave painting. One would likely interact with another ancestral human who would extol the qualities of his or her bananas, sort of like a virtual sales representative would do in a virtual world, and ask pointed questions about the quality of the spears.

Hence the need for virtual sales representatives that act like real human beings, that is, that have real human beings behind them. This would be necessary, at least initially, as users become familiar with the virtual world, after which experienced users would likely be willing to engage in trade without virtual human intervention, much like users do today through Web sites designed for e-commerce transactions. Virtual sales representatives entirely created by artificial intelligence software are not likely to do very well in that respect. The famous Turing Test suggests that human beings are exceptionally good at recognizing artificial systems trying to pass as real human beings. Another implication of this discussion is that, at least initially, C2C trade may become a stronger driver than B2C

trade in the establishment of virtual worlds as mainstream trading environments.

STUDYING HUMAN BEHAVIOR IN VIRTUAL WORLDS

As mentioned earlier, the 2007 International Conference on Information Systems had several presentations and panel discussions that focused on virtual worlds and their impact on various aspects of human behavior. Several researchers hailed virtual worlds as new and promising tools for research on human behavior in those presentations and discussions. However, in the questions and answers period that followed those presentations and discussions, virtual world users in the audience noted that, particularly in Second Life, all avatars look like beautiful people in their 20s and 30s. It was pointed out in follow-up discussions that quite a lot of deception may be going on in virtual worlds. That creates a problem for researchers, who often want to find out if there are correlations between certain types of behavioral patterns and demographic variables such as age, gender, income and country of origin. Even if virtual world users were willing to disclose demographic information about them, probably many would be inclined to lie a bit about that information.

Another difficulty of using virtual worlds to conduct behavioral research is that the multitude of possible effects on individual behavior may make isolation of specific effects difficult. Much of human technology interaction research is conducted through controlled experiments for exactly that reason. In controlled experiments, the investigators focus on one or a few particular independent variables, such as communication media naturalness (Kock, 2005), and then randomly group the subjects they are studying (i.e., the human participants in the experiment) into conditions associated with those variables. The goal is usually to isolate the effect of the independent variable (or variables) on an important dependent variable. One example of important dependent variable would be an individual's satisfaction with a trade interaction conducted in the virtual world. By employing this procedure, the investigators can study in a focused manner the effect of the independent on the dependent variable, much in the same way that pharmaceutical drug researchers do. Drug researchers often isolate the effect of certain drugs by randomly assigning their study subjects to control (placebo) and treatment (drug) groups.

On the other hand, virtual worlds can be quite useful tools for research that requires more realistic scenarios than those normally used in controlled experiments. One example is the study of large-scale human behavior in response to a disease outbreak or an environmental disaster. What differentiates this type of investigation from the controlled experiment form discussed above is that the researchers are interested primarily in large-scale group responses. In these types of responses, the characteristics and behavior of one individual, or of small groups, are not of major importance. One useful analogy is the modern study of the behavior of investors in certain markets in response to macroeconomic changes, such as changes in a country's government-regulated interest rates. In many cases, these types of studies can be credibly done even if the researchers disregard individual differences.

This is not to say that controlled experiments cannot be done in virtual worlds. They can as long as certain precautions are taken. For example, a researcher can assemble a group of human subjects prior to them creating their avatars, and collect reliable demographic information from each of them. Then each subject would create a unique avatar in a controlled manner (e.g., no major changes in appearance compared to the real world), and have his or her behavior studied over a period of time in particular circumstances in the virtual world that also contain controlled elements (e.g., virtual crowding or information overload levels).

The researcher could create sub-environments where different subjects' avatars would interact randomly; assigning different individuals to sub-environments and then comparing behavior patterns observed in each sub-environment.

CONCLUSION

As we look at the user interface problems of emergent virtual worlds, it is instructive to also look back at the early versions of online courseware like Blackboard and WebCT. Many of the problems with early online courseware suites were interface-related, and some of those problems led to dire predictions about the demise of online instruction and of the companies behind it. Those predictions were made by those at one end of a spectrum of enthusiasm regarding online learning - the very negative end of the spectrum. At the other, positive end of the spectrum, there were those who felt that online learning tools were going to revolutionize education, changing it dramatically and forever. That, in turn, led some successful enterprises to be established and flourish over the years, such as for-profit educational institutions like the University of Phoenix. It also led to some miserable failures in similar areas, such as various fully-online branches of traditional not-for-profit universities.

And where are we today with online learning? Well, after all the hype in the 1990s, the main trend seems to be to use it to deliver selected courses online and to augment more traditional forms of instruction in other courses. Most university classes are still taking place face-to-face with a slowly growing proportion of them taking place online. There are clear tradeoffs for students and instructors, and more growth is seen in contexts where the cost/benefit ratio is low; for instance, among working students in areas where high bandwidth Internet access is available.

Several empirical studies suggest that it is more cognitively demanding to interact online for both instructors and students. That is, interacting online requires more mental effort and can often lead to mental fatigue faster than face-to-face interaction. Nevertheless, online instruction also gives students who work full time, live in rural areas, or suffer from physical disabilities the opportunity to obtain the education they need to improve their professional and personal lives. Also, in spite of cognitive demands, there is evidence that learning performance is not significantly affected, either positively or negatively. This no-significant-difference effect probably is a result of compensatory adaptation to the less natural online learning media (Kock, et al., 2007).

It is difficult to predict the impact that virtual worlds will have on individuals, groups, and the society as a whole in the future. One possibility is particularly enticing though, and is related to the potential of virtual worlds to contribute to world peace. As mentioned earlier, a propensity to engage in trade appears to be a human universal, a social instinct evolved in part to reduce the chances of violent conflict among the trading parties. Trade also often has a utilitarian purpose, which is to enable the economic production and consumption of goods and services at cost and quality levels that would not otherwise be possible.

From an international trade perspective, this can lead to two main benefits: a reduction in the likelihood that individuals from different trading nations will be willing engage one another in violent conflict; and, possibly, better and cheaper products and services. Yet the trading instinct evolved in our evolutionary past, when our ancestors communicated primarily through natural face-to-face interactions. Thus, one would expect that its social catalyst effect will be realized if modern humans: (a) trade on a one-on-one basis (i.e., in a C2C mode) or in small groups; and (b) interact through communication media that have levels of naturalness that are similar to face-to-face interaction. As user interface problems are gradually resolved, virtual worlds will provide those natural communication media, and may,

in turn, help promote world peace through C2C trade.

ACKNOWLEDGMENT

The author would like to thank Arthur Kock and Monica Kock, who know a great deal about computer games, for their comments and suggestions on an earlier version of this article. Various publicly available definitions, descriptions, and multimedia materials related to virtual reality and virtual worlds have been used as a basis for this article. Particularly useful sources were the Web sites maintained by Google and Wikipedia.

REFERENCES

Anthes, G. (2007). Second Life: Is there any there there? *Computerworld*, 41(49), 30-38.

Barkow, J.H., Cosmides, L., & Tooby, J. (Eds.). (1992). *The adapted mind: Evolutionary psychology and the generation of culture*. New York, NY: Oxford University Press.

Bates, B., & Cleese, J. (2001). *The human face*. New York, NY: DK Publishing.

Buss, D.M. (1999). *Evolutionary psychology: The new science of the mind*. Needham Heights, MA: Allyn & Bacon.

Chagnon, N.A. (1977). *Yanomamo: The fierce people*. New York, NY: Holt, Rinehart and Winston.

Ho, M.S., & Su, I.J. (2004). Preparing to prevent severe acute respiratory syndrome and other respiratory infections. *The Lancet Infectious Diseases*, 4(11), 684-689.

Kock, N. (2005). Media richness or media naturalness? The evolution of our biological communication apparatus and its influence on our behavior toward e-communication tools. *IEEE*

Transactions on Professional Communication, 48(2), 117-130.

Kock, N. (Ed.). (2008). *Encyclopedia of e-collaboration.* Hershey, PA: Information Science Reference.

Kock, N., Verville, J., & Garza, V. (2007). Media naturalness and online learning: Findings supporting both the significant- and no-significant-difference perspectives. *Decision Sciences Journal of Innovative Education,* 5(2), 333-356.

McNeill, D. (1998). *The face: A natural history.* Boston, MA: Little, Brown and Company.

This work was previously published in the International Journal of e-Collaboration, edited by N. Kock, Volume 4, Issue 3, pp. 1-13, copyright 2008 by IGI Publishing, formerly known as Idea Group Publishing (an imprint of IGI Global).

Chapter XX
Socializing a Knowledge Strategy

Peter H. Jones
Redesign Research, USA

ABSTRACT

Proponents of the resource-based view of strategic management have argued for processes that align organizational knowledge resources to business strategy. In this view, a unique competitive advantage accrues from accelerating organizational learning and non-appropriable knowledge. An empirical approach known as socialization counters theories of both institutionalization and "strategic alignment." Socialization diffuses an organization's knowledge strategy through values leadership and practice-led process redesign. Consistent with structuration theory (interaction of agency and structure), socialization creates enduring, flexible process structures co-constructed by leaders and participants in a domain of practice. Socialization results in durable, accessible processes, uniquely configured to business strategy, and more resilient than acquired process structures. Values leadership orients participants toward the goals, meaning, and value of organizational knowledge inherent in indigenous processes. Socialized business processes are driven by strategic intent, are non-appropriable by competitors, and are oriented to enduring organizational values that protect process integrity. A socialization approach integrates practice-level internal knowledge networks to support business processes and strategy, leveraging and exchanging knowledge more effectively than authoritative ("top-down") institutionalization.

INTRODUCTION

Since Nonaka's (1991) concept of the knowledge-creating company, businesses have attempted to organize knowledge as a resource or asset of the firm, with the purpose of creating competitive advantage based on knowledge. Recent surveys and industry trends show that, after a decade of development of knowledge management (KM) as a technology enabler for organizational learning

Copyright © 2008, IGI Global, distributing in print or electronic forms without written permission of IGI Global is prohibited.

and knowing, few of KM's original propositions have been fulfilled. Contemporary firms have found Nonaka's model of the knowledge-creating company untenable in practice, for reasons ranging from cultural differences to the changing business climate. The originally envisioned promises of information technology have failed to harness tacit knowledge in any meaningful way, and "knowledge sharing" applications have largely reverted to document exchange within the current deployments of organizational portals. But regardless of KM technology over-reach, the significant opportunities for competitive advantage envisioned by *knowledge strategy* have been overlooked by modern organizations. Since the advantages of knowledge strategy are not associated with recognized methods for quantifying internal rates of return, consulting practice has also bypassed this opportunity. We find in knowledge strategy a strong theoretical basis with few empirical applications.

Knowledge strategy was proposed by Zack (1999) and others during the period of rapid KM technology diffusion, and remains overlooked by many strategy thinkers. Most research following Zack focuses on strategies for knowledge management, and not knowledge-based strategy. This discussion builds upon Zack's proposition and explicates the relationship of knowledge resources and processes to competitive *business strategy*. The relationship of organizational knowledge to competitive advantage is often noted, but poorly operationalized in research and practice. The following discussion presents a model for strategic management based on an organization's knowledge, processes, and values. An empirical approach known as *socialization* counters the popular theory of "strategic alignment." Instead, this treatment develops a model of enabling knowledge strategy through values leadership and practice-level socialization.

Recent research revises Nonaka's and Zack's models and suggests strategic applications of the basic theories behind knowledge management.

This body of work draws together theory and observation in applications to business strategy. Penrose's (1959) theory of strategic growth underpins the notion that superior knowledge resources enhance the firm's competitive position. A well-established line of thinking and research extends from Penrose through Nelson and Winter's (1982) evolutionary economics theory to current strategy research (Grant, 1996; Venkatraman & Tanriverdi, 2005; Zack, 1999). This school of thought views the firm as a collection of dynamic capabilities that create and integrate knowledge as a necessary resource for competition. A major goal of business strategy drawing from this *internal* perspective is to develop dynamic capabilities that effectively respond to changing, *external* market trends and competitive conditions.

While management research has explicated a meaningful association between strategic growth theory and knowledge practices, a daunting gulf of execution is found in management practices. Theoretically sound research does not necessarily inspire leadership action. The linkages between knowledge strategy and organizational leadership are rarely described empirically, with some notable exceptions (Winter, 1987). While Nonaka's (1991) research presents extraordinary observations from Japanese business culture, there are cultural determinations and organizational barriers in the application of such models in different business climates and organizational cultures.

Rescuing Strategy from Knowledge Management

Knowledge management (KM) developed within industry from the converging trends of management theories of organizational knowledge and the rapid diffusion of cost-effective information technology (IT). The influential convergence of technology overshadowed the management theories, which remain under-appreciated in firms that deployed KM, expecting to build knowledge-creating organizations. We find almost no current research or even case studies reporting the effectiveness of organizational knowledge strategies sans IT. Yet research from a sociology of knowledge perspective shows the static models of knowledge adopted by most technology frameworks are inadequate at best (Orlikowski, 2002), and may be ill-conceived for the purposes of dynamic organizations.

Failed knowledge management initiatives are common, if not legendary. Obviously failures are not as widely publicized by firms as "successes," which often are merely those projects succeeding by fact of their completion. From the very start, KM technology suffered difficulties with organizational adoption and business purpose. Chae and Bloodgood (2006) report a meta-analysis of KM-related initiatives (including IT and organizational change initiatives), finding more reports of KM failures than success. Also citing Malhotra (2004) and Mertins, Heisig, and Vorbeck (2001), they report a study across more than 1,200 European firms that fewer than 10% were satisfied with their KM initiatives.

Some critics in information science consider the appropriated concept of knowledge in KM as a meaningless glorification of "information." Wilson (2002) exhausts the published literature in a critical meta-analysis deconstructing the value and meaning of "knowledge" as found in peer-reviewed KM articles. He finds no relationship between Polanyi's (1967) concept of *tacit knowing* and the framing of *knowledge* across the business and information systems literatures. If Wilson is at least partially correct in his analysis, the emphasis on knowledge as a stock/resource may be misleading and widely misinterpreted. He places blame on its highly-visible adoption by management consultancies and the original Nonaka research itself (for misconstruing Polanyi). However, Wilson and other critics also miss the context within which Nonaka's work is presented. While Nonaka correctly cites and interprets Polanyi's tacit knowing, the knowledge-creation cycle has been lifted from context and

widely used as a general purpose model of organizational knowledge *management*. Knowledge creation is not a general process applicable to all organizational functions.

Simple explanations readily appear for the "failure" of KM to take hold. Our management theories of knowledge may be wrong, from Nonaka (1991) to Chae and Bloodgood (2006), untenable and untested. The focus on KM technology may misdirect valuable organizational attention, preventing organizations from implementing valuable knowledge management theory. Or, organizations generally lack the thoughtful leadership necessary to deploy *organizationally-centered* knowledge management, a critique that emerges between the lines in Nonaka's own explanations of the cross-cultural differences between KM as found in Japan and the U.S.

Knowledge management *as technology* cannot resolve or address the paradox of knowledge strategy. In the concept of knowledge strategy, managers recognize the competitive advantage of organizational knowing and learning, guided by strategic goals and constituted in effective internal processes. The paradox emerges when executives envision the strategic value of developing knowledge as a resource of the firm, but have no control, accounting, or valuation of knowledge as an actual asset. The top-down vantage point of (traditional) strategy is unable to generate knowledge exchange within an organization, unlike the control of other assets. Simply put, knowledge does not function as a strategic *asset* (Venkatraman & Tanriverdi, 2005); it cannot be sold or exchanged like a building or plant. Strategically, firms following this model may operate from an unworkable theory.

Another explanation accounts for these and also suggests a resolution. The development of "strategic knowing," or knowledge contributing to organizational competitiveness, is not a matter of cultivating and cataloguing knowledge assets. It is based on the dynamic capabilities orientation (Grant, 1996; Teece, Pisano & Schuen,

1997), rather than the stock assets view inherent in knowledge management. Strategic knowing is a process of organizational socialization that occurs over time, under the guidance of values-oriented leadership. (While this is not Nonaka's "socialization" as the function of transferring tacit-to-tacit knowledge, it is consistent with the notion of organizational knowledge exchange within processes.)

Reframing the Strategic Context of Knowledge

The argument for organizational investment in knowledge management is based on business strategic need, competitiveness based on innovation or market growth. But the essential promises of knowledge management have not been widely fulfilled since the widespread emergence of Nonaka's formative definitions. Management theory appropriated knowledge management as a way to implement Nonaka's theory, but only to invest in popular technological panaceas that eventually disappointed. IT deployments, KM among them, can delay the difficult changes necessary to accomplish organizational knowledge integration as people focus on the new functions routinized by information systems.

Recent research (King & Zeithaml, 2003) finds the value and leverage of knowledge resources highly variable by industry and organization, and a generic set of knowledge resources will not be competitive across industries. Competitive *specific* knowledge, non-appropriable processes and capabilities, are not amenable to development using a common method across firms. Therefore, deployment of similar technological (IT) enablers across firms also results in no competitive advantage to any one firm solely due to the change. Venkatraman and Tanriverdi (2005) note that while IT investments have been shown to improve intrafirm performance, IT fails to satisfy the competitive requirements of "rareness, inimitability, nonsubstitutability." It nearly goes without saying

that the best possible outcome with even advanced technology would be a more advanced, but still commonly available, baseline of technological infrastructure. Improving productivity does not necessarily improve competitive position and at best supports operational effectiveness and to some extent growth. They argue that knowledge resources may not be accessible using quantitative "content-free" approaches such as research and development (R&D) expenditures, patent data, or research surveys that presuppose managers' assumptions about organizational knowledge.

We should therefore concede that technology-based knowledge management made promises that were impossible to fulfill, whether due to technology or inappropriate models of knowledge. But the inability to develop a strategic approach to leveraging a firm's knowledge may have more to do with its priorities, routinized processes, and organizational values. In most firms, except the start-up and small, a vast organizational gap stretches between strategic management and knowledge-based practices. The applications of "knowledge" are very different between these organizational domains. In strategic practice, the fundamental definitions and understanding of knowledge, whether possessed by individuals or organization, relate to knowledge as *owned by the firm* as a competitive resource. At the level of *practice*, knowledge remains deeply embedded in individual expertise, localized communities of practice, and unique work processes developed in the course of everyday problem solving. How do we resolve these two differently-scaled organizational knowledge resources?

Observations of product development organizations characterized by continuous knowledge work reveal knowledge functions as an *activity*, not as an asset or collection of identifiable resources. Even the commonly-held notions of tacit and explicit *knowledge* betray this objectification of knowledge. As Orlikowski (2002) points out, Polanyi's (1967) original conception of *tacit knowing* was based in the performance of practice, of know-*how*, not know-*what*, as she claims "enacted—every day and over time—in people's practices" (p. 250). Choo (1998) also promotes the notion of the "knowing organization," based on Weick's (1995) organizational sense-making and organizational learning (Argyris & Schön, 1978). Nonaka (1991, 1996) also speaks of *knowing*, but his core model of the knowledge creation process encouraged a turn toward objectification, which neatly corresponded to the extraordinary diffusion of information technology within the same decade. While this "resource view of knowledge" may have led to the innovations known as knowledge management systems, its impact on competitive business strategy was disappointing. In recent work and interviews, Nonaka clarifies his stance toward the vision for management action as Venkatraman and Tanriverdi (2005) state in their conclusion:

The current state of clarity in this area is woefully inadequate if this is to emerge as an important anchor for new perspectives of strategic management. Time is right for making important strides in this area so that we can better understand drivers of organizational success that go beyond tangible assets. (2005, p. 59)

It is no wonder that the promise of "competing on knowledge" has proven confusing in practice. From a strategy perspective (rather than knowledge practices), it appears there are no *objects* called knowledge to manage, no levers to move "knowledge" in this way. However, adapting to the distinctions developed in the concept of "knowing" rather than knowledge fundamentally revises the strategic notion of "competing on knowledge." These are not subtle differences, but instead significant variations that should update our mental models about knowledge management, knowledge strategy, and even "knowledge work."

STRATEGY AND ORGANIZATIONAL KNOWLEDGE RESOURCES

Knowledge strategy is an application of a resource-based, internal strategy directed toward improving competitive performance, as opposed to a school or theory of strategic thought (Mintzberg, 1990, 1994). Essentially this means "competing on knowledge," as opposed to competing by position, growth, customer intimacy, or other relationships to the market that improve or maintain competitive leverage. Knowledge strategy has often been reduced to innovation strategy, under the assumption that innovation is the most knowledge-intensive process in most firms. Some accounts of knowledge strategy develop "strategies of managing knowledge" (Tierney, 1999) which, as explained, result in IT deployment for "knowledge sharing" as document management, and coordinating and cataloguing intellectual property. My account of knowledge strategy is based on the Zack (1999) definition of coordinating intangible resources (referred to as knowledge) toward a planned, sustainable competitive advantage.

But unlike most approaches to competitive strategy, knowledge (or "knowing") is exclusively a resource of the firm, and does not necessarily correspond to industry or market structures. Knowledge, as informed capability, constitutes the core of all competencies. To a great extent, knowledge strategy is a model of competency development. Organizational knowing may be the most *significant* enabler of firm capabilities and non-appropriable processes, but does any firm compete solely on its "knowledge" as a competitive strategy? Most published perspectives of knowledge strategy affirm its enabling relationship to *business strategy*.

The notion of distinguishing a knowledge strategy from business strategy suggests an inherent difficulty of mobilizing knowledge as a business resource. After all, we do not speak of human resources as a competitive strategy. But knowledge has been adopted as such, at least by innovation strategists, if not growth and market/industry strategists. While human and organizational knowledge may be core competitive resources, few firms maintain an active knowledge-based strategy as a practice in strategic management. This suggests one, or a mix of, the following situations in strategic management:

- Knowledge strategy remains insufficiently developed in theory and practice to deploy in competitive business strategy,
- Knowledge has been fully adopted as an internally managed resource and requires no exclusive attention by strategy, or
- Managers largely ignore knowledge resources in strategic thinking and typically focus on competitors, industry structures, and other externalities.

As with most applications to organizational knowledge management, Zack's (1999) approach distinguishes the value of developing tacit and explicit knowledge resources. The central contribution of this approach shows in reciprocal relationship of coordinating KM with business strategy, and aligning and developing knowledge resources as an organizational strategy. Organizational knowledge therefore follows a firm's competitive demands, as the strategic *internal* complement to an externally-facing competitive strategy.

Internally-focused approaches to business strategy (e.g., cultural, learning, organizational) adopt a resource-based view (RBV) of the firm (Barney, 1986; Penrose, 1959) as a theory of growth. Zack (1999), taking this view of "Penrose rents," expresses knowledge strategy as an *alignment* of an organization's knowledge resources to its competitive business strategy, with the aim of leveraging internal resources in the context of external competitive demands. Alignment is

viewed as a strategic selection process: "How should an organization determine which efforts are appropriate, or which knowledge should be managed and developed?" The development of the knowledge strategy approach draws from this guideline, suggesting "the most important context for guiding knowledge management is the firm's strategy," and this link, "while often talked about, has been widely ignored in practice" (Zack, 1999, p. 125).

Such a link may seem obvious to business thinkers. But the links between business strategy and knowledge are by no means direct. Business strategy is a complexity management exercise, with its focus on markets, risk, and uncertainty, growth of market share and profit, product portfolios, customer retention, alliancing, and competitor growth. Organizational knowledge represents complex human issues and practices, such as individual and team knowledge integration, organizational learning, unique and embedded routines and management processes, intellectual property and intangible capital, and incentives and benefits for knowledge sharing. Given these differential goals and drivers, knowledge strategy decision makers inhabit different organizational worlds from those setting business direction. How should decision makers identify and select investments in knowledge and organizational change with strategic goals set by executives in a completely dissociated context?

Knowledge is viewed as "the fundamental basis of competition" (Zack, 1999, p.145). But knowledge does not arise as a freely available resource; it emerges from within and makes sense within a particular organizational culture, is directed toward organizational goals, and constrained within contexts of organizational processes and values. Organizational knowledge and values represent competitive resources, since these enable cooperative behavior toward economic development, and resist appropriation or replication by competitors. Therefore, even individual knowledge ties deeply to the organizational context, and may be significantly nontransferable outside that context (Barney, 1986). To some extent, individual experts (and their knowing) are not readily transferable to other firms due to their unique expertise drawing from a co-emergence of their learning and knowledge within the organizational context of its development.

Another paradox emerges from the question of where organizational knowledge actually lives. Do we find "organizational knowing" within the person (organizational *agent*), or the organizational *structures* that motivate and generate the knowledge-producing activity of the person? This question is important from a strategic management perspective, since leadership must select the highest-leverage internal investments in an internal strategy. This account proposes a resolution of the paradox in both theoretical and pragmatic terms. The structures of organizational knowing are located in the firm's processes and related community practices. Individual know-how is deeply integrated within these processes, and is also subject to and motivated by individual and institutional *values*. We propose the link between values and processes as a significant, yet missing function in strategic management.

Organizational Functions of Knowledge Strategy

The first decade of knowledge management (1991-2000) started with observations of knowledge used as flow, as knowledge creation (Nonaka, 1991), then recognized as exchange or transfer (Zander & Kogut, 1995). The eventual reliance on IT enablers that popularized the field largely focused on knowledge as an *asset* of organizations (Hall, 1993), an approach which (by definition of asset) converts knowledge into a target of management, subject to budgeting, controls, and procedure. In practice, organizations found knowledge *as assets* to be intangible, unmanageable by classic means of control, and difficult to transfer and apply to concrete situations requiring expertise or innova-

tion. The mistakes made in KM applications were, predictably, those of applying then-current information technologies to the emerging knowledge problems. Technology claims were often based on operationalizing subtle cognitive concepts, such as the "conversion of tacit to explicit knowledge." Other claims, such as searching for unrealized knowledge through data mining, were based on emerging IT capabilities, but were unsupported by empirical research or the original theories leading to such operationalized approaches. This divergence of KM technology from its originating theory eventuated in significant disconnects between claim and operational system.

A more critical perspective of the knowledge management literature reveals knowledge treated as a property contained within individuals, and as a manageable resource expressed in similar terms as information. The common dichotomy of tacit and explicit knowledge as referring to "types" signifies this model in use. The knowledge *creation* cycle (Nonaka, 1991) has been detached to refer to taxonomic types of knowledge, which was not the intent of its originating context (even if Nonaka does describe knowledge creation as "stock"). Once defined as *types*, categories became appropriated as ostensible resources in information technology and asset management approaches. It remains common in practice to hear of projects attempting to encode tacit knowledge into explicit forms for organizational reuse (Drew, 1999; Tierney, 1999), implicitly referring to knowledge as a stock (Venkatraman & Tanriverdi, 2005).

Venkatraman and Tanriverdi (2005) identify three schools of thought of knowledge adoption in strategic use: as stock, as flow, and as driver of an organizational capability. While all three perspectives offer value as strategic drivers for knowledge, they attest to similar criticisms with the stocks and flow perspectives as cited here. Essentially, the value of knowledge as a strategic asset or stock (from the RBV perspective) is that strategic knowledge stock (per Penrose) are nontradable, non-imitable and nonsubstitutable

(Teece, 1998). This is often reflected by firms in measures such as research and development spending, which reflects consideration as a cumulative asset base.

From a strategic perspective, knowledge resources are better viewed as an organizational capability, as dynamic practices that create and integrate knowledge (Grant, 1996; Teece et al., 1997; Zack, 1999) and not as ostensible assets (stocks). Theoretical support for this approach draws from Penrose's (1959) resource-based view of the firm in which sustainable competitive advantages accrue to firms that leverage internal knowledge to develop unique, nonreplicable routines and processes (Grant, 1996; Spender, 1994). Here the focus is on continuous, dynamic learning practices, as embedded in routines or processes. While strategy cannot quantify the asset value of knowledge as stock, strategy should specifically select knowledge processes to be adopted or enhanced for competitive advantage. This involves the identification of missing or subperforming capabilities and selection of processes and practices that will reliably produce the required performance.

There are few good examples of firms effectively adopting knowledge strategy as business guidance. Knowledge management theories may have launched numerous experimental IT implementations, but managers may not find KM sufficiently motivating to dramatically reconfigure a firm's approach to strategy, planning, and human resources. Organizations are more likely to take incremental steps toward a knowledge-based business strategy, an approach which treats valuable human-centered knowledge as one of many "intangible" resources. Since Porter's (1980, 1998) ideas remain influential in corporate strategy, we might also expect to find a continuing reception of resource-based strategy as a complementary or supplemental approach.

In many Western firms, adapting resources and initiatives to an emergent or learning-oriented strategic models may incur significant risks in operations and management disruption. There are several reasons for this assertion, ranging from the difficulty most organizations have in designing competitive strategies, to the disruptive shift caused by significant changes in strategic goals, to the need to re-educate or replace management to accomplish and execute a knowledge-based strategy. Investment in enhancing the dynamic capability of processes (and the people participating in those processes) can be incompatible with cost drivers (as found in most process re-engineering). Although process re-engineering (Davenport, Thomas, & Short, 1990; Hammer & Champy, 1993) has been widely misapplied since its inception, cost-based process redesign continues as a common business response, arguing against a process-oriented knowledge strategy. Reviewing the originating claims of business process re-engineering (BPR), its model suggests substantial value as a type of process-based knowledge strategy. This view has been supported by current research into process redesign as strategy (Wu, 2002) and has matured to embrace knowledge-enabled BPR applications (Heusinkveld & Benders, 2001).

As with other trends in popular management, or "management fads," the originating theories and unique real-world applications of those theories had significant merit. However, general applications of such theories may often fail in practice, essentially proving the strategic knowledge claim of nontransferable processes and inimitability. Even a cursory review of the successful implementations of knowledge creation (Nonaka, 1991, 1996) and BPR reveals potential conjoint factors influencing the successful cases, such as national and organizational culture, organizational need and commitment, the fortunate coordination of such initiatives to compatible business strategy, supportive organizational values, and so on. Organizations are laboratories of social complexity, but published accounts typically distill theoretical claims beyond the pragmatic applications that proved the original claim. The real-world applications in actual firms show mixed results.

Research indicates that competitive advantages are created by the very uniqueness and embeddedness of firm-specific processes that generate market growth and are difficult to transfer. We should not expect business or knowledge strategy to be any more transferable than successful processes. In fact, strategic management is a type of knowledge-based process, subject to the same factors of uniqueness to firm leverage of specialized internal resources, uniquely motivating values and significant inimitability. Strategy is always a "custom solution" to a business problem.

Yet the purpose of research is to learn from observations and develop reliable accounts to enable further learning. We must make generalizations from particular cases that correspond closely enough to theoretical models to suggest general working theories of pragmatic strategic practice. We find, from the history of these theoretically-driven approaches to management strategy, two strategic knowledge functions of every organization: processes and values. Many organizations modify their processes to adapt to changing market drivers or strategic intent, and it may be the most common lever employed in implementation. Top-down process change, while necessary, is insufficient.

Processes carry the organizational values and expectations for the internal customer served by the process, as well as individual and practice values of process participants. Therefore, all constituents of an integrated, interconnected process are affected when the practices and routines used in that process change. But the most significant overlooked factor may be the difficulty in changing embedded organizational values within processes, which tend to maintain an operational status quo (Jones, 2000) regardless of the process mechanics. Organizational values determine the priorities upon which decisions are made (Christensen, 1997; Dose & Klimoski, 1999; Oliver, 1999), implicitly constraining the range of practices and filtering the opportunities available in new practices.

Resource-Based Strategic Perspective

Before the rise of two knowledge-based trends in business (innovation and knowledge management), popular approaches to strategic planning adapted Porter (1980) Five Forces model of strategy. Porter's model was based on competitive positioning within an industry structure to generate monopoly rents. Firms defined strategy based on five positions within their markets, based substantially on a stable, knowable field of competition.

While a resource view strongly implies a coherent internal knowledge strategy, observations and popular articles show most firms operate from and within an industry-facing, Porter's (1980, 1998) perspective based on industry structure, positioning, and external competition. The extraordinary rise of mergers and leveraged financing of global and large national firms in the first years of the twenty-first century show the Porter model is alive and well. The Five Forces perspective continues to dominate popular business thinking and, more importantly, in the guidance of execution. If we evaluate the models of knowledge strategy in the context of contemporary business conditions and even cultures, these two approaches appear to be incompatible in theory and practice.

Nelson and Winter (1982) and Teece (1984) were early critics of Porter's external "industry" view, holding to a model of strategy based on internal resources of the firm, of which knowledge can be considered among the most significant. More recently, Spender (1994), Kogut and Zander (1996), Grant (1996), and Zack (1999) further developed theories and dynamics of knowledge-based resource strategy, drawing from Penrose's (1959) theory of the growth of the firm. Penrose's observations were significant contributions to strategies of economic value, from empirical explanations of growth dynamics based on leveraging internally-managed resources. Adherents to Penrose promote a view of knowledge and learning as developing unique, non-appropriable routines from practices in the firm that lead to growth, and are sustained due to their effective adaptation to markets.

An essential Penrose notion is that a firm's only competitive advantage rests in its superior adaptation to business conditions by effectively coordinating its internal resources. Most of these resources are considered intangibles, such as competencies, employee knowledge, unique organizational routines, and ability to learn. Penrose rents (the power to extract revenues from markets) were based on the notion that a firm's unique knowledge-based capabilities were economically unfeasible to replicate. Growth is based on coordination of resources (and *learning within routines*) to develop "excess resources" that could be deployed to the market at zero marginal cost, an incentive for innovation and continued growth.

Nelson and Winter's (1982, p. 134) early proposition held that a firm's strategic knowledge capabilities are developed in collective practice, "embedded in the form of routines and operating procedures, allowed for the possibility that the collective had knowledge which is unknown to any of its members." Spender (1994) identifies how both explicit and implicit knowledge show up socially and individually, focusing on the competitive value of social collective knowledge. Collective knowledge in organizational routines can be viewed as emerging from coordination among resources, a highly context-specific property of the firm's practices, contextually embedded in practices; it cannot be appropriated by competitors or even individuals that leave the firm.

For example, Microsoft has developed unique practices in its forms of software engineering that have been described and copied by competitors. However, the coordination of resources between product lines, staff roles, and deep knowledge of product code, the operating system code, and their internal processes cannot be replicated within a competitive timeframe. To the extent that their product lines remain dominant in the marketplace, Microsoft's knowledge-based collective operations establish a powerful beachhead against competition. Both efficient and "dynamic," refreshed by research, their processes sustain advanced product lines and frustrate competitors through sheer scale of output.

As firms adapt to their markets and customers during growth periods, the predominant organizational values change, leading process changes that tend to follow. A large firm identified as Autoline (referenced as a case study in prior research (Jones, 2002a)) gained and held the dominant position in its market for two decades, through the widespread adoption of its retail management systems. What began as an external business strategy for Autoline became internally focused as the dominant product line sustained its competitive position. For two decades, Autoline's strategic perspective was oriented toward growth of its dominant product line beachhead, and its organizational values reflected that orientation. Internal resources were focused on supporting growth of the product portfolio, but not new knowledge-based practices. During the growth period, the firm reduced research and development, market research, and new product design capability, even while expanding product lines to meet the growing market.

As the market changed over time, the values espoused by executives also reverted from industry-facing positions to a customer-focused, "intimacy" perspective. This shift in strategic outlook demanded the coordination of internal responses to the strategy. New executive leadership initiated a clear position of values leadership, focused on customer needs and a radical change to product portfolio targets. This resulted in an intentional shift of values (toward a clearly-defined customer-centered values system) and processes (creating new design, sensing, and feedback practices), all as internally-developed resources of the firm.

KNOWLEDGE STRATEGY IN PRACTICE

We turn to practice to consider the feasibility of such a competitive knowledge strategy, aside from theoretical considerations. Competitive business strategy in practice answers the strategic question: "how do we compete?" In popular management thinking, one of three broad orientations toward market competition are employed, growth (or market value), operational effectiveness (or cost reduction), and customer intimacy (or market share). Market growth or overall value through products and services drives innovation; effectiveness drives internal knowledge sharing and management, to leverage use of knowledge to avoid costly reinvention and churn. Customer capture/intimacy drives innovating services for customers, leveraging internal knowledge of customer behavior, and sustaining revenues through customer retention.

Consider the interactions and possible decisions manifested by the directions of both business and knowledge strategy. If business strategy is to be used as guidance for knowledge initiatives, then which strategic goals are best supported by knowledge? What knowledge resources are best driven by business goals? An illustration of these relationships shows in Table 1, where both strategic orientations are mapped to these three fields of competition.

Table 1 portrays processes (associated with drivers or needs) for the two strategic vectors. The relationships between business and knowledge drivers are simply represented, with explicit orientation to external and internal management processes. The chart is illustrative of the difference in focus and management between knowledge and business strategies. These differences are oversimplified in the table and discussion to clarify the relationship of strategic management to process. In strategic practice, the drivers may be similar but strategies will integrate as many drivers as necessary to respond to competitive demands.

For example, *product innovation* suggests an internal converse of the external business drivers of product sales and customer needs. Knowledge creation may be a necessary internal driver associated with patent leverage or pricing strategy. An organizational learning culture (and *process innovation* in its many forms) may be cultivated to respond to the internal drivers for operational effectiveness. Because process innovation (improvement of internal routine effectiveness) is typically deployed in strategies for improving operational performance, it is more suited as a response to the cost/performance drivers underlying the selection of operational effectiveness strategy than a response to growth demands. In large, complex organizations multiple strategies are integrated as a whole. The table is meant to

Table 1. Business and knowledge strategy processes

	Growth	Operational Effectiveness	Customer Capture
Knowledge Strategy	Product Innovation Knowledge Creation Intellectual Capital	Process Innovation Developing Learning Culture Knowledge Sharing	Product Innovation Customer Knowledge Integration Branding Knowledge
Business Strategy	Product Sales Time to Market Distribution Networks Pricing Strategy Patent Leverage	Process Streamlining Supply Chain Management Financing Processes	Customer Retention Customer Product Needs Revenue Growth Alliance Strategies

distinguish the selections afforded each major driver, a simplified model of the common competitive orientations.

In a rapidly changing and globalized business environment, traditional strategic practices (planners and boards) have been jettisoned in large firms, and in many cases these roles have not been realigned to contemporary thinking or research. Reductive (if exhaustive) SWOT analyses and hybrid strategies (product innovation and cost reduction) have sufficed as practice in many organizations. We should not expect knowledge strategy to find widespread converts across boardrooms, even if justified as competitive. The traditional roles of strategy *advocacy* have been largely taken up by management consultants, who rely on quantifiable external or internal strategies, since they cannot efficiently learn and analyze internal knowledge networks.

Some strategy thinkers (Beinhocker, 1999; Collins & Porras, 1996) advocate adaptive strategies, ensuring the organization has a repertoire of action options available to it as a population of strategies. Internally-oriented knowledge strategy meets the criteria for an adaptive strategic repertoire, providing as it does a sustainable, organizationally embedded role for deploying business strategy.

For internal knowledge strategies, substantial organizational investment must be made, and new programs require time and learning of organizational members. Clearly, it is more difficult to implement programs considered as potentially "overhead" when external conditions suggest a focus on production. So how do decision makers identify the internal strategic "alignments" to processes that have the highest leverage or influence on the others? What path dependencies might be coordinated among knowledge processes, where one "informed capability" accelerates the performance of other activities in internal value chains? How do the values of decision makers determine the investment in knowledge-based processes?

Strategic Knowledge Integration

Grant (1996) identifies the goal for a knowledge-based strategy as to develop the dynamic capabilities of the firm, to establish organizational responsiveness to changing markets and competitive situations. According to Teece (1998), dynamic capabilities are "the ability to sense and then to seize new opportunities, and to reconfigure and protect knowledge assets, competencies, and complementary assets and technologies to achieve sustainable competitive advantage." Dynamic capabilities turn on *knowledge integration*, in Grant's (1996) view the core function of the firm itself. Knowledge integration is a function of incorporating the experience of knowing and learning into the processes of complex work. A core notion in this approach is the competitive effectiveness of nonreplicable routines, which Grant (1991) asserts, as scarce, idiosyncratic, nontransferable resources created and sustained largely by tacit knowledge in the context of production work. Whether by improving routines or complex processes, integration serves the firm by constructing repeatable practices that embody the learning of multiple experts and practitioners. Repeatable, yet often implicitly learned practices minimize the organizational burden of reproducing effective results in innovation or production.

The purpose of knowledge integration is defined as the achievement of flexible integration across multiple knowledge processes. The perspective on knowledge used in strategic assessment now becomes a critical choice. If knowledge is viewed as asset stock (as the KM view typically adopted), integration of stock knowledge leads to IT implementation, knowledge portals, and document management. If knowledge is viewed as flow and exchange, integration should lead to new and effective practices and accelerated organizational learning. Following the dynamic capability view, integration leads to coordinating knowledge flows within the practices of currently effective, adaptive routines that produce value for the firm.

Embedding knowledge in organizational routines is made more challenging when the critical knowledge changes rapidly, as in technology industries. Supporting dynamic capabilities requires a flexible organizational strategy, enabling responsive adaptation to market change, while furthering the development of competitive capabilities. The ability to shift the organization when market dynamics change is considered highly dependent on the firm's ability to adapt its knowledge to emerging situations, and to learn collectively.

But knowledge strategy research has not been oriented toward management guidance and practice. While a sound theoretical basis for knowledge strategy has been developed, there are few published applications, perhaps also due to the confidentiality of meaningful strategy. A significant gap remains between theories of dynamic capabilities of the firm and the decisions necessary to energize dynamic capabilities, and to motivate knowledge integration. At some point, managers require guidance for using a framework to improve knowledge-based processes and firm performance based on the theory and empirical observations developed in this field.

To further anchor knowledge strategy to practical management, guidance is required to identify the best leverage points (factors that have maximum influence with least relative effort) and dependent relationships between these variables. These can be simplified as two working models for these purposes:

1. A working model of dynamic organizational capabilities.
   A simplified model that describes the fit of organizational resources, routines, and actions to the firm's goals of knowledge integration.
2. A description of organizational interaction within this model.

A model of the functions or variables within the organizational processes that guide process decisions and practice development.

RPV: A Resource-Based Dynamic Capabilities Model

Zack (1999) outlines a framework for operationalizing knowledge strategy, but few other published examples are found, leading necessarily to question whether any published examples exist of successful deployment. The Resources-Processes-Values framework developed by Christensen (1997) to guide innovation strategy serves the same purposes of competitive knowledge strategy (within which *innovation* is a candidate strategic process). The RPV model represents a resource-based strategy framework, based on empirical research and application (with theoretical support). RPV enjoys operational credibility due to its development over numerous applications in innovation consulting with large product firms. Because management theory remains inadequate if not successfully applied, this leading *empirical* framework is offered for critical examination and "reverse engineered" back to theoretical foundations to promote a proven innovation model to knowledge strategy applications. This approach is consistent with Mahoney and Sanchez (2004), who suggest a pragmatic turn in management theory, wherein meaning and value are realized from the outcome of actions taken from the strategy. They describe the pragmatic, contextual orientation to strategy development as resolving the dissociation between strategy formulation and implementation. RPV, having been developed empirically as a response to innovation cycles found across many industries, meets the test of a pragmatic, competence-based theory, as specified by Mahoney and Sanchez (2004). Based on this "test," RPV serves as an example of strategic theory building that enables both "inquiry from the inside" as a pragmatic model based on learning from management action, *and* "inquiry from the outside" as a deductive-theoretical model applied to specific competitive contexts studied with actual firms.

Table 2 illustrates the RPV framework, identifying types in each of the three dimensions. Resources (consistent with Penrose) are assets, materials, and business instruments recognized by the firm as valuable. Resources are typically things and assets, identified and managed by common accounting practices, and can be obtained, transferred, and sold. Resources are considered fungible, and are readily obtained and transferred, as opposed to processes and values, which are embedded, nontransferable, and unique. Christensen's model does not explicitly resolve knowledge as a resource, but relies on conventional definitions.

Christensen's model provides reference to a published empirical strategy, to support two arguments: (1) the saliency of values in strategic management and (2) the relationship of processes and values to practice and leadership.

Processes encapsulate knowing and doing, both in explicit representations and tacit "tribal knowledge" of procedural knowledge within the organization. Processes constitute all the types of business, production, and knowledge work practices that are defined methods for coordinating multiple inputs, resources, and labor into internal value and products and goods for sale. They range in scale from those formal, institutionalized business processes to intermediate added-knowledge processes such as product design and development, to informal practices that have been routinized through continual use and learning. Christensen notes that processes, as dynamic organizational capabilities, reveal choices of *practices* that necessarily exclude other possible choices. The RPV process model suggests that a productive capability represents an organizational investment in a way of performing knowledge work. The development of processes represents a cumulative, expensive set of skills learned over time, which become repeatable, embedded routines, as the "mechanisms through which organizations create value are intrinsically inimical to change" (Christensen, 1997, p. 164).

RPV explicitly describes the function of values, a unique aspect of RPV compared to other models of process or knowledge management. These organizational values are not the motivational platitudes displayed on the walls in headquarters. Values are a significant type of knowledge "asset," as a valuable function for coordinating resources within the firm. Values include organizational knowledge ("how we do things"), individual

Table 2. Resources, processes, and values (Adapted from Christensen, 1997)

RESOURCES	PROCESSES	VALUES
Assets, materials that can be bought, sold, transferred.	Routines, practices that transform resource inputs into value.	Organizational criteria that underlie priorities and decisions.
People	Personnel hiring	Cost structure
Technologies	Training, organizational development	Corporate reports
Product lines	Product development	Customer interaction
Facilities & equipment	Project management	Opportunity scale & scope
Information	Manufacturing	Organizational culture
Cash & investments	Accounting, budgeting	Espoused corporate values
Brand & corporate identity	Market & customer research	Values in use, as practices
Distribution channels	Product design & testing	Ethical actions & statements

knowing, community and team-level norms, and govern the details of how processes are performed. As enduring constructs, they define a firm's identity and its style of work life. Over time, values build a significant organizational competency and shared outlook toward strategy.

An organization's values are complex and often contradictory formations of collective knowledge and organizational priorities, and can be described as "values systems" in the organization. They are a type of tacit knowledge (Jones, 2002a) and demonstrate individual action (Argyris, 1992) in the organization as *values in-use*. Being largely tacit and contextually embedded, values are difficult to self-disclose as explicit issues or as knowledge, but they influence processes, products, and technologies, and are observable in use (Johnson, 1997; Jones, 2002a). Values systems differ from "value systems," which are defined as networks of value-producing services in a production supply chain network (Normann & Ramirez, 1993).

Values perform significant, if overlooked, functions in growth, innovation, and strategy. There are several categories of values found in operation in organizational contexts (Jones, 2002a), but there are consistent *functions* of values that operate regardless of type and level. Values generally constrain and often define *how* people work within a process. For example, professional services firms support sophisticated processes, such as client development, that incorporate long-standing and tacit values that cultivate a desired type of client relationship, as well as more overt requirements relating to communication, billing, and sales. They influence the priorities of work practice and determine the style and presentation of internal deliverables and production outputs.

Values establish priorities, which are often in conflict with each other in organizational life. In everyday work, individual and organizational values may be widely inconsistent, and values systems may be internally inconsistent. They are not always productive and positive; they may be hidden and antiproductive. People value knowl-edge sharing in general, for example, but also value career advancement, and may "hoard knowledge" where it enables gain. Values also embed (and thereby both hide and sustain) counterproductive priorities within organizations, showing up in dynamics such as internal competition.

Many organizations can identify historically established values, such as cooperation and respecting peers, that persist as inviolable, similar to an individual's ethical values. Since the assessment of performance according to values is determined intersubjectively, rating values performance is notoriously relative. As with other forms of tacit knowledge, *explicated* values may find only tenuous connection to a strategic context; an individual's action is inseparable from tacit knowing or their values. The real priorities of values (*in use* as opposed to espoused) often show up in operational conflicts, and not in explicit discussion.

Christensen identifies values as the source of all prioritization decisions, which may be generalized to all decisions. From a strategic perspective, values influence cost structures, which reflect values and priorities. Markets and projects are identified and selected or disregarded, rapidly and strategically, based on the filter mechanism of organizational values. Theoretically, if an organization could renew and determine its values in practice, these values would redefine the business, its priorities, processes, and interactions with customers. If managers could direct organizational and individual values to adapt to strategy, the ideal of "alignment" could be realized. But instead, the problem of deeply embedded values prevents the very possibility of this rationalized approach to organizational dynamics.

THE STRATEGIC FUNCTION OF ORGANIZATIONAL VALUES

The concept of "values" has been used cautiously in research. Consistent with values, the closely related concept of *norms* (Giddens, 1984) is found in social research, or *principles* in leadership research, with slightly different meanings in those contexts. A value is held by an individual as a meaningful principle from which one responds with action or concern, or a strong preference for a type of behavior. Organizational values are principles and preferences explicitly communicated or espoused, while values *in use* (as theories in use, Argyris & Schön, 1978) are preferences which drive responses and action, but remain implicit.

As a strategic function, values are highly leveraged, since they have some influence on all decisions. Values direct an organization's knowing and doing, which affords them an extraordinary (and underemployed) leverage in strategy. Values constitute the underlying beliefs and core principles and priorities by which organizational and individual decisions are made. Values are the least transferable of resources, due to their embeddedness in nontransferable processes, informal practices, social/occupational networks, and history. In RPV, values are the longest duration variable and the slowest factor to change. As with individual values, organizational values are also "important to the individual, have effects in a variety of situations, and are comparatively difficult to change" (Dose & Klimoski, 1999).

Values and values systems show a bidirectional valence pattern with respect to strategic management. They *follow* strategic changes over time, as strategies based on significant business realities also change the values systems within the firm. But in immediate situations they *lead* decisions, by influencing and constraining the range of options available to business strategy. Therefore, firms rarely execute strategic decisions in conflict with their current organizational values. In both directions, the change of values systems lags other business changes, since their embeddedness ensures they are perhaps the last organizational function to release from a former enculturated pattern. But the persistence of values ensures they also lead new strategic efforts due to

their pervasive influence within current thinking as change decisions are contemplated.

Values (in-use) are resistant to change, due to their social embeddedness within the historical memory and social practices of the organization. They are difficult to change because the tacit agreement necessary to propagate new values requires a structural change not just in normative behaviors, but in meaning, power, and legitimation. Values are too embedded to be managed as organizational tools; *meaningful* changes to espoused, explicit values systems cannot be changed by a committee and just posted to the wall.

Values systems are collections of values within a process or organizational unit that exhibit dependencies or collective relationships. Independent values identified in use may regularly co-occur with similar values or specifically dependent values. When occurring as a values system, the independent priorities or principles may not be easily separable. Consider the values system of "innovativeness," nearly always an aggregate values system. The related values of innovative thinking, creativity, individual excellence, and competitiveness may co-occur in an organizational setting, and recur due to social reinforcement of their performance. Competitive strategy may require transformative change within an organization, and while process changes are often planned, the impact of historical organizational values is not typically foreseen at the level of strategic decision making. Values enable or constrain all other priorities by virtue of history and organizational culture. Values are not functions that can be changed by command.

Values also become anchored within organizational processes throughout everyday performance and enhancement cycles. In processes, the selection of specific operational routines is usually based on organizational priorities and individual work/professional values. These values systems accrue within processes to become inherent values of the process. Innovation management (product design, development, and marketing) is especially sensitive to organizationally embedded values. Barriers to radical innovation in large organizations are found in both overdeveloped product development processes and the associated values systems inherent in successful and long-standing practices. In large organizations, the risks of "creative destruction" of processes and values systems must be weighed against the foreseeable or strategic value of radical innovation. Christensen (1997) and Jones (2002b) empirically demonstrate that large product firms may be structurally unable to radically innovate, partly due to the function of inherited values systems within the current innovation practices.

Christensen (1997) describes the macrodynamics of values in innovation:

One of the bittersweet rewards of success is, in fact, that as companies become large, they literally lose the capability to enter small emerging markets. Their disability is not because of a change in the resources within the companies—their resources typically are vast. Rather, it is because their values change. (p. 190)

Organizational values both reflect and precede the changing approach to competition, shifting preferences from innovation and other knowledge-based strategies to exploiting the growing market. The organizational locus of power shifts from product managers and designers to marketing, sales, and even accounting, champions of the new values that define "success." A recent trend of "high design" in the stable and slow-growing consumer products sector (e.g., Procter and Gamble) does little to dispel this assessment, since design managers are elevated to newly created leadership positions to reflect the strategy. But it remains a continuation of an "exploitation" growth strategy, not an exploration (or radical innovation) strategy. Furthermore, while industrial design adds considerable value as an innovative knowledge *practice*, its recent contribution to corporate brands has served to raise American market design values closer to the traditionally more advanced European high design standard. The branded design strategy (while often linked with the language of innovation) largely remains a market-facing instrument of a market exploitation strategy. This current trend should engender more "positive" organizational values than found in examples of other firms deploying customer base exploitation strategies, *leading* future innovations and organizational change due to a larger scale values change.

As strategic choices and associated values spread through the firm during growth, the organization also forms large social networks. As the successful firm embraces more conservative business values over time, they embed into management processes, from market research to human resources, from R&D to sales. As both customer intimacy and margin-oriented values unify with everyday project and product management practice, these values become implicit and more resistant to change. The same values that create team loyalty, organizational purpose, and a shared sense of identity also implicitly limit types of work practices, investments, and customers. Values are considered the ultimate source of decisions (Christensen, 1997; Maslow, 1965; Oliver, 1999). However, being tacit in everyday use, managers cannot easily see these constraints, let alone question their impact.

Integrated Model of Organizational Values

The organizational researcher has multiple classifications of values from which to draw in developing workable models for strategic consideration. We do not suggest one class will produce superior strategic insights over another, since so many social and pragmatic business variables will always intervene with analysis or comparison. The selection of a valid values framework may be considered a lens for magnification of desired aspects and minimization of others. Several models have been developed in support of studying individual values, moral decisions, and orientation to work practice. For example, a human resources strategy might select the frequently-cited Rokeach (1973), or managers might review Dose's work values models (Dose, 1997; Dose & Klimoski, 1999) for guidance on productive team composition.

A small set of values models are widely-referenced across the organizational literatures (e.g., Dose, 1997; Rokeach, 1973) indicating their acceptance and applicability to continuing research. Many researchers adopt Rokeach's definition, and have developed upon this well-accepted model of human values (Braithwaite & Law, 1985; George & Jones, 1997; Rokeach, 1973; Schwartz, 1994). Some researchers have used this prior work as a basis for studying or developing "universal" approaches to human values (Ellis & Hall, 1994; Schwartz, 1994). As defined by Rokeach (1973), values are "an enduring organization of beliefs that are "general plans employed to resolve conflicts and to make decisions." Rokeach's values model shows personal choice based on appropriate behaviors (*instrumental*) or end states (*terminal*), both of which support personal or socially directed values. Instrumental values generally correspond to the values involved in organizational action, and terminal values to those inviolable or "protected" values (Baron & Spranca, 1997) which hold across transactions and display resistance to trade-offs.

Maslow's (1965, 1971) values model developed from the psychological model of the hierarchy of needs. Maslow distinguishes between "deficiency" values and the terminal values of being, B-values, which motivate individuals beyond merely personal value. Many of the B-values refer to almost Platonic ideal states, while many others represent noncontroversial human and social values such as honesty, justice, and autonomy. Maslow's work extended the notion of values to embrace a "fusion of facts and values," and left a legacy of research questions and testable propositions that even today remain unaddressed.

Nonaka (1996, 2001) has also written of the "foundation of knowledge" as the ideals of truth, goodness, and beauty (Kalthoff, Nonaka & Nueno, 2001). These represent the terminal ideal values, and correspond to Maslow's "values of being," which he asserted were experienced by people as a single fusion of all higher values. Like Maslow, Nonaka's claims represent an ideal that motivates the expression and exchange of knowledge.

In organizational values research, Jones (2000, 2002a) developed a composite model for use in data collection and analysis, including four families of composites. The composites were constructed both inductively and synthetically from empirical research rather than deductive models based on moral theory. The four families of values systems specified both *individual* (humanistic and design) and *institutional* (organizational and technical) values systems.

Individual Values

- **Design values:** Drawn from Friedman (1997), Kling (1996), Kumar and Bjorn-Andersen (1990), and several design studies. Situated in design research, this composite drew from models affecting the design of systems and products, not human values.
- **Humanistic values:** Humanistic values integrated the human values of Rokeach (1973) and incorporated Maslow's (1971) values framework.

Institutional Values

- **Organizational values:** Organizational values constructs were drawn from empirical case studies (e.g., Walsham & Waema, 1994) and mapped to well-supported values models (Crosby, Bitner & Gill, 1990).
- **Technical/engineering values:** Drawn from Kumar and Bjorn-Andersen (1990) and Banathy (1996), these values apply to sys-

Table 3. Institutional values framework: Organizational values (from Jones, 2000)

Organizational values	Range of Attributes	
1. Economic	Profit driven	Socially driven
2. Information as symbolic	Policy focus	Communicative
3. Control/power	Centralized	Distributed
4. Management style	Participative	Autocratic
5. Locus of decision making	Decentralized	Centralized
6. Leadership style	Informality	Formality
7. Communication style	Open	Closed
8. Organizational processes	Structured	Flexible
9. Task coordination	Single way	Multiple alternatives
10. Impact on work	Job enrichment	Isolation
11. Focus of work	Customer focus	Internal focus
12. Social nature of work	Participatory	Nonparticipatory
13. Team behavior	Cooperative	Competitive

tems engineering and development practice, the processes of focus in the research.

The organizational values family is of most interest to the strategic function, although the technical values have bearing on embedded values in specific organizational processes. The composition and range of the organizational values are displayed in Table 3.

Most of these values are easily identified within organizations, and are testable by self-selection within the range of attributes, and by case study and observational research. As values systems, clusters of similar value attributes often occur together within a focus organization, such as "open communication, flexible process, participative management." The attempt to produce a generalizable model negates the variety and range of values that might also be incorporated. The strategic function of values, again, should be to enhance the unique values systems that complement both strategy and organizational culture. A specific values model such as the example in Table 3 may

be used to evaluate change from a baseline, or to take measure of specific processes in question as an organizational strategy progresses.

While many researchers extol the virtue of values as positive motivating drivers in organizations, unexamined values may have a significantly negative influence on strategic change. Christensen's (1997) RPV model complements Jones' (2000, 2002a) findings of embedded values in processes mediating new practices toward the form of existing values. Jones (2000) found values function as barriers to innovation due to the resistance of either strongly-held personal values or embedded process values to adapt to organizational demands. Both models are proposed as compatible organizational perspectives on developing knowledge resources and managing innovation. Both assert, from empirical observations, that values underpin organizational decisions and processes, and strategy is guided by and depends on values espoused in decisions and statements of priority. As values are embedded in processes (and in turn are embedded in communities and social networks), *processes* are the knowledge structures affording individuals opportunity for agency and action.

But effective process change requires knowledgeable intervention and conservation of values consistent with the process participants. Processes must therefore be adapted by the organizational communities whose values are at stake in the organizational commitments and everyday operation of the process. Consistent with Nonaka's (1991) "middle-up-down" approach to management of knowledge practices, a *socialization* methodology coordinates knowledgeable participants and conserves the adaptation of their values. The socialization approach requires understanding and assent from organizational members to fully engage with and adapt the business strategy (to associate the new values inherent in the strategic intent). Socialization generates lateral relationships that support social networks for knowledge creation and maintenance. The virtuous cycle of socialization between process and values recommends a complementary function to strategic management.

SOCIALIZATION OF PROCESSES AND VALUES

How do managers effect changes to organizational functions based on this strategic perspective? We are interested in guiding the diffusion of selected values systems within the organization and within key, leveraged processes. A socialization approach asserts the necessity of process leaders and participants in defining new processes, performance metrics, and deliverables. Socialization also recognizes the need to negotiate changes to embedded values to minimize unproductive (but not necessarily *creative*) conflict. Socialization gains validity from its understood function in other organizational contexts, but also counters the passivity implied in the popular opposing construct, the notion of *strategic alignment*.

An Argument Against Strategic Alignment

A central organizing function of traditional strategic management is the alignment of organizational resources and processes to a defined strategic agenda and competitive posture. As strategic research continues to develop theoretically and empirically, the assumptions underpinning alignment break down. Two assumptions are briefly addressed:

1. That some agents in the organization perform work toward a state of *alignment* with strategic intent, based on organizational communications and leadership direction.
2. The notion that competitive strategy represents a fixed agenda to which decisions and resources can be aligned throughout the organization.

Alignment suggests that organizational structures and participants are capable of intentionally adapting to direction and to initiate activities consistent with a selected executive vision and agenda. It also assumes a top-down hierarchical diffusion of strategy toward which passive actors are expected to metaphorically "align."

Few commentators have challenged this received notion. Without belaboring the implied hierarchical, even military "command and control" model implied in the concept, observations about the function of alignment find no ability to coordinate resources "by alignment" within an established firm. The notion of "alignment to strategy" appears to have entered the vernacular as a rationalization developed from management consulting, not from business research. Consistent with both adaptive and learning strategy models, Ciborra (1998), calling for a return to empirical investigations of actual practice, finds the alignment concept "bankrupt" as a basis for research.

The Socialization of Processes to Strategy

To enable the organizational dynamics of the described virtuous cycle, we find a function that coordinates knowledge strategy through values leadership (top-down) and process adaptation (bottom-up). The notion of "socialization" displaces strategic alignment as a functional mechanism for such a resource strategy. "Strategic alignment of knowledge" fails in both practice and theory. The ideals and abstractions of strategic intent do not match the concrete demands and pragmatic motivations of organizational practice, of people working within teams and occupational communities. Concurrently, new knowledge in the organization is developed at the level of practice, in projects and production. Top-down strategy has very limited access to the contextual knowledge within processes.

Socialization as used here in the context of process agrees with the operational definition cited in most studies (Kraimer, 1997; Louis, 1980), except that typically socialization is considered a time-limited cycle of initiation or indoctrination into an organization. We extend the process of socialization to a dynamic organizational context, wherein processes and values are created and led by strategic change. The definition of Louis (1980) holds in this context: "A process by which an individual comes to appreciate the values, abilities, expected behaviors, and social knowledge essential for assuming an organizational role and for participating as an organization member" (p. 229).

Socialization of values, capabilities, and behaviors is repurposed toward modifying the routines of on-going practices, to adapt or create new processes within the organizational community that owns the process. Whereas indoctrination (e.g., of the newcomer) assumes socialization occurs at the organizational level, adaptation of work practices assumes a socialization among existing participants, each of which may display variances among expected values systems. Indoctrinating socialization involves substantial tacit knowing and tacit agreement. The social networking mechanism of process socialization also draws upon tacit knowing and interpersonal and team communication, in the recursive formation of new practices within the community of process practitioners. Socialization encourages the agency of all participants to identify congruence between their values and the proposed routines and structures of the strategic initiative or target process. It also affords an "unfreezing" period to suspend judgment on current practices, allowing for trial and error within a learning phase. Socialization provides latitude to explore the contradictions and resistances that emerge when prior process routines are challenged. Explicit process change triggers conflicts with long-standing values embedded within current practices; a socialization approach to process change must allow for dialogue among participants to ensure that critical values remain respected, or chosen, in the new functions.

Process socialization was developed empirically, as an alternative to planned, authoritative (top-down) institutionalization for the introduction of new knowledge-based practices in the organizations studied in this research. Theoretical support for socialization draws from organizational structuration (Orlikowski, 2002; Orlikowski & Robey, 1991) and social networks in knowledge practices (Liebeskind, Oliver, Zucker & Brewer, 1996). The essential claim argues for practice-level constitution of processes and the inscription of defined values, as two necessary components of process structure. Strategically-motivated processes are constructed by organizational teams and experts most closely involved with the performance of the process. Process values originate with and are owned by the communities of practice engaged in the process as an organizational structure. Unlike the expectations set by "alignment," values are not defined by management and carried into the process. Process values are not necessarily shared in kind with management values; deliberate difference between these communities should be encouraged to ensure sufficient variety of perspectives is promoted in the organizational ecology. The shared values system is mutually constructed with management in the specification of deliverables produced by the process for internal customers. The process customers, receiving these deliverables, will normally identify and negotiate requirements that reflect their values for use, which may be represented as specifications for quality, measures of performance, or economic priorities. This processual view of strategically motivated change corresponds to the recursive interplay between the agency of participants and organizational structures (recurrent practices and rules), in the perspective of structuration (Orlikowski, 2000, 2002).

The theoretical orientation of structuration, originated by Giddens (1979, 1984) and adapted as a lens for technology-adapted social systems by Orlikowski (1992) and DeSanctis and Poole (1994), explains the evolution of structures in organizations as mutually co-constructed by participants and the structures they develop and institutionalize over time. Structures, such as business processes and established practices, are conceived of as enduring yet flexible sets of rules and systems around and toward which individual *agency* intervenes and responds. Individuals and group processes recursively develop structures that produce intentional group outcomes. Both strategic management (typically executives) and practice-level leaders create structures and inscribe associated values in the communication and diffusion of those structures. Participating actors negotiate from agency (and their own values systems) to adapt their personal values and practices to new structures, or to negotiate changes to structures (e.g., business strategy or process).

Structuration further informs the notion that individual values (norms) and organizational values co-evolve with structures. Certain individual values, promoted in practice, survive organizational challenges to become "legitimated" and recognized as reinforcing the values and practices important to strategy. For example, socializing the process of user-centered design in a product organization necessitates a corresponding commitment to new values identified with a product's "user" as a significant and competing representation of the "customer." Not only are new practices introduced to study, observe, and design for the "user," but new values are socialized through distinctions made about the value of users, the business value of user data, and the competitive value of user preference. These distinctions encounter resistance from pre-existing, enduring commitments (e.g., customer) which are negotiated, not replaced. Over time, deeply held values associated with both users and customers are evidenced throughout the organization, creating an organic internal demand for the new process and technical practices associated with the values system. This socialization process may be a critical, yet overlooked, function in the distribution of new knowledge and developing values systems within organizations. As a theory of process, socialization accounts for all three key structural factors of structuration in KM as represented by Timbrell, Delaney, Chan, Yue, and Gable (2005): the signification or interpretive scheme of *strategy*, the *legitimation* of norms and values, and the distribution of *power* in values-oriented decisions.

The Socialization of Values to Strategy

The socialization of processes requires knowledge integration at the level of *practice*. Individuals in defined practices or belonging to practice communities (Brown & Duguid, 1991; Lave & Wenger, 1991) generally hold education and expertise in a skill area (e.g., engineering, design, or planning) as well as in the business domain. While values disclosure within practice communities evolves over the course of collaboration and knowledge sharing, socialization accelerates deployment across functions and communities. The opportunities to identify and disclose values in-use occur with *values conflicts* during the coordination of activities in organizational processes, working in teams with members of other organizational functions (Jones, 2002a). Both managers and practice leaders must learn to identify and communicate the values conflicts that occur in process redesign and transition.

Given the importance and leverage of embedded values (persistent values in-use), a knowledge strategy should propose alternative values systems within the context of process socialization. Alternatives are represented as new priorities and metaphors for action associated with the adapted process and clarified in the course of everyday decision making. Values alternatives sets may be identified as priorities and key process objectives. Practice leaders (as process owners) serve as stewards of both process and practice-level values, and can take responsibility for identifying competing values systems and negotiating conflicts. The resolution of values conflicts results in integrating the contribution as new learning (knowledge) in responsible processes.

Given the social leverage of values *in-use*, a function of knowledge strategy should be to develop values "alternatives" within the context of knowledge management activities, identified and clarified in the course of everyday decision making. Stewards of these practice-level values can take responsibility for identifying competing values systems and even negotiating conflicts. In management practice, this shows up as "ownership" of job functions or new processes.

While originating with individuals, knowledge and values develop *from* individual knowing and learning, becoming not so much encoded but encultured in the organization. Through numerous conversations, communication, and enacted practices in the organization (e.g., in the everyday practices within the process, design

reviews, requirements negotiation, walkthroughs, prototyping), individual knowing, methods and procedures, and values continually exchange through the course of production work. While new organizational routines and resources are introduced into teams and projects through formal training and new methods and practices, they will remain constrained or become diffused by the context within which knowledge is recognized and deployed in the organization.

CONCLUSION

The knowledge strategy perspective does not replace competitive business strategy as practiced; rather it offers complementary guidance within a resource-based strategic perspective. However, traditional strategic planning has become regarded by research as a poor instrument for long-range business strategy, due to rapid unforeseen market changes and the environmental complexity of modern business. The socialization of processes and leadership toward enhanced values systems asserts a more enduring and sustainable path to a desired competitive standing. It is argued that to deploy a knowledge strategy the firm must undergo a significant reconfiguration of the processes and values responsive to strategic intent, to achieve the dynamic capabilities realized by knowledge integration.

Organizational processes are the coordination capacities and defined routines within which individual tacit knowing is located. Processes and routines must be refreshed by knowledge creation and transfer, but not merely within projects or skillcraft practices. To develop nonreplicable, competitive knowledge processes, unique practices learned in the "art of doing" must be re-integrated within the overall schema of production and coordination.

Organizational values are institutionalized guiding principles and priorities that influence behavior and decision making. Changing embedded values systems requires identifying the values in-use throughout the organization or the processes of strategic interest. As opposed to changing explicit company "slogans," the espoused values on a wall plaque, cannot be easily accomplished directly. Consistent with the definition of institutionalization, over time people accept the underlying culture and its values as given. Values in-use might be accessible to intervention if they were not deeply embedded, but they would also be much less powerful in the social functions they also serve, the purpose of orienting action and simplifying decisions based on understood (yet often unexplicated) priorities.

This model proposes a strategic function for values, following a methodology known as socialization, complementary to organizational authority. Overt programs and actions taken by new managers often fail due to the resistance inherent in deeply socialized, highly stable values systems. Any successful attempt to leverage deep knowledge as a competitive strategic resource must acknowledge the existing values systems that reward, enable, and deploy organizational knowing within an intact social system.

Socialization as a management function involves values leadership, including the introduction of new opportunities (career, project, organizational) aligned with values oriented toward the outcome of knowledge practices. The embedded organizational values anticipated to follow socialization should also be considered, since these underlying values systems will persist after socialization, and theoretically until business strategy significantly shifts. While this requires an authentic, long-term commitment, the returns to the organizational culture from the commitment to change accrue immediately.

Given the ever-increasing complexity and interconnectedness of business and technology, strategic management must become more collaborative and draw on the collective knowledge of many contributors. A socialization approach mitigates the problem of analyzing complex

relationships by distributing the sensing and opportunity/threat analysis across the organization. Socialization delegates strategic intent and attention, while locating individual responsibility firmly in the processes within which one has expertise and experience.

Values leadership and socialization have the potential to significantly enhance organizational effectiveness and competitiveness. Organizationally, a strong values consensus establishes a set of decision criteria for management and resource deployment. Without the pragmatic direction of management (i.e., leadership and socialization), the historically embedded (sedimented) values of the organizational culture will bend vulnerable practices back toward the status quo. Redesigned processes tend to revert to prior states of practice, due to prior ad hoc socialization created as recurrent social practices (Giddens, 1984). Therefore, values offer a pivotal standpoint for leadership, allowing managers to identify and orchestrate examples of behavioral and practice in reference to competitive strategy.

By managing *to values* and not processes, managers empower practice leaders (across processes and project teams) to intellectually invest in their processes and continually integrate new learning to ensure competitive renewal. Disclosing and exchanging values that emerge within the context of process coordination allows participants to understand the organizational commitment to strategic goals. People do not respond emotionally to strategies, but they are motivated by and respond immediately to values, and can identify values conflicts. Values conflicts reveal meaningful opportunities for engagement, dialogue, and reconfiguration of organizational practices. From a strategic perspective, values conflicts return organizational feedback to managers from the distributed, delegated attention inherent in socialization. Strategic intent becomes socially meaningful when values differences are honored, becoming instruments of organizational learning and listening rather than merely positions in decision making.

FUTURE RESEARCH DIRECTIONS

An approach is described for developing a knowledge strategy that attempts to resolve the contradictions between the management concerns of organizational strategy and values, and the everyday concerns for action based on knowledge. This approach synthesizes both theoretical research and practical management concerns, with a dual intent of dispelling unworkable orientations to knowledge management strategies and improving strategic management practice. Both of these intents are supported by seminal foundation studies and current research, as well as experience and empirical observations over the course of organizational consulting projects.

Profitable future research directions should support both of these intents. The most valuable research contributions will be those that strengthen the theoretical and empirical bases for the organizational practices of strategy building and process design and deployment. Yet the most valuable pragmatic contributions are those that enable practical, effective management action.

The most profitable directions for knowledge strategy, and knowledge management, are those that extend our collective learning from organizational and management sciences. The KM literature has developed from a strong focus on enabling information technology. We now have a sufficient number of studies of knowledge management in actual organizational practice to offset the far-reaching claims of information technology enabling knowledge practices. New research should balance the predominance of technology with studies of organizational cognition and the successful development of new knowledge practices. And given the interdisciplinary nature of all research in knowledge, management, and organization, we must do a better job of integrat-

ing our knowledge across the social sciences and management disciplines.

The reported research did not deliberately exclude information technology from its treatment of organizational knowledge management; it was merely unnecessary given the focus and structure of the claims. While some studies of IT integration make well-founded claims for practice and process transformation, knowledge management research should advance management practice. As an interdisciplinary research area, KM researchers should evaluate and integrate current thinking in cognitive science (e.g., distributed cognition and cognitive engineering), cognitive anthropology (e.g., activity theory research), organizational sociology (e.g., structuration and institutionalization), as well as information science (e.g., contextual information practices).

A significant direction of pursuit may be to examine and validate in theory and organizational settings the empirically-developed approaches to strategy making and deployment. To better inform and enable management practice, we should be eliciting the most empirically effective models and identifying their core relationships to identify generalizable functions expressed by the model. Strategic design models such as Christensen's RPV have been developed through iterations and observations in practice. These should be rigorously "reverse-engineered," returning their empirical claims and mechanisms to theoretical form, to learn from the process to understand its connection to management practice and organizational dynamics.

Moreover, the directionality of research and practice can be profitably reversed in strategic research, similar to the research trajectories of many human sciences (clinical psychology), practices (medicine, law), and interdisciplinary research (human-computer interaction). In all these domains, theory-led proposals have often failed, and yet many scholars resist drawing from practice due to concerns for originality or academic "rigor." Mahoney and Sanchez (2004) have argued for a stronger integration of pragmatic and deductive theory. Researchers should go further than this, and conduct ethnographies of firms that successfully demonstrate the principles of strategic thinking and deployment as an organizational practice.

Strategic management itself is a creative and collaborative organizational *practice*. Strategy building requires experientially-grounded theory-creation and theory-testing within a complex fusion of business and organizational domains. The purpose of competitive business strategy is essentially to construct descriptive and predictive models of business dynamics to inform executive decision making. Organizational strategy that follows a theory-of-competition model must be deployed based on human, not economic, theories. Therefore motivation (values), productivity and innovation (cognitive effectiveness), and reorganization (process and practice) emerge as the foremost lever-variables. These are the internal resources available within the organization, all forms of knowledge and knowing. Knowledge resources will be created and sustained by people performing within the context of these process structures. Research should be conducted on the relationship between these strategy-related variables and the development of competitive knowledge resources as an outcome of organizational process and structure.

Research in knowledge strategy, in particular, should progress beyond the theoretical dimensions of strategic resource economics and identify effective relationships between strategy building and the collective intelligence available from within organizations, their people, and processes.

REFERENCES

Argyris, C. (1992). Why individuals and organizations have difficulty in double loop learning. In *On organizational learning* (pp. 7-38). Cambridge: Blackwell Publishers.

Argyris, C., & Schön, D. (1978). *Organizational learning: A theory of action perspective.* New York: McGraw-Hill.

Banathy, B.H. (1996). *Designing social systems in a changing world.* New York: Plenum Publishing Co.

Barney, J.B. (1986). Organizational culture: Can it be a source of sustained competitive advantage? *The Academy of Management Review, 11*(3), 656-665.

Baron, J., & Spranca, M. (1997). Protected values. *Organizational Behavior and Human Decision Processes, 70*(1), 1–16.

Beinhocker, E.D. (1999, March). Robust adaptive strategies. *Sloan Management Review,* p. 22.

Braithwaite, V.A., & Law, H.G. (1985). Structure of human values: Testing the adequacy of the Rokeach Value Survey. *Journal of Personality and Social Psychology, 49,* 250-262.

Brown, J.S., & Duguid, P. (1991). Organizational learning and communities of practice: Toward a unified view of working, learning and innovation. *Organization Science, 2,* 40-57.

Chae, B., & Bloodgood, J.M. (2006). The paradoxes of knowledge management: An eastern philosophical perspective. *Information and Organization, 16*(1), 1-26.

Choo, C.W. (1998). *The knowing organization: How organizations use information to construct meaning, create knowledge, and make decisions.* New York: Oxford University Press.

Christensen, C.M. (1997). *The innovator's dilemma.* Boston: Harvard Business School Press.

Ciborra, C.U. (1998). Crisis and foundations: An inquiry into the nature and limits of models and methods in the information systems discipline. *Journal of Strategic Information Systems, 7,* 5-16.

Collins, J.C., & Porras, J.I. (1996, September-October). Building your company's vision. *Harvard Business Review,* pp. 65-88.

Crosby, L.A., Bitner, M.J., & Gill, J.D. (1990). Organizational structure of values. *Journal of Business Research, 20*(2), 123-134.

Davenport, T., Thomas, H., & Short, J.E. (1990, Summer). The new industrial engineering: Information technology and business process redesign. *Sloan Management Review,* pp. 11–26.

DeSanctis, G., & Poole, M.S. (1994). Capturing the complexity in advanced technology use: Adaptive structuration theory. *Organization Science, 5*(2), 121-145.

Dose, J.J. (1997). Work values: An integrative framework and illustrative application to organizational socialization. *Journal of Occupational and Organizational Psychology, 70,* 219 -240.

Dose, J.J., &. Klimoski, R.J. (1999). The diversity of diversity: Work values effects on formative team processes. *Human Resource Management Review, 9*(1), 83-108.

Drew, S. (1999). Building knowledge management into strategy: Making sense of a new perspective. *Long Range Planning, 32*(1), 130-136.

Ellis, R.K., & Hall, M.L.W. (1994). Systems and values: An approach for practical organizational intervention. *Proceedings of the ISSS, 94.*

Friedman, B. (1997). *Human values and the design of computer technology.* Cambridge, UK: Cambridge University Press.

George, J.M., & Jones, G.R. (1997). Experiencing work: Values, attitudes, and moods. *Human Relations, 50*(4), 393-417.

Giddens, A. (1979). *Central problems in social theory: Action, structure, and contradiction in social analysis.* London: MacMillan Press, Ltd.

Giddens, A. (1984). *The constitution of society: Outline of the theory of structuration.* Berkeley, CA: University of California Press.

Grant, R.M. (1991). The resource-based theory of competitive advantage: Implications for strategy formulation. *California Management Review, 33*(3), 114-135.

Grant, R.M. (1996). Prospering in dynamically competitive environments: Organizational capability as knowledge integration. *Organization Science, 7*(4), 375-387.

Hall, R. (1993). A framework linking intangible resources and capabilities to sustainable competitive advantage. *Strategic Management Journal, 14,* 607–618.

Hammer, M., & Champy, J. (1993). *Reengineering the corporation.* New York: Harper Collins.

Heusinkveld, S., & Benders, J. (2001). Surges and sediments: Shaping the reception of reengineering. *Information & Management, 38*(4), 239-251.

Johnson, D.G. (1997). Is the global information infrastructure a democratic technology? *ACM SIGCAS Computers and Society, 27*(3), 20-26.

Jones, P.H. (2000). *Embedded values in innovation practice: Toward a theory of power and participation in organizations.* Ann Arbor, MI: Dissertation Abstracts International.

Jones, P.H. (2002a, June). Embedded values in process and practice: Interactions between disciplinary practice and formal innovation processes. In *Proceedings of the 11th International Forum on Design Management Research,* Boston, Massachusetts.

Jones, P.H. (2002b). When successful products prevent strategic innovation. *Design Management Journal, 13*(2), 30-37.

Kalthoff, O., Nonaka, I., & Nueno, P. (2001). *The light and the shadow: How breakthrough inno-*

vation is shaping European business. Oxford: Capstone Publishing Ltd.

King, A.W., & Zeithaml, C.P. (2003). Measuring organizational knowledge: A conceptual and methodological framework. *Strategic Management Journal, 24*, 763-772.

Kling, R. (1996). The centrality of organizations in the computerization of society. In R. Kling (Ed.), *Computerization and controversy: Value conflicts and social choices* (2nd ed., pp. 108-112). New York: Academic Press.

Kogut, B., & Zander, U. (1996). What firms do: Coordination, identity and learning. *Organization Science, 7*, 502-518.

Kraimer, M.L. (1997). Organizational goals and values: A socialization model. *Human Resource Management Review, 7*(4), 425-447.

Kumar, K., & Bjorn-Anderson, N. (1990). A cross-cultural comparison of IS designer values. *Communications of the ACM, 33*(5), 528-538.

Liebeskind, J.P., Oliver, A.L., Zucker, L.G., & Brewer, M.B. (1996). Social networks, learning and flexibility: Sourcing scientific knowledge in new biotechnology firms. *Organization Science, 7*(4), 428–443.

Lave, J., & Wenger, E. (1991). *Situated learning: Legitimate peripheral participation.* Cambridge, UK: Cambridge University Press.

Louis, M.R. (1980). Surprise and sense making: What newcomers experience in entering unfamiliar organizational settings. *Administrative Science Quarterly, 25*, 226–248.

Mahoney, J.T., & Sanchez, R. (2004). Building new management theory by integrating processes and products of thought. *Journal Of Management Inquiry, 13*(1), 34-47.

Malhotra, Y. (2004). Why do knowledge management systems fail? Enablers and constraints of knowledge management in human enterprises. In

M.E. Koenig & T.K. Srikantaiah (Eds.), *Knowledge management lessons learned: What works and what doesn't* (pp. 87-112). Silver Spring MD: Information Today (ASIST Monograph Series).

Maslow, A.H. (1965). *Eupsychian management: A journal.* Homewood, IL: The Dorsey Press.

Maslow, A.H. (1971). *The farther reaches of human nature.* New York: Viking Press.

Mertins, K., Heisig, P., & Vorbeck, J. (2001). *Knowledge management: Best practices in Europe.* Springer-Verlag.

Mintzberg, H. (1990). The design school: Reconsidering the basic premises of strategic management. *Strategic Management Journal, 11*, 171-1965.

Mintzberg, H. (1994). *The rise and fall of strategic planning.* New York: Free Press.

Nelson, R., & Winter, S. (1982). *An evolutionary theory of economic change.* Cambridge, MA: Harvard University Press.

Nonaka, I. (1991, November-December). The knowledge-creating company. *Harvard Business Review*, pp. 14-36.

Nonaka, I. (1996, February 23). *Knowledge has to do with truth, goodness, and beauty: A conversation with Professor Ikujiro Nonaka.* Claus Otto Scharmer. Tokyo.

Nonaka, I., & Nishiguchi, T. (2001). *Knowledge emergence: Social, technical, and evolutionary dimensions of knowledge creation.* Oxford, UK: Oxford University Press.

Normann, R., & Ramirez, R. (1993, July-August). From value chain to value constellation: Designing interactive strategy. *Harvard Business Review,* pp. 65-77.

Oliver, B.L. (1999). Comparing corporate managers' personal values over three decades, 1967-1995. *Journal of Business Ethics, 20*(2), 147-161.

Orlikowski, W.J. (1992). The duality of technology: Rethinking the concept of structure in organizations. *Organization Science, 3*(3), 398-427.

Orlikowski, W.J. (2000). Using technology and constituting structures: A practice lens for studying technology in organizations. *Organization Science, 11*(4), 404-428.

Orlikowski, W.J. (2002). Knowing in practice: Enacting a collective capability in distributed organizing. *Organization Science, 13*(4), 249-273.

Orlikowski, W.J., & Robey, D. (1991). Information technology and the structuring of organizations. *Information Systems Research, 2*(2), 143-169.

Penrose, E.T. (1959). *The theory of the growth of the firm.* New York: Wiley & Sons.

Polanyi, M. (1967). *The tacit dimension.* New York: Doubleday and Co.

Porter, M.E. (1980). *Competitive strategy: Techniques for analyzing industries and competitors.* New York: Free Press.

Porter, M.E. (1998). *Competitive advantage: Creating and sustaining superior performance.* New York: Free Press.

Rokeach, M. (1973). *The nature of human values.* New York: Free Press.

Schwartz, S.H. (1994). Are there universal aspects in the structure and contents of human values? *Journal of Social Issues, 50*(4), 19-46.

Spender, J.-C. (1994). Organizational knowledge, collective practice, and Penrose rents. *International Business Review, 3*(4), 353-367.

Teece, D.J. (1984). Economic analysis and strategic management. *California Management Review, 26*(3), 87-110.

Teece, D.J. (1998). Capturing value from knowledge assets: The new economy, markets for know-how, and intangible assets. *California Management Review, 40*(3), 55-79.

Teece, D.J., Pisano, G., & Schuen, A. (1997). Dynamic capabilities and strategic management. *Strategic Management Journal, 26*(3), 87-110.

Tierney, T. (1999). What's your strategy for managing knowledge? *Harvard Business Review, 77*(2), 106-116.

Timbrell, G., Delaney, P., Chan, T., Yue, A., & Gable, G. (2005). A structurationist review of knowledge management theories. In *Proceedings of the 26th Annual Conference on Information Systems* (pp. 247-259), Las Vegas, Nevada.

Venkatraman, N., & Tanriverdi, H. (2005). Reflecting "knowledge" in strategy research: Conceptual issues and methodological challenges. *Research Methodology in Strategy and Management, 1*, 33-65.

Walsham, G., & Waema, T. (1994). Information systems strategy and implementation: A case study of a building society. *ACM Transactions on Information Systems, 12*(2), 150-173.

Weick, K. E. (1995). *Sensemaking in organizations.* London: Sage Publications.

Wilson, T.D. (2002). The nonsense of "knowledge management." *Information Research, 8*(1), paper 144. Retrieved May 21, 2007, from http://InformationR.net/ir/8-1/paper144.html

Winter, S.G. (1987). Knowledge and competence as strategic assets. In D. Teece (ed.), *The competitive challenge: Strategies for industrial innovation and renewal.* Cambridge, MA: Ballinger Publishing Co., 159-184.

Wu, I.-L. (2002). A model for implementing BPR based on strategic perspectives: An empirical study. *Information and Management, 39*(4), 313-324.

Zack, M.H. (1999). Developing a knowledge strategy. *California Management Review, 41*(3), 125-145.

Zander, U., & Kogut, B. (1995). Knowledge and the speed of the transfer and imitation of organizational capabilities: An empirical test. *Organization Science, 6*, 76–91.

Additional Reading

Ackoff, R.L. (1994). *The democratic corporation.* New York: Oxford University Press.

Amburgey, T.L., Kelly, D., & Barnett, W.P. (1993). Resetting the clock: The dynamics of organizational change and failure. *Administrative Science Quarterly, 38*, 51-73.

Barrett, M., Cappleman, S., Shoib, G., & Walsham, G. (2004). Learning in knowledge communities: Managing technology and context. *European Management Journal, 22*(1), 1-11.

Blackler, F. (1993). Knowledge and the theory of organisations: Organisations as activity systems and the reframing of management. *Journal of Management Studies, 30*, 863-884.

Bloomfield, B.P., & Vurdubakis, T. (1997). Visions of organization and organizations of vision: The representational practices of information systems development. *Accounting, Organizations and Society, 22*(7), 639-668.

Boland, R.J., & Collopy, F. (2004). *Managing as designing.* Stanford, CA: Stanford University Press.

Christensen, C.M., & Raynor, M.E. (2003). *The innovator's solution: Creating and sustaining successful growth.* Boston: Harvard Business School Press.

Ciborra, C.U. (2004). *The labyrinths of information: Challenging the wisdom of systems.* Oxford, UK: Oxford University Press.

Cole, M., & Engeström, Y. (1991). A cultural historical approach to distributed cognition. In G.

Salamon (Ed.), *Distributed cognition* (pp. 1-47). Cambridge: Cambridge University Press.

Collins, J.C., & Porras, J.I. (1996, September-October). Building your company's vision. *Harvard Business Review,* pp. 65-88.

Eisenhardt, K. (1988). Agency and institutional theory explanations: The case of retail sales competition. *Academy of Management Journal, 30*, 488-511.

Ellingsen, G., & Monteiro, E. (2003). Mechanisms for producing a working knowledge: Enacting, orchestrating, and organizing. *Information and Organization, 13*, 203-229.

Ellis, R.K., & Hall, M.L.W. (1994). Systems and values: An approach for practical organizational intervention. *Proceedings of the ISSS, 94.*

Hannan, M.T., & Freeman, J.H. (1989). *Organizational ecology.* Cambridge. MA: Harvard University Press.

Hanseth, O., & Monteiro, E. (1997). Navigating future research: Judging the relevance of information systems development research. *Accounting, Management, and Information Technology, 6*(1/2), 77-85.

Hinings, C.R., Thibault, L., Slack, T., & Kikulis, L.M. (1996). Values and organizational structure. *Human Relations, 49*(7), 885-917.

Keeney, R.L. (1994). Creativity in decision making with value-focused thinking. *Sloan Management Review, 35*, 33-41.

Kohlberg, L. (1969). Stage and sequence: The cognitive development approach to socialization. In D.A. Goslin (Ed.), *Handbook of socialization theory and research* (pp. 347-480). Chicago: Rand McNally.

Lave, J. (1988). *Cognition in practice.* Cambridge, UK: Cambridge University Press.

Nevis, E.C., DiBella, A.J., & Gould, J.M. (1995). Understanding organizations as learning systems. *Sloan Management Review, 36*, 73-85.

Norrgren, F., & Schaller, J. (1999). Leadership style: Its impact on cross-functional product development. *Journal of Product Innovation Management, 16*(4), 377-384.

Parolini, C. (1999). *The value net: A tool for competitive strategy.* Great Britain: John Wiley & Sons Ltd.

Raynor, M. E. (2007). *The strategy paradox: Why committing to success leads to failure (and what to do about it).* New York: Doubleday.

Rouse, W. (2005). A theory of enterprise transformation. *Systems Engineering, 8*(4), 279-295.

Sauer, C., & Willcocks, L. (2003). Establishing the business of the future: The role of organizational architecture and information technologies. *European Management Journal, 21*(4), 497-508.

Star, S.L., & Ruhleder, K. (1994, October 22-26). Steps toward an ecology of infrastructure. In *Proceedings of CSCW, 94,* 253–264, Chapel Hill, North Carolina.

Storck, J., & Hill, P.A. (2000). Knowledge diffusion through "strategic communities." *Sloan Management Review, 41,* 63-74.

Thompson, M.P.A., & Walsham, G. (2004). Placing knowledge management in context. *Journal of Management Studies, 41*(5), 725-747.

Tolbert, P.S., & Zucker, L.G. (1999). The institutionalization of institutional theory. In S.R. Clegg & C. Hardy (Eds.), *Studying organization.* London: SAGE Publications.

Vaast, E., & Walsham, G. (2005). Representations and actions: The transformation of work practices with IT use. *Information and Organization, 15*(1), 65-89.

van Maanen, J., & Barley, S.R. (1984). Occupational communities: Culture and control in organizations. In B.M. Staw (Ed.), *Research in organizational behavior* (vol. 6). Greenwich, CT: JAI Press.

von Krogh, G., & Roos, J. (1995). *Organizational epistemology.* New York: St. Martin's.

Walsham, G. (2001). Knowledge management: The benefits and limitations of computer systems. *European Management Journal, 19*(6), 599-608.

Weick, K.E. (1989). Theory construction as disciplined imagination. *Academy of Management Review, 14,* 532-550.

Weick, K.E. (1990). Technology as equivoque: Sensemaking in new technologies. In P. Goodman et al. (Eds.), *Technology and organizations* (pp. 1-44). San Francisco: Jossey-Bass.

Weick, K.E., & Bougon, M.G. (1986). Organizations as cognitive maps: Charting ways to success and failure. In *The thinking organization* (pp. 102-135). San Francisco: Jossey-Bass.

Wynn, E. (1991). Taking practice seriously. In J. Greenbaum & M. Kyng (Eds.), *Design at work.* Hillsdale, NJ: Lawrence Erlbaum Associates.

Yasai-Ardekani, M., & Haug, R.S. (1997). Contextual determinants of strategic planning processes. *Journal of Management Studies, 5*(34), 729-741.

Yates, J., & Orlikowski, W.J. (1992). Genres of organizational communication: A structurational approach to studying communication and media. *The Academy of Management Review, 17*(2), 299-326.

Zuboff, S. (1988). *In the age of the smart machine.* New York: Basic Books.

This work was previously published in Knowledge Management and Business Strategies: Theoretical Frameworks and Empirical Research, edited by E. Abou-Zeid, pp. 133-163, copyright 2008 by Information Science Reference, formerly known as Idea Group Reference (an imprint of IGI Global).

Compilation of References

Aadne, J.H., von Krogh, G., & Roos, J. (1996). `Representationism, The Traditional Approach to Cooperative Strategies`. In von Krogh, G. & Roos, J. (Eds.). *Managing Knowledge: Perspectives on Cooperation and Competition,* pp. 9-31; London: Sage Publications.

Abrams, L. C., Cross, R., Lesser, E. and Levin, D.Z. (2003). Nurturing interpersonal trust in knowledge-sharing networks, *Academy of Management Executive,* 17(4), 64-77.

Acker, J. (1990). Hierarchies, Jobs, `Bodies: A Theory of Gendered Organizations´, in *Gender and Society,* 4(2) 139-158.

Ackoff, R.L. (1994). *The democratic corporation.* New York: Oxford University Press.

Adar, E., Zhang, L., Adamic, L. A, & Lukose, R. M. (2004). Implicit structure and the dynamics of blogspace. In *Workshop on the Weblogging Ecosystem,* New York, NY, USA, May 2004.

Adenfelt, M. and Lagerström, K. (2006). Knowledge development and sharing in multinational corporations: the case of a centre of excellence and a transnational team, *International Business Review,* 15(4), 381-400.

Adie, C. (2006). Report of the information services working group on collaborative tools. Retrieved May 27, 2007 from http://www.is.ed.ac.uk/content/1/c4/10/46/CollaborativeToolsAndWeb2%200.pdf

ADL, Ottobre 2001, "SCORM 1.2 – Overview, Content Aggregation Model, Run Time Environment" (http://www.adlnet.org)

Aggarwal, A. K., & Legon, R. (2006). Web-based education diffusion. *International Journal of Web-Based Learning and Teaching Technologies,* 1(1), 49-72.

Aghion, P. & Howitt, P. (1997). A Schumpeterian Perspective on Growth and Competition. In D. M. Kreps & K. F. Wallis (Eds.), *Advances in Economics and Econometrics: Theory and Applications, Vol. 2* (pp. 279-317). New York, NY: Cambridge University Press.

Agrawal, A. and Henderson, R. (2002). Putting patents in context: exploring knowledge transfer from MIT, *Management Science,* 48(1), 44-60.

Ahmed, P. K, Kok, L.K, & Loh, A.Y.E (2002). *Learning Through Knowledge Management.* Oxford: Butterworth-Heinemann.

Alexa Traffic Rankings: Global Top 500 (2007). Retrieved May 27, 2007 from http://www.alexa.com/site/ds/top_sites?ts_mode=global&lang=none

Alexander, B. (2006). Web 2.0: A new wave of innovation for teaching and learning? *Educause Review, 41*(2) (March/April). Retrieved April 19, 2007 from http://www.educause.edu/ir/library/pdf/ERM0621.pdf

Alexander, B. (2006). Web 2.0: A new wave of innovation for teaching and learning? *Educause Review, 41*(2), 32-44.

Alier, M. (2006) "A Social Constructionist Approach to Learning Communities:Moodle" in "Open Source for Knowledge and Learning Management: Strategies Beyond Tools" Militadis D. Lytras, Ambjörn Naeve (Eds). Idea Group INC.

Copyright © 2009, IGI Global, distributing in print or electronic forms without written permission of IGI Global is prohibited.

Ali-Hasan, N. F., & Adamic, L. A. (2007). Expressing Social Relationships on the Blog through Links and Comments. *Proceedings of International Conference on Weblogs and Social Media*, Boulder, Colorado, USA, March 26-28, 2007.

Alkin, M. (1997). Stakeholder Concepts in Program Evaluation. In Evaluation for Educational Productivity, edited by A.Reynolds & H.Walberg. Greenwich, CT: JAI.

Allaire, Y. & Firsirotu M.E. (1984). Theories of Organizational Culture, *Organization Studies,* 193-226.

Allan, B., Lewis, D., (2006). Virtual learning communities as a vehicle for workforce development: A case study. *Journal of Workplace Learning, 1356-5626, Vol. 18 (6) pp 367-383.*

Allen, C. (2004) Life with alacrity: Tracing the evolution of social software, http://www.lifewithalacrity.com/2004/10/tracing_the_evo.html

Alrawi, K. (2007). Knowledge management and the organization's perception: a review. *Journal of Knowledge Management Practice*, 8(1). http://www.tlainc.com/articl131.htm

Amburgey, T.L., Kelly, D., & Barnett, W.P. (1993). Resetting the clock: The dynamics of organizational change and failure. *Administrative Science Quarterly, 38,* 51-73.

American Productivity & Quality Center (APQC). (1999). *Creating a knowledge-sharing culture.* Consortium Benchmarking Study -- Best-Practice Report.

American Productivity & Quality Center (APQC). (2000). *Successfully implementing knowledge management.* Consortium Benchmarking Study -- Final Report, 2000.

Andersen, I. (1999). *The apparent reality—On knowledge production in the social sciences* (3rd ed.) [in Danish]. Copenhagen, Denmark: Samfundslitteratur.

Andersen, T., B. Eriksen, J. Lemmergaard, & L. Povlsen (2006). The Many Faces of Fit – An application to strategic human resource management, Chapter 5 (pp. 85-101). In Burton et al., 2006, *Organization Design.*

The Evolving State-of-the-Art. LLC, USA: Springer Science+Business Media.

Anderson, P. (1999). Complexity theory and organization science. *Organization Science, 10*(3), 216-232.

Anderson, T. (2004). Teaching in an Online Learning Context. In T. Anderson & F. Elloumi (Eds.), *Theory and practice in online learning* (pp. 271-296). Athabasca: Athabasca University.

Andres, Y. M. (2002). Art of Collaboration: Awesome Tools and Proven Strategies. *Journal of Computer-Mediated Communication, 8*(1), Retrieved January 2005, from http://clp.cqu.edu.au/online_articles.htm

Andrienko, N. and Andrienko, G. (2005). Exploratory Analysis of Spatial and Temporal Data -- A Systematic Approach. Springer.

Andriessen E, Soekijad M., Keasberry H.J. (2002). *Support for knowledge sharing in communities.* Delft University Press.

Andriessen, D. (2004). IC Valuation and Measurement: Classifying the State of the Art. *Journal of Intellectual Capital, 5*(2), 230-242.

Anthes, G. (2007). Second Life: Is there any there there? *Computerworld, 41*(49), 30-38.

Argyris, C. (1992). Why individuals and organizations have difficulty in double loop learning. In *On organizational learning* (pp. 7-38). Cambridge: Blackwell Publishers.

Argyris, C., & Schön, D. (1978). *Organizational learning: A theory of action perspective.* New York: McGraw-Hill.

Ariño, A., Torre, J.D.L. and Ring, P.S. (2001). Relational quality: managing trust in corporate alliances, *California Management Review,* **44(1),** 109–31.

Aristoteles (2000). "Poetics" (translated by S. H. Butcher). http://classics.mit.edu/Aristotle/poetics.html, {25.7.2006}.

Armstrong, S.J. (1997). Co-opetition, *Journal of Marketing,* 61(2), 92-95.

Ashforth, B.E. & Humphrey, R.H. (1995) Emotion in the workplace. A reappraisal`. *Human Relations*, 48. Jg. (1995) 2, S. 97–125.

Assudani, R.H. (2005). Catching the chameleon: understanding the elusive term "knowledge". *Journal of Knowledge Management, 9*(2), 31-44.

Attwell, G. (2006). *Personal learning environment.* Retrieved May 17, 2007, from http://www.knownet.com/writing/weblogs/Graham_Attwell/entries/6521819364

Augar, N., Raitman, R., & Zhou, W. (2004, December 5-8). Teaching and learning online with wikis. In R. Atkinson, C. McBeath, D. Jonas-Dwyer, & R. Phillips (Eds.), *Beyond the Comfort Zone*: *Proceedings of the 21ˢᵗ ASCILITE Conference*, Perth, Western Australia. Retrieved May 17, 2007, from http://www.ascilite.org.au/conferences/perth04/procs/contents.html

Avouris N., Komis V., Fiotakis G., Dimitracopoulou A., Margaritis M. (2004b). Method and tools for analysis of collaborative problem-solving activities. Proceedings of ATIT2004, First International Workshop on Activity Theory Based Practical Methods for IT Design , Denmark, September 2004, 5-16.

Avouris N.M., Dimitracopoulou A., Komis V., (2003). On analysis of collaborative problem solving: An object-oriented approach, Computers in Human Behavior, 19(2), 147-167.

Avouris N.M., Dimitracopoulou A., Komis V., Fidas C., (2002). OCAF: An object-oriented model of analysis of collaborative problem solving, G. Stahl (ed), Proceedings CSCL 2002, pp.92-101, Colorado, January 2002, Erlbaum Assoc. Hillsdale, NJ, 2002.

Avouris, N., Komis, V., Margaritis, M., Fiotakis, G.(2004a). An environment for studying collaborative learning activities, Journal of International Forum of Educational Technology & Society, 7(2), 34-41.

Axelrod, R. (1997). *The complexity of cooperation: Agent-based models of competition and collaboration.* New Jersey: Princeton University Press.

Axelrod, R., & Cohen, M. (1999). *Harnessing complexity: Organizational implications of a scientific frontier.* New York: The Free Press.

Babcock, M. (2007). Learning logs in introductory literature courses. *Teaching in Higher Education, 12*(4), 513-523.

Baise, M. & Stahl, H. (1999). Public Research and Industrial Innovations in Germany. *Research Policy*, 28, 397-422.

Baker M., Hansen, T., Joiner, R., & Traum, D. (1999). The role of grounding in collaborative learning tasks. In P.Dillenbourg (Ed.): Collaborative learning: Cognitive and computational approaches. UK: Elsevier Science/Pergamon.

Balester, V., Halasek, K. & Peterson, N. (1992). Sharing authority: Collaborative teaching in a computer-based writing course. *Computers and Composition, 9*(1), 25-40.

Banathy, B.H. (1996). *Designing social systems in a changing world.* New York: Plenum Publishing Co.

Barber, B.R. (2004). *Strong Democracy: Participatory Politics for a New Age.* University of California Press.

Barkow, J.H., Cosmides, L., & Tooby, J. (Eds.). (1992). *The adapted mind: Evolutionary psychology and the generation of culture.* New York, NY: Oxford University Press.

Barney, J.B. (1986). Organizational culture: Can it be a source of sustained competitive advantage? *The Academy of Management Review, 11*(3), 656-665.

Barney, J.B. (1986). Strategic factor markets: expectations, luck, and business strategy, *Management Science*, 32, 1231-1241.

Baron, J., & Spranca, M. (1997). Protected values. *Organizational Behavior and Human Decision Processes, 70*(1), 1–16.

Barrett, M., Cappleman, S., Shoib, G., & Walsham, G. (2004). Learning in knowledge communities: Managing technology and context. *European Management Journal, 22*(1), 1-11.

Barros, M., Verjedo, M., (2000). Analysing learner interaction processes in order to improve collaboration. The DEGREE approach. International Journal of Artificial Intelligence in Education, 11, 221-241.

Bates, B., & Cleese, J. (2001). *The human face.* New York, NY: DK Publishing.

Bates, T. (Forthcoming) Understanding Web 2.0 and its implications for e-learning; in *Web 2.0-Based E-Learning: Applying Social Informatics for Tertiary Teaching,* Lee, M. & McLoughlin, C. (Eds); IGI Global

Baudrillard, J. (2002). Between Difference and Singularity: An open discussion with Jean Baudrillard. Available: http://www.egs.edu/faculty/baudrillard/baudrillard-between-difference-and-singularity-2002.html. Retrieved: 02-10-07.

Baumgartner, P. (2004). The Zen art of teaching. *Communication and Interactions in eEducation.* Retrieved May 17, 2007, from http://bt-mac2.fernuni-hagen.de/peter/gems/zenartofteaching.pdf

Baumgartner, P. (2005). Eine neue lernkultur entwickeln: Komptenzbasierte ausbildung mit blogs und e-portfolios. In V. Hornung-Prähauser (Ed.), *ePortfolio Forum Austria: Proceedings of the ePortfolio Austria 2005*, Salzburg, Austria (pp. 33-38).

Baumgartner, P., Häfele, H., & Maier-Häfele, K. (2004). *Content management systeme in e-education: Auswahl, potenziale und einsatzmöglichkeiten.* Innsbruck, Austria: Studienverlag.

Bauwens, M. (2005) Peer to Peer and Human Evolution. Available online: http://integralvisioning.org/article.php?story=p2ptheory1. Retrieved: 6-04-08

Beck, U. (1999). *Individualization.* London: Sage.

Becker, B. & Gerhart, B. (1996). The Impact of Human Resource Management on Organizational Performance: Progress and prospects. *Academy of Management Journal*, 39(4), 779-801.

Bedny, G., Karwowski, W., & Bedny, M. (2001). The principle of unity of cognition and behavior: Implications of activity theory for the study of human work. International Journal of Cognitive Ergonomics, 5(4), 401-420.

Beinhocker, E.D. (1999, March). Robust adaptive strategies. *Sloan Management Review,* p. 22.

Bendel, O. (2006). Wikipedia als methode und gegenstand der lehre. In K. Hildebrand (Ed.), *HMD: Praxis der wirtschaftsinformatik: Vol. 252. Social software* (pp. 82-88). Heidelberg, Germany: dpunkt-Verlag.

Benkler, Y. (2005) Common Wisdom: Peer Production of Educational Materials, retrieved on 19. Feb. 2008 from http://www.benkler.org/Common_Wisdom.pdf

Berry, D. C. (ed.) (1997). *How Implicit is Implicit Learning?* Oxford; Oxford University Press.

Bierly, P. & Chakrabarti, A. (1996). Generic Knowledge Strategies in the US Pharmaceutical Industry. *Strategic Management Journal*, 17(1), 123-135.

Blackler, F. (1993). Knowledge and the theory of organisations: Organisations as activity systems and the reframing of management. *Journal of Management Studies, 30*, 863-884.

Blackler, F. (1995). Knowledge, Knowledge Work and Organizations: An Overview and Interpretation. *Organization Science, 16*(6), 1021-46.

Bloomfield, B.P., & Vurdubakis, T. (1997). Visions of organization and organizations of vision: The representational practices of information systems development. *Accounting, Organizations and Society, 22*(7), 639-668.

Boland, R.J., & Collopy, F. (2004). *Managing as designing.* Stanford, CA: Stanford University Press.

Bollen, K.A. (1989). A new incremental fit index for general structural equation models, *Sociological Methods and Research*, 17, 313-316.

Borgatti, S. P., Everett, M. G., & Freeman, L. C. (2002). *Ucinet 6 for Windows: Software for social network analysis.* Harvard: Analytic Technologies.

Böttger, M., & Röll, M. (2004, December 15-17). Weblog publishing as support for exploratory learning on the World Wide Web. In P. Isaias, K. Demetrios, & G. Sampson (Eds.), *Cognition and Exploratory Learning in Digital Age (CELDA 2004): Proceedings of the IADIS International Conference*, Lisbon, Portugal. IADIS Press.

Boud, D. and Miller, N. (Eds.) (1997). *Working with Experience: animating learning*, Routledge, London.

Boulos, M.N.K., Maramba, I., & Wheeler, S. (2006). Wikis, blogs and podcasts: A new generation of web-based tools for virtual collaborative clinical practice and education, *BMC Medical Education, 6*(41). Retrieved April 19, 2007 from http://www.biomedcentral.com/content/pdf/1472-6920-6-41.pdf

Boyd, S. (2003). Are you ready for social software? Retrieved April 19, 2007 from http://internettime.com/blog/archives/000554.html

Bradbury, H., & Lichtenstein, B.M.B. (2000). Relationality in organizational research: Exploring The Space Between. *Organization Science, 11,* 551-564.

Brahm, T. (2007). Social software und personal broadcasting: Stand der forschung. In S. Seufert & D. Euler (Eds.), *Ne(x)t generation learning: Wikis, blogs, mediacasts & Co. Social software und personal broadcasting auf der spur* (pp. 20-38). SCIL Arbeitsbericht.

Braithwaite, V.A., & Law, H.G. (1985). Structure of human values: Testing the adequacy of the Rokeach Value Survey. *Journal of Personality and Social Psychology, 49,* 250-262.

Brandenburger, A.M. and Nalebuff, B.J. (1996). *Co-opetition*, New York, New York, USA: Currency-Doubleday.

Brandenburger, A.M. and Stuart, H.W. (1996). Value-based business strategy, *Journal of Economics & Management Strategy*, 5(1), 5-24.

Brännström, M., & Mårtenson, C. (2006). Enhancing situational awareness by exploiting wiki technology. Proceedings of the Conference on Civil and Military Readi-

ness 2006 (CIMI 2006), Enköping, Sweden, 16-18 May, Paper S3.2. Försvarets Materielverk, Stockholm. http://www.foi.se/infofusion/bilder/CIMI_2006_S3_2.pdf

Bransford, J., Brown, A., & Cocking, R. (1999). *How people learn: Brain, mind experience and school.* Retrieved April 2005, from http://www.nap.edu/html/howpeople1

Bratitsis, T., & Dimitrakopoulou, A. (2005). Data recording and usage interaction analysis in asynchronous discussions: The DIAS system. Proceedings of the 12th International Conference on Artificial Intelligence in Education AIED, Workshop "Usage Analysis in Learning Systems", Amsterdam, The Netherlands (2005).

Braun, N. (2004). "Kontrolliertes Erzählen von Geschichten mit integrierten, Videobasierten Hyperstories". In: R. Keil-Slawik, H. Selke, and G. Szwillus (eds.), Mensch & Computer 2004: Allgegenw¨artige Interaktion, Oldenbourg. pp. 157–167.

Brin, S., & Page, L. (1998). The antaomy of a large-scale hypertextual Web search engine. *Computer Networks and ISDN Systems*(33), 107-135.

Brown J.S., Collins A., Duguid S. (1998). *Situated cognition and the culture of learning.* Educational Researcher, 1, pp. 32-42.

Brown, J. S., & Gray, E. S. (1995). *The people are the company.* Retrieved January 11, 2005, from http://www.fastcompany.com/magazine/01/people.html

Brown, J.S. and Duguid, P. (1998), "*Organizing Knowledge*", California Management Review, Vol. 40, No. 3, pp. 90 – 111.

Brown, J.S. and Duguid, P. (2000). The Social Life of Information. Harvard Business School Press. Boston, MA.

Brown, J.S., & Duguid, P. (1991). Organizational learning and communities of practice: Toward a unified view of working, learning and innovation. *Organization Science, 2,* 40-57.

Bruner, J. (1986). *Actual minds, possible worlds.* Cambridge: Harvard University Press.

Bryson, B.F. (1999). A study of individual reactions to career plateaus in the natural resources management branch of the Operations Division of the U.S. Army Corps of Engineers. *UMI Dissertation Services.*

Bukowitz, W., & Williams, R. (1999). *The knowledge management fieldbook.* London: Financial Times Prentice Hall.

Bulters, J., & de Rijke, M. (2007). Discovering Weblog Communities. *Proceedings of International Conference on Weblogs and Social Media,* Boulder, Colorado, USA, March 26- 28, 2007.

Burgoyne, J. G. & Hodgson, V. E. (1983). Natural learning and managerial action: A phenomenological study in the field setting, *Journal of Management Studies,* 20 (3): 387-399.

Buss, D.M. (1999). *Evolutionary psychology: The new science of the mind.* Needham Heights, MA: Allyn & Bacon.

Cacioppe, R., & Edwards, M. (2005). Adjusting blurred visions: a typology of integral approaches to organizations. *Journal of Organizational Change Management, 18*(3), 230-246.

Calvert, S. L. (2002). Identity Construction on the Internet. In S. L. Calvert, A. B. Jordan & R. R. Cocking (Eds.), Children in the Digital Age: Influences of Electronic Media on Development (pp. 57 - 70). Wesport, Connecticut: Praeger.

Campanini, S.E., Castagna, P., Tazzoli, R. (2004). Platypus wiki: A semantic wiki wiki web. Proceedings of Semantic Web Applications and Perspectives (SWAP) - 1st Italian Semantic Web Workshop, 10th December 2004, Ancona, Italy http://semanticweb.deit.univpm. it/swap2004/cameraready/castagna.pdf

Carayannis, E.G. and Alexander, J. (1999). Winning by co-opeting in strategic government-university-industry R&D partnerships: the power of complex, dynamic knowledge networks, J*ournal of Technology Transfer,* 24(2-3), p. 197.

Casey, C. (2000). Sensing the Body: Revitalizing a Dissociative Discourse, in Hassard, J., Holliday, R., & Wilmott, H. (2000). *Body and Organisation,* (pp. 52-70). London: Sage.

Castells, M. (1997). *The Power of Identity.* Oxford: Blackwell.

Center for Digital Storytelling (2005). Homepage, http://www.storycenter.org/index1.html, {25.7.2006}.

Chae, B., & Bloodgood, J.M. (2006). The paradoxes of knowledge management: An eastern philosophical perspective. *Information and Organization, 16*(1), 1-26.

Chagnon, N.A. (1977). *Yanomamo: The fierce people.* New York, NY: Holt, Rinehart and Winston.

Chao, J. (2007). Student project collaboration using wikis. In *Proceedings of the 20th Conference on Software Engineering Education & Training* (pp. 255-261). Washington, DC.

Chao, J. (2007). Student project collaboration using Wikis. *Proceedings of the 20th Conference on Software Engineering Education and Training (CSEE&T 2007),* Dublin, Ireland: July 3-5.

Checkland, P., & Scholes, J. (1990). *Soft systems methodology in action.* Toronto, Canada: John Wiley and Sons.

Chen, M., & Singh, J.P. (2001). *Computing and using reputations for internet ratings.* Tampa, Florida, USA : ACM Press.

Choate, M.S. (2007). *Professional Wikis.*Hoboken, NJ: Wrox Press.

Choo, C.W. (1998). *The Knowing Organization.* New York: Oxford University Press.

Choo, C.W. (1998). *The knowing organization: How organizations use information to construct meaning, create knowledge, and make decisions.* New York: Oxford University Press.

Christensen, C.M. (1997). *The innovator's dilemma.* Boston: Harvard Business School Press.

Christensen, C.M., & Raynor, M.E. (2003). *The innovator's solution: Creating and sustaining successful growth.* Boston: Harvard Business School Press.

Ciborra, C.U. (1998). Crisis and foundations: An inquiry into the nature and limits of models and methods in the information systems discipline. *Journal of Strategic Information Systems, 7,* 5-16.

Ciborra, C.U. (2004). *The labyrinths of information: Challenging the wisdom of systems.* Oxford, UK: Oxford University Press.

Clark, J. (2000). Collaboration Tools in Online Learning Environments. *ALN Magazine, 4*(2). Retrieved August 2005, from http://www.sloan-c.org/publications/magazine/v4n1/index.asp

Coates, T. (2005). *An addendum to a definition of social software.* Retrieved March 4, 2007, from http://www.plasticbag.org/archives/2005/01/an_addendum_to_a_definition_of_social_software

Cognition and Technology Group at Vanderbilt (1997). The Jasper Project. Lessons in curriculum, instruction, assessment, and professional development. Mahwah, NJ: Erlbaum.

Cohen, W. M. and Levinthal, D. A. (1990). Absorptive capacity: a new perspective on learning and innovation, *Administrative Science Quarterly,* 35(1), 128-152.

Cohen, W.M. & Levinthal, D.A. (1990). Absorptive Capacity: A New Perspective on Learning and Innovation. *Administrative Science Quarterly,* 35(1), 128-152.

COLAB: An Open Collaborative Work Environment Wiki. http://colab.cim3.net/cgi-bin/wiki.pl?WikiHomePage

Cole M. (1996). Cultural psychology: a once and future discipline. Cambridge, Mass.: Belknap Press of Harvard University Press.

Cole M., & Engeström, Y. (1993). A cultural-historical approach to distributed cognition. In Learning, working and imagining: twelve studies in activity theory. Helsinky: Orienta-Konsultit Oy.

Cole, M., & Engeström, Y. (1991). A cultural historical approach to distributed cognition. In G. Salamon (Ed.), *Distributed cognition* (pp. 1-47). Cambridge: Cambridge University Press.

Coleman, G. (2008). Toward a positive critique of the social web. Available online: http://www.re-public.gr/en/?p=288. Retrieved: 6-04-08.

Collins, J.C., & Porras, J.I. (1996, September-October). Building your company's vision. *Harvard Business Review,* pp. 65-88.

Collins, J.C., & Porras, J.I. (1996, September-October). Building your company's vision. *Harvard Business Review,* pp. 65-88.

Collison, G., Elbaum, B., Haavind, S. & Tinker, R. (2000). *Facilitating Online Learning: Effective Strategies for Moderators.* Madison, WI: Atwood Publishing.

Comas, J., & Sieber, S. (2001). Connecting knowledge management and experiential learning to gain new insights and research perspectives. In *Proceeding of the ECIS 2001,* Bled, Slowenia.

Cook, S. D. N., & Brown, J. S. (1999). Bridging epistemologies: The generative dance between organisational knowledge and organisational knowing. *Organisational Science, 4,* 381-400.

Cook, S.D., & Brown, J.S. (1999). Bridging epistemologies: The generative dance between organizational knowledge and organizational knowing. *Organization Science, 10,* 381-400.

Corso M., Giacobbe A., Martini (2008). Community and collaboration tools in the Italian banking industry. *International Journal of E-Banking,* Vol. 1, No. 1/2.

Corso, M., Giacobbe and A., Martini, A. (2008), "*Rethinking Knowledge Management: the Role of ICT and the Rise of the Virtual Workspace*", International Journal of Learning and Intellectual Capital

Corso, M., Giacobbe, A., Martini, A. and Pellegrini, L. (2006), "*What Knowledge Management for Mobile Workers?*", Knowledge and Process Management Journal,

Special Issue on Continuous Innovation and Knowledge Management, Vol. 13, No. 3, pp. 206-217.

Corso, M., Martini, A., Paolucci, E. and Pellegrini, L. (2004), "*Knowledge Management Systems in Continuous Product Innovation*", in Leondes, CT (Ed.), Intelligent knowledge-based systems. Business and Technology in the New Millennium. Volume 1 Knowledge-Based Systems, Chapter 2. Kluwer Academic Press, pp. 36-66.

Cox, S. and Daisey, P. et al. (eds.) (2005). OpenGIS Geography Markup Language (GML) Encoding Specification. Open Geospatial Consortium, Inc.

Craig, E. (2007). Changing paradigms: Managed learning environments and Web 2.0. *Campus-Wide Information Systems, 24*(3), 152-161.

Crosby, L.A., Bitner, M.J., & Gill, J.D. (1990). Organizational structure of values. *Journal of Business Research, 20*(2), 123-134.

Cross, R., & Parker, A. (2004). *The Hidden Power of Social Networks: understanding how work really gets done in organizations*. Harvard Business School Press, Boston.

Crossley, N. (1994). *The Politics of Subjectivity: Between Foucault and Merleau-Ponty*. Aldershot, England: Brookfield USA, Avebury Series in Philosophy.

Crossley, N. (1996). *Intersubjectivity: The Fabric of Social Becoming*. London: Sage.

Cunningham, W. (2007). Wiki design principles. Retrieved April 19, 2007 from http://c2.com/cgi/wiki?WikiDesignPrinciples

Dahlbom, B., & Mathiassen, L. (1993). *Computers in context—The philosophy and practice of systems design*. Cambridge, UK: Blackwell.

Dale, K. (2001). *Anatomising Embodiment and Organisation Theory*. Basingstoke: Palgrave.

Dale, K., & Burrell, G. (2000). What shape are we in? Organization theory and the organized body, in J. Hassard, R. Holliday, & H. Willmott (Eds.), (2000). *Body and organization,* (pp. 15-30). London: Sage.

Dall'Alba, G. & Barnacle, R. (2005). Embodied knowing in online environments. *Educational Philosophy. and Theory*, 37(5), 719–744.

Damiani E., Corallo A., Elia G., Ceravolo P.,"Standard per i learning objects: Interoperabilità ed integrazione nella didattica a distanza" , Convegno internazionale: "eLearning: una sfida per l'Universita' - Strategie Metodi Prospettive", 11-13 Nov., 2002.

Daugherty, M., & Turner, J. (2003). Sociometry: An approach for assessing group dynamics in web-based courses. *Interactive Learning Environments, 11*(3), 263-275.

Davenport T. and Prusak L. 'Working Knowledge. How organization manage what they know', (Boston: Harward Business School Press,1998)

Davenport, T. and Prusak, L. (1998). Working Knowledge: How Organizations Manage What they Know, Cambridge, MA, Harvard Business School Press.

Davenport, T. H., & Prusak, L. (1998). *Working Knowledge: How Organizations Manage What They Know.* Harvard Business School Press, Boston, MA, USA.

Davenport, T., Thomas, H., & Short, J.E. (1990, Summer). The new industrial engineering: Information technology and business process redesign. *Sloan Management Review,* pp. 11–26.

Davies, J. (2004). Wiki brainstorming and problems with wiki based collaboration. Unpublished Masters Thesis, Department of Computer Science at the University of York, Heslington, York, UK. Retrieved May 27, 2007 from http://www-users.cs.york.ac.uk/~kimble/teaching/students/Jonathan_Davies/wiki_collaboration_and_brainstorming.pdf

Davis, V.A. (2007) "The frontier of education: Web 3D" The Coolcat teacher blog. Online http://coolcatteacher.blogspot.com/2007/03/frontier-of-education-web-3d.html Accesed 13 March 2007

De Laat, M., Lally, V, Lipponen, L. and Simons, P.R.J. (2005). Patterns of interaction in a networked learning community: Squaring the circle. Manuscript submitted for publication (Submitted) http://eprints.soton.ac.uk/17267/.

de Sousa, R. (1987). *The Rationality of Emotions.* Cambridge, MA: MIT Press.

De Souza, C., S., Preece, J. (2004). A framework for analyzing and understanding online communities. Interacting with Computers. The Interdisciplinary Journal of Human-Computer Interaction, downloadable at http://www.ifsm.umbc.edu/~preece/Papers/Framework_desouza_preece2003.pdf. Paper retrieved on May 30th, 2007.

Dearlove, D. (2004). Origins and blasphemies, *Business Strategy Review*, 15(2), 2-4.

Decker B., Ras E., Rech J., Klein B., & Hoecht C. (2005). Self-organized reuse of software engineering knowledge supported by semantic wikis. Proceedings of the Workshop on Semantic Web Enabled Software Engineering (SWESE), at the 4th International Semantic Web Conference (ISWC 2005), November 6-10, 2005, Galway, Ireland.

Delphi Consulting Group, "Delphi on knowledge management. Research and perspectives on today's knowledge landscape", Boston, MA, USA, 1997"

DeMarzo, R.C. (2003). Today's top channel execs set corporate strategy - the chief channel officer is on par with the CFO or CIO in many companies, *VARbusiness*, Mar 3, 2003, 10.

Denzin, N.K. (1984). *On understanding emotion.* San Francisco, CA: Jossey-Bass.

DeSanctis, G., & Poole, M.S. (1994). Capturing the complexity in advanced technology use: Adaptive structuration theory. *Organization Science, 5*(2), 121-145.

Despres, C., & Chauvel, D. (2000). *Knowledge Horizons. The Present and the Promise of Knowledge Management.* New York: Butterworth-Heinemann.

Desrochers, P. (2001). Local Diversity, Human Creativity, and technological Innovation. *Growth and Change*, 32, 369-394.

Deutsch, M., Krauss, R.M. (1962). Studies of Interpersonal Bargaining. *Journal of Conflict Resolution*, 6, 52-76

Dickey, M. D. (2005). "Three-dimensional virtual worlds and distance learning: two case studies of Active Worlds as a medium for distance education." British Journal of Educational Technology 36(3): 439-451.

Diehl, W. (2007) The new social networking technologies: educators get a Second Life; in The Twelfth Cambridge Conference on Open and Distance Learning, www2.open.ac.uk/r06/conference/CambridgeConferencePapers2.pdf

Dieng, R., Corby, O., Giboin, A., Ribiere, M. (1999). Methods and tools for corporate knowledge management. *Int. J. Human-Computer Studies,* 51 (567-598).

Digital Storytelling Organization (DSA). (2002). "Defining Digital Storytelling". http://www.dsaweb.org/01associate/ds.html {25.7.2006}.

Dillenbourg, P. (1999). Collaborative Learning: Cognitive and Computational Approaches. Elsevier Science, Oxford.

Dillenbourg, P. (1999). What do you mean by collaborative learning?. In P. Dillenbourg (Ed) *Collaborative-learning: Cognitive and Computational Approaches.* (pp.1-19). Oxford: Elsevier.

Dillenbourg, P., & Schneider, D. (1995, March 7-10). Collaborative learning and the internet. Paper presented at the *International Conference on Computer Assisted Instruction (ICCAI'95).* National Chiao Tung University, Hsinchu, Taiwan. Retrieved January 2005, from http://tecfa.unige.ch/tecfa/research/CMC/colla/iccai95_1.html

Dillenbourg, P., & Traum, D. (1999). Does a shared screen make a shared solution? Paper presented at the Computer Supported Collaborative Learning Conference (CSCL'99), December 1999.

Dillenbourg, P., Baker, M., Blaye, A. & O'Malley, C. (1996). The evolution of research on collaborative learning. In E. Spada & P. Reiman (Eds) *Learning in Humans and Machine: Towards an interdisciplinary learning science.* (pp. 189-211). Oxford: Elsevier.

Doherty, P., Rothfarb, R., Barker, D. (2006) Building an Interactive Science Museum in Second Life http://www.simteach.com/SLCC06/slcc2006-proceedings.doc

Dooley, K. E., & Wickersham, L. E. (2007). Distraction, domination and disconnection in whole-class online discussions. *Quarterly Review of Distance Education, 8*(1), 1-8.

Dose, J.J. (1997). Work values: An integrative framework and illustrative application to organizational socialization. *Journal of Occupational and Organizational Psychology, 70,* 219 -240.

Dose, J.J., &. Klimoski, R.J. (1999). The diversity of diversity: Work values effects on formative team processes. *Human Resource Management Review, 9*(1), 83-108.

Downes, S. (2007). E-Learning 2.0 in Development. Brandon Hall Conference, San Jose, September 25, 2007. Available: http://www.downes.ca/. Retrieved: 02-10-07.

Drew, S. (1999). Building knowledge management into strategy: Making sense of a new perspective. *Long Range Planning, 32*(1), 130-136.

Drew. S. (1999). Building knowledge management into strategy: Making sense of a new perspective, *Long Range Planning*, 32(1), 130-136).

Drucker, P. F. (1989). *The New Realities: In Government and Politics, in Economics and Business, in Society and World View.* Harper & Row, New York.

Drucker, P. F. (1999). *Knowledge Worker Productivity: The Biggest Challenge.* California Management Review, Vol.1 No. 2, pp. 79-94.

Drucker, P.F. (2002), Management Challenges for the 21st Century, HarperBusiness, New York.

Druskat, V. U. and Pescosolido, A. T. (2002). The content of effective teamwork mental models in self-managing teams: Ownership, learning, and heedful interrelating, *Human Relations*, Vol 55, pp. 283-314

Du, H. S., & Wagner, C. (2005). Learning with Weblogs: An empirical investigation. In *Proceedings of the 38th Annual Hawaii International Conference on System Sciences (HICSS'05): Track 1* (p. 7b). Washington, DC: IEEE Computer Society.

Du, H. S., & Wagner, C. (2007). Learning with Weblogs: Enhancing cognitive and social knowledge construction. *IEEE Transactions on Professional Communication, 50*(1), 1-16.

Dublin Core Metadata Initiative (1999). "Dublin core metadata element set, version 1.1: Reference description". Technical report, Dublin Core Metadata Initiative. http://dublincore.org/documents/dces/ {25.7.2006}.

Duffy, P. & Bruns, A. (2006). The use of blogs, wikis and RSS in education: A conversation of possibilities. Proceedings of the Online Learning and Teaching Conference 2006, Brisbane: September 26. Retrieved April 19, 2007 from https://olt.qut.edu.au/udf/OLT2006/gen/static/papers/Duffy_OLT2006_paper.pdf

Duffy, P. D., & Bruns, A. (2006). The use of blogs, wikis and RSS in education: A conversation of possibilities. In *Proceedings of the Online Learning and Teaching Conference 2006*, Brisbane, Australia (pp. 31-38).

Duffy, T. M., & Jonassen, D. H. (1992). Constructivism: New implications for instructional technology. In T. M. Duffy & D. H. Jonassen (Eds.), *Constructivism and the technology of instruction: A conversation.* New Jersey: Lawrence Erlbaum.

Dyer, J.H. and Nobeoka, K. (2000). Creating and managing a high-performance knowledge-sharing network: the Toyota case, *Strategic Management Journal*, 21(3), 345-367.

Easterby-Smith, M., & Lyles, M.A, (Eds.), (2003). *The Blackwell Handbook of Organizational Learning and Knowledge Management.* Malden, MA; Oxford: Blackwell Publishing.

Edelson, D. C., Pea, R. D., & Gomez, L. (1996). Constructivism in the collaboratory. In B. G. Wilson (Ed.), *Constructivist learning environments: Case studies in instructional design* (pp. 151-164). Englewood Cliffs, New Jersey: Educational Technology Publications.

Edmondson, A. C. (1999). Psychological safety and learning behavior in work teams, *Administrative Science Quarterly*, Vol 4 No 2, pp. 350-383

Edwards, M.G. (2005). The integral holon: A holonomic approach to organisational change and transformation. *Journal of Organizational Change Management, 18*(3), 269-288.

Efimova, L. (2004). Discovering the iceberg of knowledge work: a weblog case. Proceedings of Fifth European Conference on Organizational Knowledge, Learning and Capabilities (OKLC04), Innsbruck, 2-3 April 2004.

Efimova, L. and S. Hendrick (2005). In Search for a virtual settlement: An exploration of weblog community boundaries. Communities and Technologies 05. Available: https://doc.telin.nl /dscgi/ds.py/Get/File-46041. Retrieved: 07-09-07.

Efimova, L., & Fiedler, S. (2004, March 24-26). Learning webs: Learning in Weblog networks. In P. Kommers, P. Isaias, & M. B. Nunes (Eds.), *Web based communities: Proceedings of the IADIS International Conference 2004*, Lisbon, Portugal (pp. 490-494). IADIS Press. Retrieved May 17, 2007, from https://doc.telin.nl/dscgi/ds.py/Get/File-35344

Eide F., and Eide B. (2005). Brain of the Blogger. Available: . Retrieved: 03-09-07.

Eisenhardt, K. (1988). Agency and institutional theory explanations: The case of retail sales competition. *Academy of Management Journal, 30*, 488-511.

Eisenhardt, K. M. (1989). Building theories from case study research. *Academy of Management Review, 14*(4), 532-550.

Ellingsen, G., & Monteiro, E. (2003). Mechanisms for producing a working knowledge: Enacting, orchestrating, and organizing. *Information and Organization, 13*, 203-229.

Ellis, R.K., & Hall, M.L.W. (1994). Systems and values: An approach for practical organizational intervention. *Proceedings of the ISSS, 94*.

Ellis, R.K., & Hall, M.L.W. (1994). Systems and values: An approach for practical organizational intervention. *Proceedings of the ISSS, 94*.

Engeström, Y. (1987). Learning by expanding: An activity theoretical approach to developmental research. Helsinki: Orienta-Konsultit Oy.

Engeström, Y. (1999). Innovative Learning in Work Teams: Analysing cycles of knowledge creation in Practice. In Y. Engeström, R. Miettinen, & R.L. Punamaki (Eds.): Perspectives on Activity Theory, Cambridge University Press.

Engeström, Y., Engeström, R., & Vähäaho, T. (1999). When the Center Doesn't Hold: The Importance of Knotworking. In: S. Chaiklin, M. Hedegaard, and U. Jensen (editors). *Activity Theory and Social Practice: Cultural-Historical Approaches*. Aarhus, Denmark: Aarhus University Press, 1999.

Epstein, M., & Axtell, R. (1996). *Growing artificial societies: Social science from the bottom up*. Washington D.C.: The Brookings Institution.

Erickson, R. J. (1997). Putting emotions to work, in Erickson, R. J. and Cuthbertson-Johnson, B. (Eds.), *Social Perspectives on Emotion*, JAI Press, Greenwich, CT, pp. 3-18.

Ericsson, K. A. & Simon, H. A. (1980). Verbal reports as data. Psychological Review, 87, 215-251.

Erikson, E. H. (1993). Childhood and Society. New York: W.W. Norton & Company.

Evans, C., & Sadler-Smith, E. (2006). Learning styles in education and training: Problems, politicisation and potential. *Education + Training, 48*(2/3), 77-83.

Evans, P. & Wolf, B. (2005). Collaboration rules. *Harvard Business Review*, July-Aug, *83*(7): 96-104. Retrieved April

19, 2007 from http://custom.hbsp.com/b02/en/implicit/viewFileNavBeanImplicit.jhtml?_requestid=34699

Evans, P. (2006). The wiki factor. *BizEd*, January/February, 28-32. Retrieved May 27, 2007 from http://www.aacsb.edu/publications/Archives/JanFeb06/p28-33.pdf

Everard, J. (2001). Virtual states: the Internet and the boundaries of the nation state. Routledge.

Farkas, M. (2005). Using wikis to create online communities. WebJunction. Retrieved May 27, 2007 from http://eprints.rclis.org/archive/00006130/01/wikiarticle_mfarkas.pdf

Fiedler, S. (2004). Personal Webpublishing as a reflective conversational tool for self-organized learning. In T. Burg (Ed.), *BlogTalks* (pp. 190-216). Retrieved May 7, 2007, from http://seblogging.cognitivearchitects.com/stories/storyReader$963

Fineman, S. (2000). *Emotion in organizations*. London: Sage.

Fineman, S. (2003). *Understanding emotion at work.* London: Sage.

Fiol, C.M. & Lyles, M.A. (1985). Organizational Learning. *Academy of Management Review*, 10(4), 803-813.

Fiske, J. (1990). *Introduction to communication studies* (2nd ed.). London: Routledge.

Fogarty, M., & Bahls, C. (2002). Information Overload : Feel the pressure? *The Scientist*, *16*(16).

Fohrmann, J. and Schüttpelz, E. (eds.) (2004). "Die Kommunikation der Medien". Niemeyer, Tübingen (in German).

Ford, D. (2003). Trust and knowledge management: The seeds of success. In *Handbook on Knowledge Management 1: Knowledge Matters* (pp. 553-575). Heidelberg: Springer-Verlag.

Francq, P. (2007). *The GALILEI Platform: Social Browsing to Build Communities of Interests and Share Relevant Information and Expertise*. In M.D. Lytras & A. Naeve (Editors), *Open source for knowledge and*

learning management : strategies beyond tools. Idea Group Publishing (319-342).

Franz, K. and Nischelwitzer, A. (2004). "Adaptive Digital Storytelling: A Concept for Narrative Structures and Digital Storytelling build on Basic Storytelling Principles, Adaptive Story Schemas and Structure Mapping Techniques". In L. Zimmermann (ed.): Multimedia Applications in Education Conference (MApEC) Proceedings. Graz. pp. 28-33.

Freud, S. (1989). Civilization and Its Discontents. New York: W.W. Norton & Company.

Frey, K. (1987). *The project method.* Thessaloniki: Kyriakidis (in Greek).

Friedman, B. (1997). *Human values and the design of computer technology.* Cambridge, UK: Cambridge University Press.

Friedrichs Grangsjo, von, Y. (2003). Destination networking: co-opetition in peripheral surroundings, *International Journal of Physical Distribution & Logistics Management,* 33(5), 427-449.

Friesen, N. (2002). Is There a Body in this Class? in: M. van Manen (ed.), Writing in the Dark: Phenomenological studies in interpretive inquiry, Ontario: Althouse Press.

Fromm, E. (2003). Man for Himself, an Inquiry into the Psychology of Ethics. Routledge

Fuchs-Kittowski, F., Köhler, A., & Fuhr, D. (2004). Roughing up processes the wiki way – Knowledge communities in the context of work and learning processes. Proceedings of the International Conference on Knowledge Management (I-KNOW '04) Graz, Austria, June 30 - July 2. 484-493. Retrieved May 27, 2007 from http://publica.fraunhofer.de/eprints/N-25285.pdf

Fugini M., Maio F., Plebani P., "Sicurezza dei sistemi informatici", Milano, Apogeo, 2001

Gammelgaard, J. (2007). Why not use incentives to encourage knowledge sharing? Journal of Knowledge Management Practice, 8(1). http://www.tlainc.com/articl127.htm

Garrison, D. R., Anderson, T., & Archer, W. (2001). Critical thinking, cognitive presence, and computer conferencing in distance education. *American Journal of Distance Education 15*(1), 7-23.

Garton, L., Haythornthwaite, C., & Wellman, B. (1999). Studying on-line social networks. In S. Jones (Ed.), *Doing Internet research: Critical issues and methods for examining the net* (pp. 77-105). Thousand Oaks: Sage Publications.

Garton, L., Haythornthwaite, C., & Wellman, B. (1999). Studying on-line social networks. In S. Jones (Ed.), *Doing Internet research: Critical issues and methods for examining the net* (pp. 77-105). Thousand Oaks: Sage Publications.

Gee, J. P. (1999). *An introduction to discourse analysis: theory and method.* London: Routledge

George, J.M., & Jones, G.R. (1997). Experiencing work: Values, attitudes, and moods. *Human Relations, 50*(4), 393-417.

Gergen, K.J. (1994). *Realities and Relationships. Soundings in Social Construction.* Cambridge: Harvard University Press.

Gherardi S. (2001). From organizational learning to practice-based knowing. *Human Relations, 54*(1), 131-139.

Gherardi, S. (2000). Practice-based Theorizing on Learning and Knowing in Organizations. *Organization, 7*(2), 211-223.

Gibson, W. (1984). Neuromancer. New York: Ace Books.

Giddens, A. (1979). *Central problems in social theory: Action, structure, and contradiction in social analysis.* London: MacMillan Press, Ltd.

Giddens, A. (1984). *The constitution of society: Outline of the theory of structuration.* Berkeley, CA: University of California Press.

Giddens, A. (1991). Modernity and Self-identity: Self and Society in the Late Modern Age. Cambridge, UK: Polity Press

Giles, J. (2005). Internet encyclopedias go head to head. Nature, 438(7070), 900-901 (15 Dec 2005). Retrieved May 27, 2007 from http://www.nature.com/news/2005/051212/full/438900a.html

Gill, J.H. (2000). *The Tacit Mode.* Albany: State University of New York Press.

Giorgi, A. (1997), The theory, practice, and evaluation of the phenomenological method as a qualitative research procedure. *Journal of Phenomenological Psychology,* 28(2), 235-260.

Gladwell, M., (2002). *The Tipping Point.* Boston: Back Bay Books.

Gonzalez-Reinhart, J. (2005). Wiki and the wiki way: Beyond a knowledge management solution. Information Systems Research Center, Bauer College of Business, University of Houston, 1-22. Retrieved May 27, 2007 from http://www.uhisrc.com/FTB/Wiki/wiki_way_brief%5B1%5D-Jennifer%2005.pdf

Good, D. (1988). Individuals, Interpersonal Relations, and Trust. In Gambetta, D. (Ed.): *Trust: Making and Breaking Cooperative Relations* (pp. 31-48). Basil Blackwell: New York.

Goodall, A. Taylor, R. & Pollack, S. (2004). Towards Integral Culture Change Initiative to support Knowledge Management In: Truch, E. (ed) (2004) *Leveraging Corporate Knowledge,* (pp. 158-177) Aldershot, Gower.

Goodyear, P. (2002). Psychological foundations for networked learning. In C. Steeples & C. Jones (Eds.): Networked learning: Perspectives and issues. London, Springer-Verlag.

Grant, R.M. (1991). The resource-based theory of competitive advantage: Implications for strategy formulation. *California Management Review, 33*(3), 114-135.

Grant, R.M. (1996). Prospering in dynamically competitive environments: Organizational capability as knowledge integration. *Organization Science, 7*(4), 375-387.

Grant, R.M. (1996). Toward a knowledge-based theory of the firm, *Strategic Management Journal*, 17(1), 109-122.

Grant, R.M. (1996). Toward a Knowledge-Based Theory of the Firm. *Strategic Management Journal, 17,* 109-122.

Griliches, Z. (1992). The Search for R&D Spillovers. *Scandinavian Journal of Economics*, 94(Supplement), 29-47.

Gröger, G., Kolbe, T. H. and Czerwinski, A. (eds.) (2006). Candidata OpenGIS CityGML Implementation (City Geography Markup Language). OGC 06-057rl. Open Geospatial Consortium, Inc.

Gunnlaugson, O. (2005), Toward Integrally Informed Theories of Transformative Learning, Journal of Transformative Education, Vol. 3, No. 4, 331-353 (2005).

Guskey, T. R. (2002). Does It Make a Difference? Evaluating Professional Development. Educational Leadership, 59(6), 45-51.

Habermas, J. (1991). The Structural Transformation of the Public Sphere: An Inquiry Into a Category of Bourgeois Society. The MIT Press.

Hall, R. (1993). A framework linking intangible resources and capabilities to sustainable competitive advantage. *Strategic Management Journal, 14,* 607–618.

Hammer, M., & Champy, J. (1993). *Reengineering the corporation.* New York: Harper Collins.

Hammond, M. Howarth, J. & Kent, R. (1995). *Understanding Phenomenology,* Oxford: Blackwell.

Hammond, T., Hannay, T., & Lund, B. (2004, December). The role of RSS in science publishing: Syndication and annotation on the Web. *D-Lib Magazine.* Retrieved April 20, 2007, from http://www.dlib.org/dlib/december04/hammond/12hammond.html

Hannan, M.T., & Freeman, J.H. (1989). *Organizational ecology.* Cambridge. MA: Harvard University Press.

Hänninen, S. (2007). The 'perfect technology syndrome': sources, consequences, and solutions, *International Journal of Technology Management*, 39(1-2), 20-32.

Hänninen, S. and Kauranen, I. (2007). Product innovation as micro-strategy, *International Journal of Innovation and Learning*, 4(4), 425-443.

Hansen M. T., Nohria N., Tierney T., "What's Your Strategy for Managing Knowledge?", Harvard Business Review, March-April 1999.

Hansen, M. T., Nohria, N., & Tierney, T. (1999). What is your strategy for managing knowledge? *Harvard Business Review, 77*(2), 106-116.

Hansen, M.T. (1999). The search-transfer problem: The role of weak ties in sharing knowledge across organization subunits, *Administrative Science Quarterly*, 44(1), 82-111.

Hanseth, O., & Monteiro, E. (1997). Navigating future research: Judging the relevance of information systems development research. *Accounting, Management, and Information Technology, 6*(1/2), 77-85.

Harasim, L., Hiltz, S., Teles, L. & Turoff, M. (1995). *Learning networks: A field guide to teaching and learning online.* Cambridge: MIT Press.

Hardin, R. (1993). The Street-Level Epistemology of Trust. *Politics and Society*, 21, 505–529.

Harmon, M. M (1990). Applied phenomenology and organization. *Public Administration Quarterly, 14* (1): 10-17.

Harry, Keith, John Magnus, Keegan, Desmond. (1993). Distance Education: New Perspectives. Rutledge in London and New York.

Hartwig, R.J. (1998). Cooperation and competition: a comparative review, *The Journal of Business and Economic Studies,* 4(2), 71-76.

Hassard, J., Holliday, R., & Wilmott, H. (2000). *Body and Organisation.* London: Sage.

Hauben, M., & Hauben, R. (1997). *Netizens: On the History and Impact of Usenet and the Internet.* IEEE Computer Society Press.

Haythornthwaite, C. (1996). Social network analysis: An approach and set of techniques for the study of information exchange. *Library and Information Science Research, 18*(4), 323-342.

Haythornthwaite, C. (1996). Social network analysis: An approach and set of techniques for the study of information exchange. *Library and Information Science Research, 18*(4), 323-342.

HBSP. (1998). *Harvard Business review on knowledge management.* Cambridge, MA: Harvard Business School Press.

Heeren, E. (1996). *Technology support for collaborative distance learning.* Doctoral thesis, University of Twente, Twente.

Heiden, W., Frühling, C. and Deuer, H. (2001). "Hypermedia Novel - Hymn. A New Storytelling Paradigm". Proceedings of CAST '01. pp. 345-348.

Heisig P., Mertins K., Vorbeck J., (2001), "Knowledge Management – Best Practices in Europe", Springer

Heusinkveld, S., & Benders, J. (2001). Surges and sediments: Shaping the reception of reengineering. *Information & Management, 38*(4), 239-251.

Hildreth, P.J., & Kimble, C. (2002). The duality of knowledge. *Information Research*, 8(1), paper no. 142.

Hill, K.A., & Hughes, J.E. (1998). *Cyberpolitics: Citizen Activism in the Age of the Internet.* Rowman & Littlefield Publishers, Inc.

Hiltz, S. (1995, March 7-10). Teaching in a virtual classroom. Paper presented at the *International Conference on Computer Assisted Instruction (ICCAI'95).* National Chiao Tung University, Hsinchu, Taiwan.

Hinings, C.R., Thibault, L., Slack, T., & Kikulis, L.M. (1996). Values and organizational structure. *Human Relations, 49*(7), 885-917.

Ho, M.S., & Su, I.J. (2004). Preparing to prevent severe acute respiratory syndrome and other respiratory infections. *The Lancet Infectious Diseases*, 4(11), 684-689.

Hoisl, B., Aigner, W., & Miksch, S. (2006). Social rewarding in wiki systems – Motivating the community. 2nd Austrian Symposium on Wiki Systems and Applications (Wikiposium 2006), Vienna, Austria November 25. Retrieved May 27, 2007 from http://www.donau-uni.ac.at/imperia/md/content/department/ike/ike_publications/2006/hoisl_2006_wikiposium_social_rewarding.pdf

Holland, J. (1995). *Hidden order: How adaptation builds complexity.* MA: Perseus Books Reading.

Holsapple, C.W. (Ed). (2003). *Handbook on knowledge management 2: Knowledge directions.* Heidelberg: Springer-Verlag.

Holsapple, C.W. (Ed.). (2003). *Handbook on knowledge management 1: Knowledge matters.* Heidelberg: Springer-Verlag.

Hosking, D.M., Dachler, H.P., & Gergen, K.J. (1995). *Management and Organization. Relational Alternatives to Individualism.* Averbury: Aldershot.

Howley, D. (2007). What is a wiki? MindTouch White Paper. Retrieved April 19, 2007 from http://www.mindtouch.com/sites/mindtouch.com/themes/mt2/resources/Mindtouch%20What%20Is%20A%20Wiki.pdf

Hrastinski, S. (2006a). Introducing an informal synchronous medium in a distance learning course: How is participation affected? *Internet and Higher Education, 9*(2), 117-131.

Hrastinski, S. (2006b). The relationship between adopting a synchronous medium and participation in online group work: An explorative study. *Interactive Learning Environments, 14*(2), 137-152.

Huber, G.P. (1991). Organizational Learning: The Contributing Processes and a Review of the Literature. *Organization Science*, 2, 88-117.

Huettner, B., Brown, M.K., & James-Tanny, C. (2007). *Managing Virtual Teams: Getting the Most from Wikis, Blogs, and Other Collaborative Tools.* Plano, TX: Wordware Publishing, Inc.

Huffaker, D. (2004). Gender similarities and differences in online identity and language use among teenage bloggers. Unpublished MA Thesis. Available online:

Hughes, J., & Jones, S. (2003). Reflections on the use of grounded theory in interpretive information systems research. In *Proceedings of the ECIS 2003 Conference,* Naples, Italy.

Hurst, B. (2005). My journey with learning logs. *Journal of Adolescent & Adult Literacy, 49*(1), 42-46.

IEEE LTSC, Luglio 2002, "Draft Standard for Learning Object Metadata" (http://ltsc.ieee.org)

Immon W. H., "Building the Data Warehouse", New York, Wiley, 1996.

Innes, R.B. (2007). Dialogic communication in collaborative problem solving groups. International Journal of the Scholarship of Teaching and Learning, 1(1), 1-19.

Ipe, M. (2003). *The praxis of knowledge sharing in organizations: A case study.* Doctoral dissertation. University Microfilms.

ISO (2003). "Information Technology – Multimedia Content Description Interface – part 5: Multimedia description schemes". Technical Report ISO/IEC TR 15938-5:2003.

ISO. (2002). "Information technoloy – Multimedia content description interface – Part 8: Extraction and use of MPEG-7 descriptions". Technical Report ISO/IEC TR 15938-8: 2002(E).

Ives, W., Torrey, B., & Gordon, C. (2000). Knowledge sharing is human behavior. In *Knowledge management: Classic and contemporary works* (pp. 99-129).

Jäger, L. and Stanitzek, G. (eds.) (2002). "Transkribieren - Medien/Lektüre". Wilhelm Fink Verlag, Munich (in German).

Jaldemark, J., Lindberg, J. O., & Olofsson, A. D. (2006). Sharing the distance or a distance shared: Social and individual aspects of participation in ICT-supported distance-based teacher education. In M. Chaib & A. K. Svensson (Eds.), *ICT in teacher education: Chal-*

lenging prospects (pp. 142-160). Jönköping: Jönköping University Press.

Jenkins, H. et al. (2006). Confronting the challenges of participatory culture. *MacArthur Foundation,* 2006.

Jennex, M. E., & Olfman, L. A. (2005). Assessing knowledge management success. *International Journal of Knowledge Management, 1*(2), 33-49.

Jennex, M. E., & Olfman, L. A. (2006). A Model of knowledge management success. *International Journal of Knowledge Management, 2*(3), 51-68.

Jermann, P., (2004). Computer support for interaction regulation in collaborative problem solving, Phd Thesis, Switzerland.

Jick, T. D. (1979), Mixing Qualitative and Quantitative Methods: Triangulation in Action," *Administrative Science Quarterly,* 24,4 (1979),602-611

Johnson, D.G. (1997). Is the global information infrastructure a democratic technology? *ACM SIGCAS Computers and Society, 27*(3), 20-26.

Johnson, P., & Lancaster, A. (2000). *Swarm users guide.* Swarm Development Group.

Johnson, S., Aragon, S., Najmuddin Shaik, Palma-Rivas, N. (2000). Comparative analysis of learner satisfaction and learning outcomes in online and face-to-face learning environments. *Journal of Interactive Learning, 11*(1), 29-49.

Johnston, C.G., James, R.H., Lye, J.N., & McDonald, I.M. (2000). An evaluation of collaborative problem solving for learning economics. Journal of Economic Education, Winter 2000, 13-29.

Jonassen, D. (2002). *Computers as mindtools for schools.* Upper Saddle River, NJ: Merrill.

Jonassen, D. H., & Land, S. M. (2000). Preface. In D. H. Jonassen & S. M. Land (Eds.), *Theoretical foundations of learning environments* (pp. iii-ix). New Jersey: Lawrence Erlbaum.

Jonassen, D. H., Mayes, T., & McAleese, R. (1993, May 14-18). A manifesto for a constructivist approach to uses of technology in higher education. In T. M. Duffy, J. Lowyck, D. H. Jonassen, & T. Welsh (Eds.), *Xpert. press: Vol. 105. Designing Environments for Constructive Learning: Proceedings of the NATO Advanced Research Workshop on the Design of Constructivist Learning Environments Implications for Instructional Design and the Use of Technology*, Leuven, Belgium (pp. 231-247). Berlin, Germany: Springer.

Jonassen, D., Peck, K., & Wilson, B. (1999). *Learning with technology: A constructivist perspective.* Upper Saddle River, NJ: Prentice Hall.

Jonassen, D.H., Howland, J., Moore, J., & Marra, M. (2003). Learning to solve problems with technology: A Constructivist Approach. (2nd Ed.), NJ: Merill Prentice Hall.

Jonassen, D.H., Peck, K.L., & Wilson, B.G. (1999). *Learning with technology: A constructivist perspective.* Columbus, OH: Prentice Hall.

Jonassen, D.H., Peck, K.L., & Wilson, B.G. (1999). *Learning with Technology: A Constructivist Perspective.* Columbus, OH: Prentice Hall.

Jones, P.H. (2000). *Embedded values in innovation practice: Toward a theory of power and participation in organizations.* Ann Arbor, MI: Dissertation Abstracts International.

Jones, P.H. (2002a, June). Embedded values in process and practice: Interactions between disciplinary practice and formal innovation processes. In *Proceedings of the 11th International Forum on Design Management Research*, Boston, Massachusetts.

Jones, P.H. (2002b). When successful products prevent strategic innovation. *Design Management Journal, 13*(2), 30-37.

Kahn, J. (2007) Wayne Gretzky-Style 'Field Sense' May Be Teachable, Wired Magazine, 15.06 http://www.wired.com/science/discoveries/magazine/15-06/ff_mind-games

Kalthoff, O., Nonaka, I., & Nueno, P. (2001). *The light and the shadow: How breakthrough innovation is shaping European business.* Oxford: Capstone Publishing Ltd.

Kantel, J. (2003). *Vom Weblog lernen: Community, peer-to-peer und eigenständigkeit als ein modell für zukünftige wissenssammlungen.* Retrieved March 12, 2007, from http://static.userland.com/sh4/gems/schock-wellenreiter/blogtalktext.pdf

Kaplan, R.S. & Norton D.P. (2001). *The strategy-focused organization: How balanced scorecard companies thrive in the new business environment.* Boston: Harvard Business School Press.

Karlöf, B., Lundgren, K., & Froment, M. E. (2001). *Benchlearning – forbilleder som løftestang for udvikling.* København: Børsens Forlag A/S.

Katz, Jeffrey P. (1996). Co-opetition, *The Academy of Management Executive*, 10(4), 118-119.

Kautz, K., & Thaysen, K. (2001). Knowledge, learning and IT Support in a small software company. *Journal of Knowledge Management, 5*(4), 349-357.

Kearsley, G. (2000). *Online education: Learning and teaching in cyberspace.* Belmont, CA: Wadsworth.

Keefer, M., Zeitz, C., & Resnick, L. (2000). Judging the quality of peer-led student dialogues. *Cognition and Instruction, 18*(1), 53-81.

Keeney, R.L. (1994). Creativity in decision making with value-focused thinking. *Sloan Management Review, 35*, 33-41.

Kenis, D.G.A. (1995). *Improving group decisions: designing and testing techniques for group decision support systems applying Delphi principles.* Universiteit Utrecht.

Kerres, M. (2006). Web 2.0 and its implications to e-learning. In T. Hug, M. Lindner, & P. A. Bruck (Eds.), *Micromedia & E-Learning 2.0: Gaining the Big Picture: Proceedings of Microlearning Conference 2006*, Innsbruck, Austria. University Press.

Kerres, M. (2007). Microlearning as a challenge for instructional design. In T. Hug & M. Lindner (Eds.), *Didactics of microlearning*. Münster, Germany: Waxmann. Retrieved March 10, 2007, from http://mediendidaktik. uni-duisburg-essen.de/files/Microlearning-kerres.pdf

Kerzner H., "Project Management: A Systems Approach to Planning, Scheduling, and Controlling", Wiley, 2003.

King, A.W., & Zeithaml, C.P. (2003). Measuring organizational knowledge: A conceptual and methodological framework. *Strategic Management Journal, 24*, 763-772.

Kirkpatrick, M. (2006). The flu wiki: A serious application of new web tools. Retrieved May 27, 2007 from http://marshallk.blogspot.com/2005/07/flu-wiki-serious-application-of-new.html

Klamma, R., et al. (2006). Social software for professional learning: Examples and research. In B. Kinshuk, R. Koper, P. Kommers, P. Kirschner, D. Sampson, & W. Didderen (Eds.), *Advanced Learning Technologies: ICALT 2006*, Los Alamitos, CA (pp. 912-917). IEEE Computer Society.

Klein, B., Hoecht, C., & Decker, B. (2005). Beyond capturing and maintaining software engineering knowledge - „Wikitology" as shared semantics. Workshop on Knowledge Engineering and Software Engineering, at Conference of Artificial Intelligence 2005, Koblenz.

Klein, H., & Myers, M. (1999). A set of principles for conducting and evaluating interpretive field studies in information systems. *MIS Quarterly, 23*(1), 67-93.

Kleinginna, P.R., & Kleinginna, A.M. (1981). A categorized list of emotion definitions, with suggestions for a consensual definition. *Motivation and Emotion, 5*(4), 345-379.

Kling, R. (1996). The centrality of organizations in the computerization of society. In R. Kling (Ed.), *Computerization and controversy: Value conflicts and social choices* (2nd ed., pp. 108-112). New York: Academic Press.

Klobas, J. (2006). *Wikis: Tools for Information Work and Collaboration*. Oxford, UK: Chandos Publishing.

Knowledge Management Working Group Wiki. http://colab.cim3.net/cgi-bin/wiki.pl?KnowledgeManagementWorkingGroup

Kock, N. (2005). Media richness or media naturalness? The evolution of our biological communication apparatus and its influence on our behavior toward e-communication tools. *IEEE Transactions on Professional Communication, 48*(2), 117-130.

Kock, N. (Ed.). (2008). *Encyclopedia of e-collaboration*. Hershey, PA: Information Science Reference.

Kock, N., Verville, J., & Garza, V. (2007). Media naturalness and online learning: Findings supporting both the significant- and no-significant-difference perspectives. *Decision Sciences Journal of Innovative Education, 5*(2), 333-356.

Koestler A. (1967). *The Ghost in the Machine*. London: Hutchinson.

Kogut, B. and Zander, U. (1992). Knowledge of the firm, combinative capabilities, and the replication of technology, *Organization Science, 3*(3), 383-397.

Kogut, B., & Zander, U. (1996). What firms do: Coordination, identity and learning. *Organization Science, 7*, 502-518.

Kohlberg, L. (1969). Stage and sequence: The cognitive development approach to socialization. In D.A. Goslin (Ed.), *Handbook of socialization theory and research* (pp. 347-480). Chicago: Rand McNally.

Kolb, D. A. (1984). *Experiential learning—Experience as source of learning and development*. New Jersey: Prentice Hall.

Köllinger, P. (2002). *Report e-learning in deutschen unternehmen: Fallstudien, konzepte, implementierung* (1. Aufl.). Düsseldorf, Germany: Symposion.

Korfiatis, N., & Naeve, A. (2005). Evaluating wiki contributions using social networks: A case study on wikipedia. Proceedings of the First on-Line Conference on Metadata and Semantics Research (MTSR'05). Rinton Press.

Kosch, H. (2003). Distributed Multimedia Database Technologies Supported by MPEG-7 and MPEG-21. Auerbach Publication.

Koschmann, T. (1996). Paradigm shifts and instructional technology: An introduction, In T. Koschmann (Ed.), CSCL: Theory and practice of an emerging paradigm, 1-23, Mahwah, NJ: Lawrence Erlbaum Associates.

Kotter, J. P. (1995). Leading change: Why transformation efforts fail. *Harvard Business Review, 73*(March/April), 59–67.

Kotter, J.P. (1996). *Leading change.* Boston: Harvard Business School Press.

Kotzab, H. and Teller, C. (2003). Value-adding partnerships and co-opetition models in the grocery industry, *International Journal of Physical Distribution & Logistics Management, 33*(3), 268-282.

Kraak, M.-J. and Ormeling, F. (2003). Cartography. Pearson Education Limited, England.

Kraimer, M.L. (1997). Organizational goals and values: A socialization model. *Human Resource Management Review, 7*(4), 425-447.

Kreijns, K., Kirschner, P., & Jochems, W. (2003). Identifying the pitfalls for social interaction in computer-supported collaborative learning environments: A review of the research. *Computers in Human Behaviour, 19*, 335-353.

Kuldip Kaur & Zoraini Wati Abas (2004). Implementation of a collaborative online learning project at Open University Malaysia. *2004 Southeast Asia Association for Institutional Research (SEAAIR) Conference* (pp. 453-462). Wenzhou, China: SEAAIR.

Kumar, K., & Bjorn-Anderson, N. (1990). A cross-cultural comparison of IS designer values. *Communications of the ACM, 33*(5), 528-538.

Kumar, R., Novak, J., Raghavan, P., & Tomkins, A. (2005). On the bursty evolution of blogspace. *World Wide Web,* 8 (2):159–178, June 2005.

Küpers, W. & Weibler, J. (2005). *Emotion in Organisationen.* Stuttgart: Kohlhammer

Küpers, W. (2004). Learning Organization and Leadership, in Burns, J.M., Goethals, R.R., & Sorenson, G.J. (2004). *Encyclopaedia of Leadership,* (pp. 881-886). Thousand Oaks: Sage.

Küpers, W. (2005). Phenomenology and Pheno-Practice of Embodied Implicit and Narrative Knowing. *Journal of Knowledge Management, 9*(6), 113-133.

Küpers, W. (2006). "Integrales Lernen in und von Organisationen" ("Integral Learning in and of Organisations"), In: *Integral Review,* 2, pp. 43-77.

Küpers, W. (2007), *"Inter-Practice - Perspectives on an Integral "Pheno-Practice" in Responsive Organisations",* paper presented at stream "Practice, Practicing and Practising" at EURAM Conference, Paris, 05. 2007.

Küpers, W. (2008). Phenomenology and Integral Pheno-Practice of responsive Organizations and Management. In: Barry, D., & Hansen, H. (Eds.), (2008). *New Approaches to Management and Organization.* London: Sage (forthcoming).

Kutscher, N., Klein, A., & Iske, S. (2005). Differences in Internet usage: Social inequality and informal education. *Social Work & Society, 3*, 215-233.

Kvale, S. (1983). The qualitative research interview: A phenomenological and a hermeneutical mode of understanding. *Journal of Phenomenological Psychology, 14* (2), 171-196.

Lamb, B. (2004). Wide open spaces: Wikis, ready or not. EDUCAUSE Review, 39(5) (September/October), 36-48. Retrieved May 27, 2007 from http://www.educause.edu/pub/er/erm04/erm0452.asp?bhcp=1

Lambe, P. (2002). *Autism of knowledge management.* see: www.straitsknowledge.com.

Lambert, J. (ed.) (2003). "Digital Storytelling Cookbook and Travelling Companion". Digital Diner Press, 4.0 edition, (Excerpt).

Lambropoulos, N., Kampylis, P., Papadimitriou, S., Vivitsou M., Gkikas, A. Minaoglou, N. & Konetas, D. (2008). Hybrid Synergy for Virtual Knowledge Working. In Salmons, J. & Wilson L. (Eds) (2008), Handbook of Research on Electronic Collaboration and Organizational Synergy, Hershey, PA, USA: IGI Global Publications.

Lanzara, G. F. & Patriotta, G. (2001). Technology and the courtroom: An inquiry into knowledge making in organizations, *Journal of Management Studies*, 38(7): 943-971.

Laubacher R, Malone TW. (2003) Retreat of the firm and the rise of guilds: the employment relationship in an age of virtual business. In Inventing the Organization of the 21st Century, Malone TW, Laubacher R, Scott–Morton MS (eds). MIT Press: Boston.

Laurillard, D. (1993). *Rethinking university teaching: A framework for the effective use of educational technology*. London: Routledge.

Lave, J. (1988). *Cognition in practice*. Cambridge, UK: Cambridge University Press.

Lave, J. and Wenger E. (1991). Situated Learning: Legimate Peripheral Participation. Cambridge University Press, Cambridge, UK.

Lave, J., & Wenger, E. (1991). *Situated learning: Legitimate peripheral participation.* Cambridge, UK: Cambridge University Press.

Lave, J., & Wenger, E. (1991). *Situated learning: Legitimate peripheral participation.* Cambridge, UK: Cambridge University Press.

Leder, D. (1990). *The absent body.* Chicago: University of Chicago Press.

Leidner, D. E., & Jarvenpaa, S. L. (1995). The use of information technology to enhance management school education: A theoretical view. *MIS Quarterly, 19*(3), 265-291.

Lenhart, A., & Madden, M. (2005). Teen content creators and consumers. In *Pew Internet Project Data Memo*. Retrieved June 21, 2007, from http://www.pewinternet.org/pdfs/PIP_Teens_Content_Creation.pdf

Leonard, D., & Straus, S. (1998). Putting your company's whole brain to work. In *Harvard Business Review on Knowledge Management* (pp. 109-136). Boston: Harvard Business School Press.

Leuf, B. & Cunningham, W. (2001). *The Wiki Way: Quick collaboration on the Web.* Boston, MA: Addison Wesley.

Leuf, B. & Cunningham, W. (2001). The Wiki Way: Quick Collaboration on the Web. Boston, MA: Addison Wesley.

Levinas, E. (1969). *Totality and Infinity: An Essay on Exteriority. Translated by Alphonso Lingis.* Pittsburgh: Duquesne University Press.

Levy, M., Loebbecke, C. and Powell, P. (2003). SMEs, co-opetition and knowledge sharing: the role of information systems, *European Journal of Information Systems*, 12(1), 3-18.

Levy, P. (1999). *Collective Intelligence: Mankind's Emerging World in Cyberspace.* New York: Perseus.

Lewinson, J. (2005). Asynchronous discussion forums in the changing landscape of the online learning environment. *Campus-Wide Information Systems, 22*(3), 162-167.

Li, L. (2005). The effects of trust and shared vision on inward knowledge transfer in subsidiaries' intra- and inter-organizational relationships, *International Business Review*, 14(1), 77-95.

Liao, S., Chang, J., Shih-chieh, C., & Chia-mei, K. (2004). Employee relationship and knowledge sharing: A case study of a Taiwanese finance and securities firm. *Knowledge Management Research & Practice, 2*, 24-34.

Liao, T. T. (Ed.). (1996). *Advanced educational technology: Research issues and future technologies.* Berlin: Springer-Verlag.

Licklider, J.C.R & Taylor, R.W. (1968). The computer as a communication device, Science and Technology, 76, 21-31.

Lieberman, A. (2000). Networks as learning communities: Shaping the future of teacher development. *Journal of Teacher Education, Vol. 51, No. 3, May/June 2000, 221-227.* American Association of Colleges for Teacher Education

Liebeskind, J.P., Oliver, A.L., Zucker, L.G., & Brewer, M.B. (1996). Social networks, learning and flexibility: Sourcing scientific knowledge in new biotechnology firms. *Organization Science, 7*(4), 428–443.

Lin, C.Y. and Zhang Z. (2005). Changing structures of SME networks: lessons from the publishing industry in Taiwan, *Long Range Planning*, 38(2), 145-162.

Linstone, H.A., & Turoff, M. (1975). *The Delphi Method: Techniques and Applications.* Addison-Wesley Pub. Co., Advanced Book Program.

List of Wikipedias (2007). Retrieved April 19, 2007 from http://meta.wikimedia.org/w/index.php?title=List_of_ Wikipedias&oldid=517497

Littleton, K., & Häkkinen, P. (1999). Learning together: Understanding the processes of computer-based collaborative learning. In P. Dillenbourg (Ed.), *Collaborative learning: Cognitive and computational approaches* (pp. 20-30). Oxford: Elsevier Science Ltd.

Lombardo, T. (2007). The Pursuit of Wisdom and the Future of Education [Electronic Version]. Retrieved 28.May.2007 from http://www.mcli.dist.maricopa.edu/ dd/wisdom05/pursuit_of_wisdom.pdf.

Louis, M.R. (1980). Surprise and sense making: What newcomers experience in entering unfamiliar organizational settings. *Administrative Science Quarterly, 25*, 226–248.

Louridas, P. (2006). Using wikis in software development. IEEE Software, 23(2), 88-91. Retrieved May 27, 2007 from http://ieeexplore.ieee.org/Xplore/login. jsp?url=/iel5/52/33727/01605183.pdf

Luo, Y. (2005). Toward coopetition within a multinational enterprise: a perspective from foreign subsidiaries, *Journal of World Business*, 40(1), 71-90.

Lynch, K. (1960). The Image of the City. The MIT Press.

M'Chirgui, Z. (2005). The economics of the smart card industry: towards Coopetitive Strategies, *Economics of Innovation & New Technology*, 14(6), 455-477.

Macann, C. (1993). *Four Phenomenological Philosophers: Husserl, Heidegger, Sartre, Merleau-Ponty,* New York: Routledge

Macintosh, A., Malina, A., & Farrell, S. (2002). Digital Democracy through Electronic Petitioning. *Digital Government. Dordrecht: Kluwer.*

Macmurray, J. (1957). *The Self as Agent.* London: Faber.

Mader, S. (2006). Wiki vs. Blog. Retrieved April 19, 2007 from http://www.businessblogwire.com/2006/03/ stewart_mader_wiki_vs_blog.html

Magnusson M., Davidsson N. (2001). *Creating and managing communities of knowing.* International Conference on Entrepreneurship and Learning, 21-24 June 2001, Naples, Italy.

Mahoney, J.T., & Sanchez, R. (2004). Building new management theory by integrating processes and products of thought. *Journal Of Management Inquiry, 13*(1), 34-47.

Maier R., 'Knowledge Management Systems, information and communication technologies for Knowledge Management, (Springer-Verlag Heidelberg, 2002).

Majchrzak, A., Wagner, C., & Yates, D. (2006). Corporate wiki users: Results of a Survey, Proceedings of the 2006 international symposium on Wikis (WikiSym'06), August 21–23, Odense, Denmark. 99-104. Retrieved May 27, 2007 from http://www.wikisym.org/ws2006/ proceedings/p99.pdf

Makela, K., Kalla, H.K. and Piekkari, R. (2007). Interpersonal similarity as a driver of knowledge sharing within multinational corporations, *International Business Review*, 16(1), 1-22.

Malhotra, Y. (2004). Why do knowledge management systems fail? Enablers and constraints of knowledge management in human enterprises. In M.E. Koenig & T.K. Srikantaiah (Eds.), *Knowledge management lessons learned: What works and what doesn't* (pp. 87-112). Silver Spring MD: Information Today (ASIST Monograph Series).

March, J. G. & Simon, H. A. (1958). *Organizations*. New York: John Wiley & Sons.

Marlow, C. (2004). Audience, structure and authority in the weblog community. Paper presented at the *International Communication Association Conference*, May 27-June 1, New Orleans, LA.

Marshal Poe. "The Hive". The Altantic Monthly. Magazine September 2006. Online:http://www.theatlantic.com/doc/200609/wikipedia Accessed Setembre 2007

Marshall, C., Prusak, L., & Shpilberg, D. (1997). Financial Risk and the Need for Superior Knowledge Management. In Prusak, L., *Knowledge in Organizations* (pp. 227-251). USA: Butterworth-Heinemann.

Martínez, A., Dimitriadis, Y., & De La Fuente, P. (2003). Contributions to analysis of interactions for formative evaluation in CSCL. In Llamas, M., Fernandez, M.J., & Anido, L.E. (Eds.): Computers and education. Towards of lifelong learning society, The Netherlands: Kluwer Academic, 227-238.

Martínez, J.M., Gonzández, C., García, C. and de Ramón, J. (2002). "Towards Universal Access to Content using MPEG-7". Multimedia '02. December 1-6, Juan-les-Pins, France.

Martinsons, M. G. (1997). Human Resource Management Applications of Knowledge-based Systems. *International Journal of Information Management*, 17(1), 35-53.

Maslow, A.H. (1965). *Eupsychian management: A journal*. Homewood, IL: The Dorsey Press.

Maslow, A.H. (1971). *The farther reaches of human nature*. New York: Viking Press.

Mason, H., Moutahir, M. (2006) Multidisciplinary Experiential Education in Second Life: A Global Approach http://www.simteach.com/SLCC06/slcc2006-proceedings.doc

Mazis, G.A. (1993). *Emotion and Embodiment: Fragile Ontology*. New York: Lang.

McAfee, A.P., & Sjoman, A.. (2006). Wikis at Dresdner Kleinwort Wasserstein: (A). Harvard Business School Case 606-074.

McGill, L., Nicol, D., Littlejohn, A., Grierson, H., Juster, N., & Ion, W. J. (2005). Creating an information-rich learning environment to enhance design student learning: Challenges and approaches. *British Journal of Educational Technology, 36*(4), 629-642.

McKendree, J. (2002). The Role of Discussion in Learning. Poster Presentation at *AMEE 2002*, 29 Aug-1 Sep, Lisbon, Portugal.

McLuhan, M., & Fiore, Q. (1967). *The Medium is the Massage : An Inventory of Effects* (G. Press, Éd.). Jerome Agel.

McNeill, D. (1998). *The face: A natural history*. Boston, MA: Little, Brown and Company.

Merleau-Ponty, M. (1962). *Phenomenology of Perception*. London: Routledge.

Merleau-Ponty, M. (1995). *The Visible and the Invisible*. Evanston: Northwestern University Press.

Mertins, K., Heisig, P., & Vorbeck, J. (2001). *Knowledge management: Best practices in Europe*. Springer-Verlag.

Metaxiotis, K., Ergazakis, K., & Psarras, J. (2005). Exploring the world of knowledge management: agreements and disagreements in the academic/practitioner community. *Journal of Knowledge Management, 9*(2), 6-18.

Meyer, J. W. & Rowan, B. (1977). Institutionalized Organizations: Formal Structure of Organizations as Myth and Ceremony. *American Journal of Sociology*, 83(2), 340-363.

Mezirow, J. (2003). Transformative Learning as Discourse. *Journal of ransformative Education, Vol.1, No 1, Jan. 2003, 58-63*. London: Sage publications.

Minar, N., Burkhar, R., Langton C., & Askemnazi, M. (1996). *The Swarm Simulation System: A toolkit for building multi-agent simulations*. Retrieved from http://alumni.media.mit.edu/~nelson/research/ swarm/.

Mintzberg, H. (1990). The design school: Reconsidering the basic premises of strategic management. *Strategic Management Journal, 11*, 171-1965.

Mintzberg, H. (1994). *The rise and fall of strategic planning*. New York: Free Press.

Monjon, S. & Waelbroech, P. (2003). Assesing Spillovers from Universities to Firms: Evidence from French Firm-Level Data. *International Journal of Industrial Organizations*, 21, 1255-1270.

Moore, M. G. (1989). Three types of interaction. The American Journal of Distance Education, 3(2), 1-6.

Moreno, J. L. (1934). *Who shall survive? A new approach to the problems of human interrelations*. Washington, DC: Nervous and Mental Disease Publishing Company.

Muchinsky, P.M. (2000). Emotions in the workplace: The neglect of organizational behaviour. *Journal of Organizational Behavior, 21*, 801-805.

Murray, S. (2003). *A quantitative examination to determine if knowledge sharing activities, given the appropriate richness lead to knowledge transfer, and if implementation factors influence the use of these knowledge sharing activities*. Doctoral dissertation. University Microfilms.

Naeve, A. (2005). The Human Semantic Web – Shifting from Knowledge Push to Knowledge Pull. *International Journal of Semantic Web and Information Systems (IJSWIS)*, 1(3), pp. 1-30.

Nardi, B., Whittaker, S., & Schwarz, H. (2002). NetWORKers and their Activity in Intensional Networks. In: *Computer Supported Cooperative Work* 11: 205–242, 2002.

Nelson, R., & Winter, S. (1982). *An evolutionary theory of economic change*. Cambridge, MA: Harvard University Press.

Nevis, E.C., DiBella, A.J., & Gould, J.M. (1995). Understanding organizations as learning systems. *Sloan Management Review, 36*, 73-85.

Newman, M. & Robey, D. (1992). A social process model of user-analyst relationships. MIS Quarterly (16:2), 249-266.

Nicol, D. J., & MacLeod, I. A. (2005). Using a shared workspace and wireless laptops to improve collaborative project learning in an engineering design class. *44*(4), 459-475.

Nicolini, D., Gherardi, S., & Yanow, D., (Eds.), (2003). *Knowing in Organizations: A Practice-Based Approach*. Armonk: Sharpe.

Nielsen, J. (1994). Ways to Knowledge [in Danish]. In M. Brorup, L. Hauge, & U.L. Thomsen (Eds.). *Pieces of psychology* (pp. 65-86). Copenhagen, Denmark: Gyldendah.

Nielsen, K., & Kvale, S. (1999). Master-apprenticeship learning: Learning as social practice [in Danish]. Copenhagen, Denmark: Hans Reitzel.

Nonaka I. and Takeuchi H., 'The Knowledge Creating Company', (New York: Oxford University Press ,1995).

Nonaka, I. & Takeuchi, H. (1995). *The Knowledge-Creating Company – How Japanese Companies Create the Dynamics of Innovation*. Oxford, UK: Oxford University Press.

Nonaka, I. (1991, November-December). The knowledge-creating company. *Harvard Business Review*, pp. 14-36.

Nonaka, I. (1994). A dynamic theory of organisational knowledge creation. *Organisation Science, 5*(1), 14-37.

Nonaka, I. (1996, February 23). *Knowledge has to do with truth, goodness, and beauty: A conversation with Professor Ikujiro Nonaka*. Claus Otto Scharmer. Tokyo.

Nonaka, I. and Takeuchi, H. (1995). "The Knowledge-creating Company". In: Oxford University Press, Oxford.

Nonaka, I. and Takeuchi, H. (1995). *The knowledge-creating company: how Japanese companies create the dynamics of innovation*, New York, New York, USA: Oxford University Press.

Nonaka, I., & Konno, N. (1998). The concept of "Ba": Building foundation for Knowledge Creation. *California Management Review, 40*(3).

Nonaka, I., & Konno, N. (1998). The concept of Ba: Building a foundation for knowledge creation. *California Management Review (Special Issue on Knowledge and the Firm), 40*(3), 40-54.

Nonaka, I., & Nishiguchi, T. (2001). *Knowledge emergence: Social, technical, and evolutionary dimensions of knowledge creation*. Oxford, UK: Oxford University Press.

Nonaka, I., & Takeuchi H. (1995). *The Knowledge-Creating Company: How Japanese Companies Create the Dynamics of Innovation*, New York: Oxford University.

Nonaka, I., & Takeuchi, H. (1995). *The Knowledge-creating Company.* New York: Oxford University Press.

Nonaka, I., & Takeuchi, H. (1995). *The knowledge-creating company: How Japanese companies create the dynamics of innovation.* New York: Oxford University Press.

Nonaka, I., & Takeuchi, H. (1995). *The knowledge-creating company.* Oxford, UK: Oxford University Press.

Norman, D. (2004). *Emotional Design:* New York: Basic-Books.

Normann, R., & Ramirez, R. (1993, July-August). From value chain to value constellation: Designing interactive strategy. *Harvard Business Review,* pp. 65-77.

Norrgren, F., & Schaller, J. (1999). Leadership style: Its impact on cross-functional product development. *Journal of Product Innovation Management, 16*(4), 377-384.

O'Dell, C. (2008). *Web 2.0 and knowledge management.* American Productivity & Quality Center (APQC). Retrieved from http://www.apqc.org.

O'Reilly, T. (2005). "What Is Web 2.0 - Design Patterns and Business Models for the Next Generation of Software". http://www.oreillynet.com/pub/a/oreilly/tim/news/2005/09/30/ what-is-web-20.html {3.7.2006}

O'Reilly, T. (2005). *Web 2.0: Compact definition?* Retrieved May 17, 2007, from http://radar.oreilly.com/archives/2005/10/web_20_compact_definition.html

Oatley, K., & Johnson-Laird, P.N. (1987). Towards a cognitive theory of emotions. *Cognition and Emotion, 1,* 29-50.

Oblinger, D., & Oblinger, J. (2005). Is it age or IT: First steps towards understanding the Net generation. In D. Oblinger & J. Oblinger (Eds.), *Educating the Net generation.* Educause. Retrieved June 12, 2007, from http://www.educause.edu/educatingthenetgen/

OECD (2003). *Promise and Problems of E-democracy: Challenges of Online Citizen Engagement.*

Öhman, A. (1992). Fear and anxiety as emotional phenomena: clinical, phenomenological, evolutionary perspectives, and information-processing mechanisms, in: Lewis, M./Haviland, J. M. (Eds.): *Handbook of the Emotions*, New York, S. 511-536.

Oliver, B.L. (1999). Comparing corporate managers' personal values over three decades, 1967-1995. *Journal of Business Ethics, 20*(2), 147-161.

Oliver, R., & Herrington, J. (2003). Exploring technology-mediated learning from a pedagogical perspective. Interactive Learning Environments, 11(2), 111-126.

Olson, G. (2006). New tools for learning. Retrieved April 19, 2007 from http://faculty.eicc.edu/golson/tools.htm

Ontoworld.org (2007). Semantic wiki. Retrieved April 27, 2007 from http://ontoworld.org/wiki/Semantic_wiki

Organizational uses of wiki technology. (2006). Proceedings of Wikimania 2006, Retrieved April 27, 2007 from http://wikimania2006.wikimedia.org/wiki/Proceedings: KL1

Orlikowski, W.J. (1992). The duality of technology: Rethinking the concept of structure in organizations. *Organization Science, 3*(3), 398-427.

Orlikowski, W.J. (2000). Using technology and constituting structures: A practice lens for studying technology in organizations. *Organization Science, 11*(4), 404-428.

Orlikowski, W.J. (2002). Knowing in practice: Enacting a collective capability in distributed organizing. *Organization Science, 13,* 249-273.

Orlikowski, W.J. (2002). Knowing in practice: Enacting a collective capability in distributed organizing. *Organization Science, 13*(4), 249-273.

Orlikowski, W.J., & Robey, D. (1991). Information technology and the structuring of organizations. *Information Systems Research, 2*(2), 143-169.

Orr, J. E., (1996). *Talking about machines: An ethnography of a modern job*, Ithaca and London: Cornell University Press.

Otto, H.-U., Kutscher, N., Klein, A., & Iske, S. (2005). *Social inequality in the virtual space: How do young people use the Internet? Results from empirical research about online use differences and acquiring patterns of young people.* Retrieved January 16, 2008, from http://www.kib-bielefeld.de/externelinks2005/Social_Inequality%20KIB.pdf

Owen, M., Grant L., Sayers S., & Facer K. (2006). Social Software and Learning. *FutureLab*: Bristol, UK.

Paavola, S., Lipponen, L., & Hakkarainen, K. (2002). Epistemological Foundations for CSCL: A Comparison of Three Models of Innovative Knowledge Communities. *Proceedings of the Computer-supported Collaborative Learning 2002 Conference,* Hillsdale, N.J.; Erlbaum (2002), pp. 24-32.

Packwood, N. (2004). Geography of the Blogosphere: Representing the Culture, Ecology and Community of Weblogs. In *Into the blogosphere: Rhetoric, community,*

and culture of weblogs, eds. L.J. Gurak, S. Antonijevic, L. Johnson, C. Ratliff, & J. Reyman.

Paolillo, J.C., & Penumarthy, S. (2007). The Social Structure of Tagging Internet Video on del. icio. us. *System Sciences, 2007. HICSS 2007. 40th Annual Hawaii International Conference on*, 85-85.

Parker, K.R. & Chao, J. (2007). Wiki as a teaching tool. International Journal of Knowledge and Learning Objects, (3), 57-72. Retrieved April 27, 2007 from http://ijklo.org/Volume3/IJKLOv3p057-072Parker284.pdf

Parkin, W. (1993). The public and the private: Gender, sexuality and emotion, in Fineman, S. (Eds.). *Emotion in organizations,* (pp. 167-189). London: Sage.

Parolini, C. (1999). *The value net: A tool for competitive strategy.* Great Britain: John Wiley & Sons Ltd.

Patriotta, G. (2003a), *Organization knowledge in the making: How firms create, use, and institutionalise knowledge*, Oxford & New York: Oxford University Press.

Patriotta, G. (2003a). *Organization knowledge in the making: How firms create, use, and institutionalise knowledge*, Oxford & New York: Oxford University Press.

Patriotta, G. (2003b), Sensemaking on the shop floor: Narratives of Knowledge in organizations, *Journal of Management Studies*, 40(2): 349-375.

Patriotta, G. (2003b). Sense-making on the shop floor: Narratives of Knowledge in organizations, *Journal of Management Studies*, 40(2): 349-375.

Patton, M. Q. (2002). Qualitative Research & Evaluation Methods. (3rd Ed)Sage Publications.

Paul, Binker, Adamson, & Martin. (1989). Critical thinking on the web: Definitions [Electronic Version]. Retrieved 29.May.2007 from http://www.austhink.org/critical/pages/definitions.html.

Pawlowski, S.D., & Robey, D. (2004). Bridging user organizations: Knowledge brokering and the work of information technology professionals. MIS Quarterly (28:4), 645-672.

Penrose, E.T. (1959). *The theory of the growth of the firm.* New York: Wiley & Sons.

Pentland, B. T. (1992). 'Organizing moves in software support hot lines'. *Administrative Science Quarterly,* 37, 4, 527–48.

Perrone, J. and Vickers, M. H. (2004). Emotions as Strategic Game in a Hostile Workplace: An Exemplar Case, *Employee Responsibilities and Rights Journal* Volume 16, Number 3 / September 2004 167-178Polanyi, M. (1966). *The Tacit Dimension.* London: Routledge.

Pfeffer, J. (1997). Pitfalls on the Road to Measurement: The Dangerous Liaison of Human Resources With the Ideas of Accounting and Finance. *Human Resource Management,* 36(3), 357-365.

Philip, D. (2007). The Knowledge Building paradigm: A model of learning for Net Generation students. *Innovate* 3 (5). Available: http://www.innovateonline.info /index.php?view=article&id=368. Retrieved: 06-07-07.

Phillips, J. (1996). *Accountability in Human Resource Management.* Houston: Gulf Publishing.

Phillips, M. A. and Huntley, C. (2001). "Dramatica—A New Theory Of Story". Screenplay Systems Inc., 4th edition, 2.

Polanyi M., & Prosch H. (1975). *Meaning.* Chicago: Univ. of Chicago Press.

Polanyi, M (1985). "Implizites Wissen". Suhrkamp, Frankfurt/Main (in German).

Polanyi, M. (1966). *The tacit dimension.* London: Routledge.

Polanyi, M. (1967). *The Tacit Dimension.* New York, Anchor books (based on the 1962 Terry lectures).

Polanyi, M. (1967). *The tacit dimension.* New York: Doubleday and Co.

Polanyi, M. (1969). *Knowing and Being.* Chicago: The University of Chicago Press.

Porter, M. (1985). *Competitive advantage: creating and sustaining superior performance,* New York, New York, USA: The Free Press.

Porter, M.E. (1980). *Competitive strategy: Techniques for analyzing industries and competitors.* New York: Free Press.

Porter, M.E. (1998). *Competitive advantage: Creating and sustaining superior performance.* New York: Free Press.

Potter, J. W. (2005). Media Literacy. Sage Publications: London.

Powell, W. W., Koput, K. W., and Smith-Doerr, L. (1996). Interorganizational Collaboration and the Locus of innovation: Networks of Learning in Biotechnology. *Administrative Science Quarterly* (41), 116-145

Prensky, M. (2001a). *Digital natives, digital immigrants: Part 1.* Retrieved April 13, 2007, from http://www.marcprensky.com/writing/Prensky -Digital Natives, Digital Immigrants-Part1.pdf

Prensky, M. (2001b). *Digital natives, digital immigrants: Part 2.* Retrieved April 13, 2007, from http://www.marcprensky.com/writing/Prensky -Digital Natives, Digital Immigrants-Part2.pdf

Propp, V. (1958). "Morphology of the Folktale". International Journal of American Linguistics, 24(4, Part II).

Propst, D.B., Sales, K., Iyer, V., Perales, M.K., Bryson, B.F. (2006). Extending the Army Corps of Engineers Natural Resource Management Gateway to non-Corps of Engineers audiences: results and recommendations. (In publication).

Pruitt, D.G., Kimmel, M.J. (1976). Twenty Years of Experimental Gaming: Critique, Synthesis and Suggestion for the Future. *Annual Review of Psychology,* 28, 363–392.

Putnam, L.L., & Mumby, D.K. (1993). Organisations, emotions and the myth of rationality, in Fineman, S. (Eds.). *Emotion in Organisations,* (pp. 36-57). London: Sage.

Quintana-Carcias, C. and Benavieds-Velasco, C.A (2004). Cooperation, competition, and innovative capability: a panel data of European dedicated biotechnology firms, *Technovation*, 24(12), p. 927.

Radding A., (1998), "Knowledge Management – Succeding in the Information based Global Economy", Computer Technology Research Corp.

Raymond, E.S. (2001). *The Cathedral and the Bazaar: Musings on Linux and Open Source by an Accidental Revolutionary*. O'Reilly & Associates.

Raynor, M. E. (2007). *The strategy paradox: Why committing to success leads to failure (and what to do about it)*. New York: Doubleday.

Reber, A.S. (1993). *Implicit learning and tacit knowledge*. Oxford University Press.

Resnick, M. (2002). Rethinking learning in the digital age. In G. S. Kirkman, P. K. Cornelius, J. D. Sachs, & K. Schwab (Eds.), *Global information technology report 2001-2002: Readiness for the networked world* (pp. 32-37). New York: Oxford University Press.

Retalis S., Psaromiligkos, Y., & Siassiakos K. (2005). The 'why', 'what', 'when' and 'how' of a summative evaluation method about the learning effectiveness of web-based learning systems. THEMES in Education, Universiy of Ioannina. Athens: Ellinika Grammata 6(2), 207-222.

Retalis, S., Papasalouros, A., Psaromiligkos, Y., Siscos, S., & Kargidis, T., (2006). Towards Networked Learning Analytics – A concept and a tool, Proceedings of the 5th International Conference on Networked Learning 2006, Lancaster UK.

Reus, T.H. (2004). Rhyme and Reason: Emotional Capability and the Performance of Knowledge-Intensive Work Groups. *Human Performance, 17*(2), 245-266.

Rheingold, H. (1993). *The Virtual Community*. Reading: Addison-Wesley.

Rheingold, H. (2000). *The Virtual Community*. MIT Press.

Rheingold, H. (2002). Smart Mobs: The Next Social Revolution. Perseus Books Group.

Richardson, W. (2006). *Blogs, Wikis, Podcasts, and Other Powerful Web Tools for Classrooms*. Thousand Oaks, CA: Corwin Press.

Richter, A., & Koch, M. (2007). *Social software: Status quo und zukunft* (Tech. Rep. No. 2007-01). Fakultät für Informatik, Universität der Bundeswehr München. Retrieved June 1, 2007, from http://www.unibw.de/wow5_3/forschung/social_software/

Rodwell, J.J., Lam, J. & Fastenau, M. (2000). Benchmarking HRM and the Benchmarking of Benchmarking. Best Practices from outside the Square in the Australian Finance Industry. *Employee Relations*, 22(4), 356-374.

Rogers, E.M., Collins-Jarvis, L., & Schmitz, J. (1994). The PEN project in Santa Monica: Interactive communication, equality, and political action. *Journal of the American Society for Information Science*, 45(6), 401-410.

Rokeach, M. (1973). *The nature of human values*. New York: Free Press.

Roschelle, J. & Teasley S.D. (1995). The construction of shared knowledge in collaborative problem solving. In C.E. O'Malley (Ed), *Computer-Supported Collaborative Learning*. (pp. 69-197). Berlin: Springer-Verlag.

Rosen, T. (2001). E-Democracy in Practice: Swedish Experiences of a New Political Tool. *Stockholm, Swedish Association of Local Authorities and Swedish Federation of County Councils and Regions, Department of Democracy and Self-Government*.

Roth, G. and Kleiner, A. (1999). "Car Launch: The Human Side of Managing Change". Oxford University Press, New York.

Rotter, J.B. (1980). Interpersonal Trust, Trustworthiness, and Gullibility. *American Psychologist*, 35, 1–7.

Rouse, W. (2005). A theory of enterprise transformation. *Systems Engineering, 8*(4), 279-295.

Roy Rosenzweig. (1998). Wizards, Bureaucrats, Warriors, and Hackers: Writing the History of the Internet. *The American Historical Review, 103*(5), 1530-1552.

Royrvik, E.A. and Bygdas, A.L. (2002). "Knowledge Hyperstories — The Use of ICT Enhanced Storytelling in Organizations". 3rd European Conference on Organizational Knowledge, Learning and Capabilities. Athens, Greece. http://www.alba.edu.gr/OKLC2002/Proceedings/pdf files/ID260.pdf {2.10.2006}.

Ruggles R., "Knowledge Tools: Using Technology to Manage Knowledge Better", 1997.

Rummel, N., & Spada, H. (2005). Learning to Collaborate: An Instructional Approach to Promoting Collaborative Problem Solving in Computer-Mediated Settings. Journal of the Learning Sciences, 14(2), 201-241.

Russi, J. (2005). *An evaluation of the use and perceived value of the Natural Resource Management Gateway.* Unpublished master's thesis, University of California at Sacramento, Sacramento, CA.

Saint-Onge H., Wallace D., "Leveraging Communities of Practices for Strategic Advantage", Butterworth Heinemann, 2003.

Säljö, R. (2000). *Lärande i praktiken: Ett sociokulturellt perspektiv (Learning in practice: A sociocultural perspective.* Stockholm: Prisma.

Saltz, J.S., Hiltz, S.R., Turoff, M., & Passerini, K. (2007). Increasing participation in distance learning courses. IEEE Internet Computing, 11(3), 36-44.

Sampler, J. L. (1997). Information Specificity and Environmental Scanning: An Economic Perspective. *MIS Quarterly*, 21(1), 25-53.

Sanders, P. (1982). Phenomenology; A New Way of Viewing Organizational Research', *Academy of Management Review,* 7 (3): 353-360.

Sandholtz, J., Rngstaff, C., Dwyer, D. (1997) *Teaching with technology.* NY: Teachers College Press.

Sauer, C., & Willcocks, L. (2003). Establishing the business of the future: The role of organizational architecture and information technologies. *European Management Journal, 21*(4), 497-508.

Scardamalia, M., & Bereiter, C. (1991). Higher levels of agency in knowledge building: A challenge for the design of new knowledge media. *Journal of the Learning Sciences, 1,* 37-68.

Schaffert, S., Gruber, A. & Westenthaler, R. (2006). A semantic wiki for collaborative knowledge formation. In S. Reich, G. Güntner, T. Pellegrini, A. & Wahler (Eds.): *Semantic Content Engineering*, Austria: Trauner Verlag. Retrieved May 27, 2007 from http://www.salzburgresearch.at/research/gfx/SemWikiForCollKnowForm_20060120.pdf

Schatzki, T.R., Knorr-Cetina, K., & von Savigny, E. (Eds.), (2001). *The Practice Turn in Contemporary Theory.* London: Routledge.

Scherer, U., & Tran, V. (2001). Effects of emotions on the process of organizational learning, in Dierkes, M., Antal, A.B., Child, J., & Nonaka, I. (Hrsg.): *Handbook of organizational learning and knowledge,* (pp. 369-394). Oxford: OUP.

Schipper, F. (1999) ´Phenomenology and the Reflective Practitioner´. *Management Learning,* 30 (4): 473-485.

Schneider, O., Braun, N. and Habinger G. (2003). "Storylining suspense: An authoring environment for structuring non-linear interactive narratives". In WSCG, http://wscg.zcu.cz/wscg2003/Papers_2003/I53.pdf {25.7.2006}.

Schoenfeld, A.H. (2006). Mathematics teaching and learning. In P.A. Alexander & P.H. Winne (Eds.), Handbook of Educational Psychology (2nd Ed.). Mahwah, NJ: Lawrence Erlbaum Associates, 479-495.

Scholz, T. & Hartzog, P. (2008). Toward a critique of the social web. Online interview available: http://www.re-public.gr/en/?p=201. Retrieved: 6-04-08.

Schön, D. A. (1983). *The Reflective Practitioner,* Basic Books.

Schulmeister, R. (2004). Diversität von studierenden und die konsequenzen für elearning. In D. Carstensen

& B. Barrios (Eds.), *Kommen die digitalen medien in die jahre? Medien in der wissenschaft* (Vol. 29, p. 133-144). Münster, Germany: Waxmann.

Schulmeister, R. (2005). *Lernplattformen für das virtuelle lernen: Evaluation und didaktik* (2. Aufl.). München, Germany: Oldenbourg.

Schütz, A. (1972). *The Phenomenology of the Social World*, New York. Humanities Press.

Schwartz P., Kelly E., Boyer N., "The emerging global knowledge economy", in "The Future of the Global Economy: Towards a Long Boom?", Parigi, OECD, 1999.

Schwartz, D.L. (1995). The emergence of abstract dyad representations in dyad problem solving. The Journal of the Learning Sciences, 4(3), 321-354.

Schwartz, S.H. (1994). Are there universal aspects in the structure and contents of human values? *Journal of Social Issues, 50*(4), 19-46.

Scott, J. (1991). *Social network analysis: A handbook.* Newbury Park, CA: Sage Publications.

Seely Brown, J., & Duguid, P. (1998). Organizing knowledge. *California Management Review*, 40(3), 90-111.

Semantic Interoperability Community of Practice Wiki. http://colab.cim3.net/cgi-bin/wiki.pl?SICoP

Senge, P.M. (1990), "The Leader's New Work: Building learning organizations", Sloan Management Review, Fall, pp. 7-23.

Sessums, C. (2006). Weblogging and teacher learning: getting the most out of the online social networks. Available: http://eduspaces.net/csessums/weblog/134953.html. Retrieved: 31-08-07.

Seufert, S. (2007). Ne(x)t generation learning: Was gibt es neues über das lernen? In S. Seufert & D. Euler (Eds.), *Ne(x)t generation learning: Wikis, blogs, mediacasts & Co. Social software und personal broadcasting auf der spur* (pp. 2-19). SCIL Arbeitsbericht.

Severin, W., & Tankard, J. (1997). *Communication theories* (4th ed.). New York: Longman.

Seybert, H. (2007). *Gender differences in the use of computers and the Internet.* Retrieved January 15, 2008, from http://epp.eurostat.ec.europa.eu/portal/page?_pageid=1073,46587259&_dad=portal&_schema=PORTAL&p_product_code=KS-SF-07-119

Shannon, C., & Weaver, W. (1949). *The mathematical theory of communication.* Urbana: University of Illinois Press.

Shapiro, S. P. (1987). The Social Control of Impersonal Trust. *American Journal of Sociology*, 93(3), 623–658.

Sharda, N. (2005). "Movement Oriented Design: A New Paradigm for Multimedia Design". International Journal of Lateral Computing (IJLC), 1(1):7–14, 2005.

Sharma, P., & Fiedler, S. (2004, June 30-July 2). Introducing technologies and practices for supporting self-organized learning in a hybrid environment. In K. Tochterman & H. Maurer (Eds.), *Proceedings of I-Know '04*, Graz, Austria (pp. 543-550).

Sharma, P., & Maleyeff, J. (2003). Internet education: Potential problems and solutions. *17*(1), 19-25.

Shaw, A. (1994). Neighborhood Networking and Community Building. In S. Cisler (Ed.), *Ties that bind: Building community networks.* Cuppertino, CA: Apple Computer.

Shi, X., Tseng, B., & Adamic, L. A. (2007). Looking at the Blogosphere Topology through Different Lenses. *Proceedings of International Conference on Weblogs and Social Media*, Boulder, Colorado, USA, March 26-28, 2007.

Shilling, C. (1993). *The Body and Social Theory.* London: Sage.

Shirky, C. (2003). *Social software and the politics of groups.* Retrieved May 3, 2007, from http://shirky.com/writings/group_politics.html

Shotter, J. (1993). *Cultural Politics of Everyday Life: Social Contructionism, Rhetoric, and Knowing of the Third Kind.* Toronto: Open University Press.

Siemens, G. (2004). Connectivism: A Learning Theory for the Digital Age. Available: http://www.elearnspace.org/Articles/connectivism.htm (updated: 05-04-2005). Retrieved: 02-10-07.

Siemens, G. (2005). Connectivism: Learning as Network-Creation. *Elearnspace.* Retrieved May 24, 2007, from http://www.elearnspace.org/Articles/networks.htm

Siemens, G. (2006). *Knowing Knowledge*, Lulu.com, ISBN: 978-1-4303-0230-8.

Simon, H. A. (1996). Sciences of the artificial (3rd edition): MIT.

Sirkin, H.L., Keenan, P., and Jackson, A. (2005) The hard side of change management. *Harvard Business Review,* (October): 108-118.

Skyrme D. J., "Developing a Knowledge Strategy: From Management to Leadership", in "Knowledge Management Classic and Contemporary Works", Boston, MIT Press, 2000.

Small, C. (2006). *An enterprise knowledge-sharing model: A complex adaptive systems perspective on improvement in knowledge sharing.* Doctoral dissertation, George Mason University. University Microfilms.

Small, C., & Sage, A. (2006). Knowledge management and knowledge sharing: A review. *Information, Knowledge, and Systems Management, 5*(3), 153-169.

Smolnik, S., Kremer, S., & Kolbe, L. (2005). Continuum of context explication: Knowledge discovery through process-oriented portals. *International Journal of Knowledge Management, 1*(1), 27-46.

Snow, C. P. (1959). "The Two Cultures". Cambridge University Press, Cambridge.

Snyder, W.M. & Briggs, X.S. (2003). Communities of Practice: a new tool for government managers. http://www.businessofgovernment.org/pdfs/Snyder_report.pdf (accessed May 3, 2007)

Software Engineering Institute (SEI). (1996). *IDEAL^SM: A user's guide for software process improvement* (Hand-book CMU/SEI-96-HB-001). Pittsburgh, PA: Software Engineering Institute, Carnegie Mellon University.

Soller, A., Martinez, A., Jermann, P., & Muehlenbrock, M., (2005). From mirroring to guiding: a review of state of the art technology for supporting collaborative learning. International Journal on Artificial Intelligence in Education. 15(4), 261-290.

Solomon, R.C. (1980). Emotions and choice, in Rorty, A. (Eds.). *Explaining emotions, Berkeley,* (pp. 251-281). University of California Press.

Solop, F.I. (2002). Digital Democracy Comes of Age: Internet Voting and the 2000 Arizona Democratic Primary Election. *PS: Political Science and Politics, 34*(02), 289-293.

Soo, C., Devinney, T., Midgley, D., and Deering, A. (2002). Knowledge management: Philosophy, processes, and pitfalls. *California Management Review,* 44(4), 129-150.

Spaniol, M., Klama, R., Sharda, N. and Jarke, M. (2006). "Web-Based Learning with Non-Linear Multimedia Stories", 5th International Conference on Web-based Learning (ICWL 2006), July 19-21. Penang, Malaysia.

Spatariu, A., Hartley, K. & Bendixen, L. D. (2004). Defining and measuring quality in on-line discussion. *Journal of Interactive Online Learning, 2*(4). Retrieved January 2005, from http://www.ncolr.org/jiol/issues/PDF/2.4.2.pdf

Spender, J.-C. (1994). Organizational knowledge, collective practice, and Penrose rents. *International Business Review, 3*(4), 353-367.

Spender, J.C. (1996). Making the knowledge basis of a dynamic theory of the firm, *Strategic Management Journal,* 17(1), 45-62.

Spender, J.-C. (1998), Pluralist Epistemology and the Knowledge-Based Theory of the Firm, *Organization,* Vol. 5, No. 2, pp. 233-256.

Spender; J.C. (2003). Exploring uncertainty and emotion in the knowledge-based theory of the firm. *Information Technology and People Volume, 16,* 266-288.

Spiegelberg, H. (1975). *Doing phenomenology.* The Hague/Netherlands: Martinus Nijhoff.

Stacey, R. (2001). *Complex Responsive Processes in Organizations: Learning and Knowledge Creation.* London: Routledge.

Stahl, G. (2005). *Group Cognition: Computer Support for Collaborative Knowledge Building.* Cambridge, MA: MIT Press.

Stanic, G.M.A., & Kilpatrick, J. (2003). A history of school mathematics. Reston, VA: National Council of Teachers of Mathematics, Vols.1–2.

Star, S.L., & Ruhleder, K. (1994, October 22-26). Steps toward an ecology of infrastructure. In *Proceedings of CSCW, 94,* 253–264, Chapel Hill, North Carolina.

Stein, N.L., & Trabasso, T. (1992). The organization of emotional experience: Creating links among emotion, thinking and intentional action. In N. Stein, & K. Oatley (Eds.). *Cognition and Emotion (special issue), 6,* 225-244.

Stenmark, D. (2000). Leveraging tacit organisational knowledge. *Journal of Management Information Systems, 17*(3), 9-24.

Stephenson ,N. (1992) Snowcrash. New York: Spectra.

Sternstein, A. (2005a). Online collaborative sites open to everyone enable the sharing of ideas. FCW.com. Retrieved May 27, 2007 from http://www.fcw.com/article88467-04-04-05-Print

Sternstein, A. (2005b). Wiki advocate sees government uses. FCW.com. Retrieved May 27, 2007 from http://www.fcw.com/article89069-06-03-05-Web

Storck, J., & Hill, P.A. (2000). Knowledge diffusion through "strategic communities." *Sloan Management Review, 41,* 63-74.

Styhre, A. (2003). *Understanding Knowledge Management: Critical and Postmodern Perspectives.* Copenhagen: Copenhagen Business School Press.

Styhre, A. (2004). Rethinking Knowledge: A Bergsonian Critique of the Notion of Tacit Knowledge. *British Journal of Management, 15*(2), 177-188.

Surowiecki, J. (2004). *The wisdom of crowds: Why the many are smarter than the few and how collective wisdom shapes business, economies, societies, and nations* (1st ed.). New York: Doubleday.

Swan, J., Scarbrough, H., & Preston, J. (1999). Knowledge management—The next fad to forget people. In *Proceedings of the ECIS 1999,* Copenhagen, Denmark.

Swarm Development Group. (2004). *Chris Langton, Glen Ropella.* Retrieved from http://wiki.swarm.org/.

Szybalski, A. (2005). Why it's not a wiki world (yet). Retrieved April 19, 2007 from http://andy.bigwhitebox.org/papers/wiki_world.pdf

Tangney, B., FitzGibbon, A., Savage, T., Mehan, S., & Holmes, B. (2001). Communal constructivism: Students constructing learning for as well as with others. In C. Crawford, D. A. Willis, R. Carlsen, I. Gibson, K. McFerrin, J. Price, & R. Weber (Eds.), *Proceedings of Society for Information Technology and Teacher Education International Conference 2001* (pp. 3114-3119). Norfolk, VA: AACE.

Tapscott, D. & Williams, A.D. (2006). *Wikinomics: How Mass Collaboration Changes Everything.* New York, NY: Penguin Group.

Tapscott, D., Williams, A. D. (2006). "Wikinomics: How Mass Collaboration Changes Everything" Portfolio Hardcover.

Teece, D.J. (1984). Economic analysis and strategic management. *California Management Review, 26*(3), 87-110.

Teece, D.J. (1998). Capturing value from knowledge assets: The new economy, markets for know-how, and intangible assets. *California Management Review, 40,* 55-79.

Teece, D.J. (1998). Capturing value from knowledge assets: The new economy, markets for know-how, and intangible assets. *California Management Review, 40*(3), 55-79.

Teece, D.J., Pisano, G., & Schuen, A. (1997). Dynamic capabilities and strategic management. *Strategic Management Journal, 26*(3), 87-110.

TELL Project. (2005). Introducing a Framework for the Evaluation of Network Supported Collaborative Learning, WP1 Deliverable, Project number: EAC/61/03/ GR009 eLearning Initiative, EU: European Commission Downloadable at: http://cosy.ted.unipi.gr/tell/media/ WP1_deliverable.pdf

Tennyson, R.D., & Schott, F. (1997). Instructional design theory, research, and models. In R.D.Tennyson, F.Schott, N.M.Seel, & S.Dijkstra (Eds.), Instructional design: International perspective. Mahwah, NJ: Lawrence Erlbaum Associates, Inc, 1-18.

Thijssen, T., & Vernooij, F. (2002). Breaking the boundaries between academic degrees and lifelong learning. In T. A. Johannessen (Ed.), *Educational innovation in economics and business: Vol. 6. Teaching today: The knowledge of tomorrow* (pp. 137-156). Dordrecht, The Netherlands: Kluwer Academic.

Thompson, M., & Walsham, G. (2001). Learning to value the Bardi tradition: Culture, communication, and organisational knowledge. In *Proceeding of the ECIS 2001,* Bled, Slowenia.

Thompson, M.P.A., & Walsham, G. (2004). Placing knowledge management in context. *Journal of Management Studies, 41*(5), 725-747.

Tierney, T. (1999). What's your strategy for managing knowledge? *Harvard Business Review, 77*(2), 106-116.

Tilley, P.A., & Giordano, G.A. (2003). Knowledge management strategies and cultural dimensions. Proceedings of the Ninth Americas Conference on Information Systems, 2003, pp. 2618. Retrieved April 19, 2007 from http://aisel.isworld.org/password.asp?Vpath=AMCIS/ 2003&PDFpath=03HE20.pdf

Timbrell, G., Delaney, P., Chan, T., Yue, A., & Gable, G. (2005). A structurationist review of knowledge management theories. In *Proceedings of the 26th Annual Conference on Information Systems* (pp. 247-259), Las Vegas, Nevada.

Tiwana A. 'The Knowledge Management Tool Kit' (Prentice- Hall Upper Side River , 2000)

Tolbert, P.S., & Zucker, L.G. (1999). The institutionalization of institutional theory. In S.R. Clegg & C. Hardy (Eds.), *Studying organization.* London: SAGE Publications.

Tonkin, E. (2005). Making the case for a wiki. Ariadne, Issue 42, January. Retrieved April 19, 2007 from http:// www.ariadne.ac.uk/issue42/tonkin/

Tracey, B.J. and Nathan, A.E. (2002). The Strategic and Operational Roles of Human Resources: An emerging model. *Cornell Hotel and Restaurant Administration Quarterly,* 43(4), 17-26.

Tran, V. (1998). The role of the emotional climate in learning organizations. *The Learning Organization,* 5(2) 99-103.

Truong, Q.S., Herber, N., Liguori, C., & Barroso Jr., H. (2005). Using wikis as a low-cost knowledge sharing tool. Institute of Nuclear Materials Management 46th Annual Meeting in Phoenix, Arizona. Retrieved May 27, 2007 from http://saturn.eton.ca/wiki/index.php/ INMM2005/Paper231

Tsai, W. (2002). Social structure of "coopetition" within a multiunit organization: coordination, competition, and intraorganizational knowledge sharing, *Organization Science,* 13(2), 179-190.

Tsoukas, H. (1996). The firm as a distributed knowledge system: a constructionist approach. *Strategic Management Journal, 17,* 11-25.

Tsoukas, H. (1996). The firm as a distributed knowledge system: A constructionist approach [Winter special issue]. *Strategic Management Journal, 7,* 11-25.

Tsoukas, H. (1998). The word and the world: A critique of representationalism in management research. *International Journal of Public Administration, 21*(5), 781-817.

Tulving, E. (1978). "Episodic and semantic memory". In E. Tulving and W. Donaldson (Eds.), Organization of Memory, New York: Academic Press, pp. 381-403.

Turkle, S. (1995). *Life on the Screen: Identity in the Age of the Internet.* New York: Simon and Schuster.

Turoff, M. (1999). An end to student segregation: No more separation between distance learning and regular courses. *Telelearning 99 Symposium,* Montreal, Canada. Retrieved January 2005, from http://eies.njit.edu/~turoff/Papers/canadapres/segregation.htm

Twigg, C. (2001). Innovations in online learning: Moving beyond no significant difference. *The Pew Symposia in Learning and Technology 2001.* Retrieved January 2005, from http://www.center.rpi.edu/PewSym/mono4.html

U.S. Army Corps of Engineers (2003). USACE 2012 final report. http://www.hq.usace.army.mil/stakeholders/Final.htm (accessed May 3, 2007)

U.S. Army Corps of Engineers. (1996). *Project operations – Recreation operations and maintenance policies,* Engineer Regulation 1130-2-550, Washington, DC.

U.S. Army Corps of Engineers. (2006a). *The Community of Practice (CoP) in the U.S. Army Corps of Engineers (USACE),* Engineer Regulation 25-1-8, Washington, DC.

U.S. Army Corps of Engineers. (2006b). Natural Resources Management System (NRMS) historical data. Natural Resources Management Gateway, Mike Owen, Subject Matter Expert, CESWF-OD-R. *http://CorpsLakes.usace.army.mil/employees/nrms/nrms.html* (accessed July 10, 2006).

U.S. Army Corps of Engineers. (2006c). Operations and Maintenance Business Information Link (OMBIL) historical data. Natural Resources Management Gateway, Mike Owen, Subject Matter Expert, CESWF-OD-R. *http://corpslakes.usace.army.mil/employees/ombil-rec/ombil.html* (accessed May 6, 2006).

U.S. Army Corps of Engineers. 2005. Project Management Plan Natural Resources Management (NRM) Gateway Website Initiative. *http://corpslakes.usace.army.mil/employees/gateway/pdfs/05pmp-gateway.pdf* (accessed May 1, 2006).

Ullman, M. T. (2004). "Contributions of memory circuits to language: the declarative/procedural model". Cognition, 92:231 – 270.

Ulrich, D. & Brockbank, W. (2005). *HR The Value Proposition.* United States of America: Harvard Business School Press.

Ulrich, D. (1997). *Human ressource Champions - The next agenda for adding value and delivering results.* London: Harvard Business School Press.

Ulrich, D., Brockbank, W., & Yeung, A. (1989). Beyond Belief: A Benchmark for Human Resources. *Human Resource Management, 28*(3), 311-335.

US Government Services Administration, Intergovernmental Communities. (http://www.gsa.gov/collaborate)

Uses of a wiki. (2007). Wikia, Inc. Retrieved May 27, 2007 from http://www.wikia.com/wiki/Uses_of_a_wiki

Vaast, E., & Walsham, G. (2005). Representations and actions: The transformation of work practices with IT use. *Information and Organization, 15*(1), 65-89.

van der Zalm, J. & Bergum, V. (2000). Hermeneutic-phenomenology: providing living knowledge for nursing practice Journal of Advanced Nursing 31 (1), 211–218.

van Maanen, J., & Barley, S.R. (1984). Occupational communities: Culture and control in organizations. In B.M. Staw (Ed.), *Research in organizational behavior* (vol. 6). Greenwich, CT: JAI Press.

van Maanen, J., & Kunda, G. (1989). Real Feelings: Emotional expression and organizational culture. *Research in Organizational Behavior, 11,* 43-103.

Vapola, T.J. (2000). *Technological leadership and competitive strategy: A case of shaping the future,* M.Sc. Thesis, Helsinki, Finland: Helsinki School of Economics.

Vapola, T.J. and Seppälä, T.T. (2006). The performance impact of membership in a global alliance: evidence on the revenue growth rate of mobile operators, Benito G. & Greve, H.R. (eds), *Progress in International Business Research*, London, United Kingdom: MacMillan.

Vapola, T.J., Tossavainen, P. and Gabrielsson, M. (2008). The battleship strategy: the complementing role of born globals in MNC's new opportunity creation, *Journal of International Entrepreneurship,* 6(1), 1–21.

Vedel, T. (2003). L'idée de démocratie électronique: Origines, Visions, Questions. *Le désenchantement démocratique, La Tour d'Aigues: Editions de l'Aube,* 243-266.

Veerman, A.L. (2000). Computer-supported collaborative learning through argumentation. Enschede: Print Partners Ipskamp. Downloadable at: http://eduweb.fss. uu.nl/arja/

Venkatraman, N., & Tanriverdi, H. (2005). Reflecting "knowledge" in strategy research: Conceptual issues and methodological challenges. *Research Methodology in Strategy and Management, 1,* 33-65.

Vince, R. (2001). Power and Emotion in Organizational Learning. *Human Relations, 54*(10), 1325-1351.

Vince, R. (2002). The Impact of Emotion on Organizational Learning, in: *Human Resource Development International*, 5. Jg. (2002): 1:73–85

Vivitsou, M., Lambropoulos, N., Konetas, D., Paraskevas, M., Grigoropoulos, E. (2008). The Project Method e-course: the use of tools towards the evolution of the Greek teachers' online community. *Int. J. Cont. Engineering Education and Lifelong Learning,* Inderscience Enterprises Ltd.

Von Hippel, E. (1987). Co-operation between rivals: informal know-how trading, *Research Policy,* **16**, 291–302.

Von Hippel, E. (1988). The source of innovation, New York, New York, USA: Oxford University Press.

von Hippel, E. (1998). Economics of Product Development by Users: The impact of "sticky" local information. *Management Science*, 44, 629-644.

Von Krogh, G. (2002), *"The communal resource and information systems"*, Journal of Strategic Information Systems, Vol. 11, pp. 85-107.

von Krogh, G., & Roos, J. (1995). *Organizational epistemology.* New York: St. Martin's.

Voyiatzaki E., Christakoudis Ch., Margaritis M., Avouris N. (2004). Teaching algorithms using a collaborative computer environment. Proceedings 4th ETPE Conf., Athens, vol B, pp. 641-647, October 2004 (in GREEK).

Vygotsky, L. (1978). *Mind in society.* Cambridge, MA: Harvard University Press.

Vygotsky, L. S. (1978). *Mind in society: The development of higher psychological processes.* Cambridge, Massachusetts: Harvard University Press.

Vygotsky, L.S. (1962). Thought and language. Cambridge, MA: MIT Press. (Original work published in 1934).

Vygotsky, L.S. (1978). Mind in Society: The development of higher psychological processes. Cambridge, MA: Harvard University Press.

Waldron, V. (1994). One more, with Feeling: Reconsidering the Role of Emotion in Work, in Deetz, S. A. (Eds.). *Communication Yearbook, 17,* (pp. 388-416). Thousands Oaks: Sage.

Wales, J. (2006). Wikipedia, wikia and free culture [Electronic Version]. University of Bergen. Retrieved 29.05.06 from http://academicfeeds.friwebteknologi. org/index.php?id=25

Wall, M. (2005). 'Blogs of war': Weblogs as news. *Journalism, 6*(2), 153.

Wallace, R. (2003). Online learning in higher education: a review of research on interactions among teachers and students. Education, Communication & Information, 3(2), 241-280.

Walsh, J. P., & Ungson, G. R. (1991). Organisational memory. *Academy of Management Review, 16,* 57-91.

Walsham, G. (2001). Knowledge management: The benefits and limitations of computer systems. *European Management Journal, 19*(6), 599-608.

Walsham, G., & Waema, T. (1994). Information systems strategy and implementation: A case study of a building society. *ACM Transactions on Information Systems, 12*(2), 150-173.

Warlick, D. (2005). Four reasons why the blogsphere might make a better professional collaborative environment than discussion forums. Available: http://davidwarlick.com/2cents/ 2005/08/15/four-reasons-why-the-blogsphere-might-make-a-better-professional-collaborative-environment-than-discussion-forums/. Retrieved: 31-08-07.

Wasserman, S., & Faust, K. (1994). *Social network analysis: Methods and applications.* Cambridge University Press, Cambridge, United Kingdom, 1994.

Wasserman, S., & Faust, K. (1994). *Social network analysis: Methods and applications.* Cambridge: Cambridge University Press.

Wasserman, S., & Faust, K. (1994). *Social network analysis: Methods and applications.* Cambridge: Cambridge University Press.

Watson, J. B. (1925/1997). *Behaviorism.* New Jersey: Transaction Publishers.

Weeks, M. (2004). Knowledge management in the wild. *Business Horizons,* 47(6), 15-24.

Wegerif, R. (2006). A Dialogic Understanding of the Relationship between CSCL and Teaching Thinking Skills. Computer Supported Learning, Springer Science and Business Media, Inc.

Weick, K. E. (1995). *Sensemaking in organizations.* London: Sage Publications.

Weick, K.E. (1989). Theory construction as disciplined imagination. *Academy of Management Review, 14,* 532-550.

Weick, K.E. (1990). Technology as equivoque: Sensemaking in new technologies. In P. Goodman et al. (Eds.), *Technology and organizations* (pp. 1-44). San Francisco: Jossey-Bass.

Weick, K.E., & Bougon, M.G. (1986). Organizations as cognitive maps: Charting ways to success and failure. In *The thinking organization* (pp. 102-135). San Francisco: Jossey-Bass.

Wenger E. C., "Communities of Practice", Cambridge University Press, Cambridge, 1998.

Wenger E., Snyder W. (2000) *Communities of practice: The organizational frontier,* Harvard Business Review, 1, pp. 139-145.

Wenger, E. (1998), Communities of practice. Learning, Meaning and Identity, Cambridge University Press, Cambridge

Wenger, E. (1999). *Communities of practice: learning, meaning and identity.* Cambridge: Cambridge University Press.

Wenger, E. C., & Snyder, W. M. (2000). Communities of practice: The organisational frontier. *Harvard Business Review, 78,* 139-145.

Wenger, E. C., McDermott, R., & Snyder, W. M. (2002). *Communities of practice—A guide to managing knowledge.* Boston: Harvard Business School.

Wenger, E., McDermott, R. A., and Snyder, W. (2002). *Cultivating communities of practice: a guide to managing knowledge.* Boston, Mass: Harvard Business School Press.

Wenger, E.C. and Snyder, W.M. (2000), "*Communities of practice: The organizational frontier*", Harvard Business Review, January - February, pp. 139–145.

Wernerfelt, B. (1984). A resource-based View of the Firm, *Strategic Management Journal*, 5(2), 171-180.

Wheeler, S., Kelly P., & Gale, K. (2005). The influence of online problem-based learning on teachers' professional practice and identity. ALT-J 2005, 13(2):125-137.

White, J. D. (1990). Phenomenology and Organizational development, *Administrative Science Quaterly*, Spring.

White, N. (2005). *How Some Folks Have Tried to Describe Community*. Retrieved May 21, 2007, from http://www.fullcirc.com/community/definingcommunity.htm

White, N. (2006). Blogs and Community - launching a new paradigm for online community? *The Knowledge Tree e-Journal of Learning Innovation*. Edition 11, September 2006.

Wichman, H. (1970). Effects of Isolation and Communication on Cooperation in a Two Person Game. *Journal of Personality and Social Psychology*, 16, 114–120.

Wiener, N. (1965). *Cybernetics:: Or Control and Communication in the Animal and the Machine*. Mit Pr.

Wiig, K.M. (1997). Knowledge management: Where did it come from and where will it go? *Expert Systems with Applications*, 13(1), 1-14.

Wiki's wild world (2005). Nature. 438(7070), 890 Retrieved April 15, 2007 from http://www.nature.com/nature/journal/v438/n7070/pdf/438890a.pdf

WikiMatrix - Compare Them All. (2007). Retrieved April 19, 2007 from http://www.wikimatrix.org/

Wilber, K. (1999). *Collected Works of Ken Wilber: Volumes 1-4*. Boston: Shambhala.

Wilber, K. (2000). *Collected Works of Ken Wilber: Volumes 5-8*. Boston: Shambhala.

Williams, S. (2004). The brave new world of co-opetition, *CircuiTree*, 17(11), 40-41.

Wilson, T.D. (2002). The nonsense of "knowledge management." *Information Research, 8*(1), paper 144.

Retrieved May 21, 2007, from http://InformationR.net/ir/8-1/paper144.html

Winston, W.L. (2003). *Operations Research*. Duxbury P.,U.S.

Winter, S.G. (1987). Knowledge and competence as strategic assets. In D. Teece (ed.), *The competitive challenge: Strategies for industrial innovation and renewal*. Cambridge, MA: Ballinger Publishing Co., 159-184.

Wiszniewski, D., & Coyne, R. (2002). Mask and Identity: The Hermeneutics of Self-Construction in the Information Age. In K. Ann Renninger & Wesley Shumar (Ed.) Building Virtual Communities (pp. 191-214). New York, New York: Cambridge Press.

Wittel, A. (2001). Toward a Network Sociality. *Theory, Culture & Society, Vol. 18(6): 51–76*. London: SAGE

Woolf, B. (2006). Wiki vs. Blog. *IBM developerWorks*. Retrieved April 19, 2007 from http://www-03.ibm.com/developerworks/wikis/display/woolf/Wiki+vs.+Blog

Wu, I.-L. (2002). A model for implementing BPR based on strategic perspectives: An empirical study. *Information and Management, 39*(4), 313-324.

Wynn, E. (1991). Taking practice seriously. In J. Greenbaum & M. Kyng (Eds.), *Design at work*. Hillsdale, NJ: Lawrence Erlbaum Associates.

Yasai-Ardekani, M., & Haug, R.S. (1997). Contextual determinants of strategic planning processes. *Journal of Management Studies, 5*(34), 729-741.

Yates, J., & Orlikowski, W.J. (1992). Genres of organizational communication: A structurational approach to studying communication and media. *The Academy of Management Review, 17*(2), 299-326.

Yee, N. (2007) The Daedalus Project: Psychology of MMOTPGG's. Online http://www.nickyee.com/daedalus/ Accessed 12 March 2008

Yin, R.K. (1994). *Case study research: Design and methods* (2nd ed.). Thousand Oaks, California: Sage Publications.

Zack M. H., 'Developing a Knowledge Strategy', (California Management Review, Vol. 41, N° 3, Spring 1999)

Zack, M.H. (1999). Developing a knowledge strategy. *California Management Review, 41*(3), 125-145.

Zager, D., Whittaker, S., & Schwarz, H. (2002). Collaboration as an Activity. In: *Computer Supported Cooperative Work* 11: 181–204, 2002.

Zander, U. and Kogut, B. (1995). Knowledge and the speed of the transfer and imitation of organizational capabilities: an empirical test, *Organization Science*, 6(1), 76-92.

Zander, U., & Kogut, B. (1995). Knowledge and the speed of the transfer and imitation of organizational capabilities: An empirical test. *Organization Science, 6*, 76–91.

Ziff Davis Media Speeds Projects Cycles, Slashes Group Email. (2007) SocialText Enterprise Wiki. Retrieved May 27, 2007 from http://www.socialtext.com/node/37

Zineldin, M. (2004). Total relationship and logistics management, *International Journal of Physical Distribution & Logistics Management*, 34(3-4), 286-301.

Zuboff, S. (1988). *In the age of the smart machine.* New York: Basic Books.

Zucker, L.G. (1986). Production of Trust: Institutional Sources of Economic Structure, 1846-1920. In: B.M. Staw, and L.L. Cunnings (Eds.), *Research in Organizational Behaviour* (pp. 53-111). JAI Press: Greenwich, CT *8*, 53-111.

About the Contributors

Miltiadis D. Lytras is an Assistant Professor in the Computer Engineering and Informatics Department-CEID (University of Patras). His research focuses on semantic web, knowledge management and e-learning, with more than 100 publications in these areas. He has co-edited / co-edits, 25 special issues in International Journals (e.g. IEEE Transaction on Knowledge and Data Engineering, IEEE Internet Computing, IEEE Transactions on Education, Computers in Human Behaviour etc) and has authored/[co-]edited 12 books [e.g. Open Source for Knowledge and Learning management, Ubiquitous and Pervasive Knowledge Management, Intelligent Learning Infrastructures for Knowledge Intensive Organizations, Semantic Based Information systems] . He is the founder and officer of the Semantic Web and Information Systems Special Interest Group in the Association for Information Systems (http://www.sigsemis.org). He serves as the (Co) Editor in Chief of 12 international journals [e.g. International Journal of Knowledge and Learning, International Journal of Technology Enhanced Learning, International Journal on Social and Humanistic Computing, International Journal on Semantic Web and Information Systems, International Journal on Digital Culture and Electronic Tourism, International Journal of Electronic Democracy, International Journal of Electronic Banking, International Journal of Electronic Trade] while he is associate editor or editorial board member in seven more.

Robert D. Tennyson is currently a professor of educational psychology and technology in the learning and cognition. In addition to his faculty position, he is a the program coordinator for psychological foundations of education. His published works ranges from basic theoretical articles on human learning to applied books on instructional design and technology.He is editor of the scientific journal, Computers in Human Behavior, published by Elsevier Science and now in its 17th year, as well as serving on several editorial boards for professional journals. His research and publications include topics such as cognitive learning and complex cognitive processes, intelligent systems, complex-dynamic simulations, testing and measurement, instructional design, and advanced learning technologies. At the present time, he is working with a German colleague on basic research in learning complex-advanced knowledge. His international activities include directing a NATO-sponsored advanced research workshop in Barcelona and a NATO advanced study institute in Grimstad, Norway—both on the topic of automated instructional design and delivery. He has recently directed an institute on technology in Athens and Kuala Lumpur. His other international activities include twice receiving a Fulbright Research Award to Germany and once to Russia. His teaching interests include psychology of learning, technology-based systems design, evaluation, and management systems.

Copyright © 2009, IGI Global, distributing in print or electronic forms without written permission of IGI Global is prohibited.

Patricia Ordóñez de Pablos is professor in the Department of Business Administration and Accountability, at the Faculty of Economics of The University of Oviedo (Spain). Her teaching and research interests focus on the areas of strategic management, knowledge management, intellectual capital measuring and reporting, organizational learning and human resources management. She is Executive Editor of the International Journal of Learning and Intellectual and the International Journal of Strategic Change Management.

* * *

Marc Alier received an engineering degree in computer science. He then worked in software development and e-learning industry. He has participated in the development of several LMS and authoring tools, and has been an online teacher. Since 2001, he has taught project management and computing ethics at the Universitat Politecnica de Catalunya (http://www.upc.edu), in computer science studies. He is director of a master's program in software for organization management, and a post-degree course on software development for PDA's and smart phones. He is the technical advisor and teacher in the Sciences of Education Institute, UPC (http://www.ice.upc.edu) in the implantation of Moodle. Since early 2004, he has been a member of http://moodle.org, where he developed the spell check integration and the modules Internalmail (http://appserv.lsi.upc.es/palangana/moodle/course/view.php?id=18), DFWiki (http://appserv.lsi.upc.es/palangana/moodle/course/view.php?id=15), and the future new Wiki module. He hopes to finish his PhD before 2008.

Dr. Bonnie F. Bryson is a Research Biologist with the U.S. Army Engineer Research and Development Center. Dr. Bryson conducts research and development in the areas of natural resources stewardship and related outdoor recreation management of Corps of Engineers water resource projects. Bonnie serves as Technical Coordinator for the Operations Community of Practice (CoP) Gateway website and coordinates overall Gateway activities, serving as the Recreation Technical Coordinator within the Natural Resources Management component and coordinating activities of the other Technical Coordinators for Environmental Stewardship, Environmental Compliance, Partnerships, as well as other Operations Sub-CoPs. Dr. Bryson is a three-time University of Kentucky graduate with a bachelor's degree in 1975, master's degree in 1990, and doctor of education (Ed.D.) degree in Recreation Administration in 1999. Dr. Bryson is a Certified Knowledge Manager through the International Knowledge Management Institute. Contact information: Dr. Bonnie F. Bryson, CEERD-EE-E, 3909 Halls Ferry Road, Vicksburg, MS 39180, Bonnie.F.Bryson@erdc.usace.army.mil

Dipl.-Inform. Yiwei Cao is a doctoral researcher in the Information Systems group at RWTH Aachen University. She receives a diploma in computer science from RWTH Aachen University and a bachelor in architecture from Shanghai Tongji University. She works on the interdisciplinary research cluster "Ultra-High Speed Mobile Information and Communication" within the German Excellence Cluster. She is member of the Data Management and Data Exchange Group of German Institution for Standardizations (DIN). Her research interests are (mobile) community information systems and social software across communities for cultural heritage management and technology-enhanced learning, with focus on data quality, multimedia, and metadata standards.

Dr. Joseph T. Chao has taught courses in all aspects of the software development lifecycle including programming, systems analysis and design, database systems, usability engineering, software enginee-ring, and agile software development at Bowling Green State University. Prior to entering academia, Dr. Chao has seven years of industry experience in software development, including three years as Director of Software Development. His research focus is on software engineering with special interests in agile software development, programming languages, and object-oriented analysis and design. He has published in such journals as Journal of Information Technology Education, International Journal of Knowledge and Learning, Academe: Bulletin of the American Association of University Professors, and Journal of Manufacturing Systems. Dr. Chao holds an M.S. in Operations Research from Case Western Reserve University and a Ph.D. in Industrial and Systems Engineering from The Ohio State University.

Mohamed Amine Chatti has a diploma degree in Computer Science from the Technical University of Kaiserslautern, Germany. Currently, he is working as a doctoral researcher at the Chair of Computer Science 5 – Information Systems, RWTH Aachen University, Germany. His research interests include learning and knowledge management, collaborative adaptive learning, personal learning environments, metadata, communities and networks, Web 2.0/social software, and social network analysis. In his PhD thesis "Social Media for Knowledge Management and Technology Enhanced Learning", he is working on a new vision of blended learning defined by the convergence of learning, knowledge management, and Web 2.0 concepts into one integrated solution toward a new model of network learning through active participation in knowledge ecologies.

Angelo Corallo is Researcher and Assistant Professor at the Department of Innovation Engineering at the University of Salento (Lecce, Italy). He graduated in Physics at the University of Salento. He teaches within the Master and PhD of Scuola Superiore ISUFI (University of Salento). His research interests encompass mainly the co-evolution of technological and organizational innovation, with specific focus on business ecosystem, extended enterprise and on knowledge management and collaborative working environment; in this research areas he has many scientific publications. He has been also involved in the Business Enterprise Integration Domain Task Force of OMG in order to define an organizational metamodel supporting the Architecture of Business Modelling framework. Currently he is involved in research activities related with technologies and methodologies supporting the new product development process improvement in complex domains such as the aerospace and automotive industries.

Mariano Corso, PhD, is full professor of Organization at the Polytechnic of Milano where he chairs the course of Management Engineering at the Cremona site. He is director of the Master in "Management and Organisation Development" and of the Observatory on Enterprise 2.0. He promoted and coordi-nated national and international researches on Knowledge Management and is author of more than 70 publications at the international level.

Virginia L. Dickerson is a web and database manager with the Environmental Laboratory of the U.S. Army Engineer Research and Development Center (ERDC). Virginia is responsible for the deve-lopment and maintenance of the Operations Community of Practice Gateway website. She supports the workshops and training to maintain and develop this knowledge management system. Ms. Dickerson is a graduate of Millsaps College with a Bachelor of Business Administration degree in 1994 and a

Masters of Business Administration degree, with an emphasis in marketing and information systems, in 1997. Contact information: Virginia L. Dickerson, CEERD-EV-B, 3909 Halls Ferry Road, Vicksburg, MS 39180, Virginia.L.Dickerson@erdc.usace.army.mil

Gianluca Elia is Researcher and Assistant Professor at Faculty of Engineering and Department of "Engineering for Innovation" of University of Salento (Lecce, Italy). He collaborates also with "Scuola Superiore ISUFI", specifically with the e-Business Management Section (eBMS), for the educational activities (Master and PhD programs) and research programs. His research interests are mainly focused on Collaborative Learning, integration of Knowledge Management and Web Learning, Social Computing. In this research area, he has several publications in conferences, journals and books. He also realized the "Virtual eBMS" platform, a system integrating natively Knowledge Management and Web Learning services, that received in October 2006 an awards in "Learning Technology" category from "Brandon Hall Research". Currently, he is responsible of several national research projects in his research areas, with a specific contextualization in Southern Mediterranean Countries. He also coordinates the Mediterranean School of Advanced Studies in e-Business Management research program.

Pascal Francq earned his master's degree in applied science at the Université Libre de Bruxelles (ULB) in 1996. After a 2-year experience in a private company, he came back to the Université Libre de Bruxelles (ULB) where he earned his Phd in 2003. Since 2004, he has been Professor and currently holds the Digital Information Chair. His main research topic is the Internet: its technologies, its social aspects and its support as a knowledge sharing platform. Since 1997, he has been working on automatic communities—detection and is the main contributor of the open source platform GALILEI for information management. He is currently involved in research on social networks analysis, search technologies, genetic algorithms and software design. His current research focuses on a mathematical framework for computing an authority rating for documents and an expert rating for social software contributors.

Alexandros Gkikas was born in Trikala, Greece. He holds a degree from the Theological Department of Aristotelian University in Thessaloniki. He also graduated from the OEEK, Department of the Information Technology being Technician of Computer Systems. He holds a Masters degree from the School of Humanitarian Studies of the Greek Open University. Since 1989 he teaches in Secondary Education and has worked on school projects using Information and Communication Technologies in Education and innovative educational processes to promote the equality of sexes in the educational system as well as to support students with learning difficulties.

Dr Seppo J. Hänninen is Researcher at Helsinki University of Technology Department of Industrial Engineering and Management. He holds a Doctor of Science in Technology degree from the Helsinki University of Technology with distinction. Dr Hänninen's research and teaching activities focus on the areas of new product development, commercializing technological inventions, micro-strategy management, entrepreneurship, and networks. He cooperates with several Finnish firms that develop innovations in technology programs. Before joining the research team at Helsinki University of Technology, he worked eight years in advertising industry and ten years as entrepreneur in international business. He has an extensive teaching experience at the HAMK University of Applied Sciences.

Stefan Hrastinski has a PhD in Informatics from Lund University, Sweden. He is currently a Research Fellow in Computer and Systems Science at Uppsala University, and member of The Swedish Research School of Management and IT. Stefan's research interests include e-learning, computer-mediated communication, online communities, social software, collaborative learning and work, and design science research. His recent publications appear in the Journal of Educational Computing Research, Internet and Higher Education, Interactive Learning Environments, Educational Media International, the International Journal of Knowledge and Learning, in the edited books Encyclopedia of E-Collaboration, Knowledge Networks and Principles of Effective Online Teaching, and in the proceedings of the International Conference on Information Systems and the European Conference on Information Systems.

R. Scott Jackson is a Research Biologist with the U.S. Army Corps of Engineers stationed at the Engineer Research and Development Center, Waterways Experiment Station in Vicksburg, Mississippi. He is the Manager, Recreation Management Support Program (RMSP). The RMSP conducts research and provides technical support to over 2,000 Corps of Engineers natural resource managers and rangers at over 450 sites nationwide. Mr. Jackson's professional experience includes conducting research in the following areas: recreation and natural resource management; regional economics effects of recreation; large-scale river basin management; recreation carrying capacity; and recreation monitoring techniques. Scott received a Bachelor of Science degree in Resource Conservation from Northern Michigan University and a Master's degree in Natural Resources Development from Texas A&M University. Scott is currently a doctoral candidate in Recreation Management and Policy Evaluation at Michigan State University. Contact information: R. Scott Jackson, CEERD-EE-E, 3909 Halls Ferry Road, Vicksburg, MS 39180, Scott.Jackson@erdc.usace.army.mil

Matthias Jarke is professor of Information Systems at RWTH Aachen University and Director of the Fraunhofer FIT Institute of Applied IT in Sankt Augustin, Germany. In his research, he investigates IS support for knowledge-intensive cooperative processes in business, engineering, and culture. He has coordinated several IST projects, served as program chair of leading information systems conferences. Jarke is founding director of the endowment-funded Bonn-Aachen International Centre of Information Technology (B-IT) for advanced graduate studies and continuing education in applied computer science, jointly operated by two universities and Fraunhofer. As president of the German computer society (GI), he was responsible for the definition of Germany's IT accreditation guidelines. Both his university group and Fraunhofer FIT have been involved in numerous eLearning activities, ranging from the high school level to entrepreneurship training. Jarke serves on a number of national and international advisory boards.

Dr Ilkka Kauranen is Visiting Professor at the School of Management in the Asian Institute of Technology which is an international university. He has professorship in Development and Management in Industry at Helsinki University of Technology Department of Industrial Engineering and Management. Professor Ilkka Kauranen's research and teaching activities focus on the areas of technology-based companies, commercializing technological inventions, research & development management, entrepreneurship, and regional development. In addition to his academic career, Professor Kauranen has vast experience in the top management of companies. He has been a board member in several publicly traded companies and entrepreneurial private companies. He has been a founder of several knowledge-intensive companies. He has worked as a full-time management consultant, acting as the president and one of the senior partners in the company.

Dr. Ralf Klamma is a senior researcher in the Information Systems group at RWTH Aachen University. He owns a diploma degree and a doctoral degree both in computer science from RWTH Aachen University. He has visited the Massachusetts Institute of Technology, Cambridge and has been a substitute professor at the universities of Chemnitz and Passau. He is project manager in the collaborative research center "Media and Cultural Communication" and several other cluster projects within German Science Foundation (DFG), and core member of the EU Network of Excellence PROLEARN in professional training. His research interests include theory and utilization of information systems, organizational memories and workflow management, virtual community support, social software, electronic learning and professional training.

Dimitris Konetas is the Secretary of the board of directors of the Greek Union of Computer Scientists. He received his diploma from the Computer Engineering & Informatics Department of the University of Patra, in 1992 and he is currently a PhD student at the ICT and Distance Education Laboratory of the Preschool Education Department of the University of Ioannina. He has been working as an Information Technology consultant and a System (Librarian) Administrator. He has also participated in a variety of E.C. projects and personnel training programs. He is currently teaching Computer Science in 4th TEE of Ioannina and the Technological Educational Institution of Epirus, Greece.

Dr. Wendelin Küpers works as Senior Lecturer at the Department of Management & International Business at Massey University in Auckland, New Zealand. Before working at the Institute for Leadership and Human Resource Management at the University of St. Gallen, Switzerland, and as Senior Lecturer at the Chair of Business Administration, Leadership, & Organization at the University in Hagen, Germany he studied economics and business administration at the University of Witten/Herdecke, Germany and received his PhD from the same university. Furthermore he studied philosophy at the Ruhr-University Bochum, Germany. In his research he focuses on integral leadership and followership, as well as emotional and aesthetic dimensions related to knowing, learning and communicating in organisations. Being involved in advanced phenomenological research, he is developing an integral "pheno-practice", i.e. the practical relevance of phenomenology for questions related to integral ways of organizing and managing.

Niki Lambropoulos is a PhD student at the Centre for Interactive Systems Engineering, London South Bank University with Dr Xristine Faulkner, and Professor Fintan Culwin. She holds two BAs and a Diploma in Education from the University of Athens, Greece and an MA in ICT in Education from the Institute of Education, University of London. Now she works as an e-learning consultant, and operational researcher and analyst in e-business. She has widely published in the field. She is located in London and enjoys working collaboratively over the Net.

Georgia Lazakidou is a Ph.D. student at the Department of Technology Education and Digital Systems, University of Piraeus since June 2003. Her research interests scale from collaborative learning methods and tools to interaction analysis. She works as a teacher in Primary Education since September 2001.

Jeanette Lemmergaard is assistant professor and project manager of strategic human resource management at the University of Southern Denmark. She graduated from Odense University with an M.Sc. in International Business and Modern Languages in 1997, and received her PhD in business economics from the University of Southern Denmark in 2003. She is best known professionally for her work on the influence of organizational norms and values on the decision-making processes. Her current research includes strategic human resource management, strategic corporate social responsibility, diversity management and knowledge management.

Antonella Martini, PhD, is assistant professor of management at the University of Pisa where she teaches Innovation Management and Business Economics and Organisation. Her main research interests concern Knowledge & Community Management, and Continuous Innovation: she is actively involved in national and international projects on the fields and member of the international board of the Continuous Innovation Network (CINet). She is author of 50 publications at the international level.

Sofia Papadimitriou was born in Athens and studied Mathematics in Athens University. She has a Master Degree in Computer Science since 1986 from Athens University too. She is an ICT Secondary teacher since 1990, teaching Computer Science in Gymnasium and Technical Schools. Currently she is on secondment at the Greek Educational Television since September 2007.

Dr. Kevin R. Parker is a Professor of Computer Information Systems at Idaho State University, having previously held an academic appointment at Saint Louis University. He has taught both computer science and information systems courses over the course of his fifteen years in academia. Dr. Parker's research interests include competitive intelligence, knowledge management, the Semantic Web, and information assurance. He has published in such journals as Journal of Information Technology Education, Journal of Information Systems Education, and Communications of the AIS. Dr. Parker's teaching interests include web development technologies, programming languages, data structures, and database management systems. Dr. Parker holds a B.A. in Computer Science from the University of Texas at Austin (1982), an M.S. in Computer Science from Texas Tech University (1991), and a Ph.D. in Management Information Systems from Texas Tech University (1995).

M. Kathleen Perales is a Research Biologist with the U.S. Army Corps of Engineers stationed at the Engineer Research and Development Center, Waterways Experiment Station in Vicksburg, Mississippi. She designed and is the Project Leader of the Natural Resources Management Gateway, the Operations Gateway and the Corps Lakes Gateway. Ms Perales' professional experience includes conducting research in: facility design day evaluation, economic impact studies, and use estimation surveys in developed and dispersed-use areas. Kathleen holds a B.S. in Marine Sciences from Texas A&M in Galveston and an M.Ag. in Natural Resources Management from A&M in College Station. She is ABD on a PhD in Parks Recreation and Tourism at Michigan State University. Ms. Perales is currently serving her second term as a Trustee for the National Recreation and Park Association representing the Armed Forces Recreation Society. Contact information: Kathleen Perales, CEERD-EE-E, 3909 Halls Ferry Road, Vicksburg, MS 39180, Kathleen.Perales@erdc.usace.army.mil

Ourania Petropoulou is a Ph D. student at the Department of Technology Education and Digital Systems, University of Piraeus since September 2005. Her research interests scale from interaction analysis to adult learning. She works as a public servant in Biomedical Engineering Laboratory, School of Electrical and Computer Engineering, National Technical University of Athens (NTUA).

Alessandro Piva is researcher at the School of Management, Polytechnic of Milano, where he is the project manager for the banking area of Observatory on Enterprise 2.0. His main research interests concern Intranet and Enterprise 2.0.

Dr. Symeon Retalis is an Associate professor at the Department of Technology Education & Digital Systems, University of Piraeus. He holds a diploma of Electrical and Computer Engineer from the Department of Electrical and Computer Engineering studies, National Technical University of Athens, Greece, a MSc degree in Information Technology-Knowledge Based Systems from the Department of Artificial Intelligence, University of Edinburgh, Scotland, and a PhD diploma from the Department of Electrical and Computer Engineering, National Technical University of Athens, Greece. His research interests lie on the development of web-based learning systems, design of adaptive hypermedia systems, web engineering, and human computer interaction. He has coordinated and participated in various European R & D projects. He serves in the editorial board of many international journals. He participates to the ACM Web Engineering special interest group, to the CEN/ISSS learning technologies workshop. He is also director of the CoSy LLab (Computer Supported Learning Engineering Laboratory) [http://cosy.ted.unipi.gr].

Dr. Max Senges is a knowledge entrepreneur working on trans-disciplinary research dealing predominantly with cyberspace, entrepreneurship and knowledge practices. He has published in various fields ranging from philosophy and ethics, to knowledge management, or internet governance. He is an associate researcher at the Internet Interdisciplinary Institute (UOC-Barcelona). Dr. Senges currently lives and works in Stanford California where he engages in research, entrepreneurship and freelance consulting.

Dr. Marc Spaniol is a senior researcher in the Databases and Information Systems (Department D5) at Max Planck Institute for Computer Science. He holds a diploma and a doctoral degree in computer science from RWTH Aachen University. Within the Collaborative Research Center on "Media and Cultural Communication", he worked on the project on "Capacity to Act in Digital Social Networks by Visualization of Multidimensional Disturbance Patterns". His research interests include e-Learning & multimedia information systems for communities, multimedia metadata standards such as MPEG-7, and cross-media analysis.

Dr Pekka Stenholm is Visiting Research Scholar at the School of Public Policy in the George Mason University. He is on a leave from his post of Senior Researcher at Turku School of Economics' TSE Entre unit. His research activities focus on entrepreneurship and small business management, growth and competitiveness of firms, innovativeness, and family businesses.

T. J. Vapola is a Researcher at Helsinki School of Economics and Director, Business Development & Strategic Projects at Nokia. Her research interests include global innovation alliance constellations, business strategy, international entrepreneurship, and the ICT industries.

Marianna Vivitsou is a PhD student at the Department of Applied Sciences of Education, University of Helsinki. She holds a BA from Athens University and a MEd from the Hellenic Open University, specialising in TEFL with a focus on Educational Technology. She was Secretary General of the Board of Directors of the Panhellenic Association of Greek State School Teachers of English. Currently she is on secondment at the Greek Pedagogical Institute. She has participated in e-learning courses both as course designer and e-tutor. Her main academic interests lie in the area of adult learning and of media education.

Dr. Charalambos Vrasidas is an Associate Professor of Learning Technologies at the School of Education at University of Nicosia, Cyprus. He is the co-founder and Executive Director of CARDET (Center for the Advancement of Research and Development in Educational Technology), a Non-Governmental (NGO) non-profit research and development center based in Cyprus with partners around the world. He currently serves on the Executive Committee of the International Council of Educational Media, a UNESCO affiliated organisation and he is the Editor-in-Chief of the scholarly journal Educational Media International. He has conducted research on networked learning for the over 15 years, and has advised NGOs, companies, schools, and Ministries of Education in Asia, Europe, and the United States. He has published 4 books and more than 60 articles in journals and edited volumes. His upcoming book is titled ICT for Education, Development and Social Justice.

Index

Copyright © 2009, IGI Global, distributing in print or electronic forms without written permission of IGI Global is prohibited.